Contemporary Strategy Analysis

Concepts, Techniques, Applications

Fourth Edition

Robert M. Grant

BLACKWELL
Business

Copyright © Robert M. Grant, 1991, 1995, 1998, 2002

The right of Robert M. Grant to be identified as author of this work has been asserted in accordance with the Copyright, Designs and Patents Act 1988.

First edition published 1991
Second edition published 1995
Reprinted 1995, 1996 (twice), 1997 (twice)
Third edition published 1998
Reprinted 1998, 1999 (twice), 2000 (twice), 2001

Fourth edition published 2002

Blackwell Publishers Inc.
350 Main Street
Malden, Massachusetts 02148
USA

Blackwell Publishers Ltd
108 Cowley Road
Oxford OX4 1JF
UK

British Library Cataloguing-in-Publication Data
A CIP catalogue record for this book is available from the British Library.

Library of Congress Cataloging-in-Publication Data has been applied for

ISBN 0-631-23135-8 (hbk)
ISBN 0-631-23136-6 (pbk)

Typeset by Graphicraft, in 10/12pt Galliard
Printed and bound in Great Britain by TJ International, Padstow, Cornwall

This book is printed on acid-free paper.

Contents

Preface

The purpose of *Contemporary Strategy Analysis* is to equip managers and students of management with the core concepts, frameworks, and techniques of strategic management. To achieve this I have endeavored to combine rigor with relevance and applicability.

The approach is analytical. If strategic management is all about managing the enterprise to achieve superior performance, then the essence of strategic management is to identify the sources of profit available to the business enterprise, and to formulate and implement strategies that exploit these sources of profit. The result is a book that is simultaneously theoretical and practical. It is theoretical to the extent that it concentrates upon the fundamental factors that determine business success. It is practical to the extent that acquiring deep insight into the determinants of business success is the basis for developing sound strategy.

This fourth edition of the book reflects the impact of two key forces reshaping today's business environment: competition and speed of change. Globalization, new technologies, the formation of new enterprises, and dissolving industry boundaries all increase the intensity of competition. As a result, the quest for competitive advantage becomes critical for survival – let alone prosperity. My primary goal for the fourth edition has been to sharpen and develop the analysis of competitive advantage through a stronger focus upon the need to identify, develop, and exploit the resources and capabilities of the enterprise. The new edition gives increased prominence to the tools of knowledge management, to the development of new organizational capabilities, and the creation and management of industry standards.

As the rate of change of the business environment continues to accelerate – driven by technology, deregulation, and market turbulence – the implications for strategic management are far reaching. At the most basic level, strategy making extends beyond questions of resource deployment and market position to address fundamental questions such as: What is our business? What are we trying to achieve? What is our identity as an organization? Managing under conditions of rapid change also requires new approaches to strategy analysis. In this new edition I explore the analysis of real options, patterns of industry evolution, the sources of strategic innovation, and the implications of complexity theory.

The fourth edition gives particular prominence to the impact of digital technologies on the strategic management, notably the rapid development of e-commerce. The book shows that the fundamental tools of strategy analysis are as applicable to the "New Economy" as they are to the "Old Economy." Our analysis casts doubt on the potential for the New Economy to usher in a new era of business prosperity. Not only are most e-commerce sectors subject to intense price competition, but the growth of internet-based transactions and information flows will also increase competitive pressure on "bricks and mortar" businesses.

In response to customer feedback, the fourth edition places increased emphasis upon strategy implementation. There is a broader treatment of knowledge management and the development of organizational capability, fuller consideration of the design of organizational structures and management systems, and expanded treatment of strategic planning and performance management processes. Unlike other strategy texts, I do not split the book into separate sections for strategy formulation and strategy implementation. I offer an integrated approach to strategy formulation and implementation in the belief that these cannot be treated in isolation from one another. A strategy that is formulated without regard to its implementation is likely to be fatally flawed. At the same time, it is through their implementation that strategies adapt and emerge. Hence, I introduce organization structure and management systems as basic tools of strategy analysis (Part II of the book). Subsequent chapters that explore different types of strategy and different types of business then provide an integrated treatment of strategy formulation and implementation. However, I draw limits as to how far down the path of strategy implementation it is sensible to travel. Ultimately, strategy implementation takes us into the functional areas of the business – finance, marketing, operations, human resource management, and information systems. I leave these functions to their own specialists.

There is very little in this book that is original – I have plundered mercilessly the ideas, theories, and evidence of fellow scholars of strategic management. My greatest debts are to my colleagues and students at the business schools where this book has been developed and tested – University of British Columbia, California Poly, University of California at Los Angeles, City University, and Georgetown University. Also, to those in other schools who have used the book and provided me with feedback and ideas. I continue to learn and look forward to sharing that learning with you.

Robert M. Grant
Washington DC
April 2001

I
Introduction

1 The Concept of Strategy

1

The Concept of Strategy

Strategy is the great work of the organization. In situations of life or death, it is the Tao of survival or extinction. Its study cannot be neglected.
—*Sun Tzu*, **The Art of War**

OUTLINE

INTRODUCTION AND OBJECTIVES

Strategy is about winning. This chapter investigates the role of strategy in organizational and personal success – not only in its business context, but also in relation to other fields of human endeavor, including warfare, entertainment, politics, and sport. We examine the nature of strategy and we distinguish strategy from planning. Strategy is not a detailed plan or program of instructions; it is a unifying theme that gives coherence and direction to the actions and decisions of an individual or an organization.

We go on to examine the role of analysis in strategy formulation. If strategy is purely a matter of intuition and experience, then there is little point in studying this book – the only way to learn is to go and do. The key premise that underlies this book is that there are concepts, frameworks, and techniques that are immensely useful in formulating and implementing effective strategies.

By the time you have completed this chapter, you will be able to:

- Identify the contribution that strategy can make to successful performance, both for individuals and for organizations.

- Perceive strategy as a link between the firm and its environment, and recognize external analysis (understanding the industry environment) and internal analysis (understanding the firm's resources and capabilities) as the two primary ingredients into formulating strategy.

- Describe the origins and development of business strategy.

- Recognize the multiple roles of strategy within an organization.

My intention in this chapter is to familiarize you with what strategy is and how strategic analysis and formal processes of strategy making can help organizations achieve superior performance. At the same time, I shall be outlining a framework for strategy analysis that will form the organizing framework for the whole of the book. The basis of this framework is the role of strategy as the essential link between the firm and its business environment.

Since the purpose of strategy is to help us to win, we start by looking at the role of strategy in success.

THE ROLE OF STRATEGY IN SUCCESS

Exhibits 1.1, 1.2, and 1.3 outline examples of success in three very different fields of endeavor: Madonna in popular entertainment, General Giap and the North Vietnamese armed forces in warfare, and Alex Ferguson and Manchester United in soccer. Can the success of these diverse individuals and the organizations they led be attributed to any common factors?

EXHIBIT 1.1 Madonna

Despite a new relationship (with actor Guy Ritchie) a move to London, a second pregnancy, and her 42nd birthday, the new millennium saw little evidence of a slowdown in the career of Madonna Louise Veronica Ciccone. Year 2000 saw the release of her movie *The Next Best Thing*, a major hit with her recording of Don Michelin's "American Pie," a Grammy award for her song "Beautiful Stranger," and a new album, *Music*. Meanwhile, at her production company Maverick, her stable of recording artists continued to grow in size and success. After two and a half decades at the top of her profession, Madonna continues to be the world's highest earning female entertainer and one of the best-known women on the planet.

Born in Bay City, Michigan on August 16, 1958, Madonna studied dance at University of Michigan, but left after a year to pursue a career as a dancer in New York. After a succession of small-time dancing jobs, she turned to music and eventually landed a recording contract. *Madonna*, released in 1983, ultimately sold close to 10 million copies worldwide and her second album, *Like a Virgin*, topped 12 million copies. Between 1985 and 1990, six further albums, three world tours, and five movie roles had established Madonna with an image and persona that transcended any single field of entertainment: she was rock singer, actor, author, and pinup. Yet, she was more than this – as her website proclaims, she is "icon, artist, provocateur, diva, and mogul." She has also made a great deal of money: between 1985 and 1999 she was easily the world's top earning female entertainer and has a net worth estimated at close to $200 million.

So, what is the basis of Madonna's incredible and lasting success? As an entertainer there is little evidence of outstanding natural talent. Although she has evoked comparison with stars of the past – Monroe, Garbo, and Mae West – her endowments seem modest: she lacks the voice of Whitney Houston, the dancing ability of Janet Jackson, and the songwriting talent of Sinead O'Connor. While she is undoubtedly attractive, few would regard her as outstandingly beautiful.

To understand her success, it is first worth noting that she is not the product of any media organization or the protégée of any entertainment entrepreneur. Madonna's success is the result of her own efforts and she has always directed her own career. To launch her music career, she flew to Los Angeles in 1982 to persuade Freddie De Mann, Michael Jackson's manager, to take her on and eventually to drop Jackson. Since then she has forged alliances and drawn on the resources of a wide range of individuals and organizations. Yet, she has never compromised her independence or relinquished control over her career.

Madonna's drive and purposefulness are evident throughout her life. Her wide range of activities – records, concerts, music videos, movies, books, and charity events – belies a remarkable dedication to a single goal: the quest for superstar status. For close to 20 years, Madonna has worked relentlessly to market herself and to maintain and renew her popular appeal. She is widely regarded as a workaholic who survives on little sleep and rarely takes vacations.

> I am a very disciplined person. I sleep a certain number of hours each night, then I like to get up and get on with it. All that means that I am in charge of everything that comes out.

Her career has been largely undeflected by other goals. Many of her personal relationships have been stepping stones to career transitions. Her transition from dancing into music was assisted by relationships, first with a rock musician and later with disc jockey John Benitex. Her move into Hollywood followed her brief marriage to actor Sean Penn and an affair with Warren Beatty. As Jeff Katzenberg of Deamworks observed:

> She has always had a vision of exactly who she is, whether performer or businesswoman, and she has been strong enough to balance it all. Every time she comes up with a new look it is successful. When it happens once, OK, maybe it's luck, but twice is a coincidence, and three times it's got to be a remarkable talent. And Madonna's on her fifth or sixth time.

EXHIBIT 1.1 *(cont'd)*

Like Evita Perón, whom Madonna portrayed in the movie *Evita*, Madonna has shown a determination to climb out of her humble origins, ambition to reach a pinnacle of achievement, astuteness in making the right connections, mastery of the strategic use of sex, and a knack for being in the right place at the right time.

She was quick to learn how to play the game both in Tin Pan Alley and in Hollywood. As a self-publicist she is without equal. In using sex as a marketing tool, she has followed a tradition that extends back thousands of years: her innovation has been to go further in the subtle and not-so-subtle suggestions of sexual deviance, the portrayal of pornographic imagery (often under the banner of "art"), and the juxtaposition of sexual and religious themes. But she is also astute at walking the fine line between the shocking and the unacceptable. She has had concerts banned for indecency, videos pulled from MTV because of their sexual content, and a sponsorship deal with Pepsi canceled once Pepsi discovered that the advertising video featured Madonna making love on an altar (Madonna pocketed $3 million from the deal). Yet, she has carefully nurtured relationships with key producers and promoters, and never risked being exiled from the major channels of distribution that she needs to link her to her audience.

Most striking has been her continuous renewal of her image. From her street kid look of the early 1980s, her fans have been treated to multiple reincarnations. These have included her glam-rock look of the late 1980s, a Marilyn Monroe retro look, her hard-core sexuality of the early 1990s, to her softer and more spiritual image that has accompanied motherhood. Not all her projects have been successful – several of her films have been outright failures, with her performances described as "wooden" and "one-dimensional." Yet, every time her career appears to be in decline, she has shown a remarkable ability to stage publicity coups and renew her image and appeal.

Her approach involves very careful exploitation of her own talents and endowments. Her foremost ability is designing and projecting images that combine music, dance, theater, physical presence, and her sense of style. Her weaknesses as an entertainer are compensated for by her heavy reliance on technology, sexual suggestion, and an array of support personnel, including musicians, dancers, and designers. These are effectively integrated through her own creative vision and design capability.

In all her activities, Madonna shows obsessive attention to detail. Her insistence on control is reflected in the organization of her business interests. Most of her entertainment ventures have been owned and operated by her own companies, including Boy Toy Inc. (publishing), Siren films, and Slutco Inc. (video). In 1992 she formed the recording and management company Maverick Inc., a joint venture with Time Warner. Her Maverick deal guaranteed her a base salary of $8 million a year plus a share of profits. This represented a significant shift in Madonna's business base. Rather than rely on revenues from her music and acting output, she has increasingly become a developer and promoter of younger talent. Maverick provides a vehicle focusing her creative and promotional intuition and experience and the wealth of talented specialists that she has gathered around her to develop new entertainers and enterprises. The company has recording contracts with the Deftones, William Orbit, Cleopatra, and No Authority. Madonna has also been active in launching the international careers of singer Donna De Lory, the French band Mirwais, and comedian Ali G. As Madonna noted:

> I've met these people along the way in my career and I want to take them everywhere I go. I want to incorporate them into my little factory of ideas. I also come into contact with a lot of young talent that I feel entrepreneurial about.

While Madonna's musical career continues to flourish, her business development activities occupy an increasing part of her life and provide a growing share of her income, despite the increasing dominance of the global media sector by a few mega-conglomerates: AOL-Time

EXHIBIT 1.1   *(cont'd)*

Warner, Sony, Disney, Bertelsmann, and Vivendi Universal. Madonna has maintained her independence while expanding her influence. As Harry Scolinos, a Los Angeles attorney, observes: "I would take her street-smart business sense over someone with a Harvard MBA any day."

Sources: "Madonna Is America's Smartest Business Woman," *Business Age*, June 1992: 66–9; www.madonnafanclub.com; www.maverickrc.com.

EXHIBIT 1.2   General Giap and the Vietnam Wars, 1948–75

> As far as logistics and tactics were concerned, we succeeded in everything we set out to do. At the height of the war the army was able to move almost a million soldiers a year in and out of Vietnam, feed them, clothe them, house them, supply them with arms and ammunition and generally sustain them better than any army had ever been sustained in the field . . . On the battlefield itself, the army was unbeatable. In engagement after engagement the forces of the Vietcong and the North Vietnamese Army were thrown back with terrible losses. Yet, in the end, it was North Vietnam, not the United States that emerged victorious. How could we have succeeded so well yet failed so miserably?[1]

Despite having the largest army in Southeast Asia, North Vietnam was no match for South Vietnam so long as the South was backed by the world's most powerful military and industrial nation. South Vietnam and its United States ally were defeated not by superior resources but by a superior strategy. North Vietnam achieved what Sun Tzu claimed was the highest form of victory: the enemy gave up.

The prime mover in the formulation of North Vietnam's military strategy was General Vo Nguyen Giap. In 1944, Giap became head of the Vietminh guerrilla forces. He was commander-in-chief of the North Vietnamese Army until 1974 and Minister of Defense until 1980. Giap's strategy was based on Mao Tse Tung's three-phase theory of revolutionary war: first, passive resistance during which political support is mobilized; second, guerrilla warfare aimed at weakening the enemy and building military strength; finally, general counteroffensive.[2] In 1954, Giap began the final phase of the war against the French and the brilliant victory at Dien Bien Phu fully vindicated the strategy. Against South Vietnam and its US ally, the approach was similar. Giap explained his strategy as follows:

> Our strategy was . . . to wage a long-lasting battle . . . Only a long-term war could enable us to utilize to the maximum our political trump cards, to overcome our material handicap, and to transform our weakness into strength. To maintain and increase our forces was the principle to which we adhered, contenting ourselves with attacking when success was certain, refusing to give battle likely to incur losses.[3]

The strategy built on the one resource where the communists had overwhelming superiority: their will to fight. As Clausewitz, the nineteenth-century military theorist, observed: war requires

[1]   Col Harry G. Summers Jr., *On Strategy* (Novato, CA: Presidio Press, 1982): 1.
[2]   G. K. Tanham, *Communist Revolutionary Warfare* (New York: Praeger, 1961): 9–32.
[3]   Vo Nguyen Giap, *Selected Writings* (Hanoi: Foreign Language Publishing House, 1977).

EXHIBIT 1.2 *(cont'd)*

unity of purpose between the government, the military, and the people. Such unity was never achieved in the United States. The North Vietnamese, on the other hand, were united in a "people's war." Capitalizing on this strength necessitated "The Long War." As Prime Minister Pham Van Dong explained: "The United States is the most powerful nation on earth. But Americans do not like long, inconclusive wars . . . We can outlast them and we can win in the end."[4] Limited military engagement and the charade of the Paris peace talks helped the North Vietnamese prolong the conflict, while diplomatic efforts to isolate the United States from its Western allies and to sustain the US peace movement accelerated the crumbling of American will to win.

The effectiveness of the US military response was limited by two key uncertainties: what were the objectives and who was the enemy? Was the US role one of supporting the South Vietnamese regime, fighting Vietcong terrorism, inflicting a military defeat on North Vietnam, or combating world communism? Lack of unanimity over goals translated into confusion as to whether America was fighting the Vietcong, the North Vietnamese, or the communists of Southeast Asia, or whether the war was military or political in scope. Diversity of opinion and a shifting balance of political and public opinion were fatal for establishing a consistent long-term strategy.

The consistency and strength of North Vietnam's strategy allowed it to survive errors in implementation. Giap was undoubtedly premature in launching his general offensive. Both the 1968 Tet Offensive and 1972 Easter Offensive were beaten back, inflicting heavy losses on North Vietnamese regulars and Vietcong. Giap was replaced as commander-in-chief by General Van Tien Dung, who recognized that the Watergate scandal had so weakened the US presidency that an effective American response to a new communist offensive was unlikely. On April 29, 1975, Operation Frequent Wind began evacuating all remaining Americans from South Vietnam, and the next morning North Vietnamese troops entered the Presidential Palace in Saigon.

[4]   J. Cameron, *Here Is Your Enemy* (New York: Holt, Rinehart, Winston, 1966).

EXHIBIT 1.3 Alex Ferguson and Manchester United

In terms of revenues and audience, soccer is the world's biggest sport. The sport's international governing body, FIFA, presides over the national soccer associations in over 200 countries, and estimates that there are over 200 million registered players of the game and well over a billion fans. Among the thousands of professional soccer clubs worldwide, by the end of 1999 one team was widely acknowledged as the best in the world. After achieving the unprecedented feat of winning the English league championship, the English FA Cup, and the European Cup, Manchester United went on to win the world title by beating the Brazilian champions Palmeiras in Tokyo. The club, which had long been haunted by an aircraft crash in Munich in 1957 that wiped out its brilliant cup-winning side, had exorcized old ghosts and reached a pinnacle of achievement never before realized by a British football team.

Behind this success lay planning, development, and relentless encouragement and pressure by Manchester United's manager Alex Ferguson, the quiet Scotsman who had guided the team's efforts since 1986.

With a determination and dedication to work forged by his childhood in a tenement block in Govan, a tough, shipbuilding community close to Glasgow, Ferguson's life was built around soccer. After a playing career that started in boys' club teams and continued in the Scottish professional league with St. Johnston, Glasgow Rangers, and Aidrie, Ferguson took to coaching and management. He began with bottom-of-the-league East Stirlingshire, then moved to

EXHIBIT 1.3 *(cont'd)*

St. Mirren and later Aberdeen. There, Ferguson succeeded in breaking the duopoly held by the Glasgow teams Rangers and Celtic, and won the Scottish league championship, Scottish Cup, and European Cup Winners' Cup.

It was Ferguson's 14 years at Manchester United, however, where his ambitions were finally realized. After a period of gradual building, the club won the league championship in 1993 – a feat that had eluded it for 26 years. During the following seven seasons, Manchester United dominated English football, coming top of the league in all but two seasons.

Understanding why some managers and coaches achieve outstanding success with particular teams remains a mystery. In American football, for example, how did Tom Landry at the Dallas Cowboys, Vince Lombardi at the Green Bay Packers, and Mike Ditka at the Chicago Bears drive these teams to such heights of performance? In the case of Alex Ferguson, we do have some indications of the key ingredients.

Underlying Ferguson's career has been a remarkable drive for achievement. His life has been built around the exhilaration of winning and the dread of losing. His desire to win is reflected in the determination and aggressiveness that he displayed, as a footballer on the soccer field, and as a manager in the dressing room and the boardroom. His dedication is evident in his modest and sequestered life outside of football and, while devoted to his family, their role appears to mainly lie in offering a support system to help him withstand the rigors of his career.

His approach to management is based on team building:

> The best teams stand out because they are teams, because the individual members have been so truly integrated that the team functions with a single spirit. There is a constant flow of mutual support among the players, enabling them to feed off strengths and compensate for weaknesses. They depend on one another, trust in one another. A manager should engender that sense of unity. He should create a bond among his players and between him and them that raises performance to heights that were unimaginable when they started out as disparate individuals.

Creating unity and integration is at the heart of Ferguson's approach to management. His coaching places huge emphasis on training. His training sessions build individual and team skills through continuous repetition: "refining technique to the point where difficult skills become a matter of habit." Allied to rigorous training is tight discipline. In return for nurturing, developing, and mentoring his players, Ferguson demands total commitment. Some of his biggest showdowns with his players have been over alcohol – long a tradition of British soccer players, but inconsistent, says Ferguson, with professional play at world level.

However, building an outstanding team also requires outstanding players. Here, Ferguson has used a dual approach of identifying and nurturing young players through youth programs and a network of talent scouts, and buying star players from other teams. At both Aberdeen and Manchester United, Ferguson placed significant emphasis on "home-grown" talent. At the same time, he has drawn heavily on his clubs' financial resources to pay top prices for key players. In 1998 alone, Ferguson spent £24 million ($36 million) on just three players: Dwight Yorke from Aston Villa, Jaap Stam from Eindhoven, and Jesper Blomqvist from Parma. At Manchester United, Ferguson has built a team with a depth of talent that is unrivaled in British soccer.

Yet, Ferguson recognizes that individual skills and team capability are not enough. His tactical planning for each game is meticulous. This often includes a visit to watch opponents play as well as the analysis of videoed games to highlight the playing styles and individual strengths and weaknesses. His team composition and tactics are all adjusted to take advantage of the vulnerabilities of different opponents.

Sources: Alex Ferguson, *Managing My Life* (London: Hodder & Stoughton, 1999); www.manutd.com.

For none of these three examples can success be attributed to overwhelmingly superior resources:

■ Madonna possesses vitality, intelligence, and a tremendous capacity for work, but lacks outstanding talents as a vocalist, musician, actress, or any other of the principal vocations within popular entertainment.

■ The military, human, and economic resources of the Vietnamese communists were dwarfed by those of the United States and South Vietnam. Yet, with the evacuation of US military and diplomatic personnel from Saigon in 1975, the world's most powerful nation was humiliated by one of the world's poorest.

■ Alex Ferguson was a boilermaker's son brought up in the tough shipbuilding community of Scotland's Clydeside. His progress from a child kicking a ball in the street where he lived to becoming the world's leading soccer manager was entirely due to his own efforts.

Nor can their success be attributed either exclusively or primarily to luck. For all three, lucky breaks provided opportunities at critical junctures. None, however, was the beneficiary of a consistent run of good fortune. More important than luck was the ability to recognize opportunities when they appeared and to have the clarity of direction and the flexibility necessary to exploit these opportunities.

My contention is that the key common ingredient in all these success stories was the presence of a soundly formulated and effectively implemented *strategy*. These strategies did not exist as a plan; in several cases the strategy was not even made explicit. Yet, in all three, we can observe a consistency of direction based on a clear understanding of the "game" being played and an acute awareness of how to maneuver into a position of advantage.

■ Madonna's phenomenal decade and a half as a superstar has been based on a multimarket strategy, where she has positioned herself as style leader and sex goddess, while continually keeping in the public eye through continual image renewal.

■ The victory of the Vietnamese communist forces over the French and then the Americans is a classic example of how a sound strategy pursued with total commitment over a long period can succeed against vastly superior resources. The key was Giap's strategy of a protracted war of limited engagement. With American forces constrained by domestic and international opinion from using their full military might, the strategy was unbeatable once it began to sap the willingness of the US government to persevere with a costly, unpopular foreign war.

■ Manchester United's success between 1992 and 2000 was based on Alex Ferguson's strategy of building depth of talent through investing in youth and procuring the best available players worldwide, undertaking meticulous competitor analysis, developing team coordination, and instilling determination and discipline within his players.

FIGURE 1.1   Common elements in successful strategies

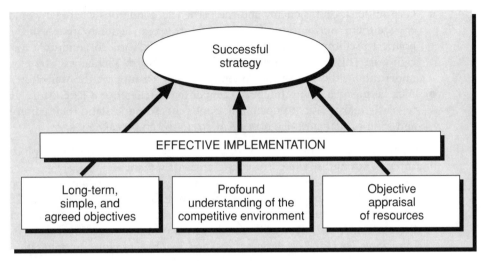

We can go further. What do these examples tell us about the characteristics of a strategy that are conducive to success? Four common factors stand out, which are illustrated in Figure 1.1.

1. *Goals that are simple, consistent, and long term.* All three individuals displayed a single-minded commitment to a clearly recognized goal that was pursued steadfastly over a substantial part of their lifetime.
    - Madonna's career featured a relentless drive for stardom in which other dimensions of her life were either subordinated to or absorbed within her career goals.
    - North Vietnamese efforts were unified and focused on the ultimate goal of reuniting Vietnam under communist rule and expelling a foreign army from Vietnamese soil. By contrast, US efforts in Vietnam were bedeviled by confused objectives. Was the United States supporting an ally, stabilizing Southeast Asia, engaging in a proxy war against the Soviet Union, or pursuing an ideological struggle against world communism?
    - Alex Ferguson's dedication to success on the football field is legendary. A steadfast husband and committed father, outside of soccer his only significant interest is his family.

2. *Profound understanding of the competitive environment.* All three individuals designed their strategies around a deep and insightful appreciation of the arena in which they were competing.
    - Fundamental to Madonna's continuing success has been a shrewd understanding of the ingredients of stardom and the basis of popular appeal. This extends from the basic marketing principle that "sex sells" to recognition of the need to manage gatekeepers of the critical media distribution channels.

Her periodic reincarnations reflect an acute awareness of changing attitudes, styles, and social norms.

■ Giap understood his enemy and the battlefield conditions where he would engage them. Supporting the military effort was an acute awareness of the political predicament of US presidents in their efforts to conduct a foreign war. This was key to the core element of North Vietnamese strategy: undermining the will of the American people to support the war effort.

■ Alex Ferguson's commitment to competitive intelligence is legendary. He regularly makes visits to upcoming opponents to understand their pattern and style of play and diagnose their strengths and weaknesses.

3. *Objective appraisal of resources.* All three strategies were effective in exploiting internal strengths, while protecting areas of weakness.

■ By positioning herself as a "star," Madonna exploited her abilities to develop and project her image, to self-promote, and to exploit emerging trends, while avoiding being judged simply as a rock singer or an actress. Her live performances rely heavily on a large team of highly qualified dancers, musicians, vocalists, choreographers, and technicians, thus compensating for any weaknesses in her own performing capabilities.

■ Giap's strategy was carefully designed to protect against his army's deficiencies in arms and equipment, while exploiting the commitment and loyalty of his troops.

■ In creating a world-class soccer team, Ferguson has shown an acute understanding of the need for depth of talent and versatility. As new players are acquired and existing players build new skills, so Ferguson has been able to adapt Manchester United's style of play to exploit these resources.

4. *Effective implementation.* Without effective implementation, the best-laid strategies are of little use. Critical to the success of Madonna, Giap, and Ferguson was their effectiveness as leaders in terms of capacity to reach decisions, energy in implementing them, and effectiveness in instilling loyalty and commitment among subordinates. All three built organizations that allowed effective marshaling of resources and capabilities, and quick responses to changes in the competitive environment.

These observations about the role of strategy in success can be made in relation to most fields of human endeavor. Whether we look at warfare, chess, politics, sport, or business, the success of individuals and organizations is seldom the outcome of a purely random process. Nor is superiority in initial endowments of skills and resources typically the determining factor. Strategies that build on the basic four elements almost always play an influential role.

Look at the "high achievers" in any competitive area. Whether we review the 43 American presidents, the CEOs of the Fortune 500, or our own circles of friends and acquaintances, it is apparent that those who have achieved outstanding success in their careers are seldom those who possessed the greatest innate abilities. Success has gone to those who managed their careers most effectively – typically by combining the four strategic factors. They are goal focused; their career goals have taken primacy over the multitude of life's other goals – friendship, love, leisure, knowledge, spiritual fulfillment – which the majority of us spend most of our lives juggling and reconciling. They know the environments within which they play and tend to be fast learners in terms of understanding the keys to advancement. They know themselves in terms of both strengths and weaknesses. And they implement their career strategies with commitment, consistency, and determination.

While focusing on a few, clearly delineated career goals is conducive to outstanding career success, such success may be matched by dismal failure in other areas of life. Many people who have achieved remarkable success in their careers have led lives scarred by poor relationships with friends and families and stunted personal development. These include Howard Hughes and John Paul Getty in business, Richard Nixon and Charles de Gaulle in politics, Marilyn Monroe and Elvis Presley in entertainment, Joe Louis and O. J. Simpson in sport, and Bobby Fischer in chess. Peter Drucker has pointed to the role of effective strategizing in career management (see Exhibit 1.4).

These same ingredients of successful strategies – clear goals, understanding the competitive environment, resource appraisal, and effective implementation – form the key components of our analysis of business strategy. These principles are not new. Over 2,000 years ago, Sun Tzu wrote:

> Know the other and know yourself:
> Triumph without peril.
> Know Nature and know the Situation:
> Triumph completely.[1]

A Framework for Analyzing Business Strategy

The same four principles that are critical to the design of successful strategies form the analytical foundations on which this book is based. Our framework views strategy as forming a link between the firm and its external environment (see Figure 1.2). The firm embodies three sets of key characteristics:

- Its goals and values.

- Its resources and capabilities.

- Its organizational structure and systems.

The external environment of the firm comprises the whole range of economic, social, political, and technological factors that influence a firm's decisions and its performance. However, for most strategy decisions, the core of the firm's external environment is its *industry*, which is defined by its relationships with customers, competitors, and suppliers.

The task of business strategy, then, is to determine how the firm will deploy its resources within its environment and so satisfy its long-term goals, and how to organize itself to implement that strategy.

---

[1] Sun Tzu, in *The Art of Strategy: A New Translation of Sun Tzu's Classic "The Art of War,"* trans. R. L. Wing (New York: Doubleday, 1988).

EXHIBIT 1.4   Peter Drucker on Managing Oneself

If we are to be successful in life, we must learn how to manage ourselves: how to develop ourselves, where to place ourselves to make the biggest contribution, and how and when to change the work we do. To manage ourselves effectively we need to ask some probing questions about ourselves:

What are my strengths? We need to assess our strengths and weaknesses through *feedback analysis* – when taking a key decision or action, write down the expected results and, nine or 12 months later, compare outcomes with expectations. Practiced consistently, this will show, over two or three years, where your strengths lie, and where you are not particularly competent. Use this understanding, first, to put yourself where your strengths can produce results, second, work on improving your strengths and addressing those weaknesses that deprive you of deriving full benefit from your strengths.

How do I perform? Understanding the processes through which one achieves results is essential to performing at one's best. Some people absorb information through reading rather than through listening (Dwight Eisenhower for example), others are better listeners than readers (Lyndon Johnson for example). By what means do I learn best: by formal instruction, by writing, by talking, or by practicing? Do I perform better individually or as part of a team? What degree of stress is ideal for me?

What are my values? Our values are a critical test of who we are and what we believe in. Organizations have values too and an individual's values must be compatible with those of the organization within which he or she works.

The answers to these three questions can help guide the key choices that we make in managing our careers and our lives.

■ *Where do I belong?* Although some people have a mission to become a mathematician or a musician, most of us do not. We must progress first by identifying where we do not belong, and then by recognizing the types of opportunity that are fitted to our strengths, method of work, and values.

■ *What should I contribute?* The degree of control we can exert over our own jobs has increased greatly over the years. How can I make a difference and what sort of difference do I want to make? How can I translate this into specific targets?

■ *What kinds of relationships do I need?* Few of us work on our own, and the kinds of people we work with and how we relate to them have a huge impact on our own performance. Choosing the people we want to work with and managing our relationship with them requires that we need to know about our co-workers' strengths, values, and how they perform.

In the new knowledge economy, each of us becomes our own chief executive officer. As with any chief executive, doing the analysis is not enough. Knowing our strengths, our method of work, and our values is the starting point, but the key is to act on this knowledge.

Source: Peter F. Drucker, "Managing Oneself," *Harvard Business Review*, March–April 1999: 65–74.

FIGURE 1.2   The basic framework: strategy as a link between the firm and its environment

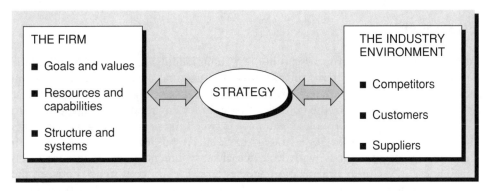

Beyond SWOT

Distinguishing between the external and the internal environment of the firm is common to most approaches to the design and evaluation of business strategies. One well-known approach is the SWOT framework: Strengths, Weaknesses, Opportunities, and Threats. This framework distinguishes between two features of the internal environment, strengths and weaknesses, and two features of the external environment, opportunities and threats. However, the SWOT framework is handicapped by difficulties in distinguishing strengths from weaknesses and opportunities from threats. For instance:

- Is Michael Eisner a strength or a weakness for Walt Disney Company? To the extent that he has masterminded Disney's revival over the past 17 years, he is an outstanding strength. Yet, his quadruple heart-bypass surgery and inability to implement a management succession plan suggest that he is also a weakness.

- Was the emergence of networked computing during the late 1990s a threat or an opportunity to Dell Computer? To the extent that computer networks shift computing power from PCs to servers, their expansion represented a threat to Dell's core business. However, while PCs have fallen in price and their margins have narrowed, so Dell moved strongly into servers (by mid-2000 it was US market leader), and it has simultaneously expanded into computer servers. It would seem, therefore, that computer networking represented both a threat and an opportunity for Dell.

The lesson here is that an arbitrary classification of external factors into opportunities and threats, and internal factors into strengths and weaknesses, is less important than a careful identification of these external and internal factors followed by an appraisal of their implications. Our approach to strategy analysis is therefore based on a simple two-way classification of *internal* and *external* factors. What will characterize our strategic appraisal will be the rigor and depth of our analysis of these factors, rather than a superficial classification of whether they are strengths or weaknesses, and opportunities or threats.

Strategic Fit

At the same time, strategy analysis is not just about identifying and understanding the various characteristics of the firm's internal and external environment. Developing strategies and appraising strategy are all about seeing "the big picture" – looking at the firm as a whole within the context of its industry environment. Thus, central to our view of strategy as forming an interface between the firm and its environment is the concept of *strategic fit*. For a strategy to be successful, it must be consistent with the firm's goals and values, with its external environment, with its resources and capabilities, and with its organization and systems. Lack of consistency between the strategy pursued by a firm and its external and internal environments is a common source of failure. The difficulties faced by many companies when they expand into a foreign market – Laura Ashley in the US, Disney with EuroDisney, General Motors in Japan – typically result when a strategy that worked well in the home market is applied to the different circumstances of an overseas market. Failure to match a strategy to the resources and capabilities of the organization can be equally disastrous. What did the fast-growing Korean auto makers Daewoo and Kia have in common with the high-profile e-commerce startups eToys and WebVan? Both sets of companies were forced into bankruptcy by strategies that overstretched their limited resources.

A BRIEF HISTORY OF BUSINESS STRATEGY

Enterprises need business strategies for much the same reasons that armies need military strategies – to give direction and purpose, to deploy resources in the most effective manner, and to coordinate the stream of decisions being made by different members of the organization.

Origins and Military Antecedents

The concepts and theories of business strategy have their antecedents in military strategy. Indeed, the term *strategy* derives from the Greek word *strategia*, meaning "generalship," itself formed from *stratos*, meaning "army," and -*ag*, "to lead."[2] However, the concept did not originate with the Greeks: Sun Tzu's classic *The Art of War*, written about 500 BC, is regarded as the first treatise on strategy. The military associations with strategy are apparent from dictionary definitions (see Table 1.1).

Military strategy and business strategy share a number of common concepts and principles, the most basic being the distinction between strategy and tactics. *Strategy*

---

[2] Roger Evered, "So What Is Strategy?," *Long Range Planning* 16 no. 3 (June 1983): 57–72.

TABLE 1.1   Some Definitions of Strategy

- Strategy. The art of war, especially the planning of movements of troops and ships etc., into favorable positions; plan of action or policy in business or politics etc.

  —Oxford Pocket Dictionary

- The determination of the long-run goals and objectives of an enterprise, and the adoption of courses of action and the allocation of resources necessary for carrying out these goals.

  —Alfred Chandler, *Strategy and Structure* (Cambridge, MA: MIT Press, 1962)

- A strategy is the pattern or plan that integrates an organization's major goals, policies and action sequences into a cohesive whole. A well-formulated strategy helps marshal and allocate an organization's resources into a unique and viable posture based upon its relative internal competencies and shortcomings, anticipated changes in the environment, and contingent moves by intelligent opponents.

  —James Brian Quinn, *Strategies for Change: Logical Incrementalism*
  (Homewood, IL: Irwin, 1980)

- Strategy is the pattern of objectives, purposes, or goals and the major policies and plans for achieving these goals, stated in such a way as to define what business the company is in or is to be in and the kind of company it is or is to be.

  —Kenneth Andrews, *The Concept of Corporate Strategy*
  (Homewood, IL: Irwin, 1971)

- What business strategy is all about is, in a word, *competitive advantage* . . . The sole purpose of strategic planning is to enable a company to gain, as efficiently as possible, a sustainable edge over its competitors. Corporate strategy thus implies an attempt to alter a company's strength relative to that of its competitors in the most efficient way.

  —Kenichi Ohmae, *The Mind of the Strategist*
  (Harmondsworth: Penguin Books, 1983)

- Lost Boy: "Injuns! Let's go get 'em!"
  John Darling: "Hold on a minute. First we must have a strategy."
  Lost Boy: "Uhh? What's a *strategy*?"
  John Darling: "It's, er . . . It's a plan of attack."

  —Walt Disney's *Peter Pan*

is the overall plan for deploying resources to establish a favorable position; a *tactic* is a scheme for a specific action. Whereas tactics are concerned with the maneuvers necessary to win battles, strategy is concerned with winning the war.[3] Strategic decisions, whether in the military or the business sphere, share three common characteristics:

- They are important.

- They involve a significant commitment of resources.

- They are not easily reversible.

---

[3] For a review of the concepts and principles of military strategy, see B. H. Liddell Hart, *Strategy* (New York: Praeger, 1968).

Many of the principles of military strategy have been applied to business situations. These include the relative strengths of offensive and defensive strategies; the merits of outflanking over frontal assault; the roles of graduated responses to aggressive initiatives; the benefits of surprise; and the potential for deception, envelopment, escalation, and attrition.[4] At the same time, the differences between business competition and military conflict must be recognized. The objective of war is (usually) to defeat the enemy. The purpose of business rivalry is seldom so aggressive: most business enterprises limit their competitive ambitions, seeking coexistence rather than the destruction of competitors.

The tendency for the principles of military and business strategy to develop as separate bodies of knowledge reflects the absence of a general theory of strategy. The publication of Von Neumann and Morgenstern's *Theory of Games* in 1944 gave rise to the hope that a general theory of competitive behavior would emerge. During the subsequent half-century, game theory revolutionized the study of competition and collaboration both between firms and within firms, and has been applied widely in military and political analysis.[5] Nevertheless, as we shall see in Chapters 3 and 4, despite offering striking conceptual insights into competition and bargaining, game theory has yet to fulfill its potential as a widely applicable and practical basis for strategy formulation by firms.[6]

From Corporate Planning to Strategic Management

The evolution of business strategy has been driven more by the practical needs of business than by the development of theory. The emergence of corporate planning was associated with the problems faced by managers during the 1950s and 1960s in coordinating decisions and maintaining control in increasingly large and complex enterprises. The development of financial budgeting procedures provided a basic control mechanism, but coordinating capital investment decisions required a longer planning horizon than the standard annual budgeting process. The emphasis on longer-term planning during the 1960s reflected concern with achieving coordination and consistency in investment planning during a period of stability and expansion. As companies sought to exploit the efficiencies of large size while controlling risks, so long-term planning based on economic and market forecasts became a central task of top management. The typical format was a

---

[4]   On the links between military and business strategy, see Roger Evered, op. cit. For a survey, see Nigel Campbell, "Lanchester Market Structures: A Japanese Approach to the Analysis of Business Competition," *Strategic Management Journal* 7 (1986): 189–200.

[5]   On the contribution of game theory to business strategy analysis, see Franklin M. Fisher, "Games Economists Play: A Noncooperative View," *RAND Journal of Economics* 20 (Spring 1989): 113–24; and Colin F. Camerer, "Does Strategy Research Need Game Theory?," *Strategic Management Journal* 12, Special Issue (Winter 1991): 137–52.

[6]   For practical and accessible introductions to the application of game theory, see Thomas C. Schelling, *The Strategy of Conflict*, 2nd edn (Cambridge, MA: Harvard University Press, 1980); A. K. Dixit and B. J. Nalebuff, *Thinking Strategically: The Competitive Edge in Business, Politics, and Everyday Life* (New York: W. W. Norton, 1991); and A. Brandenburger and B. J. Nalebuff, *Co–opetition* (New York: Doubleday, 1996).

EXHIBIT 1.5 Corporate Planning in a Large US Steel Company, 1965

The first step in developing long-range plans was to forecast the product demand for future years. After calculating the tonnage needed in each sales district to provide the "target" fraction of the total forecast demand, the optimal production level for each area was determined. A computer program that incorporated the projected demand, existing production capacity, freight costs etc., was used for this purpose.

When the optimum production rate in each area was found, the additional facilities needed to produce the desired tonnage were specified. Then the capital costs for the necessary equipment, buildings, and layout were estimated by the Chief Engineer of the corporation and various district engineers. Alternative plans for achieving company goals were also developed for some areas, and investment proposals were formulated after considering the amount of available capital and the company debt policy. The Vice President who was responsible for long-range planning recommended certain plans to the President, and after the top executives and the Board of Directors reviewed alternative plans, they made the necessary decisions about future activities.

Source: Harold W. Henry, *Long Range Planning Processes in 45 Industrial Companies* (Englewood Cliffs, NJ: Prentice-Hall, 1967): 65.

five-year corporate planning document that set goals and objectives, forecast key economic trends (including market demand, the company's market share, revenue, costs, and margins), established priorities for different products and business areas of the firm, and allocated capital expenditures. In 1963, SRI found that the majority of the largest US companies had set up corporate planning departments.[7] Exhibit 1.5 provides an example of such formalized corporate planning. The diffusion of corporate planning was accelerated by a flood of articles and books addressing this new science.[8]

The primary emphasis of corporate planning during the 1960s and early 1970s was on the diversification strategies through which large corporations pursued growth and security. Igor Ansoff, widely recognized as one of the founding figures of the new discipline of corporate strategy, went as far as to define strategy in terms of diversification decisions:

> Strategic decisions are primarily concerned with external rather than internal problems of the firm and specifically with the selection of the product-mix that the firm will produce and the markets to which it will sell.[9]

---

[7] Frank F. Gilmore, *Formulation and Advocacy of Business Policy*, rev. edn (Ithaca, NY: Cornell University Press, 1970): 16.

[8] For example, during the late 1950s, a number of articles on corporate planning appeared in *Harvard Business Review*: D. W. Ewing, "Looking Around: Long-range Business Planning" (*Harvard Business Review*, July–August 1956): 135–46; B. Payne, "Steps in Long-range Planning," *Harvard Business Review* (March–April 1957): 95–101; W. J. Platt and N. R. Maines, "Pretest Your Long-range Plans," *Harvard Business Review* (January–February 1959): 119–27; H. E. Wrap, "Organization for Long-range Planning," *Harvard Business Review* (January–February 1957): 37–47.

[9] Igor Ansoff, *Corporate Strategy* (London: Penguin, 1985): 18.

The creation of corporate planning departments by the vast majority of large companies was part of a wider enthusiasm among both companies and governments for "scientific" techniques of decision making, including cost–benefit analysis, discounted cash flow appraisal, linear programming, econometric forecasting, and macroeconomic demand management. Many economists and social commentators argued that scientific decision making and rational planning by corporations and governments were superior to the haphazard workings of the market economy.[10]

During the 1970s, circumstances changed. Not only did diversification fail to deliver the anticipated synergies, but the oil shocks of 1974 and 1979 ushered in a new era of macroeconomic instability, combined with increased international competition from resurgent Japanese, European, and Southeast Asian firms. Faced with a more turbulent business environment, firms no longer had the ability to plan their investments, product introductions, market initiatives, and personnel requirements three to five years ahead, simply because they couldn't forecast that far into the future.

The result was a shift in emphasis from *planning* to *strategy making*, where the focus was less on the detailed management of companies' growth paths as on positioning the company in markets and in relation to competitors in order to maximize the potential for profit. This transition from *corporate planning* to what became termed *strategic management* was associated with increasing focus on competition as the central characteristic of the business environment and competitive advantage as the primary goal of strategy. As Bruce Henderson, founder of the Boston Consulting Group, observed:

> Strategy is a deliberate search for a plan of action that will develop a business's competitive advantage and compound it. For any company, the search is an iterative process that begins with a recognition of where you are now and what you have now. Your most dangerous competitors are those that are most like you. The differences between you and your competitors are the basis of your advantage. If you are in business and are self-supporting, you already have some kind of advantage, no matter how small or subtle . . . The objective is to enlarge the scope of your advantage, which can only happen at someone else's expense.[11]

This shift of attention toward strategy as a quest for performance focused attention on the sources of profitability. Initially (during the late 1970s and into the 1980s), the focus was on firms' external environments through the analysis of industry structure and competition. Michael Porter of Harvard Business School pioneered the application of industrial organization economics to analyzing the determinants of firm profitability.[12] Meanwhile, at the Boston Consulting Group, the determinants of profitability differences within industries were under investigation – their studies pointed to the critical role of market share and economies of experience.[13] These two lines of inquiry – industry themes and the cost advantages of market share –

---

[10] J. K. Galbraith was a leading advocate of the view that planning by large corporations closely linked with governments would supersede markets in allocating resources, see his *New Industrial State* (London: Penguin, 1968).

[11] Bruce D. Henderson, "The Origin of Strategy," *Harvard Business Review* (November–December 1989): 139–43.

[12] Michael E. Porter, *Competitive Strategy* (New York: Free Press, 1980).

[13] Boston Consulting Group, *Perspectives on Experience* (Boston: Boston Consulting Group, 1978).

were developed and empirically refined in the Strategic Planning Institute's PIMS (Profit Impact of Market Strategy) project.[14]

During the late 1980s and early 1990s, interest in the role of strategy in building competitive advantage resulted in a shift of interest toward the internal aspects of the firm. Developments in the resource-based view of the firm and organizational competencies and capabilities pointed to the firm's resources and capabilities as the primary source of its profitability and the basis for formulating its longer-term strategy.[15] This emphasis on the internal resources and capabilities of the firm represented a substantial shift in thinking about strategy. Prior to the 1990s, the emphasis of strategy was a quest for optimal positioning: companies needed to locate within the most attractive markets where they should seek to become market leaders. However, if all companies attempted to achieve market share leadership in the same sectors, the result would be a competitive bloodbath. The focus on internal resources and capabilities has emphasized the *differences* between companies and their need to exploit these differences in order to establish unique positions of competitive advantage. Michael Porter makes the point: "Competitive strategy is about being different. It means deliberately choosing a different set of activities to deliver a unique mix of value."[16]

At the beginning of a new decade, the field continues its rapid evolution. Key theoretical developments include interest in the dynamics of competition through applying game theory and complexity theory to business,[17] probing the disruptive effects of technology,[18] diagnosis of the "new economy",[19] the strategic use of knowledge within the firm,[20] and the application of real options thinking to strategic choice.[21] At the practical level, companies continue to battle with the core dilemma of strategy formulation: how can companies take long-term decisions concerning new products, new technologies, and investments in physical and human capital when their business environments are changing at an ever accelerating pace? Resolving this dilemma calls for new approaches to strategy formulation and new tools of decision making.[22] As managers seek new strategies to exploit new sources of profitability, new approaches to strategy formulation that can generate strategic innovation, and new

[14]   R. D. Buzzell and B. T. Gale, *The PIMS Principles* (New York: Free Press, 1987).

[15]   R. M. Grant, "The Resource-based Theory of Competitive Advantage: Implications for Strategy Formulation," *California Management Review* 33 (Spring 1991): 114–35; D. J. Collis and C. Montgomery, "Competing on Resources: Strategy in the 1990s," *Harvard Business Review* (July–August 1995): 119–28.

[16]   Michael E. Porter, "What is Strategy?," *Harvard Business Review* (November–December 1996): 64.

[17]   On game theory, see A. K. Dixit and S. Skeat, *Games of Strategy* (New York: W. W. Norton, 1999); on chaos and complexity see S. Brown and K. Eisenhardt, *Competing on the Edge: Strategy as Structured Chaos* (Boston: Harvard Business School Press, 1998) and P. Anderson "Complexity Theory and Organization Science," *Organization Science* 10 (May–June 1999): 243–57.

[18]   Clayton Christensen, *The Innovator's Dilemma* (Boston: Harvard Business School Press, 1997).

[19]   Carl Shapiro and Hal R. Varian, *Information Rules* (Boston: Harvard Business School Press, 1998); Philip Evans and Thomas S. Wurster, *Blown to Bits: How the New Economics of Information Transformed Strategy* (Boston: Harvard Business School, 1999).

[20]   G. Von Krogh, K. Ichijo and I. Nonaka, *Enabling Knowledge Creation* (New York: Oxford University Press, 2000).

[21]   T. Copeland and V. Antikarov, *Real Options: A Practitioner's Guide* (Texere, 2001); E. S. Schwartz and L. Trigeorgis, *Real Options and Investment under Uncertainty: Classical Readings and Recent Contributions* (Cambridge: MIT Press, 2001).

[22]   Gary Hamel, *Leading the Revolution* (Boston: Harvard Business School Press, 2000).

TABLE 1.2 The Evolution of Strategic Management

PERIOD	1950s	1960s	EARLY-MID 1970s	LATE 1970s AND EARLY 1980s	LATE 1980s AND EARLY 1990s	LATE 1990s AND EARLY 2000s
Dominant Theme	Budgetary planning and control	Corporate planning	Corporate strategy	Analysis of industry and competition	The quest for competitive advantage	Strategic innovation and the new economy
Main Issues	Financial control through operational and capital budgeting	Planning growth	Diversification and portfolio planning	Choice of industries, markets, and segments, and positioning within them	Sources of competitive advantage within the firm	Competitive advantage through strategic innovation Competing on knowledge Adapting to the new, digital, networked economy
Principal Concepts and Techniques	Financial budgeting Investment planning Project appraisal	Business forecasting Investment planning models	Synergy Strategic business units Portfolio planning matrices	Experience curve and returns to market share Analysis of industry structure Competitor analysis PIMS analysis	Resource analysis Analysis of core competencies	Organizational flexibility and speed of response Knowledge management and organizational learning Competing for standards Early-mover advantage
Organizational Implications	Financial management the key	Rise of corporate planning departments and medium-term formal planning	Diversification Multidivisional structures Quest for global market share	Greater industry and market selectivity Industry restructuring Active asset management	Corporate restructuring and business process reengineering Refocusing and outsourcing	The virtual organization The knowledge-based firm Alliances and networks The quest for critical mass

organizational forms capable of implementing these strategies, so we business school academics search for concepts and theories that can offer insight into these complex issues. Applications of evolutionary biology, cognitive psychology, complexity theory, options theory and fractal mathematics to the practical issues of strategy have resulted in this being one of the most intellectually exciting and fast-developing fields of business management.

Table 1.2 summarizes the development of strategic management over time.

THE DISTINCTION BETWEEN CORPORATE AND BUSINESS STRATEGY

As the focus of strategic management has shifted from planning processes to the quest for profit, so the theoretical foundations of the field have been driven by analysis of the sources of profit and the factors that result in differences in profitability between firms. If we accept that the fundamental goal of the firm is to earn a return on its capital that exceeds the cost of that capital, what determines the ability of the firm to earn such a rate of return? There are two routes. First, the firm may locate in an industry where favorable conditions result in the industry earning a rate of return above the competitive level. Second, the firm may attain a position of advantage *vis-à-vis* its competitors within an industry, allowing it to earn a return in excess of the industry average (see Figure 1.3).

These two sources of superior performance define the two basic levels of strategy within an enterprise: corporate strategy and business strategy. *Corporate strategy* defines

FIGURE 1.3   The sources of superior profitability

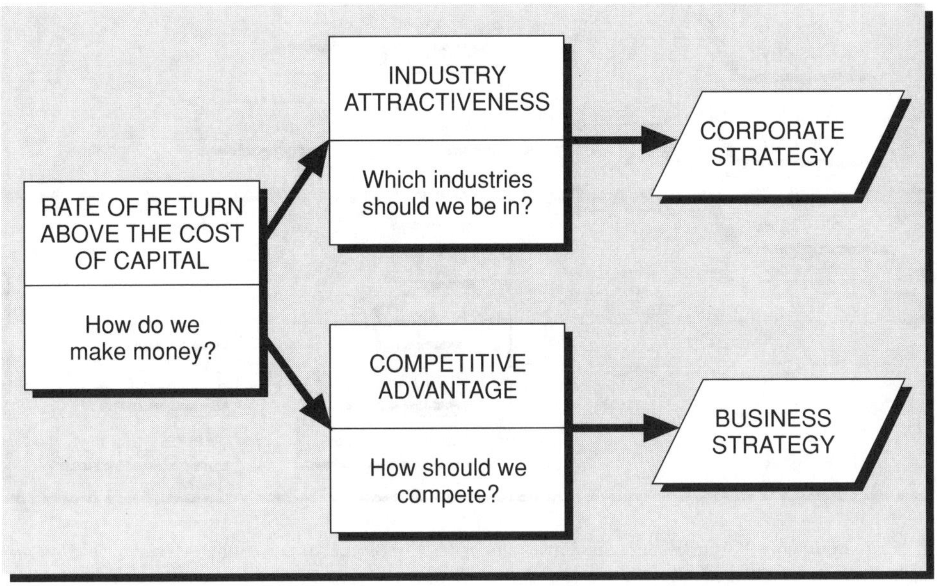

the scope of the firm in terms of the industries and markets in which it competes. Corporate strategy decisions include investment in diversification, vertical integration, acquisitions, and new ventures; the allocation of resources between the different businesses of the firm; and divestments.

Business strategy is concerned with how the firm competes within a particular industry or market. If the firm is to prosper within an industry, it must establish a competitive advantage over its rivals. Hence, this area of strategy is also referred to as *competitive strategy*. Using slightly different terminology, Jay Bourgeois has referred to corporate strategy as the task of *domain selection* and business strategy as the task of *domain navigation*.[23]

The distinction between corporate and business strategy and their connection to the two basic sources of profitability may be expressed in even simpler terms. The purpose and the content of a firm's strategy are defined by the answer to a single question: "How can the firm make money?" This question can be elaborated into two further questions: "What business or businesses should we be in?" And, within each business: "How should we compete?" The answer to the first question describes the corporate strategy of the company, the answer to the second describes the primary themes of business (or competitive) strategy.

The distinction between corporate strategy and business strategy corresponds to the organization structure of the typical multibusiness corporation. Corporate strategy is the responsibility of the top management team, supported by corporate strategy staff. Business strategy is formulated and implemented primarily by the individual businesses (typically organized as divisions or business units). Figure 1.4 also shows

FIGURE 1.4   Levels of strategy and organizational structure

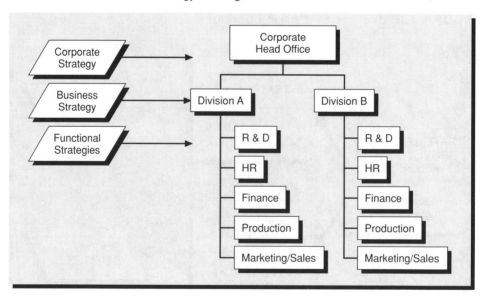

[23]   L. J. Bourgeois, "Strategy and the Environment: A Conceptual Integration," *Academy of Management Review* 5 (1980): 25–39.

a third level of strategy: functional strategy. *Functional strategies* are the elaboration and implementation of business strategies through individual functions such as production, R&D, marketing, human resources, and finance. They are primarily the responsibility of the functional departments. In single-business firms there is no distinction between corporate and business strategy.

The primary emphasis of this book is business rather than corporate strategy. This is justified by the conviction that the key to the success of an enterprise is establishing competitive advantage. Hence, from an analytical standpoint, issues of business strategy precede those of corporate strategy. Yet, these two dimensions of strategy are closely linked: the scope of a firm's business has implications for the sources of competitive advantage, whereas the nature of a firm's competitive advantage is relevant to the range of businesses and markets within which a firm can be successful.

DIFFERENT APPROACHES TO STRATEGY: *DESIGN* VERSUS *PROCESS*

As indicated by its title, the concern of this book is developing an analytical approach to strategic management. The implicit belief is that the senior managers of an organization are able objectively to appraise the enterprise and its environment, to formulate a strategy that maximizes the chances for success in an uncertain future, and to implement that strategy. The emphasis is the formulation of strategy, although, as we shall see, formulation and implementation cannot be separated: a well-formulated strategy must take account of the means by which it will be implemented, and it is through its implementation that a strategy is refined and reformulated.

How organizations formulate strategy has emerged as one of the main areas of debate within strategic management. What has become termed the "design school" of strategy views strategic decision making as a logical process, in which strategy is formulated through rational analysis of the firm, its performance, and the external environment. The strategy is then communicated to the organization and implemented down through successive organizational layers.

Such a picture is mostly a fiction: the real process is less structured, more diffused, and the dichotomization of formulation and implementation is less apparent. Consider the case of Madonna that we discussed earlier. It is doubtful whether Madonna ever formulated any explicit career strategy, even less likely that she wrote it down. She made up her strategy as she went along. What we are saying is that, as we look back on Madonna's career, we can see a consistency and direction in her decisions and actions that we can label "strategy." It is similar with most successful companies: Wal-Mart's brilliantly successful chain of discount stores based on its unique distribution system and small-town locations was not the result of grand design. It was the result of Sam Walton's hunch that discount stores could do well in small, rural towns, then finding that he needed to do his own distribution because manufacturers and wholesalers would not.

Studies by Henry Mintzberg and his colleagues at McGill University into the process of strategy making distinguish between intended, realized, and emergent strategies. *Intended strategy* is strategy as conceived of by the top management team. Even here, rationality is limited and the intended strategy is the result of a process of negotiation, bargaining, and compromise, involving many individuals and groups within the organization. However, the *realized strategy* that we observe tends to be only about 10–30 percent of the intended strategy. The primary determinant of a firm's realized strategy is what Mintzberg terms *emergent strategy* – the patterns of decisions that emerge from individual managers adapting to changing external circumstances and the ways in which the intended strategy was interpreted.[24]

The case of Honda's successful entry into the US motorcycle market has provided a well-defined battleground for the two schools to debate.[25] According to the Boston Consulting Group, Honda exemplified the rational, analytic approach to strategy formation. US entry was part of Honda's strategy aimed at exploiting volume-based economies to attain an unassailable position of cost leadership in the world motorcycle industry.[26] However, Richard Pascale's interviews with the Honda managers in charge of US market entry revealed a different story.[27] The initial decision to enter the US market was based on little analysis and included no clear plan of how the company would build a market position. The outstanding success of the Honda 50cc Supercub was a surprise to the company; Honda had believed that its main opportunities lay with its larger bikes. As Mintzberg observes: "Brilliant as its strategy may have looked after the fact, Honda's managers made almost every conceivable mistake until the market finally hit them over the head with the right formula."[28]

The debate over the Honda story and its implications continues.[29] The key point, however, is not whether it is the "design school" or the "process school" that is right, but recognizing that different approaches are suited to answering different questions. The "process school" of strategy research focuses on the realities of how strategies emerge. The central issues are the means by which strategic decisions are made in practice. The "design school" is normative: its goal is to uncover the factors that determine success to provide managers with the analytic tools needed to develop performance-enhancing strategies.

However, Henry Mintzberg goes further: not only is rational design an inaccurate account of how strategies are actually formulated, it is a poor way of making strategy. "The notion that strategy is something that should happen way up there, far removed from the details of running an organization on a daily basis, is one of the great fallacies of conventional strategic management." The problem is that a

[24] See Henry Mintzberg, "Patterns of Strategy Formulation," *Management Science* 24 (1978): 934–48; "Of Strategies: Deliberate and Emergent," *Strategic Management Journal* 6 (1985): 257–72; and *Mintzberg on Management: Inside Our Strange World of Organizations* (New York: Free Press, 1988).
[25] The two views of Honda are captured in two Harvard cases: *Honda [A]* (Boston: Harvard Business School, Case 384049, 1989) and *Honda [B]* (Boston: Harvard Business School, Case 384050, 1989).
[26] Boston Consulting Group, *Strategy Alternatives for the British Motorcycle Industry* (London: Her Majesty's Stationery Office, 1975).
[27] Richard T. Pascale, "Perspective on Strategy: The Real Story Behind Honda's Success," *California Management Review* 26, no. 3 (Spring 1984): 47–72.
[28] Henry Mintzberg, "Crafting Strategy," *Harvard Business Review* 65 (July–August 1987): 70.
[29] Henry Mintzberg, Richard T. Pascale, M. Goold, and Richard P. Rumelt, "The Honda Effect Revisited," *California Management Review* 38 (Summer 1996): 78–117.

divide between formulation and implementation precludes learning. In practice, the two must go hand in hand, with strategy constantly being adjusted and revised in light of experience. Mintzberg argues that strategy development is more about *crafting* than *planning*:

> *Crafting* strategy . . . is not so much [about] thinking and reason as involvement, a feeling of intimacy and harmony with the materials at hand, developed through long experience and commitment. Formulation and implementation merge into a fluid process of learning through which creative strategies emerge.[30]

The approach of this book is to follow a rationalist, analytic approach to strategy formulation in preference to the crafting approach advocated by Mintzberg. This is not because planning is necessarily superior to crafting – we have already noted that strategy is about identity and direction rather than planning. Nor is it because we wish to downplay the role of skill, dedication, involvement, harmony, or creativity. These qualities are essential ingredients of successful strategies and successful enterprises. Strategy development is a multidimensional process that must involve both rational analysis and intuition, experience, and emotion. Nevertheless, whether strategy formulation is formal or informal, whether strategies are deliberate or emergent, there can be little doubt as to the importance of systematic analysis as a vital input into the strategy process. Without analysis, the process of strategy formulation, particularly at the senior management level, is likely to be chaotic, with no basis for comparing and evaluating alternatives. Moreover, critical decisions become susceptible to the whims and preferences of individual managers, to contemporary fads, and to wishful thinking. Concepts, theories, and analytic frameworks are not alternatives or substitutes for experience, commitment, and creativity. But they do provide useful frames for organizing and assessing the vast amount of information available on the firm and its environment and for guiding decisions, and may even act to stimulate rather than repress creativity and innovation.

Central to the rational approach to strategy analysis is the idea that we can systematically analyze the reasons for business success and failure and apply this learning to formulating business strategies. The problem of the rationalist approach, as emphasized in Mintzberg's attacks on strategic planning, is that the analysis is too narrow – it has tended to be overformalized and has emphasized quantitative over qualitative data.[31] The danger of the Mintzberg approach is that by downplaying the role of systematic analysis and emphasizing the role of intuition and vision, we move into a world of new-age mysticism in which there is no clear basis for reasoned choices and in which disorder threatens the progressive accumulation of knowledge.

The goal of this book is to promote analysis that is sound, relevant, and applicable. If strategy analysis does not take account of experiential learning and the practicalities of implementation, it is poor analysis. Similarly, the process of strategy formulation must involve intuition, reflection, and the interaction between thought

[30] Henry Mintzberg, "Crafting Strategy," *Harvard Business Review* 65 (July–August 1987): 66.
[31] Henry Mintzberg, "The Rise and Fall of Strategic Planning," *Harvard Business Review* (January–February 1994): 107–14.

and action. Good analysis should encourage the development of intuition and promote creativity. Analysis can also greatly facilitate the process of strategy formulation.
It provides a conceptual framework for rational discussion of alternative ideas and a
vocabulary for communicating the strategy throughout the organization.

THE DIFFERENT ROLES OF STRATEGY WITHIN THE FIRM

An important realization that emerges from this discussion of strategy making as a
decision-making process is a recognition that strategic management fulfills multiple
roles within the organization. We can view strategy as a vehicle for achieving three
key managerial purposes.

Strategy as Decision Support

At the outset of this chapter, we identified strategy as a key element in success. But
why is this so? Strategy is a pattern or theme that gives coherence to the decisions
of an individual or organization. But why can't individuals or organizations make
optimal decisions in the absence of such a unifying theme? Consider the 1997
"man-versus-computer" chess epic in which Gary Kasparov was defeated by IBM's
"Deep Blue." Deep Blue did not need strategy. Because of its phenomenal memory
capacity and computing power, it could identify its optimal moves based on a huge
decision tree that computed the implications of every possible move. Kasparov, in
contrast, was subject to the cognitive limitations that constrain all human beings.
Bounded rationality – decision making that is intentionally rational, but is constrained
by human beings' limited search and information-processing capacity – creates the
need for a strategy to establish a set of guidelines and criteria for how individual
decisions will be made.[32]

Even in the smallest enterprise, many hundreds of decisions are likely to be made
every day. Decisions range from whether to give a discount to a particular customer,
to the choice of sending mail by express or regular delivery. It is not possible or
desirable to optimize every single decision by considering the full implications of
every permutation of decision choices. In these circumstances, strategies such as "We
will seek technological leadership in military applications of wireless communication,"
or "We shall provide the lowest-priced gasoline in Ohio" simplify decision making
by *constraining* the range of decision alternatives considered, and by acting as a
heuristic – a rule of thumb that reduces the search required to find an acceptable
solution to a decision problem.

The benefit of strategy is not just offering simplification and consistency to decision making; the identification of strategy as the commonality and unity of all the

[32]   The concept of bounded rationality was developed by Herbert Simon and James March: J. G. March
and H. A. Simon, *Organizations* (New York: Wiley, 1956); J. G. March, "Bounded Rationality, Ambiguity and the Engineering of Choice," *Bell Journal of Economics* 9 (1978): 587–608.

enterprise's decisions also permits the application of powerful analytic tools to help companies create and redirect their strategies. The tools of performance appraisal, industry analysis, and resource analysis with which you will become familiar as you work through the first few chapters of this book will result in your designing better strategies that will result in better decisions, and improved performance.

Strategy as a Process for Coordinating and Communicating

So, strategy helps achieve consistency in decisions. One aspect of this is consistency over time – strategy can help the firm establish long-term direction in its development and behavior. Equally important, a strategy serves as a vehicle for achieving consistent decision making across different departments and individuals. Organizations are composed of many individuals – 388,000 in the case of General Motors – all of whom are engaged in making decisions that must be coordinated.

For strategy to provide such coordination requires that the strategy process acts as a communication mechanism within the firm. Such a role is increasingly recognized in the strategic planning processes of large companies. The shift of responsibility of strategic planning from corporate planning departments to line managers, and the increased emphasis on discussion between the businesses and the corporate headquarters (as opposed to the formal approval of written plans), are part of this increased emphasis on strategic planning as a process for achieving coordination and consensus within companies.[33] Increasingly, strategic planning processes are becoming part of companies' *knowledge management* systems: as management becomes more and more concerned with how companies create, store, transfer, and deploy knowledge assets, so strategic planning becomes an integral part of how deeply embedded understanding of businesses and their environments is transferred between business units, divisional, and corporate levels, and how the knowledge of many different managers and functional experts becomes integrated within strategy.

Strategy as Target

Strategy is forward looking. A fundamental concern is what the firm (or the individual or the organization more generally) wants to be in the future. Such a view is often made explicit in a statement of company *vision*. The purpose of such goal setting is not just to establish a direction to guide the formulation of strategy, but also to set aspirations for the company that can create the motivation for outstanding

[33] Studies of strategic planning that identify these trends include: R. M. Grant, "Strategic Planning Among Large Corporations: Evidence from the Oil Sector," working paper (McDonough School of Business, Georgetown University, 1999); I. Wilson, "Strategic Planning Isn't Dead – It Changed", *Long Range Planning* 27, no. 4 (1994): 12–24. See also the changes in General Electric's strategic planning system: R. Slater, *Jack Welch and the GE Way* (New York: McGraw Hill, 1999), "General Electric: The Jack Welch Era, 1981–1998," in R. M. Grant and K. E. Neupert, *Cases in Contemporary Strategy Analysis* (Oxford: Blackwell, 1999).

EXHIBIT 1.6 Coca-Cola's Project Infinity

Coca-Cola has 43 percent of the US market for carbonated soft drinks. In the United States Coca-Cola products are sold through 2 million stores, 450,000 restaurants, and 1.4 million vending machines. A dominant player with limited growth prospects? Not according to Chairman Roberto Goizueta, who calculated Coca-Cola's market share as 3 percent. Why the discrepancy? Goizueta identifies the relevant market as the human race's total consumption of fluids. The purpose of Project Infinity is to galvanize the company into exploiting its infinite opportunities for market growth.

How will this ambitious goal be translated into sales? Rather than looking at Coke's overall share of the US and world market, the company will break down its market share data to identify discrepancies in market share between countries, localities, and specific outlets. In Bismarck, North Dakota, consumption per person averages 566 eight-ounce servings each year; in nearby Jamestown, consumption is only 314. In Memphis, Tennessee, consumption per head is 50 percent higher than in nearby Hot Springs, Arkansas.

Standing in a shopping center in Atlanta, Jack Stahl, head of Coke's US operations, can see a grocery store, three restaurants, and three vending machines, all of which sell Coke. Saturated market? No, a "microcosm of opportunity," says Stahl. "Nearby apartment buildings and office complexes could support more vending machines. I bet 150 people come into that hair salon each day – why shouldn't it sell Coke?"

Source: "A Coke and a Perm?," *Wall Street Journal*, May 8, 1997: A1.

performance. Hamel and Prahalad argue that a critical ingredient in the strategies of outstandingly successful companies is what they term "strategic intent" – an obsession with achieving leadership within the field of endeavor.[34] Examples of organizational strategic intent include the goal of the Apollo program "To put a man on the moon by the end of the decade," McDonald's pronouncement that "Our vision is to dominate the global food service industry," Komatsu's intent to "Encircle Caterpillar," and Coca-Cola's "Project Infinity" (see Exhibit 1.6). A similar point was made by James Collins and Jerry Porras in their book *Built to Last*.[35] A common feature of US companies that were preeminent in their sectors for 50 years or more, such as Merck, Walt Disney, 3M, IBM, and Ford, was the presence of "Big, Hairy, Ambitious Goals" that generated long-term commitment and drive at all levels of the companies. Sir Brian Pitman, chairman of Lloyds TSB, Britain's most profitable retail bank, argues:

> A big benefit to be derived from setting ambitious goals is that the status quo is never enough. The challenge itself brings forth new ideas and new excitement. It encourages out-of-the-box thinking.[36]

[34] Gary Hamel and C. K. Prahalad, "Strategic Intent," *Harvard Business Review* (May–June 1989): 63–77.
[35] J. C. Collins and J. I. Porras, *Built to Last: Successful Habits of Visionary Companies* (New York: HarperCollins, 1995).
[36] Sir Brian Pitman, "In My Opinion," *Management Today* (June 2000): 14.

Hamel and Prahalad extend their argument further. In a dynamic environment, the conventional approach to strategy formulation, which emphasizes the fit between internal resources and external opportunities, may be insufficient to drive long-run competitiveness. Critical to the success of upstart companies such as CNN in television, Apple in computers, Yamaha in pianos, and Southwest Airlines and Virgin Atlantic in air travel was a mismatch between resources and aspirations, in which unreasonable ambition became the driving force for innovation, risk taking, and continuous improvement. In place of *strategic fit* and *resource allocation*, Hamel and Prahalad emphasize *stretch* and *resource leverage*.[37] What we seem to be observing here is conflict between a firm's resource strength and the commitment and the intensity with which it implements its strategy. Resource scarcity may engender ambition, innovation, and a "success-against-the-odds" culture, while resource abundance may engender complacency and sloth.

THE ROLE OF ANALYSIS IN STRATEGY FORMULATION

Recognition of the multiplicity of purposes that a company's strategy fulfills – and, in particular, strategy's role in communicating purpose and setting aspirations – raises further questions about the analytical approach to strategy. Ever since Abernathy and Hayes identified "modern management techniques" as instrumental in American firms' declining international competitiveness in many sectors,[38] analytical approaches to management have been castigated for being static, conservative, risk averse, inflexible, short term, and detrimental to innovation.

The purpose of this book is not to defend conventional approaches to business strategy analysis, but to do better. Management's approach to strategy must be dynamic, flexible, and innovative. It must recognize the powerful role that values and goals play in organizations, and the importance of the strategy process in facilitating communication and coordination. It must recognize the importance of intuition, tacit knowledge, and learning-by-doing in complementing more "scientific" analysis.

It is vital that we recognize the limitations of analysis in guiding strategic management. Unlike mathematics, chemistry, or even economics, strategic management lacks an agreed, internally consistent, empirically validated body of theory. Though it employs theory and theoretical concepts, these are drawn mainly from economics, psychology, ecology and sociology, principally on an *ad hoc* basis. Even as applied science, strategic management differs substantially from more technically oriented managerial disciplines such as finance and production management. Strategy analysis does not generate solutions in the same way that scheduling algorithms or discounted cash flow analysis or the sampling frameworks of market research provide. A major feature of the techniques introduced in this book is that they do not provide solutions. Just as strategic decisions in our personal lives are not amenable to

[37]   Gary Hamel and C. K. Prahalad, "Strategy as Stretch and Leverage," *Harvard Business Review* (March–April 1993): 75–84.
[38]   W. J. Abernathy and R. H. Hayes, "Managing Our Way to Economic Decline," *Harvard Business Review* (July–August 1980): 67–77.

quantitative decision techniques (Should I get married? Have children? Change my career from bond trading to brain surgery? Move to a new location?), the same is true in business. There are simply too many variables to reduce strategy analysis to programmed algorithms.

The purpose of strategy analysis is not to provide answers but to help us understand the issues. Many of the analytic techniques introduced in this book are simply frameworks to identify, classify, and understand the principal factors that influence strategic decisions. Such frameworks are invaluable in understanding the complexities of strategy decisions: the infinite richness of the firm's environment and the tangle of people, resources, structures, and traditions that make up the business enterprise. In some instances, the most useful contribution may be in assisting us to make a start on the problem: by guiding us to the questions we need to answer, and by providing a framework for organizing the information gathered, we are in a superior position to a manager who relies exclusively on experience and intuition. Finally, analytic frameworks and techniques can improve our flexibility as managers. The analysis in this book is general in its applicability; it is not specific to particular industries, companies, or situations. Hence, it can help increase our confidence and effectiveness in understanding and responding to new situations and new circumstances. By encouraging depth of understanding in fundamental issues concerning competitive advantage, customer needs, organizational capabilities, and the basis of competition, the concepts, frameworks, and techniques in this book will encourage rather than constrain innovation, flexibility, and opportunism.

SUMMARY

This chapter has covered a great deal of ground. We have introduced the concept of strategy, explained its role in success, traced its development over time, and examined its purposes and limitations.

The fundamental premise of this chapter is that strategy is an important determinant of success in most areas of human activity. In identifying some common features of successful strategies, we have presented a framework for studying strategic choices that views strategy as a link between an organization and its environment.

In Part II, we examine each of the separate components of this framework: goals, values, and performance; the industry environment; the resources and capabilities of the firm; organization structure; and management systems. These chapters comprise the basic tools of strategy analysis. We then deploy these tools in the analysis of competitive advantage (Part III), in the formulation and implementation of business strategies in different industry contexts (Part IV), and then in the development of corporate strategy (Part V). Figure 1.5 shows the framework for the book.

FIGURE 1.5 The framework for the book

I INTRODUCTION

Chapter 1 The Concept of Strategy

II TOOLS OF STRATEGY ANALYSIS

Analysis of Industry and Competition Chapter 3 Analyzing the Industry Environment Chapter 4 Intra-Industry Analysis	*Analysis of the Firm* Chapter 2 Goals, Values, and Performance Chapter 5 Analyzing Resources and Capabilities Chapter 6 Organization Structure and Management Systems

III THE ANALYSIS OF COMPETITIVE ADVANTAGE

Chapter 7 The Nature and Sources of Competitive Advantage	
Chapter 8 Cost Advantage	Chapter 9 Differentiation Advantage

IV BUSINESS STRATEGIES IN DIFFERENT INDUSTRY CONTEXTS

Chapter 10 Industry Evolution	Chapter 11 Technology-based Industries and the Management of Innovation	Chapter 12 Competitive Advantage in Mature Industries

V CORPORATE STRATEGY

Chapter 13 Vertical Integration and the Scope of the Firm	Chapter 14 Global Strategies and the Multinational Corporation	Chapter 15 Diversification Strategy
Chapter 16 Managing the Multibusiness Corporation	Chapter 17 Current Trends in Strategic Management	

II

Tools of Strategy Analysis

2

Goals, Values, and Performance

The strategic aim of a business is to earn a return on capital, and if in any particular case the return in the long run is not satisfactory, then the deficiency should be corrected or the activity abandoned for a more favorable one.

—*Alfred P. Sloan Jr.*,
My Years with General Motors

OUTLINE

INTRODUCTION AND OBJECTIVES

The first chapter established what strategy is and what it can do. It also provided a framework for developing and appraising business strategies. In this framework, strategy is viewed as linking four sets of factors: the goals and values of the firm, the industry environment, the resources and capabilities of the firm, and its structure and management systems. Hence, strategy may be viewed as the way in which the firm deploys its resources and capabilities within its business environment in order to achieve its goals. In this chapter we explore the first of these topics: the goals and values of the firm and the performance of the firm in attaining them.

Firms possess multiple goals. Their choices of goals and the ways in which they pursue them are influenced and constrained by the values to which the firm adheres. Nevertheless, this chapter assumes that the primary goal of the firm is profit maximization – or, equivalently, maximizing shareholder value. This assumption of profit maximization underlies the analysis of the book as a whole. Most of the frameworks and techniques of strategy with which you will become familiar are based on analysis of the sources of profitability and the determinants of differences in profitability between firms. Indeed, for most practical purposes, strategic management can be defined as a quest for profitability.

By the time you have completed this chapter you will be able to:

- Evaluate the arguments for shareholder versus stakeholder approaches to the goals of the firm.

- Translate goals of profit maximization and value maximization into measurable performance targets defined by accounting returns, cash flows, economic profit, and operating targets.

- Apply the principles of valuing companies, business units, and strategies.

- Appreciate the role of values in the formulation and implementation of strategy.

STRATEGY AS A QUEST FOR VALUE

Business is about creating value. Value can be created in two ways: by production and by commerce. Production creates value by the physical transformation of products that are less valued by consumers into products that are more valued by consumers, e.g., the transformation of clay into pottery. Commerce creates value not by the physical transformation of materials, but by repositioning them in space and time. Trade involves transferring products from individuals and places where they are valued less to individuals and locations where they are valued more. Similarly, speculation involves transferring products from a point in time where the product is valued less to a point in time where it is valued more. Thus, the essence of commerce is creating value through arbitrage across time and space.

The difference between the value of a firm's output and the cost of its material inputs is its *value added*. Value added is equal to the sum of all the income paid to the suppliers of factors of production. Thus:

Value Added = Sales revenue from output *less* Cost of material inputs
 = Wages/Salaries + Interest + Rent + Royalties/License fees
 + Taxes + Dividends + Retained profit

In Whose Interest? Shareholders vs. Stakeholders

The value created by firms is distributed among different parties. Value added is distributed among employees (wages and salaries), lenders (interest), landlords (rent), government (taxes), and owners (profit). Firms also create value for their customers to the extent that they pay prices below the utility they derive from the goods and services they acquire (i.e., they benefit from *consumer surplus*). It is tempting, therefore, to think of the business enterprise as operating for the benefit of multiple constituencies. This view, which sees the business enterprise as a coalition of interest groups with different (often conflicting) interests, is referred to as the *stakeholder* approach to the firm. A key role of top management is to balance the interests of the different stakeholders. Even within each stakeholder group, diversity of goals is likely. For instance, managers tend to identify with the interests of their particular division or functional department.[1]

The case for the stakeholder approach to defining the goals of the firm is based on the recognition that the business enterprise is a social institution pursuing the interests of multiple groups. In Japan and continental Europe, the notion of corporations balancing the interests of multiple interest groups has a long tradition. These differences between *stakeholder capitalism* and the *shareholder capitalism* of Anglo-Saxon countries are reflected in international differences in companies' legal obligations. Thus, while in the US, Canada, the UK, and Australia company boards are required to act in the interests of shareholders, French boards are required to pursue the national interest, Dutch boards are required to ensure the continuity of the enterprise rather than pursue shareholder value, and German supervisory boards are constituted to include representatives of both shareholders and employees.

Whether companies should operate exclusively in the interests of their owners or should also pursue the goals of other stakeholders is an ongoing debate throughout the capitalist world. It raises issues of ethics and the broader social responsibility of business that are centrally important to our society and to our individual lives. However, it is a debate in which we do not wish to engage. The approach to strategy outlined in this book is founded on the simplifying assumption that companies operate in the interests of their owners by seeking to maximize their profits over the long term. Why do we make this assumption and how do we justify it? Let us point to four key considerations:

---

[1] R. Cyert and J. March, *A Behavioral Theory of the Firm* (Englewood Cliffs, NJ: Prentice-Hall, 1964).

1. Under conditions of increasing competition, firms may have little alternative to pursuing profitability. Increasing pressure of competition – international competition in particular – has caused the interests of different stakeholders to converge. The underlying common interest of all stakeholders is the firm's survival. Survival requires that, over the long term, the firm earns a rate of profit that covers its cost of capital. Despite the upswing in corporate profits during the 1990s, many companies fail to earn a return on capital that covers their cost of capital. During 1997–99, in the midst of unprecedented prosperity and a stock market boom, almost a year of increasing profitability and rising stock market values in the United States, almost one half of the largest 1,000 US corporations earned a net, after-tax operating profit that was less than their cost of capital.[2] Across broad sectors of industry, the heat of international competition is such that few companies have the luxury of pursuing goals that diverge substantially from profit maximization. In the fiercely competitive automobile industry, the key issue for companies such as Fiat, Hyundai, and Honda is not the whether they should focus on shareholders rather than other stakeholders, but whether their efforts to create value will be sufficient to pay creditors and reward shareholders to a degree that will permit their very survival. If a company is unable – over the long term – to earn a return on its capital that covers its cost of capital, then it will be unable to attract the capital needed to replace its assets.

2. Managers who do not serve the interests of shareholders will be replaced by those who do. A feature of the corporate financial environment of the past 20 years has been a more active "market for corporate control." Increased numbers of corporate acquisitions, many of them hostile, have meant that any company that depresses its share price by failing to maximize profits risks being acquired by owners anxious to operate the company in a more profit-focused manner. During the 1980s a whole new breed of acquisition-hungry financial groups emerged. Corporate raiders such as James Goldsmith, Frank Lorenzo, and Kirk Kerkorian, and investment companies such as Kohlberg Kravis Roberts, used high levels of debt financing to acquire large, under-performing industrial companies and then release value through restructuring. KKR's acquisition of RJR Nabisco made it clear that no company was too big to ignore its shareholders. During the new century it has been private investment groups – Hicks, Muse, Tate & Furst, and Texas Pacific – that have been most active in acquiring underperforming public companies. Even outside the Anglo-Saxon world, underperforming public companies have become vulnerable to hostile takeover. Vodafone's acquisition of Mannesmann in early 2000 was the first hostile takeover of a German by a non-German company. External pressure on top management to operate in the shareholder interest has also come through more active institutional shareholders. A large pension

---

[2] *The Stern Stewart Performance 1000: A Ranking of America's Most Value-Adding Companies* (New York: Stern Stewart, 1996).

fund, California Public Employees' Retirement System, has been especially prominent in pressuring the boards of directors of companies that have failed to generate satisfactory shareholder return. Shareholder pressure is evident in the insecurity of chief executives. During the first 10 months of 2000, 39 Fortune 500 corporations had replaced their CEO.

3. Even beyond a common interest of stakeholders in the survival of the firm, it is likely that there is more community of interests than conflict of interests among different stakeholders. The quest for profits over the long term is likely to require that a company treats its employees well and develops their full potential, acts fairly and honorably toward suppliers and customers, and conducts itself responsibly in relation to the environment and society's values. The long-term success of principled companies that are responsive to their customers, employees, and communities where they do business – companies such as Merck, Royal Dutch/Shell, McDonald's, and Kao Corporation – underlines the adage that good ethics are good business.

4. Finally, there is the question of simplicity. One of the most compelling reasons for assuming that firms exist to make profit is simply that such a goal allows us to subject strategic decision making to rational analysis. The key problem of a stakeholder approach where different groups desire different goals is the need to establish priorities and tradeoffs between these goals. The result is vastly increased complexity.[3] Virtually all the major tools of business decision making, from pricing rules to discounted cash flow analysis, are founded on the notion that more profit is better than less: the assumption that the predominant goal of the business enterprise is to earn profit opens up to us a whole arsenal of management techniques.

Accepting that company strategies are directed primarily toward the goal of making profit is not to deny that businesses and business people are driven solely by profit. The motives driving the architects of great businesses extend well beyond the simple desire to make money. Whether we are looking at Henry Ford or Bill Gates, dominant driving forces tend to be creativity, making a difference in the world, and fulfilling a vision. But accepting that enterprises and their leaders have motives that are both diverse and high-minded does not mean that we must reject profit and wealth creation as appropriate goals for enterprises. The strategy of the Walt Disney Company continues to reflect Walt Disney's desire to provide the "best in family entertainment" and to communicate the values of "happiness, optimism, and fellowship," yet the company also recognizes that Disney's overriding objective is "To create shareholder value by continuing to be the world's premier entertainment company from a creative, strategic, and financial standpoint."[4]

---

[3] See Kenneth R. MacCrimmon, "An Overview of Multiple Objective Decision Making," in J. L. Cochrane and M. Zeleny (eds), *Multiple Criteria Decision Making* (Columbia, SC: University of South Carolina Press, 1973).
[4] www.waltdisney.com.

What Is Profit?

Thus far, we have referred to firms' quest for profit and shareholder value loosely and synonymously. It is time to look a little more carefully at what we mean by profit and how it relates to shareholder value.

Profit is the surplus of revenues over costs available for distribution to the owners of the firm. If the firm is to maximize profit, it must be clear about what profit is and how it is measured. Otherwise, instructing the managers of a firm to maximize profit will create uncertainty and wide latitude for individual interpretation. What is the firm to maximize: total profit, margin on sales, return on equity, return on invested capital, or what? Over what time period? With what kind of adjustment for risk? And what is profit anyway: are we concerned with accounting profit, cash flow, or economic surplus? The ambiguity of the concept is apparent once we consider the profit performance of companies. Table 2.1 shows that any ranking of companies by performance depends critically on how profitability is measured. Among the issues that we need to consider are:

- Does profit maximization mean maximizing total profit or rate of profit? If the latter, are we concerned with profit as a ratio to sales (return on sales), total assets (return on assets), or shareholders' equity (return on equity)? As

TABLE 2.1 Performance of Leading US Companies Using Different Profitability Measures (1998 data)

COMPANY	NET INCOME[1] ($M)	RETURN ON SALES[2] (%)	RETURN ON EQUITY[3] (%)	ECONOMIC VALUE ADDED[4] ($M)	MARKET VALUE ADDED[5] ($M)	RETURN TO SHAREHOLDERS[6] (%)
General Motors	2,956	1.8	19.7	−5,525	−17,943	21.4
General Electric	6,573	9.4	22.2	4,370	285,320	45.3
Exxon	6,370	6.3	14.6	−2,262	114,774	22.4
Philip Morris	5,450	10.3	39.0	5,180	98,657	64.8
IBM	6,328	7.7	32.6	2,541	−5,878	77.5
Coca-Cola	3,533	18.8	42.0	2,194	157,356	1.3
Wal-Mart	4,430	3.2	21.0	1,159	159,444	107.7
Procter & Gamble	3,780	10.2	12.2	61,661	102,379	15.9
Microsoft	4,490	31.0	27.0	3,776	328,257	37.5
Hewlett-Packard	2,945	6.3	17.4	−593	45,464	10.7

Notes:
[1] Net after-tax profits.
[2] Net income as a percentage of sales revenues.
[3] Net income as a percentage of shareholders' equity.
[4] Economic Value Added = Net operating profits after tax less cost of capital.
[5] Market Value Added = Total market value (equity + debt), less total investment in assets by investors.
[6] Dividend in 1998 + Increase in market price of the shares during 1998/Price of shares at beginning of 1998.
Source: Fortune, April 26, 1999; Stern Stewart Performance 1000, 2000.

an objective, each will lead to perverse results. The instruction to "maximize total profit" is likely to encourage investment in activities that are profitable but where the return falls below the cost of capital. Maximizing the rate of profit encourages the firm to divest assets to the point where it is reduced to a rump of a few exceptionally profitable activities.

- Over what time period is profitability being maximized? Whatever measure of profitability is chosen, the specification of time period is critical. The instruction to "maximize next year's profit" will lead to a very different strategy from the instruction to "maximize profit over the next 10 years."

- How is profit to be measured? Accounting profit is defined by the accounting principles under which a company's financial statements are drawn up. Not only does a company's profit varies according to the accounting rules of its country of domicile, but a company has considerable discretion with regard to which items it expenses and which it capitalizes, the depreciation schedule it chooses, how it values its assets, and how it deals with exceptional and extraordinary items.[5]

From Accounting Profit to Economic Profit

One of the biggest problems with profit as measured by a firm's financial statements is that it combines two types of returns: the *normal return to capital* that rewards investors for the use of their capital; and *economic profit*, which is the pure surplus available after all inputs (including capital) have been paid out. In recent years, a number of companies and their financial advisers have encouraged firms to distinguish these two elements and to focus on economic profit as a measure of performance. To distinguish pure or economic profit from conventional accounting notions of profit, economists and business strategists use the term *rent* or *economic rent* to refer to economic profit.

The most widely used measure of economic profit is Economic Value Added (EVA), devised and popularized by the New York consulting company Stern Stewart & Company.[6] EVA is measured as Net Operating Profit After Tax (NOPAT) less Weighted Average Cost of Capital (WACC). Thus, for Anheuser-Busch, EVA is calculated as follows:

	Operating Profit	$1,756m
less	Taxes	$617m
less	Cost of Capital	$904m
=	Economic Value Added	$235m

---

[5] For discussion of the problems of accounting-based measures of profitability, see F. M. Fisher and J. J. McGowan, "On the Misuse of Accounting Rates of Return to Infer Monopoly Profit," *American Economic Review* 73 (1983): 82–7. For a more conciliatory view, see John Kay and Colin Meyer, "On the Application of Accounting Rates of Return," *Economic Journal* 96 (1986): 199–207.

[6] Shawn Tully, "EVA: The Real Key to Creating Wealth," *Fortune* (September 20, 1993): 38–50.

Where cost of capital is calculated as:

- Cost of equity 14.3 percent.

- Cost of debt (adjusted for the tax deductibility of interest payments) 5.2 percent.

- Weighted average cost of capital 11.3 percent.

- Total capital employed $8.0 billion.[7]

The advantages of economic profit over accounting profit lie both in setting performance targets for companies and business units and in evaluating performance achieved. As a target, economic profit overcomes the problems associated with instructing managers either to maximize accounting earnings (which encourages firms to overinvest through accepting projects that generate returns at less than the cost of capital) or to maximize rate of return on capital (which encourages underinvestment and the divestment of profitable assets). Thus, maximizing economic profit is consistent with maximizing shareholder value. In evaluating profit performance, economic profit has the virtue of imposing a tighter financial discipline than does accounting profit, by clarifying the fact that businesses earning less than their cost of capital are really making a loss. James Meenan, chief financial officer of AT&T, reported:

> The effect of adopting EVA on AT&T's businesses is staggering. "Good" is no longer a positive operating earnings. It's only when you beat the cost of capital.[8]

The approach has had a particularly dramatic effect on those businesses that suddenly found that, under the new rules, they had been posting negative profitability for years. Adopting EVA, or equivalent measures of economic profit, as the centerpiece of a company-wide system for imposing tight financial discipline has allowed companies to reorient their strategies and operations around the goals of maximizing shareholder value. Robert Goizueta, the former CEO of Coca-Cola, claimed that using EVA enabled Coca-Cola to "shed far-flung businesses, squeeze more Coke syrup from fewer plants, and generally build a hoard of value."[9] Exhibit 2.1 comments on the experience of Varity Corporation in implementing EVA.

Linking Profit to Shareholder Value

Profit is the surplus that accrues to the owners of a business. Hence, owners are interested in maximizing profits. Since these profits accrue over many years, it follows

---

[7] Although I focus on Stern Stewart's EVA analysis, there is nothing new or proprietary about the concept of economic profit. A similar approach has been proposed by John Kay in *Foundations of Corporate Success: How Corporate Strategies Add Value* (Oxford: Oxford University Press, 1993). Kay uses the term *added value*, which is defined as "the difference between the (comprehensively accounted) value of a firm's output and the (comprehensively accounted) cost of the firm's inputs. In this specific sense, adding value is both the proper motivation of corporate activity and the measure of its achievement" (19).

[8] Shawn Tully, "EVA: The Real Key to Creating Wealth," *Fortune* (September 20, 1993): 42.

[9] Shawn Tully, "America's Greatest Wealth Creators," *Fortune* (November 8, 2000): 68.

EXHIBIT 2.1 Deployment of EVA by Varity Corporation

Varity Corp. was built from the struggling farm-machinery manufacturer Massey-Ferguson, and is now a profitable supplier of auto components and diesel engines. Chairman and CEO Victor Rice adopted EVA in 1993 in an effort to link Varity's business objectives more closely with investor interests and to create a more financially driven corporate culture. Rice reports as follows:

> EVA permeates every level at Varity from the boardroom to the shop floor. My bonus as well as all senior managers' bonuses are determined solely by whether Varity achieves its EVA target . . . We believe that this approach enables us to directly align management and shareholder interests . . . Here are some of the specific ways we've applied EVA:

- Varity's EVA was negative $150 million in 1992. We set a five-year target to reach positive EVA in annual increments using a pre-tax cost of capital of 20 percent. By 1995 we were approaching 80 percent of our target.

- EVA caused us to take a closer look at our capital structure, recognizing the relatively higher cost of equity versus debt. This was an important factor in our decision to embark on a stock buyback program in which we purchased 10 percent of our outstanding common stock.

- EVA identifies operations and projects that earn more than the cost of capital. EVA analysis confirmed our decision to build twenty-first century manufacturing facilities for our Kelsey-Hayes antilock brake business.

- We use the EVA model to evaluate potential joint ventures. In 1994, for example, we determined that a joint venture between our UK Perkins diesel-engine business and Ishikawajima-Shibaura in Japan would generate returns in excess of cost of capital.

- As part of our annual strategic planning process we use EVA analysis to quantify business initiatives such as expansion in new markets and acquisitions.

- EVA provides a means of determining whether the sale of businesses or assets is in the best interests of shareholders.

- Almost every business process in our 80 plants and offices is influenced by EVA. For example, improvements in cycle times and inventory turns reduce capital needs and, in turn, create value.

- Using incentives to create a positive return on capital, EVA encourages managers to behave as if they are shareholders. We link employee bonuses directly to EVA improvement . . . All 4,000 Perkins employees, including union members, are tied to an EVA-based compensation plan.

Source: Victor Rice, "Why EVA Works for Varity," *Chief Executive*, September 1996.

that owners are interested in maximizing the net present value of the profits of their company over its lifetime.

In the case of publicly listed companies, owners do not receive profits directly, they receive part of the profits of the firm in dividend payments on their shares. So, are shareholders interested in maximizing dividends? Not really, since most companies pay only a fraction of net profits in dividends and many pay none at all (including most high-tech firms). Shareholders' primary interest is in the total return on their shares, of which the major part is the appreciation on the market value of those shares. Hence, shareholders are interested in maximizing the stock market value of their company.

How is this determined? Essentially, the value of the firm is calculated in the same way as for any other asset: it is the net present value (NPV) of the cash flows to that asset. Hence, the value of an enterprise is the NPV of its cash flows. This means that shareholder value maximization uses the same discounted cash flow (DCF) methodology that applies to the analysis of investment projects. In essence, shareholder value maximization views the firm as a collection of investment projects: in the same way that we calculate the NPV of an individual project, we can calculate the NPV of the firm as a whole. Thus, the value of an enterprise (V) is the sum of its free cash flows (C) in each year t, discounted at the enterprise's cost of equity capital (r).[10] The relevant cost of capital is the weighted average cost of capital (r_{e+d}) that averages the cost of equity (r_e) and the cost of debt (r_d). Hence:

$$V = \sum_t \frac{C_t}{(1 + r_{e+d})^t}$$

where *free cash flow* is measured as:

> Net Operating Profit *plus* Depreciation *less* Taxes *less* Investment
> in Fixed and Working Capital.

To calculate the value of shareholders' equity, we then subtract the value of debt and preferred stock.[11]

Thus, for a firm to maximize shareholder value means that its management must work to maximize its future net cash flows (often referred to as *free cash flow*) while also managing its finances to minimize the cost of capital at which these cash flows are discounted. However, how does this concept of shareholder value maximization relate to our concept of profit maximization?

The problem of profit maximization as a goal for the firm is that profit is a flow – it is measured over a single time period. Since companies are (hopefully) long-living organizations, they are interested in maximizing profit over multiple periods, hence the need to capitalize profits through discounting distant profit flows to the present.

---

[10] Note that the cost of equity is calculated using the Capital Asset Pricing Model: Firm X's cost of equity = the risk-free rate of interest + risk premium. The risk premium is the excess of the stock market rate of return over the risk-free rate multiplied by Firm X's beta coefficient (its measure of *systematic risk*). See T. Copeland, T. Koller, and J. Murrin, *Valuation: Measuring and Managing the Value of Companies*, 3rd edn (New York: Wiley, 2000): 214–17.

[11] This approach is what Copeland, Koller and Murrin (op. cit.: Chapter 8) refer to as the "Enterprise DCF Model." A more direct way to calculate the value of a firm's equity is the "Equity DCF Model," which discounts the cash flows to shareholders (free cash flow less interest payments) at the cost of equity. However, though seemingly simpler, the Equity DCF Model "provides less information about the sources of value creation and is not as useful in identifying value-creation opportunities" (151).

The DCF approach to company valuation implies that *cash flow* rather than *profit* is the relevant performance measure. In practice, valuing companies by discounting economic profit gives the same result as by discounting net cash flows. The difference is in the treatment of the capital consumed by the business. The cash flow approach deducts capital at the time when the capital expenditure is made; the EVA approach follows the accounting convention of charging capital as it is consumed (through charging depreciation). In principle, a full DCF approach is the most satisfactory approach to valuing companies and implementing a system of management based on shareholder value maximization. In practice, however, a DCF approach involves problems of forecasting cash flows many years ahead. Despite the claim by finance experts that "cash is king," this faith is based mainly on the recognition that cash flows are less easily manipulated by company managers for cosmetic purposes than are accounting profits. Forecasting cash flows far into the future is a particular problem for growth companies whose medium-term cash flows are depressed by heavy capital investment and whose eventual profit bonanzas are too far ahead to recognize adequately.

The case for using economic profit as a performance measure rests mainly on simplicity and practicality. First, since managers are more familiar with accounting-based measures of profitability than with cash flows, it may be easier to wean managers off accounting profit on to economic profit than on to cash flow. Second, economic profit provides a useful measure for assessing a firm's performance in a single year, whereas free cash flow does not.[12]

Applying DCF Analysis to Valuing Companies, Businesses, and Strategies

The DCF approach outlined above is widely used as a means of valuing companies and individual business units. The key difficulty is in forecasting cash flows: if the company has survived for 50 years and is expected to continue for another 50, how can we possibly forecast cash flows over that period? One approach is to assume that the current year's cash flow (C_0) will grow at a constant rate (g) into infinity. In this case, the above equation becomes:

$$V = \frac{C_0}{(1 + r_{e+d} - g)}$$

An alternative approach is to forecast free cash flow over the medium term – say five years – then to calculate a horizon value (H) based either on the book value of the firm at that time or on some more arbitrary forecast of cash flows beyond the medium term:

$$V = C_0 + \frac{C_1}{(1 + r)} + \frac{C_2}{(1 + r)^2} + \frac{C_3}{(1 + r)^3} + \frac{C_4}{(1 + r)^4} + \frac{C_5}{(1 + r)^5} + \frac{H}{(1 + r)^5}$$

---

[12]   As Copeland, Kohler and Murrin (ibid: 143) note: "Management could easily improve free cash flow in a single year at the expense of long-term value creation simply by delaying investments."

The same principles used to value companies and businesses can be applied to evaluating alternative strategies. Thus, for a business or for a whole company, the impact of different strategies can be compared by forecasting the cash flows to the business (or company) under each strategy and then selecting the strategy that produces the highest NPV.[13] Since the early 1990s, companies have increasingly integrated shareholder value analysis into their strategic planning processes. At PepsiCo, for example, shareholder value has long been used as a performance criterion. It is used to provide targets for each division and business unit against which performance is continually monitored, is a basis for evaluating strategies and investment proposals, and is the foundation for incentivizing managers. The key merit of the shareholder value approach is its consistency. The same methodology of DCF analysis and the same objective of shareholder value maximization is used to value individual investment projects, individual business units, alternative business strategies, and the corporation as a whole.

The main steps in applying shareholder value analysis to appraise business strategies are as follows:

■ Identify strategy alternatives (the simplest approach is to compare the current strategy with the preferred alternative strategy).

■ Estimate the cash flows associated with each strategy.

■ Estimate the implications of each strategy for the cost of capital: if a strategy involves increased capital expenditure (requiring borrowing), this may raise the company's cost of debt and also its cost of equity, since the equity will be viewed as more risky.

■ Select the strategy that generates the highest net present value.

Compared to the appraisal of individual investment projects, special problems arise from applying DCF analysis to strategies. To the extent that a strategy is an overall direction for the business rather than a detailed plan, it may be difficult to specify precisely the investment expenditures and the profit returns associated with a particular strategy. The problem is compounded by the length of time over which a strategy may operate: whereas individual investment projects have finite lives, businesses – and the strategy that guide them – are likely to be long living. Given the difficulties of forecasting with any precision the cash flows associated with a particular strategy, the dominant approach to the analysis of strategy in this book is *qualitative* rather than *quantitative*. While it is a desirable goal to quantify the impact on a firm's value of following strategy X rather than strategy Y, in practice such precision is elusive. A more feasible approach is to recognize and understand the

[13]   Alfred Rappaport has been prominent in developing and disseminating the "shareholder value" approach to strategy appraisal. See Rappaport, *Creating Shareholder Value: The New Standard for Business Performance* (New York: Free Press, 1986); also Rappaport, "Selecting Strategies That Create Shareholder Value," *Harvard Business Review* (May–June 1981): 139–49; Rappaport, "Linking Competitive Strategy and Shareholder Value Analysis," *Journal of Business Strategy* (Spring 1987): 58–67; Enrique R. Arzac, "Do Your Business Units Create Shareholder Value?," *Harvard Business Review* (January–February 1986): 121–6; and Rappaport, "CFOs and Strategists: Forging a Common Framework," *Harvard Business Review* (May–June 1992): 84–91.

factors that determine a firm's profits in order to select the strategy that offers the best prospect of maximizing profits, even if we are unable to quantify them.

Some of the most useful applications of shareholder value analysis are in relation to corporate strategy decisions involving acquisition, diversification, and divestment. We shall return to these issues in Chapter 15.

Taking Account of Option Values

Recent interest in the problems of uncertainty and resulting developments in finance theory have identified fundamental theoretical weaknesses in DCF approaches to strategy analysis. The result has been the development of a whole new approach to valuing investments and strategies using *real option analysis*. The technical details of valuing real options are complex. However, the underlying principles are intuitive and important. Let me outline the basic ideas of real options theory and what they mean for strategy analysis.

During the 1990s, a number of western oil majors were making multimillion-dollar investments in oil and gas projects in the energy-rich but infrastructure-poor former soviet republics, Azerbaijan and Kazakhstan. Such investments were highly risky. In addition to the usual geological and engineering uncertainties, the region lacked political and economic stability, and no reliable pipeline system existed to transport oil and gas to western markets. Discounts applied to exploration and production projects in these countries tended to be high and the resulting net present value for most of these upstream projects was negative. Yet, Chevron, ENI, BP, and Mobil invested heavily in acquiring exploration leases and forming joint ventures with local petroleum companies.

The key to understanding these investments is recognizing that they were not investments in the production of oil and gas. In acquiring exploration leases and equity stakes in local production companies, the western companies were acquiring opportunities to make later investments in oilfield development, pipelines, and downstream facilities that would be needed to exploit any oil and gas finds. However, these opportunities were *options* for the companies; by making initial investments in these projects, they retained the option of making larger, subsequent investments in developing their oil and gas finds. However, such investments would only be made if they were justified by the price of oil, the political situation, and access to markets.

In a world of uncertainty, where investments, once made, are irreversible, flexibility is valuable. Instead of committing to an entire project, there is virtue in breaking the project into a number of phases, where the decision of whether and how to embark on the next phase can be made in the light of prevailing circumstances and the learning gained from the previous stage of the project. Thus, in the case of Airbus's proposed A380 superjumbo, the company could commit to the $14 billion development program with precise design specifications and a fixed time frame. However, the value of the project is increased if Airbus approaches the project as a series of phases, from basic research and initial concept design through to more detailed design and engineering, where, at each stage, the company retains the options of delaying the project, modifying the plane's design, or even canceling the project.

Calculating Option Value

The principles of option valuation were developed by Fischer Black and Myron Scholes[14] and Robert Merton.[15] The *Black-Scholes option-pricing model* provides a formula for pricing financial options. The value of securities options was shown to depend on six variables: the price of the security, the exercise price of the option, uncertainty, the time to expiry, dividend payments, and the risk-free rate of interest.[16] Stewart Myers, Avinash Dixit, and Robert Pindyck showed that the same principles could be used to value *real options* – capital investments by firms that embodied flexibility.[17] The same factors that determine the value of a financial option also determine the value of a real option (see Figure 2.1).

Calculating real option values is complex: modeling uncertainty and incorporating the range of managerial options at different stages of a project typically soon immerses the analyst in complex mathematics. However, the basic process is logical and straight-forward. McKinsey & Company outline a four-stage process:

1. Apply a standard DCF analysis to the project without taking account of any flexibility options.

2. Model uncertainty in the project using event trees. Thus, if the project is exploiting oil reserves under the Caspian Sea in Azerbaijan, the key uncertainties would be the chances of finding oil within the exploration lease; the amount and quality of the oil found; the cost of developing the field; the chances of a pipeline being built to the Black Sea or across Iran; the price of crude oil; and the levels of taxes imposed by the Azerbaijan government. Under different outcomes for each of these uncertainties, DCF values can be calculated.

3. Identify the key managerial decisions that can be made at different points of the project's development so as to convert the event tree into a decision tree. Key aspects of managerial flexibility are the potential to defer investment in the next stage of the project, the potential to expand or contract the scale of the project, and the ability to abandon the project altogether.

---

[14]   F. Black and M. Scholes, "The Pricing of Options and Corporate Liabilities," *Journal of Political Economy* 81 (1993): 637–54.

[15]   R. C. Merton, "The Theory of Rational Option Pricing," *Bell Journal of Economics and Management Science* 4 (1973): 141–83.

[16]   None of these financial theorists was an "ivory tower" academic: Scholes and Merton were awarded the Nobel prize for economics in 1995, by which time they had founded, together with John Merriweather, Long Term Capital Management, a hedge fund that put their theories to work through using sophisticated computer models to seek out valuation anomalies. The Southeast Asian financial crisis and Russian bond default of 1998 caused the collapse of LTCM, which brought the global financial system to the brink of collapse.

[17]   A. Dixit and R. Pindyck, *Investment under Uncertainty* (Princeton, NJ: Princeton University Press, 1994); A. Dixit and R. Pindyck, "The Options Approach to Capital Investment," *Harvard Business Review* (May–June 1995): 105–15; Stewart C. Myers, "Finance Theory and Financial Strategy," *Interfaces* 14 (January–February 1984): 134–6.

FIGURE 2.1   The six levers of financial and real options

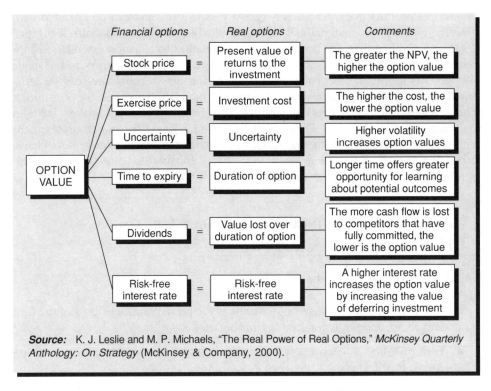

Financial options		Real options	Comments
Stock price	=	Present value of returns to the investment	The greater the NPV, the higher the option value
Exercise price	=	Investment cost	The higher the cost, the lower the option value
Uncertainty	=	Uncertainty	Higher volatility increases option values
Time to expiry	=	Duration of option	Longer time offers greater opportunity for learning about potential outcomes
Dividends	=	Value lost over duration of option	The more cash flow is lost to competitors that have fully committed, the lower is the option value
Risk-free interest rate	=	Risk-free interest rate	A higher interest rate increases the option value by increasing the value of deferring investment

OPTION VALUE

Source: K. J. Leslie and M. P. Michaels, "The Real Power of Real Options," *McKinsey Quarterly Anthology: On Strategy* (McKinsey & Company, 2000).

4. The total project with managerial flexibility can then be valued using what is known as the "replicating portfolio" approach: this replicates the cash flows of the project by a portfolio of priced securities and equates the value of the project to that of the replicating portfolio.[18]

Strategy as Options Management

From the viewpoint of strategy formulation, our primary interest is not the technicalities of options valuation, but how we can use the principles of option valuation to create shareholder value. The key observation is that creating options, by increasing the strategic flexibility of the firm, increases the value of the firm. For individual projects, this means avoiding commitment to the complete project and introducing decision points at multiple stages, where the options to delay, modify, or abandon the project are retained. Merck, an early adopter of option pricing, notes, "When you make an initial investment in a research project, you are paying an entry fee for a right, but you are not obligated to continue that research at a later stage."[19]

---

[18]   See Copeland, Koller and Murrin, op. cit.: 406–19.
[19]   Nancy Nichols, "Scientific Management at Merck: An Interview with CFO Judy Lewent," *Harvard Business Review* (January–February 1994): 89–105.

In designing projects, options thinking implies comparing the costs of flexibility with the options value that such flexibility creates. New plants that allow the assembly of multiple product lines, permit easy capacity expansion, and can be operated with different types of raw material will be more valuable than more specialized plants.

Options thinking has also been influential in relation to collaborative relationships between firms. The increased propensity for firms to form joint ventures and strategic alliances when entering new markets and exploring new technologies can be attributed, in part, to the desire to create options in relation to these opportunities. Thus, General Motors' network of strategic alliances with other automakers includes Fiat, Suzuki, and Daewoo. These alliances create options for closer involvement with these partners. Thus, with Suzuki, GM has invested in several joint-venture plants; it had the option of acquiring Daewoo in 2000, but decided not to exercise this option.[20]

APPLYING THE PRINCIPLES OF VALUE CREATION TO STRATEGIC MANAGEMENT

So far, we have established the following:

- The maximization of shareholder value is the primary financial goal of the firm and the proper basis for strategy formulation.

- Free cash flow and economic profit are better indicators of the firm's efforts to create shareholder value than is accounting profit.

- Discounted cash flow approaches to valuing companies, business units, projects, and strategies will tend to underestimate their value where significant option values are present.

These principles are straightforward, yet their application raises complex issues of measurement and forecasting. In particular, maximizing shareholder value requires maximizing cash flows over the life of the firm, yet hard financial data is available only for the past, not the future. It is hardly surprising that companies tend to persist with familiar and time-honored approaches to performance measurement. While financial purists decry the use of accounting-based measures of performance, in practice the gulf between cash flow and accounting profit approaches to analyzing performance is narrower than is often recognized. Different measures of profit tend to be highly correlated. The longer the period of time, the greater the convergence. Which measure of profit is used is less important than recognizing the limitations and biases inherent in that measure. John Kay has shown that, under

---

[20] The application of option theory to strategic management is discussed by Bruce Kogut and Nalin Kulatilaka, "Options Thinking and Platform Investments: Investing in Opportunity," *California Management Review* (Winter 1994): 52–69; and E. H. Bowman and D. Hurry, "Strategy Through the Option Lens: An Integrated View of Resource Investments and the Incremental-Choice Process," *Academy of Management Review* 18, no. 4 (1993): 760–82.

certain circumstances, accounting measures of profit approximate economic profit.[21] Over the life of the firm, the net present value of net cash flows from operations, economic profit based on historic cost accounting profit, economic profit based on replacement cost measures, and excess returns to shareholders are the same.[22]

Because expected cash flows far into the future are unobservable and difficult to estimate, practical approaches to implementing shareholder value maximization tend to resort to profitability measures relating to much shorter periods of time that utilize the accounting data available both within the firm and to outside analysts. Thus, as we have already recognized, EVA is firmly rooted in the concept of shareholder value maximization, yet it is essentially a single-period measure that adapts standard accounting earnings data. The approach to value-based management outlined by McKinsey & Co. starts from the premise of maximization of company value and the assertion that "cash is king." Yet, when it comes to estimating the value of a business or appraising past performance, the McKinsey methodology relies heavily on accounting-based measures. For example, DCF valuation techniques are translated into economic profit formulae (equivalent to the EVA approach), past performance is evaluated in terms of return on invested capital (defined as net operating income after tax as a percentage of net operating assets), and estimates of future cash flows are based on assumptions about the return on invested capital and return on sales that the firm will earn in the future.[23]

For the purposes of formulating value-creating strategies, the key tasks for financial analysis are first, appraising the current performance of the business; second, analyzing the potential for a new strategy to improve performance; third, setting performance targets for the manager whose task it is to implement the strategy. Let us look at some practical approaches for undertaking these tasks.

Appraising Current Performance

Appraising the performance of a firm requires assessing the extent to which the top management team is maximizing the net present value of future cash flows. The stock market value of the firm is the only reliable estimate of this. While shareholder return (dividends and increased stock market valuation) provides an indicator of the success of the management team in increasing the DCF value of the firm, such returns are strongly influenced by perceptions, "market psychology," and market dynamics. Moreover, stock market performance indicators are only available for public listed companies, so such measures cannot be used either for private companies or individual business units. Hence, most approaches to appraising past performance rely heavily on *ex post* measures of performance: How effective has management been in generating profits out of the firm's asset base?

[21]   John A. Kay, "Accountants, Too, Could Be Happy in a Golden Age: The Accountant's Rate of Profit and the Internal Rate of Return," *Oxford Economic Papers* 28 (1976): 447–60; and John A. Kay and Colin Meyer, "On the Application of Accounting Rates of Return," *Economic Journal* 96 (1986): 199–207.
[22]   John A. Kay, *Foundations of Corporate Success: How Business Strategies Create Value* (Oxford: Oxford University Press, 1993): 207.
[23]   Copeland, Koller, and Murrin, op. cit.: Chapters 9 and 11.

FIGURE 2.2 Disaggregating return on capital employed

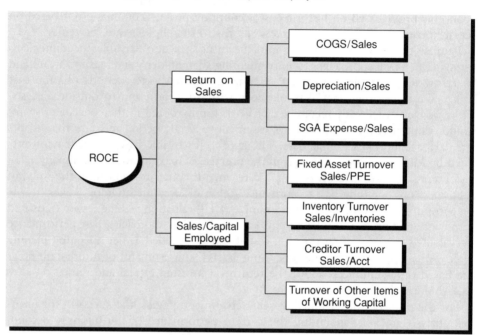

Return on invested capital (or, equivalently, return on capital employed) remains the predominant measure of the past performance of companies or individual businesses. By comparing the rate of return to the cost of capital, we can determine the extent to which the business is earning economic profit. However, for the purposes of strategy formulation, we need to go further. If profit performance is unsatisfactory, we need to diagnose the sources of poor performance so that management can take corrective action. Such diagnosis requires that we disaggregate overall return on capital into its constituent elements in order to identify the fundamental "value drivers." Figure 2.2 shows such a disaggregation.

Using the "DuPont formula," we can disaggregate return on capital into sales margin and capital turnover. But we can go further: as Figure 2.2 shows, sales margin and capital productivity can be further disaggregated into their constituent items. This analysis allows us to identify the sources of poor performance. For example, to diagnose the causes of Compaq's low return on capital, a disaggregated comparison of Compaq's financial ratios against those of Dell Computer would reveal a much lower level of capital turnover caused by lower inventory turnover, a longer collection period for receivables, and lower fixed capital turnover. It would also show lower sales margins caused by a higher cost of goods sold; higher sales, general, and administrative expenses; lower customer support and warranty costs; and an inferior sales mix (i.e., greater proportions of low-margin products and services). Many of these differences could be traced to the inferiority of Compaq's sales and distribution system as compared with Dell's direct sales model.

Evaluating Alternative Strategies

The concept and practicality of a DCF approach to evaluating alternative strategies were discussed earlier. The data problems of forecasting a firm's cash flows under alternative strategies are considerable. In practice, therefore, appraising a proposed new strategy is likely to rely primarily on qualitative tools of analysis. Thus, having identified the sources of poor performance in the past, we can look to changes in market positioning, resource deployment, and operational policies that can address these problem areas and hence contribute to increasing future profitability. To be more precise about the potential performance impact of a change in strategy, it is useful to distinguish between profit increases arising from the superior returns to existing assets and profit increases arising from new investments. On existing assets, the key task for management is to maximize the rate of return that it generates. On new investments, the key task is to earn a rate of return in excess of the cost of capital. Estimating the returns to new investments requires looking at the returns that the firm has earned on similar investments in the past and the returns that other firms have earned on similar types of investment, and making adjustments for changed industry circumstances and differential managerial efficiency.

Setting Performance Targets

As discussed in Chapter 1, a key element of a strategic planning system is a set of performance aspirations combined with a procedure for monitoring and assessing results against targeted performance. This performance management system needs to be company wide. As such, it needs to set targets for managers at different levels of the company. The key here is to match performance targets to the variables over which different managers exert some control. Thus, for the CEO, it may make sense to set the overall goal of maximizing shareholder value. For the chief operating officer and divisional heads, it makes more sense to set specific goals, such as maximizing return on capital employed on the existing asset base and investing in projects where the rate of return exceeds the cost of capital. For functional, departmental, and unit managers, more specific operating targets are preferable. Thus, in a retailing company, store managers might be given targets with regard to sales per square foot and gross margins. Warehouse managers might be required to achieve target levels of inventory turns. Purchasing managers might be required to reduce the cost of goods purchased as a percentage of sales revenue. The chief financial officer might be required to minimize average cost of capital and reduce cash balances.

The same procedure that we used to disaggregate return on capital for appraising past performance can be used to set performance targets appropriate to different levels and functions within the organization. Figure 2.3 uses the same breakout of the drivers of return on capital as Figure 2.2. The difference is that Figure 2.3 provides a basis for identifying the financial ratios appropriate to managers at the different levels and in the different functions of the company.

FIGURE 2.3 Linking value drivers to performance

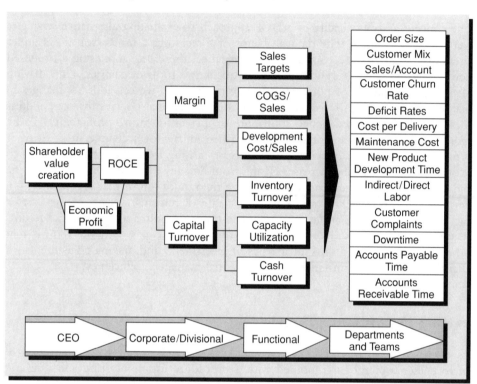

Balanced Scorecards

The problem with the above approach of disaggregating return on capital into constituent ratios is one of time period. The goal of maximizing return on capital is only consistent with maximizing shareholder value when it is pursued over a number of years, but a system of performance management must be able to identify deviations from targeted performance on an annual, preferably a quarterly, basis. The risk, however, is that setting financial targets that are monitored on a short-term basis encourages short-term optimization to the detriment of longer-term profitability (and corporate value). One solution to this dilemma is to link the overall corporate goal of maximizing shareholder value to more specific strategic and operating targets. One approach for doing this is the so-called *balanced scorecard* developed by Robert Kaplan and David Norton.[24] The balanced scorecard methodology provides an

---

[24] The methodology is outlined in a number of books and articles by R. S. Kaplan and D. P. Norton. See "The Balanced Scorecard: Measures That Drive Performance," *Harvard Business Review* (January–February 1992); *Balanced Scorecard: Translating Strategy into Action* (Boston: Harvard Business School Press, 1996); "Using the Balanced Scorecard as a Strategic Management System," *Harvard Business Review* (January–February 1996).

integrated framework for balancing shareholder and strategic goals, and extending these balanced performance measures down the organization, from corporate to divisional to individual units and departments. The performance measures combine the answers to four questions:

1. *How do we look to shareholders?* The financial perspective is composed of measures such as cash flow, sales and income growth, and return on equity.

2. *How do customers see us?* The customer perspective comprises measures such as goals for new products, on-time delivery, and defect and failure levels.

3. *What must we excel at?* The internal business perspective relates to internal business processes such as productivity, employee skills, cycle time, yield rates, and quality and cost measures.

4. *Can we continue to improve and create value?* The innovation and learning perspective includes measures related to new product development cycle times, technological leadership, and rates of improvement.

By balancing a set of strategic and financial goals, the scorecard methodology allows the strategy of the business to be linked with the creation of shareholder value while providing a set of measurable targets to guide this process. Thus, at machinery and chemicals conglomerate FMC, Kaplan and Norton report:

> Strategists came up with 5 and 10-year plans, controllers with one-year budgets and near-term forecasts. Little interplay occurred between the two groups. But the scorecard now bridges the two. The financial perspective builds on the traditional function performed by controllers. The other three perspectives make the division's long-term strategic objectives measurable.[25]

Mobil Corporation's North American Marketing and Refining business (NAM&R) was a pioneer of the balanced scorecard during the 1990s. Faced with pressures of unsatisfactory profit performance, the business adopted the scorecard methodology as a means of linking strategy with financial performance goals and translating these into operating objectives tailored to the specific performance requirements of individual business units and functional departments. The scorecard provided a mechanism for "cascading down" divisional strategy into specific operating goals. The result was an integrated system where scorecards provided the measurements by which the performance of each unit and department was appraised and against which performance-related pay bonuses were determined.[26] Figure 2.4 shows NAM&R's scorecard.

---

[25] R. Kaplan and D. Norton, "Putting the Balanced Scorecard to Work," *Harvard Business Review* (September–October 1993): 147.

[26] R. Kaplan and D. Norton, *The Strategy-focused Organization* (Boston: Harvard Business School Press, 2001): Chapter 2, "How Mobil Became a Strategy-focused Organization."

FIGURE 2.4 Balanced scorecard for Mobil North American Marketing and Refining

		Strategic Objectives	Strategic Measures
Financially Strong	Financial	F1 Return on Capital Employed F2 Cash Flow F3 Profitability F4 Lowest Cost F5 Profitable Growth F6 Manage risk	■ ROCE ■ Cash Flow ■ Net Margin ■ Full cost per gallon delivered to customer ■ Volume growth rate vs. industry ■ Risk index
Delight the Consumer **Win–Win Relationship**	Customer	C1 Continually delight the targeted consumer C2 Improve dealer/distributor profitability	■ Share of segment in key markets ■ Mystery shopper rating ■ Dealer/distributor margin on gasoline ■ Dealer/distributor survey

Safe and Reliable
 	
Competitive Supplier
 	
Good Neighbor
 	
On Spec
On time
	Internal	I1 Marketing
		  1. Innovative products and services
		  2. Dealer/distributor quality
		
		I2 Manufacturing
		  1. Lower manufacturing costs
		  2. Improve hardware and performance
		I3 Supply, Trading, Logistics
		  1. Reducing delivered cost
		  2. Trading organization
		  3. Inventory management
		
		I4 Improve health, safety, and environmental performance
		I5 Quality
			■ Non-gasoline revenue and margin per square foot
			■ Dealer/distributor acceptance rate of new programs
			■ Dealer/distributor quality ratings
			■ ROCE on refinery
			■ Total expenses (per gallon) vs. competition
			■ Profitability index
			■ Yield index
			Delivered cost per gallon vs. competitors
			■ Trading margin
			■ Inventory level compared to plan and to output rate
			■ Number of incidents
			■ Days away from work
			■ Quality index

Motivated and Prepared	Learning and growth	L1 Organization involvement L2 Core competencies and skills L3 Access to strategic information	■ Employee survey ■ Strategic competitive availability ■ Strategic information availability

VALUES, MISSION, AND VISION

There is more to business than making money. Profit maximization (shareholder value maximization, to be more precise) provides the foundation for strategy analysis, yet it is not the goal that inspired Henry Ford to build a business that profoundly changed twentieth-century lifestyles; nor is it the one that causes Bill Gates to continue working at Microsoft rather than retiring to enjoy his billions of dollars of personal wealth; nor does it provide such motivation or direction to the thousands of employees of both companies. Most successful companies are fired with a sense of purpose that extends well beyond the desire for wealth. Dennis Bakke, CEO of international electricity generating company AES, argues:

> Profits are to business as breathing is to life. Breathing is essential to life, but it not the purpose for living. Similarly, profits are essential for the existence of the corporation, but they are not the reason for its existence.

There are three concepts that have become highly influential in helping companies think about their identity, their purpose, and the fundamental features of their strategy. These are *values*, *mission*, and *vision*.

The Role of Values

All companies possess broader organizational values that are integral to their sense of who they are, what they represent, what they want to achieve, and how they intend to achieve it. These values constrain, augment, and may even transcend the fundamental requirement of profitability. Values such as providing opportunities for employees' development and self-realization, pursuing unmatched product quality, creating a safe working environment, and working for the improvement of the natural environment may constrain the pursuit of profitability, but they also play a vital role in building strategic intent and forming consensus and commitment within the organization. For example:

- The Royal Dutch/Shell Group has long been committed to a set of business principles based on core values of honesty, integrity, and respect for people, and the promotion of trust, openness, teamwork, professionalism, and pride. Shell argues that its values "mean we take pride in what we do . . . gives us clarity when making decisions, unifies and motivates staff, and allows society to measure our performance beyond the generation of wealth."

- At Body Shop, the enthusiasm and loyalty of customers and the zeal of employees and franchisees are nourished by the principles of environmental and social responsibility espoused by the founder Anita Roddick.

- The ability of McDonald's to sell 60 billion hamburgers in 86 countries and to generate vast profits for itself and its franchisees cannot be explained exclusively by a profit-driven strategy of low costs, standardization, and marketing. McDonald's is sustained by a philosophy that transcends social class and national culture and is enshrined in the principles of "quality, consistency, cleanliness, and value."

What we observe is that linking strategy to the broader pursuit of social and moral purpose may facilitate rather than impede profit performance over the long term. The values a firm embraces can assist in building relationships between the firm and others with whom it does business, can help build employee commitment and loyalty, and may offer the basis for differentiation. If human beings are ultimately concerned more with the pursuit of meaning in their lives than with material rewards, organizations that can help instill within their employees and customers a sense of purpose will have an advantage over those that do not.[27]

The Role of Mission and Vision

On its own, neither the goal of profit (or shareholder value) maximization nor the values to which the firm aspires can play much role in defining its strategy. The starting point for strategy is some underlying idea of why the business exists. The propensity for companies to articulate and disseminate statements of their vision and mission may be a recent trend, but some concept of business purpose underlies the creation of every new enterprise. What emerges is that the goals of the firm extend beyond the basic performance variables that the firm is pursuing: profit, growth, or the balanced interest of stakeholders. Though profit is the overriding performance objective of the firm, the goals of the firm typically embody a sense of overall purpose that directly shapes strategy and unifies the efforts of the many organizational members. This sense of purpose sometimes takes the form of a vision that motivates the founding of the company and sustains its development. Examples include Henry Ford's vision of a car for every family; Steve Jobs' vision of one person–one computer; Walt Disney's desire to provide family entertainment that enshrined the values of warmth, brotherhood, joy, and family unity; and at Southwest Airlines, Herb Kelleher's vision of opening air travel to a wider group of leisure travelers while infusing the whole organization with a sense of fun.

As we noted in our discussion of strategic intent in Chapter 1, a recognized sense of purpose provides a foundation for a company's strategy. A *mission statement* is a statement of a company's purpose. It typically comprises a statement of what the company is trying to achieve and very often defines, in broad terms, the business that it is in. If mission outlines what the company is attempting to achieve at the present time, its *vision* offers a view of what the enterprise might become. Bennis and Nanus describe vision as central to strategic leadership:

> To choose a direction, a leader must first have developed a mental image of a possible and desirable future state of the organization . . . which we call a vision. A vision articulates a view of a realistic, credible, attractive future for the orgnization . . . With a vision, the leader provides an all-important bridge from the present to the future.[28]

---

[27]   Abraham Maslow, "A Theory of Human Motivation," *Psychological Review* 50 (1943): 370–96, postulated that human beings have a hierarchy of needs, the highest being that of "self-actualization": the realization of one's distinctive psychological potential that goes beyond economic and social fulfillment.

[28]   W. Bennis and B. Nanus, *Leaders: The Strategies for Taking Charge* (New York: Harper and Row, 1985); quoted by G. Saloner, A. Shepard, and J. Poldolny, *Strategic Management* (New York: Wiley, 2000): 27.

Exhibit 2.2 reproduces AOL and Chevron Corporation's statements of mission and vision.

EXHIBIT 2.2   Statements of Mission and Vision: AOL and Chevron

---

America Online, Inc.

Mission Statement: To build a global medium as central to people's lives as the telephone or television . . . and even more valuable.

Vision Statement: To build an interactive medium that improves the lives of people and benefits society as no other medium before it.

Chevron: "The Chevron Way"

Mission: We are an international company providing energy and chemical products vital to the growth of the world's economies. Our mission is to create superior value for our stockholders, our customers, and our employees.

Vision: Our vision is to be Better than the Best, which means:
- Employees are proud of their success as a team
- Customers, suppliers, and government prefer us
- Competitors respect us
- Communities welcome us
- Investors are eager to invest in us

Our primary objective is to exceed the financial performance of our strongest competitors. Our goal is to be No. 1 among our competitors in total Stockholder Return for the period 1994–1998. We will balance long-term growth and short-term results in the pursuit of this objective.

Our approach to the business is based on:
- Committed team values
- Total quality management
- Protecting People and the Environment

We will be guided by the Strategic Intents in our Corporate Strategic Plan and will measure progress with the Vision Metrics.

Vision Metrics:

■ Superior Stockholder Return	*Metric*: Total Stockholder Return
■ Superior Financial Performance	*Metrics*: Return on Capital Employed
	Earnings Growth
■ Delighted Customers	*Metric*: Customer Satisfaction
■ Competitive Operating Advantage	*Metric*: Operating Expense per Barrel
■ Public Favorability	*Metric*: Public Favorability Index
■ Committed Team	*Metrics*: Worldwide Employee Survey Results
	Safety Performance

Sources: http://corp.aol.com/careers/2/aolinside/changing.html; *Chevron Corporation 1995 Annual Report*, 6.

SUMMARY

Chapter 1 established that strategy is about success and that a successful strategy is one that deploys a firm's resources and capabilities within its industry environment in order to achieve its goals. This raises the issue of what the goals of the firm are. The major assumption in this chapter is that the firm operates in the interests of its owners – its shareholders – through maximizing their wealth. This implies profit maximization, which, we have seen, raises some complex issues with regard to the meaning and measurement of profit, the relevant time period, and the appropriate rate of discount. Clarifying these issues is vital in setting targets for the firm and evaluating its performance.

The fundamental role of strategy analysis is in identifying and understanding the fundamental drivers of profitability (and hence shareholder value). Figure 2.5 shows the overall value metrics framework. Analyzing financial data to separate broad profitability measures into constituent financial and operational ratios can help us to identify the areas where profits and/or losses are being generated. Ultimately, however, we need to address the underlying value drivers. This requires careful analysis and deep insight into the economics of the industry and characteristics of the firm. This is the task of the remaining chapters in Part II.

FIGURE 2.5   A comprehensive value metrics framework

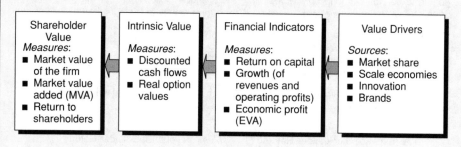

Despite our focus on the drivers of profit, we need to remember that understanding the goals of the firm is not simply proclaiming the supremacy of profit and shareholder value. Chapter 1 noted that the role of strategy is not only to access the sources of profit, it is also about communicating, coordinating, and motivating the organization. It is in these roles that values and vision are important. Whereas profit objectives relate to the material goals of a firm's owners, the quest for creativity, recognition, and making a difference in the world may be far more powerful motivating forces, not just for the entrepreneurs that start up new enterprises but for all who work in them.

While acknowledging the power of values and a sense of vision, we return to the theme of strategy as a quest for profit. Why give the values, vision, and mission such limited attention? Not because they are unimportant – as we have seen, they are likely to be fundamental in providing direction for strategy and building organizational purpose. The point here is that there is little left to say. Goals, values, and vision are not topics for analysis but for discovery. They need to be recognized, but once their leading role in shaping strategic direction is accepted, the firm still needs to acknowledge that it is unlikely to prosper on values alone. Given its values and purpose in the world, how does the firm survive and ensure a prosperous future? Hence, we proceed by exploring the drivers of firm profitability. Our next port of call is the industry environment of the firm.

3

Analyzing the Industry Environment

When a management with a reputation for brilliance tackles a business with a reputation for poor fundamental economics, it is the reputation of the business that remains intact.

—**Warren Buffett, Chairman,**
Berkshire Hathaway

The reinsurance business has the defect of being too attractive-looking to new entrants for its own good and will therefore always tend to be the opposite of, say, the old business of gathering and rendering dead horses that always tended to contain few and prosperous participants.

—**Charles T. Munger, Chairman,**
Wesco Financial Corp.

OUTLINE

- INTRODUCTION AND OBJECTIVES
- FROM ENVIRONMENTAL ANALYSIS TO INDUSTRY ANALYSIS
- THE DETERMINANTS OF INDUSTRY PROFIT: DEMAND AND COMPETITION
- ANALYZING INDUSTRY ATTRACTIVENESS
    Porter's Five Forces of Competition
       Framework
    Competition from Substitutes
    Threat of Entry
    Rivalry Between Established Competitors
    Bargaining Power of Buyers
    Bargaining Power of Suppliers

INTRODUCTION AND OBJECTIVES

In this chapter and the next we explore the external environment of the firm. In Chapter 1 we observed that profound understanding of the competitive environment is a critical ingredient of a successful strategy. We further noted that for business enterprises, strategy is essentially a quest for profit. The primary task for this chapter is to identify the sources of profit in the business environment.

The distinction between corporate-level and business-level strategy is relevant here. Corporate strategy is concerned with deciding which businesses the firm should be engaged in and with the allocation of corporate resources among them. To make such decisions, it is vital that the firm evaluates the attractiveness of different industries in terms of their potential to yield profit in the future. The main objective of this chapter is to analyze how competition determines industry profitability. Once the determinants of industry profitability are understood, it is possible to forecast the future profit potential of an industry.

Business strategy is concerned with establishing competitive advantage. Identifying the basis of and opportunities for competitive advantage requires an understanding of competition within the industry. It also requires that we understand customers, their needs and motivations, and the means by which these needs are satisfied.

By the time you have completed this chapter you will be able to:

- Identify the main structural features of an industry that influence competition and profitability.

- Use structural analysis to explain why in some industries competition is more intense and profitability lower than in other industries.

- Use evidence on structural trends within industries to forecast changes in competition and profitability in the future.

- Develop strategies to influence industry structure in order to improve industry profitability.

- Appreciate the roles of both competitive and cooperative behavior in seeking profit within an industry.

- Analyze competition and customer requirements in order to identify opportunities for competitive advantage within an industry.

FROM ENVIRONMENTAL ANALYSIS TO INDUSTRY ANALYSIS

The business environment of the firm consists of all the external influences that affect its decisions and performance. The problem here is that, given the vast number and range of external influences, how can managers hope to monitor, let alone analyze, environmental conditions? The starting point is some kind of system or framework for organizing information. For example, environmental influences can be classified by source into political, economic, social, and technological factors ("PEST analysis"); or by proximity: the "micro-environment" or "task environment" can be distinguished from the wider influences that form the "macro-environment."[1] Though systematic, continuous scanning of the whole range of external influences might seem desirable, such extensive environmental analysis is unlikely to be cost effective and creates information overload.

The prerequisite for effective environmental analysis is to distinguish the vital from the merely important. To do this, let's return to first principles. For the firm to make profit it must create value for customers. Hence, it must understand its customers. Second, in creating value, the firm acquires goods and services from suppliers. Hence, it must understand its suppliers and how to form business relationships with them. Third, the ability to generate profitability from value-creating activity depends on the intensity of competition among firms that vie for the same value-creating opportunities. Hence, the firm must understand competition. Thus, the core of the firm's business environment is formed by its relationships with customers, suppliers, and competitors. This is its industry environment.

This is not to say that macro-level factors such as general economic trends, changes in demographic structure, or social and political trends are unimportant to strategy analysis. These factors may be critical determinants of the threats and opportunities a company will face in the future. The key issue is how these more general environmental factors affect the firm's industry environment (Figure 3.1). For most firms, for example, global warming is not a critical issue. For the producers of automobiles, however, the implications of global warming for the use of fossil fuels and possible government measures to tax fuels and regulate automobile use mean that global

---

[1]   For a review of macroenvironmental ("PEST") analysis, see V. K. Narayanan and L. Fahey, "Macroenvironmental Analysis: Understanding the Environment Outside the Industry," in L. Fahey and R. M. Randall (eds), *The Portable MBA in Strategy*, 2nd edn (New York: Wiley, 2001): 189–214.

FIGURE 3.1   From environmental analysis to industry analysis

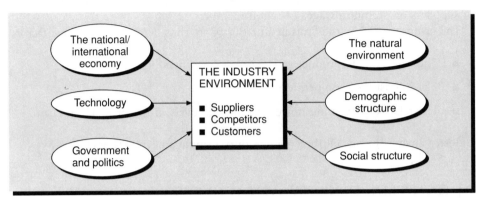

warming is a vital issue. However, in analyzing its potential impact, the task for the auto companies is to trace the possible implications of global warming on their industry environment, specifically the impact on customers and market demand, the impact on suppliers, and the impact on competition, not just among the existing auto companies, but also on potential entrants and the suppliers of substitutes such as public transport. By focusing on the industry environment, we can determine which macro-level influences are important for the firm and how they are likely to affect the firm's relations with customers, suppliers, and competitors.

THE DETERMINANTS OF INDUSTRY PROFIT: DEMAND AND COMPETITION

If the purpose of strategy is to help a company to survive and make money, the starting point for industry analysis is: What determines the level of profit in an industry?

As already noted, business is about the creation of value for the customer. Firms create value by production (transforming inputs into outputs) or arbitrage (transferring products across time and space). Value creation requires that the price the customer is willing to pay the firm exceed the costs incurred by the firm. But value creation does not translate directly into profit. The surplus of value over cost is distributed between customers and producers by the forces of competition. The stronger the competition among producers, the lower the price actually paid by customers compared with the maximum price they would have been willing to pay. In other words, the greater the proportion of the surplus gained by customers (consumer surplus), the less earned by producers (producer surplus or economic rent). A single supplier of bottled water at an all-night dance party can charge a price that fully exploits the dancers' thirst. If there are many suppliers of bottled water, then, in the absence of collusion, competition causes the price of bottled water to fall toward the cost of supplying it.

The surplus earned by producers over and above the minimum costs of production is not entirely captured in profits. Where an industry has powerful suppliers

– monopolistic suppliers of components or employees united by a strong labor union – a substantial part of the surplus may be appropriated by these suppliers (the profits of suppliers or premium wages of union members).

The profits earned by the firms in an industry are thus determined by three factors:

- The value of the product or service to customers.

- The intensity of competition.

- The relative bargaining power at different levels in the production chain.

Industry analysis brings all three factors into a single analytic framework.

ANALYZING INDUSTRY ATTRACTIVENESS

Table 3.1 shows the average rate of profit earned in different US industries. Some industries (such as tobacco and pharmaceuticals) consistently earn high rates of profit; others (such as iron and steel, nonferrous metals, airlines, and basic building materials) have failed to cover their cost of capital. As noted in the last chapter, accounting profits include both economic profit and the normal return on capital. Hence, Table 3.2 provides profit measures based on Economic Value Added. The

TABLE 3.1   The Profitability of US Industries Measured by Return on Equity, 1986–97

INDUSTRY	RETURN ON EQUITY (1985–97)
Pharmaceuticals	20.28%
Food and kindred products	14.76%
—of which Tobacco products	19.60%
Instruments and related products	11.26%
Electrical and electronic equipment	10.95%
Printing and publishing	10.59%
Rubber and misc. plastics products	10.70%
Fabricated metal products	9.87%
Aircraft, guided missiles, and parts	9.71%
Petroleum and coal products	9.58%
Retail trade corporations	8.86%
Paper and allied products	8.47%
Textile mill products	7.63%
Stone, glass and clay products	6.78%
Wholesale trade corporations	6.50%
Machinery, exc. electrical	5.98%
Nonferrous metals	5.65%
Motor vehicles and equipment	5.53%
Mining corporations	2.72%
Iron and steel	2.61%
Airlines	1.08%

Sources: Federal Trade Commission, Fortune 500.

Table 3.2 The Profitability of US Industries Measured by EVA, Valuation Ratio, and Return on Assets, 1986–97

INDUSTRY	EVA/CE	MV/CE	ROA
Tobacco	0.0936	3.2314	14.3979
Computer Software and Services	0.0590	4.0331	10.3530
Entertainment	0.0442	2.8240	8.4403
Personnel-Supply Services	0.0402	2.8095	–
Personal Care	0.0281	2.8700	8.005
Medical Products	0.0276	3.0987	9.5384
Food Processing	0.0251	1.7090	8.5306
Food Retailing	0.0248	1.9880	6.5234
IT Consulting Services	0.0206	2.7136	6.5260
Business Machine and Services	0.0149	2.0492	8.2812
Apparel	0.0106	2.0114	10.6866
Games and Toys	0.0083	2.3755	–
Packaging	0.0075	1.7197	4.9736
Drugs and Research	0.0065	3.3807	7.6439
Chemicals	0.0029	1.8195	7.9589
Beverages	0.0018	2.1688	5.5960
Eating Places	0.0014	2.3246	6.8867
Industrial Distribution	0.0012	2.5401	5.3783
Car Parts and Equipment	−0.0003	1.5767	4.5989
Textiles	−0.0012	1.9392	7.4093
Fashion Retailing	−0.0039	1.9829	9.2833
Food Distribution	−0.0056	2.3515	–
Building Materials	−0.0056	1.5521	5.6250
Drug Distribution	−0.0067	1.6614	5.5325
Metals	−0.0101	1.7447	–
Telephone Companies	−0.0124	1.3680	4.6181
Discount Retailing	−0.0126	1.7803	6.3501
Semiconductors and Components	−0.0126	2.0560	5.9906
Aluminum	−0.0128	1.4844	–
Pollution Control	−0.0140	1.7691	–
Paper and Products	−0.0149	1.2902	5.2342
Broadcasting and Publishing	−0.0149	1.8042	6.0059
Cars and Trucks	−0.0150	0.9473	2.1660
Healthcare Services	−0.0169	2.4681	3.2672
Machine and Hand Tools	−0.0174	1.4356	6.0154
Appliances and Home Furnishing	−0.0191	1.5416	5.8016
Transportation Services	−0.0195	1.5836	3.1847
Printing and Advertising	−0.0196	1.5565	2.3386
Telephone Equipment and Services	−0.0206	2.0647	7.0432
Plastics and Products	−0.0261	1.8394	5.3089
General Engineering	−0.0303	1.7353	5.1617
Computers and Peripherals	−0.0306	1.7332	3.1143
Electrical Products	−0.0327	1.3056	4.6276
Aerospace and Defense	−0.0331	1.3982	4.8390
Railroads	−0.0340	1.0257	3.7780
Hotel and Motel	−0.0362	0.5391	–
Machinery	−0.0406	1.0974	–
Instruments	−0.0415	1.5443	5.1271
Airlines	−0.0416	1.1676	0.9866

TABLE 3.2 *(cont'd)*

INDUSTRY	EVA/CE	MV/CE	ROA
Construction and Engineering	−0.0458	1.6749	–
Oil and Gas	−0.0461	1.3604	2.5455
Steel	−0.0647	1.2967	2.2646
Cable Television	−0.0720	1.6966	−3.2513
Electronics	−0.0921	1.6542	3.4505
Petroleum Services	−0.0980	1.7189	−0.5861
Mean (all industries)	*−0.0110*	*1.8930*	*5.5989*
Standard Deviation	*0.0335*	*0.6550*	*3.0364*

Notes:
1. EVA/CE measures the ratio of Economic Value Added (as estimated by Stern Stewart) to capital employed for the companies in each industry.
2. MVA/CE meures the ratio of market value of equity and debt to capital employed for the companies in each industry.
3. ROA measures the percentage of net income to total assets for each industry.
Source: Gabriel Hawawini, Venkat Subramanian, and Paul Verdin, "Is Firms' Profitability Driven by Industry or Firm-Specific Factors? A New Look at the Evidence," paper presented to the Strategic Management Society Conference (Vancouver, October 2000).

basic premise that underlies industry analysis is that the level of industry profitability is neither random nor the result of entirely industry-specific influences, but is determined, in part at least, by the systematic influence of industry structure. As an example of how an attractively structured industry can support superior profitability, consider the cases of the sausage skin manufacturer, Devro, and tobacco products supplier, UST (see Exhibit 3.1).

The underlying theory of how industry structure drives competitive behavior and determines industry profitability is provided by industrial organization (IO) economics. The two reference points are the theory of monopoly and the theory of perfect competition, which represent the two ends of a spectrum of industry structures. A single firm protected by barriers to the entry of new firms forms a monopoly in which it can appropriate in profit the full amount of the value it creates. By contrast, many firms supplying an identical product with no restrictions on entry or exit constitutes perfect competition: the rate of profit falls to a level that just covers firms' cost of capital. In the real world, industries fall between these two extremes. The US market for chewing tobacco is close to being a monopoly; the Chicago grain markets are close to being perfectly competitive. Most manufacturing industries and many service industries tend to be oligopolies: they are dominated by a small number of major companies. Table 3.3 identifies some key points on the spectrum. By examining the principal structural features and their interactions for any particular industry, it is possible to predict the type of competitive behavior likely to emerge and the resulting level of profitability.

EXHIBIT 3.1   Sausage Skins and Chewing Tobacco: In Praise of Niche Markets

Devro International plc is a Scottish company with headquarters in the village of Moodiesburn, near Glasgow. With plants in Scotland, Belgium, the Czech Republic, Australia, and the United States, Devro holds over 60 percent of the world market for collagen sausage skins. The company was listed on the London Stock Exchange in 1993, two years after a management buyout from its parent, Johnson & Johnson. During the 1990s operating profits averaged 20 percent of sales revenue. Devro holds 94 percent of the UK market, 83 percent of the Australian market, and 40 percent of the US market. Although collagen casings are a substitute for natural gut sausage casings, collagen possesses some clear advantages that have resulted in the steady displacement of natural gut. Scale economies, technology, and Devro's absolute cost advantages pose substantial barriers to would-be entrants. Because casings account for only a small proportion of a sausage manufacturer's total costs, these companies are relatively insensitive to the price of casings and do not exert substantial bargaining power.

UST Inc. (formerly US Tobacco) has the distinction of earning the highest return on equity of any company in the Fortune 500 listings (over 100 percent over the period 1995–99). UST dominates the US market for "smokeless tobacco" (chewing tobacco and snuff), with a market share of 78 percent (in a range of brands including Skoal, Copenhagen, Long Cut, and Red Seal). Despite its association with a bygone era of cowboys and rural poverty, chewing tobacco has been a growth market over the past two decades with a surprisingly large number of young consumers. UST's long-established brands, its distribution through tens of thousands of small retail outlets, and the unwillingness of major tobacco companies to enter this market (due to the poor image and social unacceptability of the product) have supported the company's unassailable market position. Federal controls on the advertising of smokeless tobacco products introduced in 1986 have buttressed UST's market position by limiting the opportunities for would-be entrants to market their products.

Sources: James Buxton, "A Leaner Business that Has More Bite," *Financial Times* (April 16, 1993): 33; www.devro.plc.uk; Standard & Poor's Stock Reports.

TABLE 3.3   The Spectrum of Industry Structures

	Perfect Competition	Oligopoly	Duopoly	Monopoly
Concentration	Many firms	A few firms	Two firms	One firm
Entry and Exit Barriers	No barriers	Significant barriers		High barriers
Product Differentiation	Homogeneous product	Potential for product differentiation		
Information	Perfect information flow	Imperfect availability of information		

Porter's Five Forces of Competition Framework

Table 3.3 identifies four structural variables influencing competition and profitability. In practice, there are many features of an industry that determine the intensity

FIGURE 3.2 Porter's Five Forces of Competition Framework

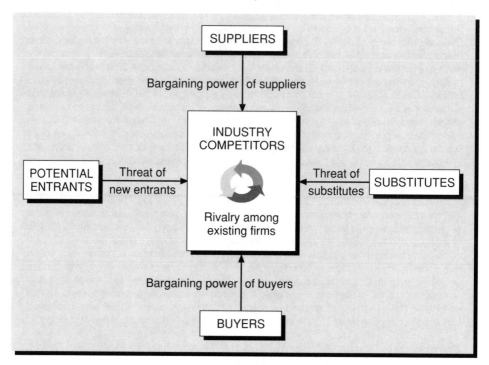

of competition and the level of profitability. A helpful, widely used framework for classifying and analyzing these factors is the one developed by Michael Porter of Harvard Business School.[2] Porter's Five Forces of Competition framework views the profitability of an industry (as indicated by its rate of return on capital relative to its cost of capital) as determined by five sources of competitive pressure. These five forces of competition include three sources of "horizontal" competition: competition from substitutes, competition from entrants, and competition from established rivals; and two sources of "vertical" competition: the bargaining power of suppliers and buyers (see Figure 3.2).

The strength of each of these competitive forces is determined by a number of key structural variables, as shown in Figure 3.3.

Competition from Substitutes

The price customers are willing to pay for a product depends, in part, on the availability of substitute products. The absence of close substitutes for a product, as in

---

[2] Michael E. Porter, *Competitive Strategy: Techniques for Analyzing Industries and Competitors* (New York: Free Press, 1980): Chapter 1. For a summary, see his article, "How Competitive Forces Shape Strategy," *Harvard Business Review* 57 (March–April 1979): 86–93.

FIGURE 3.3 The structural determinants of the Five Forces of Competition

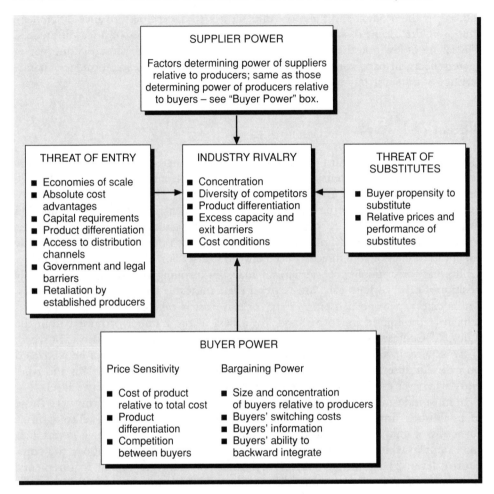

the case of gasoline or cigarettes, means that consumers are comparatively insensitive to price, i.e., demand is inelastic with respect to price. The existence of close substitutes means that customers will switch to substitutes in response to price increases for the product, i.e., demand is elastic with respect to price. During the past decade, express delivery companies such as Federal Express, DHL, and UPS have faced increasing substitute competition from alternative document transfer media, including e-mail and fax machines. Substitute competition has caused margins to narrow in the express document delivery industry and encouraged companies to seek growth in distributing goods for manufacturers and online retailers.

The extent to which substitutes limit prices and profits depends on the propensity of buyers to substitute between alternatives. This, in turn, is dependent on their price–performance characteristics. If city-center to city-center travel between Washington and New York is 90 minutes quicker by air than by train and the average traveler values time at $30 an hour, the implication is that the train will be competitive at fares of $45 below those charged by the airlines. The more complex the needs being fulfilled by the product and the more difficult it is to discern performance differences, the lower the extent of substitution by customers on the basis of price differences. The failure of low-priced imitations of leading perfumes to establish significant market share reflects, in part, consumers' difficulty in recognizing the performance characteristics of different fragrances.

Threat of Entry

If an industry earns a return on capital in excess of its cost of capital, that industry acts as a magnet to firms outside the industry. Unless the entry of new firms is barred, the rate of profit will fall toward its competitive level. The US bagel industry, for example, faced a flood of new entrants in 1996, which caused a sharp diminution of profit prospects.[3] The threat of entry rather than actual entry may be sufficient to ensure that established firms constrain their prices to the competitive level. Only American Airlines offers a direct service between Dallas/Fort Worth and Santa Barbara, California, for example. Yet, American may be unwilling to exploit its monopoly position if other airlines can easily extend their routes to cover the same two cities. An industry where no barriers to entry or exit exist is *contestable*: prices and profits remain at the fully competitive level, regardless of the number of firms within the industry.[4] Contestability depends on the absence of sunk costs. Sunk costs exist where entry requires investment in industry-specific assets whose value cannot be recovered on exit. An absence of sunk costs makes an industry vulnerable to "hit-and-run" entry whenever established firms raise their prices above the competitive level.

In most industries, however, new entrants cannot enter on equal terms with those of established firms. The size of the advantage of established over entrant firms (in terms of unit costs) measures the height of barriers to entry, which determines the extent to which the industry can, in the long run, enjoy profit above the competitive level. The principal sources of barriers to entry are capital requirements, economies of scale, cost advantages, product differentiation, access to channels of distribution, governmental and legal barriers, and retaliation.

Capital Requirements

The capital costs of getting established in an industry can be so large as to discourage all but the largest companies. The duopoly of Boeing and Airbus in large passenger

---

[3] The *Wall Street Journal* ("For Bagel Chains, Investment May Be Money in the Hole," December 30, 1997: B8) reported that the influx of new bagel chains, including Einstein/Noah Bagel Corp., Manhattan Bagel, BAB Holdings (Big Apple Bagels), Uncle B's Bakery, Bruegger's Bagel, Big City Bagels, and a host of others, resulted in widespread losses as prices were cut and margins fell.

[4] W. J. Baumol, John C. Panzar, and Robert D. Willig, *Contestable Markets and the Theory of Industry Structure* (New York: Harcourt Brace Jovanovitch, 1982). See also Michael Spence, "Contestable Markets and the Theory of Industry Structure: A Review Article," *Journal of Economic Literature* 21 (September 1983): 981–90.

jets is protected by the prohibitive costs of establishing such a venture. In satellite television broadcasting in Britain, Rupert Murdoch's Sky TV incurred almost $1 billion in capital costs and operating losses and Robert Maxwell's British Satellite Broadcasting spent some $1.8 billion before the two merged in 1991. In other industries, entry costs can be modest. Startup costs for franchised fast-food restaurants are around $350,000 for a Wendy's and close to $1 million for a Burger King.[5]

Economies of Scale

In industries that are capital or research or advertising intensive, efficiency requires large-scale operation. The problem for new entrants is that they are faced with the choice of either entering on a small scale and accepting high unit costs, or entering on a large scale and running the risk of drastic underutilization of capacity while they build up sales volume. In automobiles, it is generally reckoned that to be a low-cost producer, sales of over four million vehicles a year are necessary. These economies of scale have deterred entry into the industry so that the only recent entrants have either been state-supported companies (e.g., Proton of Malaysia and Maruti of India) or companies that have gambled that low labor and material costs would offset their scale inefficiency (e.g., Samsung and Ssangyong of Korea, both of which had exited by mid-2000). In aerospace, the costs of developing a new passenger jet are so great that a company can only cover these costs by obtaining a major share of world orders. Airbus's proposed A380 superjumbo will cost an estimated $12–16 billion, requiring sales of over 800 planes to break even. The economics of the business mean that new entry into large commercial jets is unthinkable.

Absolute Cost Advantages

Apart from economies of scale, established firms may have a cost advantage over entrants simply because they entered earlier. Absolute cost advantages tend to be associated with the acquisition of low-cost sources of raw materials or economies of learning.

Product Differentiation

In an industry where products are differentiated, established firms possess the advantages of brand recognition and customer loyalty. The percentage of US consumers loyal to a single brand varies from under 30 percent in batteries, canned vegetables, and garbage bags, up to 61 percent in toothpaste, 65 percent in mayonnaise, and 71 percent in cigarettes.[6] New entrants to such markets must spend disproportionately heavily on advertising and promotion to gain levels of brand awareness and brand goodwill similar to that of established companies. One study found that, compared to early entrants, late entrants into consumer goods markets incurred additional

---

[5] "Annual Franchise 500," *Entrepreneur* (January 1999).
[6] "Brand Loyalty Is Rarely Blind Loyalty," *Wall Street Journal* (October 19, 1989): B1.

advertising and promotional costs amounting to 2.12 percent of sales revenue.[7] Alternatively, the new entrant can accept a niche position in the market or can seek to compete by cutting price.

Access to Channels of Distribution

Whereas lack of brand awareness among consumers acts as a barrier to entry to new suppliers of consumer goods, a more immediate barrier for the new company is likely to be gaining distribution. Limited capacity within distribution channels (e.g., shelf space), risk aversion by retailers, and the fixed costs associated with carrying an additional product result in retailers being reluctant to carry a new manufacturer's product. The battle for supermarket shelf space between the major food processors (typically involving lump-sum payments to retail chains in order to reserve shelf space) means that new entrants scarcely get a look in.

Governmental and Legal Barriers

Some economists (notably those of the Chicago School) claim that the only effective barriers to entry are those created by government. In taxicabs, banking, telecommunications, and broadcasting, entry usually requires the granting of a license by a public authority. In knowledge-intensive industries, patents, copyrights, and trade secrets are major barriers to entry. Xerox Corporation's near-monopoly position in the world plain-paper copier business until the mid-1970s was protected by a wall of over 2,000 patents relating to its xerography process. Regulatory requirements and environmental and safety standards often put new entrants at a disadvantage to established firms, because compliance costs tend to weigh more heavily on newcomers.

Retaliation

The effectiveness of barriers to entry also depends on the entrants' expectations as to possible retaliation by established firms. Retaliation against a new entrant may take the form of aggressive price cutting, increased advertising, sales promotion, or litigation. The airline industry has a long history of retaliation against low-cost entrants. Laker Air, one of the first cut-price transatlantic airlines, was ultimately driven out of business by established airlines' aggressive price cutting. British Airways launched a "dirty tricks" campaign against Virgin Atlantic that included accessing Virgin's computer system and poaching its customers. Southwest has alleged that selective price cuts by American and other major airlines amounted to predatory pricing designed to prevent its entry into new routes.[8] The likelihood of retaliation is influenced by the scale of entry. When Japanese firms first entered the US car and consumer electronics

---

[7] Robert D. Buzzell and Paul W. Farris, "Marketing Costs in Consumer Goods Industries," in Hans Thorelli (ed.), *Strategy + Structure = Performance* (Bloomington, IN: Indiana University Press, 1977): 128–9.
[8] "U.S. Probes Whether Airlines Colluded on Fare Increases," *Wall Street Journal* (December 14, 1989): B1; "A Tank Full of Trouble," *Economist* (December 16–22, 1989): 57.

markets, they sought to avoid retaliation by introducing small products in segments that were deemed unprofitable by US producers. A successful retaliatory strategy is one that deters entry by using a threat that is credible enough to intimidate would-be entrants.[9]

The Effectiveness of Barriers to Entry

Studies by Bain[10] and Mann[11] found that profitability was higher in industries with "very high entry barriers" than in those with "substantial" or "moderate to low" barriers. Capital intensity and advertising are key variables that increase entry barriers and raise industry profitability.[12]

Whether barriers to entry are effective in deterring potential entrants depends on the resources of those potential entrants. Barriers that are effective for new companies may be ineffective for firms that are diversifying from other industries. George Yip found no evidence that entry barriers deterred new entry.[13] His research showed that entrants were able successfully to overcome entry barriers for one of two reasons. Some possessed resources and capabilities that permitted them to surmount barriers and compete against incumbent firms using similar strategies. Mars used its strong position in confectionery to enter the ice cream market.[14] Virgin has used its brand name to enter a wide range of industries from airlines to telecommunications. Other companies circumvented entry barriers through innovative strategies, different than those of incumbent firms.[15] Dell Computer's business model based on direct sales and telephone support by-passed the barrier to entry posed by established distribution channels.

Rivalry between Established Competitors

For most industries, the major determinant of the overall state of competition and the general level of profitability is competition among the firms within the industry. In some industries, firms compete aggressively – sometimes to the extent that prices are pushed below the level of costs and industry-wide losses are incurred. In others, price competition is muted and rivalry focuses on advertising, innovation,

[9] Martin B. Lieberman, "Excess Capacity as a Barrier to Entry," *Journal of Industrial Economics* 35 (June 1987): 607–27, argues that to be credible the threat of retaliation needs to be supported by excess capacity.

[10] J. S. Bain, *Barriers to New Competition* (Cambridge, MA: Harvard University Press, 1956).

[11] H. Michael Mann, "Seller Concentration, Entry Barriers, and Rates of Return in Thirty Industries," *Review of Economics and Statistics* 48 (1966): 296–307.

[12] See, for example, the studies by W. S. Comanor and T. A. Wilson, *Advertising and Market Power* (Cambridge: Harvard University Press, 1974); and L. Weiss, "Quantitative Studies in Industrial Organization," in M. Intriligator (ed.), *Frontiers of Quantitative Economics* (Amsterdam: North Holland, 1971).

[13] George S. Yip, "Gateways to Entry," *Harvard Business Review* 60 (September–October 1982): 85–93.

[14] Guy de Jonquieres, "Europe's New Cold Warriors," *Financial Times* (May 19, 1993): 18.

[15] R. M. Grant, "Richard Branson and the Virgin Group of Companies," in R. M. Grant, *Cases in Contemporary Strategy Analysis*, 3rd edn (Oxford: Blackwell, 2002).

and other nonprice dimensions. Six factors play an important role in determining the nature and intensity of competition between established firms: concentration, the diversity of competitors, product differentiation, excess capacity, exit barriers, and cost conditions.

Concentration

Seller concentration refers to the number and size distribution of firms competing within a market. It is most commonly measured by the concentration ratio: the combined market share of the leading producers. For example, the four-firm concentration ratio (conventionally denoted "CR4") is the market share of the four largest producers. A market dominated by a single firm, e.g., Microsoft in PC operating systems, or UST in the US smokeless tobacco market, displays little competition and the dominant firm can exercise considerable discretion over the prices it charges. Where a market is dominated by a small group of leading companies (an oligopoly), price competition may also be restrained, either by outright collusion, or more commonly through "parallelism" of pricing decisions.[16] Thus, in markets dominated by two companies, such as alkaline batteries (Duracell and Eveready), color film (Kodak and Fuji), and soft drinks (Coke and Pepsi), prices tend to be similar and competition focuses on advertising, promotion, and product development. As the number of firms supplying a market increases, coordination of prices becomes more difficult, and the likelihood that one firm will initiate price cutting increases. However, the effect of seller concentration on profitability has been hard to pin down empirically. Richard Schmalensee concluded that: "The relation, if any, between seller concentration and profitability is weak statistically and the estimated effect is usually small."[17]

Diversity of Competitors

The ability of firms in an industry to avoid price competition also depends on their similarities in terms of origins, objectives, costs, and strategies. The cozy atmosphere of the US auto industry prior to the advent of import competition was greatly assisted by the similarities of the companies in terms of cost structures, strategies, and top management mindsets. The intense competition of the past two decades is partly due to the fact that there are more companies competing in the US market, but also because these companies have different national origins, costs, strategies, and management styles. Similarly, the difficulties of OPEC in agreeing and enforcing oil prices and output quotas are increased by differences among member countries in objectives, costs, politics, and religion.

---

[16] F. M. Scherer and D. R. Ross, *Industrial Market Structure and Economic Performance*, 3rd edn (Boston: Houghton Mifflin, 1990); R. M. Grant, "Pricing Behavior in the UK Wholesale Market for Petrol. A 'Structure-Conduct Analysis'," *Journal of Industrial Economics* 30 (March 1982).
[17] Richard Schmalensee, "Inter-Industry Studies of Structure and Performance," in Richard Schmalensee and Robert D. Willig, *Handbook of Industrial Organization*, 2nd edn (Amsterdam: North Holland, 1988): 976. For evidence on the impact of concentration in banking, airlines, and railroads, see D. W. Carlton and J. M. Perloff, *Modern Industrial Organization* (Glenview, IL: Scott, Foresman, 1990): 383–5.

Product Differentiation

The more similar the offerings among rival firms, the more willing customers are to substitute and the greater the incentive for firms to cut prices to increase sales. Where the products of rival firms are virtually indistinguishable, the product is a commodity and price is the sole basis for competition. Commodity industries such as agriculture, mining, and petrochemicals tend to be plagued by price wars and low profits. By contrast, in industries where products are highly differentiated (perfumes, pharmaceuticals, restaurants, management consulting services), price competition tends to be weak, even though there may be many firms competing.

Excess Capacity and Exit Barriers

Why does industry profitability tend to fall so drastically during periods of recession? The key is the balance between demand and capacity. Unused capacity encourages firms to offer price cuts to attract new business in order to spread fixed costs over a greater sales volume. Excess capacity may be cyclical (e.g., the boom–bust cycle in the semiconductor industry); it may also be part of a structural problem resulting from overinvestment and declining demand. In these latter situations, the key issue is whether excess capacity will leave the industry. Barriers to exit are costs associated with capacity leaving an industry. Where resources are durable and specialized, and where employees are entitled to job protection, barriers to exit may be substantial.[18] Exit barriers in the European oil refining industry resulting from the high costs of dismantling refineries, environmental cleanup, and employee layoffs have resulted in a continuing overhang of excess capacity that has kept profits at a very low level. Conversely, rapid demand growth creates capacity shortages that boost margins, though cash flows can be negative due to high rates of investment (see Figure 3.4).

Cost Conditions: Scale Economies and the Ratio of Fixed to Variable Costs

When excess capacity causes price competition, how low will prices go? The key factor is cost structure. Where fixed costs are high relative to variable costs, firms will take on marginal business at any price that covers variable costs. The consequences for profitability can be disastrous. From 1990 to 1995, the total losses of the US airline industry exceeded total profits during the previous three decades. The willingness of airlines to offer heavily discounted tickets on flights with low bookings reflects the very low variable costs of filling empty seats. The devastating impact of excess capacity on profitability in petrochemicals, tires, steel, and memory chips is a result of high fixed costs in these businesses and the willingness of firms to accept additional business at any price that covers variable costs.

---

[18]   The problems caused by excess capacity and exit barriers are discussed in Charles Baden-Fuller (ed.), *Strategic Management of Excess Capacity* (Oxford: Basil Blackwell, 1990).

FIGURE 3.4 The impact of growth on profitability

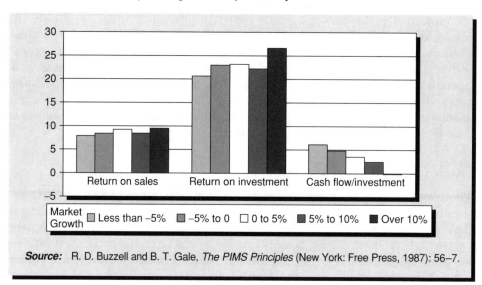

Source: R. D. Buzzell and B. T. Gale, *The PIMS Principles* (New York: Free Press, 1987): 56–7.

Scale economies may also encourage companies to compete aggressively on price in order to gain the cost benefits of greater volume. If scale efficiency in the auto industry means producing four million cars a year, a level that is achieved by only six of the nineteen international auto companies, the implication is that industry will see a battle for market share as each firm tries to achieve critical mass.[19]

Bargaining Power of Buyers

The firms in an industry operate in two types of markets: in the markets for inputs and the market for outputs. In input markets firms purchase raw materials, components, and financial and labor services. In the markets for outputs firms sell their goods and services to customers (who may be distributors, consumers, or other manufacturers). In both markets the transactions create value for both parties to the transaction. How this value is shared between them in terms of profitability depends on their relative economic power. Let us deal first with output markets. The strength of buying power that firms face from their customers depends on two sets of factors: buyers' price sensitivity and relative bargaining power.

Buyers' Price Sensitivity

The extent to which buyers are sensitive to the prices charged by the firms in an industry depends on four main factors:

[19] R. M. Grant, "Daimler Chrysler and the World Automobile Industry," in R. M. Grant, *Cases in Contemporary Strategy Analysis,* 3rd edn (Oxford: Blackwell, 2002).

- The greater the importance of an item as a proportion of total cost, the more sensitive buyers will be about the price they pay. Beverage manufacturers are highly sensitive to the costs of metal cans because this is one of their largest single cost items. Conversely, most companies are not sensitive to the fees charged by their auditors, since auditing costs are such a small proportion of overall company expenses.

- The less differentiated the products of the supplying industry, the more willing the buyer is to switch suppliers on the basis of price. The manufacturers of T-shirts, lightbulbs, and blank videotapes have much more to fear from Wal-Mart's buying power than have the suppliers of perfumes.

- The more intense the competition among buyers, the greater their eagerness for price reductions from their sellers. As competition in the world automobile industry has intensified, so component suppliers are subject to greater pressures for lower prices, higher quality, and faster delivery.

- The greater the importance of the industry's product to the quality of the buyer's product or service, the less sensitive are buyers to the prices they are charged. The buying power of personal computer manufacturers relative to the manufacturers of microprocessors (Intel, Motorola, Advanced Micro Devices) is limited by the critical importance of these components to the functionality of their product.

Relative Bargaining Power

Bargaining power rests, ultimately, on refusal to deal with the other party. The balance of power between the two parties to a transaction depends on the credibility and effectiveness with which each makes this threat. The key issue is the relative cost that each party sustains as a result of the transaction not being consummated. A second issue is each party's expertise in leveraging its position through gamesmanship. Several factors influence the bargaining power of buyers relative to that of sellers:

- Size and concentration of buyers relative to suppliers. The smaller the number of buyers and the bigger their purchases, the greater the cost of losing one. Because of their size, health maintenance organizations (HMOs) can purchase health care from hospitals and doctors at much lower cost than can individual patients.

- Buyers' information. The better informed buyers are about suppliers and their prices and costs, the better they are able to bargain. Doctors and lawyers do not normally display the prices they charge, nor do traders in the bazaars of Tangier and Istanbul. Keeping customers ignorant of relative prices is an effective constraint on their buying power. But knowing prices is of little value if the quality of the product is unknown. In the markets for haircuts, interior design, and management consulting, the ability of buyers to bargain over price is limited by uncertainty over the precise attributes of the product they are buying.

■ Ability to integrate vertically. In refusing to deal with the other party, the alternative to finding another supplier or buyer is to do it yourself. Large food-processing companies such as Heinz and Campbell Soup have reduced their dependence on the manufacturers of metal cans by manufacturing their own. The leading retail chains have increasingly displaced their suppliers' brands with their own-brand products. Backward integration need not necessarily occur – a credible threat may suffice.

Empirical evidence points to the tendency for buyer concentration to depress prices and profits in supplying industries.[20] PIMS data show that the larger the average size of customers' purchases and the larger the proportion of customers' total purchases the item represents, the lower the profitability of supplying firms.[21]

Bargaining Power of Suppliers

Analysis of the determinants of relative power between the producers in an industry and their suppliers is precisely analogous to analysis of the relationship between producers and their buyers. The only difference is that it is now the firms in the industry that are the buyers and the producers of inputs that are the suppliers. The key issues are the ease with which the firms in the industry can switch between different input suppliers and the relative bargaining power of each party.

Because raw materials, semi-finished products, and components are often commodities supplied by small companies to large manufacturing companies, their suppliers usually lack bargaining power. Hence, commodity suppliers often seek to boost their bargaining power through cartelization, e.g., OPEC, the International Coffee Organization, and farmers' marketing cooperatives. A similar logic explains labor unions. However, the suppliers of complex, technically sophisticated components may be able to exert considerable bargaining paper. The supplier power of Intel in microprocessors, Microsoft in operating systems, Sharp in flat screens, and Seagate in disk drives has been a powerful factor depressing the profitability of the PC manufacturers. Forward integration by suppliers into a customer industry increases their supplier power and depresses profitability in the customer industry.[22]

A common source of supplier power is labor unions. Where is an industry has a high percentage of its employees unionized, its profitability is reduced (see Table 3.4).

[20] S. H. Lustgarten, "The Impact of Buyer Concentration in Manufacturing Industries," *Review of Economics and Statistics* 57 (1975): 125–32; and Robert M. Grant, "Manufacturer-Retailer Relations: The Shifting Balance of Power," in G. Johnson (ed.), *Business Strategy and Retailing* (Chichester: John Wiley, 1987).

[21] Robert D. Buzzell and Bradley T. Gale, *The PIMS Principles: Linking Strategy to Performance* (New York: Free Press, 1987): 64–5.

[22] Ibid.

TABLE 3.4 The Impact of Unionization on Profitability

		PERCENTAGE OF EMPLOYEES UNIONIZED			
	none	1 to 35%	35 to 60%	60 to 75%	over 75%
ROI (%)	25	24	23	18	19
ROS (%)	10.8	9.0	9.0	7.9	7.9

Source: R. D. Buzzell and B. T. Gale, *The PIMS Principles: Linking Strategy to Performance* (New York: Free Press, 1987): 67.

APPLYING INDUSTRY ANALYSIS

Once we understand how industry structure drives competition, which, in turn, determines industry profitability, we can apply this analysis, first to forecasting industry profitability in the future, and second to devising strategies for changing industry structure.

Forecasting Industry Profitability

Decisions to commit resources to a particular industry must be based on anticipated returns five to ten years in the future. Over these periods, profitability cannot be accurately forecast by projecting current industry profitability. However, we can predict changes in the underlying structure of an industry with some accuracy. Structural changes are driven by current changes in product and process technology, the current strategies of the leading players, the changes occurring in infrastructure and in related industries, and government policies. If we understand how industry structure affects competition and profitability, we can use our projections of structural change to forecast the likely changes in competition and profitability.

The first stage is to understand how past changes in industry structure have influenced competition and profitability. The next stage is to identify current structural trends and determine how these will affect the five forces of competition and resulting industry profitability. Exhibit 3.2 considers how the changing structure of the US casino gambling industry is likely to influence competition and profitability in the industry. A key issue in all attempts to forecast the future of competition and profitability in an industry is that some structural changes are likely to be beneficial to profitability, while others depress profitability. Thus, a key issue in the casino industry is whether the current merger wave will offset the tendency for increasing excess capacity to depress profitability. Determining the net effect of conflicting forces is a matter of judgment.

EXHIBIT 3.2 Prospects for the US Casino Industry

The 1990s were a period of rapid development for the US casino gambling industry. The perception of the industry as a gold mine was shared not just by the existing casino operators, but also by municipalities, states, and entertainment companies. The result was unprecedented expansion.

In terms of new entry, casino gambling expanded well beyond its traditional centers in Las Vegas, Nevada, and Atlantic City, NJ. The municipalities and state governments saw gambling as offering new tax revenue sources and economic development opportunities. The result was the introduction of riverboat casinos and the licensing of casinos in Mississippi and seven other states (in addition to Nevada and New Jersey). The 1988 Indian Gaming Regulatory Act opened the way for casinos on Indian reservations. By early 2000 there were 100 casinos on Indian reservations across 17 states. One of the biggest was Foxwood's, owned by the Mashantucket Pequot tribe in Ledyard, CT. During 2000, the relaxation of gambling restrictions on the Indian reservations in California encouraged a new wave of casino projects.

The period 1996–2000 saw a battle among the major casino companies to build the "biggest and best" hotel/casino complexes in Las Vegas and Atlantic City. Between 1996 and 2000, the number of hotel rooms at Las Vegas casinos doubled. New "mega-casinos" in Vegas included the $390 million Luxor, the $450 million Treasure Island, the $1 billion MGM Grand resort, the $1.6 billion Bellagio, the $1.4 billion New York, and the 6000-room, $1.5 billion Venetian Hotel. Personal rivalry between Donald Trump and Mirage Resorts' Steve Wynn helped fuel capacity expansion in Atlantic City, where the impact of excess capacity was exacerbated by the high fixed costs of operating casinos.

Competition between casino companies involved ever more ambitious differentiation. The new casinos in Las Vegas broke fresh ground in spectacle, entertainment, theming, and sheer scale. Price competition was also evident in terms of subsidized travel packages, free rooms and other perks for "high rollers."

Growing substitute competition included an increasing number of state lotteries, offshore gambling on cruiseships, the installation of slot machines at horsetracks, and, most significantly, the growth of internet gambling.

Increasing competition encouraged increasing industry concentration. The consolidation wave of the mid and late 1990s saw the emergence of a small number of major hotel/casino chains. Hilton Hotels acquired Bally Entertainment, Sharwoods acquired ITT's Sheraton chain (which included Caesar's Palace). Mirage Resorts, Circus Circus, and MGM Grand all acquired smaller players. Consolidation was facilitated by the desire of the many hotel/casino chains to split their hotel and casino operations. Park Place entertainment was formed from the casino activities of Hilton Hotel and Starwood Hotels and Resorts sold off its casinos. During the early months of 2000, consolidation accelerated. MGM Grand acquired Mirage Resorts to create the second largest gaming company in the US behind Park Place Entertainment.

The impact of new entry, excess capacity, and substitute competition upon industry margins depends on the extent to which new supply will create its own demand and the ability of the industry leaders to keep their instincts for aggressive competition under control. During the 1990s increased demand for gambling was able to absorb the rapid increase in casino capacity and the growth in alternative gambling media. Total US gambling revenues rose from $124 billion in 1982, to $304 billion in 1991, $509 billion in 1996, and over $700 billion in 1999. Nevertheless, as the data below show, industry profitability remained low.

	Average profit ratios, 1995–99 (%)	
	Return on Equity	Operating Profit/Sales
Park Place Entertainment	2.5	11.5
MGM Grand	9.1	21.1
Hurrah's Entertainment	15.4	14.3
Mirage Resorts	12.0	17.9
Industry average	5.7	11.4

The critical issue for the early years of the new decade was whether the economic expansion would continue to fuel increased demand for casino gambling, or whether the huge investments of the late 1990s would ultimately undermine the industry economics.

Sources: www.ft.com; *Wall Street Journal*; aol.marketguide.com.

Strategies to Alter Industry Structure

Understanding how the structural characteristics of an industry determine the intensity of competition and the level of profitability provides a basis for identifying opportunities for changing industry structure in order to alleviate competitive pressures. The first issue is to identify the key structural features of an industry that are responsible for depressing profitability. The second is to consider which of these structural features are amenable to change through appropriate strategic initiatives. For example:

- In the European and North American oil refining industry, most firms have earned returns well below their cost of capital due to many competitors, excess capacity, and commodity products. Efforts to restore profitability in the downstream sector of the oil industry have focused mainly on consolidation to increase industry concentration and facilitate capacity rationalization. In Europe BP and Mobil merged their downstream activities, and in the US Shell and Texaco created a downstream joint venture. In the subsequent wave of megamergers, cost reduction and competition reduction in downstream markets were a major goal. Thus, BP acquired first Amoco, then Arco. Exxon merged with Mobil. In Europe the merger of Total, Fina, and Elf significantly reduced the intensity of competition in the oil products markets in France, Belgium, and the Netherlands.

- Excess capacity has also been a major problem in the European petrochemicals industry. Through a series of bilateral plant exchanges, the number of companies producing each product group has been reduced and capacity rationalization has been facilitated.[23] During 1993, ICI initiated a program of plant swaps with BASF, Bayer, and Dow to reduce excess capacity in European polyurethane production.[24]

- In the US airline industry, the major airlines have sought to offset an unfavorable industry structure by a number of strategies. In the absence of significant product differentiation, the airlines have used frequent-flier schemes as a means of recreating customer loyalty. Through hub-and-spoke route systems, the companies have achieved dominance of particular airports: American at Dallas-Fort Worth, US airways at Charlotte NC, and Northwest at Detroit and Memphis, for example. Mergers and alliances have reduced the numbers of competitors on many routes.

- Building entry barriers is a vital strategy for preserving high profitability in the long run. A primary goal of the American Medical Association has been to maintain the incomes of its members by controlling the numbers of doctors trained in the United States and imposing barriers to the entry of doctors from overseas.

---

[23] See Joe Bower, *When Markets Quake* (Boston: Harvard Business School Press, 1986).

[24] Paul Abrahams, "ICI Seeks Restructure of Polyurethane Industry," *Financial Times* (July 1, 1993): 28.

DEFINING INDUSTRIES: WHAT'S THE RELEVANT MARKET?

A key challenge in industry analysis is defining the relevant industry. Suppose Jaguar, a subsidiary of Ford Motor Company, is assessing its future prospects. In forecasting the profitability of its industry, should Jaguar consider itself part of the "motor vehicles and equipment" industry (SIC 371), the automobile industry (SIC 3712), or the luxury car industry? Should it view its industry as national (UK), regional (Europe), or global?

The first issue is clarifying what we mean by the term "industry." Economists define an industry as a group of firms that supplies a market.[25] Hence, the key to defining industry boundaries is identifying the relevant market. By focusing on the relevant market, we do not lose sight of the critical relationship among firms within an industry: competition.

A market's boundaries are defined by substitutability, both on the demand side and the supply side. Thus, in determining the appropriate range of products to be included in Jaguar's market, we should look first at substitutability on the demand side. If customers are unwilling to substitute trucks for cars on the basis of price differences, Jaguar's market should be viewed as automobiles rather than all motor vehicles. Again, if customers are willing to substitute among different types of automobiles – luxury cars, sports cars, family sedans, sport utility vehicles, and station wagons – on the basis of relative price, Jaguar's relevant market is the automobile market rather than just the luxury car market.

Even if there is limited substitution by customers between different types of automobile, if manufacturers find it easy to switch their production from luxury cars to family sedans to sports cars and the like, such supply-side substitutability would suggest that Jaguar is competing within the broader automobile market. The ability of Toyota, Nissan, and Honda to penetrate the luxury car market suggests that supply-side substitutability between mass-market autos and specialty autos is moderately high. Similarly, the automobile industry is frequently defined to include vans and light trucks, since these can be manufactured at the same plants as automobiles (often using the same platforms and engines). So too with "major appliance" manufacturers. They tend to be classified as a single industry, not because consumers are willing to substitute between refrigerators and dishwashers, but because the manufacturers can use the same manufacturing plants and distribution channels for different major appliances.

The same considerations apply to the geographical boundaries of markets. Should Jaguar view itself as competing in a single global market or in a series of separate national or regional markets? The criterion here again is substitutability. If customers are willing and able to substitute cars available on different national markets, and/or

---

[25]   The economist's definition of an industry may differ from normal usage of the term. For example, the US automobile industry tends to be viewed either as comprising US-owned carmakers (GM, Ford, Chrysler) or US-located carmakers (the Big Three plus the US subsidiaries of foreign-owned auto companies such as Honda, Nissan, and BMW). A market-based definition would comprise all auto companies that supply the US car market whether they have plants in the US, or supply the US market through imports.

if manufacturers are willing and able to divert their output among different countries to take account of differences in margins, then a market is global. The key test of the geographical boundaries of a market is price: if there are no significant differences between the prices of the same product between different locations, then these locations lie within a single market.

Whereas the market for jet aircraft is clearly global and that for dairy products clearly national (or local), automobiles are an especially difficult case. To the extent that most auto manufacturers are multinational corporations, there is considerable supply-side substitutability. However, to the extent that national markets are separated by trade restrictions, regulations, and the manufacturers' tightly controlled distribution channels, the international auto market may be seen as a conglomeration of many national markets with imperfect demand and supply-side substitutability among them. This is indicated by the substantial price differentials between the same model of car in the different countries of the European Union.[26]

Shiv Mathur and Alfred Kenyon go further.[27] They argue that, if we are to understand the realities of competition and the formulation of competitive strategy, we must rethink the conventional concepts of industries and markets and begin from first principles (see Exhibit 3.3).

We draw two conclusions from this discussion. First, drawing boundaries around industries and markets is a matter of judgment that must account for the purposes and context of the analysis. If Ford is considering the pricing and market positioning of its Jaguar cars, it must take a micro-level approach that defines markets around each model, in each country, and in relation to different categories of customer (e.g., distinguishing between sales to car rental companies and sales to individual consumers). In considering decisions over investments in fuel cell technology, the location of engine plants, and which new products to develop over the next five years, Ford will probably view its market as global and extending across its full range of models. The longer term the decisions are that it is considering, the more broadly it will wish to consider its markets, since substitutability is higher in the long run than in the short term.

Second, the precise delineation of the boundaries of a market or industry is seldom critical to the outcome of our analysis so long as we remain wary of external influences. Mathur and Kenyon's view of the market in which an offering competes is a continuum rather than a bounded space. Disneyland, Anaheim, may compete most closely with Universal Studios Tour and more distant competitors may include Sea World and Six Flags, but the broader arena of competitive offerings might include a trip to Las Vegas, a skiing weekend, or even playing on a PlayStation II. The Five Forces framework defines an industry "box" within which industry rivals compete, but because competitive forces outside the industry box are included – entrants and substitutes – the precise boundaries of the industry box are not greatly important. Thus, whether we view BMW as competing in the world automobile market or the luxury car

---

[26] In the UK, a car can cost up to 65 percent more than a nearly identical model in Denmark or Italy. See European Commission, "Car Price Differentials in the EU," Brussels, May 2000 (www.europea.ui.int/competition/car_sector).

[27] Shiv Mathur and Alfred Kenyon, *Creating Value: Shaping Tomorrow's Business* (Oxford: Butterworth-Heinemann, 1997).

EXHIBIT 3.3 Mathur and Kenyon's Approach to Competitive Analysis

Mathur and Kenyon argue that our conventional concept of industry is fundamentally flawed, since entities such as the automobile industry or the banking industry do not correspond to the realities of competition. Their starting point is customer choice. Customers do not choose a product or a company, their unit of choice is the single *offering*. Competitive strategy is "the triangular positioning of a single offering vis-à-vis a unique set of potential customers and competitors." Thus:

- Land Rover's Discovery and Defender models are a separate offerings because they compete for different groups with different preferences and with different competing offerings from other companies. To the extent that customer preferences and the range of competitors are different in France from Canada or Malaysia, then we can regard each model in each country as a separate offering competing in a separate market.

- London's Dorchester Hotel comprises a number of separate offerings: luxury hotel accommodation, restaurant services, cocktail bar drinks, and various personal services and retail products. The customers for these may be much the same, but each will have a separate set of competitors.

The result is a much more micro view of the external environment and competitive strategy than that associated with the conventional industry analysis of Porter and others. Not only are *offerings* much more narrowly defined than *products*, but each offering has its own unique market. Given such a finely grained analysis of competition and strategy, a critical issue for the business is the strategic management of *clusters* of offerings.

Does the Mathur and Kenyon approach require us to abandon our conventional industry analysis? It is clear that the more macro-level analysis of markets and industries associated with industrial economics and Michael Porter fails to take account of the specifics of competition at the level of the individual offering. Mathur and Kenyon offer us a far more precise and realistic approach to understanding and analyzing competition in the marketplace. For decisions relating to marketing strategy – including those of product design, pricing, advertising, and distribution – this micro-level analysis of individual offerings in relation to specific groups of customers and competitors is essential.

The case for retaining a more macro-level industry analysis based on a more conventional sectoral analysis rests on two principal grounds. First, if we return to the criterion of *substitution*, even though products (offerings) may not be close substitutes on the demand side, they may be close substitutes on the supply side. Thus, even though customers may be unwilling to substitute between a four-door sedan, a minivan, and a pick-up truck, if they can all be built using common platforms, drivetrains, and components, then for a wide range of strategic decisions they may be regarded as competing in the same market. Second, this concept of the industry allows us to consider competition in two types of market: in the market for goods and services (output markets) and in the markets for resources (input markets). As we will see when we introduce the *value chain* as an analytic tool, the vertical structure of an industry is an important dimension of strategy analysis.

Source: Shiv Mathur and Alfred Kenyon, *Creating Value: Shaping Tomorrow's Business* (Oxford: Butterworth-Heinemann, 1997).

market is not critical to the outcome of our analysis. Within the world auto market we consider Fiat and Hyundai as rivals within the industry; within the luxury car market we consider Fiat and Hyundai as suppliers of substitute products that are also potential entrants into the luxury car market.

EXTENDING THE FIVE FORCES FRAMEWORK

Limits of the Five Forces Framework

Further criticisms of Porter's Five Forces of Competition have come from economists who question the theoretical foundations of the model. Its basis is the structure–conduct–performance approach to industrial organization, which has been largely displaced in microeconomics by game theory. Apart from unease over its dubious theoretical foundations, the Five Forces model is also limited by its static nature. It views industry structure as stable and externally determined. Industry structure drives intensity of competition, which in turn determines the level of industry profitability. In practice, this is not a linear process that leaves industry structure unchanged. Competition is a dynamic process where strategy also transforms industry structure. What we are observing in telecommunications, banking, airlines, and a host of other industries is structural transformation as companies vie for advantage through acquisitions, new ventures, new technologies, and novel approaches to distribution and segmentation. The primary focus of this section is on dynamic aspects of competition.

There is also a lack of empirical evidence as to the importance of industry environment as a determinant of firm profitability. A series of studies have compared the relative importance of industry-level and firm-level influences on firm profitability. Schmalensee found that industry membership accounted for almost 20 percent of the differences in business unit return on assets.[28] A more sophisticated study by Rumelt, however, found that industry effects were dominated by firm-level effects: only 8 percent of differences in business unit profitability could be attributed to long-term industry effects, while corporate membership was responsible for 46 percent of profitability differences.[29] A recent study by Hawawini, Subramanian, and Verdin also shows industry effects as having a negligible impact on firms' EVA. However, once most profitable and least profitable firms in each industry were excluded, industry effects were substantially greater.[30]

Let us proceed by exploring some extensions of the Five Forces model.

[28] R. Schmalensee, "Do Markets Differ Much?," *American Economic Review*, 75 (1985): 341–51. Schmalensee's findings were broadly confirmed by Wernerfelt and Montgomery who used Tobin's q (the ratio of stock market valuation to replacement cost of assets) as their measure of performance (B. Wernerfelt and C. A. Montgomery, "Tobin's q and the Importance of Focus in Firm Performance," *American Economic Review* 78 (1988): 246–50).

[29] Richard P. Rumelt, "How Much Does Industry Matter?," *Strategic Management Journal* 12 (1991): 167–85.

[30] Gabriel Hawawini, Venkat Subramanian, and Paul Verdin, "When Does Industry Matter? An Empirical Study using EVA and MVA," discussion paper (Catholic University of Leuven, April 2000).

FIGURE 3.5   The value net

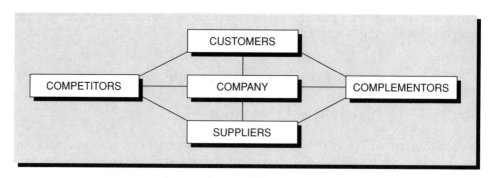

Complements: A Missing Dimension of the Five Forces Model?

The Porter framework identifies the suppliers of substitute goods and services as one of the forces of competition that reduces the profit available to the firms within an industry. However, economic theory identifies two types of relationship between different products: substitutes and complements. While substitutes have a negative impact on value, complements have a positive impact on value. The availability of ink cartridges for my ink-jet printer increased its value, and the more competition there is between suppliers of ink cartridges (and, hence, the lower their price), the greater the value I derive from my printer.

In their influential book *Co-opetition*, Brandenburger and Nalebuff introduce complementors as playing a key role in a firm's competitive environment.[31] The Brandenburger-Nalebuff *value net* is a framework for analyzing a firm's industry environment that is very similar to the Porter Five Forces framework. The main differences are first, the introduction of complementors and second, the lumping together of industry rivals, potential entrants, and suppliers of substitutes as "competitors" (see Figure 3.5). The simplest way to combine the two models is to add a sixth force to the Porter framework (see Figure 3.6). However, unlike the other five forces, complementors are not a competitive force; on the contrary, the more complements there are and the closer their relationship to the products supplied by the industry, the greater the potential profit within the industry.

However, a key point of the Brandenburger-Nalebuff analysis is the need to manage relationships with the suppliers of complements. Where products are close complements, they have little value to customers individually; customers value the whole system. But how is the value shared between the producers of the complements? Bargaining power and its deployment are the key. During early 1991, Nintendo's market value was greater than that of either Nissan or Sony, a result of Nintendo's

---

[31]   Adam Brandenburger and Barry Nalebuff, *Co-opetition* (New York: Doubleday, 1996).

FIGURE 3.6   Five Forces, or Six?

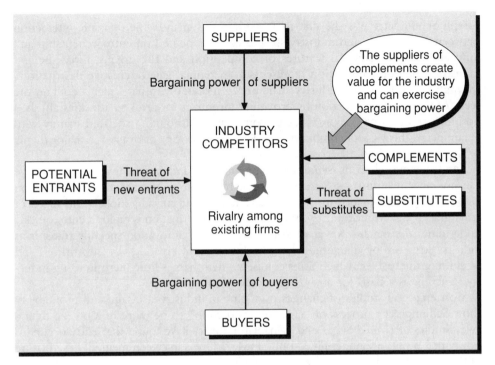

remarkable ability to generate profit out of its video game consoles. Although it is the software (blockbuster games such as Super Mario Brothers) rather than the hardware that creates the customer appeal of video game systems, Nintendo's strategic genius was in the management of its relationships with games developers. Nintendo established a dominant relationship with games developers by establishing an in-house software unit and issuing licenses to developers that permitted developers to supply games only to Nintendo. Nintendo controlled manufacture and distribution of games and earned a royalty on all Nintendo games sold.[32]

The role of complementary products and strategies toward their suppliers is just one aspect of Brandenburger and Nalebuff's framework for the application of game theory to competitive strategy. We shall return to their analysis in the next chapter.

---

[32]   The Nintendo example is outlined in Adam Brandenburger and Barry Nalebuff, "The Right Game: Use Game Theory to Shape Strategy," *Harvard Business Review* (July–August 1995): 63–4. See also A. Brandenburger, J. Kou, and M. Burnett, *Power Play (A): Nintendo in 8-bit Video Games* (Harvard Business School Case #9-795-103, 1995).

Dynamic Competition: The Process of Creative Destruction

Joseph Schumpeter was the first to recognize and analyze the dynamic interaction between competition and industry structure.[33] He focused on entrepreneurship and innovation as fundamental features of competition and the driving forces behind industry evolution. Innovation represents a "perennial gale of creative destruction" through which favorable industry structures – monopoly in particular – contain the seeds of their own destruction by providing incentives for firms to attack established positions through new approaches to competing. Although associated mainly with Schumpeter, this view of competition as a dynamic process of rivalry is a major theme of the Austrian school of economics.[34]

The key issue raised by Schumpeter for our basic industry analysis is whether we can use current industry structures as a reliable guide to the nature of competition and industry performance in the future. The relevant consideration is the speed of structural change in the industry. If the pace of transformation is rapid, if entry quickly undermines the market power of dominant firms, if innovation speedily transforms industry structure by changing process technology, by creating new substitutes, and by shifting the basis on which firms compete, then there is little merit in using industry structure as a basis for analyzing competition and profit.

Most empirical studies of changes over time in industry structure and profitability show Schumpeter's process of "creative destruction" to be more of a breeze than a gale. Studies of United States and Canadian industry have found that entry occurs so slowly that profits are undermined only slowly.[35] One survey commented: "the picture of the competitive process . . . is, to say the least, sluggish in the extreme."[36] Overall, the studies show a fairly consistent picture of the rate of change of profitability and structure. Both at the firm and the industry level, profits tend to be highly persistent in the long run.[37] Structural change – notably concentration, entry, and the identity of leading firms – also appears to be, on average, slow.[38]

Some industries, however, conform closely to Schumpeter's model. Jeffrey Williams identifies "Schumpeterian industries" as those subject to rapid product innovation

---

[33] J. A. Schumpeter, *The Theory of Economic Development* (Cambridge, MA: Harvard University Press, 1934).

[34] See Robert Jacobson, "The Austrian School of Strategy," *Academy of Management Review* 17 (1992): 782–807; and Greg Young, Ken Smith, and Curtis Grimm, "Austrian and Industrial Organization Perspectives on Firm-Level Competitive Activity and Performance," *Organization Science* 7 (May–June 1996): 243–54.

[35] R. T. Masson and J. Shaanan, "Stochastic Dynamic Limit Pricing: An Empirical Test," *Review of Economics and Statistics* 64 (1982): 413–22; R. T. Masson and J. Shaanan, "Optimal Pricing and Threat of Entry: Canadian Evidence," *International Journal of Industrial Organization* 5 (1987).

[36] P. A. Geroski and R. T. Masson, "Dynamic Market Models in Industrial Organization," *International Journal of Industrial Organization* 5 (1987): 1–13.

[37] Dennis C. Mueller, *Profits in the Long Run* (Cambridge: Cambridge University Press, 1986).

[38] Richard Caves and Michael E. Porter, "The Dynamics of Changing Seller Concentration," *Journal of Industrial Economics* 19 (1980): 1–15; P. Hart and R. Clarke, *Concentration in British Industry* (Cambridge: Cambridge University Press, 1980).

with relatively steep experience curves.[39] Here, structure tends to be unstable. In these circumstances, using current trends in industry structure to forecast profitability several years ahead is unreliable for two reasons: the relationship between competition and industry structure is unstable, and changes in industry structure are rapid and difficult to predict. We return to the issues of industry evolution and forecasting industry structure in Chapter 10.

Schumpeter's ideas of competition as a process of creative destruction have been developed in Rich D'Aveni's concept of "hypercompetition":

> Hypercompetition is an environment characterized by intense and rapid competitive moves, in that competitors must move quickly to build advantages and erode the advantages of their rivals. This speeds up the dynamic strategic interactions among competitors.
>
> Hypercompetitive behavior is the process of continuously generating new competitive advantages and destroying, obsoleting, or neutralizing the opponent's competitive advantage, thereby creating disequilibrium, destroying perfect competition, and disrupting the status quo of the marketplace. This is done by firms moving up their escalation ladders faster than competitors, restarting the cycles, or jumping to new arenas.[40]

The driving force of competition is the quest for profit through establishing competitive advantage. However, rivalry for competitive advantage means that competitive advantage is transitory. Only by continually recreating and renewing competitive advantage can firms sustain market dominance and superior performance over the long haul.

Competition in the New Economy

During the latter half of the 1990s, a number of fundamental changes became apparent in the economy of the United States and, to a lesser extent, other advanced industrialized countries, which have been described as the "New Economy." At the macroeconomic level, the most noticeable feature of these new economic circumstances has been an acceleration of productivity growth that has produced the remarkable combination of low unemployment and low inflation that was described by economic commentators as the "Goldilocks economy" (not too hot and not too cold). Underlying the upsurge in productivity have been structural changes in the economy caused by the information revolution. Although the information economy is closely associated with the development and diffusion of microelectronic technologies, the Stanford economist Paul Romer argues that the transition from

[39] Jeffrey R. Williams, "The Productivity Base of Industries," working paper (Carnegie-Mellon Graduate School of Industrial Administration, 1994) and *Renewable Advantage: Crafting Strategy through Economic Time* (New York: Free Press, 1999).

[40] Richard D'Aveni, *Hypercompetition: Managing the Dynamics of Strategic Maneuvering* (New York: Free Press, 1994): 217–18.

a mechanized economy to a software-based economy was a feature of the twentieth century as a whole. Among the different types of software, the most important in terms of contributing to productivity growth have been "recipes" for producing goods and services. These include Henry Ford's mass manufacturing system, the system at McDonald's for producing fast food in thousands of locations throughout the world, and Wal-Mart's system of retailing. A key feature of software – whether it is a movie, a book, a computer program, or a business system – is that its initial cost of creation is very high, but subsequent copies cost much less. Increasing returns in the modern economy are also a consequence of the fact that new knowledge complements older knowledge, and every investment in knowledge makes us better at discovering new knowledge.[41]

The key feature of the information revolution of the past decade is its digital foundation. Digital technologies exhibit extreme levels of scale economy: the initial cost of creating a product such as Microsoft Windows, a Pentium chip, or Pixar's *Toy Story* is very high but, once created, the product can be replicated at negligible cost.[42]

As we know from the Five Forces analysis, one implication of economies of scale is strong rivalry for market share. If the fixed costs of developing the product can only be amortized over a huge sales base, firms will compete vigorously for market share. The intensity of competition between Netscape and Microsoft in the market for internet browsers resulted in the price falling to zero – the companies gave the product away.

The effect of extreme scale economies in driving competition has been exacerbated by two further factors. First, a key feature of many information-based markets is networks of consumers and producers. Where consumers are connected in networks, *network externalities* are often present: the value of a product and service to a consumer depends on the number of other users of the product. These network effects provide further incentives for market dominance. They encourage convergence around a single technical standard. Competition for standards is a dominant feature of many new, technology-based industries. Thus, the markets for digital music, wireless telephony, operating systems for handheld computers, and digital image storage all feature competition between rival standards.[43]

Second, rates of technological change have accelerated remarkably. One implication is rapidly declining costs. Nowhere is this more evident than in semiconductors, where Moore's Law predicts a doubling of the density of transistors on a integrated circuit every two years. Since market leaders, such as Intel in microprocessors and

[41] Paul Romer, "Increasing Returns and Long-run Growth," *Journal of Political Economy* 54 (1986): 897–908; Romer, "The Origins of Endogenous Growth," *Journal of Economic Perspectives* 8 (Winter 1994): 3–22; Romer, "The Soft Revolution," *Journal of Applied Corporate Finance* (Summer 1998).
[42] Carl Shapiro and Hal Varian, *Information Rules* (Boston: Harvard University Press, 1998), discuss the economics of information-based products.
[43] On the role of networks and competition for standards, see Carl Shapiro and Hal Varian, "The Art of Standards Wars," *California Management Review* (Winter 1999); and Kevin Kelly, *New Rules for the New Economy* (New York: Viking, 1998).

Cisco in internet hardware, are better placed to drive technological progress and new product development, shortening life spans for technologies and new products further intensify competitive pressures.[44]

The result of these factors is intense competition in emerging markets for information-based products. The combination of extreme scale economies, network externalities, and rapid technological innovation creates "winner-take-all" markets where each competitor is willing to incur substantial losses to gain the chance to emerge as the industry winner. The browser wars between Netscape and Microsoft, the online auction battle in Europe between eBay and QXL, and the competition between Palm, Symbian, and Microsoft in operating systems for handheld digital devices are instances of such extreme competition.

Thus, despite the differences between "old" and "new" economies, industry, structure drives competition and profitability in both. The collapsing share prices of many new-economy companies during the latter part of 2000 and early 2001 reflected a recognition of these realities. Thus, most online retail markets – whether for books, airline tickets, or securities trading – are subject to low entry barriers, excess capacity, and low differentiation between rival companies, all of which suggest low margins. In wireless telecommunications, the combination of multiple competitors, excess network capacity, and a monopoly supplier of spectrum (government) has ensured that the sector will generate low rates of return for years to come. The primary beneficiaries of this industry structure are governments. In their auctions for third-generation licenses, the British and German governments succeeded in sucking out virtually all of the potential profits from the telecom operators in their respective counties.

THE EXTERNAL SOURCES OF COMPETITIVE ADVANTAGE: IDENTIFYING KEY SUCCESS FACTORS

The Five Forces framework allows us to determine an industry's potential for profit. But how is industry profit shared between the different firms competing in that industry? As we have noted in our discussion of industry dynamics, competition between industry participants is ultimately a battle for competitive advantage in which firms rival one another to attract customers and maneuver for positional advantage. The purpose of this section is to look explicitly at the sources of competitive advantage within an industry. In subsequent chapters, we develop a more comprehensive analysis of competitive advantage. Our goal is to identify those factors within the firm's market environment that determine its ability to survive and prosper – its

---

[44] Larry Downes, Chunka Mui, and Nicholas Negroponte (*Unleasing the Killer App*, Boston: Harvard Business School Press, 1998) argue that the combination of Moore's Law and Metcalfe's Law (that the value of a network increases exponentially with the number of its nodes) have transformed competition in the digital economy, particularly in relation to the growing significance of market-dominating products and services ("killer apps").

EXHIBIT 3.4   Probing for Key Success Factors

As a consultant faced with an unfamiliar business or industry, I make a point of first asking the specialists in the business, "What is the secret of success in this industry?" Needless to say, I seldom get an immediate answer, and so I pursue the inquiry by asking other questions from a variety of angles in order to establish as quickly as possible some reasonable hypotheses as to key factors for success. In the course of these interviews it usually becomes quite obvious what analyses will be required in order to prove or disprove these hypotheses. By first identifying the probable key factors for success and then screening them by proof or disproof, it is often possible for the strategist to penetrate very quickly to the core of a problem.

Traveling in the United States last year, I found myself on one occasion sitting in a plane next to a director of one of the biggest lumber companies in the country. Thinking I might learn something useful in the course of the five-hour flight, I asked him, "What are the key factors for success in the lumber industry?" To my surprise, his reply was immediate: "Owning large forests and maximizing the yield from them." The first of these key factors is a relatively simple matter: purchase of forest land. But his second point required further explanation. Accordingly, my next question was: "What variable or variables do you control in order to maximize the yield from a given tract?"

He replied: "The rate of tree growth is the key variable. As a rule, two factors promote growth: the amount of sunshine and the amount of water. Our company doesn't have many forests with enough of both. In Arizona and Utah, for example, we get more than enough sunshine but too little water, and so tree growth is very low. Now, if we could give the trees in those states enough water, they'd be ready in less than fifteen years instead of the thirty it takes now. The most important project we have in hand at the moment is aimed at finding out how to do this."

Impressed that this director knew how to work out a key factor strategy for his business, I offered my own contribution: "Then under the opposite conditions, where there is plenty of water but too little sunshine – for example, around the lower reaches of the Columbia River – the key factors should be fertilizers to speed up the growth and the choice of tree varieties that don't need so much sunshine."

Having established in a few minutes the general framework of what we were going to talk about, I spent the rest of the long flight very profitably hearing from him in detail how each of these factors was being applied.

Source: Kenichi Ohmae, *The Mind of the Strategist* (Harmondsworth: Penguin, 1982): 85.

---

key success factors.[45] In Exhibit 3.4, Kenichi Ohmae of McKinsey and Co. in Tokyo discusses key success factors in forestry and their link with strategy.

Like Ohmae, our approach to identifying key success factors is straightforward and common sense. To survive and prosper in an industry, a firm must meet two criteria: first, it must supply what customers want to buy, second, it must survive competition. Hence, we may start by asking two questions:

---

[45]   The term was coined by Chuck Hofer and Dan Schendel, *Strategy Formulation: Analytical Concepts* (St. Paul: West Publishing, 1977): 77, who defined key success factors as "those variables that management can influence through its decisions and that can affect significantly the overall competitive positions of the firms in an industry . . . Within any particular industry they are derived from the interaction of two sets of variables, namely, the economic and technological characteristics of the industry . . . and the competitive weapons on which the various firms in the industry have built their strategies."

- What do our customers want?

- What does the firm need to do to survive competition?

To answer the first question we need to look more closely at customers of the industry and to view them not so much as a source of bargaining power and hence as a threat to profitability, but more as the basic rationale for the existence of the industry and as the underlying source of profit. This implies that the firm must identify who its customers are, determine their needs, and establish the basis on which they select the offerings of one supplier in preference to those of another. Once we have identified the basis of customers' preference, this is merely the starting point for a chain of analysis. As Table 3.4 will show, if consumers select supermarkets primarily on the basis of price and if low prices depend on low costs, the interesting questions concern the determinants of low costs.

The second question requires that the firm examine the basis of competition in the industry. How intense is competition and what are its key dimensions? If competition in an industry is intense, then, even though the product may be highly differentiated and customers may choose on the basis of design and quality rather than price, low cost may be essential for survival. Retailers such as Harrods, Nordstrom, and Tiffany's do not compete on low prices, but in a fiercely competitive retailing sector, their prosperity depends on rigorous cost control.

A basic framework for identifying key success factors is presented in Figure 3.7. Application of the framework to identify key success factors in three industries is outlined in Table 3.5.

Key success factors can also be identified through the direct modeling of profitability. In the same way that our Five Forces analysis models the determinants of

FIGURE 3.7 Identifying key success factors

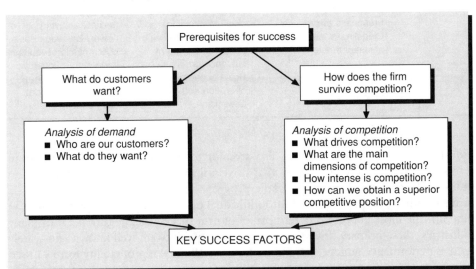

TABLE 3.5 Identifying Key Success Factors: Some Examples

	WHAT DO CUSTOMERS WANT? (Analysis of demand)	HOW DOES A FIRM SURVIVE COMPETITION? (Analysis of competition)	KEY SUCCESS FACTORS
Steel	Customers include auto, engineering, and container industries. Customers acutely price sensitive. Customers require product consistency and reliability of supply. Specific technical specifications required for special steels.	Competition primarily on price. Competition intense due to declining demand, high fixed costs, excess capacity, low-cost imports, and exit barriers high. Transport costs high. Scale economies important.	Cost efficiency through scale-efficient plants, low-cost location, rapid adjustment of capacity to output, efficient use of labor. Scope for differentiation through quality service and technical factors.
Fashion clothing	Demand fragmented by garment, style, quality, color. Customers' willingness to pay price premium for fashion, exclusivity, and quality. Mass market highly price sensitive. Retailers seek reliability and speed of supply.	Low barriers to entry and exit. Low seller concentration. Few scale economies. International competition strong. Retail chains exercise strong buying power.	Need to combine effective differentiation with low-cost operation. Key differentiation variables are speed of response to changing high fashions, style, reputation and quality.
Supermarkets	Low prices. Convenient location. Wide range of products. Product range adapted to local customer preferences. Freshness of produce. Cleanliness, service, and pleasant ambience.	Markets localized and concentration normally high. But customer price sensitivity encourages vigorous price competition. Exercise of bargaining power an important influence on input cost. Scale economies in operation and advertising.	Low-cost operation requires operational efficiency, scale-efficient stores, large aggregate purchases to maximize buying power, low wage costs. Differentiation requires large stores (to allow wide product range), convenient location, easy parking.

industry-level profitability, we can also attempt to model firm-level profitability in terms of identifying the key factors that drive a firm's relative profitability within an industry. In Chapter 2, we made some progress on this front. By disaggregating a firm's return on capital employed into individual operating factors and ratios, we can pinpoint the most important determinants of firm success (see Figure 2.2). In many industries, these primary drivers of firm-level profitability are well known and widely used as performance targets. Exhibit 3.5 gives a well-known profitability formula used

EXHIBIT 3.5 Identifying Key Success Factors Through Modeling Profitability: The Airline Business

Profitability, as measured by operating income per available seat-mile (ASM), is determined by three factors: yield which is total operating revenues divided by the number of revenue passenger miles (RPM); load factor which is the ratio between RPMs and APMs; and unit cost which is total operating expenses divided by ASMs (available seat miles). Thus:

$$\frac{\text{Income}}{\text{ASMs}} = \frac{\text{Revenue}}{\text{RPMs}} \times \frac{\text{RPMs}}{\text{ASMs}} \;less\; \frac{\text{Expenses}}{\text{ASMs}}$$

Some of the primary determinants of each of these measures are the following:

- Revenue/RPMs
  - Intensity of competition on routes flown.
  - Effective yield management to permit quick price adjustment to changing market conditions.
  - Ability to attract business customers.
  - Superior customer service.

- Load factors
  - Competitiveness of prices.
  - Efficiency of route planning (e.g., through hub-and-spoke systems).
  - Building customer loyalty through quality of service, frequent-flier programs.
  - Matching airplane size to demand for individual flights.

- Expenses/ASMs
  - Wage rates and benefit levels.
  - Fuel efficiency of aircraft.
  - Productivity of employees (determined partly by their job flexibility).
  - Load factors.
  - Level of administrative cost.

In their quest for survival and competitive advantage, the airlines have sought to optimize as many of these factors as possible in order to improve their profitability. In terms of revenue enhancement, several airlines have withdrawn from the most intensely competitive routes, and others have sought to achieve a fare premium over the cut-price airlines through punctuality, convenience, comfort, and services (e.g., in-flight telephones, personal video monitors with choice of movies). To improve load factors, companies have sought flexibility in allocating plane capacity to routes, and used their computer reservation systems and internet sales to achieve more flexible pricing. Most notably, companies have sought cost economies through increasing employee productivity, reducing administrative overhead through outsourcing, investing in fuel-efficient aircraft, and reducing wages and benefits.

in the airline industry, then identifies the factors that drive the profitability ratios. More generally, the approach introduced in Chapter 2 to disaggregate return on capital into its component ratios can be extended to identify the specific operational and strategic drivers of superior profitability. Figure 3.8 applies this analysis to identifying success factors in retailing.

FIGURE 3.8   Identifying key success factors through analyzing profit drivers: the case of retailing

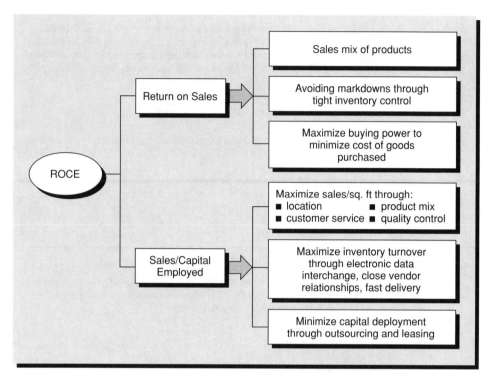

The value of success factors in formulating strategy has been scorned by some strategy scholars. Pankaj Ghemawat observes that the "whole idea of identifying a success factor and then chasing it seems to have something in common with the ill-considered medieval hunt for the philosopher's stone, a substance that would transmute everything it touched into gold."[46] The objective here in identifying key success factors is less ambitious. There is no universal blueprint for a successful strategy, and even in individual industries, there is no "generic strategy" that can guarantee superior profitability. However, each market is different in terms of what motivates customers and how competition works. Understanding these aspects of the industry environment is a prerequisite for an effective business strategy. Nevertheless, this does not imply that firms within an industry adopt common strategies. Since every firm comprises a unique set of resources and capabilities, every firm must pursue unique key success factors.

---

[46]   Pankaj Ghemawat, *Commitment: The Dynamic of Strategy* (New York: Free Press, 1991): 11.

SUMMARY

In Chapter 1, we observed that understanding one's competitive environment is a key ingredient of a successful strategy. In this chapter, we have examined concepts and frameworks that can assist our understanding of the firm's business environment. This approach rests on the assumption that, to understand competition and the determinants of profitability within an industry, we are limited to acquiring experience-based, industry-specific learning over a long period of time. Instead, we can draw on concepts, principles, and theories that can be applied to any industry. Although every industry is unique, the patterns of competitive behavior can be explained and explored using common analytic frameworks.

The underlying premise of this chapter is that the structural characteristics of an industry play a key role in determining the nature and intensity of the competition within it and the rate of profit it earns. Our framework for linking industry structure to competition and profitability is Porter's Five Forces of Competition model. This provides a simple, yet powerful organizing framework for classifying the relevant features of an industry's structure and predicting their implications for competitive behavior. The framework is particularly useful for:

- predicting industry profitability;
- indicating how the firm can influence industry structure in order to moderate competition and improve profitability.

The Porter framework suffers from some critical limitations, however. In particular, it does not take adequate account of the dynamic character of competition. Competition is a powerful force that changes industry structure. In hypercompetitive industries, competing strategies create a process of "creative destruction" that continually transforms industry structure. Nowhere are the features of hypercompetition more clearly exhibited than in the seemingly chaotic industries that have developed in the wake of the internet – internet service providers and online financial services, for example. Even here, however, we can use our structural analysis to effect. The intense price competition and huge losses being made in many of these online businesses reflect the competitive intensity created by vast economies of scale combined with low levels of product differentiation and relatively easy entry.

Nevertheless, we need to develop our basic tools of industry and competitive analysis further. In particular, we need a better understanding of the process of competitive rivalry between small groups of players within a market. To do this we shall draw on the concepts of game theory and competitor analysis. This will also help us to address some of the theoretical weaknesses of the Porter framework to which I have already alluded.

In the next chapter we take a more detailed look inside the industry environment in order to explore competitive rivalry in greater depth. We shall also take up the issue raised by Mathur and Kenyon concerning the need to analyze competition at a more micro level. We shall do this through showing how, for the purposes of analyzing competition at a more detailed level, industries can be segmented into more specific markets. Subsequent chapters will draw extensively on the frameworks, concepts, and techniques introduced here. In particular, we shall develop our industry analysis through considering the evolution of industry structure (Chapter 10) and the characteristics of technology-based industries (Chapter 11), mature industries (Chapter 12), and global industries (Chapter 14).

4

Intra-Industry Analysis

OUTLINE

INTRODUCTION AND OBJECTIVES

The analysis of industries and competition outlined in the previous chapter takes a simplified view of both industry and competition. The odd feature about competition within the Porter model is that it bears little relationship to the dynamic process of rivalry that characterizes competitive behavior in business, sport, and politics. Competition in real markets is described less by industry-level structures and outcomes as by the competitive interactions between firms. Pepsi-Cola's competitive environment is defined less by the structure of the world soft drink industry than by the strategy and marketing tactics of Coca-Cola. We may consider Airbus Industrie as competing in the world aerospace industry, but the dominant feature of the industry is the competitive behavior of Boeing. Our Five Forces analysis tells us little about competitive interaction between particular players. To explore competitive behavior further, we shall explore a body of theory known as *game theory*, which for more than half a century has sought to model and predict competitive (and cooperative) behavior between specified players. At a less theory-based level, we shall also see how the tools of *competitor analysis* can help predict the strategic initiatives and responses by a rival company.

We shall also extend our competitive analysis in other ways. In the previous chapter, I noted that firms do not compete within clearly defined industries. If we follow Mathur and Kenyon's analysis, markets are defined by a set of customers (and their preferences) and a set of competitors. American Airlines competes in the world airline industry. However, each route comprises a different market with a different set of competitors. Between New York and Milan, American's closest competitor is Alitalia, but between New York and Montreal it is Air Canada. Even within a market, competitive relationships are differentiated by the distance of the relationship. Between the east and west coasts of the US, American Airlines' closest competitors are United Airlines and Delta, slightly more distant competitors are America West and Southwest, even more distant competitors are Amtrak and Greyhound. Standard industry classifications seldom correspond closely to groups of competing firms. The US retailing sector includes Safeway food stores, Shell gas stations, and Blockbuster video. Each of these retailers inhabits a different competitive environment. Yet, all three offer video tapes and candy. Clearly, competitive relationships are complex and markets are difficult to define.

To take account of the internal heterogeneity of industries and the fact that the companies within an industry may compete within a number of distinct markets, we shall disaggregate industries in order to understand competition and the determinants of profitability at a more detailed level. Such segmentation can help us understand why within the highly competitive microcomputer industry, gross margins on desktop PCs are in the 15–20 percent range, while gross margins on servers and portables are twice that level. It can also help us to understand why Chrysler, because of its heavy involvement in the minivan and sport-utility segments of the auto industry, was the world's most profitable carmaker during the 1990s. We shall also use strategic group analysis to explore the strategic positioning of firms within an industry.

By the time you have completed this chapter, you will be able to:

■ Appreciate the insights that game theory offers into the nature of competitive interaction between firms – in particular, the balance of competitive and cooperative behavior and the use of threats, commitments, signaling, deterrence, and preemption to gain competitive advantage.

- Use competitor analysis to predict the behavior of individual companies, including the competitive moves a rival is likely to initiate, and the rival's responses to our own initiatives.

- Segment an industry into its constituent markets and identify the relative attractiveness of the different segments and the differences in key success factors among them.

- Classify the firms within an industry into strategic groups based on similarities in their strategies.

THE CONTRIBUTION OF GAME THEORY

Central to the criticisms of Porter's Five Forces as a static framework is its failure to take full account of competitive interactions among firms. In Chapter 1, we noted that the essence of strategic competition is the interaction among players, such that the decisions made by any one player are dependent on the actual and anticipated decisions of the other players. By relegating competition to a mediating variable that links industry structure with profitability, the Five Forces analysis offers little insight into firms' choices of whether to compete or cooperate; sequential competitive moves; and the role of threats, promises, and commitments. Game theory has two especially valuable contributions to make to strategic management:

1. *It permits the framing of strategic decisions.* Apart from any theoretical value of the theory of games, game theory provides a structure, a set of concepts, and a terminology that allows us to describe a competitive situation in terms of:
   - identity of the players;
   - specification of each player's options;
   - specification of the payoffs from every combination of options;
   - the sequencing of decisions using game trees.

   This permits us to understand the structure of the competitive situation and facilitates a systematic, rational approach to decision making.

2. *It can predict the outcome of competitive situations and permit the selection of optimal strategic choices.* Through the insight it offers into situations of competition and bargaining, game theory can predict the equilibrium outcomes of competitive situations and the consequences of strategic moves by any one player. Game theory provides penetrating insights into central issues of strategy that go well beyond pure intuition. Simple game models (e.g., "Prisoners' Dilemma") predict cooperative versus competitive outcomes, whereas more

complex games permit analysis of the effects of reputation,[1] deterrence,[2] information,[3] and commitment[4] – especially within the context of multiperiod games. Particularly important for practicing managers, game theory can indicate strategies for improving the structure and outcome of the game through manipulating the payoffs to the different players.[5]

Despite the explosion of interest in game theory during the 1980s, practical applications, especially in the area of strategic management, remained limited until the 1990s. Interest in game theory has grown recently as a result of a number of practical guides to the application of game theory's tools and insights.[6] Game theory has provided illuminating insights into a wide variety of situations, including the Cuban missile crisis of 1962,[7] President Reagan's 1981 tax cut,[8] subsidies for Airbus Industrie,[9] the problems of OPEC in agreeing to production cuts, the competitive impact of Philip Morris's "Marlboro Monday" price cut,[10] decisions over investments in new production capacity,[11] and the airwaves auctions in the US, New Zealand, the UK, and Germany.[12]

Cooperation

One of the greatest benefits of game theory is its ability to view business interactions as comprising both competition and cooperation. A key deficiency of the Five Forces framework is in viewing rivalry and bargaining as competitive in nature. The

---

[1] Keith Weigelt and Colin F. Camerer, "Reputation and Corporate Strategy: A Review of Recent Theory and Applications," *Strategic Management Journal* 9 (1988): 137–42.

[2] A. K. Dixit, "The Role of Investment in Entry Deterrence," *Economic Journal* 90 (1980): 95–106.

[3] P. Milgrom and J. Roberts, "Informational Asymmetries, Strategic Behavior and Industrial Organization," *American Economic Review* 77, no. 2 (May 1987): 184–9; J. Tirole, *The Theory of Industrial Organization* (Cambridge, MA: MIT Press, 1990).

[4] Pankaj Ghemawat, *Commitment: The Dynamic of Strategy* (New York: Free Press, 1991).

[5] There are two outstanding introductions to the principles of game theory and their practical applications: Thomas C. Schelling, *The Strategy of Conflict*, 2nd edition (Cambridge: Harvard University Press, 1980); and A. K. Dixit and B. J. Nalebuff, *Thinking Strategically: The Competitive Edge in Business, Politics, and Everyday Life* (New York: W. W. Norton, 1991).

[6] Avinash K. Dixit and Barry Nalebuff, op. cit.; John McMillan, *Games, Strategies, and Managers* (New York: Oxford University Press, 1992); M. D. Morton, *Game Theory: A Nontechnical Introduction* (Dover, 1997); A. Malthoo, *Bargaining Theory with Applications* (Cambridge: Cambridge University Press, 1999); A. Dixit and S. Skeath, *Games of Strategy* (New York: Norton, 1999).

[7] Graham Allison, *Essence of Decision: Explaining the Cuban Missile Crisis* (Boston: Little, Brown, 1971).

[8] A. K. Dixit and B. J. Nalebuff, op. cit.: 131–5.

[9] M. Lynn, *Birds of Prey: Boeing Vs. Airbus, A Battle for the Skies* (New York: Four Walls Eight Windows, 1997).

[10] "Business War Games Attract Big Warriors," *Wall Street Journal* (December 22, 1994): B1.

[11] Michael E. Porter and A. M. Spence, "The Capacity Expansion Process in a Growing Oligopoly: The Case of Corn Wet Milling," in J. McCall (ed.), *The Economics of Information and Uncertainty* (Chicago: University of Chicago Press, 1982).

[12] "Learning to Play the Game," *Economist* (May 17, 1997): 93; "The Price is Right," *Economist* (July 29, 2000): 34; "Game Theory in Action: Designing the US Airwaves Auction," *Financial Times* Mastering Strategy Supplement (October 11, 1999): 4.

central message of Adam Brandenburger and Barry Nalebuff's book *Co-opetition* is recognizing the competitive/cooperative duality of business relationships. Whereas Coca-Cola's relationship with Pepsi-Cola is essentially competitive, that between Intel and Microsoft is primarily complementary. Thus:

■ A player is your complementor if customers value your product more when they have the other player's product than when they have your product alone.

■ A player is your competitor if customers value your product less when they have the other player's product than when they have your product alone.

However, there is no simple dichotomy between competition and cooperation: a player may occupy multiple roles. Microsoft and Netscape competed fiercely to dominate the market for Internet browsers. At the same time, the two companies cooperate in establishing security protocols for protecting privacy and guarding against credit card fraud on the internet. The desire of competitors to cluster together – antique dealers in London's Bermondsey Market and movie studios in Hollywood – points to the complementary relations among competitors in growing the size of their market and developing its infrastructure. Similarly, with customers and suppliers, though these players are essentially partners in creating value, they are also bargaining over sharing that value.

In many business relationships, competition results in an inferior outcome for the players than would cooperation. The classic Prisoners' Dilemma game is one where a pair of suspects to a crime are arrested and each is offered an incentive to "grass" on the other. The dominant strategy is for each to implicate the other, even though, if both had remained silent, there would have been insufficient evidence for a conviction and the pair would have avoided conviction. Examples of Prisoners' Dilemmas include:

■ A price war between evenly matched competitors that results in no change in market share and only lower profits all round.

■ Competitive bidding between rival art collectors at an auction of old masters.

■ Bargaining between a buyer and seller for a product where the quality cannot be easily discerned prior to purchase (e.g., a used car). The seller has an incentive to offer low quality; the buyer has an incentive to offer a low price in the likelihood that quality will be poor. The equilibrium is a low-priced, low-quality product, though both parties would benefit from a better-quality, higher-price product.

How can such Prisoners' Dilemmas be resolved? One answer is to change a one-period game (single transaction) into a repeated game. In the case of the supplier–buyer relationship, moving from a spot transaction to a long-term vendor relationship gives the supplier the incentive to offer a better-quality product and the buyer to offer a price that offers the seller a satisfactory return. In the case of price competition, markets dominated by two or three suppliers tend to converge toward patterns of price leadership where price competition is avoided.

A second solution is to change the payoffs in the game. The Mafia has been successful in changing the payoffs in the classic Prisoners' Dilemma game such that confessing and implicating accomplices is no longer a dominant strategy. It achieves this by imposing draconian reprisals on those who break the code of silence.

Deterrence

The idea of influencing rivals' behavior by means of changing the payoffs in a game[13] is a key lesson of game theory. The principle behind deterrence is to impose costs on the other players for actions that we deem to be undesirable. By establishing the certainty that deserters would be shot, the British army provided a strong incentive to its troops to participate in advances on heavily fortified German trenches during World War I.

The key to the effectiveness of any deterrence is that it must be credible. The problem here is that if administering the deterrent is costly or unpleasant for the threatening party, the deterrent is not credible. Incumbents in a market may threaten a would-be entrant with aggressive price cuts. However, the entrant may rationalize that, once it has entered the market, it is no longer in the incumbent firm's best interest to engage in a costly price war. The key then is for the incumbent to make a credible commitment to price cutting. One example would be a clause in customer commitments that it will match any price cuts offered by a rival. Thus, a retailer's price guarantee that it will make a refund to any customer able to purchase an equivalent item at a lower cost is in effect providing a deterrent to any competitor cutting its prices. Firms may deliberately overinvest in order to have available capacity that can be used to flood a competitor's market, to deter competitive initiatives by the competitor. The classic example is Alcoa's use of capacity expansion as a warning to potential entrants into the US aluminum industry (*United States versus Alcoa*, 1945). Anita McGahan argued that, because Philips was reluctant to make an early investment in US manufacturing capacity for compact discs, it failed to deter entrants into the US CD market.[13] However, Marvin Lieberman has cast doubt on the effectiveness of excess capacity in deterring new entry.[14]

Deterrence has provided a central theme in defense strategy. The nuclear arms race between the US and the then Soviet Union was based on the logic of "mutual assured destruction": any nuclear aggression would be automatically retaliated against, risking destruction of the human race. The stability of the Cold War between 1946 and 1990 is evidence of the effectiveness of this deterrent.

[13] A. M. McGahan, "The Incentive Not to Invest: Capacity Commitments in the Compact Disk Introduction," in R. A. Burgelman and R. S. Rosenbloom (eds), *Research on Technological Innovation Management and Policy*, vol. 5 (Greenwich, CT: JAI Press, 1994).
[14] Marvin B. Leiberman, "Excess Capacity as a Barrier to Entry: An Empirical Appraisal," *Journal of Industrial Economics* 35 (1987): 607–27.

Commitment

For deterrence to be effective it must be credible, which means being backed by some kind of commitment. Commitment is an interesting strategy since it is seemingly irrational – it involves the elimination of strategic options. When Hernan Cortes sank most of his ships on arrival in Mexico in 1519, he achieved, first, motivation for his men to conquer the Aztec empire, second, a signal to Montezuma that any Aztec aggression could not lead to Spanish withdrawal. The commitment that Airbus is making to the A380 superjumbo in terms of investments in technology, supplier contracts, and advertising is to signal commitment both to the airlines and to Boeing, such that the airlines will be encouraged to place orders, and Boeing will be discouraged from developing a rival plane.

These commitments to aggressive competition have been described as "hard commitments." A company may also make a commitment to avoid aggressive competition, what are called "soft commitments."[15] The airlines' frequent-flier programs are a commitment by the airlines to redeem miles flown with free tickets. They also signal to other airlines a shift of competition away from price competition and carry the message that the airline is less vulnerable to a rival's price cuts. However, how these different types of commitment affect the profitability of the firm making the commitment depends on the type of game being played. Where companies compete on price, game theory shows that they tend to match one another's price changes.[16] Hence, under price adjustments, hard commitments (e.g., a commitment by Coca-Cola to cut price) tend to have a negative profit impact and soft commitments (e.g., a commitment to raise prices) have a positive impact. Conversely, where companies compete on output, game theory shows that increases in output by one result in output reductions by the other.[17] Hence, under quantity adjustments, a hard commitment (e.g., a commitment by Samsung to build several large new plants for producing a new generation of DRAM chips) will tend to have a positive effect on the committing firm's profitability, since it will tend to be met by other firms reducing their output.[18]

Changing Industry Structure

There are many ways in which a player can change the structure of the game it is playing. A company may seek to change the structure of the industry within which it is competing in order to increase the profit potential of the industry or to

---

[15] J. Chevalier, "When It Can Be Good to Burn Your Boats," *Financial Times* Mastering Strategy Supplement (October 25, 1999): 2–3.

[16] Games where price is the primary decision variable are called Bertrand models after the nineteenth-century French economist Joseph Bertrand.

[17] Games where quantity is the primary decision variable are called Cournot models after the nineteenth-century French economist Augustin Cournot.

[18] Fiona Scott Morton, "Strategic Complements and Substitutes," *Financial Times* Mastering Strategy Supplement (November 8, 1999): 10–13.

appropriate a greater share of the profit available. Thus, establishing alliances and agreements with competitors can increase the value of the game by increasing the size of the market and building joint strength against possible entrants. There may be many opportunities for converting win–lose (or even lose–lose) games into win–win games. A cooperative solution was found to Norfolk Southern's competition with CSX for control of Conrail, for example. The 1997 bidding war was terminated when CSX and Norfolk Southern agreed to dismember and share Conrail.

In some cases, it may be advantageous for a firm to create competition for itself. When Intel developed its 8086 microprocessor, it gave up its potential monopoly by offering second-sourcing licenses to AMD and IBM. Although Intel was creating competition for itself, it was also encouraging the adoption of the 8086 chip by computer manufacturers (including IBM) who were concerned about overdependence on Intel. Once Intel had established its technology as the industry standard, it developed its family of 286, 386, 486, and Pentium processors and became much more restrictive over licensing.

Signaling

How a competitor will react to a company's strategic initiative depends not just on what that initiative is, but how the competitor perceives the initiative. The term *signaling* is used to describe the selective communication of information to competitors designed to influence their perception and hence to provoke or avoid certain types of reaction.[19] The use of diversionary attacks and misinformation is well developed in military warfare. In 1944, Allied deception was so good that even during the D-Day landings in Normandy, the Germans believed that the main invasion would occur near Calais. The principal role of signaling is to deter competitors. But, as noted in discussing deterrence, information on its own is not enough: signals need to be credible. Thus, Allied misinformation concerning the invasion of Europe included the marshaling of a phantom army designed to convince the German high command that the Normandy invasion was merely a diversionary mission.

The credibility of threats is critically dependent on the company's reputation.[20] Even though carrying out threats against rivals is costly and depresses short-term profitability, such threats can build a reputation for aggressiveness that deters competitors in the future. The benefits of building a reputation for aggressiveness may be particularly great for diversified companies where reputation can be transferred from one market to another.[21] Hence, Procter & Gamble's protracted market share wars in disposable diapers and household detergents have established a reputation

[19] For a review of theory and research on competitive signaling, see O. Heil and T. S. Robertson, "Toward a Theory of Competitive Market Signaling: A Research Agenda," *Strategic Management Journal* 12 (1991): 403–18.

[20] For a survey of the strategic role of reputation, see Keith Weigelt and Colin Camerer, "Reputation and Corporate Strategy: A Review of Recent Theory and Applications," *Strategic Management Journal* 9 (1988): 443–54.

[21] P. Milgrom and J. Roberts, "Predation, Reputation, and Entry Deterrence," *Journal of Economic Theory* 27 (1982): 280–312.

for toughness that protects it from competitive attacks in other markets. *Fortune* magazine identifies Gillette in razors and razor blades, Anheuser-Busch in beer, and Emerson Electric in sink disposal units as examples of companies whose aggressive quest for market share has gained them reputations as "killer competitors," which has encouraged a number of rivals to give up the fight.[22]

Signaling may also be used to maintain a cozy industry environment of cooperation and restrained competition among firms. One means of avoiding price competition in an industry is for firms to follow a pattern of price leadership. In the UK gasoline market, the initiation of a price increase by a firm is normally preceded by a period of consensus building, during which the firm tests the water by press releases that announce "the unsatisfactory level of margins in the industry," the "need for a price increase to recoup recent cost increases," and the likelihood that "a price increase will become necessary in the near future."[23]

Is Game Theory Useful?

The value of game theory has been a topic of considerable debate in the field of strategy. For economists and mathematicians this seems paradoxical, since to them game theory is the theory of strategy. As one economist states: "The essence of strategic thinking is to anticipate your competitor's moves in advance. Knowledge of your competitor's reaction, or likely reaction, dramatically improves your ability to choose a strategy that will be successful."

The great virtue of game theory is its rigor. In microeconomics, the game theory revolution of the past quarter-century has revolutionized the analysis of markets and firm behavior, putting it on a much more secure theoretical foundation. However, the cost of game theory's mathematical rigor has been narrowness of application. Game theory provides clear prediction in highly stylized situations involving few external variables and highly restrictive assumptions. The result is a mathematically sophistic-ated body of theory that suffers from unrealistic assumptions, lack of generality, and an analysis of dynamic situations through a sequence of static equilibria.[24] When applied to more complex (and more realistic) situations, game theory frequently results in

---

[22]   "Companies That Compete Best," *Fortune* (May 22, 1989): 36–44.

[23]   Robert M. Grant, "Pricing Behavior in the UK Wholesale Market for Petrol," *Journal of Industrial Economics* 30 (1982): 271–92.

[24]   There are numerous critiques of the usefulness of game theory. F. M. Fisher, "The Games Economists Play: A Noncooperative View," *Rand Journal of Economics* 20 (Spring 1989): 113–24, points to the ability of game theory to predict almost any equilibrium solution. Colin Camerer describes this as the "Pandora's Box Problem," see C. F. Camerer, "Does Strategy Research Need Game Theory?," *Strategic Management Journal*, special issue, 12 (Winter 1991): 137–52. Steve Postrel illustrates this problem by developing a game theory model to explain the rationality of bank presidents setting fire to their trousers; see S. Postrel, "Burning Your Britches Behind You: Can Policy Scholars Bank on Game Theory," *Strategic Management Journal*, special issue, 12 (Winter 1991): 153–5. Michael E. Porter, "Toward a Dynamic Theory of Strategy," *Strategic Management Journal*, special issue, 12 (Winter 1991): 95–117, notes that game theory "stops short of a dynamic theory of strategy . . . these models explore the dynamics of a largely static world."

either no equilibrium or multiple equilibria, and outcomes that are highly sensitive to small changes in the assumptions. In general, game theory has not developed to the point where it permits us to model real business situations in a level of detail that can generate precise predictions.

In terms of empirical application, game theory has done a much better job of explaining the past than of predicting the future. In diagnosing the Cuban missile crisis, Nintendo's domination of the video games industry in the 1980s, and Nutrasweet's efforts to retain its domination of the world market for aspartame, game theory has proved a remarkable illumination of the situation and the strategies of the different players. It provided valuable decision support in negotiations and in simulating competitive patterns of action and reaction. However, in predicting outcomes and designing strategies, game theory has been much less impressive. The most direct and explicit application of game theory was in the US Federal Communications Commission's auctioning of licenses for digital wireless spectrum during 1995–97. Despite employing leading game theorists to design the auction, the results were viewed as a disaster. Licenses for some cities were sold for $1 and there were widespread allegations of collusion among bidders.[25]

So, where can game theory assist business managers? As with all our theories and frameworks, game theory is useful not because it gives us answers, but because it can help us understand business situations. Game theory provides a set of tools that allows us to structure our view of competitive interaction. If we identify the players in a game, identify the decision choices available to each player, specify the performance implications of each combination of decisions, and predict how each player is likely to react to the decision choices of the other, then we have made huge progress in understanding the dynamics of competition. Most importantly, by describing the structure of the game we are playing, we have a basis for suggesting ways of changing the game and thinking through the likely outcomes of such changes.

Although game theory continues its rapid development, it is nevertheless far from providing the central theoretical foundation for strategic management. Though we draw on game theory in several places in this book, particularly in exploring the interaction between firms in markets dominated by a handful of major competitors, our emphasis in strategy formulation will be less on achieving advantage through influencing the behavior of competitors and much more on transforming competitive games through building positions of unilateral competitive advantage. The competitive market situations with which we shall be dealing will, for the most part, be different from those considered by game theory. Game theory typically deals with competitive situations with closely matched players where each has a similar range of strategic options (typically relating to price changes, advertising budgets, capacity decisions, and new product introductions). The outcome of these games is highly dependent on order of moves, signals, bluffs, and threats. Our emphasis in strategy analysis will be less on the similarities between firms and their strategic options than on their differences. The key to competitive advantage and superior performance will be exploiting uniqueness.

---

[25]   "Learning to Play the Game," *Economist* (May 17, 1997): 93.

COMPETITOR ANALYSIS

We have argued that in highly concentrated industries, the key characteristics of a company's external environment are determined by the behavior of a few rivals – possibly a single firm. In household detergents, Unilever's industry environment is dominated by the strategy of Procter & Gamble. The same is true in soft drinks (Coke and Pepsi), jet engines (GE, United Technologies, and Rolls-Royce), and networking software (Oracle and Microsoft). Similar circumstances exist in more local markets. For the owner of the Shell gas station in the British village of Coalpit Heath, the dominant feature of the local gasoline market is the competitive behavior of the Texaco station across the road. Game theory provides the primary theoretical apparatus for understanding these situations of competitive interaction between small numbers of rivals. However, as we have seen, in its application to everyday business situations, the promise of game theory has yet to be fulfilled. Given the limitations of formal game theory, more informal approaches to analyzing competitors and predicting their behavior have been adopted. Conventional approaches to competitor analysis focus on two major issues: acquiring information about competitors and predicting their behavior.

Competitor Intelligence

Competitor intelligence involves the systematic collection and analysis of public information about rivals for informing decision making. It has three main purposes:

- To forecast competitors' future strategies and decisions.

- To predict competitors' likely reactions to a firm's strategic initiatives.

- To determine how competitors' behavior can be influenced to make it more favorable.

For all three purposes, the key requirement is to understand competitors in order to predict their choices of strategy and tactics and their reactions to environmental changes and our own competitive moves. To understand competitors, it is important to be informed about them. A growing area of corporate activity in recent years has been competitor intelligence. This interest has been accompanied by a flood of books,[26] a journal devoted to competitive intelligence,[27] and a host of consulting firms specializing in intelligence activities. Almost one-fifth of large US corporations are

---

[26] Larry Kahaner, *Competitive Intelligence: How to Gather, Analyze, and Use Information to Move Your Business to the Top* (Carmichael, CA: Touchstone Books, 1998); Jerry P. Miller (ed.), *Millennium Intelligence: Understanding and Conducting Competitive Intelligence in the Digital Age* (Medford, NJ: Information Today, 2000); Michelle and Curtis Cook, *Competitive Intelligence* (London: Kogan Page, 2000).

[27] *Competitive Intelligence Review* (New York: John Wiley).

estimated to have competitor intelligence units, a proportion that has quadrupled since 1988. *Business Week* reports that Anne Selgas, Eastman Kodak's director of competitive intelligence, reads particularly widely:

> (She) regularly reads an extensive list of publications that even she considers a tad bizarre. Her favorite is the *Transylvania Times*, a semi-weekly out of tiny Brevard in North Carolina's Transylvania County. A medical film rival – Sterling Diagnostic Imaging Inc. – has a plant there, and Selgas says the paper has lots of hiring and layoff news that helps her understand what's going on.[28]

Increased competitive pressures, including the growth of international competition, and greater need for fast responses to changing competitive circumstances have intensified interest in competitors' activities. Discount broker Charles Schwab created its competitor intelligence program in 1994, tracking both traditional and new competitors by paying consultants to visit rivals' offices, hiring competing firms' employees, and quizzing customers. The distinction between public and private information is not always clear; the application of trade secrets law to the information carried by an employee moving between firms is especially murky. As a result, competitor intelligence always runs the risk of degenerating into industrial espionage. General Motors' litigation against Volkswagen over the alleged theft of confidential information by its former manager Jose Ignacio Lopez was a particularly prominent example. And in June 1996, Boehringer Mannheim Corp. sued Johnson & Johnson's Lifescan Inc. for obtaining confidential information relating to its AccuEasy blood-monitoring device through eavesdropping on a sales meeting. A key motivation behind the establishment of associations for professionals specializing in competitive intelligence has been to establish and enforce ethical standards in this shadowy area of competitive activity.[29]

A Framework for Predicting Competitor Behavior

Competitor intelligence is not simply about collecting information. The problem is likely to be too much rather than too little information. The key is a systematic approach that makes clear what information is required and for what purposes it will be used. The objective is to *understand* one's rival. A characteristic of great generals from Hannibal to Patton has been their ability to go beyond military intelligence and to "get inside the heads" of their opposing commanders. A starting point for understanding is a simple framework that states the key questions and a basis for organizing the relevant information (see Figure 4.1). There are four main inputs into the analysis.

---

[28] "They Snoop to Conquer," *Business Week* (October 28, 1996): 172–6.
[29] See, for example, the Society of Competitive Intelligence Professionals (www.scip.org) and the Canadian Institute for Competitive Intelligence (www.cici-icic.ca).

FIGURE 4.1 A framework for competitor analysis

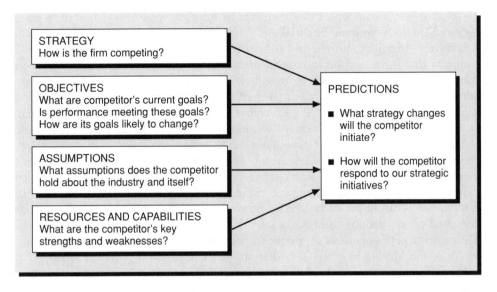

1. Identifying Current Strategy

The starting point is identifying the competitor's current strategy. In the absence of any forces for change, a reasonable assumption is that the company will continue to compete in the future in much the same way as it competes at the present. A competitor's strategy may be identified on the basis of what the firm says and what it does. These two are not necessarily the same. As Mintzberg has pointed out, there may be a divergence between intended strategy and realized strategy.[30] Major sources of explicit statements of strategy intentions can be found in the annual reports of companies, particularly in the chairman's message to shareholders, and in other statements by senior managers, especially in meetings with investment analysts. With regard to emergent strategy, emphasis must be given to competitors' actions and decisions: what capital investment projects are being undertaken, what hiring is taking place, what new products are in the pipeline, what acquisitions or strategic alliances have recently been undertaken or rumored, what new advertising and promotional campaigns have been planned? Because of the importance of communicating both to employees who implement the strategy and to the investment community who need to appraise the company, organizations are becoming more explicit about their strategic plans. Thus, most corporate web sites include not only company reports, financial statements, and press releases, but also copies of presentations and speeches to analysts.

[30] Henry Mintzberg, "Opening up the Definition of Strategy," in James Brian Quinn and Henry Mintzberg (eds), *The Strategy Process: Concepts, Contexts and Cases* (Englewood Cliffs, NJ: Prentice-Hall, 1988).

2. Identifying the Competitor's Objectives

To forecast how a competitor might change its strategy, some knowledge of its goals is crucial. Identifying basic financial and market objectives is particularly important. A company driven by short-term profitability is a very different competitor from a company that is focused on long-term market share goals. A company with market share goals is likely to be much more aggressive in responding to a rival's competitive initiative than one that is mainly interested in the bottom line. The collapse of the British motorcycle industry and the US consumer electronics industry can be attributed, in part, to the willingness of domestic companies to cede market share to Japanese competition in the interests of maintaining short-term profitability.[31] By comparison, Procter & Gamble and Coca-Cola are obsessed with market share and tend to react much more aggressively when a newcomer threatens to take away market share. When a rival is not subject to profitability disciplines at all, this can cause destructive price competition. During the early 1990s, the world aluminum industry was plagued by depressed prices resulting from heavy sales by Russian producers on to world markets. The prices of petrochemicals are frequently depressed by sales from state-owned companies in the Middle East and Asia that are interested more in revenue than profit.

If the competitor is a subsidiary of a larger corporation, it is important to comprehend the goals of the parent, since these goals affect the strategy of the subsidiary. The means by which the parent controls the subsidiary is also important. How much autonomy does the subsidiary have? A subsidiary's ability to respond to competitive assaults may be restricted by corporate control mechanisms.

The level of current performance in relation to the competitor's objectives is important in determining the likelihood of strategy change. The more a company is satisfied with present performance, the more likely it is to continue with the present strategy. If, on the other hand, the competitor's performance is falling well short of target, the likelihood of radical strategic change, possibly accompanied by a change in top management, is increased.

3. Competitors' Assumptions about the Industry

A competitor's strategic decisions are conditioned by its perceptions (of the outside world and of itself) and by assumptions concerning the industry and about business in general. Both are likely to reflect the theories and beliefs that senior managers hold about their industry and the determinants of success within it. Evidence suggests that not only do these systems of belief tend to be stable over time, they also tend to converge within an industry. These industry-wide beliefs about the determinants of success have been described by J.-C. Spender as "industry recipes."[32]

---

[31] Boston Consulting Group, *Strategy Alternatives for the British Motorcycle Industry* (London: Her Majesty's Stationery Office, 1975); M. Dertouzos, R. Lester, and R. Solow, *Made in America: Regaining the Productive Edge* (Cambridge, MA: MIT Press, 1989).

[32] J.-C. Spender, *Industry Recipes: The Nature and Sources of Managerial Judgement* (Oxford: Basil Blackwell, 1989). The propensity for social interaction to result in a convergence of perceptions and beliefs is commonly referred to as "groupthink" and has been discussed by Anne Huff, "Industry Influences on Strategy Reformulation," *Strategic Management Journal* 3 (1982): 119–31.

EXHIBIT 4.1 Motorcycle Myopia

During the 1960s, the motorcycle markets in Britain and the United States were dominated by BSA and Harley-Davidson, respectively. At the beginning of the 1960s, Japanese manufacturers, spearheaded by Honda, began to make inroads into the market for small bikes in both countries. The leading British and US manufacturers discounted the Japanese threat, principally because of their disregard for smaller motorcycles.

Eric Turner, chairman of BSA Ltd. (manufacturer of Triumph and BSA motorcycles), commented in 1965:

> The success of Honda, Suzuki, and Yamaha has been jolly good for us. People start out by buying one of the low-priced Japanese jobs. They get to enjoy the fun and exhilaration of the open road and they frequently end up buying one of our more powerful and expensive machines.

Similar complacency was expressed by William Davidson, president of Harley-Davidson:

> Basically, we do not believe in the lightweight market. We believe that motorcycles are sports vehicles, not transportation vehicles. Even if a man says he bought a motorcycle for transportation, it's generally for leisure time use. The lightweight motorcycle is only supplemental. Back around World War I, a number of companies came out with lightweight bikes. We came out with one ourselves. We came out with another in 1947 and it just didn't go anywhere. We have seen what happens to these small sizes.

By the end of the 1970s, BSA and Triumph had ceased production and Harley-Davidson was barely surviving. The world motorcycle industry, including the large bike segments, was dominated by the Japanese.

Sources: *Advertising Age* (December 27, 1965); *Forbes* (September 15, 1966); Richard T. Pascale, *Honda A* (Harvard Business School, Case 9-384-049, 1983).

Industry recipes may limit the ability of a firm, and indeed an entire industry, to respond rationally and effectively to external change. The result may be that established firms have a "blindspot" to the competitive initiatives of a newcomer. During the 1960s, the Big Three US automobile manufacturers firmly believed that small cars were unprofitable. This belief was based on their own experiences – which were, in part, a consequence of their own cost allocation procedures. As a result, they were willing to yield the fastest-growing segment of the US automobile market to Japanese and European imports. Similar beliefs explain the complacency of British and US motorcycle manufacturers in the face of Japanese competition (see Exhibit 4.1).

4. Identifying the Competitor's Resources and Capabilities

Predicting a competitor's future strategy is not enough. The key issue for a firm is evaluating the seriousness of a potential challenge. The extent to which a competitor threatens a company's market position depends on the competitor's capabilities. Detailed analysis of resources and capabilities is deferred to the next chapter. At this stage, the key elements are an examination of the firm's principal categories of resources, including financial reserves, capital equipment, work force, brand loyalty, and management skills, together with an appraisal of capabilities within each of the major functions: R&D, production, marketing, distribution, and so on.

Circumspection in evaluating a competitor's capabilities is essential before embarking on a strategy that may provoke an aggressive response. Many brilliant and innovative new companies have failed to withstand the aggressive reactions of established, well-financed incumbents. In the US airline industry, most of the new entrants of the early 1980s had been forced out of business by the end of the decade. Conversely, the trepidation felt by established companies in network software, internet browsers, and online information and entertainment over Microsoft's entry to these markets is a result of Microsoft's huge financial resources, its marketing muscle, and its fearsome reputation for market dominance.

Applying the Results of Competitor Analysis

For the purpose of strategy formulation, competitor analysis is useful both in predicting how competitors are likely to behave, and in influencing their behavior. In predicting competitors' behavior, the first question we seek to answer is: "What strategy shifts is the competitor likely to make?" This requires that we carefully identify current forces that are likely to provoke a change in strategy. These may be external – a shift in consumer preferences or regulatory change that may have important consequences for the firm – or they may be internal – a failure to achieve current financial or market share targets, or divisive conflict within the company. Whatever the sources, a careful identification of current strategy and goals and the company's assumptions about the industry and its capabilities provides a sound basis on which to forecast the direction of change.

Second, we may wish to forecast a competitor's likely reactions to a proposed strategy change that our own company is initiating. If this strategy change involves an attack on the competitor's market base, its reactions may be crucial in determining the desirability of the competitive move. The same four elements together provide useful guidance as to the nature, likelihood, and seriousness of a defensive reaction by the competitor. When Honda first attacked BSA/Triumph and Harley-Davidson with the introduction of a large-capacity motorcycle, Honda knew the following:

- Both companies pursued medium-term financial goals rather than market share goals.

- Both firms were benefiting from an upsurge in motorcycle demand; hence, they were not unduly sensitive to losses in market share.

- Both firms believed that, due to their own customer loyalty and brand image, the Japanese producers were not a serious threat in the big bike market.

- Even if BSA/Triumph and Harley-Davidson did react aggressively, the effectiveness of their response would be limited by their weak financial positions and by their lack of innovation and manufacturing capabilities.

Once we understand our competitor, we can explore opportunities for influencing its behavior. Here we draw on the tools of game theory outlined above: deterrence, commitment, signaling, and changing the structure of the game.

SEGMENTATION ANALYSIS[33]

The Uses of Segmentation

Conventionally, industries are defined broadly: the automobile industry, the computer software industry, the airline industry. As we have acknowledged, however, competition tends to occur at a more localized level – within specific product groups and specific national or regional markets. Hence, if our competitive analysis begins at an aggregated level, it is likely that we shall need to disaggregate in order to develop carefully targeted competitive strategies. To do so we need to segment industries and markets. Such segmentation is particularly important if the nature and intensity of competition varies among the different submarkets that an industry serves. Such analysis is useful for the new entrant in determining the most attractive part of a market to enter, and for established firms in deciding how to allocate resources among different segments. The ability to identify and shift resources to attractive segments can help a company outperform the industry average by a significant margin. In the PC industry, Dell Computer has been highly effective in focusing on products and customer groups that offer higher margins. Its direct distribution model allows it to analyze profability on a customer-by-customer basis: "We cut the market and then cut it again, looking for the most profitable customers to serve," says vice chairman Kevin Rollins.[34]

Differences in customers and competition between segments may also mean differences in key success factors. In the US beer industry, competing effectively in the market for standard, packaged beer requires cost-efficient operation in the form of large-scale, automated production, national distribution through a network of franchised distributors, and heavy investment in advertising and promotion. However, in the market for specialty beers, success is far more dependent on a carefully crafted, high-quality, flavorful product; local mystique; and localized distribution that emphasizes freshness and careful handling.

Stages in Segmentation Analysis

Segmentation analysis proceeds in five principal stages. Exhibit 4.2 summarizes these stages and applies them to the European metal container industry.

---

[33] This section draws heavily on the approach used by Michael E. Porter, *Competitive Advantage* (New York: Free Press, 1985): Chapter 7.
[34] O. Gadiesh and J. L. Gilbert, "Profit Pools: A Fresh Look at Strategy," *Harvard Business Review* (May–June 1998): 146.

EXHIBIT 4.2   Segmenting the European Metal Can Industry

1. Identify Key Segmentation Variables and Categories

- Identify possible segmentation variables

  Raw material, can design, can size, customer size, customer's industry, location

- Reduce the number of segmentation variables: Which are most significant? Which are closely correlated and can be combined?

  Type of can, customer industry, customer location

- Identify discrete categories for each segmentation variable.

  Type of can: steel 3-piece, steel 2-piece, aluminum 2-piece, general cans, composite cans, aerosols. Type of customer: food processing, fruit juice, petfood, soft drink, toiletries, beer, oil. Location: France, Germany, Spain/Portugal, Italy, UK, Benelux/Netherlands).

2. Construct a Segmentation Matrix

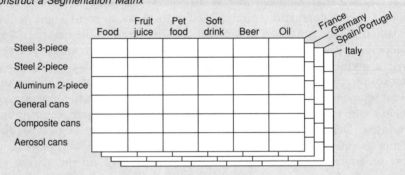

3. Analyze Segment Attractiveness

Apply Five Forces analysis to individual segments. For example, the market for aluminum 2-piece cans to soft drink canners in Italy may be analyzed as follows:

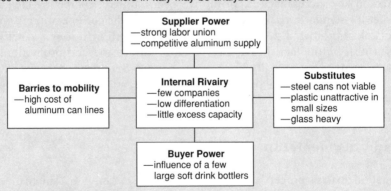

4. Identify Key Success Factors in Each Segment

Within each segment, how do customers choose, and what is needed to survive competition?

5. Analyze Attractions of Broad versus Narrow Segment Scope

- What is the potential to share costs and transfer skills across segments?
- How similar are key success factors between segments?
- Are there benefits of segment specialization?

1. Identify Key Segmentation Variables

The first stage of segmentation analysis is to determine the basis of segmentation. Segment decisions essentially are choices about products and customers, hence segmentation variables relate to the characteristics of the product or characteristics of customers. Figure 4.2 lists a number of segmentation variables. The most appropriate segmentation variables are those that partition the market most distinctly in terms of substitutability among customers (demand-side substitutability) and producers (supply-side substitutability). Market segments tend to be recognizable from price differentials. A classic example of price-based segmentation was by General Motors during the 1920s. In contrast to Henry Ford's single-model strategy, Alfred Sloan identified six market segments ranging from the lowest price category, $450–$600, to the highest, $2,500–$3,500. Each of GM's divisions targeted a separate price segment, with Chevrolet at the bottom and Cadillac at the top.[35]

Typically, there are many customer and product characteristics that can be used as a basis for segmentation. In order for a segmentation analysis to be manageable, we need to reduce these to two or three. This requires that we do the following:

FIGURE 4.2   The basis for segmentation: the characteristics of buyers and products

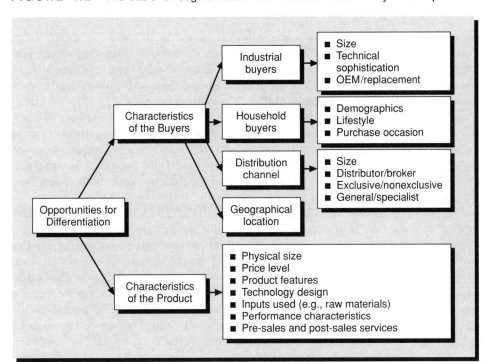

---

[35]   Alfred P. Sloan, *My Years with General Motors* (London: Sidgwick & Jackson, 1963): 65, 67.

- Identify the most *strategically significant* segmentation variables. Which variables are most important in creating meaningful divisions in a market? In the case of metal containers, location is critical (cans are expensive to transport over long distances), as is raw material (influences both demand-side and supply-side substitutability).

- Combine segmentation variables that are closely correlated. In the case of restaurants, possible segmentation variables such as price level, service (waiter service/self-service), cuisine (fast-food/full meals), and alcohol license (wine served/soft drinks only) could be combined into a single variable, restaurant type, with three categories: full-service restaurants, cafés, and fast-food outlets.

2. Construct a Segmentation Matrix

Once the segmentation variables have been selected and discrete categories determined for each, the individual segments may be identified using a two- or three-dimensional matrix. Thus, the European metal container industry might be analyzed in a three-dimensional segmentation matrix (see Exhibit 4.2), whereas the world automobile industry might be segmented simply by vehicle type and geographical region (see Exhibit 4.3).

3. Analyze Segment Attractiveness

Profitability within an industry segment is determined by the same structural forces that determine profitability within an industry as a whole. As a result, Porter's Five Forces of Competition framework is equally effective in relation to a segment as to an entire industry. Exhibit 4.3 outlines some implications of a Five Forces analysis for certain segments of the world automobile industry.

There are, however, a few differences. First, when analyzing the pressure of competition from substitute products, we are concerned not only with substitutes from other industries, but, more importantly, substitutes from other segments within the same industry. For example, in deciding whether to introduce a station wagon version of its Mondeo/Contour sedan, Ford's analysis of the station wagon market must consider substitute competition from passenger minivans.

Second, when considering entry into the segment, the main source of entrants is likely to be producers established in other segments within the same industry. Thus, the threat of entry into a segment depends on whether there are barriers that restrict the entry of firms from other segments. These are termed *barriers to mobility* to distinguish them from the barriers to entry that offer protection from outside the industry. Barriers to mobility are key factors in determining the ability of a segment to offer superior returns to those available elsewhere in the industry. Unless there are significant barriers to the mobility of firms from other segments, a segment will be unable to maintain superior profitability to that of the industry.[36] In most industries, the increased flexibility of design and production made possible by computer-aided design and flexible manufacturing

---

[36] For a formal analysis of mobility barriers, see Richard E. Caves and Michael E. Porter, "From Entry Barriers to Mobility Barriers: Conjectural Decisions and Contrived Deterrence to New Competition," *Quarterly Journal of Economics* 91 (1977): 241–62.

EXHIBIT 4.3 Segmenting the World Automobile Market

A global automobile producer such as Ford or Toyota might segment the world auto market by product type and geography. A first-cut segmentation might be along the following lines:

REGIONS

		North America	Western Europe	Eastern Europe	Asia	Latin America	Australasia	Africa
P R O D U C T S	Luxury cars							
	Full-size sedans							
	Mid-size sedans							
	Small sedans							
	Station wagons							
	Minivans							
	Sports cars							
	Sport-utility							
	Pickup trucks							

To identify segments with the best profit prospects for the future, we need to understand why, in the past, some segments have been more profitable than others. For example, during the 1990s:

■ The North American market for small sedans was unprofitable due to many competitors (all the world's major auto producers were represented), lack of clear product differentiation, and customers' price sensitivity.

■ The North American/European markets for passenger minivans have been highly profitable segments due to strong demand relative to capacity, and comparatively few participants. Chrysler's survival during the 1980s was primarily owing to its strong position within this segment. The influx of companies into minivans was eroding margins by the late 1990s.

■ The luxury car segment is traditionally a high-margin segment due to few players, high product differentiation, and price insensitivity of buyers. However, margins in the 1990s were low: the small size of the segment made it difficult to spread the fixed costs of new model development; the new entry by Honda (Acura), Toyota (Lexus), and Nissan (Infiniti) and the acquisition of Jaguar by Ford increased competition.

Once we understand the factors that determined segment profitability in the past, we can predict segment profitability in the future.

systems has had the effect of reducing barriers to mobility. In the automobile industry, high-margin segments such as luxury cars, passenger vans, and sport-utility vehicles have seen a sharp rise in competition as volume car manufacturers have entered them.

Segmentation analysis can also be useful in identifying unexploited opportunities in an industry. For example, a segmentation matrix of the restaurant industry in a town or locality might reveal a number of empty segments. The interesting question is whether such empty segments represent unexploited opportunities or whether they reflect a lack of customer demand. Consider the market for kitchen appliances. In the early 1960s, microwave ovens and dishwashers were manufactured almost exclusively for the catering trade. A segmentation analysis of the appliance industry might have alerted the firms established in these segments to opportunities for developing these products for the consumer market.

4. Identify the Segment's Key Success Factors

Differences in competitive structure and in customer preferences between segments imply differences in the basis of competitive advantage. Using the same analysis of buyers' purchase criteria and the basis on which firms compete that was outlined in Chapter 3 (see Figure 3.8), we can identify key success factors for individual segments.

For example, the US bicycle industry can be segmented on the basis of the age group of the customer (infants, children, youths, adults), price, branding, and distribution channel. Combining and categorizing these segmentation variables results in four major segments, each with different key success factors (see Figure 4.3).

5. Select Segment Scope

A final issue relating to the choice of which segments to enter concerns the relative advantages of segment specialization versus segment diversity. The advantages of a

FIGURE 4.3   Segmentation and key success factors: the US bicycle industry

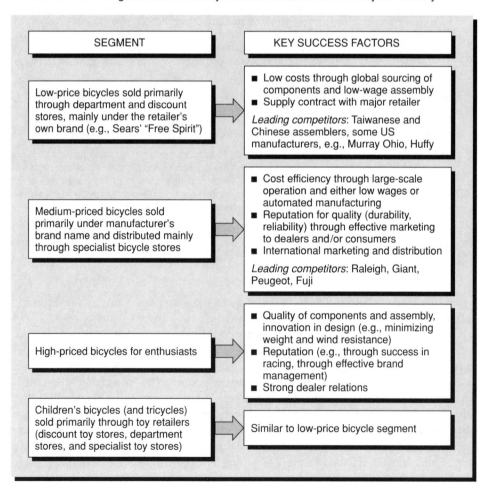

broad over a narrow segment focus depend on two main factors: similarity of key success factors and the presence of shared costs. In an industry where key success factors are similar across segments, a firm can adopt a similar strategic approach in relation to different segments. If different strategies need to be adopted for different segments, not only does this pose organizational difficulties for the firm, but also the credibility of the firm in one segment may be adversely affected by its strategy in another. Harley-Davidson's introduction of a range of lightweight motorcycles during the early 1970s was a failure, not only because Harley-Davidson could not compete with the Japanese in this segment, but also because of the damage to the firm's reputation in the heavyweight motorcycle segment. During 1999–2000, Mercedes-Benz suffered a similar fate with its A-class compact car.

Shared costs mean that broad-segment suppliers can achieve lower costs than their narrow-segment competitors. The vulnerability of narrow-segment specialists to competition from broad-line competitors is constantly being revealed.

- In soft drinks, Seven Up's reliance on a single lemon-lime drink made it vulnerable to competition from broad-line competitors such as Coca-Cola and Pepsi. Ultimately, Seven Up, together with Dr. Pepper, was acquired by Cadbury Schweppes.

- The acquisition of specialist auto producers Saab, Lancia, Jaguar, AMC-Jeep, Maserati, Audi, Alfa-Romeo, and Rolls-Royce by broad-segment car makers was a result of the inability of these specialists to spread their development costs over a large enough sales volume.

The relative merits of focused and broad-segment strategies vary among industries. The critical issue concerns the benefits of specialization versus those of sharing joint costs. In service industries, William Davidow and Bro Uttal have argued that economies from specialization and differences in key success factors in different customer segments favor a narrow segment focus. By specializing in hernia surgery, for example, Shouldice Hospital near Toronto achieves remarkable levels of productivity and quality.[37] In audio equipment, specialists (such as Bose and Bang & Olufsen) have continued to dominate the high-quality segment against the major consumer electronics companies such as Sony, Matsushita, and Philips.

The issues of specialization versus spreading common costs over multiple markets are similar to diversification decisions. We return to this discussion in Chapter 15.

Vertical Segmentation: Profit Pools

Segmentation is usually thought of in terms of segmenting markets according to customer characteristics. However, from an industry viewpoint we can also segment an industry vertically in terms of its value chain activities. Bain & Company argues that profitability varies greatly across the range of vertical activities within an industry. It proposes *profit pool mapping* as a technique for analyzing the vertical structure

---

[37] William H. Davidson and Bro Uttal, "Service Companies: Focus or Falter," *Harvard Business Review* (July–August 1989): 77–84.

FIGURE 4.4   The US auto industry profit pool

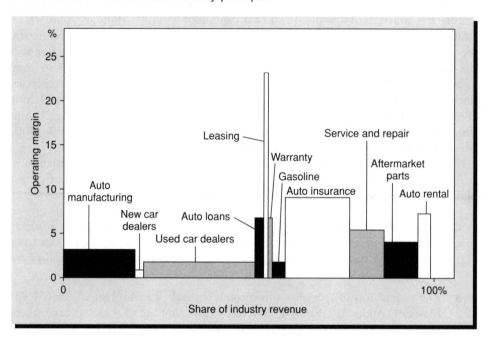

of profitability.[38] Thus, in the US automobile industry, downstream activities such as finance, leasing, insurance, and service and repair are more profitable than manufacturing (see Figure 4.4). In response to these differences, Ford has scaled back its manufacturing investments and invested increasingly in finance and parts. During the 1990s, about half of Ford's profits came from its financing activities. It is similar with the PC industry. The manufacture of personal computers accounts for a small proportion of the total profit pool. Microprocessors, other components, peripherals, and services each contribute significantly more.

To map an industry's profit pool, Bain & Company identifies four steps:

1. *Defining the pool's boundaries.* What is the range of value-adding activities that your business sector encompasses? The Bain consultants argue that it may be desirable to look beyond conventional industry boundaries.

2. *Estimating the pool's overall size.* Total industry profit may be available from industry reports or by applying the average margin earned by a sample of companies to an estimate of industry total revenues.

3. *Estimating the size of each value chain activity in the pool.* Here is the key challenge. It requires gathering data from companies that are "pure players"

---

[38]   O. Gadiesh and J. L. Gilbert, "Profit Pools: A Fresh Look at Strategy," *Harvard Business Review* (May–June 1998): 139–47; O. Gadiesh and J. L. Gilbert, "How to Map Your Industry's Profit Pools," *Harvard Business Review* (May–June 1998): 149–62.

– specialized in the single value chain activity – and disaggregating data for "mixed players" – those performing multiple activities.

4. *Checking and reconciling the calculations.* Comparing the aggregation of profits in each activity (stage 3) with the total for the industry (stage 2) provides opportunities for reconciling differences and refining the estimates.

STRATEGIC GROUPS

Whereas segmentation analysis concentrates on the characteristics of markets as the basis for disaggregating industries, strategic group analysis uses the characteristics of firms as the basis for division. A strategic group is "the group of firms in an industry following the same or a similar strategy along the strategic dimensions."[39] Strategic dimensions include those decision variables that best distinguish the business strategies and competitive positioning of the firms within an industry. These may include product market scope (in terms of product range and geographical breadth), choice of distribution channels, level of product quality, degree of vertical integration, choice of technology, and so on. By selecting the most important strategic dimensions and locating each firm in the industry along them, it is usually possible to identify one or more groups of companies that have adopted more or less similar approaches to competing within the industry. Figure 4.5 identifies strategic groups within the world automobile industry, and Figure 4.6 strategic groups within the oil industry.[40]

Strategic groups were developed as a result of empirical analysis of the domestic appliance[41] and brewing industries.[42] Most of the empirical research into strategic groups has been concerned with analyzing differences in profitability among firms.[43] The basic argument is that mobility barriers between strategic groups permit some groups of firms to be persistently more profitable than other groups. In general, the proposition that profitability differences *within* strategic groups are less than differences *between* strategic groups has not received robust empirical support.[44] The inconsistency of empirical findings may reflect the fact that the members of a strategic

[39] Michael E. Porter, *Competitive Strategy* (New York: Free Press, 1980): 129.

[40] For further discussion of strategic groups and their role in strategy analysis, see John McGee and Howard Thomas, "Strategic Groups: Theory, Research, and Taxonomy," *Strategic Management Journal* 7 (1986): 141–60.

[41] Michael Hunt, *Competition in the Major Home Appliance Industry*, doctoral dissertation (Harvard University, 1973); and Michael E. Porter, "Structure Within Industries and Companies' Performance," *Review of Economics and Statistics* 61 (1979): 214–27.

[42] Ken Hatten, Dan Schendel, and Arnold Cooper, "A Strategic Model of the US Brewing Industry," *Academy of Management Journal* 21 (1978): 592–610.

[43] Karl Cool and Dan Schendel, "Strategic Group Formation and Performance: The Case of the US Pharmaceutical Industry," *Management Science* 33 (1987): 1102–24; A. Feigenbaum and H. Thomas, "Strategic Groups and Performance: The US Insurance Industry," *Strategic Management Journal* 11 (1990): 197–215.

[44] K. Cool and I. Dierickx, "Rivalry, Strategic Groups, and Firm Profitability," *Strategic Management Journal* 14 (1993): 47–59.

FIGURE 4.5 Strategic groups within the world automobile industry

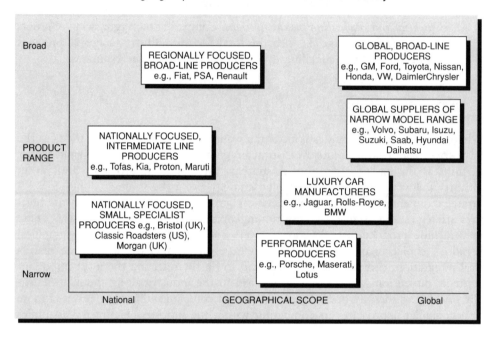

FIGURE 4.6 Strategic groups within the world petroleum industry

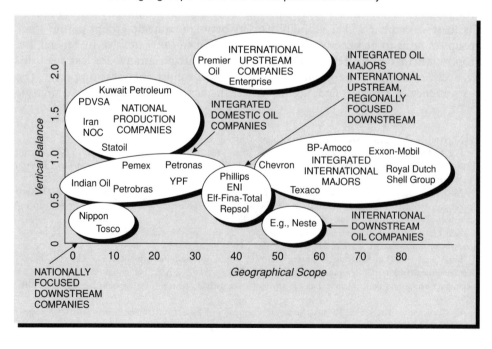

group, though pursuing similar strategies, are not necessarily in competition with one another. For example, within the world oil industry, the nationally based integrated oil companies such as Petrobras (Brazil), Indian Oil, Mitsubishi Oil (Japan), and Petronas (Indonesia) are located within the same strategic group, but do not compete directly with one another. Results from the US airline industry suggest that, though strategic group analysis may not tell us much about profitability differences, it can be useful in helping us understand the types of competitive responses by different firms within an industry.[45]

For our purposes, strategic group analysis is more valuable as a descriptive than a predictive tool. Because strategic group analysis focuses on strategic similarities rather than competitive relationships, its potential for explaining inter-firm profitability differences is limited. However, as a means of gaining a broad picture of the types of firms within an industry, the kinds of strategies that have proved viable, and how different firms are positioned in relation to one another, strategic group analysis can contribute substantially to the understanding of industry structure, firm strategy, and industry evolution. This view of strategic groups as a valuable descriptive device is supported by Reger and Huff's evidence that managers within an industry have consistent perceptions of groupings of similar firms.[46]

SUMMARY

The purpose of this chapter has been to go beyond the industry-level analysis of Chapter 3. In this chapter we recognize that competition is not simply a description of the state of the extenal environment, it is an interactive process of strategic initiatives and responses. We have used game theory to explore competition as an process of dynamic interaction and to recognize how strategy choices must take account of the reactions of other firms. At a less formal level, we have introduced a practical approach to appraising cometitors and predicting their behavior. "Getting inside" competitors in order to understand and influence competitive interaction lies at the heart of strategy analysis. An essential characteristic of successful strategists, whether corporate chief executives, military commanders, political leaders, or chess players, is their ability insightfully to analyze their opponents.

Because most industires, as conventionally defined, are too broad an entity for formulating competitive strategy at a detailed level, we have shown how segmentation analysis can disaggregate industries and markets, permitting a company to identify segments with the greatest profit potential, recognize differences in key success factors across segments, and evaluate niche strategies as compared with multisegment strategies.

[45]   Ken Smith, Curtis Grimm, and Stefan Wally, "Strategic Groups and Rivalrous Firm Behavior: Toward a Reconciliation," *Strategic Management Journal* 18 (1997): 149–57.

[46]   R. K. Reger and A. S. Huff, "Strategic Groups: Cognitive Perspective," *Strategic Management Journal* 14 (1993): 103–24.

5

Analyzing Resources and Capabilities

Analysts have tended to define assets too narrowly, identifying only those that can be measured, such as plant and equipment. Yet the intangible assets, such as a particular technology, accumulated consumer information, brand name, reputation, and corporate culture, are invaluable to the firm's competitive power. In fact, these invisible assets are often the only real source of competitive edge that can be sustained over time.

—**Hiroyuki Itami,** Mobilizing Invisible Assets

You've gotta do what you do well.
—**Lucino Noto, Vice Chairman, Exxon Mobil**

OUTLINE

INTRODUCTION AND OBJECTIVES

In Chapter 1, we observed that a major change in strategy thinking over the past decade has been a shift in focus from the industry environment to internal aspects of the firm. In this chapter, we will make the same transition. In concentrating attention on the resources and capabilities of the firm, we shall also encounter ideas, concepts, and techniques that will form the foundation for our analysis of competitive advantage.

By the time you have completed this chapter you will be able to:

■ Appreciate the role of a company's resources and capabilities as a basis for formulating strategy.

■ Identify and appraise the resources and capabilities of a firm.

■ Evaluate the potential for a company's resources and capabilities to confer sustainable competitive advantage, and hence earn a stream of economic rents for the firm.

■ Use the results of resource and capability analysis to formulate strategies that exploit internal strengths while defending against internal weaknesses.

■ Recognize the challenge and the opportunities for developing the firm's base of resources and capabilities.

We begin by explaining why a company's resources and capabilities are so important to its strategy.

FIGURE 5.1 Analyzing resources and capabilities: the interface between strategy and the firm

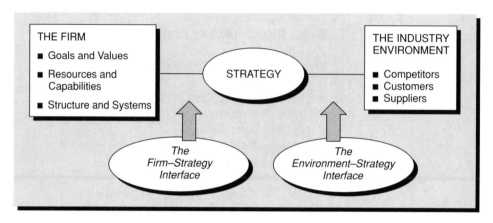

THE ROLE OF RESOURCES AND CAPABILITIES IN STRATEGY FORMULATION

Strategy is concerned with matching a firm's resources and capabilities to the opportunities that arise in the external environment. So far, the emphasis of the book has been the interface between strategy and the external environment of the firm. With this chapter, our emphasis shifts to the interface between strategy and the internal environment of the firm, and, more specifically, to the resources and capabilities of the firm (see Figure 5.1).

This shift of focus parallels the changing emphasis within strategic management during the 1990s. In the 1980s, most developments in strategy analysis concentrated on the industry environment of the firm and its competitive positioning in relation to rivals; the work of Michael Porter is especially prominent in this area. By contrast, strategic analysis of the firm's internal environment remained underdeveloped. Analysis of the internal environment was, for the most part, concerned with issues of strategy implementation – the design of structure, control systems, and management style – all of which were viewed as consequences of the strategy adopted.[1] The comparative neglect of internal resources by business strategists contrasted sharply with military strategy, which had been dominated by the analysis of relative resource strength. From seventeenth-century Europe until the collapse of the Soviet Union, international diplomacy had been based on the resource-based notion of *balance of*

---

[1] Analysis of the internal environment of the firm has also been given prominence by researchers who have investigated the process of strategy formulation. Researchers who have approached strategy formulation from a behavioral science perspective view it not as rational optimizing decisions made with objective information, but either as an evolving pattern of decisions and actions, e.g., Henry Mintzberg, "Crafting Strategy," *Harvard Business Review* (July–August 1987): 66–75, or as a political process within the firm, e.g., Andrew M. Pettigrew, "Strategy Formulation as a Political Process," *International Studies of Management and Organization* 7, no. 2 (1977): 78–87.

power. The unease among the German High Command over Hitler's military strategy throughout World War II reflected recognition that Germany did not possess the resources simultaneously to wage war on the Eastern, Western, and North African fronts as well as in the sky and sea. Military historian Liddell Hart has gone so far as to argue that there is only one underlying principle of military strategy: "concentration of strength against weakness."[2]

Basing Strategy on Resources and Capabilities

During the 1990s, ideas concerning the role of a firm's resources and capabilities as the principal basis for its strategy and the primary source of its profitability coalesced into what has become known as the *resource-based view of the firm*.[3] Central to this "resource-based view" is the idea that the firm is essentially a pool of resources and capabilities, and that these resources and capabilities are the primary determinants of its strategy.

To understand why this is a radical idea, let us go back to the starting point for strategy formulation, which is typically some statement of the firm's identity and purpose (typically a mission statement). Fundamental to this identity and purpose is an answer to the question: "What is our business?" Traditionally, firms have defined their businesses in terms of the market they serve: "Who are our customers?" and "Which of their needs are we seeking to serve?" However, in a world where customer preferences are volatile and the identity of customers and the technologies for serving them are changing, a market-focused strategy may not provide the stability and constancy of direction needed as a foundation for long-term strategy. When the external environment is in a state of flux, the firm itself, in terms of its bundle of resources and capabilities, may be a much more stable basis on which to define its identity. Hence, a definition of the firm in terms of what it is capable of doing may offer a more durable basis for strategy than a definition based on the needs that the business seeks to satisfy.[4]

Theodore Levitt's solution to the problem of external change was that companies should define their markets broadly (in terms of underlying customer needs) rather than narrowly (in terms of specific products): railroads should have seen themselves as being in the transportation business, not the railroad business.[5] However, such broadening of the target market is of little value if the company cannot easily develop the capabilities required for serving customer requirements across a wide front. Although railroad companies have entered into the airlines, shipping, and trucking

---

[2]   B. H. Liddell Hart, *Strategy* (New York: Praeger, 1954): 365.

[3]   The "resource-based view" is described in J. B. Barney, "Firm Resources and Sustained Competitive Advantage," *Journal of Management* 17 (1991): 99–120; J. Mahoney and J. R. Pandian, "The Resource-Based View within the Conversation of Strategic Management," *Strategic Management Journal* 13 (1992): 363–80; M. A. Peterlaf, "The Cornerstones of Competitive Advantage: A Resource-Based View," *Strategic Management Journal* 14 (1993): 179–92; David Collis and Cynthia Montgomery, "Competing on Resources: Strategy in the 1990s," *Harvard Business Review* (July–August 1995): 119–28.

[4]   J. B. Quinn emphasizes the need for companies to focus their strategies around the activities of their key internal strengths in *Intelligent Enterprise* (New York: Free Press, 1992).

[5]   Theodore Levitt, "Marketing Myopia," *Harvard Business Review* (July–August 1960): 24–47.

FIGURE 5.2   Resource-based strategy: Honda

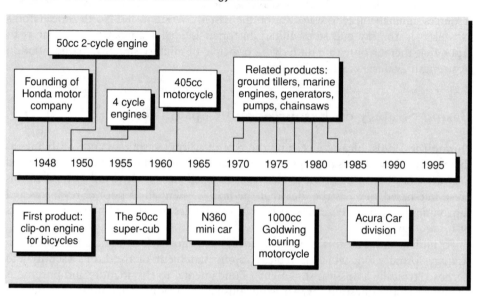

industries, their performance in these markets was generally poor. Perhaps the resources and capabilities of the railroad companies were better suited to real-estate development, pipelines, telecommunications, or oil and gas exploration – businesses where several of these railroad firms did, in fact, prosper.

Many of the companies that have sought to serve broadly defined customer needs have experienced considerable difficulties:

- Efforts by Merrill Lynch, American Express, and Sears Roebuck to "serve the full range of financial needs of our customers" by diversifying across stock-broking, retail banking, investment banking, insurance, and real-estate brokerage gave rise to serious problems and resulted in disappointing profitability.[6]

- Allegis Corporation's attempt to "serve the needs of the traveler" through combining United Airlines, Hertz car rental, and Westin Hotels was a costly failure.

By contrast, several companies whose strategies have been based on developing and exploiting clearly defined internal capabilities have successfully adjusted to and exploited external change:

- Honda's strategy since its founding in 1948 has been built around its expertise in the development and manufacture of engines; this capability has successfully carried it from motorcycles to a number of gasoline-engined products (see Figure 5.2).

---

[6]   Robert M. Grant, "Diversification in Financial Services: Why Are the Benefits So Elusive?," in A. Campbell and K. Luchs (eds), *Strategic Synergy* (London: Heinemann, 1994).

FIGURE 5.3   The evolution of capabilities and products: 3M

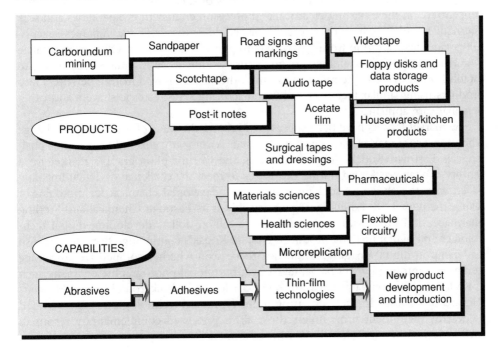

■   3M Corporation has expanded from sandpaper, into adhesive tapes, audiotapes and videotapes, road signs, medical products, and floppy disks. Its product list comprises over 30,000 separate products. Is it a conglomerate? Certainly not, claims 3M. Its vast product range rests on a foundation of key technologies relating to adhesives and thin-film coatings, and its remarkable ability to manage the development and marketing of new products (see Figure 5.3).

In general, the greater the rate of change in a firm's external environment, the more likely it is that internal resources and capabilities will provide a secure foundation for long-term strategy. In fast-moving, technology-based industries, new companies are built around specific technological capabilities. The markets where these capabilities are applied are a secondary consideration. Motorola, the Texas-based supplier of wireless telecommunications equipment, semiconductors, and direct satellite communications, has undergone many transformations, from being a leading provider of TVs and car radios to its current focus on telecom equipment. Yet, underlying these transformations has been a consistent focus on technological leadership in electronic components – semiconductors in particular.

When a company faces the imminent obsolescence of its core product, does it orient its strategy around external customer needs or internal resources and capabilities? Consider the typewriter manufacturers facing the microcomputer revolution of the 1980s. As microcomputers displaced typewriters, should companies pursue their traditional market focus and attempt to acquire the electronic technology necessary to continue to serve the word-processing needs of their customers? Or should they concentrate on their existing electrical and precision engineering capabilities and seek alternative markets where these capabilities could be used? Few companies successfully made this transition from typewriters to personal computers. Olivetti, the Italian typewriter and office equipment manufacturer, built up substantial losses trying to establish itself in PCs.[7] Remington, on the other hand, moved from typewriters into products using similar technical and manufacturing skills: electric shavers and other personal care appliances.[8]

Few market leaders have been successful in riding the wave of technological change when their core market has been transformed. A company currently facing this challenge is Eastman Kodak. After dominating the world's photographic market for a century, Kodak was forced during the 1990s to meet the challenge of digital imaging. Faced with the choice of sticking with its well-developed chemical technologies or taking the plunge into digital imaging, it sold off its Eastman Chemical and Sterling pharmaceutical businesses, and spent over a billion dollars developing digital technologies and digital imaging products. Despite Kodak's continuing efforts to establish leadership in digital imaging, it remains to be seen whether competitive advantage in digital photography will be achieved by a traditional photographic company such as Kodak, or by a company with a strong microelectronics background such as Hewlett-Packard or Canon.[9] In the typesetting industry, radical technological change tended to destroy incumbent firms unless those firms possessed complementary resources such as reputation and close links with customers.[10]

Resources and Capabilities as Sources of Profit

In Chapter 1, we noted that superior profitability might derive from two sources: location within an attractive industry, and achieving a competitive advantage over rivals. Industry analysis emphasizes the former: superior profitability is the result of market power conferred by favorable industry structures. The implication is that strategic management is concerned with locating within attractive industries and industry segments, and adopting strategies that modify industry conditions and competitor behavior in order to moderate competition. This approach has been undermined by two factors. First, now that internationalization, deregulation, and other forces have increased competitive pressure within most sectors, few industries (or segments) offer cozy refuges from vigorous competition. Second, empirical research

---

[7]   "Olivetti: On the Ropes," *Economist* (May 20, 1995): 60–61; "Olivetti Reinvents Itself Once More," *Wall Street Journal* (February 22, 1999): A.1.
[8]   www.remington-products.com.
[9]   "Blurred Image: Kodak Moment Came Early for CEO Fisher, Who Takes a Stumble," *Wall Street Journal* (July 25, 1997): A1; "Eastman Kodak: Meeting the Digital Challenge," in R. M. Grant and K. E. Neupert, *Contemporary Strategy Analysis* (Oxford, Blackwell, 1999): 90–112.
[10]   M. Tripsas, "Unraveling the Process of Creative Destruction: Complementary Assets and Incumbent Survival in the Typesetter Industry," *Strategic Management Journal*, 18, Summer special issue (1997): 119–42.

suggests that industry factors account for only a small proportion of inter-firm profit differentials.[11] Hence, establishing competitive advantage through the development and deployment of resources and capabilities, rather than seeking shelter from the storm of competition, has become the primary goal for strategy.

The distinction between industry attractiveness and competitive advantage based on superior resources as the primary determinant of a firm's performance corresponds to the distinction that economists make between different types of profit (or *rent*). The profits associated with lack of competition are referred to as *monopoly rents*; those associated with the possession of superior resources are *Ricardian rents*, after the nineteenth-century British economist David Ricardo. Ricardo explained why fertile land was able to earn high returns even when the market for wheat was competitive. Ricardian (or scarcity) rent is the return earned by a resource over and above that required to bring it into production.[12]

In practice, distinguishing the profits associated with industry attractiveness from those associated with owning superior resources and capabilities is difficult. A closer look at Porter's Five Forces frameworks suggests that monopoly rents derive ultimately from the ownership of resources. Barriers to entry, for example, are the result of patents, brands, distribution channels, learning, or some other resource that incumbent firms possess but that entrants can acquire only slowly over time or at disproportionate expense. A monopoly or oligopoly position in an industry is founded on the possession of reputation, know-how, manufacturing capacity, or distribution facilities that other firms in the industry cannot match.

The resource-based view of the firm has had a profound impact on our understanding of strategy formulation. When the primary concern of strategy was industry selection and positioning for cost and differentiation advantage, the tendency was for companies to adopt similar strategies. The resource-based view emphasizes the uniqueness of each company and suggests that the key to profitability is not through doing the *same* as other firms, but rather through exploiting *differences*. Establishing competitive advantage involves formulating and implementing a strategy that exploits the unique features of each firm's collection of resources and capabilities. Thus, although Southwest Airlines, Wal-Mart, and YKK (in zip fasteners) all pursue strategies of cost leadership, each does so through the deployment of unique sets of resources and capabilities and through distinctive strategies and organizational systems. Other companies can learn from their experiences, but any attempt to replicate the strategy of any of these companies would almost certainly be both impossible and undesirable.

---

[11]   Richard P. Rumelt, "How Much Does Industry Matter?," *Strategic Management Journal* 12 (1991): 167–85, found that among 2,180 business units, only 4 percent of the variance of return on assets was attributable to the influence of industry. A. J. Mauri and M. P. Michaels, "Firm and Industry Effects with Strategic Management: An Empirical Examination," *Strategic Management Journal*, 19 (1998): 211–19 also found that industry membership accounted for only a small part of interfirm profit differentials. However, A. M. McGahan and M. E. Porter, "How Much Does Industry Matter, Really?," *Strategic Management Journal* 18, Summer special issue (1997), found that industry effects accounted for 19 percent of variation in business unit profitability.

[12]   For a discussion of different types and sources of profit, see Jeff W. Trailer, "On the Theory of Rent and the Mechanics of Profitability," working paper #00-1 (Pennsylvania State University, Erie, 2000).

The remainder of this chapter outlines a resource-based approach to strategy formulation. The basic requirement is that the firm seeks a thorough and profound understanding of its resources and capabilities. Such understanding then provides a basis for:

1. Selecting a strategy that exploits a firm's key strengths. Walt Disney's turn-around under Michael Eisner's leadership was the result of exploiting its underlying resources more effectively (see Exhibit 5.1).

2. Developing the firm's resources and capabilities. Resource analysis is not just about deploying existing resources, it is also concerned with filling resource gaps and building capability for the future. Toyota, Microsoft, Johnson

---

EXHIBIT 5.1 Resource Utilization: Revival at Walt Disney

When Michael Eisner arrived at Walt Disney Productions in 1984 to take over as president, the company was in its fourth consecutive year of declining net income and its share price had fallen to a level that was attracting predators. Between 1984 and 1988, Disney's sales revenue increased from $1.66 billion to $3.75 billion, net income from $98 million to $570 million, and the stock market's valuation of the company from $1.8 billion to $10.3 billion. Yet, during Eisner's first three years at Disney, there was no major shift of strategy. All Disney's major initiatives of the 1980s – the Epcot Center, Tokyo Disneyland, Touchstone Films, the Disney Channel, and the acquisition of Arvida Corporation – had been launched by the previous management.

The key to the Disney turnaround was the mobilization of Disney's considerable resource base. Prominent among Disney's underutilized resources were 28,000 acres of land in Florida. With the help of the Arvida Corporation, a land development company acquired in 1984, Disney began hotel, resort, and residential development of these landholdings. New attractions were added to the Epcot Center, and a new theme park, the Disney-MGM Studio Tour, was added. Disney World expanded beyond theme parks into resort vacations, the convention business, and residential housing.

In exploiting its huge film library, Disney went far beyond its usual practice of periodic re-releases of its classic movies. It introduced videocassette sales of Disney movies and licensed packages of movies to TV networks. A single package of films licensed to a European TV network raised $21 million. The huge investments in the Disney theme parks were more effect-ively exploited through heavier marketing effort and increased admission charges. Encouraged by the success of Tokyo Disneyland, Disney embarked on further international duplication of its US theme parks with Euro Disneyland just outside Paris, France.

The most ambitious feature of the turnaround was Disney's regeneration as a movie studio. As well as maintaining the company's commitment to high-quality family movies (and cartoons in particular), Eisner began a massive expansion of its Touchstone label, which had been established in 1983 with the objectives of putting Disney's film studios to fuller use and estab-lishing the company in the teenage and adult markets. To achieve fuller utilization, Disney Studios quickly doubled the number of movies in production. Simultaneously, it engaged in aggress-ive recruiting of leading producers, directors, filmmakers, actors, and scriptwriters. In 1988, it became America's leading studio in terms of box office receipts. Studio production was further boosted by Disney's increasing TV presence, both though the Disney Channel and programs for network TV.

Above all, the new management team was exploiting Disney's most powerful and endur-ing asset: the affection of millions of people of different nations and different generations for the Disney name and the Disney characters.

& Johnson, and BP Amoco are all companies whose long-term success owes much to their commitment to nurturing talent, developing technologies, and building capabilities to permit adaptability to change within their business environments.

Our starting point is to identify and assess the resources and capabilities available to the firm.

THE RESOURCES OF THE FIRM

It is important to distinguish between the resources and the capabilities of the firm. The basic units of analysis are the individual resources of the firm: capital equipment, human resources, intellectual capital, and so on. But, in most instances, these resources do not create value for the firm on their own. In order for the firm to establish competitive advantage, resources must work together in order to create *organizational capability*. On their own, Ford's engineers, designers, labs, studios, and IT resources are of limited value. Together, they can provide the new product development capability needed to create new models such as the Ford Focus and the 2002 Thunderbird. Figure 5.4 shows the relationship among resources, capabilities, and competitive advantage.

Drawing up an inventory of a firm's resources can be surprisingly difficult. No such document exists within the accounting or management information systems of

FIGURE 5.4 The links among resources, capabilities, and competitive advantage

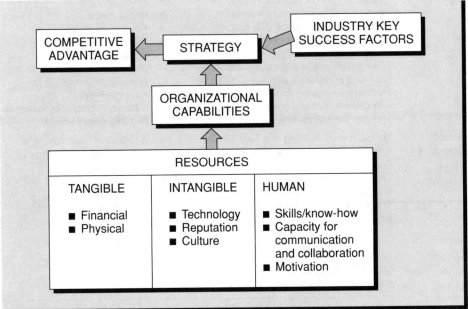

TABLE 5.1 Classifying and Assessing the Firm's Resources

RESOURCE	RELEVANT CHARACTERISTICS	KEY INDICATORS
Tangible Resources Financial Resources	The firm's borrowing capacity and its internal funds generation determine its resilience and capacity for investment.	■ Debt/equity ratio ■ Operating cash flow/free cash flow ■ Credit rating
Physical Resources	Physical resources constrain the firm's set of production possibilities and impact its cost position. Key characteristics include: ■ The size, location, technical sophistication, and flexibility of plant and equipment ■ Location and alternative uses for land and buildings ■ Reserves of raw materials	■ Market values of fixed assets ■ Vintage of capital equipment ■ Scale of plants ■ Flexibility of fixed assets
Intangible Resources Technological Resources	Intellectual property: patent portfolio, copyright, trade secrets Resources for innovation: research facilities, technical and scientific employees	■ Number and significance of patents ■ Revenue from licensing patents and copyrights ■ R&D staff as a percent of total employment ■ Number and location of research facilities
Reputation	Reputation with customers through the ownership of brands and trademarks; established relationships with customers; the reputation of the firm's products and services for quality and reliability. The reputation of the company with suppliers (including component suppliers, banks and financiers, employees and potential employees), with government and government agencies, and with the community.	■ Brand recognition ■ Brand equity ■ Percent of repeat buying ■ Objective measures of comparative product performance (e.g., Consumers' Association ratings, J. D. Power ratings) ■ Surveys of corporate reputation (e.g., *Business Week*)
Human Resources	The education, training and experiences of employees determine the skills available to the firm. The adaptability of employees contributes to the strategic flexibility of the firm. The social and collaborative skills of employees determine the capacity of the firm to transform human resources into organizational capabilities. The commitment and loyalty of employees determine the capacity of the firm to attain and maintain competitive advantage.	■ Educational, technical, and professional qualifications of employees ■ Compensation relative to industry ■ Percentage of days lost through stoppages and industrial disputes ■ Absentee rates ■ Employee turnover rate

most corporations. The corporate balance sheet provides a limited view of a firm's resources; its emphasis is almost entirely based on financial and physical resources. A useful starting point to identify a firm's resources is to classify principal types of resources into tangible, intangible, and human resources. Table 5.1 describes the principal categories.

Tangible Resources

Tangible resources are the easiest to identify and evaluate: financial resources and physical assets are identified and valued in the firm's financial statements. Yet, balance sheets are renowned for their propensity to obscure strategically relevant information, and to under- or overvalue assets. Historic cost valuation can provide little indication of an asset's market value. Disney's movie library had a balance sheet value of $2.49 billion on September 30, 1999. But this valuation was based on production cost less amortization – Disney's classic animated movies were almost certainly ascribed no balance sheet value, despite their continuing potential to generate revenue.

However, our goal of resource analysis is not simply to value a company's assets; it is to understand the potential for creating competitive advantage. Information that Bethlehem Steel has fixed assets with a book value of $480 million is of little use in assessing their strategic value. In order to assess Bethlehem's ability to compete effectively in the US steel industry, we need to know where the company's plants are located, their capacities, the age and type of the equipment, and how flexible the plants are with regard to both inputs and outputs. To identify how we can create value from tangible resources, we must address two key questions:

1. *What opportunities exist for economizing on the use of finance, inventories, and fixed assets?* It may be possible to use fewer resources to support the same level of business, or to use the existing resources to support a larger volume of business. ConAgra, NationsBank, and Emerson Electric are masters of making horizontal acquisitions, then pruning the assets needed to support the turnover of the acquired businesses.

2. *What are the possibilities for employing existing assets more profitably?* US railroad companies have become adept at using their rail networks to route gas pipelines and fiber-optic telecommunication cables.

Intangible Resources

For most companies, intangible resources contribute much more than do tangible resources to total asset value. Yet, in relation to company financial statements, intangible resources remain largely invisible – even more for US companies than for European ones. The exclusion or undervaluation of intangible resources from company balance sheets is a major reason for the large and growing divergence between companies' balance sheet valuations ("book values") and stock market valuations (see

TABLE 5.2　Large Companies* with the Highest Ratio of Share Price to Book Value per Share

COMPANY	MARKET-TO-BOOK RATIO	INDUSTRY
Juniper Networks (US)	58.5	Computer software and services
Oracle (US)	56.2	Computer software and services
TIM (Italy)	45.0	Telecommunications
Broadcom (US)	42.6	Computer software and services
Nokia (Finland)	42.0	Telecom equipment
Yahoo! (US)	41.3	Computer software and services
Cisco Systems (US)	31.9	Telecom equipment
America Online (US)	34.0	Telecommunications
US West (US)	28.9	Telecommunications
Glaxo Wellcome (UK)	25.4	Drugs
Sun Microsystems (US)	24.4	Computers
Charles Schwab (US)	24.2	Financial services
L. M. Ericsson (Sweden)	24.1	Telecom equipment
Warner-Lambert (US)	23.0	Drugs
EMC (US)	21.5	Electronics
Amgen (US)	21.4	Drugs
Dell Computer (US)	21.0	Computers
Colgate-Palmolive (US)	20.8	Personal care products
SmithKline Beecham (US)	20.6	Drugs
SAP (Germany)	19.4	Computer software and services
Pfizer (US)	19.4	Drugs
Eli Lilly (US)	18.8	Drugs
Sprint PCS Group (US)	18.3	Telecommunications
Softbank (Japan)	18.2	Computer software and services

*　Companies with a stock market valuation in excess of $270 billion on May 31, 2000.
Source:　"*Business Week* Global 1000," *Business Week* (July 10, 2000).

Table 5.2). Among the most important of these undervalued or unvalued intangible resources are brand names. Table 5.3 shows companies owning brands valued at $20 billion or more.

Brand names and other trademarks are a form of *reputational assets*: their value is in the confidence they instill in customers. This value is reflected in the price premium that customers are willing to pay for the branded product over that for an unbranded or unknown brand. Brand value (or "brand equity") can be estimated by taking the price premium attributable to a brand, multiplying it by the brand's annual sales volume, then calculating the present value of this revenue stream. The brand valuations in Table 5.3 involve estimating the operating profits for each brand (after taxation and a capital charge), estimating the proportion of net operating income attributable to the brand, then capitalizing these returns. The value of a company's brands can be increased by extending the product/market scope over which the company markets its brands. Philip Morris is an expert at internationalizing its brand franchises. Harley-Davidson's brand strength has not only permitted the company to obtain a price premium of about 40 percent above that of comparable motorcycles,

TABLE 5.3   The World's Most Valuable Brands, 2000

RANK	COMPANY	BRAND VALUE ($BN)	RANK	COMPANY	BRAND VALUE ($BN)
1	Coca-Cola	72.5	8	Disney	33.6
2	Microsoft	70.2	9	McDonald's	27.9
3	IBM	53.2	10	AT&T	25.5
4	Intel	39.0	11	Marlboro	22.1
5	Nokia	38.5	12	Mercedes	21.1
6	General Electric	38.1	13	Hewlett-Packard	20.6
7	Ford	36.4	14	Cisco Systems	20.0

Source: Interbrand/*Financial Times* (July 18, 2000): 17.

but also to license its name to the manufacturers of clothing, coffee mugs, cigarettes, and restaurants.

Reputation may be attached to a company as well as to its brands. In discontinuing the St. Michael label from its clothing products, Marks & Spencer acknowledged that its company name carried a much stronger reputation than its brand name. Company reputation is a valuable resource, not just in relation to customers, but also in relation to employees, suppliers (including financial institutions), and governments.

Like reputation, technology is an intangible asset whose value is not evident from most companies' balance sheets. Intellectual property – patents, copyrights, and trade secrets – comprise technological and artistic resources where ownership is defined in law. Once we stray into the broad area of know-how, what is owned by the company and what is owned by employees is less clear. Over the past 20 years, companies have become more attentive to the value of their intellectual property. Texas Instruments was one of the first companies to begin managing its patent portfolio in order to maximize its licensing revenues. The largest single contributor to Qualcomm's $49.4 billion market value (at September 2000) was its patents relating to CDMA digital wireless telephony.

Human Resources

Human resources are the *productive services* that human beings offer to the firm in terms of their skills, knowledge, and reasoning and decision-making abilities. Human resources do not appear on corporate balance sheets for the simple reason that people cannot be owned: companies contract with their employees to purchase their time and expertise. Identifying and appraising the stock of human resources within a firm is complex and difficult. Human resources are appraised at the time of recruitment, where qualifications and experience are used as indicators of performance potential, and in employment, typically through annual performance reviews.

Companies are continually seeking more effective methods to assess the perform-ance abilities and performance potential of their employees (and potential employees). Over the past decade, human resource appraisal has become far more systematic and sophisticated. Organizations are relying less on formal qualifications and more on flexibility, learning potential, and the ability to work collaboratively in teams. Many have established assessment centers specifically for the purpose of providing comprehensive, quantitative assessments of the skills and attributes of individual employees. *Competency modeling* involves identifying the set of skills, content knowledge, attitudes, and values associated with superior performers within a particular job category, then assessing each employee against that profile.[13] The results of such competency assessments can then be used to identify training needs, make selections for hiring or promotion, and determine compensation. The technique was pioneered by David McClelland of Harvard University and developed subsequently by McBer & Co. and the Hay Group.[14] A central feature of competency modeling is the emphasis it gives not just to technical and professional abilities, but also to the psychological and social aptitudes so critical in linking technical and professional abilities to overall job performance. Recent interest in *emotional intelligence* reflects growing recognition of the importance of social and emotional skills and values.[15] In a study of international business development at Amoco Corporation, the individual competencies most closely associated with superior performance were achievement motivation, impact and influence, self-confidence, analytical thinking, and conceptual thinking.[16]

The ability of employees to harmonize their efforts and integrate their separate skills depends not only on their interpersonal skills but also the organizational context. This organizational context as it affects internal collaboration is determined by a key intangible resource: the *culture* of the organization. The term *organizational culture* is notoriously ill defined. It relates to an organization's values, traditions, and social norms. Building on the observations of Peters and Waterman that "firms with sustained superior financial performance typically are characterized by a strong set of core managerial values that define the ways they conduct business," Jay Barney identifies organizational culture as a firm resource that is potentially very valuable and of great strategic importance.[17]

ORGANIZATIONAL CAPABILITIES

Resources are not very productive on their own. A brain surgeon is close to useless without a radiologist, anesthetist, nurses, surgical instruments, imaging equipment,

---

[13] Edward Lawler, "From Job-Based to Competency-Based Organizations," *Journal of Organizational Behavior* 15 (1994): 3–15.

[14] See Lyle Spencer, David McClelland, and S. Spencer, *Competency Assessment Methods: History and State of the Art*, Hay/McBer Research Group (1994); Kathryn Cofsky, "Critical Keys to Competency-Based Pay," *Compensation and Benefits Review* (November–December 1993): 46–52; Lyle Spencer and Sigune Spencer, *Competence At Work: Models for Superior Performance* (New York, Wiley: 1993).

[15] D. Goleman, *Emotional Intelligence* (New York: Bantam, 1995).

[16] G. J. Mount, "What Role Does Emotional Intelligence Play for Superior Performers in the International Business of a Capital-Intensive, Asset-Based Industry?," Ph.D. dissertation (Benedictine University, Chicago, 2000).

[17] Jay Barney, "Organizational Culture: Can It Be a Source of Sustained Competitive Advantage?," *Academy of Management Review* 11 (1986): 656–65.

and a host of other resources. We use the term *organizational capabilities* to refer to a firm's capacity for undertaking a particular productive activity. Just as an individual may have the capability to play the violin, ice skate, and speak Mandarin, so the organization may have the capability to manufacture widgets, distribute them throughout the Baltic states, and hedge its resulting foreign exchange exposure. The literature uses the terms "capability" and "competence" interchangeably.[18] The key differences are the adjectives used to modify the terms. Thus, Selznick used *distinctive competence* to describe those things that an organization does particularly well relative to its competitors,[19] and Igor Ansoff used the same term to analyze the basis of firms' growth strategies.[20] Hamel and Prahalad coined the term *core competences* to distinguish those capabilities fundamental to a firm's performance and strategy.[21] Core competences, according to Hamel and Prahalad, are those that:

1. Make a disproportionate contribution to ultimate customer value, or to the efficiency with which that value is delivered, and

2. Provide a basis for entering new markets.[22]

The value of the terms "distinctive competence" and "core competence" is that they direct our attention toward competitive advantage. Our interest is not in capabilities *per se*, but in capabilities *relative to other firms*. Many companies can produce personal computers; the critical issue is whether they can produce PCs with a cost, quality, and speed that can match Dell Computer. Establishing competitive advantage requires that a firm identify what the firm can do *better* than its competitors.

Prahalad and Hamel criticize US companies for emphasizing product management over competence management. They compare the strategic development of Sony and RCA in consumer electronics. Both companies were failures in the home video market. RCA introduced its videodisk system, Sony its Betamax videotape system. For RCA, the failure of its first product marked the end of its venture into home video systems and heralded a progressive retreat from various segments of the consumer electronics industry. RCA was eventually acquired by GE, and the combined consumer electronics division was sold to Thomson of France. Sony, on the other hand, acknowledged the failure of Betamax, but continued to develop its capabilities in video technology. Sony's continuous development and upgrading of its video capabilities have resulted in a string of successful video products, including the camcorder and the PlayStation game console.

A strategic focus on capabilities rather than products is also observable in Canon's development. Canon's technological capabilities lie in the integration of

---

[18]   While some attempts have been made to differentiate the two, Gary Hamel and C. K. Prahalad argue in, *Harvard Business Review* (May–June 1992): 164–5, that "the distinction between competencies and capabilities is purely semantic."

[19]   P. Selznick, *Leadership in Administration: A Sociological Interpretation* (New York: Harper & Row, 1957).

[20]   Igor Ansoff, *Corporate Strategy* (Harmondsworth: Penguin, 1965).

[21]   C. K. Prahalad and Gary Hamel, "The Core Competences of the Corporation," *Harvard Business Review* (May–June 1990): 79–91.

[22]   Gary Hamel and C. K. Prahalad, letter, *Harvard Business Review* (May–June 1992): 164–5.

FIGURE 5.5 Canon: products and capabilities

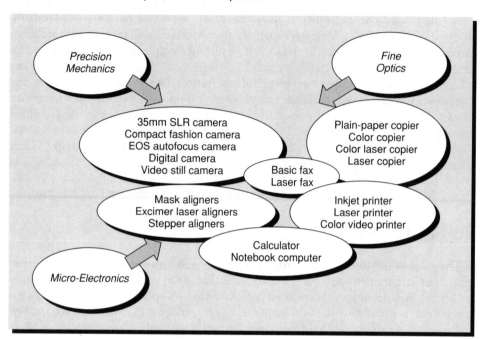

microelectronics, fine optics, and precision engineering. Figure 5.5 shows how these technologies are common to most of Canon's product introductions during the late 1980s.

Classifying Capabilities: Functions and Value Chain Activities

To identify a firm's capabilities, we need to have some basis for classifying and dis-aggregating its activities. Two approaches are commonly used:

1. A *functional analysis* identifies organizational capabilities in relation to each of the principal functional areas of the firm. Table 5.4 classifies the principal functions of the firm and identifies organizational capabilities pertaining to each function.

2. A *value chain analysis* separates the activities of the firm into a sequential chain. McKinsey & Co.'s "business system" – a chain of activities flowing from research and product development through to marketing and customer after-sales services – was elaborated by Michael Porter.[23] His value chain

---

[23] The McKinsey business system is outlined in C. F. Bates, P. Chatterjee, F. W. Gluck, D. Gogel, and A. Puri, "The Business System: A New Tool for Strategy Formulation and Cost Analysis," in R. Bauron, "New Game Strategies," *McKinsey Staff Paper* (March 1980), reprinted in *McKinsey on Strategy* (Boston: McKinsey & Company, 2000). Porter's value chain is the main framework of his *Competitive Advantage* (New York: Free Press, 1984).

TABLE 5.4   A Functional Classification of Organizational Capabilities

FUNCTIONAL AREA	CAPABILITY	EXEMPLARS
CORPORATE FUNCTIONS	Financial control Strategic management of multiple businesses Strategic innovation Coordinating divisional and business unit management Acquisition management	Exxon, Coca-Cola General Electric, ABB Enron, AOL Shell, Unilever ConAgra, Cisco Systems
MANAGEMENT INFORMATION	Comprehensive, integrated MIS network linked to managerial decision making	Wal-Mart Federal Express
RESEARCH & DEVELOPMENT	Research Innovative new product development Fast-cycle new product development	IBM, Merck Sony, Kao Canon
MANUFACTURING	Efficiency in volume manufacturing Continual improvements in production processes Flexibility and speed of response	Briggs & Stratton, YKK Toyota, Komatsu Benetton, Nucor
PRODUCT DESIGN	Design capability	Swatch, Nokia
MARKETING	Brand management and brand promotion Promoting and exploiting reputation for quality Identifying and responding to market trends	P&G, Philip Morris American Express, LVMH MTV, Campbell Soup
SALES AND DISTRIBUTION	Effective sales promotion and execution Efficiency and speed of order processing Speed of distribution Quality and effectiveness of customer service	Rubbermaid Glaxo L. L. Bean Amazon.com Federal Express Singapore Airlines Shangri-La Hotels

distinguishes between *primary activities* (those involved with the transformation of inputs and interface with the customer) and *support activities*. Figure 5.6 shows Porter's conceptualization of the value chain. The value chain permits disaggregation of the firm first at the level of broad categories of activities (e.g., inbound logistics, marketing) and then at a finer level (thus, outbound logistics may be broken down into warehousing, inventory control, packing, and distribution).

Architecture of Capability

Although the concept of an organization possessing the capability (or competence) to perform certain activities is straightforward, understanding the structure and determinants of capability is much more complex. Why is Enron so good at developing new products for trading energy and managing their risks? How is Wal-Mart able to combine relentless cost focus and high levels of flexibility and adaptability?

FIGURE 5.6   Porter's value chain

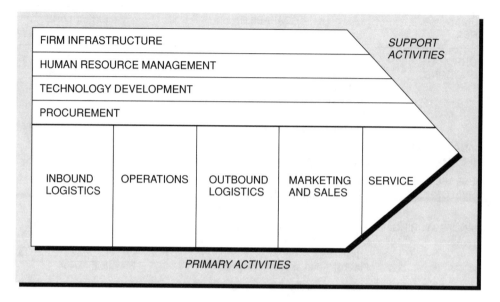

Why has Exxon-Mobil been so much better at financial management than the Royal Dutch/Shell Group? We can hypothesize about the answers to these questions, but the fact remains: We don't really know how organizational capabilities are created, how they are performed, and why some companies perform a capability to a much higher standard than another. Let us look more closely at the structure of organizational capability.

Capability as Routine

Organizational capability requires the expertise of various individuals to be integrated with capital equipment, technology, and other resources. But how does this integration occur? Virtually all productive activities involve teams of people undertaking closely coordinated actions without significant direction or verbal communication. Richard Nelson and Sidney Winter have used the term *organizational routines* to refer to these regular and predictable patterns of activity made up of a sequence of coordinated actions by individuals.[24] Such routines form the basis of most organizational capabilities. At the manufacturing level, a series of routines govern the passage of raw materials and components through the production process to the factory gate. Sales, ordering, distribution, and customer service activities are similarly organized through a number of standardized, complementary routines. Even top management activity includes routines: monitoring business unit performance, capital budgeting, and strategic planning.

[24]   R. R. Nelson and S. G. Winter, *An Evolutionary Theory of Economic Change* (Cambridge, MA: Belknap, 1982).

Routines are to the organization what skills are to the individual. Just as the individual's skills are carried out semi-automatically, without conscious coordination, so organizational routines are based on firm-level tacit knowledge that can be observed in the operation of the routine, but cannot be fully articulated by any member of the team, not even the manager. Just as individual skills become rusty when not exercised, so it is difficult for organizations to retain coordinated responses to contingencies that arise only rarely. Hence, there may be a tradeoff between efficiency and flexibility. A limited repertoire of routines can be performed highly efficiently with near-perfect coordination – all in the absence of significant intervention by top management. The same organization may find it extremely difficult to respond to novel situations.[25]

We have said little about the role of managers. Can organizational capabilities operate purely through management direction? In every McDonald's hamburger restaurant the operating manuals provide precise directions for the conduct of every activity undertaken, from the placing of the pickle on the burger to the maintenance of the milk-shake machine. Yet, the fact that every McDonald's employee, from restaurant manager to counter hand, goes through extensive on-the-job and off-the-job training, and that the operating manuals are seldom referred to in the course of day-to-day operation, is indicative of the fact that the capabilities of McDonald's in producing and serving fast food are dependent mainly on organizational routines.

The Hierarchy of Capabilities

Whether we approach capabilities from a functional or value chain approach, it is evident that broad functions or value chain segments can be disaggregated into more specialist capabilities performed by smaller teams of resources. What we observe is a hierarchy of capabilities where more general, broadly defined capabilities are formed from the integration of more specialized capabilities. For example:

■ A hospital's capability in treating heart disease depends on its integration of capabilities pertaining to a patient's diagnosis, cardiovascular surgery, pre- and post-operative care, as well as capabilities relating to various administrative and support functions.

■ Toyota's manufacturing capability – generally referred to as its system of "lean production" – is a highly complex organizational capability requiring the integration of a large number of more specific capabilities relating to the manufacture of particular components and subassemblies, supply-chain management, production scheduling, assembly processes, quality control procedures, systems for managing innovation and continuous improvement, and inventory control mechanisms. Within the firm, specialized capabilities relating to

[25] This observation is supported by John Freeman and Michael Hannan, "Niche Width and the Dynamics of Organizational Populations," *American Journal of Sociology* 88 (1984): 1116–45, who observe that in the restaurant industry, specialists survived better than generalists (except where the environment was highly variable, in which case generalists displayed greater adaptability).

FIGURE 5.7 The hierarchical nature of capabilities: a manufacturer of PBXs

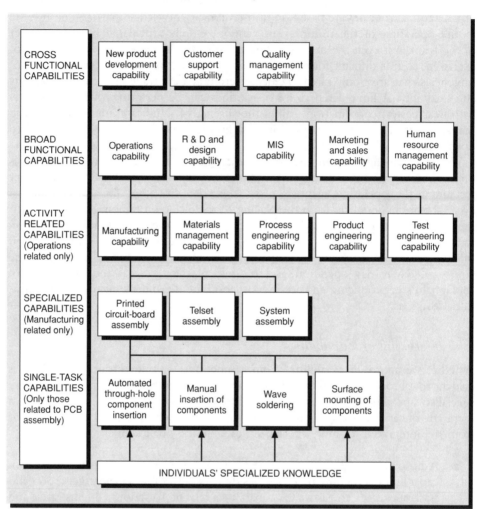

individual tasks are integrated into broader functional capabilities: marketing capabilities, manufacturing capabilities, R&D capabilities, and the like. At the highest level of integration are capabilities that require wide-ranging cross-functional integration. Thus, new product development capability requires the integration of R&D, marketing, manufacturing, finance, and strategic planning.[26] Figure 5.7 shows a hierarchy of capabilities for a manufacturer of telecommunication switching equipment.

---

[26] For an illuminating description of the integration of functional and technical capabilities to develop new automobiles, see K. B. Clark and T. Fujimoto, *Product Development Performance* (New York: Free Press, 1991).

Although higher-level capabilities involve the integration of lower-level capabilities, it is important to recognize that capabilities cannot be integrated directly. Capabilities can only be integrated through the knowledge of individual persons. This is precisely why higher-level capabilities are so difficult to perform. New product development requires the integration of a wide diversity of specialized knowledge and skill, yet communication constraints mean that the number of individuals who can be directly involved in the process is limited. A common solution has been the creation of cross-functional product development teams. Though setting up such teams would appear to be a straightforward task, research into new product development confirms that a key problem is the team's ability to access and integrate the vast range of specialized knowledge that needs to be imbedded within the product.[27] A major achievement of Japanese industrial corporations has been the establishment of the structures and patterns of coordination needed to integrate knowledge across a broad spectrum, and greatly to reduce the cycle time for new product development. Companies such as Toyota, Sony, Matsushita, and Canon have been models for US and European corporations seeking to accelerate new product development. Chrysler's revival during the 1990s owed much to the restructuring of its new product development processes to imitate those of Honda.

Leveraging Resources into Capabilities

The linkage between resources and capabilities is complex. Hamel and Prahalad observe that outstanding capabilities are not always the result of superior resource endowments. They pose the questions:

- If GM outspends Honda four-to-one on R&D, why is GM not the undisputed world leader in power train chassis technology?

- Why has Sony, with a much smaller research budget than Philips, produced so many more successful innovations?

A firm's resource base has only an indirect link with the capabilities that that firm can generate. The key, according to Hamel and Prahalad, is the firm's ability to *leverage* its resources.[28] Resources can be leveraged in the following ways:

- *Concentrating resources* through the processes of *converging* resources on a few clearly defined and consistent goals; *focusing* the efforts of each group, department, and business unit on individual priorities in a sequential fashion; and *targeting* those activities that have the biggest impact on customers' perceived value.

[27] Clark and Fujimoto, op. cit.; and K. Imai, I. Nonaka, and H. Takeuchi, "Managing the New Product Development Process: How Japanese Companies Learn and Unlearn," in K. Clark, R. Hayes, and C. Lorenz (eds), *The Uneasy Alliance* (Boston: Harvard Business School Press, 1985).
[28] Gary Hamel and C. K. Prahalad, *Competing for the Future* (Boston: Harvard Business School Press, 1994).

- *Accumulating resources* through *mining experience* in order to achieve faster learning, and *borrowing* from other firms – accessing their resources and capabilities through alliances, outsourcing arrangements, and the like.

- *Complementing resources* involves increasing their effectiveness through linking them with complementary resources and capabilities. This may involve *blending* product design capabilities with the marketing capabilities needed to communicate these to the market, and *balancing* to ensure that limited resources and capabilities in one area do not hold back the effectiveness of resources and capabilities in another.

- *Conserving resources* involves utilizing resources and capabilities to the fullest by *recycling* them through different products, markets, and product generations; and *co-opting* resources through collaborative arrangements with other companies.

- *Recovering resources* by increasing the speed with which investments in resources generate cash returns to the firm. A key determinant of resource recovery is new product development cycle time.

APPRAISING THE PROFIT-EARNING POTENTIAL OF RESOURCES AND CAPABILITIES

So far, we have established what resources and capabilities are, how they can provide a long-term focus for a company's strategy, and how we can go about identifying them. However, if the focus of this book is the pursuit of profit, we also need to appraise the potential for resources and capabilities to earn profits for the company.

The profit returns to resources and capabilities ("rents") depend on the extent to which a firm deploys its resources and capabilities to establish and sustain a competitive advantage. We examine this issue in greater detail in the next chapter. In this section, we identify key characteristics of a firm's resources and capabilities that determine their profit-earning potential.

The profits that a firm obtains from its resources and capabilities depend on three factors: their abilities to *establish* a competitive advantage, to *sustain* that competitive advantage, and to *appropriate* the returns to that competitive advantage. Each of these depends on a number of resource characteristics. Figure 5.8 shows the principal relationships.

Establishing Competitive Advantage

For a resource or capability to establish a competitive advantage, two conditions must be present. First, a resource or capability must be *scarce*. If it is widely available within the industry, then it may be essential in order to play, but not a sufficient basis for winning. In oil and gas exploration, new technologies such as directional drilling and 3-D seismic analysis are critical to reducing the finding costs of new reserves. The

FIGURE 5.8   The rent-earning potential of resources and capabilities

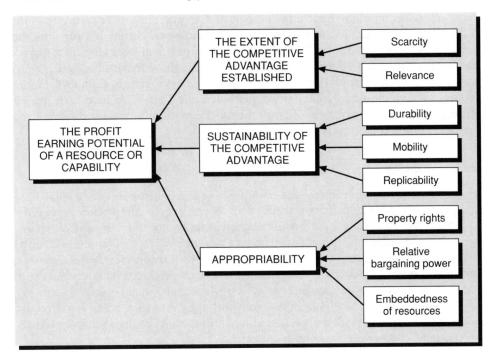

problem for firms is that these technologies are widely available from oilfield drilling and IT companies. The situation is similar for automobiles. Quality remains critical, but, with the diffusion of total quality management, it is no longer an obvious source of competitive advantage; it is a "needed to play" rather than a "needed to win" criterion.

Second, the resource or capability must be *relevant*. British coal mines produced some wonderful brass bands. Unfortunately, these bands did little to assist the mines in meeting competition from cheap South African and American coal and North Sea gas. As retail banking shifts toward automated teller machines and online transactions, so the retail branch networks of the banks become less relevant for customer service. Thus, resources and capabilities are valuable only if they can be linked to one or more of the key success factors within an industry: they must assist the firm in creating value for its customers, or in surviving competition.

Sustaining Competitive Advantage

The profits earned from resources and capabilities depend not just on their ability to establish competitive advantage, but also on how long that advantage can be sustained. This depends on whether resources and capabilities are *durable* and whether rivals can *imitate* the competitive advantage they offer. Resources and capabilities are imitable if they are *transferable* or *replicable*.

Durability

Some resources are more durable than others and, hence, are a more secure basis for competitive advantage. The increasing pace of technological change is shortening the useful life span of most resources; both capital equipment and technological resources such as patents. Reputation, on the other hand, can show remarkable resilience to the passage of time. Brands such as Heinz sauces, Kelloggs' cereals, Campbell's soup, Hoover vacuum cleaners, Singer sewing machines, and Coca-Cola have been market leaders for periods of a century or more. Corporate reputation is similarly long-lived – unless tarnished by misdeeds or ineptitude.

Transferability

The simplest means of acquiring the resources and capabilities necessary for imitating another firm's strategy is to buy them. If rivals can acquire the resources required to imitate the strategy of a successful company, that company's competitive advantage will be short lived. The ability to buy a resource or capability depends on its transferability – the extent to which it is mobile between companies. Some resources, such as finance, raw materials, components, machines produced by equipment suppliers, and employees with standardized skills (such as short-order cooks and auditors), are transferable and can be bought and sold with little difficulty. Some resources are not easily transferred – either they are entirely firm specific, or their value depreciates on transfer.[29] Sources of immobility include:

- Geographical immobility of natural resources, large items of capital equipment, and some types of employees may make it difficult for firms to acquire these resources without relocating themselves.

- Imperfect information concerning the quality and productivity of resources creates considerable risks for firms seeking to acquire those resources. Such imperfections are especially important in relation to human resources. People are exceptionally heterogeneous and their performance is highly context specific, particularly within team-based production.[30] The superior information of established firms concerning the characteristics of their resources creates risks for the firm seeking to acquire resources – the so-called "lemons problem."[31] Jay Barney has shown that different valuations of resources by firms can result

---

[29]   This concept of resources being specific to the firm is developed in Richard Caves' discussion of "specific assets" (see "International Corporations: The Industrial Economics of Foreign Investment," *Economica* 38, 1971: 1–27). This differs from Oliver Williamson's use of the same term, which refers to assets that are specific to a particular transaction not a particular firm (see *The Economic Institutions of Capitalism* New York: Free Press, 1985: 52–6).

[30]   A. A. Alchian and H. Demsetz, "Production, Information Costs, and Economic Organization," *American Economic Review* 62 (1972): 777–95.

[31]   G. Akerlof, "The Market for Lemons: Qualitative Uncertainty and the Market Mechanism," *Quarterly Journal of Economics* 84 (1970): 488–500.

in their being either underpriced or overpriced, giving rise to differences in profitability between firms.[32]

- Complementarity between resources such that the detachment of a resource from its "home team" causes it to lose productivity and value. Thus, if brand reputation is associated with the company that created it, a change in ownership of the brand erodes its value. The acquisition of Harrods department store by the Al Fayed brothers raised concerns over the possible detriment of foreign ownership to Harrods' reputation as the quintessential English department store. Employees may also be unable to replicate their former performance with a new employer. Gilbert Amelio was less effective as Apple Computer's CEO from 1996 to 1997 than he was as National Semiconductor's CEO. George Fisher was also unable to lead Eastman Kodak as effectively as he did Motorola.

Organizational capabilities, because they are based on teams of resources, are less mobile than individual resources. Even if the whole team can be transferred (in investment banking it has been commonplace for whole teams of analysts or M&A bankers to defect from one bank to another), the dependence of the team on a wider network of relationships and corporate culture may pose difficulties for recreating the capability in the new company.

Replicability

If a firm cannot buy a resource or capability, it must build it. In financial services, innovations such as interest rate swaps, stripped bonds, electricity futures, weather options and most other derivatives can similarly be imitated easily by competitors – unlike mechanical or chemical innovations, few financial innovations can be patented. In retailing, competitive advantages that derive from store layout, point-of-sale technology, charge cards, and extended opening hours can be copied easily by competitors.

Less easily replicable are capabilities based on complex organizational routines. Federal Express's national, next-day delivery service and Nucor's system for steel manufacturing that combines efficiency with flexibility are complex capabilities based on unique corporate cultures. Some capabilities appear simple but prove difficult to replicate. Just-in-time scheduling and quality circles are relatively simple techniques used effectively by Japanese companies. Although neither require advanced manufacturing technologies or sophisticated information systems, their dependence on high levels of collaboration through communication and trust meant that many American and European firms had difficulty implementing them.

Even where replication is possible, incumbent firms may benefit from the fact that resources and capabilities that have been accumulated over a long period are often less costly and more productive than the same assets that have been accumulated quickly by would-be imitators. Dierickx and Cool identify several sources

---

[32] Barney, op. cit.

of incumbent advantage from accumulated stocks of resources and capabilities.[33] "Asset mass efficiencies" occur where a strong initial position in technology, distribution channels, or reputation facilitates the subsequent accumulation of these resources. "Time compression diseconomies" are the additional costs incurred in quickly accumulating a resource or capability. Thus, "crash programs" of R&D and "blitz" advertising campaigns tend to be less productive than similar expenditures made over a longer period.

Appropriating the Returns to Competitive Advantage

Who gains the returns generated by a resource or capability? We should normally expect that such returns accrue to the owner of that resource or capability. However, ownership is not always clear-cut. The boundary between the human capital owned by the employee and the know-how and trade secrets of the company is particularly difficult to define. When General Motors' cost-cutting genius José Ignacio Lopez de Arriortua and his colleagues left Opel for Volkswagen in March 1993, to what extent were they transferring their individual knowledge and expertise, and to what extent were they stealing GM's trade secrets?[34] When Charles and Maurice Saatchi were ejected from the chaotically mismanaged Saatchi & Saatchi plc and went on to form their own advertising agency, M&C Saatchi, to what extent were they taking with them know-how and client relations that were really owned by Saatchi & Saatchi plc?[35] The lack of ownership of critical human resources is a critical problem in the acquisition of human capital-intensive firms (see Exhibit 5.2). Charles Ferguson claims that when engineers and managers leave an IT company to form their own business startup, this is not simply high-tech entrepreneurship, it is really the exploitation of corporate knowledge for private gain. This continual leakage of the technological assets of leading US companies impedes their global leadership.[36] The prevalence of partnerships (rather than stockholder-owned corporations) in many professional services (lawyers, accountants, and management consultants) reflects the desire to avoid conflicts over company versus employee ownership of knowledge, reputation, and customer relationships.

The less clearly defined are property rights in resources and capabilities, the greater the importance of relative bargaining power in determining the division of returns between the firm and its individual members. In the case of team-based

---

[33]   Ingemar Dierickx and Karel Cool, "Asset Stock Accumulation and Sustainability of Competitive Advantage," *Management Science* 35 (1989): 1504–13.

[34]   "Court orders VW to stop recruiting Opel executives," *Financial Times* (April 3, 1993): 7.

[35]   K. Goldman, *Conflicting Accounts: The Creation and Crash of the Saatchi & Saatchi Advertising Empire* (New York: Simon & Schuster, 1997).

[36]   Charles Ferguson, "International Competition, Strategic Behavior, and Government Policy in Information Technology Industries," Ph.D. thesis (MIT, 1987). For a summary and critique see George Gilder, "The Revitalization of Everything: The Law of the Microcosm," *Harvard Business Review* (March–April 1988): 49–61. For a reply see Charles Ferguson, "From the People Who Brought You Voodoo Economics," *Harvard Business Review* (May–June 1988).

EXHIBIT 5.2   Our Assets Just Walked Out On Us!

In the summer of 1987, Martin Sorrell, CEO of WPP Group plc, purchased Lord, Geller, Fredrico, Einstein (LGFE), one of New York's most respected advertising agencies, best known for its advertisements for IBM. The acquisition followed WPP's purchase of J. Walter Thompson and a string of other agencies that established WPP as the world's largest advertising agency.

Friction between LGFE and its British parent WPP over issues of business and creative independence reached a climax in March 1988. The chairman, president, and four top executives from LGFE left to establish a new agency, Lord, Einstein, O'Neill & Partners. They were joined on March 22 by over a dozen other key employees. The exit of employees was followed by the defection of clients. One client, the president of the *New Yorker* magazine, explained: "If you're used to working with someone who is generating ideas and helping you, you stay with them. This is a matter of personal loyalties." Meanwhile, the parent company, WPP, was busy taking legal action against the new agency, contending that the former LGFE employees had conspired to take away Lord Geller's business, while at the same time trying to quash rumors that Lord Geller was about to close.

WPP obtained a temporary injunction against Richard Lord and Arthur Einstein Jr. from soliciting or accepting business from any of LGFE's clients. The new firm also took to the courts, charging Martin Sorrell and WPP with libel and slander.

By the end of 1988, WPP's LGFE subsidiary was in a sorry state. Despite loyalty from a few clients – LGFE kept Hennessy cognac's $8 million advertising account – many of its largest clients switched to other agencies. Sears, Roebuck and Pan Am withdrew their business from LGFE; IBM awarded part of its $120 million account to the new agency, Lord, Einstein, O'Neill & Partners. While this new agency prospered, LGFE was forced to lay off one-third of its employees.

Source: *Wall Street Journal* (March 23, 1988): A1, 21; and subsequent issues.

---

organizational capabilities, this balance of power between the firm and an individual employee depends crucially on the relationship between individuals' skills and organizational routines. The more deeply embedded individual skills and knowledge are within organizational routines, and the more they depend on corporate systems and reputation, the weaker the employee is relative to the firm.

Conversely, the closer an organizational capability is identified with the expertise of individual employees, and the more effective those employees are at deploying their bargaining power, the better able employees are to appropriate rents. If the individual employee's contribution to productivity is clearly identifiable, if the employee is mobile, and if the employee's skills offer similar productivity to other firms, the employee is in a strong position to appropriate a substantial proportion of his or her contribution to the firm's value added. If the improvements in team performance, game attendance, and TV ratings that Patrick Ewing brings to the New York Knicks would work for any basketball team, then it is likely that the $17 million a year that Ewing receives in salary is close to the full value of these benefits. In recent years investment banks and consulting companies have emphasized the team-based nature of their capabilities. In downplaying the role of individual expertise, they can improve their firm's potential for appropriating the returns to their capabilities.

PUTTING RESOURCE AND CAPABILITY ANALYSIS TO WORK: A PRACTICAL GUIDE

A problem with recent work on organizational capability and the resource-based view of the firm is that, while rich in insightful concepts, its application to strategic decisions is often unclear. This is unfortunate. If resources and capabilities are to be the foundation for company strategy and the primary source of profitability, it is essential for us to be able to put these concepts and ideas to practical use. Let me provide a step-by-step guide to appraising a company's resources and capabilities and then apply the result of that appraisal to strategy formulation.

Step 1 Identify the Key Resources and Capabilities

Drawing up an initial list of key resources and capabilities can be done from both the demand side and the supply side. On the demand side, we can begin with key success factors (see Chapter 3). What factors determine why some firms in an industry are more successful than others and on what resources and capabilities are these success factors based? Suppose we are evaluating the resources and capabilities of Volkswagen AG, the German-based automobile manufacturer. From the demand side we would start with its success factors in the world automobile industry: low-cost production, attractively designed new models embodying the latest technologies, and the financial strength to weather the cyclicality and heavy investment requirements of the industry. What capacities and resources do these key success factors imply? These would include manufacturing capabilities, new product development capability, effective supply chain management, global distribution, band strength, scale-efficient plants with up-to-date capital equipment, a strong balance sheet, and so on. To organize and categorize these various resources and capabilities, it is helpful to switch our attention to the supply side and look at the company's value chain. What is the chain of activities in which the company is engaged, from new product development to purchasing, to supply chain management, to component manufacture, assembly, and right the way through to dealership support and after-sales service? We can then look at the capabilities at each stage of the chain and the resources that underpin these capabilities. On the supply side, we could start with the value chain and identify the key capabilities at each stage of the value chain and the resources on which these capabilities are based.

Step 2 Appraising Resources and Capabilities

Resources and capabilities need to be appraised against two key criteria. First is their *importance*: Which resources and capabilities are most important in conferring sustainable competitive advantage? Second, where are our strengths and weaknesses as compared with competitors?

Assessing Importance

The temptation in assessing which resources and capabilities are most important is to concentrate on customer choice criteria. What we must bear in mind, however, is that our ultimate objective is not to attract customers, but to make superior profit through establishing a sustainable competitive advantage. For this purpose we need to look beyond customer choice to the underlying strategic characteristics of resources and capabilities. To do this we need to look at the set of appraisal criteria outlined in the previous section on "Appraising the Profit-Earning Potential of Resources and Capabilities." In the case of Volkswagen, and the auto industry generally, many resources and capabilities are essential to compete in the business, but several of them are not scarce (for example, total quality management capability and technologically advanced assembly plants have become widely diffused within the industry), while others (such as IT capability and design capability) are outsourced to external providers – either way, they are "needed to play" but not "needed to win." On the other hand, resources such as brand strength and a global distribution network, and capabilities such as fast-cycle new product development and global logistics capability, cannot be easily acquired or internally developed – they are critical to establishing and sustaining advantage.

Assessing Relative Strengths: The Role of Benchmarking

Objectively appraising the comparative strengths and weaknesses of a company's resources and capabilities relative to competitors is difficult. In assessing their own competencies, organizations frequently fall victim to past glories, hopes for the future, and their own wishful thinking. The tendency toward hubris among companies – and their senior managers – means that business success often sows the seeds of its own destruction.[37] Among the failed industrial companies in both America and Britain are many whose former success blinded them to their stagnating capabilities and declining competitiveness:

- Sheffield, England, once supplied cutlery and silverware to the world. Its stubborn belief in its superior production skills and product quality contributed to its near extinction in the face of foreign competition.[38]

- Lack of domestic competition and easy access to sources of coal and iron ore encouraged complacency and chauvinism among US steelmakers concerning their technological prowess and the superior quality of American steel. Neglect of new process technology and customers' preferences resulted in a rapid decline in the face of competition from imports and domestic minimills.[39]

[37]   Danny Miller, *The Icarus Paradox: How Exceptional Companies Bring About Their Own Downfall* (New York: HarperBusiness, 1990).
[38]   Robert M. Grant, "Business Strategy and Strategy Change in a Hostile Environment: Failure and Success Among British Cutlery Producers," in Andrew Pettigrew (ed.), *The Management of Strategic Change* (Oxford: Basil Blackwell, 1987).
[39]   Paul R. Lawrence and Davis Dyer, *Renewing American Industry* (New York: Free Press, 1983): 60–83.

Firms may be unaware of the capabilities they possess. In the mid-1950s, Richard and Maurice McDonald owned a single hamburger restaurant in San Bernardino, California. It was Ray Kroc, then a milkshake salesman, who recognized the merits of the McDonalds' approach to fast-food and the potential for replicating their system.[40] The Starbucks chain of coffee houses has a remarkably similar history. It was a visiting housewares salesman, Howard Schultz, who saw the potential of the original Seattle shop and eventually acquired it.

To identify and appraise a company's capabilities, managers must look broadly, deeply, and from different perspectives. A starting point is internal discussion and review. Managers can form one or more focus groups to share insights and evidence and attempt to establish a consensus regarding their company's resource and capability profile. Considering the evidence of history can be useful: in reviewing the projects and activities where the company has performed well and those where it has performed poorly, do any patterns appear? Typically, internal discussion surfaces very different perceptions of the same organization. Establishing objectivity requires quantifiable measures of performance. *Benchmarking* has emerged as an important tool for appraising and developing organizational capability through detailed comparisons with other organizations.

Benchmarking has been used primarily as a technique for upgrading a company's capabilities in performing a particular function or activities through transferring best practices from companies that have been identified as "best-in-class" in that function or activity.[41] As McKinsey & Co. has shown, performance difference between top-performing and average-performing companies in most activities tends to be wide.[42] Benchmarking has played a key role in capability upgrading at many companies. For example:

■ Xerox's revitalization during the 1980s owed much to detailed comparisons that showed that its Japanese competitors made copiers at half the cost, developed new products in half the time with half as many people, and achieved defects per thousand that were 10 to 30 times fewer than Xerox. Every department within the company is encouraged to look globally to identify best-in-class companies against which to benchmark. For instance, for inventory control and customer responsiveness, Xerox benchmarked L. L. Bean, the direct-mail clothing manufacturer.

■ Bank of America's vice chairman, Martin Sheen, commented, "We have worked a lot with the Royal Bank of Canada on benchmarking because our sizes and philosophies are comparable and we're not direct competitors. We have had some particularly good exchanges with them on processes. We can also benchmark through the Research Board against an array of competitors reported in a disguised fashion. What these do is to highlight anomalies. You can't get down to a unit cost or systems task level. But if a comparable company has 22 people and we have 60, we can sit down and try to figure out what's going on."

---

[40]   www.mcdonalds.com.
[41]   "First Find Your Bench," *Economist* (May 11, 1991): 102.
[42]   S. Walleck, D. O'Halloran, and C. Leader, "Benchmarking World-Class Performance," *McKinsey Quarterly* 1 (1991).

Ultimately, appraising resources and capabilities is not about data, it's about insight and understanding. Every organization has some activity where it excels or has the potential to excel. For Federal Express, it is a system that guarantees next-day delivery anywhere within the United States. For Marks & Spencer, it is the ability to ensure a high and consistent level of product quality across a wide range of merchandise through meticulously managed supplier relationships. For McDonald's, it is the ability to supply millions of hamburgers from thousands of outlets throughout the world, with remarkable uniformity of quality, customer service, and hygiene. For General Electric, it is a system of corporate management that reconciles coordination, innovation, flexibility, and financial discipline in one of the world's largest and most diversified corporations. All these companies are examples of highly successful enterprises. One reason why they are successful is that they have recognized what they can do well and have based their strategies on it. Most other companies are not as successful. One reason for lack of success is not an absence of distinctive capabilities, but a failure to recognize what they are and to design strategy to use them most effectively.

Bringing Together Importance and Relative Strength

Putting together the two criteria – importance and relative strength – allows us to highlight a company's key strengths and key weaknesses. Returning to our example of Volkswagen AG, Table 5.5 provides a partial (and hypothetical) identification and appraisal of VW's resources and capabilities in relation to the two criteria of importance and relative strength outlined above. Figure 5.9 then brings the two criteria together into a single display. Dividing this display into four quadrants allows us to identify those resources and capabilities that we may regard as key strengths and those that we may identify as key weaknesses. For example, our assessment suggests that

FIGURE 5.9   Appraising VW's resources and capabilities

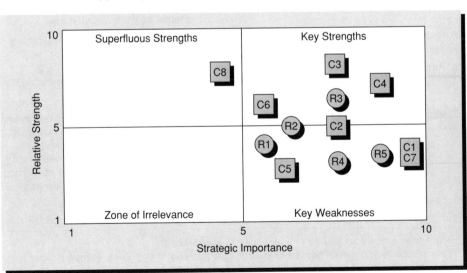

TABLE 5.5 Appraising VW's Resources and Capabilities

	IMPORTANCE[1]	VW'S RELATIVE STRENGTH[2]	COMMENTS
RESOURCES			
R1. Finance	6	4	VW's capital investments during recent years exceed operating cash flows. Debt/equity ratio is high relative to other major auto companies
R2. Technology	7	5	Despite technical strengths, VW is not a leader in automotive technology
R3. Plant and equipment	8	8	Has invested heavily in upgrading plants
R4. Location (proximity to key markets and low-cost inputs)	7	3	High costs from German manufacturing base Strong in E. Europe, Latin America, China Weak in US
R5. Distribution (dealership network)	8	4	Dealership network less geographically extensive than Ford, GM, or Toyota
CAPABILITIES			
C1. Product development	9	4	Traditional weakness of VW: Beetle (first introduced 1930s) still biggest-selling model Acquisitions of Skoda and Seat have broadened design/development capability
C2. Purchasing	7	5	Traditionally weak – strengthened by Lopez
C3. Engineering	7	9	The core technical strength of VW
C4. Manufacturing	8	7	Problems of high costs, inflexibility, and indifferent quality largely resolved
C5. Financial management	6	3	Has traditionally lacked a strong financial orientation
C6. R&D	6	6	A comparative strength of VW, but becoming less important as technology shifts increasingly to suppliers
C7. Marketing and sales	9	4	Despite traditional weakness in recognizing and meeting customer needs in different national markets, VW has increased its sensitivity to the market, improved brand management, and managed its advertising and promotion with increasing dexterity
C8. Government relations	4	8	Important in emerging markets

[1] Both scales range from 1 to 10 (1 = very low, 10 = very high).
[2] VW's resources and capabilities are compared against those of GM, Ford, Toyota, Honda, Chrysler, Nissan, Honda, Fiat, and PSA, where 5 represents parity.

plant and equipment, engineering capability, manufacturing capability, and supply chain management are key strengths of VW, while distribution (a relatively weak presence in the US and Japan), new product development (no consistent record of fast-cycle development of market-winning new models), and financial management are key weaknesses.

Step 3   Developing Strategy Implications

Our key focus is on the two right-hand quadrants of Figure 5.9. How do we exploit our key strengths most effectively? What do we do about our key weaknesses in terms of both upgrading them and reducing our vulnerability to them? Finally, what about our "inconsequential" strengths? Are these really superfluous, or are there ways in which we can deploy them to greater effect?

Exploiting Key Strengths

Having identified resources and capabilities that are important and where our company is strong relative to competitors, the key task is to formulate our strategy to ensure that these resources are deployed to the greatest effect. If engineering and manufacturing capabilities are key strengths of Volkswagen, then it may wish to maintain a stronger presence in component manufacture and assembly than some of its rivals, who are attempting to outsource as much of their manufacturing activities as possible. If VW is well positioned in China, eastern Europe, and Latin America, and these are potential growth markets, it needs to develop products that will appeal to the needs of these markets.

To the extent that different companies within an industry have different capability profiles, this implies differentiation of strategies within the industry. If Toyota's most distinctive capability is its fast-cycle new product development, the implication is that it will compete through technological and design leadership – bringing in new models with the latest designs and technologies quickly. By contrast, if VW lacks flair and creativity in new product design, the implication is that it will rely less on innovative new models, and more on upgrading and revamping its existing models – as it has done with its old favorites such as the Beetle, the Golf, and the Vanagon. Similarly, if Korean manufacturers' greatest strength lies in the cost advantages associated with their Korean location, this will favor internationalization strategies based on exporting from the home base.

IBM's revival under the leadership of Lou Gerstner is an interesting case of refocusing strategy around core strengths. During the late 1990s, IBM shifted its strategy to concentrate on two areas of business: IT consulting and components. Increasingly, it has reduced computer manufacturing (PCs in particular) and focused its resources on its fast-growing, high-margin consulting business, and the supply of components to other IT companies – Dell Computer and Cisco Systems in particular. This strategy represents a return to IBM's traditional core capabilities: its strength in customer service (IBM's mainframe business thrived on IBM's commitment to a service network committed to solving the problems of its business customers) and its strength in basic technology (IBM possesses the biggest patent portfolio of any IT company).

Managing Key Weaknesses

What does a company do about its key weaknesses? The immediate response is to think of how it can fill these resource gaps: investing in those resources and capabilities where a company is at a disadvantage to its principal competitors. We shall appraise and look at how companies can extend existing capabilities and develop new capabilities in the next section. For the time being, let us acknowledge that converting weakness into strength is likely to be a long-term task for most organizations and that, in the short to medium term, a company is likely to be stuck with the resources and capabilities that it inherits from the previous period.

Where a company has strengths in certain activities within the value chain and weaknesses in others, the predominant solution is to ask whether it can specialize in those activities where it is strong and outsource the rest. Thus, in the automobile industry, companies have gone from very high levels of vertical integration – Ford was traditionally involved in every stage of the value chain, from producing iron and steel and raw rubber through to providing finance to car buyers – to much greater selectivity. Most automakers now outsource some of their design, most of their component manufacturing, and a major part of their IT requirements. Similarly, in athletic shoes and clothing, Nike is involved in product design and product manufacturing, but manufacturing and logistics are contracted out to other companies. We shall consider the vertical scope of the firm at greater depth in Chapter 13.

A particular interesting challenge of a company is to formulate its strategy to defend against key weaknesses, or even to turn a weakness into a competitive advantage. Consider Harley-Davidson. With sales of a mere 200,000 bikes a year (compared with 4 million at Honda), it is very difficult for Harley to compete with its bigger rivals in terms of technology and new product development. How has it dealt with this problem? It has made a virtue out of its outmoded technology and traditional designs. The fact that Harley-Davidson bikes embody otherwise obsolete push-rod engines and designs that have not changed substantially since the 1950s has become central to the retro-look appeal of the "hog."

What about Superfluous Strengths?

What about those resources and capabilities where a company has particular strengths, but these don't appear to be important sources of sustainable competitive advantage? One response may be to lower the level of investment from these resources and capabilities. If a retail bank has a particularly strong branch network, but this network is increasingly unimportant in an era of ATMs and online banking, the company may wish to downsize its retail network in order to invest in technology and other more critical resources.

However, in the same way that companies can turn apparent weaknesses into competitive strengths, so it is possible to develop innovative strategies that turn apparently inconsequential strengths into really valuable resources and capabilities.

Consider Apple Computer's declining position in the market for personal computers. While Apple is weak in most key resources and capabilities (size of installed base, cost leadership, technological progressiveness, and customer support), its iMac range has effectively leveraged one of its outstanding strengths – its innovative, user-friendly design – in order to reinvigorate the company's appeal among those consumers who value aesthetics above connectivity.

In addition, consider my own institution, Georgetown's McDonough School of Business. A unique characteristic of the school is its Jesuit heritage, a resource that one would be difficult to regard as a important source of competitive advantage in the fiercely competitive MBA market. Yet, to the extent that a fundamental principle of Jesuit education is educating the whole person, and to the extent that being a successful manager is not just about what you know, it is also about who you are, then Georgetown's Jesuit tradition can provide a key differentiating factor through the program's focus on developing the values and the emotional intelligence necessary to be a successful business leader.

DEVELOPING RESOURCES AND CAPABILITIES

Let us return to the question of how companies develop their resources and capabilities. Such development is important in eliminating existing weaknesses, and building the new resources and capabilities that are required in order to adapt to external change and perpetuate competitive advantage. The conventional approach to resource building has focused on *gap analysis*. Once a company has evaluated its relative strengths in resources and capabilities (as discussed above), it can compare its desired relative position with its actual position, then determine how it will go about filling the resulting resource and capability gaps. These gaps are not always a consequence of weakness: once a firm decides to exploit its key strengths more effectively, this may reveal critical gaps in certain complementary resources and capabilities. If we consider once more the turnaround of Walt Disney between 1985 and 1988 (see Exhibit 5.1), the effort to utilize Disney's key resources more effectively required the company to acquire certain additional resources. For example, to revitalize its motion picture business and utilize its studios more fully, Disney needed to hire new creative talent: directors, actors, scriptwriters, and cartoonists. To better utilize its huge Florida land holdings, Disney acquired the Arvida Corporation to provide the real-estate development capability that it needed.

Replicating Capabilities

Exploiting capabilities to their fullest extent requires that the firm replicate them internally.[43] Some of the world's most successful corporations are those that have been able to replicate their capabilities in different product and geographical markets. Ray

---

[43]   Sid Winter, "The Four Rs of Profitability: Rents, Resources, Routines, and Replication," in Cynthia Montgomery (ed.), *Resource-Based and Evolutionary Theories of the Firm* (Boston: Kluwer, 1995): 147–78.

Kroc's genius was to take the original McDonald's formula and replicate it thousands of times over in a global chain of hamburger restaurants. Other leading service companies – Marriott, BankOne, Club Med, McKinsey & Co. – have followed similar patterns of growth through replication, as has Toyota with automobile plants throughout the world.

If routines develop through practice and perfection and if the knowledge is tacit, replication is far from easy. A critical step is to transfer the tacit knowledge embodied in the routine into explicit knowledge in the form of guidelines and operating procedures.[44] Thus, McDonald's has distilled its system into operating procedures and training manuals; Andersen Consulting (now Accenture) has embodied the systems integration and management consulting skills of its leading consultants into a set of standard techniques and procedures based on the "Andersen Way."[45]

Developing New Capabilities

Acquiring new or additional resources requires that a firm purchases the desired resources on external factor markets or, if the resources are not transferable, builds them internally. Developing resources such as company reputation or installed customer base may be difficult and long term, but at least the size and scope of the challenge can be understood. Organizational capabilities pose a bigger challenge. If capabilities are based on routines that develop through practice and learning with limited management direction, what can the firm do to establish and develop its organizational capabilities? We know that capabilities involve teams of different resources working together, but, even with the tools of business process mapping, we typically have only limited understanding of how people, machines, technology, and organizational culture fit together to achieve a particular level of performance. In the same way that we can only speculate about what makes Tiger Woods the greatest golfer of our time, we are unable fully to diagnose why Sony is so brilliant at new product development or how Dell achieves its incredible inventory turnover ratio. Evidence suggests that managers certainly know how to destroy capabilities, but know much less about building them.

Since organizational capabilities develop slowly, they are clearly *path dependent*: to understand a company's capabilities today, we must look at that company's historical development. Looking ahead, the capabilities that a company will possess in five years' time will depend on where it is now, and where it has come from. If we look at companies that possess outstanding capabilities, it is clear that these capabilities often have their origins in the circumstances that existed at the time of those companies' foundation and early development. How did Wal-Mart develop its super-efficient system of warehousing and distribution? This system was not the

---

[44] I. Nonaka and H. Takeuchi, *The Knowledge-Creating Company* (New York: Oxford University Press, 1995): Chapter 3.

[45] Sidney Winter and Gabriel Szulanski ("Replication as Strategy," *Organization Science* 12 (forthcoming, 2001)) show that replication is a complex process requiring the creation and refinement of a business model followed by stabilization and leveraging of the "template."

TABLE 5.6 Distinctive Capabilities as a Consequence of Childhood Experiences: The Oil Majors

COMPANY	DISTINCTIVE CAPABILITY	EARLY HISTORY
Exxon	Financial management	Exxon's predecessor, Standard Oil (NJ), was the holding company for Rockefeller's Standard Oil Trust
Royal Dutch/Shell Group	Coordinating a decentralized global network of 200+ operating companies	Shell Transport & Trading headquartered in London and founded to sell Russian oil in China and the Far East. Royal Dutch Petroleum headquartered in The Hague; founded to exploit Indonesian reserves
BP	"Elephant hunting"	Discovered huge Persian reserves, went on to find Forties field (North Sea) and Prudhoe Bay (Alaska)
ENI	Deal making in politicized environments	The Enrico Mattei legacy; the challenge of managing government relations in post-war Italy
Mobil	Lubricants	Vacuum Oil Co. founded in 1866 to supply patented petroleum lubricants

result of careful planning and design, but rather of the fact that, because of its rural locations, the company was unable to get reliable distribution from its suppliers, and so it established its own distribution system. How does one explain Wal-Mart's amazing commitment to cost efficiency? Its management systems are undoubtedly important, but without understanding its origins in the rural American South and the values and personality of its founder, Sam Walton, we can never hope to understand the culture that sustains this obsession with efficiency and cost cutting.

Consider too the world's largest oil and gas majors (see Table 5.6). Despite a hundred years or more of competing in the same countries with near-identical products and similar strategies, these companies have very different capability profiles. If we look at Exxon and the Royal Dutch/Shell Group, despite their parallel development during much of the twentieth century, they have very different capabilities. Exxon is known for its financial management capabilities exercised through rigorous investment controls and performance auditing. Shell is known for its decentralized, international management capabilities, in particular its adaptability to a wide variety of national environments. These differences can be traced back to the companies' nineteenth-century origins. Exxon (then Standard Oil New Jersey) was part of Rockefeller's Standard Oil Trust, where it played a key holding company role with responsibilities for the financial management of other parts of the Standard Oil empire. Shell was established to sell Russian oil in China and the Far East, while Royal Dutch was established to exploit Indonesian oil reserves. With head offices thousands of miles away in Europe, it is little wonder that the group developed a decentralized, adaptable management style.

We may go further: the more highly developed a firm's organizational capabilities are, the narrower their repertoire and the more difficult it is for the firm to adapt them to new circumstances. Dorothy Leonard's study of new product development showed that although core capabilities are essential for new product development, they also represent *core rigidities* in terms of inhibiting companies' ability to access and develop new capabilities.[46] Although some companies appear to have the capacity to continually upgrade, extend, and reconfigure their organizational capabilities, it is not clear what determines why some companies' capabilities are highly specific and rigid, while others are much more flexible and adaptable. David Teece and his colleagues have referred to *dynamic capabilities* as the "firm's ability to integrate, build, and reconfigure internal and external competences to address rapidly changing environments."[47] If established firms' existing capabilities represent barriers to acquiring new capabilities, this implies that in responding to radical change within an industry, or in exploiting entirely new business opportunities, new firms are at an advantage with respect to established firms. Whereas new firms are faced with the challenge of acquiring entirely new capabilities, established firms are faced with the dual challenges of acquiring new capabilities and dismantling existing obsolete capabilities.

In most new industries, the most successful firms tend to be startups rather than established firms. In personal computers, it was Compaq, Dell, Acer, and Gateway 2000 that emerged as most successful. Among established firms, relatively few (e.g., IBM, Hewlett-Packard, and Toshiba) went on to significant success. Many others (e.g., Xerox, GE, Texas Instruments, AT&T, and Olivetti) fell by the wayside.[48] In developing the capabilities needed to compete in a new business, startups face the "liability of newness," while established companies suffer from the "liability of oldness." The key issue facing established companies is the applicability of the capabilities they bring to the new business. In the early years of the TV industry, for example, existing producers of radios were also successful in producing TVs because of the similar types of capability required by each product.[49]

In today's e-commerce markets, the picture is less clear-cut. Startups have the advantages of flexibility and focus, and they have dominated certain sectors (Amazon

---

[46]   Dorothy Leonard-Barton, "Core Capabilities and Core Rigidities," *Strategic Management Journal*, Summer special issue (1992): 111–26.

[47]   D. J. Teece, G. Pisano, and A. Shuen, "Dynamic Capabilities and Strategic Management," *Strategic Management Journal* 18 (1997): 509–33. The nature of dynamic capability is further explored in K. M. Eisenhardt and J. A. Martin, "Dynamic Capabilities: What Are They," *Strategic Management Journal* 21 (2000): 1105–21.

[48]   A number of studies have explored the failure of established firms to survive radical innovation. See, for example, R. M. Henderson and K. B. Clark, "Architectural Innovation: The Reconfiguration of Existing Product Technologies and Failure of Established Firms," *Administrative Science Quarterly* 35 (1990): 9–30; Clay Christensen, "The Rigid Disk Drive Industry: A History of Commercial and Technological Turbulence," *Business History Review* 67 (1993): 531–88; A. Henderson, "Firm Strategy and Age Dependence: A Contingent View of the Liabilities of Newness, Adolescence and Obsolescence," *Administrative Science Quarterly* 44 (1999): 281–314. Chapter 10 will return to the issue of whether and how companies adapt to industry evolution and technological change.

[49]   S. Klepper and K. L. Simons, "Dominance by Birthright: Entry of Prior Radio Producers and Competitive Ramifications in the US Television Receiver Industry," *Strategic Management Journal* 21 (2000): 997–1016.

in books, AOL in internet service provision, eBay in online auctions). Existing firms, however, have consolidated their leadership in those sectors where established brands and operating capabilities are key success factors (Schwab in online brokerage services; Circuit City, Egghead, and Best Buy in online sales of electronic products and software; Ford, Boeing, and other industrial giants in the creation of web-based components markets).

Approaches to Capability Development

So, how do companies go about developing new capabilities? My review of company case studies suggests five main approaches.

Developing the Individual Competences Required to Develop Organizational Capability

If capabilities are founded on resources and if the most important resources are human resources, then one approach to capability development is to develop the human resources required for a particular capability. Earlier in the chapter we looked at the use of job competency assessment to appraise, select, and develop individual competencies. Such an approach can be used to develop organizational-level capabilities. Exhibit 5.3 outlines the approach taken at Amoco to link strategy formulation, organizational capability assessment, and individual competency development. The evidence suggests that developing human resource competencies can be effective in maintaining and developing existing competencies, but it is likely to be of limited help in constructing new capabilities. This is for two reasons. First, job competency assessment is essentially conservative: it establishes selection and development criteria that are based on individuals who have performed well in the past. Second, it takes no account of the problem of integrating individual-level competencies in order to produce organizational-level capability. As the history of professional sport illustrates, there are many examples of team managers who have spent heavily on acquiring the best playing talent, but have failed to build successful teams.

Corporate Acquisitions

If new capabilities can only be developed over long periods, then short-circuiting the process through acquiring a company, or business unit, that already has the desired capability is obviously attractive. It is often difficult to establish whether the primary goal of an acquisition is to acquire the business or the capabilities that are utilized in that business. However, in some instances, it is clear that the primary interest of an acquirer is using the acquiree's capabilities within its own business. For example, in acquiring Vickers' Rolls-Royce Motors, Volkswagen was interested primarily in the reputation, craftsmanship and engineering excellence long associated with Rolls Royce and Bentley cars. BMW's acquisition of the Rolls-Royce brand name from under VW's nose presents an interesting challenge for both companies. Can BMW

EXHIBIT 5.3   Developing Organizational Capabilities at Amoco

During the 1990s, Amoco Corporation, the international oil, gas, and chemical company, committed itself to strategic management as the basis on which it would develop its businesses and revitalize its financial performance. It identified itself as "a strategically managed company," and named its top management team the "Strategic Planning Committee." One feature of Amoco's strategic management focus was its emphasis on building competitive advantage through the development of organizational capability. This involved integrating strategic planning with human resource management: the strategic planning process identified the organizational capabilities needed to implement Amoco's strategy; HR was responsible for developing these capabilities through recruiting, selecting, training, and incentivizing the appropriate human resources.

The analysis and development of organizational capabilities were the responsibility of the Organizational Capability Group within Amoco's human resources department. The methods included:

■ Identifying "capability gaps" by determining the capabilities required by different businesses and functions (Amoco distinguished those capabilities "needed to win" from those capabilities "needed to play"), and assessed Amoco's performance relative to competitors in terms of superiority or inferiority.

■ Linking organizational capabilities to individual skills and aptitudes using competency modeling – identifying the combination of individual competencies required for superior performance within a particular job type, and a methodology for assessing each person's competencies against the profile created.

■ Using the results of these analyses to guide employee appraisal, training, recruitment, and promotion.

The figure below shows the organization capability-building process in terms of the link between strategy formulation and human resource management.

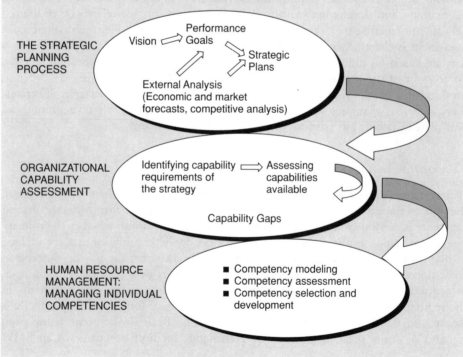

really recreate the Rolls-Royce reputation and mystique without the capabilities that have underpinned the brand's reputation?[50] Can VW build a viable luxury car business with only the Bentley brand? A similar quest for capability has lain behind Microsoft's acquisition of many companies' networking, e-commerce, and new home entertainment technologies. During Summer 2000, it acquired Pacific Microsonics for its digital audio technology, Mongo Music for its digital music distribution expertise and infrastructure, NetGames and Big Huge Games for their capabilities in developing computer games, and DriveOff.com for its capability in selling automobiles online.[51] In the US healthcare sector over an 18-year period, acquisitions played an important role in allowing companies to change their business portfolios, to reinforce their existing skills, and to make substantial jumps into new skill sets.[52]

However, using acquisitions as a means of extending a company's capability base involves major risks. On its own, acquisition does not achieve the intended goal. Once the acquisition has been made, the acquiring company must find a way to integrate the acquiree's capabilities with its own. Herein lies the main difficulty with most mergers and acquisitions:

- Compaq Computer's attempt to build competitive advantage in the corporate sector by adding DEC's sales and customer service capabilities to its own technology and product development capacities was a dismal failure.[53]

- AT&T's attempt to merge its telecommunications expertise with the computer skills of NCR was an even greater disaster. After years of fruitless attempts at managing the convergence of telecommunications and computing, AT&T eventually spun off NCR.

- The jury is still out on the merger between Daimler-Benz and Chrysler. A key objective of the merger was to combine Daimler's engineering and technological strengths with Chrysler's design flair and fast-cycle product development capability. However, this appears to be yet another merger where differences in corporate (and national) cultures have posed a barrier to knowledge transfer and organizational integration.[54]

Acquiring Capabilities through Strategic Alliances

Given the high cost of acquiring companies, it may be more cost effective to acquire another company's capability through a collaborative relationship that permits organizational learning. *Strategic alliances* refer to a range of cooperative relationships between firms that involve common goals and some degree of resource sharing. These relationships include joint ventures, technology-sharing arrangements, joint

[50] Mahen Tampoe, "Is the Goose Worth More than the Golden Egg," *Strategy* (September 1998): 13–15.

[51] www.microsoft.com/msft/invest.htm.

[52] S. Karim and W. Mitchell, "Path-Dependent and Path-Breaking Change: Reconfiguring Business Resources Following Acquisitions in the US Medical Sector, 1978–1995," *Strategic Management Journal* 21 (2000): 1016–81.

[53] "Merger Brief: The Digital Dilemma," *Economist* (July 22, 2000): 55–6.

[54] "Merger Brief: The Daimler Chrysler Emulsion," *Economist* (July 29, 2000): 57–8.

research and development, shared manufacturing, joint marketing and/or distribution arrangements, and vertical partnerships. An important motivation for such alliances is the desire to observe, evaluate, and absorb the capabilities of the alliance partner.[55] The result may well be a "competition for competence" between the alliance partners that ultimately destabilizes the relationship.[56]

Strategic alliances have played a key role in attempts by companies to extend and broaden their range of capabilities. During the 1980s, General Motors formed joint ventures with Toyota (NUMMI, Fanuc in robotics) and a number of technology-based companies in order to upgrade its manufacturing operations through computer-integrated manufacturing and improved quality.[57] Cisco Systems has also relied heavily on strategic alliances in broadening its base of technical capabilities.

Incubating Capabilities

A critical problem in developing new capabilities is that the organizational structure, management systems, and behavioral norms that support existing capabilities may be unsuitable for new capabilities. To resolve this problem, companies may need to develop new capabilities in organizationally separate units. For example:

- IBM developed its prototype personal computer at its Entry Level systems unit led by IBM veteran Bill Lowe. The unit was located in Florida, over a thousand miles away from its corporate headquarters in New York. The isolation of the unit and the protection and support it received from IBM's CEO, John Opel, were critical in allowing the PC development team to create a product design and business system that were totally different from those that characterized IBM's mainframe business.[58]

- Brown & Root, the engineering services company, developed world-beating capabilities in logistics management and emergency-response services that support a business with revenues of over $500 million. This development took place in a "protected and stimulating environment in which the new competences were able to flourish. The environment was bounded not by fire walls, but by a one-way membrane that allowed the incubator to beg, borrow or steal people and practices from the main business, while not being bound by its rules."[59]

---

[55]   See, for example, Marjorie Lyles, "Learning Among Joint-venture Sophisticated Firms," *Management International Review* 28, special issue (1988): 85–98; A. Mody, "Learning Through Alliances," *Journal of Economic Behaviour and Organisation* 20 (1993): 151–70; D. C. Mowery, J. E. Oxley, and B. S. Silverman, "Strategic Alliances and Interfirm Knowledge Transfer," *Strategic Management Journal* 17, Winter special issue (1996): 77–93; A. C. Inkpen and M. M. Crossan, "Believing Is Seeing: Joint Ventures and Organisational Learning," *Journal of Management Studies* 32 (1995): 595–618.

[56]   G. Hamel, "Competition for Competence and Inter-partner Learning within International Strategic Alliances," *Strategic Management Journal* 12, Summer special issue (1991): 83–103.

[57]   Joseph A. Badaracco, *The Knowledge Link: How Firms Compete Through Strategic Alliances* (Boston: Harvard Business School Press, 1991).

[58]   Tait Elder, "Lessons from Xerox and IBM," *Harvard Business Review* (July–August 1989): 66–71.

[59]   Kevin Coyne, Stephen Hall, and Patricia Gorman Clifford, "Is Your Core Competence a Mirage?," *McKinsey Quarterly* no. 1 (1997): 40–54.

- The innovative, fast-growing, British online financial services company Egg was established by its parent, Prudential Insurance, as a separate unit with two locations, at Dudley near Birmingham and at Derby, both well away from Prudential's London headquarters.

It can be argued that these incubator arrangements represent the best of all worlds in developing new capabilities: the new unit can establish the flexibility and autonomy of a startup, while drawing on the established resources and capabilities of the parent. However, the challenge occurs when the established organization needs to bring the new capability back into the company. As occurred at Xerox, the separate unit was very effective at developing innovative new computer technologies at its Palo Alto Research Center. However, it was much easier for these technologies to flow to nearby competitors – Hewlett-Packard, Apple, Microsoft, and Sun Microsystems – than it was for them to be absorbed by the rest of Xerox back in the East.

A similar story may be told of Saturn. The Tennessee-based subsidiary of GM has done well in developing new manufacturing and marketing capabilities, but, as yet, these seem to have had little impact on the parent organization.[60]

Product Sequencing

If we do not fully comprehend the structure of organizational capabilities, and do not know the mechanisms through which they operate or the processes that cause them to merge, it is very difficult to manage their creation and development. However, even if we cannot fully analyze them, we may be able to identify the circumstances that foster their development. For example, we may observe that when companies commit themselves to the challenge of developing new products, they typically develop the capabilities that these new products need. Hence, through managing new product development strategy, we can, in effect, create a "pull" system that draws the development of new capabilities. For product development goals to pull the development of capabilities requires a systematic approach where successive products require incremental developments of capability. Thus, Helfat and Raubitschek identify *product sequencing* as a means by which a company's products' capabilities develop and co-evolve – though it is product development that is in the lead.[61]

The development of products and capabilities at 3M (Figure 5.3) illustrates one example of this co-evolution. An even more striking example is the rapid emergence of Hyundai as a leading international supplier of automobiles. While most of the world's leading car manufacturers have been involved in the automotive industry since the early years of the twentieth century, Hyundai entered it in 1986.[62]

[60] Jack O'Toole, *Forming the Future: Lessons from the Saturn Corporation* (New York: Harper, 1996).
[61] Connie E. Helfat and Ruth S. Raubitschek, "Product Sequencing: Co-evolution of Knowledge, Capabilities and Products," *Strategic Management Journal* 21 (2000): 961–79.
[62] L. Kim, "Crisis Construction and Organizational Learning: Capability Building and Catching-up at Hyundai Motor," *Organizational Science* 9 (1998): 506–21.

The design of a strategy that achieves the parallel development of the firm's products and its base of resources and capabilities is what Hiroyuki Itami has referred to as *dynamic resource fit*. The firm's strategy not only utilizes its resources, but also augments them through the creation of skills and knowledge that are the products of experience.

> Effective strategy in the present builds invisible assets, and the expanded stock enables the firm to plan its future strategy to be carried out. And the future strategy must make effective use of the resources that have been amassed.[63]

Matsushita's multinational expansion has closely followed this principle of parallel and sequential development of strategy and resources. In developing production in a foreign country, it has typically begun with the production of batteries, then moved on to the production of products requiring greater manufacturing and marketing sophistication. Arataroh Takahashi explained the strategy:

> In every country batteries are a necessity, so they sell well. As long as we bring a few advanced automated pieces of equipment for the processes vital to final product quality, even unskilled labor can produce good products. As they work on this rather simple product, the workers get trained, and this increased skill level then permits us to gradually expand production to items with increasingly higher technology levels, first radios, then televisions.[64]

This idea that ambitious performance can create the driving force for the continual development of a firm's resources and capabilities is a common theme in the writings of several leading strategy thinkers. For example, Gary Hamel and C. K. Prahalad have emphasized the role of strategic intent, resource "leverage and stretch," and ambition to "create the future" as much more important in building sustainable competitive advantage than are initial resource advantages.[65] In a similar vein, Michael Porter argues that it is continuous investment in resources and capabilities that is the key to competitive advantage over the long haul:

> Firms create and sustain competitive advantage because of the capacity to continuously improve, innovate, and upgrade their competitive advantages over time. Upgrading is the process of shifting advantages throughout the value chain to more sophisticated types and employing higher levels of skill and technology.[66]

---

[63] Hiroyuko Itami, *Mobilizing Invisible Assets* (Boston: Harvard University Press, 1987): 125.

[64] A. Takahashi, *What I Learned from Konosuke Matsushita* (Tokyo: Jitsugyo no Nihonsha, 1980); in Japanese, quoted by Itami, op. cit.: 25.

[65] Gary Hamel and C. K. Prahalad, "Strategic Intent," *Harvard Business Review* (May–June, 1989): 45–52; Gary Hamel and C. K. Prahalad, "Strategy and Stretch and Leverage," *Harvard Business Review* (March–April, 1993): 53–62; Gary Hamel and C. K. Prahalad, *Competing for the Future* (Boston: Harvard Business School Press, 1994).

[66] Michael E. Porter, "Toward a Dynamic Theory of Strategy," *Strategic Management Journal*, Winter special issue (1991): 111.

SUMMARY

We have shifted the focus of our attention from the external to the internal environment of the firm. This internal environment comprises many features of the firm, but for the purposes of strategy analysis, the key issue is what the firm can *do*. This means looking at the resources of the firm and the way resources are brought together to create organizational capabilities. Our main interest is in identifying those resources and capabilities that have the potential to establish sustainable competitive advantage for the company. A systematic appraisal of a company's resources and capabilities then provides the basis for reconsidering strategy. How can the firm deploy its strengths to maximum advantage? How can it minimize its vulnerability to its weaknesses? How can it develop and extend its capabilities to meet the challenges of the future? Figure 5.10 provides a simplified view of the approach to resource analysis developed in this chapter.

Despite the progress that has been made in the last ten years in our understanding of resources and capabilities, there is much that remains unresolved. We know little about the microstructures of organizational capabilities and how they are established and develop. Can firms develop entirely new capabilities, or must top management accept that distinctive capabilities are the result of experience-based learning over long periods of time through processes that

FIGURE 5.10 Summary: a framework for analyzing resources and capabilities

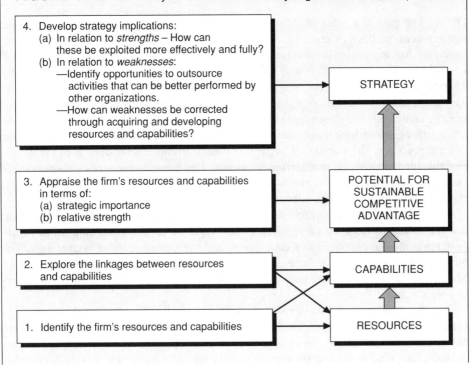

are poorly understood? If that is the case, strategy must be concerned with exploiting, preserving, and developing the firm's existing pool of resources and capabilities, rather than trying to change them. We have much to learn in this area.

Although much of the discussion has been heavy on concepts and theory, the issues are practical. The management systems of most firms devote meticulous attention to the physical and financial assets that are valued on the balance sheet, much less attention has been paid to the critical intangible and human resources of the firm, and even less to the identification and appraisal of organizational capability. Most firms are now aware of the importance of their resources and capabilities, but the techniques of identifying, assessing, and developing them are woefully underdeveloped.

Because the resources and capabilities of the firm form the foundation for building competitive advantage, we shall return again and again to the concepts of this chapter. Our next port of call is the structures and systems through which the firm deploys its resources, builds and exercises its capabilities, and implements its strategy.

Appendix: The Contribution of Knowledge Management

During the past ten years our thinking about resources and capabilities and their management has been extended and reshaped by a surge of interest in knowledge management. Among practicing managers, awareness of the need to manage companies' knowledge assets more effectively has been triggered by recognition of the woeful inefficiency with which these resources are deployed. Initial interest focused on the use of information technology, especially intranets, groupware, and databases, for storing, analyzing, and disseminating information. Subsequent developments in knowledge management have been concerned less with data and more with the transfer of best practices, the pursuit of organizational learning, the fostering of creativity, and the management of intellectual property. The broadening scope of knowledge management is indicated by the number of large corporations that have created the position of chief knowledge officer.

At the academic level, interest in the role of knowledge in economic organization has grown out of research into resources and capabilities, the economics of information, epistemology, evolutionary economics, and the management of technology. The outcome has been a *knowledge-based view of the firm* that considers the firm as a set of knowledge assets and the role of the firm in creating and deploying these assets to create value.

Yet, like all major fashions in management, it is unclear to what extent knowledge management is merely a fad, or a set of management theories and tools with real value. Certainly, many of the manifestations of knowledge management are highly dubious. *The Wall Street Journal* reports that Saatchi & Saatchi's director of knowledge management is "absorbing everything under the sun," including the implications of breakthrough products such as Japanese pantyhose "embedded with millions of microcapsules of vitamin C and seaweed extract that burst when worn to provide extra nourishment for the limbs."[67] Lucy Kellaway of the *Financial Times* notes that beyond the simple truth that "companies that are good at sharing information have an advantage over companies that are not. . . . The subject [of knowledge management] has attracted more needless obfuscation and wooly thinking by academics and consultants than any other."[68]

My approach in this appendix is to regard knowledge management and the knowledge-based view of the firm as important extensions of our analysis of resources and capabilities. In terms of resources, knowledge is acknowledged to be the overwhelming important productive resource; indeed, the value of people and machines lies primarily in the fact that they embody knowledge. From the strategic viewpoint, knowledge is a particularly interesting resource: many types of knowledge are scarce, much of it is difficult to transfer, and complex forms of knowledge may be very difficult to replicate. Capabilities may be viewed as the manifestation of the knowledge of the organization. The tools of knowledge management can offer us insight into the architecture of organizational capability and uncover fundamental issues as to how capability can be created, developed, maintained, and replicated.

Types of Knowledge

The single most useful contribution of knowledge management is the recognition that different types of knowledge have very different characteristics. A key distinction is between *knowing how* and *knowing about*. Know-how is primarily *tacit* in nature – it involves skills that are expressed through their performance (riding a bicycle, playing the piano); knowing about is primarily *explicit* – it comprises facts, theories, and sets of instructions. The primary difference between tacit and explicit knowledge lies in their transferability. Explicit knowledge is revealed by its communication: it can be transferred across individuals, across space, and across time. This ease of communication means that explicit knowledge – information especially – has the characteristics of a *public good*: once created, it can be replicated among innumerable users at very low marginal cost (IT has driven these costs to near zero for most types of information). Tacit knowledge, on the other hand, cannot be codified; it can only be observed through its application and acquired through practice, hence its transfer between people is slow, costly, and uncertain.

This distinction has huge implications for strategy and for management more broadly. If explicit knowledge can be transferred so easily, it is seldom the foundation of sustainable competitive advantage. Because explicit knowledge leaks so quickly to competitors, it is only when it is protected, either by intellectual property (patents, copyrights, trade secrets) or by secrecy ("The formula for Coca-Cola will be kept in a

---

[67]   "Saatchi's 'Manager of Knowledge' Keeps Track of What's Trendy," *Wall Street Journal* (February 28, 1997): B.16.
[68]   Lucy Kellaway column, *Financial Times* (June 23, 1999): 13.

safe in the vault of our Atlanta headquarters guarded by armed Coca-Cola executives"). The challenge of tacit knowledge is the opposite: if Ms. Jenkins is an incredibly successful salesperson, how can the skills embedded in her brain be transferred to the rest of the sales force of Acme Delights?

The tacit/explicit distinction has important implications for the distribution of decision-making authority within the company. If the knowledge relevant to decisions is explicit, it can be easily transferred and assembled in one place, hence permitting centralized decision making (treasury activities within companies are typically centralized). If knowledge is primarily tacit, it cannot be transferred and decision making needs to be located among the people where the knowledge lies. If each salesperson's knowledge of how to make sales is based on their intuition and their understanding of their customers' idiosyncrasies, such knowledge cannot be easily transferred to their sales managers. It follows that decisions about their working hours and selling strategies should be made by them, not by the sales manager.

Types of Knowledge Process

The second major component of knowledge management is the recognition of the processes through which knowledge is developed and applied. Two categories of knowledge processes can be identified: those that are concerned with increasing the stock of knowledge available to the organization, and those that are concerned with the application of the organization's knowledge. J.-C. Spender refers to the former as *knowledge generation* and the latter as *knowledge application*. James March's distinction between *exploration* and *exploitation* recognizes a similar dichotomy.[69] Within these two broad areas we can identify a number of different knowledge processes, each of which has been associated with particular techniques and approaches to knowledge management (see Figure 5.11).

The best-developed and most widely applied techniques of knowledge management have focused on some of the most basic aspects of knowledge application and exploitation. For example:

- In the area of *knowledge identification*, companies are increasingly assembling and systematizing information on their knowledge assets. These include assessments and reviews of patent portfolios and providing personnel data that allows each employee to identify the skills and experience of other employees in the organization. A key aspect of such knowledge identification is the recognition of knowledge that is being generated within the organization so that it can subsequently be stored for future use. Such knowledge identification is especially important in project-based organizations to ensure that knowledge developed in one project is not lost to the organization. Systematic post-project reviews are a central theme in the US Army's "lessons learned" procedure. At the Army's

---

[69]   J.-C. Spender, "Limits to Learning from the West," *The International Executive* 34 (September/October 1992): 389–410; J. G. March, "Exploration and Exploitation in Organizational Learning," *Organization Science* 2 (1991): 71–87.

FIGURE 5.11 Knowledge processes within the organization

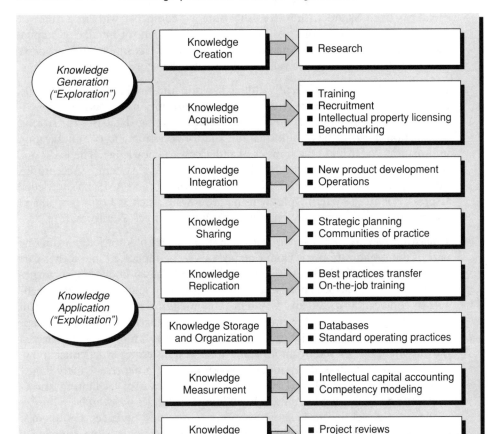

National Training Center, the results of practice maneuvers and simulated battles are quickly identified, then distilled into tactical guidelines and recommended procedures by the Center for Army Lessons Learned. A similar systematized learning process is applied to identifying knowledge generated from actual operations. During the military intervention in Bosnia in 1995, the results of every operation were forwarded to the Center for Lessons Learned to be collected and codified. Resulting lessons learned were distributed to active units every 72 hours.[70] By the late 1990s, virtually every major management consulting firm had introduced a system whereby the learnings of each consulting project had to be identified, written up, and submitted to a common database.

[70] "Lessons Learned: Army Devises System to Decide What Does and What Does Not Work," *Wall Street Journal* (May 23, 1997): A1 and A10.

- *Knowledge measurement* involves the difficult task of applying metrics to the organization's stock of knowledge and its utilization. The pioneer of measurement has been Skandia, the Swedish insurance company, with its system of intellectual capital accounting.[71] Dow Chemical's system of intellectual capital management also relies on quantitative tools to link its intellectual property portfolio to the shareholder value using a balanced scorecard approach.

- For knowledge to be efficiently utilized within the organization, *knowledge storage and organization* are critical. The key contribution of information technology to knowledge management has been in creating databases for storing information, for organizing information, and for accessing and communicating information, to facilitate the transfer of and access to knowledge. The backbone of the Booz-Allen & Hamilton's "Knowledge-On-Line" system,[72] Accenture's (formerly Andersen Consulting) "Knowledge Xchange", and AMS's "Knowledge Express"[73] is an IT system typically using groupware (such as Lotus Notes) and a company intranet to allow employees to input and access information.

- *Knowledge sharing and replication* involves the transfer of knowledge from one part of the organization (or from one person) to be replicated in another part (or by another individual). A central function of IT-based knowledge management systems is to achieve precisely that. However, tacit knowledge is not amenable to codification within an IT system. The traditional answer to the problem of replicating tacit knowledge embodied within individuals is use apprenticeships and other forms of on-the-job training. Recently, organizations have discovered the important role played by informal networks in transferring experiential knowledge. These initially self-organizing *communities of practice* are increasingly being deliberately established and managed as a means of facilitating knowledge sharing and group learning.[74] Replicating capabilities poses an even greater challenge. Gabriel Szulanski shows that transferring best practices within companies is not simply about creating appropriate incentives; it is the complexity of the knowledge involved that constitutes the most significant barrier.[75]

- *Knowledge integration* represents one of the greatest challenges to any company. Ultimately, producing a good or service requires bringing together the knowledge of many people, and establishing organizational processes that allow this to be achieved efficiently is a daunting task. The task of knowledge integration is central to many organizational processes. For example, a strategic planning system

---

[71] L. Edvinsson and S. Malone, *Intellectual Capital: Realizing Your Company's True Value by Finding its Hidden Brainpower* (New York: Harper Business, 1997); D. Marchand and J. Roos, *Skandia AFS: Measuring and Visualizing Intellectual Capital*, Case GM 624 (Lausanne: IMD, 1996).

[72] *Cultivating Capabilities to Innovate: Booz-Allen & Hamilton*, Case 9-698-027 (Boston: Harvard Business School, 1997).

[73] *American Management Systems: The Knowledge Centers*, Case 9-697-068 (Boston: Harvard Business School, 1997).

[74] E. C. Wenger and W. M. Snyder, "Communities of Practice: The Organizational Frontier," *Harvard Business Review* (January–February 2000).

[75] G. Szulanski, "Exploring Internal Stickiness: Impediments to the Transfer of Best Practices within the Firm," *Strategic Management Journal* 17, Winter special issue (1996): 27–44.

may be seen as a vehicle for integrating the different knowledge bases of managers at different levels of the organization and from different functions in order to create the best strategy for the company. Similarly with new product development, the key is to integrate the knowledge of many technical experts and across a range of functions. Our developing understanding of these processes points to the key role of project teams in achieving effective knowledge integration.[76]

In the area of knowledge generation, it is possible to distinguish between the internal creation of knowledge (*knowledge creation*) and the search to identify and absorb existing knowledge from outside the organization (*knowledge acquisition*). The mechanisms through which knowledge is acquired from outside the organization are typically well known: hiring skilled employees, acquiring companies or their knowledge resources, benchmarking companies that are recognized as "best-in-class" for certain practices, and learning through alliances and joint ventures. Creativity remains a key challenge for most companies. While most studies of creativity emphasize the role of the individual and the types of environment conducive to individual creativity, Dorothy Leonard has explored the role of groups and group processes in stimulating innovation.[77]

Knowledge Conversion

In practice, knowledge generation and application are not distinct. For example, the application of existing knowledge creates opportunities for learning that increase the stock of knowledge.[78] Nonaka's theory of knowledge creation identifies the processes of knowledge conversion – between tacit and explicit and between individual and organizational knowledge – as central to the organization's building of its knowledge base. The conversion of knowledge between the different knowledge types (the "epistemological dimension") and knowledge levels (the "ontological dimension") forms a knowledge spiral in which the stock of knowledge broadens and deepens (see Figure 5.12). Nonaka specifies four types of knowledge conversion (see Figure 5.13).

Knowledge conversion between tacit and explicit dimensions is of particular interest. Nonaka discusses the problems of sharing intuition and know-how among the members of cross-functional product development teams and notes the importance of analogy and metaphor in communicating these types of knowledge. For example, a member of Canon's mini-copier development team used a beer can to explain his

---

[76]   See, for example, Clark and Fujimoto, op. cit.; and Imai et al., op. cit.

[77]   D. Leonard and J. Rayport, "Sparking Innovation through Empathic Design," *Harvard Business Review* (November–December 1997): 102–13; D. Leonard and S. Sensiper, "The Role of Tacit Knowledge in Group Innovation," *California Management Review* 40 (Spring 1998): 112–32; Dorothy Leonard-Barton, *The Wellsprings of Knowledge* (Boston: Harvard Business School Press, 1996).

[78]   Peter McNamara argues that, in addition to *exploration* and *exploitation*, *development* needs to be regarded as a separate knowledge-building activity: P. McNamara, "Managing the Tension Between Knowledge Exploration and Exploitation: The Case of UK Biotechnology," Ph.D. thesis (City University Business School, London, 2000).

FIGURE 5.12 Nonaka's spiral of knowledge creation

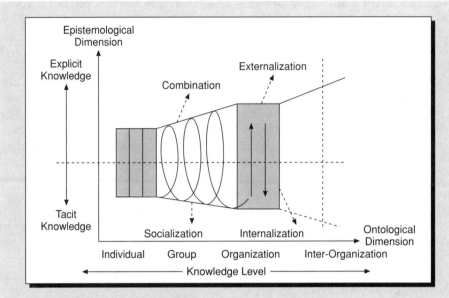

Source: I. Nonaka, "On a Knowledge Creating Organization," paper presented at AIF National Congress (Posma, October 1993).

FIGURE 5.13 Nonaka's knowledge conversion matrix

	Tacit Knowledge **TO**	Explicit Knowledge
Tacit Knowledge	SOCIALIZATION Sharing of tacit knowledge among individuals and from the organization to the individual	EXTERNALIZATION The articulation and systematization of tacit into explicit knowledge. Use of metaphor to communicate tacit concepts
FROM **Explicit Knowledge**	INTERNALIZATION Instructions and principles are converted into intuition and routines	COMBINATION A key role of information systems is to combine different units of information and other forms of explicit knowledge

Source: I. Nonaka, "On the Knowledge Creating Organization," paper presented at the AIF National Congress (Posma, October 1991).

concept of a drum cylinder. Converting tacit into explicit knowledge is also critical to companies that wish to replicate their capabilities. Several companies have created huge amounts of value from systematizing tacit knowledge and then replicating it in multiple locations:

- Henry Ford's Model T was initially produced on a small scale by skilled metal workers one car at a time. Ford's assembly-line mass-production technology systematized that tacit knowledge, built it into machines and a business process, and replicated in Ford plants throughout the world. With the knowledge built into the system, the workers no longer needed to be highly skilled, so Ford's plants were staffed by semi-skilled workers.

- When Ray Kroc discovered the McDonald brothers' hamburger stand in Riversdale, California, he quickly recognized the potential for systematizing their operation and fast-service, assembly-line meals, not just in a single location but in many McDonald's outlets. McDonald's knowledge is systematized and replicated through operating manuals, videos, and training programs. It allows its thousands of worldwide outlets to produce fast food to exacting standards by a labor force that, for the most part, possesses very limited culinary skills.

Knowledge-based View of the Firm

The emerging *knowledge-based view of the firm* regards the business enterprise as an institution for generating and applying knowledge. Its basis is a set of ideas about the knowledge processes within the firm. Most importantly, it recognizes that the processes of knowledge generation and knowledge application require different organizational arrangements. Efficiency in creating and storing knowledge requires that individuals specialize in particular types of knowledge. Yet, production requires the integration of many different types of knowledge. Hence, the fundamental challenge of business organization is to reconcile these two processes.[79] Despite the emphasis of much of the knowledge management literature on *organizational learning*, the danger of learning is that it can easily undermine the efficiencies of specialization. When Soichiro Honda and Takeo Fujisawa began their collaboration to form Honda Motor Company at the end of 1949, Honda brought his engineering genius; Fujisawa brought sound business sense and marketing expertise. For them to combine their knowledge by each learning what the other knew would be slow and inefficient. The key was to create a way of collaborating such that each could input their different expertise while avoiding the costs of large-scale knowledge transfer.

How can knowledge be integrated in ways that preserve the efficiencies of specialization? Among the processes that have been suggested are *rules*, whereby specialists translate their knowledge into rules and directives to guide the practices

---

[79] See, for example, H. Demsetz, "The Theory of the Firm Revisited," in *The Nature of the Firm* (New York: Oxford University Press, 1991): 159–78; and R. M. Grant, "Toward a Knowledge-based Theory of the Firm," *Strategic Management Journal* 17, Winter special issue (1996): 109–22.

and behavior of others, and *routines*, whereby different specialists establish ways of interacting that allow each to input their knowledge into a combined process. For knowledge integration to work efficiently, there needs to be some degree of *common knowledge* that permits different specialists to collaborate and interact. This common knowledge comprises elements such as a common language to support communication and a common culture to support compatible behaviors and cognitive processes. By recognizing the specific features of different knowledge processes, it is possible to recognize the type of organizational structure and systems needed to support each knowledge process. Awareness of these complexities of processing knowledge offers a view of the business enterprise that is richer and more sophisticated than economic theories of the firm that focus on transaction costs or efficient incentive structures. Thus, Bruce Kogut and Udo Zander argue that firms are:

> social communities in which individual and social expertise is transferred into economically-useful products and services by the application of a set of higher-order organizing principles. Firms exist because they provide a social community of voluntaristic action structured by organizing principles that are not reducible to individuals.[80]

Conclusion

At the academic level, the analysis of the characteristics of knowledge and the processes through which the firm creates value from knowledge has the potential to develop our understanding of fundamental aspects of the role of firms and the nature of management – including the architecture and operation of organizational capability.

In terms of practical techniques of knowledge management, considerable advances have been made. The key contribution is in closing the gap between the sophisticated tools of financial and operational analysis to which tangible assets have been subject (including the full panoply of financial accounting), and the gross neglect to which most intangible assets have been subject. While plant, equipment, inventories, and financial assets have long been subject to careful scrutiny and detailed valuation, it is only recently that attempts have been made even to value brands and intellectual property (patents, copyrights, trademarks, and the like). Meanwhile, more intangible – yet even more critical – assets such as capabilities and corporate reputation have received very little systematic attention.

At the same time, the field of knowledge management is vast. It could be argued that, since all management is involved with managing the knowledge embodied within human beings, machines, and business systems, knowledge management covers virtually the whole field of management. In this situation, the value of knowledge management is not merely a set of techniques for improving the efficiency with which knowledge is developed and exploited with the firm, it is also a perspective that can broaden our understanding of the firm and its management.

---

[80]   B. Kogut and U. Zander, "Knowledge of the Firm, Combinative Capabilities, and the Replication of Technology," *Organization Science* 3 (1992): 389.

Given the scope of knowledge management and the vast range of tools, techniques, and frameworks that have been developed, where does a company begin to incorporate knowledge management within its management systems? The starting point, we suggest, is to identify the linkage between knowledge and the basis through which the firm creates value. This can then highlight the key processes through which knowledge is generated and applied. Consider the following examples:

- For Dow Chemical, the core of its value creation is in generating intellectual property – patents and trade secrets – in the form of new chemical products and processes, and exploiting them through worldwide manufacturing, marketing, and sales. If the foundation of value creation is the creation and exploitation of intellectual property, this is on what its knowledge management system should concentrate. Dow's "Intellectual Capital Management" places its central emphasis on the company's patent portfolio, but links its intellectual property to a broad range of intellectual capital variables and processes and ultimately to the company's total value.[81]

- For McKinsey & Co., the key to competitive advantage and creating value for clients is to continually build on the knowledge it generates from client assignments, and to systematize and conceptualize that knowledge base. Building the knowledge base first requires a structure for allowing specialization. This was achieved through the creation of practices organized by industry group (e.g., consumer goods, financial institutions, energy, basic materials, government) and by function (e.g., strategy, organization, IT, operations). Second, it requires that knowledge generated from each project is captured, systematized, and made available for subsequent client projects.[82]

- For McDonald's restaurants, knowledge management is primarily concerned with implementing the McDonald's system. This is a detailed set of rules and operating practices that extend from the company's values down to the placing of a pickle on the bun of a Big Mac and the procedure for servicing a McDonald's milkshake machine. The essence of the McDonald's system is the systematization of knowledge into a detailed set of rules that must be followed in each McDonald's outlet. However, this is not simply a question of converting all experience and tacit knowledge into explicit operating practices, but also ensuring that these operating practices are internalized within employees' cognition and behavior through rigorous attention to training, both in formal training programs at Hamburger University, and in training at individual restaurants.

The design of every knowledge process needs also to take account of the characteristics of the knowledge being deployed. As we have already noted, the fundamental

---

[81] G. Petrash, "Dow's Journey to a Knowledge Value Management Culture," *European Management Journal* 14 (August 1996): 365–73.

[82] *McKinsey & Company: Managing Knowledge and Learning*, Case Number 9-396-357 (Boston: Harvard Business School, 1996).

distinction is between explicit and tacit knowledge. Take a simple example of the transfer of best practice between the different fabrication plants of a multinational semiconductor plant. If the knowledge is explicit, then such knowledge can be disseminated in the form of reports, or directives requiring every plant to adopt a new standard operating procedure. If the knowledge is tacit – it is the result of the experience or intuition of a single plant manager – the task is more difficult. Transferring the best practice is likely to require either visits by other plant managers to the innovating plant, or for the innovating plant manager to adopt a consulting role and visit other plants in the group for the purpose of teaching employees there.

It is in the area of managing tacit knowledge (which includes, typically, the major part of the knowledge relevant to organizational capability) that the major challenges and opportunities in knowledge management lie. Information technology has made huge strides in the storage, analysis, and systematization of explicit knowledge. However, the greater part of organizational learning is experienced based and intuitive. Identifying this knowledge, and transferring it to other parts of the organization in order to utilize it more effectively, remains a fundamental management challenge.

6

Organization Structure and Management Systems

Ultimately, there may be no long-term sustainable advantage other than the ability to organize and manage.

—*Jay Galbraith and Ed Lawler*

OUTLINE

INTRODUCTION AND OBJECTIVES

One of the most pernicious misconceptions in the history of strategic management is the idea that the formulation of strategy can be separated from its implementation. The convention articulated in numerous strategic management texts was that strategy formulation required identifying the organization's goals and analyzing its external environment and internal resources and capabilities. Once formulated, the strategy was then implemented by selecting the appropriate organizational structure and management systems. The dictum *structure follows strategy* was also evident in the strategic planning processes of many companies. Strategy formulation was the responsibility of top management advised by specialist corporate planners. Implementation was the responsibility of functional and business-level middle managers.

This supposed division between formulation and implementation is fiction. At the most obvious level, formulating a strategy without taking into account the conditions under which it will be implemented will result in a poorly designed strategy. The comment "Great strategy, lousy implementation" gives unjustified credit to the strategist. If the strategy has been designed without taking account of the organization's capacity for implementation, it's a lousy strategy. More fundamentally, we saw in the previous chapter that a firm's capabilities depend on how it organizes its resources. Indeed, the organization of the firm – the way in which individuals relate to one another in productive activities – is fundamental to its very existence. If capabilities are the primary basis of the firm's strategy, and if capabilities are a product of the structure that coordinates teams of resources to work together, then it might be argued that *strategy follows structure*. The key point, however, is not whether strategy or structure takes precedence, but the recognition that the two are closely interdependent.[1] Consider, for example, Benetton, with its closely coordinated network of local suppliers and worldwide network of franchised retailers; or General Electric, with its 17 business groups coordinated and controlled by its corporate headquarters; or Amway, with its

---

[1]   The complementarity of strategy, structure, and management systems is emphasized in R. Whittington, A. Pettigrew, S. Peck, E. Fenton, and M. Conyon, "Change and Complementarities in the New Competitive Landscape," *Organization Science* 10 (1999): 583–96.

pyramid of commission-based, independent distributors. These companies reinforce Tom Peters' dictum that "Strategy *is* structure."

Having established that how companies organize themselves is fundamental to their strategy and their performance, the goal of this chapter is to introduce the key concepts and ideas necessary to understand and design companies' structures and systems. The approach is concise and selective. I do not intend to offer a potted overview of organizational theory. My aim is to introduce some basic principles of organizational design and to apply these to key aspects of firm structure. The principles outlined here will be further developed in later chapters when we consider strategies within particular business contexts. For example, Chapter 11 considers the organizational conditions conducive to innovation; Chapter 12 considers organization and organizational change within mature industries; Chapter 13 discusses vertical structures and outsourcing; Chapter 14 examines the structure and management systems of the multinational corporation; and Chapter 16 deals with organizing the multidivisional company.

By the time you have completed this chapter you will be able to:

- Recognize the key organizational innovations that have shaped the evolution of the modern corporation.

- Understand the basic principles that determine the structural characteristics of complex human organizations.

- Apply the principles of organizational design to recommend the types of organizational structure suited to particular tasks and particular business environments.

- Understand the role of information systems, strategic planning, financial control, and human resource management in the coordination and control of corporations.

- Appreciate the forces that are causing companies to seek new organizational structures and management systems.

THE EVOLUTION OF THE CORPORATION

Most of the world's production of goods and services is undertaken by corporations. The main exceptions include agriculture and crafts in the developing world, where family-based production predominates, and services such as defense, policing, and education that are usually provided by government organizations.

This has not always been so. Until the nineteenth century, the only large corporations were colonial trading companies such as the Dutch East India Company, Hudson's Bay Company, and the United Africa Company. As late as the 1840s, the largest enterprises in the US in terms of numbers of workers were agricultural plantations.[2] Most manufacturing was organized through networks of self-employed, home-based workers. The English woolen industry consisted of home-based spinners who purchased raw wool (on credit) from a merchant to whom they sold the yarn; the merchant resold the yarn to home-based weavers from whom he purchased cloth. This "putting-out" system survived until the onset of the Industrial Revolution. With the advent of water-powered looms, weavers moved to factories where, initially, they rented looms from the factory owner by the hour. Factory-based manufacture made this system of independent contractors inefficient – it was difficult to schedule machine time, and there was little incentive for the independent workers to look after their rented machines. The emergence of firms where market relationships among workers, machine owners, and merchants were replaced by employment relationships between the owner of capital and the workers was a more efficient means of organizing production.

This issue of the relative roles of *firms* and *markets* is a central aspect of economic organization. In the capitalist economy, production is organized in two ways: in markets (by the price mechanisms) and in firms (by managerial direction). The relative roles of firms and markets is determined by efficiency: if the *administrative costs* of firms are less than the *transaction costs* of markets (as occurred in the English textile industry after the introduction of the factory system), transactions will tend to be organized within firms rather than across markets. We shall revisit the *theory of transaction costs* when we consider the scope and boundaries of the firm in Chapter 13.

Initially, most companies were small. Lack of transportation limited each firm's market to its immediate vicinity, while lack of communication prevented the firm from operating in multiple locations. The railroad and the telegraph changed all that. While new forms of transportation and communication created the opportunity for companies to grow, developments in organizational structure and management techniques gave firms the capacity to grow. The railroad companies themselves were the first to realize the potential of the new transportation and communications technologies to establish the "first administrative hierarchies in American business" using "line and staff" structures, with line operations organized around separate geographical divisions and head offices organized in functional staff departments.

Initially, firms were small, single-establishment enterprises because of lack of transportation and communication. The advent of railroads and the telegraph changed all that. Very quickly, regional and national markets could be supplied from a single establishment in a timely manner, and the activities of multiple establishments could be coordinated from a single office. With the increasing size of firms, management developed as a specialized activity.

This emergence of the modern corporation with multiple operating units and a head office organized by function was the first of the two "critical transformations" identified by Alfred Chandler.[3] The second was the emergence during the 1920s

---

[2]   Alfred D. Chandler, *The Visible Hand: The Managerial Revolution in American Business* (Cambridge, MA: MIT Press, 1977): Chapter 2.
[3]   Alfred D. Chandler, *Strategy and Structure* (Cambridge: MIT Press, 1962); Chandler, *The Visible Hand*, op. cit.

of the divisionalized corporation, which, over time, replaced both the centralized, functional structures that characterized most industrial corporations and the loosely knit, holding companies that had been created by the wave of mergers at the beginning of the twentieth century. The pioneers were DuPont, which adopted a product division structure to replace its functional structure in 1920, and General Motors, which arrived at a similar structure but from a quite different starting point.

- At DuPont, the strain of increasing size and a widening product range stimulated the adoption of a divisionalized structure. Under its centralized, functional structure, coordination among the various functional departments for each product area became increasingly difficult, and top management became overloaded. As Chandler observed:

  > the operations of the enterprise became too complex and the problems of coordination, appraisal and policy formulation too intricate for a small number of top officers to handle both long-run, entrepreneurial and short-run, operational administrative activities.[4]

  The solution devised by Pierre Du Pont was to decentralize: to create product divisions where the bulk of operational decisions would be made, leaving to the corporate head office the task of coordination and strategic leadership and control.

- At General Motors, reorganization from a holding company to a more coordinated, divisionalized structure was a response to acute financial and organizational difficulties, including lack of inventory control, absence of a standardized accounting system, lack of information, and a confused product line. The new structure was based on two principles: the chief executive of each division was fully responsible for the operation and performance of that division, while the general office, headed by the president, was responsible for the development and control of the corporation as a whole, including:
  —monitoring return on invested capital within the divisions;
  —coordinating the divisions (including establishing terms for interdivisional transactions);
  —establishing a product policy.[5]

The primary feature of the divisionalized corporation was the separation of operating responsibilities, which were vested in general managers at the divisional level, from strategic responsibilities, which were located at the head office. The divisionalized corporation represented a reconciliation of the efficiencies associated with decentralization with those resulting from centralized coordination. Table 6.1 summarizes some of the key influences on the strategy and structure of corporations.

---

[4] Chandler, *Strategy and Structure*, op. cit.: 382–3.
[5] Alfred P. Sloan, *My Years at General Motors* (London: Sidgwick & Jackson, 1963): 42–56.

TABLE 6.1   The Evolution of the Modern Industrial Corporation

ENVIRONMENTAL INFLUENCES	STRATEGIC CHANGES	ORGANIZATIONAL CONSEQUENCES
Early nineteenth century Local markets. Transport and communication slow. Labor-intensive production.	Firms small, specialized, and focused on local market.	No complex administrative or accounting systems. No middle management.
Late nineteenth century Railroads, telegraph, and mechanization permit large-scale production and distribution.	Geographical expansion: national distribution, large-scale production. Broadening of product lines. Forward integration.	Emergence of functional organization structures with top management providing coordination. Development of accounting and control systems. Line and staff distinction.
Early twentieth century Excess capacity in distribution systems, increased availability of finance. Desire for growth.	Product diversification.	Increased difficulties of cross–functional coordination; top management overload. Functional structure replaced by multidivisional structure: operational management at the division level, strategic management at corporate head office.

THE PRINCIPLES OF ORGANIZATIONAL DESIGN

According to Henry Mintzberg:

> Every organized human activity – from making pots to placing a man on the moon – gives rise to two fundamental and opposing requirements: the division of labor into various tasks, and the coordination of these tasks to accomplish the activity. The structure of the organization can be defined simply as the ways in which labor is divided into distinct tasks and coordination is achieved among these tasks.[6]

We begin with these two fundamental organizational requirements: *division of labor* (or *specialization*) and *coordination*.

Specialization and Division of Labor

Firms exist because they are efficient institutions for the organization of economic activities, particularly the production of goods and services. The fundamental source of efficiency in production is *specialization*, especially the *division of labor* into separate

---

[6] Henry Mintzberg, *Structure in Fives: Designing Effective Organizations* (Englewood Cliffs: Prentice-Hall, 1993): 2.

tasks. The classic statement on the gains due to specialization is Adam Smith's description of pin manufacture:

> One man draws out the wire, another straightens it, a third cuts it, a fourth points it, a fifth grinds it at the top for receiving the head; to make the head requires two or three distinct operations; to put it on is a peculiar business, to whiten the pins is another; it is even a trade by itself to put them into the papers.[7]

Smith's pin makers produced about 4,800 pins per person each day. "But if they had all wrought separately and independently, and without any of them having been educated to this peculiar business, they certainly could not each have made 20, perhaps not one pin, in a day." Similarly, Henry Ford experienced huge productivity gains by installing moving assembly lines and assigning individuals to highly specific production tasks. Between the end of 1912 and early 1914, the time taken to assemble a Model T fell from 106 hours to just over six hours. More generally, the difference in human productivity between modern industrial society and primitive subsistence society is the result of the efficiency gains from individuals specializing. The gains from specialization and division of labor extend to management. The nineteenth-century owner-manager was strategic planning manager, chief financial officer, chief operating officer, head of human resources, technical director, marketing director, purchasing manager, as well as many other functional roles, all of which are specialized career tracks today.

A critical design issue for all organizations is the optimal degree of job specialization. Although increased specialization results in efficiency gains in individual job performance, there is a tradeoff between specialization gains and the increased coordination needed as the division of labor increases. The more an organization needs to adapt its outputs to changes in the external environment, the greater these coordination costs are likely to be. In general, the more stable the environment, the lower the coordination costs and the greater the optimal division of labor. This is true both for firms and for entire societies. Civilizations are built on increased division of labor, which is only possible through stability. As Bosnia, Afghanistan, and Sierra Leone have demonstrated so tragically, once chaos reigns, so societies regress toward subsistence mode where each family unit must be self-sufficient.

The Coordination Problem

Coordination is critical to the performance of any organization. No matter how great the specialist skills possessed by individuals, unless these individuals can coordinate their efforts, production doesn't happen. The challenge for every manager of a national sports team is how to coordinate the efforts of talented individuals within a limited time frame. The dismal performance of the England soccer team between 1990 and 2000 was not the result of a lack of talented players, but an inability to coordinate these skills into effective team capabilities. Conversely, the exceptional capabilities of

---

[7] Adam Smith, *The Wealth of Nations* (London: Dent, 1910): 5.

organizations such as Wal-Mart, McDonald's, the Cirque du Soleil, and the New Zealand America's Cup sailing team are primarily the result of superb coordination between organizational members. How do individuals within organizations coordinate their efforts? Let us look at the operation of four different coordination mechanisms:

- *Price.* In the market, coordination is achieved through the *price mechanism*. Price mechanisms also exist within firms. Different departments and divisions may trade on an arm's-length basis, where internal prices (*transfer prices*) are either negotiated or set by corporate headquarters.

- *Rules and directives.* The key feature of corporations and other formal organizations is the existence of employment contracts. Unlike self-employed workers who negotiate market contracts for individual tasks, employees enter general employment contracts where (within certain limits) they agree to perform a range of duties as indicated by their employer. Authority is exercised within by means of general rules ("Employees with report for work not later than 8.30 a.m.") and specific directives ("Miss Moneypenny, show Mr. Bond his new cigarette case with 3G digital communcation and concealed death ray").

- *Mutual adjustment.* The simplest form of coordination involves the mutual adjustment of individuals engaged in related tasks. In soccer or doubles tennis, each player coordinates with fellow team members without any authoritative relationship among them. Such mutual adjustment occurs in leaderless teams and work groups.

- *Routines.* Where activities are performed recurrently, coordination based on mutual adjustment and rules becomes institutionalized within organizational routines. As we noted in the previous chapter, these "regular and predictable sequences of coordinated actions by individuals" are the foundation of organizational capability. If organizations are to perform complex activities at extreme levels of efficiency and reliability, coordination by rules, directives or mutual adjustment is not enough – coordination must become embedded in routines.

The relative roles of these different coordiantion devices depends on the types of activity being performed and the intensity of collaboration that different activities require. Price mechanisms work well in situations of "arm's-length" coordination. For example, in coordinating production and sales, it may be sufficient to offer sales personnel simple price incentives such as higher commission rates on those products where inventories are high. Rules tend to work well for activities where standardized outcomes are required and the decision-making abilities of the operatives involved may be limited – most quality control procedures involve the application of simple rules. Routines form the basis for coordination in most activities where close interdependence exists between individuals, whether a basic production task (supplying customers at Starbucks) or a more complex activity (performing a heart by-pass operation or implementing a systems integration project for a multinational corporation).

The Cooperation Problem: Incentives and Control

The discussion of coordination has dealt only with the technical problem of integrating the actions of different individuals within the organization. Coordination, however, is not simply a technical issue – it is confounded by the problems of different goals among different organizational members. This is referred to as the *cooperation problem*. Coordination is about building mechanisms that link individuals together in ways that permit them to perform given tasks. However, if these mechanisms are to work individuals must have incentives to do so.

The problem of incentives that arises from different individuals having different goals is analyzed in the economics literature as the *agency problem*. An *agency relationship* exists when one party (the principal) contracts with another party (the agent) to act on behalf of the principal. The problem of such a relationship is ensuring that the agent acts in the principal's interest. Within the firm, attention has focused on the agency problem that exists between owners (shareholders) and professional managers. The problem of ensuring that managers operate companies to maximize shareholder wealth is at the center of the corporate governance debate. Changes in the way that top managers are remunerated, in particular the increasing emphasis given to stock options and profit-based bonuses, are efforts to improve the alignment of manager and shareholder interests. At the same time, such incentives impose significant costs: stock options and profit-related bonuses are absorbing a growing proportion of companies' operating profits.[8]

Agency problems exist throughout the hierarchy. For individual employees, systems of incentives, monitoring, and appraisal are designed to encourage employees to pursue organizational objectives and overcome employees' tendency either to seek their own self-interest or simply to shirk. The organization structure and its related cultures may itself create problems. Either unintentionally or by design, organizational units create their own subgoals that may not be fully aligned with the overall organizational goals. Such subgoals are typically associated with the individual functional departments of the firm.[9] Bruce Henderson, founder of the Boston Consulting Group, has observed:

> Every production man's dream is a factory that always runs at full capacity making a single product that requires no change . . . every salesman would like to give every customer whatever he wants immediately.[10]

Different mechanisms are available for achieving goal alignment within organizations:

- *Control mechanisms* typically operate on the basis of managers supervising groups of subordinates. Managerial supervision involves monitoring behavior and performance, while subordinates are obliged to seek approval for actions

---

[8]   *Long Range Planning* (Special Issue on Corporate Governance, 2000).
[9]   For a formal analysis, see R. Cyert and J. March, *A Behavioral Theory of the Firm* (Englewood Cliffs: Prentice-Hall, 1964).
[10]   Bruce Henderson, *The Logic of Business Strategy* (New York: Ballinger, 1984): 26–7.

that lie outside their area of authority. Such hierarchical supervision and control rests on both positive and negative incentives. Positive incentives are typically the reward of promotion up the hierarchy in return for compliance; negative incentives are dismissal and demotion for failing to acquiesce to rules and directives.

- *Reward incentives* operate on the basis of rewarding performance. At the bottom of the organization, production workers may be paid piece-rates – a fixed payment for every unit of output – while at the top of the organization, senior executives may be rewarded by stock options and profit bonuses. Such performance-related incentives have two main benefits: first, they are *high powered* – they relate rewards directly to output – second, they may economize on the need for a costly management structure to monitor and supervise the activities of employees. Performance-related incentives can also create problems. Where employees work closely with others doing jobs whose output cannot easily be measured – R&D managers and strategic planning managers, for example – performance-related pay is difficult to design and may provide incentives that discourage collaboration.

- *Shared values.* Some organizations are able to achieve high levels of cooperation and low levels of goal conflict without extensive control mechanisms and without performance-related incentives. Churches, charities, choral groups, indeed most voluntary organizations fall into this category. The reason is the commonality of goals between organizational members. In their study of excellent companies, Tom Peters and Bob Waterman pointed to the existence of shared values as a common feature of excellence.[11] The role of culture as a control mechanism that is an alternative to bureaucratic control or a market system of control is central to Bill Ouchi's concept of *clan control*.[12] In Japanese corporations, for example, a powerful culture results in people aligning their individual goals and behaviors with those of the organization, with companies reinforcing this identification through lifetime employment and a heavy emphasis on socializing new employees. Such control saves on monitoring costs, as self-control and informal monitoring by co-workers substitute for managerial supervision and financial incentives. Similar comments can be made about many Silicon Valley companies. At Apple Computer in the early 1980s, for example, the common belief that Apple was leading a computer revolution that would transform and democratize society permitted intense cooperation with very little formal control. As one cynic noted: "What's the difference between Apple and the Boy Scouts? In the Boy Scouts, the kids have adult supervision!" Shared values also play a key role in other companies with strong corporate cultures, such as Body Shop, Amway, Marks & Spencer, and Wal-Mart.

We shall return to these issues of incentives and control when we consider the management systems of companies.

---

[11]   T. Peters and R. Waterman, *In Search of Excellence* (New York: Harper & Row, 1982).
[12]   William G. Ouchi, *Theory Z* (Reading, MA: Addison-Wesley, 1981).

HIERARCHY IN ORGANIZATIONAL DESIGN

How have companies addressed these basic needs for specialization, coordination, and cooperation? The traditional approach to large-scale organization has been to create *hierarchy*. Despite the negative associations that currently attach to hierarchy, we shall argue that hierarchical structures are essential for creating efficient and flexible coordination in complex organizations. The critical issue is not whether or not to organize by hierarchy – there is little alternative – but how the hierarchy should be structured and how the different parts of it should relate to one another. Hierarchies come in many forms. Traditionally, hierarchy is associated with bureaucratic approaches to management control. However, hierarchical structures may also be organized along *organic* lines. The past decade has seen important changes in how companies structure and manage hierarchical structures.

Hierarchy as a Coordinating Device: Modularity

Hierarchy is fundamental to the structure of all organizations; indeed, according to Herbert Simon, hierarchy is present in virtually all complex systems. If a hierarchy is defined as a system composed of interrelated subsystems, examples of hierarchy include:

- The human body, which is composed of a hierarchy of cells, organs, and subsystems such as the respiratory system, nervous system, digestive system, and so on.

- Physical systems are composed at the macro level of planets, stars, and galaxies, and at the micro level of subatomic particles, atoms, and molecules.

- Social systems consist of individuals, families, communities, tribes or socioeconomic groups, and nations.

- A book consists of letters, words, sentences, paragraphs, and chapters.

Note that this is a broader concept of hierarchy than that encountered in most discussions of organization design, where hierarchy is identified with *administrative hierarchy*, in which organizational members are arranged in superior–subordinate relationships and authority flows downward from the top.

Viewed in this broad context of subsystems and component units, there are two key advantages to hierarchical structures. The first is adaptability. Simon argues that hierarchical forms have the capacity to evolve more rapidly than unitary systems, which are not organized into subsystems. The adaptability of hierarchical systems requires some degree of *decomposability*: the ability of component subsystems to operate with some measure of independence from other subsystems. Thus, in the case of the automobile, its modular structure permits different subassemblies (power units, brakes, air bags, and electronic guidance systems) to be developed without

FIGURE 6.1   How hierarchy economizes on coordination

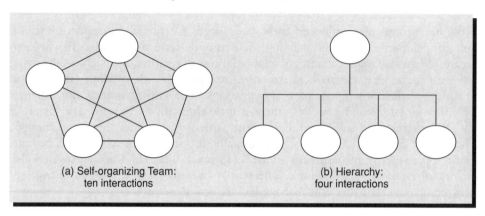

(a) Self-organizing Team:
ten interactions

(b) Hierarchy:
four interactions

constant communication and coordination with the designers of every other unit.[13] Similarly, defects can be corrected by replacing a single subunit – the engine, the gearbox, or the exhaust system – without having to scrap the entire car. These same advantages exist in modular organizations such as the multidivisional firm: strategic and operational improvements can occur in GE's domestic appliance businesses without requiring the involvement of managers in jet engines and GE Capital. Similarly, GE can acquire a new business (e.g., Honeywell) or dispose of an existing subsidiary (e.g., Kidder Peabody) without requiring organizational changes throughout the company. The benefits of modular design with *loose coupling* of organizational units is being increasingly recognized in the academic literature.[14]

The second advantage of hierarchy is in economizing on coordination. As we have noted, the gains from specialization come at the cost of coordination. Suppose there are five programmers designing a piece of customized computer software. If they are structured as a "self-organized team," where coordination is by mutual adjustment (see Figure 6.1a), ten bilateral interactions must be managed. Alternatively, suppose the programmer with the biggest feet is selected to be supervisor. In this simple hierarchy (Figure 6.1b), there are only four relationships to be managed. Of course, this says nothing about the quality of the coordination: if the programmers' work is highly interdependent, hierarchical relationships may not allow for the richness of communication and collaboration that a team structure would permit.

---

[13]   M. Sako and F. Murray, "Modular Strategies in Car and Computers," *Financial Times*, Mastering Strategy Part 11 (December 6, 1999): 4–7.

[14]   R. Sanchez and J. T. Mahoney, "Modularity, Flexibility, and Knowledge Management in Product and Organizational Design," *Strategic Management Journal* 17, Winter special issue (1996): 63–76; J.-C. Spender and P. H. Grinyer, "Organizational Renewal: Top Management's Role in a Loosely Coupled System," *Human Relations* 48 (1995): 909–26; M. A. Schilling, "Toward a General Modular Systems Theory and its Application to Interfirm Product Modularity," *Academy of Management Review* 25 (2000): 312–34.

EXHIBIT 6.1   Hierarchical Structures: The 1952 Mandela Plan for the ANC

Along with many others, I had become convinced that the government intended to declare the ANC (African National Congress) and the SAIC (South African Indian Congress) illegal organizations, just as it had done with the Communist Party. It seemed inevitable that the state would attempt to put us out of business as a legal organization. With this in mind, I approached the National Executive with the idea that we must come up with a contingency plan for such an eventuality . . . They instructed me to draw up a plan that would enable the organization to operate from underground. This strategy came to be known as the Mandela-Plan, or simply, M-Plan.

The idea was to set up organizational machinery that would allow the ANC to take decisions at the highest level, which could then be swiftly transmitted to the organization as a whole without calling a meeting. In other words, it would allow the organization to continue to function and enable leaders who were banned to continue to lead. The M-Plan was designed to allow the organization to recruit new members, respond to local and national problems and maintain regular contact between the membership and the underground leadership.

I worked on it for a number of months and came up with a system that was broad enough to adapt itself to local conditions and not fetter individual initiative, but detailed enough to facilitate order. The smallest unit was the cell, which in urban townships consisted of roughly ten houses on a street. A cell steward would be in charge of each of these units. If a street had more than ten houses, a street steward would take charge and the cell stewards would report to him. A group of streets formed a zone directed by a chief steward, who was in turn responsible to the secretariat of the local branch of the ANC. The secretariat was a subcommittee of the branch executive, which reported to the provincial secretary. My notion was that every cell and street steward would know every person and family in his area, so that he would be trusted by his people and know whom to trust. The cell steward arranged meetings, organized political classes, and collected dues. He was the linchpin of the plan.

The plan was accepted and was implemented immediately. Word went out to the branches to begin to prepare for this covert restructuring. Although it was accepted at most branches, some of the more far-flung outposts felt that the plan was an effort by Johannesburg to centralize control over the regions.

As part of the M-Plan, the ANC introduced an elementary course of political lectures for its members throughout the country. These lectures were meant not only to educate but to hold the organization together. They were given in secret by branch leaders. Those members in attendance would in turn give the same lectures to others in their homes and communities.

Source: Nelson Mandela, *Long Walk to Freedom* (London: Little, Brown, 1994): 134–5.

The flexibility advantages of modularity and efficiency advantages of hierarchical communication are evident in Nelson Mandela's restructuring of the ANC (see Exhibit 6.1). Let's look more closely at administrative hierarchies associated with *bureaucratic* or *mechanistic* organizational forms.

Hierarchy as a Control Device: Bureaucracy

If hierarchy is the basic organizational form for all complex systems, the *administrative hierarchy*, in which power is located at the apex of the hierarchy and delegated downward, has been the dominant form of most organizational hierarchies since early Chinese civilization. Administrative hierarchies operate as *bureaucracies*, the principles of which, according to Max Weber writing at the end of the nineteenth century, are:

1. *Rational-legal authority* based on "Belief in the legality of enacted rules and the right of those elevated to authority under such rules to issue commands."

2. *Specialization* through a "systematic division of labor" with clear job definitions and individual authority limited to the sphere of work responsibilities.

3. *Hierarchical structure* with "each lower office under the control and supervision of a higher one."

4. *Coordination and control* through rules and standard operating procedures.

5. *Standardized employment rules and norms.*

6. *Separation of management and ownership.*

7. *Separation of jobs and people*, where the organization is defined by positions and their associated responsibilities and authority, not by individuals; there is no ownership of the position by the individual.

8. *Formalization* in writing of "administrative acts, decisions, and rules."[15]

The bureaucratic form of organization is highly formalized, eliminating most of the features that characterize human societies and human behavior: cooperation, innovation, personality, variation, and emotion. For this reason, Burns and Stalker have described bureaucratic organizations as *mechanistic*[16] and Mintzberg terms then *machine bureaucracies.*[17]

Mechanistic and Organic Forms

For much of the twentieth century, the bureaucratic model dominated thinking about organizational structure. This was partly because of Weber's clear articulation of the principles of bureaucracy and partly because most large organizations – the military and civil service in particular – corresponded closely to the bureaucratic form. However, the study of business enterprises made it clear that bureaucracy was not the only, nor necessarily the best, basis for organization.

In studying the difficulties experienced by Scottish engineering companies responding to the challenges and opportunities provided by electronic technologies, Burns and Stalker observed two organizational forms: in addition to the bureaucratized *mechanistic form*, they identified a less formalized organizational type where

---

[15] The quotes in this section are from Max Weber, *Economy and Society: An Outline of Interpretive Sociology* (Berkeley: University of California Press, 1968).
[16] T. Burns and G. M. Stalker, *The Management of Innovation* (London: Tavistock Institute, 1961).
[17] Henry Mintzberg, op. cit.: Chapter 9.

TABLE 6.2 Mechanistic vs. Organic Organizational Forms

FEATURE	MECHANISTIC	ORGANIC
Task definition	Rigid and highly specialized	Flexible and less narrowly defined
Coordination and control	Rules and directives vertically imposed	Mutual adjustment, common culture
Communication	Vertical	Vertical and horizontal
Knowledge	Centralized	Dispersed
Commitment and loyalty	To immediate superior	To the organization and its goals
Environmental context	Stable with low technological uncertainty	Unstable with significant technological uncertainty and ambiguity

Source: Adapted from Richard Butler, *Designing Organizations: A Decision-Making Perspective* (London: Routledge, 1991): 76.

coordination was achieved primarily by mutual adjustment, jobs were less narrowly defined, and patterns of interaction were flexible and multidirectional. They described these companies as *organismic*, subsequently abbreviated to *organic*. Table 6.2 contrasts key characteristics of the two forms.

The relative merits of bureaucratic as opposed to organic organizational forms depend on the activities the organization undertakes and the environment in which it operates. Where an organization is producing standardized goods and services (beverage cans, property tax collections, haircuts for army inductees), using well-understood processes, in an environment where change is slow and predictable, the bureaucratic model with its standard operating procedures and high levels of specialization offers tremendous efficiency advantages. The problems occur when the bureaucratic model has to produce heterogeneous outputs from heterogeneous inputs, using poorly understood technologies, in an environment where change requires constant adjustment. Here, the bureaucratic system fails. In some instances, firms may attempt to retain the advantages of bureaucracy by trying to control variation in the outside environment. The business system perfected by McDonald's is highly mechanistic, including reliance on highly standardized, formalized working practices that are carefully documented in the company's operating procedures. This system can only work by McDonald's carefully controlling its inputs to reduce variation: potatoes are carefully selected for size and shape, managers are carefully selected and trained, consumer tastes and expectations are carefully managed through advertising and promotion.

In most organizations, the extent to which a department or unit corresponds to the mechanistic or organic type depends on these factors. Thus, in most companies, payroll, treasury, taxation, customer support, and purchasing activities tend to be organized along bureaucratic principles; research, new product development, marketing, and business process reengineering tend to be more organic.

Rethinking Hierarchy

The current unpopularity of bureaucracy in large companies and the movement toward delayering hierarchies can be linked to changes in the nature of the business environment. Global competition, deregulation, and accelerating technological change have made the business environment of most companies less stable and less predictable. These changes have revealed the shortcomings of administrative hierarchy organized along bureaucratic principles.

Hierarchical organizations add layers as they get bigger. Thus, with a fixed span of control of three, a firm with 4 employees (including the CEO) is organized into two layers, 5 to 13 employees require three layers, from 14 to 41 employees require four layers, and 42 to 122 employees require five layers. (Sketch this for yourself.) If the hierarchy is run as a bureaucracy with centralized power, it suffers from slower and slower decision making and increased loss of control as the size of the organization increases.[18]

In a stable environment with limited decision-making pressure on top management, such ponderousness is of little consequence. However, in a fast-paced business environment, the slow movement of information up the hierarchy and decisions down the hierarchy is likely to be fatal. The movement to reform and restructure corporate hierarchies does not amount to a rejection of hierarchy as an organizing principle – so long as there are benefits from the division of labor, hierarchy is inevitable. The critical issue is to reorganize hierarchies in order to increase responsiveness to external change. The organizational changes that have occurred in giant corporations such as Unilever, British Petroleum, ABB, and General Electric retained the basic multi-divisional structures of the companies, but reduced the number of hierarchical layers, decentralized decision making, shrank headquarters staffs, emphasized horizontal rather than vertical communication, and shifted the emphasis of control from *supervision* to *accountability*.[19]

APPLYING THE PRINCIPLES TO DESIGNING ORGANIZATIONS

We have established, so far, that the fundamental problem of organization is reconciling specialization with coordination and cooperation. The basic solution to organizing complex human organizations – whether they are business enterprises, religious orders, political associations, or criminal organizations – is hierarchy. The essence of hierarchy is the creation of specialized units coordinated and controlled by a superior unit. However, this does not take us very far. On what basis should specialized units be defined? How should decision-making authority be allocated? And what kind of relationships – both vertical and horizontal – should there be between different organizational units?

---

[18]   The control loss phenomenon in hierarchies is analyzed in O. E. Williamson, "Hierarchical Control and Optimal Firm Size," *Journal of Political Economy* 75 (1967): 123–38.
[19]   R. Whittington and A. Pettigrew, "New Notions of Organizational Fit," *Financial Times*, Mastering Strategy Part 10 (November 29, 1999): 8–10.

In this section, we will tackle the first two of these questions: the basis of grouping and the allocation of decision-making power. We shall then, in the next section, look at some typical organizational structures found in business enterprises. Then, in the next section we shall look at structuring relations between units – the operation and design of management systems.

Defining Organizational Units

If the efficient operation of a complex system requires some form of hierarchy of units and subsystems, how are individuals to be formed into groups and units within the firm? This issue is fundamental to the design of the organization and is complex because it involves comparing the benefits of organizing on one basis to the benefits of organizing on an alternative basis. Multinational, multiproduct companies are continually grappling with the issue of whether they should be structured around product divisions, country subsidiaries, or functional departments, and occasionally undergo the disruption of changing from one to another. Some of the principal bases for grouping employees are common tasks, products, geography, and process:

- *Common tasks.* The most frequent basis for organizations to group employees is to departmentalize on the basis of common tasks. Thus, an engineering company might include a machine shop, an assembly line, a maintenance department, a design engineering unit, a quality control department, a finance office, and an administrative support unit.

- *Products.* Where a company offers multiple products, these can provide a basis for structure. Magazine publishing companies tend to be organized with a separate editorial group publishing each title. In a department store, departments are defined by products: kitchen goods, bedding, lingerie, and so on.

- *Geography.* Where a company serves multiple local markets, organizational units can be defined around these localities. Wal-Mart is organized by individual stores, groups of stores within an area, and groups of areas within a region. The Church of England compromises parishes, dioceses, and arch-dioceses.

- *Process.* A process is a sequence of interlinked activities. An organization may be viewed as a set of processes: the product development process, the manufacturing process, the sales and distribution process, and so on. A process may correspond closely with an individual product, or a process may be dominated by a single task. Functional organizations tend to combine task-based and process-based grouping.

Defining Organizational Units on the Basis of Intensity of Interaction

The relative merits of different approaches depend on several factors. The fundamental issue is achieving the coordination necessary to integrate the efforts of the various members of the organization. This implies grouping individuals according to the intensity of their coordination needs. Those individuals whose tasks require the most intensive coordination should work within the same organizational unit. Those whose coordination needs are less, or are infrequent, may be separated organizationally.

The principle of organizing according to intensity of coordination combined with the principle of decentralizing through loose coupling is the basis for Oliver Williamson's concept of *hierarchical decomposition*, whereby the organization is sliced vertically – grouping the operating parts into separate entities, the interactions within which are strong and between which are weak. Slicing the organization horizontally means grouping activities according to frequency of decisions: operating activities involve high-frequency decision making, strategic decisions tend to be low frequency. Hence:

> The hierarchical decomposition principle can be stated as follows: Internal organiza-
> tion should be designated in such a way as to effect quasi-independence between the
> parts, the high frequency dynamics (operating activities) and low frequency dynamics
> (strategic planning) should be clearly distinguished, and incentives should be aligned
> within and between components so as to promote both local and global effectiveness.[20]

To organize according to intensity of interaction requires some understanding of the nature of interdependence between individuals and units within an organization so that intensity of interactions can be recognized. James Thompson defined three types of interdependence. *Pooled interdependence*, the loosest form, exists where the units or individuals operate independently, but are all dependent on one another's performance for the survival of the organization. Thus, in an office equipment service company, each service engineer works individually. *Sequential interdependence* exists where the output of one individual or unit is the input of the other, as in many manufacturing processes such as an assembly line. *Reciprocal interdependence* is a mutual dependence relationship where the output of each unit is the input of the other, as in the relationship between doctors and nurses within a hospital. Thompson argued that organizations should be structured according to intensity of interdependence: first, putting together tasks involving reciprocal interdependence within the same units; second, creating links between sequentially interdependent units; finally, linking together parts of the organization with pooled interdependence.[21]

Changes in technology, strategy and the competitive environment result in changes in the patterns and extent of interdependencies between employees and organizational units that require companies to change the basis of their organizational groups leading to major structural reconfigurations. For example:

---

[20] O. E. Williamson, "The Modern Corporation: Origins, Evolution, Attributes," *Journal of Economic Literature* 19 (1981): 1537–68.

[21] J. D. Thompson, *Organizations in Action* (New York: McGraw Hill, 1967). The nature of interdependence in organizational processes is revisited in T. W. Malone, K. Crowston, J. Lee, and B. Pentland, "Tools for Inventing Organizations: Toward a Handbook of Organizational Processes," *Management Science* 45 (March 1999): 489–504.

■ Firms operating in a single industry tend to be functionally organized, since the primary coordination needs are within each type of activity. However, once firms begin to diversify, close coordination within each business becomes more important than coordination within each function. Hence, most multiproduct corporations adopt the multidivisional structure organized around businesses and product groups.

■ When country differences were substantial and transportation and communication between countries were slow and expensive, multinational corporations tended to organize around national subsidiaries. Globalization has involved convergence of national market characteristics and easier transportation and communication. The tendency has been for multinationals to move from geographically based structures to organization around worldwide product divisions.

Other Factors Influencing the Definition of Organizational Units

Coordination requirements are not the only consideration in deciding how to group together employees and activities within the firm. Additional factors that influence the efficiency of different organizational arrangements include economies of scale, economies of utilization, learning, and standardization of control systems:

■ *Economies of scale*. There may be advantages in grouping together activities where scale economies are present. Thus, it may be desirable to group together research activities even if there is little coordination among different research projects, simply to exploit scale economies in specialized facilities and technical personnel.

■ *Economies of utilization*. It may also be possible to exploit efficiencies from grouping together similar activities that result from fuller utilization of employees. Even though there may be little need for individual maintenance engineers to coordinate with one another, establishing a single maintenance department permits maintenance personnel to be utilized more fully than assigning a maintenance engineer to each manufacturing cell.

■ *Learning*. If establishing competitive advantage requires building distinctive capabilities, firms must be structured to maximize learning. Typically, it was assumed that learning was best achieved by grouping together individuals doing similar jobs – creating a manufacturing engineering department, a quality control department, and a finance function. More recently, it has been observed that the specialized functional and discipline-based knowledge may be less important than *architectural knowledge* – knowing how to link together specialized knowledge from different fields. This implies the creation of multifunctional work groups comprising experts from different knowledge bases.

■ *Standardization of control systems*. Tasks may be grouped together in order to achieve economies in standardized control mechanisms. An advantage of the typing pool and the sales department was that employees doing near-identical jobs could be subject to the same system of monitoring, performance measurement, training, and behavioral norms. In the Appendix to Chapter 5, we drew a distinction between knowledge-generating – or *exploration* – activities and knowledge-application – or *exploitation* – activities. Exploration activities are likely to require looser, more organic structures and systems, while exploitation activities are likely to require more mechanistic approaches. Reconciling such different management systems within the same company is easier if creative activities such as research and new product development are separate organizational units from the more routine activities such as manufacturing and accounting.[22]

ALTERNATIVE STRUCTURAL FORMS

On the basis of these alternative approaches to grouping tasks and activities, we can identify three basic organizational forms: the functional structure, the product division structure, and the matrix structure.

The Functional Structure

Single-business firms tend to be organized along functional lines. The benefits of functional structures are that they bring together similar activities within which interdependence tends to be high, and by centralizing these groups of activities offer advantages in scale economies, learning and capability building, and designing and deploying standardized control systems. Since cross-functional integration occurs at the top of the organization, functional structures are conducive to effective control by the CEO and top management team.

Coordination within the functional firm remains a problem, however. Different functions tend to develop their own goals, values, vocabularies, and behavioral norms. Though these may be conducive to integration and effectiveness at the functional level, they can make cross-functional integration difficult. As the size of the firm increases, the pressure on top management to achieve effective integration increases. Because the different functions of the firm tend to be *tightly coupled* rather than *loosely coupled*, to the extent that there is a continuing need for sales, distribution, manufacturing, and purchasing closely to integrate their activities, there is very limited scope for decentralization. In particular, it is very difficult to operate individual functions as semi-autonomous profit centers.

The real problems arise when the firm grows its range of products and businesses. As we noted with DuPont during the early twentieth century, once a company expands into a new product area, the critical coordination need is between functions within each product area. Similarly, when IBM entered the personal computer business, it could not build this business through its existing functional structure by asking

---

[22] The need for organizations to differentiate management and organization between different functional departments and product units is discussed in P. R. Lawrence and J. W. Lorsch, *Organization and Environment* (Boston: Harvard Business School Press, 1986).

engineers in R&D, manufacturing managers in operations, product managers in marketing, and sales personnel in sales to collaborate in bringing to market an entirely new product range. IBM established its PC division as a standalone operation in a location far from the company's headquarters.

Although the long-term trend among very large companies has been for product-based, divisionalized companies to replace functionally organized companies, the trend is not entirely one way. As companies mature, the need for strong centralized control and effective functional coordination sometimes takes precedence over tight cross-functional integration at the product level. Apple Computer and General Motors are such examples.

- When John Scully became CEO of Apple in 1984, the company was organized by product groups: Apple II, Apple III, Lisa, and Macintosh. These product divisions achieved highly effective coordination among hardware engineers, software engineers, production managers, and marketing personnel. The problem was that there was little integration across products: each product was completely incompatible with the others, and the structure failed to exploit scale economies within functions. Scully's response was to reorganize Apple along functional lines in order to gain control, reduce costs, and achieve a more coherent product strategy.

- General Motors, one of the innovators of the multidivisional structure, has, over the past 20 years, been moving toward a more functional structure. As its strategic priorities have shifted from differentiation and segmentation toward cost efficiency, it has maintained its brand names (Cadillac, Oldsmobile, Chevrolet, Buick), but merged the separate divisions into a structure that allows exploitation of functional-level scale economies and faster technical transfer (see Figure 6.2).

The Multidivisional Structure

We have seen how the product-based, multidivisional structure emerged during the twentieth century in response to the coordination problems caused by diversification. The key advantage of divisionalized structures (whether product based or geographically based) is the potential they offer for decentralized decision making. The multidivisional structure is the classic example of a loose-coupled, modular organization where business-level strategies and all operating decisions can be made at the divisional level, and the relationships with the corporate headquarters are limited to corporate planning, budgeting, and the provision of common services. Chapter 16 is devoted to the management of multidivisional companies; here we outline just a few key features.

The ability to manage divisions with a common set of management tools permits a wide span of control: at ITT, more than 50 divisional heads and functional and regional managers reported to Harold Geneen. A high level of divisional autonomy is also conducive to the development of divisional heads with well-developed general management capabilities. This facilitates top management succession.

FIGURE 6.2 General Motors Corporation: organizational structure, 1997

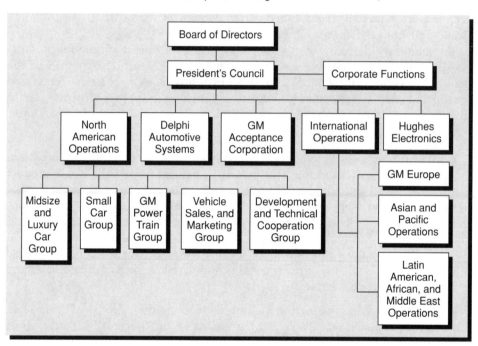

The large, divisionalized corporation is typically organized into three levels: the corporate center, the divisions, and individual business units, each representing a distinct business for which financial accounts can be drawn up and strategies formulated. Figure 6.3 shows General Electric's organizational structure at the corporate and divisional levels.

Many divisionalized companies are hybrids, a combination of product-based and geographically based divisions reflecting the varied coordination requirements of different businesses and different countries and regions. Figure 6.4 shows Mobil Corporation's divisional structure (prior to its merger with Exxon). Some of Mobil's "business groups" were defined on a business basis (e.g., Mobil Chemical Company; Supply, Trading and Transportation), some on a geographical area basis (e.g., South America, Asia/Pacific); others combined the two (e.g., North American Exploration and Production). Still other divisions were functionally defined (e.g., Mobil Technology Company). This mixed basis for grouping reflected different coordination priorities. The chemicals business was driven by technology and scale economies, since the business was essentially the same from one country to another. The key coordination requirement was *within* the chemicals business: it was more important that Mobil's chemicals business in Germany coordinated with the chemicals business in France than with Mobil's other businesses in Germany. In the former Soviet Union (FSU), on the other hand, the dominant factors influencing all Mobil's businesses in the region were the difficult business environment and the need to manage relationships with governments and public-sector authorities. Hence, all Mobil's businesses within the FSU were organized within a single business group.

FIGURE 6.3 General Electric: organization structure, 2000

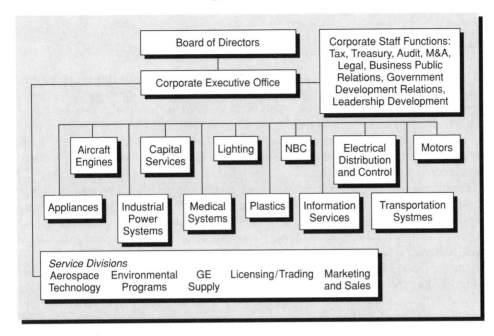

FIGURE 6.4 Mobil Corporation: organization structure, 1998

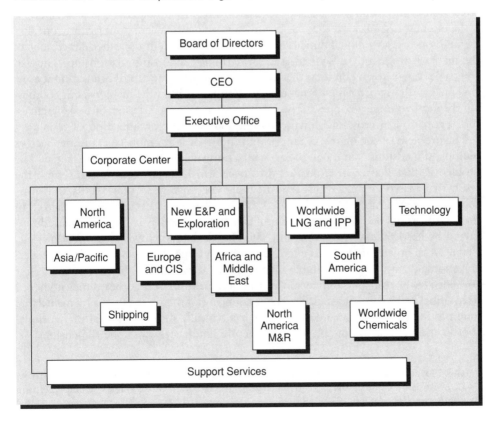

Matrix Structures

Whatever the primary basis for grouping, all multiproduct, multinational, and multi-functional companies must ultimately coordinate across all three dimensions: functions, products, and geographical areas. This is formalized within the matrix structure. Essentially, the matrix sacrifices the unity of command that characterizes most hierarchical organizations (especially the military), and that was regarded by Henri Fayol as a fundamental principle of effective management, in favor of a dual or even multidimensional authority structure.[23]

Figure 6.5 shows the Shell management matrix (up to Shell's reorganization in 1996). Within this structure, the general manager of Shell's Berre refinery in France reported to his country manager, the managing director of Shell France, but also reported to the business sector head, the coordinator of Shell's refining sector, as well as having a functional relationship with Shell's head of manufacturing.

During the 1960s and 1970s, many companies adopted matrix structures as a means of reconciling the coordination needs of businesses, functions, and geographical areas. However, few companies have attempted to give equal authority to all dimensions of the matrix. In general, most companies have retained some element of the "unity of command" principle by making one dimension of the matrix dominant in terms of budgetary authority, personnel reporting and appraisal, and strategy formulation. Thus, within the Shell matrix the geographically based structure was dominant: power centered around the country heads and regional coordinators. Under the new structure, it is the business organization that has become preeminent. Where power clearly operates through one organizational dimension, coordination through the other dimensions of the matrix is frequently described as a "dotted line" reporting relationship. Thus, in companies organized by business divisions, corporate-level functional heads cannot exercise much authority over their functional counterparts within the divisions, but coordinate through voluntary cooperation over issues such as the transfer of best practices, the negotiation of cross-divisional collaboration, and the organization of training.

The problem of the matrix organization is not that it attempts to coordinate across multiple dimensions – in a complex organization such coordination is essential. The problem is that matrix structures tend to overformalize such relationships, with the result that matrix organizations tend to build excessive head office staffs and over-complex systems. Although Shell prided itself on being one the most decentralized of the oil majors, its decentralized system of almost 200 country subsidiaries was administered by head offices in London and The Hague that employed over 3,000 people. Certainly, all organizations need effective control through the standard tools of budgetary, strategic, and human resource planning, but these control mechanisms are best concentrated within one dimension of the organization. The other dimensions can be informal and more voluntaristic. The renouncing of matrix structures by many large multiproduct, multinational corporations has typically meant that multidimensional coordination remains, but the formal structure emphasizes just one dimension.[24]

---

[23] Henri Fayol, *General and Industrial Management* (London: Pitman, 1949, first published 1916).
[24] C. A. Bartlett and S. Ghoshal, "Matrix Management: Not a Structure, a Frame of Mind," *Harvard Business Review* (July–August 1990): 138–45.

FIGURE 6.5   Royal Dutch/Shell Group: pre-1996 matrix structure

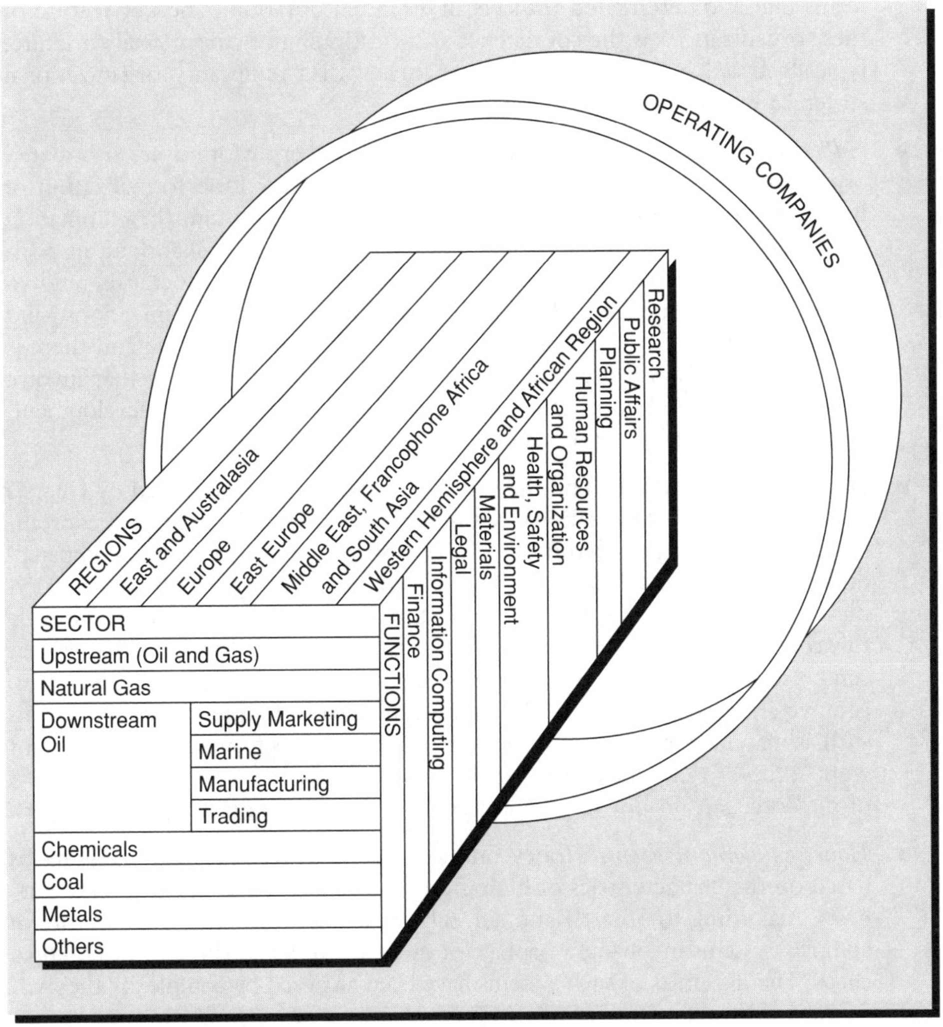

Nonhierarchical Coordination Structures

Recognition of the rigidities and costs associated with hierarchical, authority-based approaches to coordination has encouraged companies to experiment with alternatives to administrative hierarchies. A variety of organizational forms have appeared, including team-based organizations, project-based organizations, adhocracies, cluster designs, shamrock organizations, honeycomb organizations, inside-out doughnuts, and networks. Let's look at a few of these more closely.

- *Project-based organizations.* Project-based organizations have long existed in the construction industry, oil exploration, and other industries where the work forms highly differentiated projects of a limited duration. The key feature of these organizations is the coexistence of a continuing organizational structure, typically based on functional departments, with a temporary organizational structure based on project teams.

- *Adhocracies.* Adhocracies are identified by Mintzberg as innovation-oriented organizations of an extremely organic type, with very little formalization of behavior and a maximization of innovation potential through the elimination of standardization.[25] Adhocracies consist of experts who collaborate in non-routine modes, often in multifunctional project teams. Adhocracies tend to exist within new product development groups, research organizations, and consulting firms. Each specialist is valued for his or her expertise and there is little exercise of authority. Adhocracies work well with activities that involve problem solving and nonroutine operations, such as new product development, process reengineering, and crisis management.

- *Shamrock organizations.* The shamrock organization was identified by Charles Handy as another organizational response to the costs and rigidities of coordination within the large enterprise.[26] The downsizing by so many large companies during the 1980s and 1990s involved concentrating the tightly integrated activities of the firm into a professional core (the first leaf of the shamrock). Outside this core, forming the second leaf of the shamrock, are all those activities that can be contracted out to other companies, which may include not just administrative services such as payroll administration and IT, but also key functions such as manufacturing and distribution. The final leaf is formed by a contingent work force of temporary and part-time workers, who support the operation of the core, but do not require a high level of integration with core workers.

- *Honeycomb organizations.* Honeycomb organizations are self-organizing groups based on the characteristics of biological organisms such as beehives and ants' nests. According to Stuart Kaufman, self-organization is a common feature of complex systems involving a haphazard quest for order in the face of potential chaos. The dynamics of such systems have been analyzed by complexity theory.[27] Among industrial corporations, AES, the Virginia-based power producer, uses the honeycomb principle as its basis for organization. At AES's power plant at Thames, Connecticut, the key elements of the honeycomb philosophy are:
  —no employee handbooks, manuals, or rules (except safety);
  —no operating, maintenance, or technical departments;
  —no shift supervisors or maintenance supervisors;
  —no staff, except financial;
  —no "turf."[28]

---

[25] Henry Mintzberg, op. cit.: Chapter 12.
[26] Charles Handy, *The Age of Unreason* (Boston: Harvard Business School Press, 1990): Chapter 4.
[27] S. Kauffman, *At Home in the Universe* (New York: Oxford University Press, 1996); P. Anderson, "Complexity Theory and Organization Science," *Organization Science* 10 (1999): 216–32.
[28] *AES Honeycomb (A)*, Case 9-395-132 (Boston: Harvard Business School, 1995): 9.

Common features of all these nonhierarchical structures are as follows:

1. *A focus on coordination rather than control.* The administrative hierarchy combines two organizational tasks: achieving coordination between different specialists and ensuring cooperation through control. A central feature of the newer approaches is their emphasis on coordination, with cooperation being taken care of by financial or professional incentives and greater emphasis on social rather than managerial control.

2. *Reliance on coordination by mutual adjustment.* Central to all nonhierarchical structures is their dependence on voluntaristic coordination through bilateral and multilateral adjustment. The capacity for coordination through mutual adjustment has been greatly enhanced by information technology. IT eliminates each individual's reliance on the hierarchy for information flows and permits information and communication to flow horizontally at very low cost.

3. *Individuals in multiple organizational roles.* Reconciling complex patterns of coordination with high levels of flexibility and responsiveness is difficult if job designs and organizational structures are rigidly defined. Adhocracies and team-based organizations feature individuals switching their organizational roles and occupying multiple roles simultaneously. For example, AES has no finance function, no HR function, no safety or environmental affairs functions, and no public relations department. These functions are performed by teams of operating and managerial employees. Thus, at AES's Connecticut plant, a team composed of coal handlers, maintenance engineers, and other plant employees gathers each afternoon to manage the plant's finances, including cash management and short-term investments.

MANAGEMENT SYSTEMS FOR COORDINATION AND CONTROL

The relationship between organizational structure and management systems may be illustrated by analogies drawn from biology and information technology. The skeleton provides the framework for the human body, while the respiratory system, digestive system, nervous system, and other systems provide the means by which the body operates. In a computer network, the hardware provides the structure and the software provides the systems through which the hardware operates in order to make the network operational. Within business enterprises, management systems provide the mechanisms of communication, decision making, and control that allow the organization to operate and develop. These systems are the primary means through which organizations solve the basic problems of achieving both coordination – how individuals undertaking specialized tasks and groups undertaking specific activities integrate their separate actions – and cooperation – how the goals of individuals and groups are aligned with those of the organization. Whereas coordination is mainly about establishing the information and communication systems and procedures that can permit individuals to relate and adjust their separate actions, cooperation involves the establishment of incentives and penalties that encourage individuals to subjugate their goals and desires to those of the organization.

Four management systems are of primary importance in achieving control: the information systems, the strategic planning systems, the financial systems, and the human resource management systems.

Information Systems

Information is fundamental to the operation of all management systems. As the work of Chandler and other business historians has shown, the development of the telegraph, telephone, and computer had a huge impact on the practice of management and the size and structure of the firm. Accounting systems too are means by which information can be collected and organized systematically, then communicated to top management and other parts of the organization.

The administrative hierarchy is founded partly on the centralization of authority that is delegated downward through the hierarchy, and partly on vertical information flows: the ability of the manager to supervise subordinates depends on the upward flow of information to the manager, either from direct observation or from written reports, and a downward flow of instructions.

Two key aspects of increased information availability are *information feedback* to the individual on job performance, which has made self-monitoring possible, and *information networking*, which has allowed individuals to coordinate their activities voluntarily and informally without hierarchical supervision. A central element of total quality management has been recognition that providing regular, even real-time, performance feedback to employees permits them to take responsibility for quality control, reducing or eliminating the need for supervisors and quality controllers. At Wal-Mart there is continual feedback to the departmental managers for individual product sections within each store. Feedback includes information on daily sales by product line with comparisons to previous sales and to other stores. This same information system gathers and transmits data from point-of-sale scanners to monitor inventory levels, plan deliveries, and trigger reorders from suppliers. IT facilitates coordination by making information instantaneously available throughout the organization. It can achieve automatic coordination, as when electronic data interchange between Wal-Mart and Procter & Gamble results in sales information from Wal-Mart sales registers causing automatic reordering of Tide detergent.

Strategic Planning Systems

A small, entrepreneurial startup may operate without any explicit strategy. The firm's strategy is likely to exist only in the head of the founder, and apart from being articulated through verbal communications with employees, suppliers, and other interested parties, may have been made explicit only when a business plan was required by outside investors. Most corporations with an established management structure tend to have some form of strategic planning process, though in small, single-business companies the strategy process may be highly informal, with no regular cycle, and may result in little documentation. Most larger companies, especially those with multiple businesses, have more systematic strategic planning processes, the outcome of which is a documented corporate plan that integrates the business plans of the individual divisions.

Whether formal or informal, systematic or *ad hoc*, documented or not, the strategy formulation process is an important vehicle for achieving coordination within a company. As discussed in Chapter 1, the strategy process occupies multiple roles within the firm. It is in part a process for improving decision making by encouraging systematic analysis and bringing together the knowledge from individuals and locations within the company. It is in part a coordination device encouraging consistency between the decisions being made at different levels and in different parts of the organization. And it is in part a mechanism for driving performance by establishing consensus around ambitious long-term targets and by inspiring organizational members through creating vision and a sense of mission. In these roles, the strategy process can be important in achieving both coordination and cooperation.

The system through which strategy is formulated varies considerably from company to company. Even after the entrepreneurial startup has grown into a large company, strategy making may remain the preserve of the chief executive. At MCI Communications during the 1980s, strategic planning was the responsibility of the chairman and CEO: "We do it strictly top-down at MCI."[29] The first director of strategic planning was warned: "If you ever write a strategic plan, you will be fired." Medium-sized, single-business companies typically have simple strategic planning processes where functional managers provide key inputs such as financial projections and market analysis, but the key elements of strategy – goals, new business developments, capital investment, and key competitive initiatives – are decided by the chief executive.[30]

The more systematized strategic planning processes typical of large companies with separate divisions or business units traditionally follow an annual cycle. Strategic plans tend to be for three to five years and combine top-down initiatives (indications of performance expectations and identification of key strategic initiatives) and bottom-up business plans (proposed strategies and financial forecasts for individual divisions and business units). After discussion between the corporate level and the individual businesses, the business plans are amended and agreed and integrated into an overall corporate plan that is presented to and agreed by the board of directors. Figure 6.6 shows a typical strategic planning cycle.

The resulting strategic plan typically comprises the following elements:

■ *A statement of the goals* the company seeks to achieve over the planning period with regard to both financial targets (e.g., targets for revenue growth, cost reduction, operating profit, return on capital employed, return to shareholders) and strategic goals (e.g., market share, new products, overseas market penetration, and new business development). For example, the December 2000 strategy

[29] Quote by CEO, Orville Wright in 1989. See *MCI Communications: Planning for the 1990s*, Case 9-190-136 (Boston: Harvard Business School, 1990): 1.
[30] William C. Finnie, *Hands-On Strategy: The Guide to Crafting Your Company's Strategy* (New York: John Wiley, 1994).

FIGURE 6.6 The generic strategic planning cycle

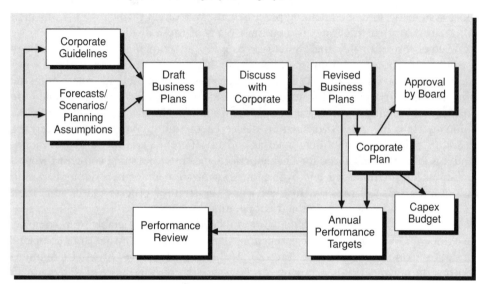

announcement by the Royal Dutch/Shell Group established a ROCE target of 15 percent and growth of hydrocarbon output of 5 percent a year.[31]

- *A set of assumptions or forecasts* about key developments in the external environment to which the company must respond. For example, Shell's plans formulated in 2000 were based on an assumed oil price of $14 a barrel (despite the fact that prevailing oil prices at the time were close to $30 a barrel).

- *A qualitative statement* of how the shape of the business will be changing in relation to geographical and segment emphasis, and the basis on which the company will be establishing and extending its competitive advantage. For example, Shell's 2000 strategy emphasized upstream investment and building on existing strengths in the Asia-Pacific region, especially in power, liquefied natural gas, and gas-to-liquids conversion.

- *Specific action steps* with regard to decisions and projects, supported by a set of mileposts stating what is to be achieved by specific dates. For example, Shell's strategy mileposts included reducing costs in chemicals by $650 million by end 2001, and introducing differentiated fuels in 40 countries by the same time.

- *A set of financial projections*, including a capital expenditure budget and outline operating budgets. For example, Shell's December 2000 strategy statement set a capital expenditure budget of $10–12 billion per year, a ratio of debt to debt and equity of 20 to 30 percent within five years, and annual operating cost reduction of $5 billion.

---

[31] Information on Royal Dutch/Shell Group is from December 18, 2000 strategy presentation. See www.shell.com.

Although directed toward making decisions that are documented in written strategic plans, the important elements of strategic planning form the strategy *process*: the dialog through which knowledge is shared and ideas communicated, the establishment of consensus, and the commitment to action and results.

Increasing turbulence in the business environment has caused strategic planning processes to become less formalized and more flexible. For example, among the world's largest petroleum majors, the key changes have been as follows:

- Strategic planning became more heavily focused on performance targets, especially on financial goals such as profitability and shareholder return. The result was a shift of emphasis from longer-term strategic planning toward shorter-term financial planning.

- Companies recognized the impossibility of forecasting the future and based their strategies less on medium- and long-term economic and market forecasts of the future and more on more general issues of strategic direction (in the form of vision, mission, and strategic intent) and alternative views of the future (e.g., using scenario analysis).

- Strategic planning shifted from a *control perspective*, in which senior management used the strategic planning mechanisms as a means of controlling decisions and resource deployments by divisions and business units and departments, toward more of a *coordination perspective*, in which the strategy process emphasized dialog involving knowledge sharing and consensus building. As a result, the process become increasingly informal and puts less emphasis on written documents.

- A diminishing role for strategic planning staff as responsibility for strategic decisions and the strategy-making process become located among senior managers.[32]

A study of strategic planning processes among "best practice" companies also pointed to an emphasis on flexible planning processes, "stretch" goals (especially those based on shareholder return and economic profit), and a strong emphasis on communication between business and corporate levels, with line managers rather than staff as the key drivers of the process.[33]

Financial Planning and Control Systems

Financial planning and control systems relate to budgeting activities and financial targets. If profitability is the primary goal of the firm, then it is inevitable that financial systems are the primary mechanism through which top management seeks to

---

[32]   Robert M. Grant, "Strategic Planning among the Oil and Gas Majors," working paper (McDonough School of Business, Georgetown University, 1999).

[33]   *Strategic Planning: Final Report* (Houston: American Productivity and Quality Center, 1996).

control performance. At the center of financial planning is the *budgetary process*. This involves setting and monitoring financial estimates with regard to income and expenditure for a fixed period, both for the firm as a whole and for divisions and sub-units. Budgets play multiple, somewhat ambiguous roles. They are in part an estimate of incomes and expenditures for the future, in part a target of required financial performance in terms of revenues and profits, and in part a set of authorizations for expenditure up to specified budgetary limits. Two types of budget are set: the capital expenditure budget and the operating budget.

The Capital Expenditure Budget

The *capital expenditure budget* grows out of the strategic planning system. In setting strategy and performance guidelines, strategic plans also forecast capital expenditure for the strategic planning period. For the first year of the plan, a precise capital expenditure budget is set in terms of actually allocating funds to each division or subsidiary. The size and content of the capital budget are determined by the approvals already given for individual capital expenditure projects, together with an estimate of the new projects likely to be approved during the budget year.

Most companies have a standardized approach to evaluating projects and approving them. Project proposals originate in the individual businesses and a request for funding is prepared according to a standardized methodology, typically based on a forecast of cash flows discounted at the relevant cost of capital (adjusted for project risk) and with indications of the sensitivities of the project's returns to key environmental uncertainties. For example, to estimate the net present value (NPV) of a new copper mine, RTZ would make different estimates for different assumptions about future copper prices; to evaluate investment in a new semiconductor plant in Malaysia, Texas Instruments would examine the sensitivity of the project's NPV to different assumptions about the exchange rate between the US dollar and the Malaysian ringgit. Capital expenditure approvals take place at different levels of a company according to their size. Projects up to $5 million might be approved by a business unit head, projects up to $25 million might be approved by divisional top management, larger projects might need to be approved by the top management committee, while the biggest projects might require approval of the board of directors.

The Operating Budget

The *operating budget* is a pro forma profit and loss statement for the company as a whole and for individual divisions and business units for the upcoming year. It is usually divided into quarters and months to permit continual monitoring and the early identification of variances. The operating budget is part forecast and part target. It is set within the context of the performance targets established by the strategic plan. Thus, the performance targets set by the Royal Dutch/Shell Group for 2001 included an ROCE of 15 percent and a reduction in operating costs of $5 billion.[34] Each business typically prepares an operating budget for the following year that is

---

[34]   Royal Dutch/Shell Group of Companies, press release (December 18, 2000).

then discussed with the top management committee and, if acceptable, approved. At the end of the financial year, business-level divisional managers are called on to review the performance of the business over the past year.

Human Resource Management Systems

Ultimately, achieving coordination and cooperation within an organization is about managing people. Even though strategic planning systems and financial planning systems are about strategies and finances, ultimately they are systems for influencing the ways in which people behave in terms of decisions and efforts. To support strategic and financial planning, companies also need systems for setting goals, creating incentives and monitoring performance at the level of the individual employee. The central role for human resource management is establishing an incentive system that supports the implementation of strategic plans and performance targets through aligning employee and company goals. The general problem, we have noted, is one of agency: How can a company induce employees to do what it wants?

The problem of aligning employee goals with those of the firm is a central problem. It is compounded by the imprecision of employment contracts. Unlike market contracts, employment contracts are imprecise about what is being delivered by the provider (the employee). The employer has the right to assign the employee to a particular category of tasks for a certain number of hours per week, but the amount of work to be performed and the quality of that work are typically unspecified. Employment contracts give the right to the employer to terminate the contract for unsatisfactory performance by the employee, but the threat of termination is an inadequate incentive: it imposes costs on the employer and only requires the employee to perform better than a new hire would. Moreover, the employer has imperfect information as to employees' work performance. To ensure that an employee is not using the firm's computer to play games and the firm's telephone to call relatives in New Zealand imposes monitoring costs. The more employees are engaged in team production activities where their individual output is not separately observable, the greater the potential for shirking.[35]

The firm can ensure the employee's compliance with organizational goals using direct supervision of the type that administrative hierarchies are designed to do. The weaknesses of such administrative supervision are, first, there is little incentive for performance in excess of minimum requirements, second, supervision imposes costs, and third, the system presupposes that the supervisor has the knowledge required to direct the employee effectively.

The key to promoting more effective cooperation is for more sophisticated incentives than the threat of dismissal. The principal incentives available to the firm for promoting cooperation are compensation and promotion. The key to designing compensation systems is to link pay either to the inputs required for effective job performance (hours of work, punctuality, effort, numbers of customers visited)

[35]   A. Alchian and H. Demsetz, "Production, Information Costs, and Economic Organization," *American Economic Review* 62 (1972): 777–97.

or to outputs. The simplest form of output-linked pay is piece-work (paying for each unit of output produced) or commission (paying a percentage of the revenue generated).

Relating pay to individual performance is suitable for tasks performed individually. However, firms exist primarily to permit complex coordination among individuals; encouraging such collaboration requires linking pay to team or departmental performance. Where broad-based, enterprise-wide collaboration is required, there may be little alternative to linking pay to company performance through some form of profit sharing.

The process of delayering and dismantling hierarchical control mechanisms has been accompanied by increased reliance on financial incentives as mechanisms for coordination and control. If the remuneration of business unit and departmental heads is linked to their unit and departmental performance, then incentives can replace direct supervision as a control device. In the past, performance-related pay was too small a proportion of total remuneration to exert powerful incentive effects. This is changing. Among the chief executives of US companies with revenues of $2 billion or more, performance bonuses frequently fall into the range of 50–70 percent of base salary.

Corporate Culture as a Control Mechanism

We earlier examined the role of shared values in helping to align the goals of different stakeholders and units within the organization. More generally, we can view the culture of the organization as a mechanism for achieving coordination and control. *Corporate culture* comprises the beliefs, values, and behavioral norms of the company that influence how employees think and behave.[36] It is manifest in symbols, ceremonies, social practices, rites, vocabulary, and dress. As with any social group, corporate cultures are complex phenomena. They are embedded within national cultures, and incorporate elements of social and professional cultures. As a result, a corporate culture may be far from homogeneous: very different cultures may be evident in the research lab, on the factory floor, and within the accounting department. To this extent, culture is not necessarily an integrating device – it can contribute to divisiveness.

The earlier discussion of shared values emphasized the role of culture in assisting cooperation; culture can also help coordination. In large, decentralized corporations such as Royal Dutch/Shell, Accenture, and Matsushita, strong corporate cultures create a sense of identity among employees that facilitates communication and the building of organizational routines, even across national boundaries. It is especially supportive of horizontal communication and coordination. The unifying influence of corporate culture is likely to be especially helpful in assisting coordination through mutual adjustment in large cross-functional teams of the type required for new product development. One of the advantages of culture as a coordinating device is that it permits substantial flexibility in the types of interactions it can support.

---

[36]   E. H. Schein, "Organizational Culture," *American Psychologist* 45 (1990): 109–19.

The extent to which corporate culture assists coordination depends on the characteristics of the culture. Salomon Brothers (now part of Citigroup) was renowned for its individualistic, internally competitive culture; this was effective in motivating drive and individual effort, but did little to facilitate cooperation. The British Broadcasting Corporation has a strong culture that reflects internal politicization, professional values, internal suspicion, and a dedication to the public good, but without a strong sense of customer focus.[37] A key problem is that cultures take a long time to develop and cannot easily be changed. As the external environment changes, a highly effective culture may become dysfunctional. The Los Angeles Police Department's culture of professionalism and militarism that made it one of the most admired and effective police forces in America has contributed to its current problems of isolation and unresponsiveness to community needs and political currents.[38]

Integrating Different Control Mechanisms

The past ten years have seen substantial progress in integrating different control systems. As strategy has become more and more focused on creating shareholder value, so financial goals, financial measures, and budgeting have become more closely integrated with strategy formulation. Indeed, preoccupation with profitability and shareholder return has caused a shift in emphasis from strategic to financial planning, with a consequent shortening of time horizons. However, for most companies, financial and strategic planning have become closely integrated, the two being seen as complementary to one another. Thus, annual performance targets for business units and departments tend to combine financial goals such as return on capital employed, and strategic goals with regard to market share, productivity, new product introduction, and the like.

Linking strategic and financial goals with human resource management has been the final stage of integrating control mechanisms. The essence of such integration is the desegregation of broad, enterprise-wide financial and strategic goals into targets for individual employees. If targets are to be effective motivators, they must be measurable. The central aspect of the "metrics" movement within management is the ability not just to establish quantitative goals for individual employees and groups, but to create mechanisms for measuring and reporting the attainment of these targets. The balanced scorecard system outlined in Chapter 2 is but one approach to this linking of employee goals to company-wide goals.

---

[37] Tom Burns, *The BBC: Public Institution and Private World* (London: Macmillan, 1977).
[38] "LAPD: Storming the Rampart," *Economist* (December 2, 2000): 72.

SUMMARY

The internal structure and systems of the firm are not simply a matter of "strategy implementation," which can be separated from the hard analytics of strategy formulation. Not only is strategy implementation inseparable from strategy formulation, but issues of structure and systems are central to the fundamental issues of competitive advantage and strategy choice – the existence of organizational capability in particular.

Despite the importance of these issues, this chapter provides only a brief introduction to some of the key issues in organization design. Although subsequent chapters develop many of the themes more fully in relation to particular areas of strategy and particular business contexts, our progress is limited by the weakness of theory in this area. Though our analysis of the industry environment has progressed substantially in recent decades – thanks especially to the contributions from industrial economics and game theory – organization theory is an exceptionally rich field that still lacks adequate integration of its component disciplines: sociology, psychology, organizational economics, systems theory, population ecology, and organizational evolution. While business enterprises continue to experiment with new organizational forms, we business school academics lag some way behind in fitting our theories to the organizational phenomena that we observe.

The chapters that follow will have more to say on the organizational structures and management systems appropriate to different strategies and different business contexts. In the final chapter (Chapter 17) we shall explore some of the new trends and new ideas that are reshaping our thinking about organizational design.

III
The Analysis of Competitive Advantage

7

The Nature and Sources of Competitive Advantage

One Saturday afternoon in downtown Chicago, Milton Friedman, the famous free-market economist, was shopping with his wife.

"Look, Milton!" exclaimed Mrs. Friedman. "There's a $20 bill on the sidewalk!"

"Don't be foolish, my dear," replied the Nobel laureate. "If that was a $20 bill, someone would have picked it up by now."

—**economist's anecdote of doubtful authenticity**

OUTLINE

INTRODUCTION AND OBJECTIVES

In this chapter, we draw together the different elements of competitive advantage that we have analyzed in prior chapters. Chapter 1 noted that a firm can earn a rate of profit in excess of its cost of capital either by locating in an attractive industry or by establishing a competitive advantage over its rivals. Of these two sources of superior profitability, competitive advantage is the more important. As competition has intensified across almost all industries, very few industry environments can guarantee secure returns; hence, the primary goal of a strategy is to establish a position of competitive advantage for the firm. Kenichi Ohmae has gone as far as to define strategy as the quest for competitive advantage (see Table 1.1).

Chapters 3 and 5 provided the two primary components of our analysis of competitive advantage. The last part of Chapter 3 analyzed the external sources of competitive advantage: key success factors are the general requirements for satisfying customer needs and surviving competition within a market. Chapter 5 analyzed the internal sources of competitive advantage: the potential offered by the firm's resources and capabilities for establishing and sustaining competitive advantage.

This chapter extends our analysis of competitive advantage. We focus on the relationship between competitive advantage and the competitive process. Competition provides the incentive for establishing advantage and is the means by which advantage is eroded. Only by understanding the characteristics of competition in a market can we identify the opportunities for competitive advantage. My goal is to draw together ideas of competition, success factors, and the returns to resources and capabilities into a broad-based analysis of the nature and sources of competitive advantage.

By the time you have completed this chapter you will be able to:

■ Identify the circumstances in which a firm can create a competitive advantage over a rival.

- Understand how responsiveness and innovation can create competitive advantage.

- Predict the potential for competition to erode competitive advantage through imitation.

- Recognize the role of resource conditions in creating imperfections in the competitive process and, therefore, opportunities for competitive advantage.

- Distinguish the two primary types of competitive advantage: cost advantage and differentiation advantage.

- Apply this analysis to formulate business strategies capable of establishing and sustaining competitive advantage in different types of industry.

THE EMERGENCE OF COMPETITIVE ADVANTAGE

To understand how competitive advantage emerges, we must first understand what competitive advantage is. It can be defined as follows:

> When two or more firms compete within the same market, one firm possesses a competitive advantage over its rivals when it earns (or has the potential to earn) a persistently higher rate of profit.

Competitive advantage, then, is the ability of the firm to outperform rivals on the primary performance goal – profitability. Note that competitive advantage may not be revealed in higher profitability: a firm may trade current profit for investment in market share or technology, or a firm may forgo profits in the interests of customer satisfaction, philanthropy, employee benefits, or executive perks.

External Sources of Change

Differences in profitability between competing firms are a disequilibrium phenomenon – the emergence of competitive advantage requires some form of change to occur. The source of the change may be external or internal to the industry: Figure 7.1 illustrates several sources. For an external change to create competitive advantage, the change must have differential effects on companies because of their different resources and capabilities or strategic positioning. For example, during 1996–98, Chrysler was the most profitable of world's major car companies, primarily a result of its successful minivan and Jeep models. However, by the third quarter of year 2000, Chrysler (now a division of DaimlerChrysler) reported a loss – a result, in part, of the rising value of the US dollar and the tripling of oil prices that hit sales of its minivan and sports-utility vehicles. Conversely, the competitive positions and profitability of Renault and Peugeot were greatly improved by these same factors.

FIGURE 7.1 The emergence of competitive advantage

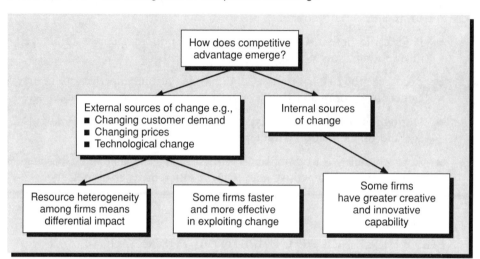

The extent to which external change creates competitive advantage and disadvantage depends on the magnitude of the change and the extent of firms' strategic differences. The more turbulent an industry's environment, the greater the number of sources of change, and the greater the differences in firms' resources and capabilities, the greater the dispersion of profitability within the industry. In the world oil industry of the 1960s, the industry environment was relatively stable and the leading firms pursued similar strategies. As a result, competitive advantages, as reflected in inter-firm profit differentials, tended to be small. The toy industry, on the other hand, experiences rapid and unpredictable changes in demand, technology, and fashion, and firms are positioned very differently with regard to capabilities and product lines. Inter-firm profitability tends to be widely dispersed.

Competitive Advantage from Responsiveness to Change

The role of external change in creating competitive advantage is not simply in conferring advantages and disadvantages on otherwise passive firms. The competitive advantage that arises from external change also depends on a firm's ability to respond to external change. Any external change creates opportunities for profit. The ability to identify and respond to opportunity lies in the core management capability that we call *entrepreneurship*.[1] To the extent that external opportunities are fleeting or subject to first-mover advantage, speed of response is critical to exploiting business opportunity. An unexpected rain shower creates an upsurge in the demand for

---

[1] Richard Rumelt, "Theory, Strategy and Entrepreneurship," in David J. Teece (ed.), *The Competitive Challenge: Strategies for Industrial Innovation and Renewal* (Cambridge, MA: Ballinger, 1987): 137, defines entrepreneurship as "the creation of new businesses." Here, we define entrepreneurship more broadly to also include the adaptation of an existing business to create and exploit a new business opportunity.

umbrellas. Those street vendors who position themselves outside a busy railroad station at the onset of rain will benefit most from this business opportunity.

As markets become increasingly turbulent, so responsiveness to external change has become increasingly important as a source of competitive advantage.

- Wal-Mart's ability consistently to outperform Kmart and other discount retailers is based on a business system that responds quickly and effectively to changes in demand. Wal-Mart's distribution and purchasing are driven by point-of-sale data in a tightly integrated system that results in low inventories, few stockouts, and few forced markdowns. However, at the heart of Wal-Mart's fast-response capability is a management system and a corporate culture that encourage and reward initiative at all levels of the company.[2]

- The highly successful textile industry of the Prato region of northern Italy is based on a business model pioneered by Massimo Menichetti in the early 1970s. The Prato model of small, specialized textile and clothing companies competing and cooperating through highly flexible, closely integrated networks is uniquely suited to the fast-paced business environment of fashion clothing.[3]

Responsiveness also involves anticipating changes in the basis of competitive advantage over time. As an industry moves through its life cycle, as customer requirements change, and as patterns of competition shift, so companies must adjust their strategies and their capabilities to take account of the key success factors of the future. Monsanto showed considerable foresight in building its competitive position to outlive the expiration in 1992 of its patents on its artificial sweetener, NutraSweet. In addition to heavy promotion of the NutraSweet brand name and its "swirl" logo, Monsanto invested in scale-efficient production facilities, signed long-term exclusive supply contracts with key customers (such as Coca-Cola), and used trade secrets to protect its production know-how.[4] DaimlerChrysler's Smart micro-car, jointly designed by Mercedes and the Swatch watchmaker SMH, anticipated increasing concerns over congestion and pollution.

Responsiveness to the opportunities provided by external change requires one key resource – information – and one key capability – flexibility of response. Information is necessary to identify and anticipate external changes. This is dependent on a firm's environmental scanning capability. As the pace of change has accelerated, environmental scanning activities have changed with it: firms are less dependent on

---

[2] Bob Ortega, *In Sam We Trust: The Untold Story of Sam Walton and How Wal-Mart is Devouring America* (New York: Times Books, 2000).

[3] H. Voss, "Virtual Organization," *Strategy and Leadership* 24 (July–August, 1996): 12–24. The Italian model of small firm networks has been documented and analyzed by Gianni Lorenzoni. See G. Lorenzoni and Charles Baden Fuller, "Creating a Strategic Center to Manage a Web of Partners," *California Management Review* 37 no. 3 (1995): 146–63; G. Lorenzoni, "Organizational Architecture, Inter-Firm Relationships and Entrepreneural Profile: Findings from a Set of SME," *Frontiers of Entrepreneurship Research* (Boston: Babson College: 1993).

[4] *Bitter Competition: The Holland Sweetener Co. vs. NutraSweet (A)*, Case No. 9-794-079 (Boston: Harvard Business School: 1998). See also David J. Teece, "Profiting from Technological Innovation: Implications for Integration, Collaboration, Licensing, and Public Policy," in David J. Teece (ed.), op. cit.

conventional analysis of economic and market research data and more dependent on "early warning systems" through direct relationships with customers, suppliers, and competitors.

Flexibility of response requires that a firm swiftly redeploys its resources to meet changes in external conditions. Traditionally associated with plant and equipment, information systems, and other aspects of "organizational hardware," flexibility is now viewed as primarily dependent on "organizational software" – organizational structure, decision-making systems, job design, and culture. Flexibility typically requires fewer levels of hierarchy, greater decentralization of decision making, and informal patterns of cooperation and coordination. Benetton's remarkable responsiveness to emerging market trends and changing customer preferences is achieved through a highly flexible network. The shifting of garment dyeing to the end of the production process is just one means by which it has redesigned its business processes to maximize flexibility.[5] At the retail level, Benetton operates through a system of country and regional agents who coordinate the franchised retail outlets within their territories. At the production level, its own production facilities are supported by over 2,000 subcontractors. A remarkable feature of this vertically integrated network is an absence of formal contracts.

The greater a company's flexibility in responding to changing market circumstances, the less dependent it is on its ability to forecast. Dell Computer is the epitome of the current trend toward speed and agility. A custom order placed at 9 a.m. on Monday can be on a delivery truck by 9 p.m. Tuesday. This permits Dell to customize each computer to the customer's specifications and to operate with under 14 days' inventory, which not only cuts costs but permits Dell to adjust rapidly and effortlessly to fluctuations in market demand and upgrade its products quickly to take advantage of technical advances in components. Between 1996 and 1999, Dell grew net income at over 50 percent a year and earned a return on equity of over 50 percent – far ahead of any other PC maker.[6]

As fast-response capability becomes an increasingly important key success factor across most industries, interest in time-based management and the role of time as a strategically important resource has grown. George Stalk of the Boston Consulting Group argued that speed through time-based manufacturing, time-based sales and distribution, and time-based innovation is the primary competitive advantage of many leading-edge Japanese companies.[7] The premise that speed is the only real source of advantage in today's economy was the primary rationale behind the founding of *Fast Company* magazine in 1995 and subsequently www.fastcompany.com. In automobiles, speed of new product development is a major advantage of Japanese companies (see Table 7.1). During the 1990s, major efforts have been made by US and European companies to increase their fast-response capabilities by reducing cycle times both in manufacturing and in new product development.

---

[5] G. Lorenzoni, "Benetton," in C. Baden Fuller and M. Pitt (eds), *Strategic Innovation* (London, Routledge, 1996): 355–88.

[6] Joan Magretta, "The Power of Vitual Integration: An Interview with Dell Computer's Michael Dell," *Harvard Business Review* (March–April 1998): 73–84.

[7] George Stalk Jr., "Time – The Next Source of Competitive Advantage," *Harvard Business Review* (July–August 1988): 41–51.

TABLE 7.1 New Product Development Performance by US, Japanese, and European Auto Producers

	JAPANESE VOLUME PRODUCER	US VOLUME PRODUCER	EUROPEAN VOLUME PRODUCER	EUROPEAN HIGH-END SPECIALIST
Average lead time (months)	42.6	61.9	57.6	71.5
Engineering hours (in millions)	1.2	3.5	3.4	3.4
Total product quality index	58	41	41	84

Source: Kim B. Clark and Takahiro Fujimoto, *Product Development Performance* (Boston: Harvard Business School Press, 1991): 73.

Competitive Advantage from Innovation: "New Game" Strategies

The source of disturbance that creates the opportunity for competitive advantage may be internal as well as external. Internal change is generated by innovation. Innovation not only creates competitive advantage, it provides a basis for overturning the competitive advantage of other firms. Schumpeter's view of the competitive process as "a gale of creative destruction" involved market leadership being eroded not by imitation but by innovation. Innovation is typically thought of in its technical sense: the embodiment of new ideas and knowledge in new products or processes. In a business context, however, innovation also embodies new approaches to doing business. Innovative strategies involve new approaches to competing within an industry. Innovative strategies tend to be the basis of most outstanding success in most industries – far more so than product innovation alone. Many creative business strategies involve little product innovation. Indeed, Gary Hamel argues that *business concept innovation* is the foundation for value creation in the new economy (see Exhibit 7.1).

What is the nature of these innovatory business concepts? Some involve creating value for customers from novel experiences, products, or product delivery or bundling. The competition in the retail sector is diven by a constant quest for new retail concepts and formats:

- In department stores, Nordstrom redefined the shopping experience through augmented customer service.

- In bookstores, Barnes and Noble have a retail environment that is conducive to browsing, relaxing, and social interaction. It offers spaciousness, a wide selection of books, and Starbuck's coffee.

- Sephora, subsidiary of the French-based luxury products firm LVMH, has redefined the retailing of cosmetics. With over 230 stores at the end of 2000, including 143 in France and 50 in the US, it "seeks to defy the traditional *selling methodology* to give you what you want – Freedom, Beauty and Pleasure."

For example, "Freedom comes to you in a hands-on, self-service shopping environment. Feel free to touch, smell and experience each and every product . . . You are also free to choose the level of assistance you desire, from individual experience and reflection, to detailed expert advice."[8] Sephora's unique layout features a "Fragrance Organ – a circular scent bar, where you can test and compare fragrances. Use a tester stick to experiment with fragrance notes and accords" and a "Lipstick Rainbow" with 365 shades of lipstick.

Other new business models have been built on new process technologies and new organizational formats.

EXHIBIT 7.1   Reconfiguring the Value Chain to Formulate New Game Strategies: Savin and Xerox

---

For most of the 1970s, Xerox possessed a near monopoly position in the North American market for plain-paper copiers. Xerox's dominance rested, first, upon the wall of patents that the company had built over several decades and, second, on the scale economies and reputation that its market dominance conferred. The first company to compete effectively with Xerox during the late 1970s was Savin. The basis of Savin's challenge was an approach that sought not to imitate Xerox's success but to compete in an entirely different manner.

Savin developed and patented a new low-cost technology. Its product design permitted the use of standardized parts that could be sourced in volume from Japan. Assembly was also undertaken in Japan. The result was a product whose cost was about half that of Xerox's. To avoid the costs of leasing and the need for a costly direct sales force, Savin distributed through existing office equipment dealers.

The principal differences between the approach of Savin and that of Xerox can be seen by comparing the main activities of the companies:

	XEROX	SAVIN
Technology and design	Dry xerography High copy speed Many features	Liquid toner Low copy speed Few features and options
Manufacture	Most manufacturing (including components) in house	Machines sourced from Ricoh in Japan
Product range	Wide range of machines	Narrow range of machines for different volumes and uses
Marketing	Machines leased to customers	Machines sold to customers
Distribution	Direct sales force	Distribution through dealers
Service	Directly operated service organization	Service by dealers and independent service engineers

---

Source: Roberto Buaron, "New-Game Strategies," *McKinsey Staff Paper* (March 1980); reprinted in *On Strategy* (McKinsey Quarterly Anthologies, 2000): 34–6.

---

[8]   www.sephora.com.

- In the US steel industry, Nucor achieved unrivaled productivity and flexibility by combining new process technologies, flat and flexible organizational structures, and innovative management systems. In 1997, it overtook USX as America's biggest steel producer.

- Wal-Mart's position as the world's biggest and most successful retailer owes much to a business model based heavily on new process technology and novel approaches to organization. Wal-Mart's supply chain, featuring its hub-and-spoke distribution system, innovatory techniques such as cross-docking, and its use of IT and communication to allow point-of-sale data to drive decision making across its whole value chain, is a model of efficiency, flexibility, and integration.

Charles Baden Fuller and John Stopford provide compelling evidence that, even in mature industries, strategic innovation is the primary basis for competitive advantage and the principal driving force of industry change. Central to such innovation is creating customer value through the combination of performance dimensions that were previously viewed as conflicting. For example, Toyota's "lean production system" combines low cost and high quality, and Richardson, a Sheffield-based manufacturer of kitchen knives, used process technology, innovatory design, and a culture of entrepreneurship to achieve performance that was unprecedented in the British cutlery industry.[9]

McKinsey and Co. has argued that innovative business concepts (what it calls "new game" strategies) typically involve reconfiguration of the industry value chain. By reconstructing and rearranging the value chain, a company can change the "rules of the game" so as to capitalize on its distinctive competencies, catch competitors off guard, and erect barriers to protect the advantage created. McKinsey cites Savin in the North American market for plain-paper copiers as an example of the potency of new game strategies in challenging an established firm with a seemingly impregnable competitive position and an illustration of the application of the value chain in formulating new game strategies (see Exhibit 7.2).

New business concepts based on redefining the industry value chain have been fundamental to business success in many established industries:

- Southwest Airlines built a business system that differs radically from that of the established airlines: it offers point-to-point routes (instead of the usual hub-and-spoke system), provides no in-flight meals, operates a single type of plane, and does not utilize either of the industry's main computerized reservations systems. Southwest's unique approach has given it some of the lowest unit costs in the industry.

- Nike built its large and successful businesses on a business system that involved a total reconfiguration of the activities of the traditional shoe manufacturing firm. To begin with, Nike does not manufacture shoes – indeed, it manufactures

---

[9] Charles Baden Fuller and John M. Stopford, *Rejuvenating the Mature Business* (London and New York: Routledge, 1992).

EXHIBIT 7.2 Gary Hamel on Business Concept Innovation and the Quest for New Business Models

In his influential book *Leading the Revolution*, Gary Hamel, chairman of the consulting firm Strategos and visiting professor at London Business School, argues that the age of continuity is over and we have now entered the age of revolution where the value of incumbency is being eroded and those companies that embrace discontinuous change will be the winners. The revolutionaries will win through innovatory business concepts embodied in new business models:

> In the new economy, the unit of analysis for innovation is not a product or a technology – it's a business concept. The building blocks of a business concept and a business model are the same – a business model is simply a business concept that has been put into practice. Business concept innovation is the capacity to imagine dramatically different business concepts or dramatically new ways of differentiating existing business concepts. Business concept innovation is thus the key to creating new wealth. Competition within a broad domain – be it financial services, communications, entertainment, publishing, education, energy, or any other field – takes place not between products or companies, but between business models.

Source: G. Hamel, *Leading the Revolution* (Boston: Harvard Business School Press, 2000).

little of anything. It designs, markets, and distributes shoes, but its primary activity is the coordination of a vast and complex global network involving design and market research (primarily in the US), the production (under contract) of components (primarily in Korea and Taiwan), and the assembly of shoes (in China, the Philippines, India, Thailand, and several other low-wage countries).

- Dell Computer established its direct-sales model initially over the telephone and subsequently the internet. Its entire logistics are outsourced. Some components are delivered to customers without passing through Dell's hands, e.g., monitors are shipped directly from supplier to customer to arrive simultaneously with the computer.

Value chain reconfiguration is also a feature of many e-commerce strategies:

- MP3.com offers a radical new approach to music distribution. With its database of 606,600 songs from over 94,200 artists (as of October 2000), it offers direct digital download and disintermediates record companies.

- Hotmail, the web-based free e-mail servce acquired by Microsoft in 1998, created a new approach to electronic mail. Not only was its service free, but it could be accessed from any computer, anywhere, without downloading any special software.

- Webvan.com offers a radical new approach to grocery distribution. Orders are submitted and paid for online and distribution is through large distribution centers and fleets of vans direct to the consumer's home.

More generally, the primary impact of the internet on conventional value chains has been *disintermediation* – the elimination of intermediaries such as wholesalers, retailers, and publishers. The classic example of such disintermediation are consumer-to-consumer businesses such as the online auctioneers eBay and QXL, which exist only to facilitate transations between individuals. In practice, the major impact of the internet has been the creation of new intermediaries. These include *infomediaries*,[10] such as Price Watch and DealPilot.com, which allow customers to search for the best deals among different online retailers, and trusted third parties (TTPs), such as Better Business Bureau Online and TRUSTe, which verify internet retailers' privacy standards.[11]

SUSTAINING COMPETITIVE ADVANTAGE

Once established, competitive advantage is subject to erosion by competition. The speed with which competitive advantage is undermined depends on the ability of competitors to challenge either by imitation or innovation. Imitation is the most direct form of competition, thus, for competitive advantage to be sustained over time barriers to imitation must exist. Rumelt uses the term *isolating mechanisms* to describe "barriers that limit the *ex post* equilibration of rents among individual firms."[12] The more effective these isolating mechanisms are, the longer competitive advantage can be sustained against the onslaught of rivals. Empirical studies show that the process through which competition destroys the competitive advantage of industry leaders is slow. Even over periods of a decade and more, inter-firm profit differentials tend to persist, with little change in the identities of the leaders and the laggards.[13]

To identify the sources of isolating mechanisms, we need to examine the process of competitive imitation. For one firm successfully to imitate the strategy of another, it must meet four conditions:

- *Identification*. The firm must be able to identify that a rival possesses a competitive advantage.

- *Incentive*. Having identified that a rival possesses a competitive advantage (as shown by above-average profitability), the firm must believe that by investing in imitation, it too can earn superior returns.

---

[10]   John Hagel and Marc Singer, *Net Worth: Shaping Markets When Customers Make the Rules* (Boston: Harvard Business School Press, 1999).

[11]   M. D. Smith, J. Bailey, and E. Brynjolfsson, "Understanding Digital Markets: Review and Assessment," in E. Brynjolfsson and B. Kahin (eds), *Understanding the Digital Economy: Data, Tools, and Research* (Cambridge: MIT Press, 2000): 122.

[12]   Richard P. Rumelt, "Toward a Strategic Theory of the Firm," in R. Lamb (ed.), *Competitive Strategic Management* (Englewood Cliffs, NJ: Prentice-Hall, 1984): 556–70.

[13]   See John Cubbin and Paul Geroski, "The Convergence of Profits in the Long Run: Interfirm and Interindustry Comparisons," *Journal of Industrial Economics* 35 (1987): 427–42; Robert Jacobsen, "The Persistence of Abnormal Returns," *Strategic Management Journal* 9 (1988): 415–30; and Dennis C. Mueller, "Persistent Profits among Large Corporations," in Lacy Glenn Thomas (ed.), *The Economics of Strategic Planning* (Lexington, MA: Lexington Books, 1986): 31–61.

FIGURE 7.2 Sustaining competitive advantage: types of isolating mechanism

REQUIREMENT FOR IMITATION	ISOLATING MECHANISM
Identification	—*Obscure* superior performance
Incentives for imitation	—*Deterrence*: signal aggressive Intentions to imitators —*Preemption*: exploit all available investment opportunities
Diagnosis	—Rely on multiple sources of competitive advantage to create "*causal ambiguity*"
Resource acquisition	—Base competitive advantage on resources and capabilities that are *immobile* and *difficult to replicate*

- *Diagnosis.* The firm must be able to diagnose the features of its rival's strategy that give rise to the competitive advantage.

- *Resource acquisition.* The firm must be able to acquire through transfer or replication the resources and capabilities necessary for imitating the strategy of the advantaged firm.

Figure 7.2 illustrates these stages and the forms of isolating mechanism that exist at each stage.

Identification: Obscuring Superior Performance

A simple barrier to imitation is to obscure the firm's superior profitability. In the 1948 movie classic *The Treasure of the Sierra Madre*, Humphrey Bogart and his fellow gold prospectors go to great lengths to obscure their find from other prospectors.[14] The most direct means of obscuring competitive advantage in order to discourage would-be competitors is simply to forgo short-term profits. The *theory of limit pricing*, in its simplest form, postulates that a firm in a strong market position sets prices at a level that just fails to attract entrants. A more attractive means of avoiding competition is for the firm to withhold information about its profitability.

[14] The film was based on the book, by B. Traven, *The Treasure of the Sierra Madre* (New York: Knopf, 1947).

Private companies and unincorporated forms of business have an advantage in this respect: they are not obliged to make public their financial results. The recent trend to take public companies private has been motivated, in part, by the advantages of nondisclosure. Among public companies, diversification and consequent consolidation of accounts can help protect highly profitable subsidiaries from competitive entry.

Incentives to Compete: Deterrence and Preemption

A firm may avoid competition by undermining the incentives for imitation. If a firm can persuade rivals that by imitating its strategy they will not achieve comparable profitability, it may be able to avoid competitive challenges. In Chapter 4 we discussed the role of signaling: the manipulation of information by a firm in order to influence the behavior of competitors. Deterrence involves making threatening signals toward competitors that encourage the competitor to believe that a strategy of imitation will not prove profitable. The key to deterrence is the promise of retaliation against a competitor that encroaches on the firm's strategic niche. For a threat to be effective in deterring a competitive challenge, it must be credible. Because carrying out a threat is usually costly to both the aggressor and the victim, it needs to be supported by commitment.[15] Thus, the threat of aggressive price cuts needs to be backed either by excess capacity or by excess inventories.

The credibility of a threat also depends on the reputation of the firm that issues it. Engaging in costly competitive battles may be advantageous if it builds a reputation for aggressiveness. Microsoft's aggressiveness in office software and internet browsers has given it a reputation that inhibits many weaker rivals from doing battle with it in the wide range of markets that it has subsequently entered. Brandenburger and Nalebuff argue that in the aspartame market, NutraSweets aggressive price war against the Holland Sweetener Company deterred other would-be entrants.[16]

A firm can also deter imitation by preemption – occupying existing and potential strategic niches in order to reduce the range of investment opportunities open to the challenger. Preemption can take many forms:

- Proliferation of product varieties by a market leader can leave new entrants and smaller rivals with few opportunities for establishing a market niche. Between 1950 and 1972, for example, the six leading suppliers of breakfast cereals introduced 80 new brands into the US market.[17]

- Large investments in production capacity ahead of the growth of market demand also preempt market opportunities for rivals. Monsanto's heavy investment in plants for producing NutraSweet ahead of its patent expiration was a clear threat to would-be producers of generic aspartame.

[15]   Thomas C. Schelling, *The Strategy of Conflict*, 2nd edn (Cambridge: Harvard University Press, 1980): 35–41.
[16]   Adam Brandenburger and Barry Nalebuff, *Co-opetition* (New York: Doubleday, 1996): 72–80.
[17]   Richard Schmalensee, "Entry Deterrence in the Ready-to-Eat Breakfast Cereal Industry," *Bell Journal of Economics* 9 (1978): 305–27.

■ Patent proliferation can protect technology-based advantage by limiting competitors' technical opportunities. In 1974, Xerox's dominant market position was protected by a wall of over 2,000 patents, most of which were not used. When IBM introduced its first copier in 1970, Xerox sued it for infringing 22 of these patents.[18]

The ability to sustain competitive advantage through preemption depends on the presence of two imperfections of the competitive process. First, the market must be small relative to the minimum efficient scale of production, such that only a very small number of competitors is viable. Second, there must be first-mover advantage that gives an incumbent preferential access to information and other resources, putting rivals at a disadvantage.

Diagnosing Competitive Advantage: "Causal Ambiguity" and "Uncertain Imitability"

If a firm is to imitate the competitive advantage of another, it must understand the basis of its rival's success. In most industries, there is a serious identification problem in linking superior performance to the resources and capabilities that generate that performance. Consider the remarkable success of Wal-Mart in the discount retailing business. It is easy for Kmart to point to the differences between Wal-Mart and itself. As one Wal-Mart executive commented: "Retailing is an open book. There are no secrets. Our competitors can walk into our stores and see what we sell, how we sell it, and for how much." The difficult task is to identify which differences are critical to the profitability differential between the two retailers. Is it Wal-Mart's store locations (typically in small towns with little direct competition)? Its tightly integrated logistics of purchasing, warehousing, and distribution? Its unique management system? The information system that supports Wal-Mart's logistics and decision-making practices? Or is it the culture that combines rural American values of thrift, simplicity, and hard work, with company traditions of family-like unity, customer attentiveness, and entrepreneurial drive?

The problem for Kmart and other wannabe Wal-Marts is what Lippman and Rumelt refer to as *causal ambiguity*.[19] The more multidimensional a firm's competitive advantage and the more each dimension of competitive advantage is based on complex bundles of organizational capabilities rather than individual resources, the more difficult it is for a competitor to diagnose the determinants of success. The outcome of causal ambiguity is *uncertain imitability*: where there is ambiguity associated with the causes of a competitor's success, any attempt to imitate that strategy is subject to uncertain success.

---

[18]   Monopolies and Mergers Commission, *Indirect Electrostatic Reprographic Equipment* (London: Her Majesty's Stationery Office, 1976): 37, 56.
[19]   S. A. Lippman and Richard P. Rumelt, "Uncertain Imitability: An Analysis of Interfirm Differences in Efficiency under Competition," *Bell Journal of Economics* 13 (1982): 418–38. The analysis of causal ambiguity has been further developed by Richard Reed and Robert DeFillippi, "Causal Ambiguity, Barriers to Imitation, and Sustainable Competitive Advantage," *Academy of Management Review* 15 (1990): 88–102.

Acquiring Resources and Capabilities

Having diagnosed the sources of an incumbent's competitive advantage, the imitator can mount a competitive challenge only by assembling the resources and capabilities necessary for imitation. As we saw in Chapter 5, a firm can acquire resources and capabilities in two ways: it can buy them or it can build them. The period over which a competitive advantage can be sustained depends critically on the time it takes to acquire and mobilize the resources and capabilities needed to mount a competitive challenge.

There is little to add here to the discussion of transferability and replicability in Chapter 5. The ability to buy resources and capabilities from outside factor markets depends on their transferability between firms. Even if resources are mobile, the market for a resource may be subject to transactions costs – costs of buying and selling arising from search costs, negotiation costs, contract enforcement costs, and transportation costs. Transactions costs are greater for highly differentiated (or "idiosyncratic") resources.[20]

The alternative to buying a resource or capability is to create it through internal investment. As we noted in Chapter 5, where capabilities are based on organizational routines, accumulating the coordination and learning required for their efficient operation can take considerable time. Even in the case of "turn-key" plants, developing the required operating capability can be a problem. Michael Polanyi observed:

> I have myself watched in Hungary a new imported machine for blowing electric lamp bulbs, the exact counterpart of which was operating successfully in Germany, failing for a whole year to produce a single flawless bulb.[21]

Businesses that require the integration of a number of complex, team-based routines may take years to reach the standards set by industry leaders. GM's attempt to transfer Toyota-style, team-based production from its NUMMI joint venture at Fremont, California, to the GM Van Nuys plant 400 miles to the south involved complex problems of learning and adjustment that remained unsolved two years after the program had begun.[22]

Conversely, where a competitive advantage does not require the application of complex, firm-specific resources, imitation is likely to be easy and fast. In financial services, many new products such as money market checking accounts, brokerage accounts with checking services, stripped bonds, interest rate swaps, and various financial derivatives typically require resources and capabilities that are widely distributed among banks. Hence, imitation of financial innovations is swift. The rapid decline of Filofax, the British manufacturer (and originator) of personal organizers, similarly reflected the ease of replicating the product.[23]

---

[20] See O. E. Williamson, "Transaction Cost Economics: The Governance of Contractual Relations," *Journal of Law and Economics* 19 (1979): 153–6.

[21] M. Polanyi, *Personal Knowledge: Toward a Post-Critical Philosophy*, 2nd edn (Chicago: University of Chicago Press, 1962): 52.

[22] C. Brown and M. Reich, "When Does Union–Management Cooperation Work? A Look at NUMMI and GM-Van Nuys," *California Management Review* 31 (Summer 1989): 26–44.

[23] "Faded Fad," *Economist* (September 30, 1989): 68.

First-mover Advantage

A firm's ability to acquire the resources and capabilities needed to challenge an incumbent firm depends on the extent and the sources of first-mover advantage in the market. The idea of first-mover advantage is that the initial occupant of a strategic position or niche gains access to resources and capabilities that a follower cannot match. The simplest form of first-mover advantage is a patent or copyright. By establishing a patent or copyright, the first mover possesses a technology, product, or design from which a follower is legally excluded. Early occupancy of a strategic niche can offer other resource advantages. The ability of advantaged firms to acquire superior resources and capabilities confirms the adage that "success breeds success."

- Where the resources required for competing are scarce, e.g., store locations in a new shopping mall or highly specialized employees, first movers can simply preempt these scarce resources.

- Initial competitive advantage offers a profit flow that permits the firm to invest in extending and upgrading its resource base. Pilkington's revolutionary float glass process – the manufacture of flat glass by floating molten glass on a bath of molten tin – was a competitive advantage whose life was limited to the term of the patent. However, the company used its profits and income from patent licenses to invest heavily in new plants, expand multinationally by acquiring overseas competitors, and finance R&D into fiber-optics and other new uses of glass.

- The first mover in a market establishes a reputation with suppliers, distributors, and customers that cannot be initially matched by the follower.

- Where proprietary standards in relation to product design and technology are important to competitive advantage, the first mover may have an advantage in setting the standard.

- Economies of learning suggest that the first mover can build a cost advantage over followers as a result of greater experience.[24]

We shall return to the issue of first-mover versus follower advantages when we consider compeititve advantage in emerging and technology-based industries (Chapter 11).

COMPETITIVE ADVANTAGE IN DIFFERENT MARKET SETTINGS

We have seen that profiting from competitive advantage requires that the firm first establish a competitive advantage, and then sustain its advantage for long enough to

[24] For an analysis of first-mover advantage, see Marvin Lieberman and David Montgomery, "First-Mover Advantages," *Strategic Management Journal* 9 (1988): 41–58; and Marvin Lieberman and David Montgomery, "First-Mover (Dis)Advantages: Retrospective and Link with the Resource-based View," *Strategic Management Journal* 19 (1998): 1111–25.

FIGURE 7.3 Competitive advantage in different industry settings: trading and production

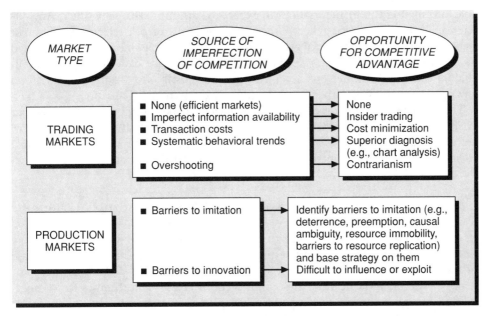

reap its rewards. To identify opportunities for establishing and sustaining competitive advantage in a business requires understanding the characteristics of the competitive process in that specific market. For competitive advantage to exist, there must be some imperfection of competition. To identify and understand these imperfections in the competitive process, we need to recognize the types of resources and capabilities necessary to compete and the circumstances of their availability.

Our initial discussion of the nature of business in Chapter 1 identified two types of value-creating activity: trading and production. Trading involves arbitrage across space (trade) and time (speculation). Production involves the physical transformation of inputs into outputs. These different types of business activity correspond to different market types: trading markets and production markets (see Figure 7.3). We begin with a discussion of a special type of trading market: an efficient market.

Efficient Markets: The Absence of Competitive Advantage

In Chapter 3, we introduced the concept of perfect competition. Perfect competition exists where there are many buyers and sellers, no product differentiation, no barriers to entry or exit, and free flow of information. In equilibrium, all firms earn the competitive rate of profit, which equals the cost of capital. The closest real-world examples of perfect competition are financial and commodity markets (for example, the markets for securities, foreign exchange, and grain futures). Electronic markets such as those that have proliferated on the internet – Covisint's online market for auto components – also approximate the conditions of perfect competition.[25] These markets are sometimes described as *efficient*. An *efficient market* is one in which prices reflect all available information. Because prices adjust instantaneously to newly available information, no market trader can expect to earn more than any other. Any differences in *ex post* returns reflect either different levels of risk selected by different traders or purely random factors (luck). Because all available information is reflected in current prices, no trading rules based on historical price data or any other available information can offer excess returns: it is not possible to "beat the market" on any consistent basis. In other words, competitive advantage is absent.

The absence of competitive advantage in efficient markets can be linked to resource availability. If financial markets are efficient, it is because only two types of resource are required to participate – finance and information. If both are equally available to all traders, there is no basis for one to gain competitive advantage over another.

Competition and Competitive Advantage in Trading Markets

In order for competitive advantage to exist, imperfections (or "inefficiencies") must be introduced into the competitive process. Focusing on the relatively simple case of trading markets, let us introduce different sources of imperfection to the competitive process, showing how these imperfections create opportunities for competitive advantage, and how the imperfections are closely related to the conditions of resource availability.

Imperfect Availability of Information

Financial markets (and most other trading markets) depart from the conditions for efficiency because of imperfect availability of information. Competitive advantage, therefore, is dependent on superior access to information. The most likely source of superior information is privileged access to private information. Trading on the basis of such information normally falls within the restrictions on "insider trading." Though insider information creates advantage, such competitive advantage tends to be of short duration. Once a market participant begins acting on the basis of insider information, other operators are alerted to the existence of the information. Even though they may not know its content, they are able to imitate the behavior of the market leader. A commonly followed strategy in stock markets is to detect and follow insider transactions by senior company executives.

Transaction Costs

If markets are efficient except for the presence of transactions costs, then competitive advantage accrues to the traders with the lowest transaction costs. In stock markets, low transactions costs are also attainable by traders who economize on research and market analysis and minimize the transactions required to attain their

---

[25]   Smith, Bailey and Brynjolfsson, op. cit.: 99–136.

portfolio objectives. Studies of mutual fund performance show that "Net of all management fees, the average managed investment fund performed worse than a completely unmanaged buy-and-hold strategy on a risk-adjusted basis. Further, the amount by that the funds fell short of the unmanaged strategy was, on average, about the same as the management cost of the funds."[26] The observation that competitive advantage is attained through minimizing transactions costs is further supported by evidence that, over the long term, market index funds outperform managed funds. During 1996–98, the S&P 500 index beat 75 percent of US fund managers. During the first half of 1997 the figure was 95 percent.

Systematic Behavioral Trends

If the current prices in a market fully reflect all available information, then price movements are caused by the arrival of new information and follow a random walk.[27] If, however, other factors influence price movements, there is scope for a strategy that uses an understanding of how prices really do move. Some stock market anomalies are well documented, notably the "small firm effect," the "January effect," and "weekend effects."[28] More generally, there is evidence that prices in financial markets follow systematic patterns that are the result of "market psychology," the trends and turning points of which can be established from past data. Chart analysis uses hypotheses concerning the relationship between past and future price movements for forecasting. Standard chartist tools include Elliott wave theory, Gann theories, momentum indicators, and patterns such as "support and resistance levels," "head and shoulders," "double tops," "flags," and "candlesticks." There is some evidence that chart analysis outperforms other forecasting techniques.[29] Hence, in markets where systematic behavioral trends occur, competitive advantage is gained by traders with superior skill in diagnosing such behavior.

Overshooting

Inefficiencies can also arise in trading markets due to the propensity of market participants to overreact to new information, with the result that prices overshoot.[30] Such overreaction is typically the result of imitative behavior resulting in the creation of bandwagon effects. On the assumption that overshooting is temporary and is eventually offset by an opposite movement back to equilibrium, then advantage can be

---

[26]   Frank J. Finn, "Evaluation of the Internal Processes of Managed Investment Funds," *Contemporary Studies in Economic and Financial Analysis, vol. 44* (Greenwich, CT: JAI Press, 1984): 6; "Index Investing: The Joys of Flying on Autopilot," *Business Week* (June 16, 1997): 128–31.

[27]   Eugene F. Fama, "Efficient Capital Markets: A Review of Theory and Empirical Work," *Journal of Business* 35 (1970): 383–417.

[28]   Simon Keane, "The Efficient Market Hypothesis on Trial," *Financial Analysts Journal* (March–April 1986): 58–63.

[29]   H. Allen and M. Taylor, "Charts, Noise, and Fundamentals in the London Foreign Exchange Market," *Economic Journal*, conference supplement, 100 (1990): 49–59.

[30]   For empirical evidence, see Werner De Bondt and Richard Thaler, "Does the Stock Market Overreact?," *Journal of Finance* 42 (1985): 793–805.

gained through a contrarian strategy: acting in the opposite direction to market swings. Warren Buffett, the billionaire chairman of Berkshire Hathaway, is a declared contrarian: "The best time to buy assets may be when it is hardest to raise money," he notes. Prince Alwaleed bin Talal bin Abdulaziz Alsaud also goes against the market tides in acquiring major interests in depressed businesses such as Canary Wharf, EuroDisney, and Apple Computer.[31]

Competition and Competitive Advantage in Production Markets

The transitory nature of competitive advantage in trading markets is a result of the characteristics of the resources required to compete: finance and information. Finance is a relatively homogeneous resource that is widely available. Information, although highly differentiated, is transferable easily and at very low cost; hence, the competitive advantage it offers tends to be fleeting.

Production markets are quite different. Production activities require complex combinations of resources and capabilities, and these resources and capabilities are highly differentiated. The result, as we have noted, is that each producer possesses a unique combination of resources and capabilities. The greater the heterogeneity of firms' endowments of resources and capabilities, the greater the potential for competitive advantage. Thus, as the players in the US steel industry became increasingly diverse during the period from 1970 to 1996, with new companies entering (Nucor, Chaparral, Birmingham Steel, and North Star) and existing companies restructuring, profit differentials widened between innovative minimills (such as Nucor and Chaparral) and the lumbering giants (such as USX and Bethlehem).[32]

Differences in resource endowments among firms also have an important impact on the process by which competitive advantage is eroded. Where firms possess very similar bundles of resources and capabilities, imitation of the competitive advantage of the encumbent firm is most likely. Where resource bundles are highly differentiated, competition is likely to be less direct. Using different resources and capability, a firm may sustitute a rival's competitive advantage.[33] For example:

- A company may use a well-developed strategic planning system to substitute for the charismatic leadership of its leading comeptitor.[34]

- Canon substituted for Xerox's technical service capability in copiers by developing high-reliability copiers that needed little service.[35]

[31] "Arabian Knight," *Business Week* (April 21, 1997): 50–2.
[32] "Why Steel Is Looking Sexy," *Business Week* (April 4, 1994): 106–8.
[33] Jay Barney, "Firm Resources and Sustained Competitive Advantage," *Journal of Management* 17 (1991): 99–120.
[34] Jay Barney, "Integrating Organizational Behavior and Strategy Formulation: A Resource-based Analysis," in P. Shrivastava, A. Huff, and J. Dutton (eds), *Advances in Strategic Management Vol. 9* (Greenwich, CT: JAI Press, 1992): 39–62.
[35] S. K. McEvily, S. Das, and K. McCabe, "Avoiding Competence Substitution Through Knowledge Sharing," *Academy of Management Review* 25 (2000): 294–311.

■ Online discount brokers have used the internet to substitute for networks of retail offices of established brokerage companies such as Merrill Lynch and Charles Schwab, and online research to substitute for the established brokers' research departments. The effectiveness of this substitute competition is indicated by the fact that all the main established brokers have set up online stock trading services.[36]

Since substitute competition can come from many directions – alternative resources, technological innovations, new business models – it is difficult to counter. The key, according to McEvily et al., is to pursuade potential competitors that substitution is unlikely to be profitable. This can be achieved through committing the firm to continuous improvement, locking in custmers and suppliers, and market deterrence.[37]

The potential for creating and sustaining advantage in production markets depends not only on inter-firm differences in resources, but also on the characteristics of the industry. Thus, building on our analysis of the processes through which competitive advantage emerges and is eroded, it is possible to identify various aspects of industry structure that may assist or constrain these forces.

Industry Conditions Conducive to Emergence of Competitive Advantage

Opportunities for competitive advantage through responding to external change depend on the extent and sources of change in the business environment. Industries subject to a wide range of unpredictable external changes, such as the telecommunications industry, which is subject to rapid regulatory and technological change, are likely to offer a multiplicity of opportunities for creating competitive advantage (even though these opportunities may not support sustainable advantages).

Competitive advantage also emerges through strategic innovation. The more complex an industry in terms of multidimensionality of customer choice criteria and the number of value chain activities, the greater the potential for creating "new game" strategies: the residential homebuilding industry, for example, offers greater scope for strategic innovation than the cement industry.

Industry Conditions Conducive to Sustaining Competitive Advantage

Early on we identified a number of barriers to the erosion of competitive advantage through imitation. Each is likely to depend on characteristics of the industry:

■ *Imperfection of information.* If the erosion of competitive advantage through imitation first requires potential imitators to identify those rivals in possession of competitive advantage and then to diagnose the basis of their advantage, then the greater the imperfection of information in an industry, the more difficult such identification and diagnosis. Therefore, in industries where competitive

---

[36] Pankaj Ghemawat, *Strategy and the Business Landscape* (Reading MA: Addison Wesley, 1999): 90–3.
[37] McEvily, Das, and McCabe, op. cit.

advantage is based on complex, multilayered capabilities, it may be difficult for poorly performing firms to comprehend the success of their better-performing rivals. Thus, in movie production, the long-established leadership of studios such as Paramount, Columbia, Universal, Fox, and Disney may reflect the difficult-to-diagnose secrets of producing "blockbuster" movies, even though the individual resources (scripts, actors, technicians, and directors) can be hired from the market.

- *Opportunities for deterrence and preemption.* Industries where valuable first-mover advantages exist because either the market is small (relative to the minimum efficient scale of production), essential resources are scarce or tightly held, industry standards can be set, or economies of learning are important, are likely to be those where competitive advantages are not easily eroded.

- *Difficulties of resource acquisition.* Finally, industries differ according to their ability to acquire the most strategically important resources. In the bicycle messenger business in London or New York, competitive advantage is easily eroded because the key resources (cyclists, wireless communication, and marketing) are easily acquired. The securities underwriting business (whether for IPOs or corporate bond issues) offers more sustainable advantages because the key resources and capabilities (market expertise, reputation, relationships, retail distribution links, and massive financial reserves) tend to be difficult to assemble. The difficulties of assembling the resources and capabilities needed to challenge the advantages of incumbents increases to the extent that initial resource advantages are cumulative. The ability of successful companies such as Microsoft, Sony, and Procter & Gamble to attract the most talented new graduates is such an advantage.

TYPES OF COMPETITIVE ADVANTAGE

A firm can achieve a higher rate of profit (or potential profit) over a rival in one of two ways: either it can supply an identical product or service at a lower cost, or it can supply a product or service that is differentiated in such a way that the customer is willing to pay a price premium that exceeds the additional cost of the differentiation. In the former case, the firm possesses a cost advantage; in the latter, a differentiation advantage. In pursuing cost advantage, the goal of the firm is to become the cost leader in its industry or industry segment. Cost leadership is a unique position in the industry that requires that the firm "must find and exploit all sources of cost advantage . . . [and] . . . sell a standard, no-frills product."[38] Differentiation by a firm from its competitors is achieved "when it provides something unique that is valuable to buyers beyond simply offering a low price."[39] Figure 7.4 illustrates these two types of advantage.

---

[38] Michael E. Porter, *Competitive Advantage* (New York: Free Press, 1985): 13.
[39] Ibid.: 120.

FIGURE 7.4 Sources of competitive advantage

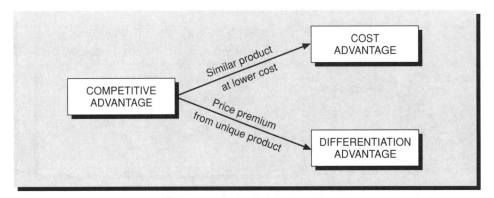

TABLE 7.2 Features of Cost Leadership and Differentiation Strategies

GENERIC STRATEGY	KEY STRATEGY ELEMENTS	RESOURCE AND ORGANIZATIONAL REQUIREMENTS
Cost leadership	Scale-efficient plants Design for manufacture Control of overheads and R&D Avoidance of marginal customer accounts	Access to capital Process engineering skills Frequent reports Tight cost control Specialization of jobs and functions Incentives for quantitative targets
Differentiation	Emphasis on branding advertising, design, service, and quality	Marketing abilities Product engineering skills Strong cross-functional coordination Creativity Research capability Qualitative performance targets and incentives

The two sources of competitive advantage define two fundamentally different approaches to business strategy. A firm that is competing on low cost is distinguishable from a firm that competes through differentiation in terms of market positioning, resource and capabilities, and organizational characteristics. Table 7.2 outlines some of the principal features of cost and differentiation strategies.

By combining the two types of competitive advantage with the firm's choice of scope – broad market versus narrow segment – Michael Porter has defined three generic strategies: cost leadership, differentiation, and focus (see Figure 7.5). Porter views cost leadership and differentiation as mutually exclusive strategies. A firm that attempts to pursue both is "stuck in the middle":

> The firm stuck in the middle is almost guaranteed low profitability. It either loses the high volume customers who demand low prices or must bid away its profits to get this business from the low-cost firms. Yet it also loses high-margin business – the

FIGURE 7.5 Porter's generic strategies

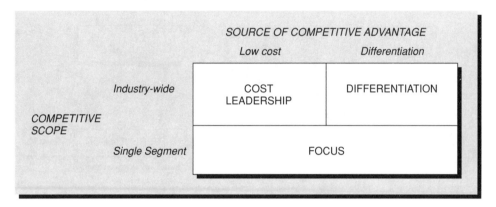

cream – to the firms who are focused on high-margin targets or have achieved differentiation overall. The firm that is stuck in the middle also probably suffers from a blurred
corporate culture and a conflicting set of organizational arrangements and motivation
system.[40]

In practice, few firms are faced with such stark alternatives. Differentiation is not
simply an issue of "to differentiate or not to differentiate." All firms must make decisions as to which customer requirements to focus on, and where to position their
product or service in the market. A cost leadership strategy typically implies a narrow-
line, limited-feature, standardized offering. However, such a positioning does not
necessarily imply that the product or service is an undifferentiated commodity. In the
case of IKEA furniture and McDonald's hamburgers, a low-price, no-frills offering
is also associated with clear market positioning and a unique brand image. The VW
Beetle is evidence that a low-cost, utilitarian, mass-market product may achieve a
highly differentiated market status. At the same time, firms that pursue differentiation
strategies cannot be oblivious to cost.

In most industries, market leadership is held by a firm that maximizes customer
appeal by reconciling effective differentiation with low cost. In many industries, the
cost leader is a smaller company that minimizes overhead and operates with cheaply
acquired assets. In US oil refining, the cost leader is not Exxon-Mobil or Shell, it is
Tosco. In automobiles, the ill-fated Daewoo and Kia rather than Ford or Toyota
achieved the lowest unit costs. In auto rental, the cost leader is more likely to be
Rent-A-Wreck Rent-A-Car (a division of Bundy American Corporation) rather than
Hertz or Avis. What characterizes market leadership in most of these, and other,
industries is the ability to reconcile relatively low cost with a level of quality and
brand awareness to create an attractive value-for-money package that effectively
differentiates the company from the no-frills cost leaders that dominate the bottom
of the market.

---

[40] Michael E. Porter, *Competitive Strategy* (New York: Free Press, 1980): 42.

Reconciling differentiation with low cost has been one of the greatest strategic challenges of the 1990s. Common to the success of Japanese companies in consumer goods industries such as cars, motorcycles, consumer electronics, and musical instruments has been the ability to reconcile low costs with high quality and technological progressiveness. The total quality management methods that they adopted exploded the myth that there is a tradeoff between high quality and low cost. Numerous studies show that innovations in manufacturing technology and manufacturing management result in simultaneous increases in productivity and quality.[41] Achieving higher quality in terms of fewer defects and greater product reliability frequently involves simpler product design, fewer component suppliers that are more closely monitored, and fewer service calls and product recalls – all of which save cost. Tom Peters observes an interesting asymmetry:

> Cost reduction campaigns do not often lead to improved quality; and, except for those that involve large reductions in personnel, they don't usually result in long-term lower costs either. On the other hand, effective quality programs yield not only improved quality but lasting cost reductions as well.[42]

Having conquered the cost/quality tradeoff, companies such as Honda, Toyota, Sony, and Canon have gone on to reconcile world-beating manufacturing efficiency and outstanding quality with flexibility, fast-paced innovation, and effective marketing.

Differentiation and cost reduction are linked in other ways. High levels of advertising and promotional expenditure can increase market share, which then permits the exploitation of scale economies across a wide range of functions. Moreover, the existence of scale economies in advertising and other differentiation activities means that a market share leader can improve its relative cost position by forcing rivals to compete on product differentiation. The heavy advertising campaign with which Apple launched its Macintosh computer in 1984 was partly motivated by the desire to "up the stakes" for smaller manufacturers of personal computers that did not possess the sales base to justify large-scale advertising. Accenture's heavy emphasis on media advertising represents a similar strategy in management and IT consulting. In the motorcycle industry, Honda's product strategy of annual model changes increased the pressure on manufacturers who lacked the sales volume to justify such heavy fixed costs of new models.[43]

In the next two chapters, I shall develop and operationalize these concepts of cost and differentiation advantage by showing how to diagnose the sources of cost and differentiation advantage and formulate strategies to exploit them.

---

[41] See, for example, Jack R. Meredith, "Strategic Advantages of the Factory of the Future," *California Management Review* (Winter 1989): 129–45.

[42] Tom Peters, *Thriving on Chaos* (New York: Knopf, 1987): 80.

[43] The potential for differentiation to assist the attainment of cost leadership is analyzed by Charles Hill, "Differentiation versus Low Cost: A Contingency Framework," *Academy of Management Review* 13 (1988): 401–12.

SUMMARY

Making money in business requires establishing and sustaining competitive advantage. Both these conditions for profitability demand profound insight into the nature and process of competition within a market. Competitive advantage depends critically on the presence of some imperfection in the competitive process – under perfect competition, profits are transitory. Our analysis of the imperfections of the competitive process has drawn us back to the resources and capabilities that are required to compete in different markets and to pursue different strategies. Sustaining competitive advantage depends on the existence of isolating mechanisms: barriers to rivals' imitation of successful strategies. The greater the difficulty that rivals face in accessing the resources and capabilities needed to imitate or substitute the competitive advantage of the incumbent firm, the greater the sustainability of that firm's competitive advantage. Hence, one outcome of our analysis is to reinforce the argument made in Chapter 5: the characteristics of a firm's resources and capability are fundamental to its strategy and its performance in decision making and long-term success.

In the next two chapters, we analyze the two primary dimensions of competitive advantage: cost advantage and differentiation advantage. In both of these areas we emphasize the importance of a deep understanding of both the firm and its industry environment. To this end, it is useful to disaggregate the firm into a series of separate but interlinked activities. A useful and versatile framework for this purpose is the value chain, which is an insightful tool for understanding the sources of competitive advantage in an industry, for assessing the competitive position of a particular firm, and for suggesting opportunities to enhance a firm's competitiveness.

8
Cost Advantage

SEARS MOTOR BUGGY: $395

For car complete with rubber tires, Timken roller bearing axles, top, storm front, three oil-burning lamps, horn, and one gallon of lubricating oil. Nothing to buy but gasoline.

. . . We found there was a maker of automobile frames that was making 75 percent of all the frames used in automobile construction in the United States. We found on account of the volume of business that this concern could make frames cheaper for automobile manufacturers than the manufacturers could make them themselves. We went to this frame maker and asked him to make frames for the Sears Motor Buggy and then to name us prices for those frames in large quantities. And so on throughout the whole construction of the Sears Motor Buggy. You will find every piece and every part has been given the most careful study; you will find that the Sears Motor Buggy is made of the best possible material; it is constructed to take the place of the top buggy; it is built in our own factory, under the direct supervision of our own expert, a man who has had fifteen years of automobile experience, a man who has for the past three years worked with us to develop exactly the right car for the people at a price within the reach of all.

—Extract from an advertisement in the Sears Roebuck & Co. catalog, 1909: 1150

OUTLINE

INTRODUCTION AND OBJECTIVES

Historically, business strategy analysis has emphasized cost advantage as the primary basis for competitive advantage in an industry. This focus on cost advantage reflects the traditional emphasis by economists on price as the principal medium of competition – competing on price depends on cost efficiency. It also reflects the strategy preoccupations of large industrial corporations. For much of the twentieth century, the strategies of large corporations were driven by the quest for economies of scale and scope through investment in mass production and mass distribution. During the 1980s and 1990s, cost efficiency remained a priority, but the focus shifted toward cost cutting through restructuring, downsizing, outsourcing, "lean production," and the quest for dynamic rather than static sources of cost efficiency. However, the current merger wave in banking, automobiles, petroleum, brewing, and many other global industries appears to be driven by a renewed quest for conventional scale economies.

For some industries, cost advantage is the predominant basis for competitive advantage: for commodity goods and services there are few opportunities for competing on dimensions other than cost. But even where competition focuses on product differentiation, intensifying competition has resulted in cost efficiency becoming a prerequisite for profitability. Some of the most dramatic examples of companies and industries being transformed through the pursuit of cost efficiency are in sectors where competition has increased sharply due to deregulation, such as airlines, telecommunications, banking, and electrical power generation.

By the time you have completed this chapter, you will be able to:

■ Identify the determinants of relative cost within the industry or activity ("cost drivers").

■ Assess a firm's cost position relative to its competitors and identify the factors responsible for cost differentials.

■ Recommend cost-reduction measures.

The analysis in this chapter is oriented around these objectives. In pursuing these objectives, we shall examine techniques for:

- Identifying the basic sources of cost advantage in an industry.

- Appraising the cost position of a firm within its industry by disaggregating the firm into its separate activities.

- Using the analysis of costs and relative cost position as a basis for recommending strategies for enhancing cost competitiveness.

ECONOMIES OF EXPERIENCE

The study of cost advantage holds a special place in the development of strategy analysis. Interest in economies derived from accumulated experience exerted a powerful influence on thinking about competitive advantage and the benefits of market share throughout the 1970s and 1980s. The development and popularization of the experience curve as a tool of strategy analysis can be attributed mainly to the Boston Consulting Group (BCG), whose *Perspectives in Experience* was published in 1968. The experience curve became one of the best-known and most influential concepts in the history of strategic management.

The Experience Curve

The experience curve has its basis in the systematic reduction in the time taken to build airplanes and Liberty ships observed during World War II.[1] The concept of economies of learning was generalized by BCG to encompass not just direct labor hours, but the behavior of all added costs with cumulative production. In a series of studies, ranging from bottle caps and refrigerators to long-distance calls and insurance policies, BCG observed a remarkable regularity in the reductions in costs (and prices) that accompanied increased production. Doubling of cumulative production typically reduced unit costs by 20 to 30 percent. BCG summarized its observations in its "Law of Experience":

> The unit cost of value added to a standard product declines by a constant percentage (typically between 20 and 30 percent) each time cumulative output doubles.

"Unit cost of value added" is total cost per unit of production less the cost per unit of production of bought-in components and materials. If suppliers of components and materials are subject to similar cost reductions as volume increases, then "unit cost" may be substituted for "unit cost of value added" in the definition.

---

[1] Louis E. Yelle, "The Learning Curve: Historical Review and Comprehensive Survey," *Decision Sciences* 10 (1979): 302–28.

FIGURE 8.1   The experience curve

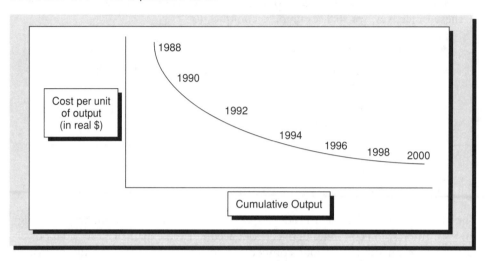

Figure 8.1 shows a typical experience curve. In logarithmic form, the curve becomes a straight line. The size of the experience effect is measured by the proportion by which costs are reduced with subsequent doublings of aggregate production. The relationship between unit cost and production volume may be expressed as follows:

$$C_n = C_1 \cdot n^{-a}$$

where C_1 is the cost of the first unit of production
C_n is the cost of the nth unit of production
n is the cumulative volume of production
a is the elasticity of cost with regard to output.

Experience curves may be drawn for either an industry or a single firm, and may use either cost or price data. An industry-level experience curve can be constructed by plotting producer price indices against industry output data. Using prices rather than costs assumes that margins are constant. Figure 8.2 shows examples of experience curves estimated by the Boston Consulting Group.

Strategy Implications: The Role of Market Share

The significance of the experience curve lies in its implications for business strategy. If costs decline systematically with increases in cumulative output, then a firm's costs relative to its competitors depend on its cumulative output relative to that of competitors. If a firm can expand its output at a greater rate than its competitors, it is then able to move down the experience curve more rapidly than its rivals and can open up a widening cost differential. The implication drawn by BCG was that a firm's

FIGURE 8.2   Examples of experience curves

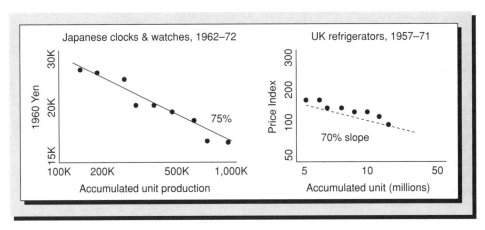

primary strategic goal should be market share. A firm's increase in cumulative output compared to a competitor's depends on their relative market shares. If Boeing holds 60 percent of the world market for large commercial jet aircraft and Airbus holds 40 percent, Boeing will reduce its costs at one-and-a-half times the rate of Airbus (other factors being equal).[2]

The quest for economies of experience also has important implications for pricing policy.[3] The firm should price its products not on the basis of current costs, but on the basis of anticipated costs.[4] In its study of the British motorcycle industry, BCG observed that British motorcycle manufacturers adopted cost-plus pricing, whereas Honda priced to meet market share objectives. Honda's assumption was that once sufficient sales volume had been achieved, costs would fall to a level that offered a satisfactory profit margin.[5] The quest for experience-based economies also points to the advantages of maximizing volume by offering a broad rather than a narrow product range and expanding internationally rather than restricting sales to the domestic market.

Empirical studies confirm the positive relationship between profitability and market share.[6] As Table 8.1 shows, the positive relationship between profit margin and market share is directly the result of greater productivity: market share leaders tend to

---

[2] A rigorous analysis of the profit gains to market share leadership under differently sloped experience curves and different competitive conditions is developed by David Ross, "Learning to Dominate," *Journal of Industrial Economics* 34 (1986): 337–53.

[3] For a discussion of the policy implications of the experience curve, see Charles Baden Fuller, "The Implications of the Learning Curve for Firm Strategy and Public Policy," *Applied Economics* 15 (1983): 541–51.

[4] This is sometimes referred to as "penetration" pricing, as opposed to "full-cost" pricing, or "skimming."

[5] Boston Consulting Group, *Strategy Alternatives for the British Motorcycle Industry* (London: Her Majesty's Stationery Office, 1975).

[6] Robert D. Buzzell, Bradley T. Gale, and Ralph Sultan, "Market Share – A Key to Profitability," *Harvard Business Review* (January–February 1975); Robert D. Buzzell and Fredrick Wiersema, "Successful Share-Building Strategies," *Harvard Business Review* (January–February 1981); Robert Jacobsen and David Aaker, "Is Market Share All That It's Cracked up to Be?," *Journal of Marketing* 49 (Fall 1985): 11–22.

TABLE 8.1 The Relationship Between Market Share, Costs, and Profitability

MARKET SHARE RANK

	#1	#2	#3	#4	#5 OR BELOW
Investment/Sales	6.3	52.1	52.5	51.4	54.9
Receivables/Sales	14.7	14.7	14.7	14.8	15.3
Inventory/Sales	18.5	19.6	20.5	20.6	22.3
Purchases/Sales	41.8	43.4	45.8	48.8	51.3
Marketing/Sales	8.9	9.5	9.5	9.3	9.2
R&D/Sales	2.1	2.3	1.9	1.8	1.9
Relative Quality (%)	69.0	51.0	47.0	45.0	43.0
Relative Price (%)	105.7	103.8	103.4	103.2	103.0
Pretax Profit/Sales	12.7	9.1	7.1	5.5	4.5

Source: R. D. Buzzell and B. T. Gale, *The PIMS Principles* (New York: Free Press, 1987): 75.

have lower rates of investment, receivables, purchases, marketing expenses, and R&D to sales. However, there are difficulties in interpreting the relationship and doubts about the wisdom of pursuing market share as a strategic goal.

- *Association is not the same as causation.* Does market share confer superior profit, or do profitable firms use their earnings to build market share? The most plausible explanation is that profitability and market share are consequences of some common underlying factor. For example, superior efficiency or innovation results in both high profits and high market share.[7]

- *The unprofitability of pursuing market share.* Even if firms with high market shares have cost advantages resulting in superior profitability, this does not necessarily imply that investments in increasing a firm's market share will increase profitability. If the relationship between market share and profitability is widely known and if all firms have the opportunity of competing for market share, then the competition for market share will erode any superior profitability resulting from increased market share.[8]

- *The fallacy of composition.* Pursuing experience economies through pricing for market share may be successful for the individual firm; it can be fatal when attempted by several competitors. During the 1970s, US and European producers of steel, petrochemicals, ships, and synthetic fibers followed the lead of their Japanese competitors by investing heavily in large-scale efficient plants while cutting margins in anticipation of lower costs. Overinvestment and aggressive pricing resulted in losses that continued for a decade or more.

---

[7] Richard Rumelt and Robin Wensley, using PIMS data, found the relationship between market share and profitability to be the result of both being joint outcomes of a risky competitive process. "In Search of the Market Share Effect," Paper MGL-63 (Graduate School of Management, UCLA, 1981).

[8] Robin Wensley, "PIMS and BCG: New Horizons or False Dawn?," *Strategic Management Journal* 3 (1982): 147–58.

FIGURE 8.3   The drivers of cost advantage

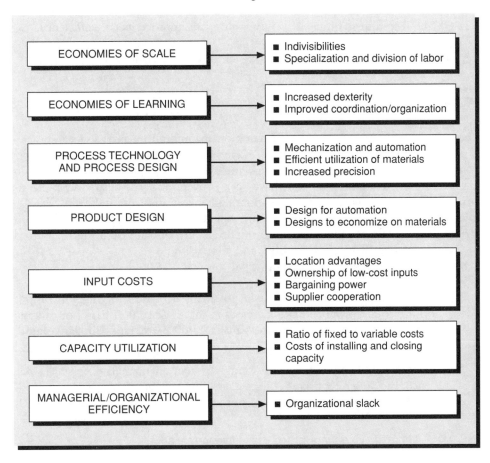

THE SOURCES OF COST ADVANTAGE

The key to cost analysis is to go beyond mechanistic and purely empirical approaches such as the experience curve and probe into the factors that determine a firm's cost position. The experience curve combines four sources of cost reduction: economies of scale, economies of learning, improved process technology and process design, and improved product design. To these we can add three more factors that influence a firm's relative cost position: capacity utilization, the cost of inputs, and residual efficiency. The determinants of a firm's unit costs (cost per unit of output) we term cost drivers (see Figure 8.3).

The relative importance of these different cost drivers varies across industries, across firms within an industry, and across the different activities within a firm. By identifying these different cost drivers, we can do the following:

- Diagnose a firm's cost position in terms of understanding why its unit costs diverge from those of its competitors.

- Make recommendations as to how a firm can improve its cost efficiency.

Let's examine the nature and the role of each of these cost drivers.

Economies of Scale

The predominance of large corporations in most manufacturing and service industries is a consequence of economies of scale. Economies of scale exist wherever proportionate increases in the amounts of inputs employed in a production process result in lower unit costs. Economies of scale have been conventionally associated with manufacturing. Figure 8.4 shows a typical relationship between unit cost and plant capacity. The point at which most scale economies are exploited is the Minimum Efficiency Plant Size (MEPS). Scale economies are also important in nonmanufacturing operations such as purchasing, R&D, distribution, and advertising.

Scale economies arise from three principal sources:

1. *Technical input–output relationships.* In many activities, increases in output do not require proportionate increases in input. A 10,000-barrel oil storage tank does not cost five times the cost of a 2,000-barrel tank. Similar volume-related economies exist in ships, trucks, and steel and petrochemical plants.

2. *Indivisibilities.* Many resources are "lumpy" – they are unavailable in small sizes. Hence, they offer economies of scale, as firms are able to spread the costs of these items over larger volumes of output. Units of capital equipment (such

FIGURE 8.4 The long-run average cost curve for a plant

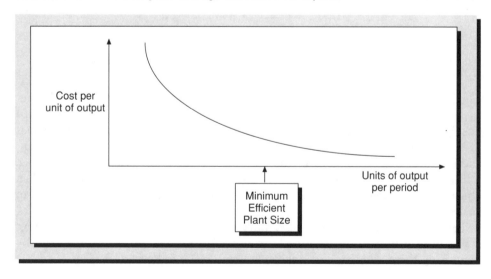

as a body press in an auto plant or a catalytic cracker in an oil refinery), research facilities, advertising campaigns, and distribution systems are available only above a certain minimum size.

3. *Specialization.* Expanding the number of inputs permits greater task specialization. *Division of labor* is particularly important in this respect. Mass production, pioneered in automobiles by Henry Ford, involves breaking down the production process into a series of separate tasks to be performed by specialized workers using specialized equipment. Specialization of labor promotes learning, avoids time loss from switching activities, and assists in mechanization and automation. Similar economies are important in knowledge-intensive industries such as investment banking, management consulting, and design engineering, where specialization of labor allows large firms to combine depth of knowledge with breadth of knowledge.

Scale Economies and Industry Concentration

Scale economies are the single most important determinant of an industry's level of concentration (the proportion of industry output accounted for by the largest firms). However, the critical scale advantages of large companies are seldom in production. In packaged consumer goods – cigarettes, household detergents, beer, and soft drinks – the tendency for markets to be dominated by a few giant companies results from scale economies in marketing. Advertising is a key indivisibility. The cost of producing and airing a TV commercial nationally is a fixed cost whether the product has a 5 percent or 50 percent market share. The 90-second commercial produced in 1996 for British Airways by M&C Saatchi cost $1.6 million to produce and formed part of a $158 million two-year advertising campaign. Figure 8.5 shows the relationship between sales volume and average advertising costs for different brands of soft drinks.

FIGURE 8.5   Economies of scale in advertising: US soft drinks

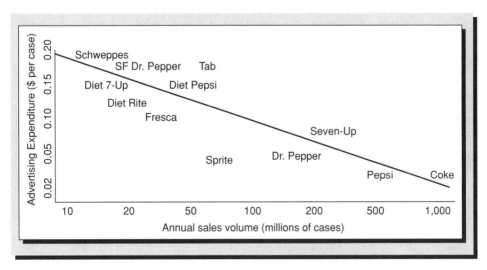

TABLE 8.2   The Development Cost (Including Plant and Tooling) of Models

Ford Escort (new model)	$2 billion
Ford Mondeo/Contour	$6 billion
GM Saturn	$5 billion
Chrysler Neon	$1.3 billion

Consolidation in the world car industry has been driven by the huge costs associated with new model development (see Table 8.2). Small and medium-sized auto companies have been acquired by larger rivals simply because they lacked the necessary volume over which to amortize the costs of developing new models. Thus, VW acquired Skoda, Seat, and Rolls-Royce, while Ford acquired Jaguar, Mazda, Land Rover, and Volvo. Remaining smaller auto producers typically license technology and designs from bigger auto companies.[9]

Costs of product development are also the driving force behind the concentration of large passenger aircraft production into just two companies: Boeing and Airbus. Boeing's cost leadership is based on its ability to amortize development costs over very long runs: over 1,000 747s were built between 1970 and 1998. Conversely, with only 16 planes built, the supersonic Concorde was a financial disaster for Aerospatiale and British Aerospace (and for their supporting governments).

The exploitation of scale economies has been a major force for globalization as companies seek to realize scale economies from consolidating activities and functions globally. During the 1980s and early 1990s, Xerox, Digital Equipment (now part of Compaq), and Coulter Electronic achieved substantial cost economies from globally consolidating product development, purchasing, production, demand management, and order fulfillment.[10]

The same sources of economies of scale drive competitive advantage in many sectors of the "new economy." A key feature of most digital products, including software such as internet browsers and video games, is that the initial development costs are very high but, once developed, they can be reproduced and distributed at negligible cost. Hence, in sectors such as computer software, browsers, search engines, and online auctions, profitability depends crucially on market dominance.

Limits to Scale Economies

The sizes of plants and firms are frequently much smaller than would be implied by the extent of scale economies. Reluctance fully to exploit economies of scale is explained by three reasons:

[9]   To be more precise, the economies of amortizing the costs of new product development are economies of volume rather than economies of scale. The product development cost per unit of production declines not on the volume of production per unit of time, but on the total volume of production over the life of the model.

[10]   M. E. McGrath and R. W. Hoole, "Manufacturing's New Economies of Scale," *Harvard Business Review* (May–June 1992): 94–102.

■ *Product differentiation.* Where customer preferences are differentiated, firms may find that the price premium of targeting a single segment with a differentiated product outweighs the higher cost of small-volume production. General Motors' rise to market leadership over Ford during the late 1920s is an example of a multimodel differentiation strategy triumphing over a single-model, scale-economy strategy.

■ *Flexibility.* Scale-efficient production is likely to involve highly specialized labor and equipment, which tends to be inflexible. In a dynamic environment, very large plants and firms have greater difficulties than smaller units in adjusting to fluctuations in demand and changes in technology, input prices, and customer preferences.[11]

■ *Problems of motivation and coordination.* Large units tend to be more complex and more difficult to manage than smaller units. Common to the some of the world's largest plants, from Crown Cork & Seal's original Philadelphia can and bottle cap plant[12] to VW's Wolfsburg Halle 54,[13] has been failure to reach maximum efficiency due to problems of strained labor relations, increased supervision costs, waste of materials, and low levels of employee motivation.

Economies of Learning

The principal source of experience-based cost reduction is learning by organization members. Repetition reduces costs by decreasing the time required for particular jobs, thus reducing waste and defects, and improving coordination between jobs.[14] For example, in 1943 it took 40,000 labor-hours to build a Convair B-24 bomber. By 1945 it took only 8,000 hours.[15] The more complex a process or product, the greater the potential for learning. Learning effects are important in complex products such as aircraft, process plant construction, and computer software. They are also important in complex processes. Japanese companies dominate the world market for active-matrix flat screens primarily because of unassailable cost leadership resulting from experience-based learning. The complexity of flat screen manufacture and the fact that a single chip defect may render an entire screen useless mean that yield rate is the key to cost advantage, and learning is the basis of high yields.[16] Learning occurs both at the individual level through improvements in dexterity and problem solving, and at the group level through the development and refinement of organizational routines.

[11] This argument was first made by David Schwartzman, "Uncertainty and the Size of the Firm," *Economica* (August 1963).
[12] Joe Bower, *Crown Cork & Seal and the Metal Container Industry*, Case 9-373-077 (Boston: Harvard Business School, 1984).
[13] Maryann Keller, *Collision* (New York: Doubleday, 1993): 173–7.
[14] Clair Brown and Michael Reich, "When Does Union–Management Cooperation Work? A Look at NUMMI and GM-Van Nuys," *California Management Review* (Summer 1989): 28–9.
[15] Leonard Rapping, "Learning and World War II Production Functions," *Review of Economics and Statistics* (February 1965): 81–6. See also Kim B. Clark and Robert H. Hayes, "Recapturing America's Manufacturing Heritage," *California Management Review* (Summer 1988): 25.
[16] "Road Toward Success at Flat Screens Is Full of Bumps," *Wall Street Journal* (April 20, 1994): B4.

Process Technology and Process Design

For most goods and services, alternative process technologies exist. A particular production method is technically superior to another when, for each unit of output, it uses less of one input without using more of any other input. Where a production method uses more of some inputs but less of others, then the relative cost efficiency of the alternative techniques depends on the relative prices of the inputs. Hence, low-cost assembly of consumer electronic products might be achieved in China using labor-intensive techniques, or in Singapore in a fully automated plant.

New process technology may radically reduce costs. Pilkington's float glass process gave it (and its licensees) an unassailable cost advantage in glass production. At the end of 1912, it took 106 hours to assemble a Ford Model T. A little over a year later, after Ford had introduced his moving-assembly line and interchangeable parts, the labor input had been cut to just over six hours. The automobile was transformed from a rich man's luxury to a form of mass transportation.

When process innovation is embodied in new capital equipment, diffusion is likely to be rapid. Those firms that are expanding the most rapidly and have the highest rates of net investment will tend to establish cost leadership over their slower-growing rivals. However, the full benefits of new processes typically require systemwide changes in job design, employee incentives, product design, organizational structure, and management controls.[17] Between 1979 and 1986, General Motors spent $40 billion on new technology and new plants with a view to becoming the world's most efficient volume manufacturer of automobiles. Yet, in the absence of fundamental changes in organization and management, the productivity gains were meager. Cadillac's state-of-the-art Hamtramck plant in Detroit was a nightmare of inefficiency, line stoppages, and robots run amok. After a tour of the plant, Toyota chairman Eiji Toyoda told a colleague, "It would have been embarrassing to comment on it."[18] By contrast, the superiority of Japanese companies in flexible manufacturing systems reflects the adaptation of their management processes to the requirements of the new technology.[19]

Indeed, the greatest productivity gains from process innovation typically are the result of organizational improvements rather than technological innovation and new hardware:

- Toyota's system of lean production combines JIT, TQM, quality circles, teamworking, job flexibility, and supplier partnerships. The principles of lean production have been extended by Dan Jones and James Womack in the philosophy and methodology of "lean thinking" in the "lean enterprise."[20]

---

[17] Robert H. Hayes and Ramchandran Jaikumar, "Manufacturing's Crisis: New Technologies, Obsolete Organizations," *Harvard Business Review* (September–October 1988): 85; and Robert M. Grant, A. B. Shani, R. Krishnan, and R. Baer, "Appropriate Manufacturing Technology: A Strategic Approach," *Sloan Management Review* 33, no. 1 (Fall 1991): 43–54.

[18] Maryann Keller, op. cit.: 169–71.

[19] Ramchandran Jaikumar, "Postindustrial Manufacturing," *Harvard Business Review* (November–December 1986): 69–76.

[20] James Womack and Dan T. Jones, *Lean Thinking* (New York: Simon & Schuster, 1996); James Womack and Dan T. Jones, "From Lean Production to Lean Enterprise," *Harvard Business Review* (March–April 1994); James Womack and Dan T. Jones, "Beyond Toyota: How to Root Out Waste and Pursue Perfection," *Harvard Business Review* (September–October 1996).

- Harley-Davidson's gains in productivity during the late 1980s and early 1990s resulted from reorganizing its production processes and management systems and philosophy, but with limited investment in automation and new manufacturing hardware.[21]

In service industries, cost advantage has been closely associated with the introduction of new systems of production that have resulted in standalone, "mom-and-pop" businesses being replaced by multi-unit corporations with standardized systems:

- In retailing, the chain store system, which originated with the Atlantic & Pacific Tea Company (later A&P) during the 1930s, has been developed by retail chains such as Wal-Mart in discount stores, The Gap in apparel, Circuit City in consumer electronics, and Home Depot in home improvement products.

- In fast-food restaurants, franchising and standardized operating systems, pioneered by McDonald's, have resulted in the sector becoming dominated by a few major corporations.

- In document and small-package delivery, Federal Express's system network of distribution centers served by its Nashville hub represented a huge leap in efficiency over traditional courier-delivery systems.

Business Process Reengineering

During the 1990s, recognition that the redesign of operational processes could achieve substantial efficiency gains stimulated a surge of interest in a new management tool called *business process reengineering* (BPR). "Reengineering gurus" Michael Hammer and James Champy defined BPR as:

> the fundamental rethinking and radical redesign of business processes to achieve dramatic improvements in critical contemporary measures of performance, such as cost, quality, service, and speed.[22]

The reengineering movement was based on the recognition that production processes involve complex interactions among many individuals and that these processes evolve over time with little conscious or consistent direction. Redesigning business processes in a logical way can fundamentally increase their efficiency. With information technology, the temptation is to automate existing processes – "paving over cowpaths," as Michael Hammer calls it.[23] The key is to detach from the way in which a process is currently organized and to begin with the question: "If we were starting afresh, how would we design this process?" Although lacking any general theory or design

---

[21]   Robert M. Grant, "Harley-Davidson in 1998," in R. M. Grant and K. E. Neupert (eds), *Cases for Contemporary Strategy Analysis*, 2nd edn (Oxford: Blackwell, 1996).

[22]   Michael Hammer and James Champy, *Reengineering the Corporation: A Manifesto for Business Revolution* (New York: HarperBusiness, 1993): 32. See also Michael Hammer, *Beyond Reengineering: How the Processed Centered Organization Is Changing our Work and our Lives* (New York: HarperBusiness, 1996).

[23]   Michael Hammer, "Reengineering Work: Don't Automate; Obliterate," *Harvard Business Review* (July–August 1990).

framework, Hammer and Champy point to the existence of a set of "commonalities, recurring themes, or characteristics" that can guide BPR. These include:

- Combining several jobs into one.

- Allowing workers to make decisions.

- Performing the steps of a process in a natural order.

- Recognizing that processes have multiple versions and designing processes to take account of different situations.

- Performing processes where it makes the most sense, e.g., if the accounting department needs pencils, it is probably cheaper for such a small order to be purchased directly from the office equipment store along the block than to be ordered via the firm's purchasing department.

- Reducing checks and controls to the point where they make economic sense.

- Minimizing reconciliation.

- Appointing a case manager to provide a single point of contact at the interface between processes.

- Reconciling centralization with decentralization in process design, e.g., via a shared database decentralized decisions can be made while permitting overall coordination simply through information sharing.

BPR has been attributed with achieving major gains in efficiency, quality, and speed (see Exhibit 8.1). At the same time, there has been widespread disappointment with the outcomes of reengineering initiatives. One of the major realizations to emerge from BPR exercises is that most production and administrative processes are exceedingly complex. To redesign a process one must first understand it. Process mapping exercises reveal that even seemingly simple business processes, such as the procurement of office supplies, involve complex and sophisticated systems of interactions among a number of organizational members. Reengineering without a complete understanding of the process is hazardous.

Product Design

Design-for-manufacture – designing products for ease of production rather than simply for functionality and aesthetics – can offer substantial cost savings, especially when linked to the introduction of new process technology.

- In automobiles, companies have sought to offset the rising cost of developing and introducing new models by means of designing their different models around a few common platforms.

- The IBM "Proprinter," one of the most successful computer printers of the 1980s, owed its low costs (and reliability) to an innovative design that:

EXHIBIT 8.1 Process Reengineering at IBM Credit

IBM Credit provides credit to customers of IBM for the purchase of IBM hardware and software. Under the old system, five stages were involved:

1. The IBM salesperson telephoned a request for financing. The request was logged on a piece of paper.

2. The request was sent to the Credit Department where it was logged onto a computer and the customer's creditworthiness was checked. The results of the credit check were written on a form and passed to the Business Practices Department.

3. There the standard loan covenant would be modified to meet the terms of customer loan.

4. The request was passed to the pricer who determined the appropriate interest rate.

5. The clerical group took all the information and prepared a quote letter, which was sent to the salesperson.

Because the process took an average of six days, it resulted in a number of lost sales and delayed the sales staff in finalizing deals. After many efforts to improve the process, two managers undertook an experiment. They took a financing request and walked it around through all five steps. The process took 90 minutes!

On this basis, a fundamental redesign of the credit approval process was achieved. The change was replacing the specialists (credit checkers, pricers, and so on) with generalists who undertook all five processes. Only where the request was nonstandard or unusually complex were specialists called in. The basic problem was that the system had been designed for the most complex credit requests that IBM received, whereas in the vast majority of cases no specialist judgment was called for – simply clerical work involving looking up credit ratings, plugging numbers into standard formulae, etc.

The result was that credit requests are processed in four hours compared to six days, total employees were reduced slightly, while the total number of deals increased one hundred times.

Source: Adapted from M. Hammer and J. Champy, *Reengineering the Corporation: A Manifesto for Business Revolution* (New York: HarperBusiness, 1993): 36–9.

—reduced the number of parts from 150, found in the typical PC printer, to 60;

—designed the printer in layers so that robots could build it from the bottom up;

—eliminated all screws, springs, and other fasteners that required human insertion and adjustment and replaced them with molded plastic components that clipped together.[24]

■ Service offerings too can be designed for ease and efficiency of production. Motel 6, cost leader in US budget motels, carefully designs its product to keep operating costs low. Its motels occupy low-cost, out-of-town locations, it uses standard motel designs, it avoids facilities such as pools and restaurants, and it designs rooms to facilitate easy cleaning and low maintenance.

---

[24] Ralph E. Gomory, "From the Ladder of Science to the Product Development Cycle," *Harvard Business Review* (November–December 1989): 103.

Capacity Utilization

Over the short and medium term, plant capacity is more or less fixed, and variations in output are associated with variations in capacity utilization. During periods of low demand, plant capacity is underutilized. This raises unit costs because fixed costs must be spread over fewer units of production. In businesses where virtually all costs are fixed (e.g., airlines, theme parks), profitability is highly sensitive to shortfalls in demand. During periods of peak demand, output may be pushed beyond the normal full-capacity operation. As Boeing discovered in 1997, pushing output beyond capacity operation increases unit costs due to overtime pay, premiums for night and week-end shifts, increased defects, and higher maintenance costs.

In declining industries, the ability speedily to adjust capacity to the current level of demand can be a major source of cost advantage. During the 1980s and early 1990s, British Steel was Europe's most profitable steel producer partly because it reduced capacity faster than its rivals. The key to such adjustment, however, is the ability to distinguish *cyclical* overcapacity – common to all cyclical industries, from semiconductors and construction to hotels and railroads – from the *structural* over-capacity that affects steel, oil refining, automobiles, and the US hospital industry.[25] However, structural overcapacity is not associated only with declining industries. In many emerging, e-commerce industries (including online stockbroking, online auctions, and internet service providers), competition to exploit scale economies and attain market leadership has resulted in capacity far outstripping demand.

Input Costs

When the firms in an industry purchase their inputs in the same competitive input markets, we can expect every firm to pay the same price for identical inputs. In most industries, however, differences in the costs incurred by different firms for similar inputs can be an important source of overall cost advantage. There are several common sources of lower input costs:

- *Locational differences in input prices.* The prices of inputs may vary between locations, the most important being differences in wage rates from one coun-try to another. In labor-intensive industries such as clothing, footwear, hand tools, and toys, low wage rates give an unassailable cost advantage to pro-ducers in developing countries. European, Japanese, and American companies typically perform such labor-intensive activities offshore. This relocation is not restricted to unskilled activities: a major US corporation might locate soft-ware development in Israel or India, the call center in Ireland, and back-office functions (such as insurance claim processing) in Scotland. Exchange rate movements exert a major influence on the prices of local inputs. The fall of

---

[25] Jim Billington, "Listening to Overcapacity – Lessons from the Auto and Health Care Industries," *Harvard Management Update* (Boston: Harvard Business School, 1998, Reprint # U98068).

TABLE 8.3 Costs per Available Seat-Mile in Short-Haul Passenger Transport, 1993

	SOUTHWEST AIRLINES (CENTS)	UNITED AIRLINES (CENTS)
Wages and benefits	2.4	3.5
Fuel and oil	1.1	1.1
Aircraft ownership	0.7	0.8
Aircraft maintenance	0.6	0.3
Commissions on ticket sales	0.5	1.0
Advertising	0.2	0.2
Food and beverage	0.0	0.5
Other	1.7	3.1
Total	7.2	10.5

Source: United Airlines.

the euro during 1999–2000 boosted the competitiveness of European firms in North America and Japan.

■ *Ownership of low-cost sources of supply.* In raw material-intensive industries, ownership or access to low-cost sources may be a key cost advantage. Prior to its acquisition by BP, Arco had cost leadership in US West Coast gasoline markets as a result of its low-cost, easily-accessible Alaskan oil reserves.

■ *Non-union labor.* In some labor-intensive industries, cost leaders are often the firms that have avoided unionization. In the US airline industry, unionization is a major source of the cost difference between low-cost carriers and the major airlines (see Table 8.3).

■ *Bargaining power.* Where bought-in products are a major cost item, differences in buying power among the firms in an industry can be an important source of cost advantage.[26] Wal-Mart's UK entry (with its acquisition of Asda) was greeted with dismay by British retailers – they recognized that Wal-Mart would be able to use its massive bargaining power to extract additional discounts from Asda's suppliers, which it could use to fuel aggressive price competition.

Residual Efficiency

In many industries, the basic cost drivers – scale, technology, product and process design, input costs, and capacity utilization – fail to provide a complete explanation for why one firm in an industry has lower unit costs than a competitor. Even after taking all these cost drivers into account, unit cost differences between firms remain.

[26] See Robert M. Grant, "Manufacturer-Retailer Relations: The Shifting Balance of Power," in G. Johnson (ed.), *Retailing and Business Strategy* (New York: John Wiley, 1987).

These residual efficiencies relate to the extent to which the firm approaches its efficiency frontier of optimal operation. Residual efficiency depends on the firm's ability to eliminate "organizational slack"[27] or "X-inefficiency"[28] – surplus costs that keep the firm from maximum efficiency operation. These costs are often referred to as "organizational fat" and build up unconsciously as a result of employees – both in management and on the shop floor – maintaining some margin of slack in preference to the rigors of operating at maximum efficiency.

Eliminating excess costs is difficult. It may take a shock to a company's very survival to provide the impetus for rooting out institutionalized inefficiencies. When faced with bankruptcy or a precipitous fall in profitability, companies can demonstrate a remarkable capacity for paring costs:

- Nissan Motor, the failing Japanese auto producer, was able to achieve a 20 percent cut in operating costs during its first year under the management of Renault's Carlos Ghosn.[29]

- The collapse of profitability at Xerox during 2000 resulted in a campaign to reduce costs by $1 billion.

In the absence of a threat to survival, high levels of residual efficiency are typically the result of an organizational culture and management style that are intolerant toward all manifestations of unnecessary costs. At Wal-Mart, for example, parsimony and frugality are virtues that take on a near-religious significance.

USING THE VALUE CHAIN TO ANALYZE COSTS

To analyze costs and make recommendations for building cost advantage, the company or even the business unit is too big a level for us to work at. As we saw in Chapter 5, every business may be viewed as a chain of activities. In most value chains each activity has a distinct cost structure determined by different cost drivers. Analyzing costs requires disaggregating the firm's value chain in order to identify:

- The relative importance of each activity with respect to total cost.

- The cost drivers for each activity and the comparative efficiency with which the firm performs each activity.

- How costs in one activity influence costs in another.

- Which activities should be undertaken within the firm and which activities should be outsourced.

[27] R. Cyert and J. March, *A Behavioral Theory of the Firm* (Englewood Cliffs, NJ: Prentice-Hall, 1963).
[28] H. Leibenstein, "Allocative Efficiency Versus X-Efficiency," *American Economic Review* 54 (June 1966).
[29] "Nissan on the Road to Recovery," *Financial Times* (October 4, 2000): 17.

The Principal Stages of Value Chain Analysis

A value chain analysis of a firm's cost position comprises the following stages:

1. *Disaggregate the firm into separate activities.* Determining the appropriate value chain activities is a matter of judgment. It requires understanding the chain of processes involved in the transformation of inputs into output and its delivery to the customer. Very often, the firm's own divisional and departmental structure is a useful guide. Key considerations are:
   - the separateness of one activity from another;
   - the importance of an activity;
   - the dissimilarity of activities in terms of cost drivers;
   - the extent to which there are differences in the way competitors perform the particular activity.

2. *Establish the relative importance of different activities in the total cost of the product.* Our analysis needs to focus on the activities that are the major sources of cost. In disaggregating costs, Michael Porter suggests the detailed assignment of operating costs and assets to each value activity. Though the adoption of activity-based costing has made such cost data more available, detailed cost allocation can be a major exercise.[30] Even without such detailed cost data, it is usually possible to identify the critical activities, establish which activities are performed relatively efficiently or inefficiently, identify cost drivers, and offer recommendations.

3. *Compare costs by activity.* To establish which activities the firm performs relatively efficiently and which it does not, benchmark unit costs for each activity against those of competitors.

4. *Identify cost drivers.* For each activity, what factors determine the level of cost relative to other firms? For some activities, cost drivers are evident simply from the nature of the activity and the composition of costs. For capital-intensive activities such as the operation of a body press in an auto plant, the principal factors are likely to be capital equipment costs, weekly production volume, and downtime between changes of dies. For labor-intensive assembly activities, critical issues are wage rates, speed of work, and defect rates.

5. *Identify linkages.* The costs of one activity may be determined, in part, by the way in which other activities are performed. Xerox discovered that its high service costs relative to competitors reflected the complexity of design of its copiers, which required 30 different interrelated adjustments. The careful tracing of defects that appear at one stage of a production process to their source

---

[30] On activity-based costing, see Robert S. Kaplan and Robin Cooper, *Cost and Effect: Using Integrated Cost Systems to Drive Profitability and Performance* (Boston: Harvard Business School Press, 1997); Jim Billington, "The ABCs of ABC: Activity-based Costing and Management," *Harvard Management Update* (Boston: Harvard Business School Publishing, May 1999).

FIGURE 8.6   Using the value chain in cost analysis: an automobile manufacturer

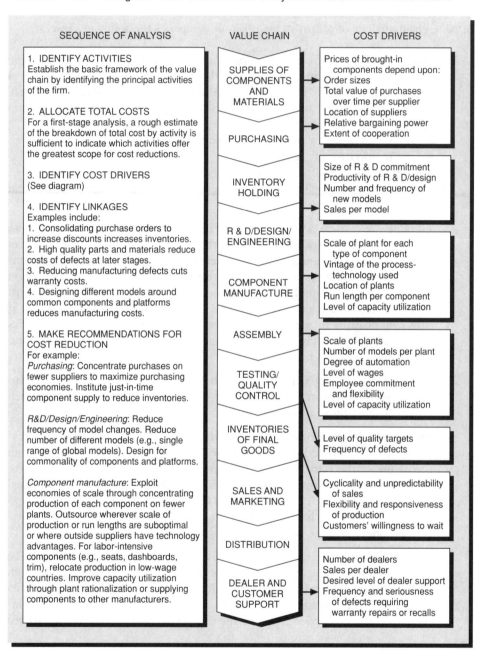

in an earlier stage is a key element of total quality management. In recent years, the optimization of activities throughout the value chain has become a major source of cost reduction, and speed enhancement has become a key challenge for computer integrated manufacturing. SAP of Germany is a leading supplier of the integration of activities within the firm, whereas Manugistics, i2 Technologies, and several other companies compete for leadership in the market for supply chain management software.

6. *Identify opportunities for reducing costs.* By identifying areas of comparative inefficiency and the cost drivers for each, opportunities for cost reduction become evident. For example:
   - If scale economies are a key cost driver, can volume be increased? One feature of Caterpillar's cost-reduction strategy was to broaden its model range and OEM (original equipment manufacture) sales of diesel engines to exploit scale economies, R&D, component manufacturing, and dealer support over a larger sales volume.
   - Where wage costs are the issue, can wages be reduced either directly or by relocating production?
   - If a certain activity cannot be performed efficiently within the firm, can the activity be contracted out, or can the component or service be bought in? Outsourcing in the auto industry has extended to the point where at VW's Brazilian plant, external suppliers not only supply components and subassemblies, they are also responsible for installing them on VW's assembly line. Outsourcing of information technology functions has fueled the growth of EDS, Accenture, and other suppliers of IT services.

Figure 8.6 shows how the application of the value chain to automobile manufacture can yield suggestions for possible cost reductions.

MANAGING COST CUTTING

As the level of competition in most markets continues, so companies are continually being forced to seek new opportunities for cost reduction. The pressure for cost reduction is strongest in those industries where price competition is fiercest due to commodity products, excess capacity, and many competitors – steel, airlines, and chemicals are classic examples. However, pressures for cost cutting are also being felt in technology-based growth industries. In telecommunications, despite rapidly growing demand, falling prices and excess capacity are forcing leading players such as AT&T, British Telecom, WorldCom and Sprint urgently to reduce their cost base. In e-commerce, the end of the dot-com boom has forced the survivors among online brokers, ISPs, and online retailers to cut back on their overheads. In the meantime, in the aftermath of the Asia crisis of 1997–98, the diversified corporations of Japan, Korea, and Southeast Asia are engaged in the same type of restructuring and cost cutting that their western counterparts went through during the 1980s and 1990s.

The approach to cost analysis outlined above – identifying cost drivers and exploring their impact on the different activities of the business – is a useful diagnostic tool, but tells us little about how companies actually implement cost-cutting measures. The experience of cost reduction by companies over the past two decades points to two important lessons in managing for cost efficiency: first, the role of dynamic approaches to cost efficiency; second, the potential for integrated approaches to restructuring and cost reduction.

Dynamic Aspects of Cost Efficiency

One of the dangers of the analytic approach to cost analysis outlined above is its static nature. The operations management experts at Harvard Business School point out that the critical advantage of Japanese over American companies in manufacturing industries such as automobiles, consumer electronics, and construction equipment was Japanese companies' emphasis on dynamic efficiency through continuous improvement (*kaizen*).[31] The total quality movement of the 1980s encouraged western corporations to adopt a continuous improvement approach to operations management that had important implications for cost management. The emphasis of TQM on the rigorous analysis of production activities, simplification of processes, training, and empowerment of shop-floor workers resulted in reducing the costs of defects and rework, supervision and maintenance, inventories and work in progress, while stimulating process innovation.[32]

Radical Cost Surgery

For underperforming companies, incremental efficiency increases are unlikely to be sufficient, and radical, short-term initiatives to achieve major cost reductions may be needed to boost financial performance and regain investor confidence. Such radical cost reduction is likely to be part of a wider program of organizational change involving committing to shareholder wealth maximization, divesting poorly performing assets, refocusing around core strengths, and organizational changes to eliminate inefficiencies and increase accountability and speed of decision making. The term *corporate restructuring* refers to these dramatic, simultaneous changes in strategy, structure, and management systems adopted by mature corporations during the 1980s and 1990s as they sought to adjust to an environment of competition, instability, and shareholder activism. The cost-reduction measures involved include:

- Plant closures to improve capacity utilization and eliminate obsolete technology.

- Outsourcing of components and services wherever internal suppliers are less cost efficient than external suppliers.

---

[31]   Robert H. Hayes, Steven C. Wheelwright, and Kim B. Clark, *Dynamic Manufacturing: Creating the Learning Organization* (New York: Free Press, 1988).
[32]   David A. Garvin, *Managing Quality: The Strategic and Competitive Edge* (New York: Free Press, 1988).

■ Reductions in employment.

■ Increasing managerial efficiency through "delayering" to reduce administrative overhead, and the application of rigorous financial targets and control to provide incentives for aggressive cost reduction.

Because of the urgency of cost reduction and the need to avoid extensive negotiation and compromise, restructuring and radical cost reduction typically involve a recentralization of power into the hands of the CEO with direct, top-down decision making and implementation. In some cases, restructuring plans may be drawn up outline the existing management structure through creating and empowering a high-level task force. Xerox Corporation's restructuring announced in 2000 involved a number of crisis measures, including the sale of its financing business, the sale of its 50 percent stake in Fuji Xerox, the quest for partners for its Palo Alto Research Center, a substantial reduction in employment, and a set of measures aimed at achieving substantial cost reductions throughout its business. Corporate restructurings have often been very successful at achieving substantial reductions in operating cost and greater efficiency of asset use. Exhibit 8.2 reports on Chevron's corporate-wide cost-reduction program of the early 1990s.

EXHIBIT 8.2   Cost Cutting at Chevron 1992–93

After several years during which Chevron's profitability and shareholder returns lagged those of most other US oil majors, in January 1992, CEO Kenneth Derr announced an "aggressive action plan" involving:

■ A company-wide program to reduce operating expenses by 50 cents a barrel sold by mid-1993.

■ Capacity reduction and efficiency increases at the Port Arthur refinery, including 700 job cuts.

■ The sale of 600 of Chevron's 1,000 remaining US oil and gas fields.

The targeted cost reduction was achieved in six months. For 1992 as a whole, operating expenses were reduced by 59 cents for each barrel of product sold, adding $570 million to pre-tax income. Total employment was cut by 6,200 during 1992. For 1993, a further cost reduction target of 25 cents per barrel was established. A key element of the proposed cuts in costs were reductions at the corporate level, where a 30 percent cost reduction was targeted. In its report for the third quarter of 1993, Chevron was able to advise that it had already exceeded its cost-reduction target for 1993: costs had been reduced by over 40 cents a barrel of product sold. After adjusting for special items, Chevron succeeded in cutting operating costs by 7 percent during the first nine months of 1993 compared to the comparable period in 1992. The principal cost economies occurred in the following areas:

1. Selling, general and administrative expenses. These were cut from $459 million during the third quarter of 1992 to $359 million during the third quarter of 1993. The biggest cost savings were incurred at corporate headquarters. Between 1992 and 1993, headquarters staff was reduced from 3,600 to 2,600, and headquarters operating costs from $670 million to $470 million. Of the 1,000 headquarters positions lost, about 550

EXHIBIT 8.2 *(cont'd)*

were by voluntary early retirement. The reductions were primarily in tax, treasury, public affairs, security, law, and human resources. Chairman K. Derr stated, "We regret that these changes will leave some employees without jobs. The cutbacks reflect a business environment that has required us to change our structure and eliminate work that's not absolutely essential to our business."

2. Chevron Information Technology Company. A combination of reorganization and outsourcing of IT services resulted in CITC's employment being cut from 2,300 in 1992 to 1,800 in 1993.

3. Exploration and production. In 1992, oilfield sales, a 23 percent reduction in employee numbers, and the implementation of efficiency measures suggested by employees, cut operating costs by $400 million, or $1.18 per barrel of oil.

4. US refining and marketing. A key to achieving the target of reducing operating costs by $300 million was capacity reduction. At its Port Arthur (Texas) and Richmond (California) refineries, capacity was cut and capacity utilization increased. In retailing, Chevron reduced its number of stations from 3,400 to 2,500, while focusing its marketing efforts on 16 key metropolitan areas in the South and West. At the end of 1993, Chevron was pursuing further capacity reduction. Its Port Arthur and Philadelphia refineries were put up for sale together with two small refineries in the Northwest and six terminals in the East.

Source: Chevron Annual Reports.

SUMMARY

Cost efficiency may no longer be a guarantee of profitability in today's fast-changing markets, but in almost all industries it is a prerequisite for success. In industries where competition has always been primarily price based – steel, textiles, and mortgage loans – increased intensity of competition requires relentless cost-reduction efforts. In industries where price competition was once muted – airlines, banking, and electrical power – firms have been forced to reconcile the pursuit of innovation, differentiation, and service quality with vigorous cost reduction.

The foundation for a cost-reduction strategy must be an understanding of the determinants of a company's costs. The principal message of this chapter is the need to look behind cost accounting data and beyond simplistic approaches to the determinants of cost efficiency, and to analyze the factors that drive relative unit costs in each of the firm's activities in a systematic and comprehensive manner.

Increasingly, approaches to cost efficiency are less about incremental efficiencies, and more about fundamentally rethinking the activities undertaken by the firm and the ways in which it organizes them. By focusing on those activities in which the firm possesses a cost advantage and outsourcing others, and by extensively reengineering manufacturing and administrative processes, firms have succeeded in achieving dramatic reductions in operating costs.

Given multiple drivers of relative cost, cost management implies multiple initiatives at different organizational levels. Careful analysis of existing activities relative to competitors can pinpoint cost-reduction opportunities by lowering input costs, accessing scale economies, and better utilizing capacity. At the same time, the firm must seek opportunities for innovation and process redesign in order to exploit new sources of dynamic efficiency.

9
Differentiation Advantage

If the three keys to selling real estate are location, location, location, then the three keys of selling consumer products are differentiation, differentiation, differentiation.

—**Robert Goizueta, former Chairman, Coca-Cola Company**

If you gave me $100 billion and said, "Take away the soft drink leadership of Coca-Cola in the world," I'd give it back to you and say, "It can't be done."

—**Warren Buffett, Chairman, Berkshire Hathaway, and Coca-Cola's biggest shareholder**

OUTLINE

INTRODUCTION AND OBJECTIVES

A firm differentiates itself from its competitors "when it provides something unique that is valuable to buyers beyond simply offering a low price."[1] Differentiation advantage occurs when a firm is able to obtain from its differentiation a price premium in the market that exceeds the cost of providing the differentiation.

Every firm has opportunities for differentiating its offering to customers, although the range of differentiation opportunities depends on the characteristics of the product. An automobile or a restaurant offers greater potential for differentiation than standardized products such as cement, wheat, or computer memory chips. These latter products are called "commodities" precisely because they lack physical differentiation. Yet, even commodity products can be differentiated in ways that create customer value: "Anything can be turned into a value-added product or service for a well-defined or newly created market," claims Tom Peters.[2]

The personal computer is essentially a commodity item: the components are standardized and PCs are identified by their technical specifications rather than by their brand name. Yet, Dell Computer's direct sales model has allowed it to differentiate its PC offerings by allowing customers to design their own computer system (which is manufactured and shipped within days) and to offer services that include, among many more, online customer support, three-year on-site warranty, web hosting, installation and configuration of customers' hardware and software. Founded in 1984 by 19-year-old Michael Dell, Dell Computer has become the world's market leader in PCs and earned a return on equity that averaged 78 percent during 1998–2000. The lesson from Dell Computer is this: differentiation is not simply about offering different product features, it is about identifying and understanding every possible interaction between the firm and its customers, and asking how the these interactions can be enhanced or changed in order to deliver additional value to the customer.

Analyzing differentiation requires looking at both the firm (the supply side) and its customers (the demand side). While supply-side analysis identifies the firm's potential to create uniqueness, the critical issue is whether such differentiation creates value for customers, and whether the value created exceeds the cost of the differentiation. Hence, in this chapter we shall be concerned especially with the demand side of the market. By understanding what customers want, how

---

[1] Michael E. Porter, *Competitive Advantage* (New York: Free Press, 1985): 120.
[2] Tom Peters, *Thriving on Chaos* (New York: Knopf, 1987): 56.

they choose, and what their motivations are, we can identify opportunities for profitable differentiation.

Differentiation strategies are not about pursuing uniqueness for the sake of being different. Differentiation is about understanding the need that our product is serving and about understanding our customers. To this extent, the quest for differentiation advantage takes us to the heart of business strategy. The fundamental issues of differentiation are also the fundamental issues of business strategy: Who are our customers? How do we create value for them? And how do we do it more effectively and efficiently than anyone else?

Because differentiation is about uniqueness, differentiation advantage cannot be achieved simply through the application of standardized frameworks, techniques, and systems of classification. This is not to say that differentiation advantage is not amenable to systematic analysis. As we have observed, there are two require-ments for creating profitable differentiation. On the supply side, the firm must be aware of the resources and capabilities through which it can create unique-ness (and do it better than competitors). On the demand side, the key is insight into customers and their needs and preferences. These two sides form the major components of our analysis of differentiation. This analysis is not intended to constrain or supplant intuition and creativity, but to provide a framework capable of stimulating and guiding novel and creative approaches to generating customer value.

By the time you have completed this chapter you will be able to:

■ Understand what differentiation is, recognize its different forms, and appreciate its potential for creating competitive advantage.

■ Analyze the sources of differentiation in terms of customers' preferences and characteristics, and of the firm's capacity for supplying differentiation.

■ Formulate strategies that create differentiation advantage by linking the firm's differentiation capability to customers' demand for differentiation.

THE NATURE OF DIFFERENTIATION AND DIFFERENTIATION ADVANTAGE

Let us begin by exploring what differentiation is and why it is such an important basis for competitive advantage.

Differentiation Variables

The potential for differentiating a product or service is partly determined by its phys-ical characteristics. For a product that is technically simple (a pair of socks, a brick), or that satisfies uncomplicated needs (a corkscrew, a nail), or that must meet specific technical standards (a spark plug, a thermometer), differentiation opportunities are constrained by technical and market factors. Products that are complex (an airplane), that satisfy complex needs (an automobile, a vacation), or that do not need to conform to stringent technical standards (wine, toys) offer much greater scope for differentiation.

Beyond these constraints, the potential in any product or service for differentiation is limited only by the boundaries of the human imagination. For simple products such as shampoo, toilet paper, and cigarettes, the proliferation of brands on any supermarket's shelves is testimony both to the ingenuity of firms and the complexity of customer preferences. Differentiation extends beyond the physical characteristics of the product or service to encompass everything about the product or service that influences the value customers derive from it. This means that differentiation includes every aspect of the way in which a company does business and relates to its customers. Thus, the differentiation advantage of McDonald's within the fast-food business depends not just on the characteristics of the food it serves or the associated services (speed of service, cleanliness), but also the values it projects such as happiness, child development, family unity, and care for communities and the natural environment.

Differentiation is not an activity specific to particular functions such as design and marketing; it infuses all activities within the organization and is built into the identity and culture of a company. As a result, companies that supply seemingly basic, no-frills offerings such as Volkswagen (with its Beetle), Southwest Airlines, and Wal-Mart may achieve highly differentiated market positions in terms of customers' perceptions.

Differentiation strategy extends beyond product differentiation to include all aspects of the relationship between a company and its customers. Ultimately, differentiation is all about a firm's responsiveness to customer requirements. Tom Peters calls for "total customer responsiveness":

> Every action, no matter how small, and no matter how far from the firing line a department may be, must be processed through the customer's eyes. Will this make it easier for the customer? Faster? Better? Less expensive? . . . Long-term profit equals revenue from continuously happy customer relationships minus cost.[3]

In analyzing differentiation opportunities, a basic distinction is between *tangible* and *intangible* dimensions of differentiation. Tangible differentiation is concerned with the observable characteristics of a product or service that are relevant to customers' preferences and choice processes. These include such characteristics as size, shape, color, weight, design, material, and technology. Tangible differentiation also includes the performance of the product or service in terms of reliability, consistency, taste, speed, durability, safety. The products and services that are complements to the product in question are also important in relation to differentiation potential. These include pre-sales services, after-sales services, accessories, availability and speed of delivery, credit, and the ability to upgrade the product in the future. For consumer products, these differentiation variables directly determine the utility that consumers gain from the product. For producer goods, differentiation variables affect the customer firms' ability to make money in their own businesses – hence these performance variables

---

[3] Ibid.: 185.

are valuable sources of differentiation if they lower customer firms' costs or increase their ability to differentiate their own products.

Opportunities for intangible differentiation arise because the value that customers perceive in a product or service is not dependent exclusively on the tangible aspects of the offering. There are few products where customer choice is determined solely by observable product features or objective performance criteria. Social, emotional, psychological, and aesthetic considerations are present in choices over all products and services. The desires for status, exclusivity, individuality, and security are extremely powerful motivational forces in choices relating to most consumer goods. Where a product or service is meeting complex customer needs, differentiation choices involve the overall image of the firm's offering. Issues of image differentiation are especially important for those products and services whose qualities and performance are difficult to ascertain at the time of purchase ("experience goods"). These include cosmetics, medical services, and education.

Differentiation and Segmentation

Differentiation is different from segmentation. Differentiation is concerned with *how* a firm competes – the ways in which it can offer uniqueness to customers. Such uniqueness might relate to consistency (McDonald's), reliability (Federal Express), status (American Express), quality (BMW), and innovation (Sony). Segmentation is concerned with *where* a firm competes in terms of customer groups, localities, and product types.

Whereas segmentation is a feature of market structure, differentiation is a strategic choice by a firm. A segmented market is one that can be partitioned according to the characteristics of customers and their demand. Differentiation is concerned with a firm's positioning within a market (or market segment) in relation to the product, service, and image characteristics that influence customer choice.[4] By locating within a segment, a firm does not necessarily differentiate itself from its competitors within the same segment. Ameritrade, E*Trade, Web Street, and Quick & Reilly are all located within the online segment of the brokerage industry, yet these firms are not significantly differentiated from one another. At the same time, a company may pursue a differentiation strategy, but position itself within the mass market and span multiple segments. Dell Computer, Amazon, McDonald's, Ford Motor Company, and Starbucks Coffee all aim at well-defined positions of differentiation within their markets, while aiming at market share leadership.

However, differentiation decisions may be closely linked to choices over the segments in which a firm competes. By offering uniqueness in its offerings, a firm may inevitably target certain market niches. By selecting performance, engineering, and style as the basis on which BMW competes in the automobile industry, it inevitably appeals to different market segments than does VW.

---

[4] These distinctions are developed in more detail by Peter R. Dickson and James L. Ginter, "Market Segmentation, Product Differentiation and Marketing Strategy," *Journal of Marketing* 51 (April 1987): 1–10.

The Sustainability of Differentiation Advantage

Although strategy analysis has traditionally emphasized cost advantage as the primary basis for establishing a competitive advantage, low cost tends to be less secure a basis for competitive advantage than is differentiation. The growth of international competition has revealed the fragility of seemingly well-established positions of domestic cost leadership. Across North America, western Europe, and Japan, companies whose competitive advantage rested on cost leadership have been outcompeted by overseas competitors with lower labor costs. In the US steel industry, former giants such as US Steel, Bethlehem, and Wheeling-Pittsburgh (WHX) are struggling for survival against low-cost imports from Korea and Latin America. The large-scale textile manufacturers of Britain and America have either failed, retreated to niche markets, or shifted production offshore. Cost advantage is highly vulnerable to unpredictable external forces. The fall of the euro against the US dollar between 1998 and 2000 shifted cost advantage in most manufacturing industries strongly in favor of European-based companies. The aluminum industry of western Europe was brought to the brink of ruin during the mid-1990s by low-cost Russian producers benefiting from government subsidies and low energy costs.

Even within a domestic context, cost advantage may be vulnerable to new technology and strategic innovation. Thus, low-cost foreign competition is only partly to blame for the decline of the US integrated iron and steel producers. Their major loss of market share has been to the minimill producers – Nucor, Chaparral Steel, Steel Dynamics, and a host of other newcomers – that have used small-scale, scrap-fed, electric arc plants to undercut their bigger brethren. In retailing, former cost leaders such as Sears Roebuck and J. C. Penney were undermined by emerging "category killers" such as Wal-Mart, Best Buy, and Home Depot.

As a result, companies that have been consistently successful over long periods tend to be those that have pursued differentiation rather than cost leadership. Table 9.1 shows that Fortune 100 companies with the highest return to stockholders tend to be those that have pursued differentiation through quality, branding, and innovation. Relatively few of these companies (Home Depot, Wal-Mart, and Target) are companies that have competed primarily on the basis of cost leadership.

ANALYZING DIFFERENTIATION: THE DEMAND SIDE

Successful differentiation involves matching customers' demand for differentiation with the firm's capacity to supply differentiation. Let's begin with the demand side. Analyzing customer demand enables us to determine which product characteristics have the potential to create value for customers, those customers' willingness to pay for differentiation, and a company's optimal competitive positioning in terms of differentiation variables.

Analyzing demand begins with understanding why customers buy a product or service. What are the needs and requirements of a person who is purchasing a personal computer? What is motivating a company when it hires management consultants?

TABLE 9.1   Companies Among the 100 Largest US
Corporations with the Highest Return to Stockholders,
1989–99

	AVERAGE ANNUAL RETURN %
Dell Computer	97.2
Microsoft	58.0
MCI WorldCom	53.0
Home Depot	44.3
Intel	44.2
Merrill Lynch	31.7
Target	23.5
General Electric	28.4
Motorola	27.0
Enron	23.1
Johnson & Johnson	22.3
Coca-Cola	21.3
Merck	20.6
Bristol Myers Squibb	20.4
IBM	19.3

Source: "The Fortune 500," *Fortune* (April 28, 2000).

Market research systematically explores customer preferences and customer perceptions of existing products. However, the key to successful differentiation is to understand customers. In gaining insight into customer requirements and preferences, simple, direct questions about the purpose of a product and its performance attributes can often be far more illuminating than objective market research data obtained from large samples of actual and potential customers. Exhibit 9.1 provides a striking example of the value of simplicity and directness in probing customer requirements.

Product Attributes and Positioning

Virtually all products and services serve multiple customer needs. As a result, understanding customer needs requires the analysis of multiple attributes. Market research has developed numerous techniques for analyzing customer preferences in relation to different product attributes. These techniques – including multidimensional scaling, conjoint analysis, and hedonic price analysis – can guide the positioning of new products, repositioning of existing products, and setting product prices.

Multidimensional Scaling

Multidimensional scaling (MDS) permits customers' perceptions of competing products' similarities and dissimilarities to be represented graphically and for the dimensions

---

EXHIBIT 9.1   Understanding What a Product Is About

Getting back to strategy means getting back to a deep understanding of what a product is about. Some time back, for example, a Japanese home appliance company was trying to develop a coffee percolator. Should it be a General Electric-type percolator, executives wondered? Should it be the same drip-type that Philips makes? Larger? Smaller? I urged them to ask a different kind of question: Why do people drink coffee? What are they looking for when they do? If your objective is to serve the customer better, then shouldn't you understand why that customer drinks coffee in the first place? Then you would know what kind of percolator to make.

The answer came back: good taste. Then I asked the company's engineers what they were doing to help the consumer enjoy good taste in a cup of coffee. They said they were trying to design a good percolator. I asked them what influences the taste in a cup of coffee. No one knew. That became the next question we had to answer. It turns out that lots of things can affect taste – the beans, the temperature, the water. We did our homework and discovered all the things that affect taste . . .

Of all the factors, water quality, we learned, made the greatest difference. The percolator in design at the time, however, didn't take water quality into account at all . . . We discovered next the grain distribution and the time between grinding the beans and pouring in the water were crucial. As a result we began to think about the product and its necessary features in a new way. It had to have a built-in dechlorinating function. It had to have a built-in grinder. All the customer should have to do is pour in water and beans . . .

To start you have to ask the right questions and set the right kinds of strategic goals. If your only concern is that General Electric has just brought out a percolator that brews coffee in ten minutes, you will get your engineers to design one that brews it in seven minutes. And if you stick to that logic, market research will tell you that instant coffee is the way to go . . . Conventional marketing approaches won't solve the problem. If you ask people whether they want their coffee in ten minutes or seven, they will say seven, of course. But it's still the wrong question. And you end up back where you started, trying the beat the competition at its own game. If your primary focus is on the competition, you will never step back and ask what the customers' inherent needs are, and what the product really is about.

Source: Kenichi Ohmae, "Getting Back to Strategy," *Harvard Business Review* (November–December 1988): 154. Copyright © 1988 by the President and Fellows of Harvard College; all rights reserved.

---

to be interpreted in terms of key product attributes.[5] For example, a survey of consumer ratings of competing pain relievers resulted in the mapping shown in Figure 9.1. MDS has also been used to classify 109 single-malt Scotch whiskies according to the characteristics of their color, nose, palate, body, and finish.[6]

---

[5]   See S. Schiffman, M. Reynolds, and F. Young, *Introduction to Multidimensional Scaling: Theory, Methods, and Applications* (Cambridge, MA: Academic Press, 1981).

[6]   F.-J. Lapointe and P. Legendre, "A Classification of Pure Malt Scotch Whiskies," *Applied Statistics* 43 (1994): 237–57. On principles of MDS, see I. Borg and P. Groenen, *Modern Multidimensional Scaling: Theory and Application* (Springer Verlag, 1997).

FIGURE 9.1   Consumer perceptions of competing pain relievers: a multidimensional scaling mapping

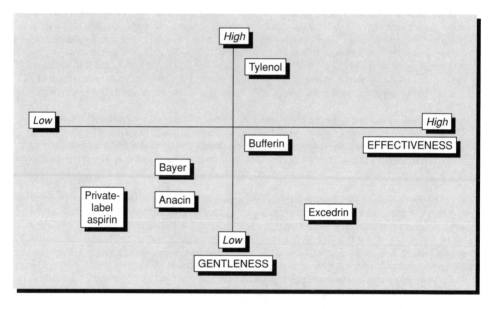

Conjoint Analysis

Conjoint analysis is a powerful means of analyzing the strength of customer preferences for different product attributes. The technique requires, first, an identification of the underlying attributes of a product and, second, market research to rank hypothetical products that contain alternative bundles of attributes. The results can then be used to estimate the proportion of customers who would prefer a hypothetical new product to competing products already available in the market.[7] A conjoint analysis undertaken by BCG of potential personal computer buyers identified price, manufacturer's reputation, portability, processing capability, memory capacity, word-processing capability, and styling as critical attributes. The data were used to predict the share of customer preferences that forthcoming IBM and Apple new models would obtain, and to simulate the effects of changing the design features and prices.[8] Conjoint analysis has been used to design new products ranging from Marriott's Courtyard hotel chain[9] to nature tourism in the Amazon basin.[10]

---

[7]   See P. Cattin and D. R. Wittink, "Commercial Use of Conjoint Analysis: A Survey," *Journal of Marketing* (Summer 1982): 44–53.

[8]   Alan Rowe, Richard Mason, Karl Dickel, and Neil Snyder, *Strategic Management: A Methodological Approach*, 3rd edn (Reading, MA: Addison-Wesley, 1989): 127–8.

[9]   J. Wind, P. Green, D. Shifflet, and M. Scarborough, "Courtyard by Marriott: Designing a Hotel Facility with Consumer-based Marketing Models," *Interfaces* 19 no. 1 (1989): 25–47.

[10]   T. Holmes, C. Zinkhan, K. Alger, and E. Mercer, "Conjoint Analysis of Nature Tourism Values in Bahia, Brazil," FPEI Working Paper 57 (SE Center for Forest Economics Research, 1996).

Hedonic Price Analysis

The demand for a product may be viewed as the demand for the underlying attributes that the product provides.[11] The price at which a product can sell in the market is the aggregate of the values derived from each of these individual attributes. Hedonic price analysis observes price differences for competing products, relates these differences to the different combinations of attributes offered by each product, and calculates the implicit market price for each attribute. For example:

- For European automatic washing machines, price differences were related to differences in capacity, spin speed, energy consumption, number of programs, and reliability (as indicated by consumer organizations' data). Using estimates of the implicit price for each attribute, it is possible to determine the price premium that can be charged for additional units of a particular attribute. In Britain, for example, a machine that spins at 1000 rpm sells at about a $200 price premium to one that spins at 800 rpm.[12]

- In the case of spreadsheets, hedonic price analysis was used to value attributes such as compatibility with a Lotus platform, links to external databases, and LAN linkage.[13]

It may not be necessary to resort to hedonic price analysis to calculate the price advantage that differentiation will support. Thus, if the introduction of high-speed trains on the New York–Boston route can reduce journey time by 45 minutes, and if the average Amtrak passenger values her time at $20 an hour, the implication is that Amtrak can raise fares by $15.

The Role of Social and Psychological Factors

The problem with analyzing product differentiation in terms of measurable performance attributes is that it does not delve very far into customers' underlying motivations. Very few goods or services are acquired to satisfy basic needs for survival: most buying reflects social goals and values in terms of the desire to find community with others, to establish one's own identity, and to make sense of what is happening in the world. Our discussion of goals in Chapter 2 referred to Maslow's hierarchy of needs: once basic needs for survival are satisfied, there is a progression from security needs, to belonging needs, to esteem needs, to self-actualization needs.[14] Most suppliers of branded goods recognize that their brand equities have much more to

---

[11]   Kelvin Lancaster, *Consumer Demand: A New Approach* (New York: Columbia University Press, 1971).
[12]   Phedon Nicolaides and Charles Baden Fuller, "Price Discrimination and Product Differentiation in the European Domestic Appliance Market," discussion paper (London: Center for Business Strategy, London Business School, 1987).
[13]   N. Gondal, "Hedonic price indexes for spreadsheets and an empirical test for network externalities," *Rand Journal of Economics* 25 (1994): 160–70.
[14]   Abraham Maslow, "A Theory of Human Motivation," *Psychological Review* 50 (1943): 370–96.

do with belonging, esteem, and self-actualization than to survival or security. Not since the far-off days of the "Pepsi Challenge" have Coke or Pepsi marketed their colas on the basis of taste. Harley-Davidson recognizes quite clearly that it is in the business of selling lifestyle, not transportation.

If the customer needs that are being satisfied by a company's offerings are concerned with self-identity and social affiliation, the implications for differentiation are far reaching. In particular, to understand customer demand and identify profitable differentiation opportunities requires that we analyze not only the product and its characteristics, but also customers, their lifestyles and aspirations, and the relationship of the product to these lifestyles and aspirations. Market research that looks behind the product and explores the demographic (age, sex, race, location), socioeconomic (income, education), and psychographic (lifestyle, personality type) characteristics of potential customers may be of some value. However, effective differentiation is likely to depend on an understanding of what customers want and how they behave rather than the results of statistical market research. The answer, according to Tom Peters, is simple: business people need to listen to their customers.

> Good listeners get out from behind their desks to where the customers are . . . Further, good listeners construct settings so as to maximize "naive" listening, the undistorted sort . . . Finally, good listeners provide quick feedback and act on what they hear.[15]

In practice, understanding customer needs and preferences is likely to require more than listening. Typically, consumers cannot clearly articulate the motives that drive them and the emotions that different products trigger. Companies must observe their customers in order to understand their lives and their use of the product. The implication is that, for companies to understand their customers, they need to become involved in them. Johansson and Nonaka show that Japanese companies emphasize intuition and relationships. Satisfying the customer is not about bundling together favored attributes, but is going beyond functionality to provide emotional and aesthetic satisfaction.[16]

Figure 9.2 summarizes some key points of this discussions by posing some basic questions that explore the potential for differentiation on the demand side of the market.

Broad-based versus Focused Differentiation

Differentiation, we have observed, may focus on a broad market appeal or on a specific market segment. The choice of market scope has important implications for the orientation of demand analysis. A firm that wishes to establish a broad-based position of differentiation advantage in an industry is primarily concerned with the general features of market demand: What general needs does a product satisfy? What do

---

[15]   Tom Peters, *Thriving on Chaos* (New York: Knopf, 1987): 149.

[16]   Johny K. Johansson and Ikujiro Nonaka, *Relentless: The Japanese Way of Marketing* (New York: HarperBusiness, 1996).

FIGURE 9.2 Identifying differentiation potential: the demand side

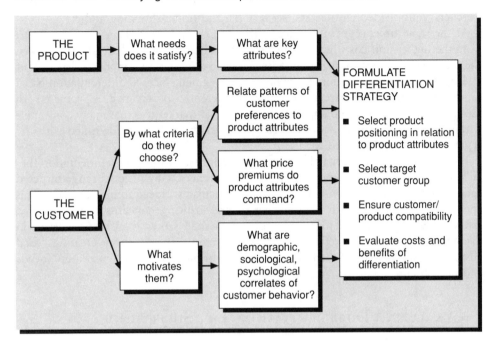

different customers have in common in terms of their motivations and choice criteria? The critical distinction between broad-based and focused differentiation is whether the company concentrates on the factors that segment a market, or the factors that all customers have in common. Establishing uniqueness while still appealing to a broad market is no easy task:

- McDonald's has extended its appeal across age groups, social groups, and national boundaries by emphasizing a few qualities with universal appeal: speed, consistency, value, hygiene, and family lifestyles.

- The British retailer Marks & Spencer has been similarly successful in establishing a reputation for product quality and fair dealing that extends across the traditional class divisions that segment British consumer markets.

- Honda has positioned itself within the US auto market to achieve a broad-based market appeal in contrast to most American and European brands, which target specific demographic and socioeconomic segments.

The challenge for broad-based differentiators is the tendency for focused differentiation to displace broad-based differentiation. In principle, a customer should prefer a targeted product offering that matches his or her particular preferences to one that is designed to appeal to a broad range of tastes. Thus, the challenge facing the US broadcast networks – NBC, ABC, CBS, and Fox – is to develop programming that maintains mass-audience appeal against the cable and satellite channels that nibble away at their viewer ratings by targeting specific groups: children, sports fans, movie watchers, music-video enthusiasts, sci-fi buffs, and home-shopping addicts.

At the same time, segment-focused approaches to differentiation run risks. Apart from the higher unit costs incurred in supplying a narrow rather than a broad market, there are dangers that market segments can change over time, or that a firm adopts an inappropriate segmentation in the first place. Segment-focused differentiation based on existing differences between customers is inherently conservative. A problem with General Motors' segmented approach to the US car market was that many consumers within the segments GM had targeted no longer wanted to be identified with the segment that it had defined for them.

Focused differentiation may be based on an approach to market segmentation that fails to acknowledge customers' needs and preferences. GM's model range targeted each brand to a specific price bracket and particular socioeconomic category. This approach encouraged it to overlook customers' growing concerns over economy, safety, reliability, and the increasing role of lifestyle rather than income levels in distinguishing customer preferences. If differentiation is really about creating "total customer responsiveness," then analysis should bring us closer to customers' needs and not obscure them.

ANALYZING DIFFERENTIATION: THE SUPPLY SIDE

Demand analysis identifies customers' demands for differentiation and their willingness to pay for it, but creating differentiation advantage also depends on a firm's ability to offer differentiation. To identify the firm's potential to supply differentiation, we examine the activities the firm performs and the resources to which it has access.

The Drivers of Uniqueness

Differentiation is concerned with the provision of uniqueness. A firm's opportunities for creating uniqueness in its offerings to customers are not located within a particular function or activity, but can arise in virtually everything that it does. Michael Porter identifies a number of drivers of uniqueness over which the firm exercises control. These include:

- Product features and product performance.

- Complementary services (e.g., credit, delivery, repair).

- Intensity of marketing activities (e.g., rate of advertising spending).

- Technology embodied in design and manufacture.

- The quality of purchased inputs.

- Procedures influencing the conduct of each activities (e.g., rigor of quality control, service procedures, frequency of sales visits to a customer).

FIGURE 9.3 Differentiation of merchandise (hardware) and support (software)

	SUPPORT (SOFTWARE)	
	Differentiated	Undifferentiated
MERCHANDISE (HARDWARE) — Differentiated	SYSTEM	PRODUCT
MERCHANDISE (HARDWARE) — Undifferentiated	SERVICE	COMMODITY

Source: Shiv Mathur and Alfred Kenyon, *Creating Value* (Oxford: Butterworth-Heinemann, 1997).

- The skill and experience of employees.

- Location (e.g., with retail stores).

- The degree of vertical integration (which influences a firm's ability to control inputs and intermediate processes).[17]

Most transactions do not involve a single product or a single service, but are a combination of products and services. In analyzing the potential for differentiation, we can distinguish between differentiation of the product ("hardware") and ancillary services ("software"). On this basis, four transaction categories can be identified (see Figure 9.3).[18]

As markets mature, so "systems" comprising both hardware and software tend to "unbundle," with products increasingly becoming commodities and services being provided by specialized companies. However, the growing sophistication of customer preferences and the quest for differentiation advantage encourage producers to repackage hardware and software into new systems. Thus, as personal computers have increasingly become commoditized, suppliers of "Wintel"-standard computers continually seek new opportunities for bundling additional products and services. Thus, Dell achieves a price premium by offering its computers with an on-site warranty, tuition, internet service, web hosting, and a number of other value-adding services.

A critical issue is whether such bundling really creates customer value. Thus, the offer of "one-stop shopping" by financial service companies that offer personal banking, brokerage services, and insurance products to customers has typically little market appeal.

---

[17] Michael E. Porter, *Competitive Advantage* (New York: Free Press, 1985): 124–5.
[18] Shiv Mathur, "Competitive Industrial Marketing Strategies," *Long Range Planning* 17 no. 4 (1984): 102–9.

Similarly, the arguments of Vivendi, Scottish Power, and other utilities that competitive advantage can be created by offering a single point of supply for electricity,
telecommunication service, gas, and TV have yet to be validated in the marketplace.
The advent of internet-based electronic commerce has greatly reduced customers'
transaction costs, allowing them easily to assemble their own bundles of goods and
services at low cost. Hence, tour companies that organize vacations comprising flights,
hotel bookings, car hire, insurance, and other services are increasingly threatened by
consumers who use internet purchases to create their own customized vacation. The
result, according to McKinsey consultants Hagel and Singer, is not just unbundling
of products, but the unbundling of the corporation itself.[19]

Product Integrity

All companies face a range of differentiation opportunities. The primary issue is likely
to be determining which forms of differentiation may be most successful in distinguishing the firm in the market and which are most valued by customers. However,
such choices cannot be made on a piecemeal basis. Establishing a coherent and
effective differentiation position requires that the firm assemble a complementary
package of differentiation measures. If Beck's beer wishes to differentiate itself on the
basis of the quality of its ingredients, then it must adopt production methods that
are consistent with quality ingredients, and packaging, advertising, and distribution
appropriate to a quality, premium-priced product.

Product integrity refers to the consistency of a firm's differentiation; it is the extent
to which a product achieves:

> total balance of numerous product characteristics including basic functions, aesthetics,
> semantics, reliability, and economy . . . Product integrity has both internal and external
> dimensions. Internal integrity refers to consistency between the function and structure of
> the product – e.g., the parts fit well, components match and work well together, layout
> achieves maximum space efficiency. External integrity is a measure of how well a product's
> function, structure, and semantics fit the customer's objectives, values, production system,
> lifestyle, use pattern, and self-identity.[20]

In their study of product development in the car industry, Clark and Fujimoto
argue that simultaneously achieving internal and external integrity is the most complex organizational challenge facing automakers, since it requires linking close interfunctional collaboration with intimate customer contact. The organizational changes
among US and European automakers, including the growing role of product managers,
have attempted to imitate the success of Toyota and Honda in achieving internal–
external integration.[21]

---

[19]   John Hagel and Marc Singer, "Unbundling the Corporation," *McKinsey Quarterly* no. 3 (2000).
[20]   Kim Clark and Takahiro Fujimoto, *Product Development Performance* (Boston: Harvard Business School
Press, 1991): 29–30.
[21]   Ibid.: 247–85.

Achieving combined internal and external product integrity is critical to all companies that seek differentiation advantage. It is especially important to those supplying "lifestyle" products whose differentiation is based on customers' social and psychological needs. Here, the credibility of the image depends critically on the consistency of the image presented. A critical factor in such differentiation is the ability of employees and customers to identify with one another. Thus:

- Harley-Davidson's ability to develop its image of ruggedness, independence, and individuality is supported by a top management team that dons biking leathers and ride its "hogs" to owners' group rallies, and a management system that empowers shop-floor workers and fosters quality, initiative, and responsibility.

- MTV's capacity to stay at the leading edge of popular culture and embody "coolness" for new generations of young people owes much to its internal culture and human resource management, which rely heavily on the ideas and enthusiasm of its youngest employees.[22]

Maintaining integrity of differentiation is ultimately dependent on a company's ability to live the values embodied in the images with which its products are associated. Exhibit 9.2 discusses the role of values in Body Shop's strategy.

EXHIBIT 9.2 Body Shop: The Role of Values in Differentiation

Though Anita Roddick scorns businessmen and management principles, the success of Body Shop reveals an insightful and sophisticated approach to differentiation strategy. In some respects, Body Shop's strategy is consistent with other manufacturers of cosmetics and toiletries – success has always been associated with the establishment of a strong product image that requires consistency among the product, the packaging, the advertising and promotion, the retail environment, and the image of the company.

To this extent, Body Shop is not novel: its products are physically differentiated. This differentiation is carried through to the packaging and to the retail environment in which the products are sold. Indeed, Body Shop goes one step further than most competitors – it only sells its products within its own franchised stores. However, in the nature of its image, Body Shop has contradicted the industry's conventions concerning differentiation advantage. The companies have sought to differentiate their products on the basis of beauty, youth, and sexual attractiveness. Body Shop rejects this "magic" – "My products can only cleanse, moisten, and protect."

Rather, Body Shop appeals to traditional notions of grooming, maintaining, and enhancing faces and bodies through the use of natural ingredients, many of them associated with the traditions of ethnic peoples throughout the world. This differentiation of the product is supported by a strong commitment to research and discovery to identify and examine the use and potential of a whole range of natural products from oatmeal to obscure vegetable oils.

Emphasis on the natural properties of the products is encouraged by packaging that emphasizes simplicity, economy, and information. A similar feeling is communicated by Body Shop's retail outlets, which are open, non-ostentatious and designed to encourage customers to look, read, sample, and interact with sales personnel. Despite the encouragement that the Body Shop gives to employees' individuality and free expression, the retail stores are uniform in their decor and display and maintain common approaches to customer service.

---

[22] John Seabrook, "Rocking in Shangri-La," *The New Yorker* (October 10, 1994): 64–78.

EXHIBIT 9.2 *(cont'd)*

In contrast to other cosmetic companies, which use advertising and promotion to identify their products with beauty, style, and the fountain of youth, Body Shop communicates its image through its values. In virtually all its words and actions, Body Shop emphasizes commitment to environmental and social responsibility. The primary medium for communication is Body Shop's employees and franchisees. Body Shop exerts special care in selecting its franchisees, rejecting those with prior business experience in favor of those with enthusiasm and commitment to Body Shop ideals. The result is that Body Shop is not simply supplying skin creams and shampoo, it is creating an identity with its customers built around the concepts of naturalness, global environmental responsibility, economic support for indigenous people through trade, and a rejection of traditional business methods (which it sees as exploiting the weak and disregarding the environment).

The problems that Body Shop has encountered in the late 1990s stem from allegations about Body Shop's ethical lapses, in terms of departures from "all natural" ingredients in its products, use of animal-tested ingredients, unfair treatment of franchisees and employees, and weaknesses of its community support and "fair trade" initiatives. Because Body Shop's values are fundamental to its image and relationships with customers, suppliers, franchisees, and employees these criticisms represent a fundamental threat to its competitive position.

Source: *Body Shop International,* Case 9-392-032 (Boston: Harvard Business School, 1992).

Signaling and Reputation

Differentiation is only effective if it is communicated to customers. But customers are not always well informed about the qualities and characteristics of the goods they purchase. The economics literature distinguishes between *search goods,* whose qualities and characteristics can be ascertained by inspection, and *experience goods,* whose qualities and characteristics are only recognized after consumption. This latter class of goods includes medical services, baldness treatments, frozen TV dinners, and wine. Even with experience goods, performance attributes may be slow in revealing themselves – only over time can we assess the reliability of a car or the competence of our dentist.

In the terminology of game theory (see Chapter 4), the market for experience goods corresponds to a classic "prisoners' dilemma." The firm can offer a high-quality or a low-quality product. The customer can pay either a high or a low price. If quality cannot be detected, then equilibrium is established, with the customer offering a low price and the supplier offering a low-quality product, even though both would be better off with a high-quality product sold at a high price (see Figure 9.4).

The resolution of this dilemma is for producers to find some credible means of signaling quality to the customer. The most effective signals are those that change the payoffs in the prisoners' dilemma. Thus, an extended warranty is effective because providing such a warranty would be more expensive for a low-quality than a high-quality producer. Brand names, warranties, expensive packaging, money-back guarantees, sponsorship of sports and cultural events, and a carefully designed retail environment in which the product is sold are all signals of quality. Their effectiveness stems from the fact that they represent significant investments by the manufacturer that will be devalued if the product proves unsatisfactory to customers.

FIGURE 9.4 The problem of quality in experience goods: a "prisoner's dilemma"

		Producer's strategies	
		High quality	Low quality
Consumer's strategies	High price	7 7	10 −5
	Low price	−5 10	3 3

Note: In each cell, the lower-left number is the payoff to the consumer and the upper-right number the payoff to the producer.

The need for signaling variables to complement performance variables in differentiation depends on the ease with which performance can be assessed by the potential buyer. The more difficult it is to ascertain performance prior to purchase, the more important signaling is.

■ A perfume can be sampled prior to purchase and its fragrance assessed, but its ability to augment the identity of the wearer and attract attention remains uncertain. Hence, the key role of branding, packaging, advertising, and lavish promotional events in establishing an identity for the perfume in terms of the implied personality, lifestyle, and aspirations of the user.

■ In financial services, the customer cannot easily assess the honesty, financial security, or competence of a broker, fund manager, or insurance company. Hence, financial service companies accord emphasis to symbols of security, stability, and competence – large, well-located head offices; conservative and tasteful office decor; smartly dressed, well-groomed employees; and stress on size and continuity over time.

Strategies for reputation building have been subjected to extensive theoretical analysis.[23] Some of the propositions that arise from this research include the following:

■ Quality signaling is primarily important for products whose quality can only be ascertained after purchase ("experience goods").

■ Expenditure on advertising is an effective means of signaling superior quality, since suppliers of low-quality products will not expect repeat buying, hence it is not profitable for them to spend money on advertising.

---

[23] For a survey, see Keith Weigelt and Colin Camerer, "Reputation and Corporate Strategy: A Review of Recent Theory and Applications," *Strategic Management Journal* 9 (1988): 443–54.

■ A combination of premium pricing and advertising is likely to be superior in signaling quality than either price or advertising alone.

■ The higher the sunk costs required for entry into a market and the greater the total investment of the firm, the greater the incentives for the firm not to cheat customers through providing low quality at high prices.

Brands

Brand names and the advertising that supports them are especially important as signals of quality and consistency – because a brand is a valuable asset it acts as a disincentive to provide poor quality. For many consumer goods' (and some producer goods') companies, their brand is their most important asset.

Brands fulfill multiple roles. Most importantly, a brand provides a guarantee by the producer to the consumer of the quality of the product. It does so in several ways. At its most basic, a brand identifies the producer of a product. This ensures that the producer is legally and morally accountable for the products supplied to market. Further, the brand represents an investment that provides an incentive to maintain quality and customer satisfaction. Hence, the brand represents a guarantee to the customer that reduces uncertainty and search costs. The more difficult it is to discern quality on inspection, and the greater the cost to the customer of purchasing a defective product, the greater the value of a brand. Thus, a well-known brand name is likely to be more important to us when we purchase a third-generation cellphone than when we buy a pair of socks.

The traditional role of the brand as a guarantor of reliability has become of particular significance in e-commerce. Internet transactions are characterized by the anonymity of buyers and sellers, lack of experience between most buyers and sellers, and lack of government regulation. As a result, well-established players in e-commerce – AOL, Amazon, Microsoft, eBay, Netscape, and Yahoo! – carry substantial brand equity in terms of reducing buyers' perceived risk. By contrast, the value conferred by leading consumer brands such as Coca-Cola, Harley-Davidson, Mercedes-Benz, Gucci, Virgin, and American Express is less a guarantee of reliability and more an embodiment of identity and lifestyle.

Although different brands may create value in different ways, common to all strong brands is the capacity to confer competitive advantage. Figure 9.5 shows that not only do firms with strong brands deliver greater returns than firms with weak brands, but firms that are capable of leveraging their brands across multiple markets (e.g., GE, Disney, and Virgin) earn more than firms whose brands are focused on a single market (Levi-Strauss, Dell, Sprint). While diversified brands create value by creating a core personality (such as Sony's product design and Disney's wholesome fun) and credible, trustworthy image, focused brands create value by establishing a clear personality and dominating and expanding a particular market (Coca-Cola and Gillette being classic examples).[24]

---

[24] D. C. Court, M. G. Leiter, and M. A. Loch, "Brand Leverage," *McKinsey Quarterly* no. 2 (1999): 100–10.

FIGURE 9.5 The impact of quality on profitability

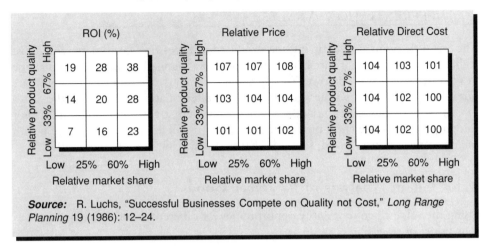

Source: R. Luchs, "Successful Businesses Compete on Quality not Cost," *Long Range Planning* 19 (1986): 12–24.

The Costs of Differentiation

Differentiation adds cost. The direct costs of differentiation include higher-quality inputs, better-trained employees, higher advertising, and better after-sales service. The indirect costs of differentiation arise through the interaction of differentiation variables with cost variables. If differentiation narrows a firm's segment scope, it also limits the potential for exploiting scale economies. If differentiation requires continual product upgrading, it hampers the exploitation of experience curve economies.

One means of reconciling differentiation with cost efficiency is to postpone differentiation to later stages of the firm's value chain. Economies of scale and the cost advantages of standardization are frequently greatest in the manufacturing of basic components. Modular design with common components permits scale economies while maintaining considerable product variety. All the major automakers have reduced the number of platforms and engine types and increased the commonality of components across their model ranges, while offering customers a greater variety of colors, trim, and accessory options.

New manufacturing technology has redefined traditional tradeoffs between efficiency and variety. Flexible manufacturing systems and just-in-time scheduling have increased the versatility of many plants, made model changeovers less costly, and made the goal of an "economic order quantity of one" increasingly realistic. More and more automobile, motorcycle, and domestic appliance plants are producing multiple models on a single assembly line.[25] Electronic commerce allows consumers the ability to design their products: through the internet I can design my own AOL portal, select components for my own edition of the *Financial Times*, and create a CD with my own selection of tracks.

---

[25] Richard J. Schonberger, *World Class Manufacturing Casebook: Implementing JIT and TQC* (New York: Free Press, 1987): 120–3.

BRINGING IT ALL TOGETHER: THE VALUE CHAIN IN DIFFERENTIATION ANALYSIS

There is little point in identifying the product attributes that customers value most if the firm is incapable of supplying those attributes. Similarly, there is little purpose in identifying a firm's ability to supply certain elements of uniqueness if these are not valued by customers. The key to successful differentiation is matching the firm's capacity for creating differentiation to the attributes that customers value most. For this purpose, the value chain provides a particularly useful framework. Let's begin with the case of a producer good, i.e., one that is supplied by one firm to another.

Value Chain Analysis of Producer Goods

Using the value chain to identify opportunities for differentiation advantage involves four principal stages:

1. *Construct a value chain for the firm and the customer.* It may be useful to consider not just the immediate customer, but also firms further downstream in the value chain. If the firm supplies different types of customers – for example, a steel company may supply steel strip to automobile manufacturers and white goods producers – draw separate value chains for each of the main categories of customer.

2. *Identify the drivers of uniqueness in each activity.* Assess the firm's potential for differentiating its product by examining each activity in the firm's value chain and identifying the variables and actions through which the firm can achieve uniqueness in relation to competitors' offerings. Figure 9.6 identifies sources of differentiation within Porter's generic value chain.

3. *Select the most promising differentiation variables for the firm.* Among the numerous drivers of uniqueness that we can identify within the firm, which one should be selected as the primary basis for the firm's differentiation strategy? On the sypply side, there are three important considerations.
   - First, we must establish where the firm has greater potential for differentiating, or can differentiate at lower cost, than rivals. This requires some analysis of the firm's internal strengths in terms of resources and capabilities.
   - Second, in order to identify the most promising aspects of differentiation, we also need to identify linkages among activities, since some differentiation variables may involve interaction among several activities. Thus, product reliability is likely to be the outcome of several linked activities: monitoring purchases of inputs from suppliers, the skill and motivation of production workers, and quality control and product testing.
   - Third, the ease with which different types of uniqueness can be sustained must be considered. The more differentiation is based on resources specific to the firm or skills that involve the complex coordination of a large number of individuals, the more difficult it will be for a competitor to imitate the particular source of differentiation. Thus, offering business-class

FIGURE 9.6 Using the value chain to identify differentiation potential on the supply side

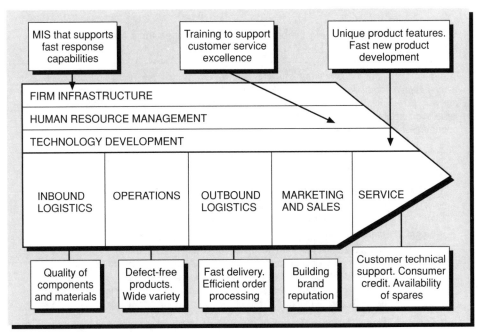

passengers wider seats and more legroom is an easily imitated source of differentiation. Achieving high levels of punctuality represents a more sustainable source of differentiation.

4. *Locate linkages between the value chain of the firm and that of the buyer.* The objective of differentiation is to yield a price premium for the firm. This requires that the firm's differentiation create value for the customer. Creating value for customers requires either that the firm lower the customers' costs, or that the customers be assisted in their own product differentiation. Thus, by completely reorganizing its system of ordering and distribution, Compaq, the world's top PC maker, has radically reduced distribution time and increased delivery reliability. This permits retailers to save inventory costs while offering computers configured to customers' specifications. To identify the means by which a firm can create value for its customers it must locate the linkages between differentiation of its own activities and cost reduction and differentiation within the customer's activities. Analysis of these linkages can also evaluate the potential profitability of differentiation. The value differentiation created for the customer represents the maximum price premium the customer will pay. If the provision of just-in-time delivery by a component supplier costs an additional $1,000 a month but saves an automobile company $6,000 a month in reduced inventory, warehousing, and handling costs, then it should be possible for the component manufacturer to obtain a price premium that easily exceeds the costs of the differentiation.

Exhibit 9.3 demonstrates the use of value chain analysis in identifying differentiation opportunities available to a manufacturer of metal containers.

EXHIBIT 9.3 Analyzing Differentiation Opportunities for a Manufacturer of Metal Containers

---

The metal container industry is a highly competitive, low-growth, low-profit industry. Cans lack much potential for differentiation and buyers (especially beverage and food canning companies) are very powerful. Clearly, cost efficiency is essential, but are there also opportunities for differentiation advantage? A value chain analysis can help a metal can manufacturer identify profitable opportunities for differentiation.

STAGE 1.   Construct value chain for firm and customers. The principal activities of the can manufacturer and its customers are shown in the diagram below.

STAGE 2.   Identify the drivers of uniqueness. For each of the can-making activities it is possible to suggest several possible differentiation variables. Examples are shown on the diagram.

STAGE 3.   Select key variables. To select the most promising differentiation variables, the company's internal strengths must be considered. If the firm has strong technical capabilities, then it might design and manufacture products to meet difficult technical and design specifications, and provide sophisticated technical services to customers. If its logistics capabilities are strong it might offer fast and reliable delivery, possibly extended to electronic data interchange with customers.

STAGE 4.   Identify linkages. To determine differentiation likely to create value for the customer, identify linkages between the can maker's potential for differentiation and the potential for reducing cost or enhancing differentiation within the customer's value chain. The diagram identifies five such linkages:
1.   Designing a distinctive can for customers may assist their own marketing activities.
2.   Consistent quality of cans lowers customers' canning costs by avoiding breakdowns and holdups on their canning lines.
3.   By maintaining high stocks and offering speedy delivery, customers can economize on their own stockholding (they may even be able to move to a just-in-time system of can supply).
4.   Efficient order processing can reduce customers' ordering costs.
5.   Capable and fast technical support can reduce the costs of breakdowns on canning lines.

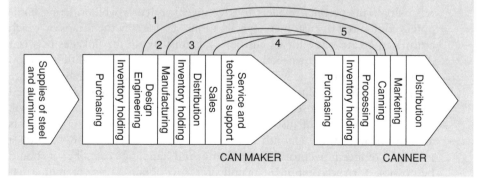

Value Chain Analysis of Consumer Goods

Value chain analysis is most readily applicable to producer goods where the customer is also a company with an easily definable value chain and where linkages between the supplier's and the customer's value chains are readily apparent. However, the same analysis can be applied to consumer goods with very little modification. Few consumer goods are consumed directly; in most cases consumers are involved in a chain of activities involving the acquisition and purchase of the product.

This is particularly evident for consumer durables where customers are involved in a long chain of activities from search, purchase, financing, acquiring accessories, operation, service and repair, and eventual disposal. Complex consumer value chains offer many potential linkages with the manufacturer's value chain, with considerable opportunity for innovative differentiation. Japanese producers of automobiles, consumer electronics, and domestic appliances have a long tradition of observing their customers and monitoring their behavior in retail outlets, then using the information of customer usage and selection processes in product design. Recent strategic changes at Ford Motor Company have been motivated by its quest for value-creating differentiation through closer linkage with its customers' value chains (see Exhibit 9.4).

EXHIBIT 9.4   Ford Motor Company: Looking Downstream for Differentiation Opportunity

---

Competition between Ford and General Motors during the 1920s was a classic battle of cost leadership versus differentiation. While GM produced a "car for every pocketbook," Ford stuck resolutely to its standard Model T – producing a total of 15 million over its lifetime. Color? "You can have any color you like so long as it's black!" Henry Ford retorted.

In 2000, Ford's mass production tradition was finally buried by its new CEO, Jac Nasser. From three brands (Ford, Mercury, and Lincoln), Ford had grown to eight with the addition of Jaguar, Aston Martin, Volvo, Land Rover, and Mazda. To focus the company on serving customers, its "Consumer Insight Experience" brought together customers with cross-functional groups of Ford employees. Closer customer understanding led to a new initiative for enhancing customers' experience with Ford vehicles. For example, recognition of the role of sound in consumers' driving experiences encouraged Ford to establish its Acoustic Center in Germany where, on the basis of customer responses to auditory signals such as the sound of the car doors closing and the clicking sound of turn signals, acoustic engineering was used to enhance customers' auditory experiences.

Ford also placed greater emphasis on after-sales services to its customers. Financing customer vehicle purchases had long been one of the company's most profitable activities. By 2000 its four "aftermarket" businesses – Ford Credit, Quality Care, Hertz, and Kwik-Fit – were brought together under Ford's Consumer Service Group. New services included Ford's Telematics communications business supplying in-car information and entertainment.

New technology played a key role in involving the company more closely with its customers. CarPoint – a joint venture with Microsoft – allowed consumers to design and order the car they wanted, when they wanted it. Teaming with Yahoo!, Ford offered personalized services for its owners, including online chat with its engineers. Through its web sites OwnerConnection.com and Ford.com, it offered information and services aimed at making it easier for consumers to own and operate its products over their lifetime. To involve all Ford employees more closely with customers, all employees were offered home computers and internet access for a monthly fee of $5.

Source: Ford Annual Report, 1999.

Even nondurables involve the consumer in a chain of activities. Consider a frozen TV dinner: it must be purchased, taken home, removed from the package, heated, and served before it is consumed. After eating, the consumer must clean any used dishes, cutlery, or other utensils. A value chain analysis by a frozen foods producer would identify ways in which the product could be formulated, packaged, and distributed to assist the consumer in performing this chain of activities.

SUMMARY

The attraction of differentiation over low cost as a basis for competitive advantage is its potential for sustainability. It is less vulnerable to being overturned by changes in the external environment, and it is more difficult to replicate.

The potential for differentiation in any business is vast. It may involve physical differentiation of the product, it may be through complementary services, it may be intangible. Differentiation extends beyond technology, design, and marketing to include all aspects of a firm's interactions with its customers.

The essence of differentiation advantage is to increase the perceived value of the offering to the customer either more effectively or at lower cost than do competitors. This requires that the firm match the requirements and preferences of customers with its own capacity for creating uniqueness.

The value chain provides a useful framework for analyzing differentiation advantage. By analyzing how value is created for customers and by systematically appraising the scope of each of the firm's activities for achieving differentiation, the value chain permits matching demand-side and supply-side sources of differentiation.

Successful differentiation requires a combination of astute analysis and creative imagination. The two are not antithetical. A systematic framework for the analysis of differentiation can act as a stimulus to creative ideas.

IV

Business Strategies in Different Industry Contexts

10

Industry Evolution

No company ever stops changing . . . Each new genera-
tion must meet changes – in the automotive market,
in the general administration of the enterprise, and
in the involvement of the corporation in a changing
world. The work of creating goes on.
—*Alfred P. Sloan Jr., president of General*
Motors 1923–37, chairman 1937–56

OUTLINE

INTRODUCTION AND OBJECTIVES

The analysis of competitive advantage in Part III emphasized competition as a dynamic process in which firms vie to gain competitive advantage, only to see it eroded through imitation and innovation by rivals. The outcome of this process is an industry environment that is continually being reshaped by the forces of competition. This view of competition as a dynamic process contrasts with the static approach of the Porter Five Forces of Competition framework (see Chapter 3), which views industry structure as a stable determinant of the intensity of competition in an industry. In practice, industry structures continually evolve, driven both by the forces of competition and by fundamental changes in technology and economic growth. Firms that develop the capabilities and strategies suited to emerging industry circumstances prosper and grow; those that do not are eliminated. In this chapter we consider whether industry evolution can be anticipated. My central thesis is that, although every industry follows a unique development path, it is possible to detect some common patterns that are the result of common driving forces. Our task is to identify these patterns of industry evolution, the forces that drive them, and their implications for competition and competitive advantage.

We will examine the industry life cycle as a framework for viewing industry development and for classifying industries according to their stage of development. This raises two questions. First, is the industry life cycle a valid and useful description of how industries evolve? Second, does categorization of industries according to their stage of development (or on some other basis) serve any useful purpose? On this latter question, I argue that the purpose of classifying industries is not to ignore their unique features, but to help us recognize the key factors that determine the strategic character of an industry.

We study industry evolution to help us manage change. This requires that we predict future changes in the firm's external environment in order to *adapt* to change, but also that we identify opportunities to *shape* the firm's environment.

By the time you have completed this chapter, you will be able to:

- Recognize the different stages of industry development and understand the factors that drive the process of industry evolution.

- Identify the key success factors associated with industries at different stages of their development.

- Identify the strategies, organizational structures, and management systems appropriate to different stages of industry development.

- Use scenarios to explore industry futures.

- Recognize the challenges that managers face when adapting their organizations to industry evolution.

FIGURE 10.1   The industry life cycle

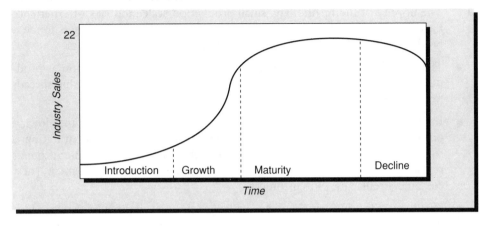

THE INDUSTRY LIFE CYCLE

One of the best-known and most enduring marketing concepts is the product life cycle.[1] Products are born, their sales grow, they reach maturity, they go into decline, and they ultimately die. If products have life cycles, so too do the industries that produce them. The industry life cycle is the supply-side equivalent of the product life cycle. To the extent that an industry produces a range and sequence of products, the industry life cycle is likely to be of longer duration than that of a single product. For example, though the 128-bit video game consoles produced by Nintendo, Sega, and Sony have a probable life cycle of a few years, the life cycle of the electronic games industry extends back to the release of the Atari 2600 in 1977.

The life cycle comprises four phases: *introduction* (or *emergence*), *growth*, *maturity*, and *decline* (see Figure 10.1). Before we examine the features of each of these stages, let us examine the forces that are driving industry evolution. Two factors are fundamental: demand growth and the production and diffusion of knowledge.

Demand Growth

The life cycle and the stages within it are defined primarily by changes in an industry's growth rate over time. The characteristic profile is an S-shaped growth curve.

[1]   The concept of the product life cycle is associated with the work of Everett M. Rogers, *The Diffusion of Innovations* (New York: Free Press, 1962); and Theodore Levitt, "Exploit the Product Life Cycle," *Harvard Business Review* (November–December 1965): 81–94. For a contemporary discussion, see Philip Kotler, *Marketing Management: Millennium Edition*, 10th edn (Upper Saddle River, NJ: Prentice-Hall, 2000): Chapter 10.

- In the *introduction stage*, sales are small and the rate of market penetration is low because the industry's products are little known and customers are few. The novelty of the technology, small production scale, and lack of experience mean that costs and prices are high, while quality is low. Customers for new products tend to be affluent, innovation oriented, and risk tolerant.

- The *growth stage* is characterized by accelerating market penetration as product technology becomes more standardized and prices fall. Ownership spreads from higher-income customers to the mass market.

- Increasing market saturation causes the onset of the *maturity stage* and slowing growth as new demand gives way to replacement demand. Once saturation is reached, demand is wholly for replacement, either direct replacement (customers replacing old products with new products) or indirect replacement (new customers replacing old customers).

- Finally, as the industry becomes challenged by new industries that produce technologically superior substitute products, the industry enters its *decline stage*.

Creation and Diffusion of Knowledge

The second key force driving the industry life cycle is the creation and diffusion of knowledge. New knowledge in the form of product innovation is responsible for an industry's birth, and the dual processes of knowledge creation and knowledge diffusion have a major influence on its pattern of development.

In the introduction stage, product technology advances rapidly. There is no dominant product technology, and rival technologies compete for attention. Competition is primarily between alternative technologies and design configurations. Although technology and design are linked, the primary competitive battle tends to be between rival technologies:

- The early years of the automobile industry featured competition between different power sources (steam vs. gasoline-powered internal combustion), transmission systems, cooling mode (air vs. water), and steering and braking systems.

- The early years of the home computer industry saw competition between different data storage systems (audio tapes vs. floppy disks), visual displays (TV receivers vs. dedicated monitors), operating systems (CPM vs. DOS vs. Apple II), and microprocessors.

The outcome tends to be convergence around a dominant technology, which may involve particular technical standards. Such standards may be imposed by governments and public authorities (e.g., standards for television broadcasting and wireless telecommunications established by the FCC) or they may be *de facto* standards that emerge out of competitive rivalry, e.g., the establishment of the VHS format as the industry standard for video recording during the early 1980s.[2]

---

[2]   Richard S. Rosenbloom and Michael A. Cusumano, "Technological Pioneering and Competitive Advantage: The Birth of the VCR Industry," *California Management Review* 29 no. 4 (1987).

The convergence process also involves the emergence of a *dominant design* – a generally adopted configuration of components that defines the look, functionality, and production criteria for the product. Such dominant designs have included the following:

■ The IBM PC launched in 1981 established the basic design parameters of the personal computer as well as the key technical standard that was eventually to dominate the industry (the so-called "Wintel" standard).

■ Leica's Ur-Leica 35mm camera developed by Oskar Barnack and launched in Germany in 1924 established what would become the dominant design for cameras, though it was not until Canon began mass producing cameras based on the Leica design that the 35mm camera came to dominate still photography.[3]

Dominant designs also extend to the design of strategy. In many e-commerce markets, competition is between rival *business models* – configurations of strategy relating to the sources of revenue and profit. In internet access, competition is between subscription-based ISPs (such as AOL), nonsubscription ISPs (such as Freeserve in the UK, where revenue is derived from advertising and revenue sharing with telephone companies), companies offering internet access through video game consoles (e.g., Sega.com), and interactive TVs offering web service (e.g., Gemstar and TiVo in the US, BSkyB/Open in the UK, and TPS in France).[4]

The transition from heterogeneity of technologies and designs toward greater increased standardization typically marks a shift from radical to incremental innovation. Such a transition may be necessary to inaugurate the industry's growth phase. Greater standardization reduces risks to customers and encourages firms to invest in manufacturing. The result is a shift from product innovation to process as firms seek to reduce costs and increase product reliability through large-scale manufacturing methods (see Figure 10.2). The combination of process improvements, design

FIGURE 10.2 Product and process innovation over time

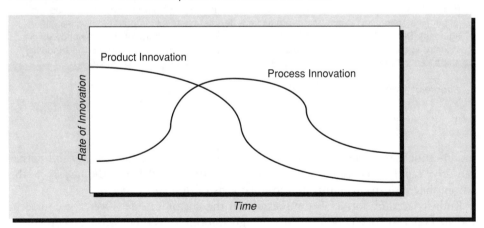

[3] Thanks to Bob Edwards for information on the development of camera design.
[4] "ISPs May Be Topped by the Interactive Box," *Financial Times* (November 13, 2000): 20.

EXHIBIT 10.1 Evolution of the Automobile Industry

The period 1890–1910 was one of rapid product innovation in the auto industry. After 1886 when Karl Benz received a patent on his three-wheel motor carriage, a flurry of technical advances occurred in Germany, France, the US, and Britain. Developments included:

- The first four-cylinder four-stroke engine (by Karl Benz in 1890).

- The honeycomb radiator (by Daimler in 1890).

- The speedometer (by Oldsmobile in 1901).

- Automatic transmission (by Packard in 1904).

- Electric headlamps (by General Motors in 1908).

- The all-steel body (adopted by General Motors in 1912).

Ford's Model T, introduced in 1908, with its front-mounted, water-cooled engine and transmission with a gearbox, wet clutch, and rearwheel drive, acted as a dominant design for the industry. During the remainder of the twentieth century automotive technology and design converged. A key indicator of this was the gradual elimination of nonconventional technologies and designs. Volkswagen's Beetle was the last mass-produced car with a rear-mounted, air-cooled engine. Citroën abandoned its distinctive suspension and braking systems. Four-stroke engines with four or six inline cylinders became dominant. Distinctive national differences eroded as American cars became smaller and Japanese and Italian cars became bigger. The fall of the Iron Curtain extinguished the last outposts of nonconformity: by the mid-1990s, East German two-stroke Wartburgs and Trabants were collectors' items. Increasing similarity between cars meant that by 2000, GM introduced a wireless telephone-activated device to help motorists locate their cars within car parks.

As product innovation slowed, so process innovation took off. In October 1913, Ford opened its Highland Park Assembly Plant with its revolutionary production methods based on interchangeable parts and a moving assembly line. In the space of one year, chassis assembly time was cut from 12 hours and 8 minutes to 1 hour and 33 minutes. The price of the Model T fell from $628 in 1908 to $260 in 1924. Between 1908 and 1927 over 15 million Model Ts had been produced.

The second revolutionary process innovation in automobile manufacturing was Toyota's system of "lean production," involving a tightly integrated "pull" system of production embodying just-in-time scheduling, team-based production, flexible manufacturing, and total quality management. During the 1970s and 1980s, lean production diffused throughout the world vehicle industry in the same way that Ford's mass-production system had transformed the industry half a century before.

Sources: www.daimlerchrysler.com; www.ford.com.

modifications, and scale economies results in falling costs and greater availability that can drive rapidly increasing market penetration. Exhibit 10.1 uses the history of the automobile industry to illustrate these patterns of development.

Knowledge diffusion is also important on the customer side. Over the course of the life cycle, customers become increasingly informed. As they become more knowledgeable about the performance attributes of rival manufacturers' products, so they are better able to judge value for money and become more price sensitive.

How General Is the Life Cycle Pattern?

To what extent do industries conform to this life cycle pattern? To begin with, the duration of the life cycle varies greatly from industry to industry:

- The life cycle of the US railroad industry extended from the 1840s to the 1950s before entering its decline phase.

- The introduction stage of the US automobile industry lasted about 25 years, from the 1890s until growth took off in 1913–15. The growth phase lasted about 40 years. Maturity, in terms of slackening growth, set in during the mid-1950s.

- In personal computers, the introduction phase lasted only about four years before growth took off in 1978. Between 1978 and 1983 a flood of new and established firms entered the industry. Toward the end of 1984, the first signs of maturity appeared: growth stalled, excess capacity emerged, and the industry began to consolidate around a few companies; however, it remained strong until the end of the 1990s.

- Compact discs, introduced in 1984, passed almost immediately from introduction to growth phase. By 1988, they outsold conventional record albums in the United States. The market matured during the 1990s and went into decline in 2000, threatened by direct on-line distribution.

The tendency over time has been for life cycles to become compressed. This is evident for all consumer electronic products, communication products, and also pharmaceuticals. In e-commerce, life cycles have become even more compressed. Businesses such as online gambling, business-to-business online auctions, and online travel services have gone from initial introduction to apparent maturity with a few years. Such time compression has required a radical rethink of strategies and management processes – "competing on internet time" is how Michael Cusumano and David Yoffie refer to the challenge.[5]

Patterns of evolution also differ. Industries supplying basic necessities such as residential construction, food processing, and clothing may never enter a decline phase because obsolescence is unlikely for such needs. Some industries may experience a rejuvenation of their life cycle. In the 1960s, the world motorcycle industry, in decline in the US and Europe, re-entered its growth phase as the influx of new Japanese bikes stimulated the recreational use of motorcycles. The TV monitor industry has experienced successive revivals: maturity of the market for black and white sets was followed by the color TV boom, the demand for computer monitors and video games spurred another cycle, and high-definition TV promises a further cycle. Similar waves of innovation have revitalized retailing (see Figure 10.3). These rejuvenations of the product life cycle are not natural phenomena – they are typically the result of

[5]   M. A. Cusumano and D. B. Yoffie, *Competing on Internet Time: Lessons From Netscape and Its Battle with Microsoft* (New York: Free Press, 1998).

FIGURE 10.3   Innovation and renewal in the industry life cycle: retailing

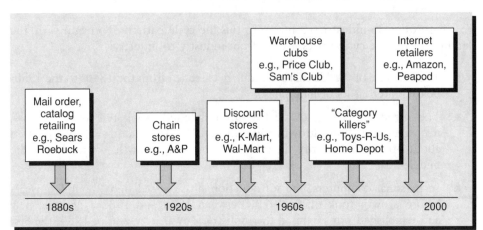

companies resisting the forces of maturity through breakthrough product innovations or developing new markets.

An industry is likely to be at different stages of its life cycle in different countries. Although the US auto market is in the early stages of its decline phase, markets in China, India, and Russia are in their growth phases. Multinational companies can exploit such differences: developing new products and introducing them into the advanced industrial countries, then shifting attention to other growth markets once maturity sets in. In the automobile and can-making industries, pursuing market growth phases is accompanied by shipping whole plants from North America and western Europe to Latin America, eastern Europe, and Asia.[6]

STRUCTURE, COMPETITION, AND SUCCESS FACTORS OVER THE LIFE CYCLE

Changes in demand growth and technology over the cycle have implications for industry structure, competition, and the sources of competitive advantage (key success factors). Table 10.1 summarizes the principal features of each stage of the industry life cycle.

Product Differentiation

Emerging industries are characterized by a wide variety of product types that reflect the diversity of technologies and designs – and the lack of consensus over customer

[6]   In metal containers, Crown Cork & Seal followed this strategy (see *Crown Cork and Seal and the Metal Container Industry* (Boston: Harvard Business School, 1978).

TABLE 10.1   The Evolution of Industry Structure and Competition over the Life Cycle

	INTRODUCTION	GROWTH	MATURITY	DECLINE
Demand	Limited to early adopters: high-income, avant-garde.	Rapidly increasing market penetration.	Mass market, replacement/repeat buying. Customers knowledgeable and price sensitive.	Obsolescence.
Technology	Competing technologies. Rapid product innovation.	Standardization around dominant technology. Rapid process innovation.	Well-diffused technical know-how: quest for technological improvements.	Little product or process innovation.
Products	Poor quality. Wide variety of features and technologies. Frequent design changes.	Design and quality improve. Emergence of dominant design.	Trend to commoditization. Attempts to differentiate by branding, quality, bundling.	Commodities the norm: differentiation difficult and unprofitable.
Manufacturing and distribution	Short production runs. High-skilled labor content. Specialized distribution channels.	Capacity shortages Mass production. Competition for distribution.	Emergence of overcapacity. Deskilling of production. Long production runs. Distributors carry fewer lines.	Chronic overcapacity. Re-emergence of specialty channels.
Trade	Producers and consumers in advanced countries.	Exports from advanced countries to rest of world.	Production shifts to newly industrializing then developing countries.	Exports from countries with lowest labor costs.
Competition	Few companies.	Entry, mergers, and exits.	Shakeout. Price competition increases.	Price wars, exits.
Key success factors	Product innovation. Establishing credible image of firm and product.	Design for manufacture. Access to distribution. Building strong brand. Fast product development. Process innovation.	Cost efficiency through capital intensity, scale efficiency, and low input costs. High quality.	Low overheads. Buyer selection. Signaling commitment. Rationalizing capacity.

requirements. Standardization during growth and maturity phases increases product uniformity, with the result that a product may evolve toward commodity status unless producers are effective in developing new dimensions for differentiation, such as marketing variables, ancillary services (e.g., credit facilities, after-sales service), and product options.[7] A feature of the markets for personal computers, credit cards, securities broking, and internet access is their increasing commodity status in which buyers select primarily on price.

Industry Structure and Competition

Market growth and technological change are major determinants of the structure of manufacturing and distribution, although it is difficult to generalize about resulting industry structures. In most industries, the introduction phase is associated with a fragmented structure and diversity of products and technologies. Thus, the automobile, aircraft, and personal computer industries all went through their "garage stages" involving numerous small startups and entry by established companies from different industries. The growth stage may also attract further new entry, but soon fragmentation is counteracted by pressures for lower costs through scale-efficient production. Rapid consolidation around fewer players is certainly a feature of the transition to maturity, when the slowdown of market growth causes excess capacity and a "shakeout" phase for the industry. This shakeout period may mark the onset of aggressive price competition in the industry.[8]

Typically, new industries attract a flood of new entrants where the different origins of the entrants add to the diversity of technologies and business models deployed.[9] The US automobile industry featured many hundreds of producers in the early years of the twentieth century,[10] while in TV receivers there were 92 companies in 1951.[11] Large companies (with bigger R&D budgets) and companies with more successful R&D projects tend to grow, causing other firms to decline and exit.[12] The general trend, therefore, is for concentration to increase over time. The shakeout phase of intensive acquisition, merger, and exit occurs, on average, 29 years into the life cycle and results in the number of producers being halved.[13] In the US tire

[7]   In Shiv Mathur and Alfred Kenyon's "transaction cycle," differentiation re-emerges as products and service are recombined into new systems. See "Competitive System Dynamics," in *Creating Wealth: Shaping Tomorrow's Business* (Oxford: Butterworth-Heinemann, 1997): Chapter 9.

[8]   High rates of entry and exit may continue well into maturity. In US manufacturing industries in any given year, it was found that 39 percent of larger companies were not industry participants five years earlier and 40 percent would not be participants five years later. See T. Dunne, M. J. Roberts, and L. Samuelson, "Patterns of Firm Entry and Exit in US Manufacturing Industries," *Rand Journal of Economics* 19 (1988): 495–515.

[9]   On the early development of the semiconductor industry see D. Holbrook, W. M. Cohen, D. A. Hounshell, and S. Klepper, "The Nature, Sources, and Consequences of Firm Differences in the Early History of the Semiconductor Industry," *Strategic Management Journal* 21 (2000): 1017–41.

[10]   G. R. Carroll, L. S. Bigelow, M.-D. Seidel, and B. Tsai, "The Fates of *de novo* and *de alio* Producers in the American Automobile Industry, 1885–1981," *Strategic Management Journal* 17, Summer special issue (1996): 117–37.

[11]   S. Klepper and K. L. Simons, "Dominance by Birthright: Entry of Prior Radio Producers and Competitive Ramifications in the US Television Receiver Industry," *Strategic Management Journal* 17 (2000): 997–1016.

[12]   This process is modeled in S. Klepper, "Firm Survival and the Evolution of Oligopoly," working paper (Pittsburgh: Carnegie Mellon University, 1999).

[13]   S. Klepper and E. Grady, "The Evolution of New Industries and the Determinants of Industry Structure," *Rand Journal of Economics* (1990): 27–44.

industry, the number of players increased during the first 25 years, before waves of consolidation typically triggered by technological and strategic changes within the industry.[14]

However, generalization is dangerous. Other industries, especially those where the first mover achieves substantial patent protection, may start out as near-monopolies, then become increasingly competitive. Plain-paper copiers were initially monopolized by Xerox Corporation and it was not until the early 1980s that the industry was transformed by the entry of many competitors. Scale economies and entry barriers play a key role in different paths of evolution between industries. Where entry barriers rise due to increasing scale economies and capital requirements (automobiles, commercial aircraft, telecommunications equipment) or product differentiation and access to distribution channels (soft drinks, ice cream, cosmetics), seller concentration increases substantially over the life cycle. Where entry barriers fall because technology becomes more accessible or product differentiation declines, concentration may decline (credit cards, television broadcasting, frozen foods).

Location and International Trade

The industry life cycle is associated with changes in the pattern of trade and direct investment that together result in international migration of production.[15] The life cycle theory of trade and direct investment is based on two assumptions. First, that demand for new products emerges first in the advanced industrialized countries of North America, western Europe, and Japan and then diffuses internationally. Second, that with maturity, products require fewer inputs of technology and sophisticated skills. The result is the following development pattern:

1. New industries begin in high-income countries (traditionally the United States, but increasingly in Japan and western Europe) because of the presence of a market and the availability of technical and scientific resources.

2. As demand grows in other markets, they are serviced initially by exports.

3. Continued growth of overseas markets and reduced need for inputs of technology and sophisticated labor skills make production attractive in newly industrialized countries. The advanced industrialized countries begin to import.

4. With maturity, a reduced need for skilled production workers, and an increased perception of the product as a commodity, the production activity shifts increasingly to developing countries in search of low-cost labor.

---

[14] S. Klepper and K. Simons, "The Making of an Oligopoly: Firm Survival and Technological Change in the Evolution of the US Tire Industry," *Journal of Political Economy* 108 (2000).

[15] R. Vernon, "International Investment and International Trade in the Product Cycle," *Quarterly Journal of Economics* 80 (1966): 190–207.

For example, consumer electronics were initially dominated by the United States and Germany. During the early 1960s, production shifted towards Japan. The 1980s saw the rise of Korea, Hong Kong, and Taiwan as leading exporters. By the mid-1990s, assembly had moved to lower-wage countries such as China, the Philippines, Thailand, Mexico, and Brazil. We return to these issues of national-level competitiveness in Chapter 14.

The Nature and Intensity of Competition

Competition changes in two ways over the course of the industry life cycle. First, there is a shift from nonprice to price competition. Second, the intensity of competition grows causing margins to narrow. During the introduction stage, competitors battle for technological leadership and competition focuses on technology and design. Gross margins can be high, but heavy investments in innovation and market development tend to depress return on capital. The growth phase is more conducive to profitability as market demand outstrips industry capacity – especially if incumbents are protected by barriers to entry. With the onset of maturity, increased product standardization increases the emphasis on price competition. How intense this is depends a great deal on the capacity/demand balance and the extent of international competition. In food retailing, airlines, motor vehicles, metals, oil refining, and insurance, maturity was associated with strong price competition and slender profitability. In household detergents, breakfast cereals, cosmetics, and investment banking, high levels of seller concentration and successful maintenance of product differentiation resulted in positive economic profits. The decline phase is almost always associated with strong price competition (and may degenerate into destructive price wars) and dismal profit performance. Changes in profitability over the industry life cycle are shown in Figure 10.4.

Key Success Factors and Industry Evolution

The changes in industry structure, demand, and technological requirements over the industry life cycle have important implications for the primary sources of competitive advantage at each stage of industry evolution:

- During the introductory stage product innovation is the basis for initial entry and for subsequent success. Soon, however, knowledge alone is not enough. As the industry begins its evolution and technological competition intensifies, other requirements for success emerge. In moving from the first generation of products to subsequent generations, investment requirements tend to grow, and financial resources become increasingly important. Capabilities in product development soon need to be matched by capabilities in manufacturing, marketing, and distribution. Hence, in an emerging industry, firms need to support their innovation with a broad array of vertically integrated capabilities.

FIGURE 10.4 Return on invested capital at different stages of the industry life cycle

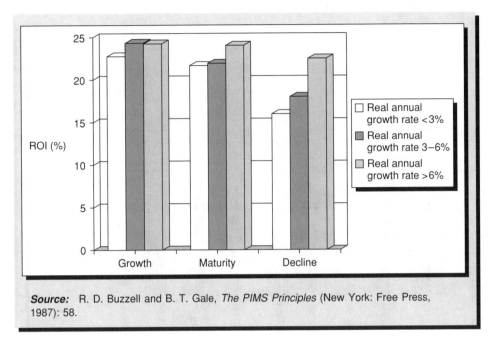

Source: R. D. Buzzell and B. T. Gale, *The PIMS Principles* (New York: Free Press, 1987): 58.

- Once the growth stage is reached, the key challenge is scaling up. As the market expands, the firm needs to adapt its product design and its manufacturing capability to large-scale production. As Figure 10.5 shows, investment in R&D, plant and equipment, and sales tends to be high during the growth phase. To utilize increased manufacturing capability, access to distribution becomes critical. At the same time, the tensions that organizational growth imposes create the need for internal administrative and strategic skills. We consider these issues in Chapter 11.

- With the maturity stage, competitive advantage is increasingly a quest for cost efficiency – or, at least, this is the case in those mature industries that tend toward commoditization. Cost efficiency through scale economies, low wages, and low overheads become the key success factors. Figure 10.5 shows that R&D, capital investment, and marketing are lower in maturity than during the growth phase.

- The transformation to the decline phase raises the potential for destructive price competition. Whether a firm has a competitive advantage is secondary to the importance of maintaining a stable industry environment. Hence, company strategies focus on encouraging the orderly exit of industry capacity and building a strong position in relation to residual market demand. We consider the strategic issues presented by mature and declining industries more fully in Chapter 12.

FIGURE 10.5 Differences in strategy and performance between businesses at different stages of the industry life cycle

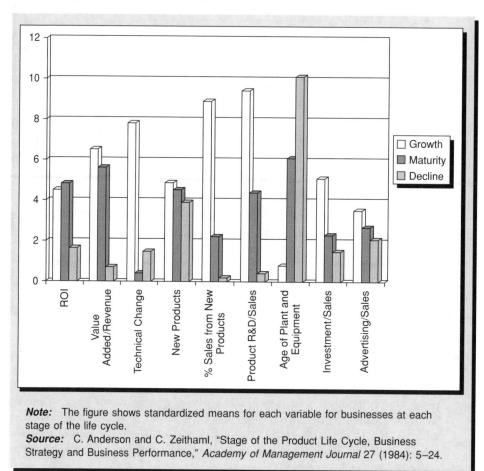

Note: The figure shows standardized means for each variable for businesses at each stage of the life cycle.
Source: C. Anderson and C. Zeithaml, "Stage of the Product Life Cycle, Business Strategy and Business Performance," *Academy of Management Journal* 27 (1984): 5–24.

ADAPTING TO CHANGE AND SHAPING THE FUTURE

In Chapter 1, we introduced the notion of *fit*. For companies to be successful, their strategies and organizational structures need to be aligned with their industry environments. This concept of fit has its origin in *contingency* approaches to organization theory.[16] Industry evolution poses a huge challenge to managers: How can the organization adapt to keep pace with the rate of change in the external environment?

---

[16] Contingency theory has its origins in P. R. Lawrence and J. W. Lorsch's book *Organization and Environment* (Boston: Harvard Business School, 1967). See also A. Ginsberg and N. Venkatraman, "Contingency Perspectives of Organizational Strategy," *Academy of Management Review* 10 (1985): 421–34.

Organizational Change

Organizations adjust to external change in two ways: *selection* and *adaptation*.

Selection

Although new entry is associated primarily with the introduction and growth phases of the life cycle and exit with a period of shakeout, entry and exit occur throughout the life span of every industry. Organizational ecologists view the competitive process as a *selection mechanism*, in which competition results in the survival of those organizations whose characteristics match the requirements of their environment, and the failure (through acquisition or liquidation) of those organizations that do not fit their environment. The result is that different companies tend to be industry leaders at different stages of an industry's life cycle.

The assumption here is that companies do not adapt easily to change. This can be explained by the role of *organizational routines*, discussed in Chapter 5. If organizational capabilities are based on complex routines, and if success at any one stage of the life cycle requires highly developed, finely honed routines, then companies successful at one stage of industry development will find it difficult to adapt to the next stage of development that requires new capabilities. Companies get caught in "*competency traps*"[17] where their "core capabilities become core rigidities."[18]

Adaptation

Companies can and do adapt to change. General Motors has led the world automobile industry since the mid-1920s. General Electric has been the biggest supplier of heavy electrical equipment since 1910. Exxon (now Exxon-Mobil) and Royal Dutch/Shell have dominated the petroleum industry for almost the whole of the twentieth century. Nevertheless change is difficult. Organizational change requires building new capabilities, it threatens the existing power structure, and it is likely to require changes in top management teams.[19]

The ability to adapt to external change depends very much on the implications of change for the existing capabilities of the company. Some technological changes may enhance a company's existing capabilities, others may be "competence destroying."[20] The ability to adapt to technological change is likely to depend on whether its impact is at the "component" or the "architectural" level.[21] Thus, in determining whether

[17] J. G. March, "Exploration and Exploitation in Organizational Learning," *Organizational Science* 2 (1991): 71–87.
[18] D. Leonard-Barton, "Core Capabilties and Core Rigidities: A Paradox in Managing New Product Development," *Strategic Management Journal*, Summer special issue (1992): 111–25.
[19] M. Wiersema and K. Bantel, "Top Management Team Turnover as an Adaptation Mechanism," *Strategic Management Journal* 14 (1993): 485–504.
[20] M. L. Tushman and P. Anderson, "Technological Discontinuities and Organizational Environments," *Administrative Science Quarterly* 31 (1986): 439–65.
[21] R. M. Henderson and K. B. Clark, "Architectural Innovation: The Reconfiguration of Existing Systems and the Failure of Established Firms," *Administrative Science Quarterly* (1990): 9–30.

startups such as Webvan and Peapod or established retailers such as Safeway and Kroger will dominate the market for online grocery retailing, a critical issue is whether online ordering and direct home delivery can be "bolted on" to existing supermarkets' current operations (i.e., component-level innovation), or whether it requires them to reconfigure their value chains completely (i.e., architectural innovation).

While some scholars identify the potential for companies to adapt through a series of discrete changes ("*logical incrementalism*"[22]), most observers suggest that gradual, adaptive change is too slow for organizational change to keep pace with change in the external environment. Elaine Romanelli and Michael Tushman identify a process of *punctuated equilibrium* in which organizational inertia prevents adaptation to external change, up to the point where the widening misalignment between the organization and its environment forces radical and comprehensive change on the company.[23] During the 1970s and 1980s, the oil majors maintained their top-heavy, vertically integrated structures despite increasing competition and market turbulence, but, by the mid-1980s, the fall in crude prices forced almost all of them to radical restructuring.[24]

Andy Grove of Intel has pointed to the necessity for top management to be alert to the need for radical strategic change. His experience at Intel suggests that continuous and adaptive change is effective only to a point. Then, at what Grove refers to as a *strategic inflection point*, a company must be willing to make a radical strategic shift. For Intel, such an inflection point occurred when it recognized that its future lay in microprocessors rather than its traditional business of designing and fabricating memory chips.[25]

The Challenge of Disruptive Technologies

Technological change presents a particularly important source of change within industries. *Disruptive technologies*, according to Clay Christensen, are those that offer a very different package of attributes from the existing technology. Thus,

> Sony's early transistor radios sacrificed sound fidelity but created a market for portable radios by offering a new and different package of attributes – small size, light weight and portability.[26]

Established leaders in the older technology typically fail to make the transition to the new wave of technology:

[22] J. B. Quinn, "Strategic Change: Logical Incrementalism," *Sloan Management Review* 20 (Fall 1978): 7–21.
[23] M. L. Tushman and E. Romanelli, "Organizational Evolution: A Metamorphosis Model of Convergence and Reorientation," in L. L. Cummins and B. M. Staw (eds) *Research in Organizational Behavior* 7 (1985): 171–222; E. Romanelli and M. L. Tushman, "Organizational Transformation as Punctuated Equilibrium: An Empirical Test," *Academy of Management Journal* 37 (1994): 1141–66.
[24] R. Cibin and R. M. Grant, "Restructuring among the World's Leading Oil Companies," *British Journal of Management* 7 (1996): 283–308.
[25] A. Grove, *Only the Paranoid Survive* (New York: Doubleday, 1996).
[26] J. Bower and C. M. Christensen, "Disruptive Technologies: Catching the Wave," *Harvard Business Review* (January–February 1995): 43–53.

- In steel, it was newcomer Nucor using minimill technology that became the most successful steelmaker in the US. US Steel and Bethlehem Steel are still struggling to make money from their blast furnaces.

- In personal computers, not one of the leading minicomputer makers made a successful transition into PCs.

- Only one of the existing department store companies, Dayton Hudson, became successful in discount retailing.

The tendency for established industry leaders to succumb to stealth attacks by newcomers armed with disruptive technologies is not simply the result of ignorance of internal rigidities among incumbent firms. Based on detailed analysis of technological change in hard-disk drives, Christensen notes that the critical barriers to established companies developing a new technology are, first, customers don't want the new technology; second, the new technology doesn't perform as well as the existing technology. In hard disks, at every transition from 14" to 8" to 5.25" to 3.5" drives, the established companies were an average of two years behind new companies in launching the new category of products.

Even when established companies recognize the potential of a new technology, the problem is that they can't develop the capabilities needed to be successful in adopting and developing it. The problem, according to Christensen and Overdorf, is that, as a company matures, so its capabilities become embedded in processes and values that tend to be inflexible. With regard to processes, Digital Equipment's failure in PCs stemmed from processes that were oriented toward internal development and sourcing of most major components, in contrast to the outsourcing model that dominated PC manufacture. With regard to values, Digital's belief that a 40 percent margin on its products was necessary in order to generate a reasonable return on capital meant that PCs were always a low strategic priority.[27] The solution, according to Christensen and Overdorf, is for established companies to develop products and businesses that embody disruptive technologies in organizationally separate units.

Managing with Dual Strategies

Adapting to change requires that companies must simultaneously compete in two time periods. Strategy is about maximizing performance under today's circumstances; it is also about developing and deploying resources and capabilities for competing in the future. Whereas strategies for the present are primarily concerned with maximizing the effectiveness of current resources and capabilities, competing in the future is concerned with redeploying existing resources and capabilities and developing, extending, and augmenting them. Derek Abell identifies the pursuit of "dual strategies" – optimizing present performance while adapting to the future

---

[27] C. M. Christensen and M. Overdorf, "Meeting the Challenge of Disruptive Change," *Harvard Business Review* (March–April 2000): 66–76.

– as a critical strategic change.[28] Managing dual strategies requires dual planning systems:

■   Short-term planning that focuses on strategic fit and performance over a one- or two-year period.

■   Longer-term planning to develop vision, reshape the corporate portfolio, redefine and reposition individual businesses, develop new capabilities, and redesign organizational structures over periods of five years or more.

Competing for the Future

Gary Hamel and C. K. Prahalad argue that for most companies, emphasis on competing in the present means that too much management energy is devoted to preserving the past and not enough to creating the future.[29] They challenge managers with seven questions:

1.   How does senior management's point of view about the future compare with that of your competitors: conventional and reactive, or distinctive and far sighted?

2.   Which business issue absorbs more senior management attention: reengineering core processes or regenerating core strategies?

3.   How do your competitors view your company: mostly as a rule follower or mostly as a rule maker?

4.   What is your company's strength: operational efficiency or innovation and growth?

5.   What is the focus of your company's advantage-building efforts: mostly catching up or mostly getting out in front?

6.   What has set your transformation agenda: your competitors or your foresight?

7.   Do you spend the bulk of your time as a maintenance engineer preserving the status quo or as an architect designing the future?[30]

Hamel and Prahalad develop what they describe as a "new strategy paradigm" that emphasizes the role of strategy as a systematic and concerted approach to redefining both the company and its industry environment in the future. This compares with the conventional, more static approach, which emphasizes the fit between the firm's strategy and, on the one hand, the industry environment and, on the other, the firm's resources and capabilities. The key is not to anticipate the future, but to *create* the future. We shall return to this point in Chapter 12, when we

[28]   Derek F. Abell, *Managing with Dual Strategies* (New York: Free Press, 1993).
[29]   Gary Hamel and C. K. Prahalad, *Competing for the Future* (Boston: Harvard Business School Press, 1995).
[30]   Gary Hamel and C. K. Prahalad, "Competing for the Future," *Harvard Business Review* (July–August 1994): 122–8.

FIGURE 10.6 Competing for the future: Hamel and Prahalad's "new strategy paradigm"

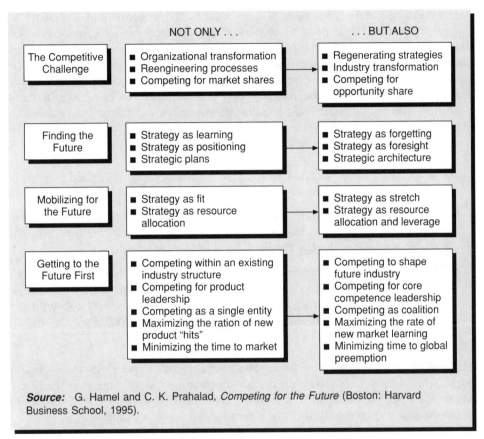

	NOT ONLY . . .	. . . BUT ALSO
The Competitive Challenge	■ Organizational transformation ■ Reengineering processes ■ Competing for market shares	■ Regenerating strategies ■ Industry transformation ■ Competing for opportunity share
Finding the Future	■ Strategy as learning ■ Strategy as positioning ■ Strategic plans	■ Strategy as forgetting ■ Strategy as foresight ■ Strategic architecture
Mobilizing for the Future	■ Strategy as fit ■ Strategy as resource allocation	■ Strategy as stretch ■ Strategy as resource allocation and leverage
Getting to the Future First	■ Competing within an existing industry structure ■ Competing for product leadership ■ Competing as a single entity ■ Maximizing the ration of new product "hits" ■ Minimizing the time to market	■ Competing to shape future industry ■ Competing for core competence leadership ■ Competing as coalition ■ Maximizing the rate of new market learning ■ Minimizing time to global preemption

Source: G. Hamel and C. K. Prahalad, *Competing for the Future* (Boston: Harvard Business School, 1995).

discuss strategic innovation. The main features of Hamel and Prahalad's paradigm are summarized in Figure 10.6.

The idea that adapting to change requires *strategic* rather than *incremental* change has also been made by Michael Porter. He points to a growing tendency for companies to confuse measures and programs to promote efficiency and effectiveness with strategic decisions. Strategic decisions involve difficult-to-reverse choices over the allocation of the company's resources. The essence of strategy is choice. Operational effectiveness issues such as cutting administrative staff, reducing inventories, pressing suppliers for lower component prices, reengineering processes, and implementing TQM may be vital, but they are not strategic. Efficiency is desirable whichever strategy is adopted, but it will be insufficient to save a company from a competitor's fundamental strategic innovation.[31]

---

[31] Michael E. Porter, "What Is Strategy?," *Harvard Business Review* (November–December 1996): 61–80.

In his most recent book, *Leading the Revolution*, Gary Hamel goes much further. In an age of revolution, "the company that is evolving slowly is already on its way to extinction."[32] What answer does Hamel offer? Revolution must be met by revolution. Established companies must give up incremental improvement and adapt to a nonlinear world. They need to recognize that competition is between business concepts rather than products, blow up their old business models, and create new ones. Most of Hamel's message is about changing the psychological and sociological aspects of organizations and their members. How can we think differently about the future: embracing novelty and rejecting convention? How can companies ferment revolution: encouraging individual activists and visionaries and creating the conditions that can foster insurrection? Yet, when it comes to formulating innovative business concepts, Hamel turns to some basic elements of strategy analysis:

- At the heart of the business model is *core strategy*, which is defined by *business mission*, *product/market scope*, and a *basis for differentiation*.

- *Strategic resources* provide the foundations for competitive advantage. These comprise what the firm knows (its *core competencies*), what the firm owns (its *strategic assets*), and what the firm does (its *core processes*).

- To *boost profits* companies need to take advantage of *increasing returns* through network externalities, learning, and positive feedback, *competitor lockout* through preemption and customer locking, *strategic economies* through economies of scale and scope, and *strategic flexibility* through agility, portfolio breadth, and low breakeven levels.

The upshot is this: Adapting to faster rates of change will require new mindsets and organizational processes. However, the basis for competitive advantage in the future will be the result of strategies based on the concepts that we have covered so far in this book and will continue to introduce in the subsequent chapters.

Preparing for the Future: Scenario Analysis

Whether a company is seeking to adapt to changes in its industry environment or to shape industry evolution, a profound understanding of the forces driving industry change is critical. We cannot predict the future. "Only a fool would make predictions – especially about the future," remarked movie mogul Samuel Goldwyn. But although we cannot predict the future, we can think about what might happen. And we can do so in a systematic way that builds on what we know about current trends and signals to future developments. This is what *scenario analysis* does. Scenario analysis is not a forecasting technique, but a process for thinking and communicating about the future.

Herman Kahn, who pioneered their use first at the Rand Corporation and subsequently at the Hudson Institute, defined scenarios as "hypothetical sequences

---

[32] G. Hamel, *Leading the Revolution* (Boston: Harvard Business School Press, 2000): 5.

of events constructed for the purpose of focusing attention on causal process and decision points."[33] The multiple scenario approach constructs several – typically three or four – distinct and internally consistent views of how the future may look 10 to 25 years ahead (shorter in the case of fast-moving sectors). Its key value is in combining the interrelated impacts of a wide range of economic, technological, demographic, and political factors into a few distinct alternative stories of how the future might unfold. Scenarios are good exercise for the imagination and are valuable in identifying possible threats and opportunities, generating flexibility of thinking by managers, and developing highly practical approaches to the management of risk. Applied to particular industries, scenarios can help clarify and develop alternative views of how changing customer requirements, emerging technologies, and new firm strategies may influence industry structure, and what the implications for competition and competitive advantage might be.

However, as with most strategy techniques, the value of scenario analysis is not in the results, but in the process. Scenario analysis is a powerful tool for knowledge management in terms of bringing together different ideas and insights about the business environment and building consensus about possible outcomes. Most importantly, however, scenarios can help evaluate alternative strategic options. By assessing how a strategy might perform under different scenarios, they can help a firm identify which strategies are most robust and can assist in contingency planning by forcing managers to address a series of "What if?" questions. Exhibit 10.2 outlines the use of scenarios at Shell.

EXHIBIT 10.2   Multiple Scenario Development at Shell

The Royal Dutch/Shell group of companies has pioneered the use of multiple scenario development as a basis for long-term strategic planning in an industry known for its high risks and very long-term investment projects. In 1967, a "Year 2000" study was inaugurated and scenario development soon became fundamental to Shell's planning process. Mike Pocock, Shell's former chairman, observed: "We believe in basing planning not on single forecasts, but on deep thought that identifies a coherent pattern of economic, political, and social development."

Shell views its scenarios as critical to its transition from planning toward strategic management, in which the role of the planning function is not so much to produce a plan, but to manage a process, the outcome of which is improved decision making by managers. This involves continually challenging current thinking within the group, encouraging a wider look at external influences on the business, promoting learning, and forging coordination among Shell's 200-odd subsidiaries.

---

[33] See C. A. R. NcNulty, "Scenario Development for Corporate Planning," *Futures* (April 1977). R. E. Linneman and H. E. Klien, "The Use of Multiple Scenarios by US Industrial Companies: A Comparison Study," *Long Range Planning* (December 1983): 94–101, found that over half of Fortune 500 companies were using multiple scenario analysis by the beginning of the 1980s. P. Malaska, "Multiple Scenario Approach and Strategic Behavior in European Companies," *Strategic Management Journal* 6 (1985): 339–55, found scenario analysis used most widely in petroleum, transportation equipment, and electricity industries.

EXHIBIT 10.2 (cont'd)

Shell's global scenarios are prepared about every four years by its corporate-level planning staff. Economic, political, technological, and demographic trends are analyzed and two alternative scenarios are constructed for the development of the world economy over the following 20 years. Thus, Shell's 1984–2005 scenarios were:

- *Next Wave*, which envisaged near-term crisis breaking down structural barriers to change and propelling the global economy into rapid technological progress and strong growth, but accompanied by increasing power of the oil-producing nations and stronger competition to oil from gas and electricity.

- *Divided World*, in which the barriers to change – protectionism and regulation – stunt growth and technological progress, result in a divide between stagnation in Europe and the developing world and economic development in Asia-Pacific, and are accompanied by weak oil prices.

Once approved by top management, the scenarios are disseminated by reports, presentations, and workshops, where they form the basis for long-term strategy discussion by business sectors and operating companies.

Shell is adamant that its scenarios are not forecasts. They represent carefully thought-out stories of how the various forces shaping the global energy environment of the future might play out. Their value is in stimulating the social and cognitive processes through which managers think about the future. For example:

- The formulation of scenarios involves bringing out the assumptions and mental models through which managers view their world. All too often these remain hidden and mis-understood – most importantly, by the individuals who hold them. This identification and sharing of implicit assumptions and theories is an important vehicle for mutual learning among different managers.

- The scenario development process permits a deeper and broader understanding of the various forces driving change and how they interact. This can be assisted by sophisticated computer modeling, including simulation.

- The incorporation of scenarios into the strategy formulation process encourages managers to build flexibility into their strategies by envisaging responses to hypothetical situations. Thus, in 1984, Shell had a scenario in which oil was $15 a barrel – which most viewed as inconceivable at a time when oil was $28 a barrel. When the price of oil fell precipitously to $10 in 1986, Shell was able to adjust more easily than most oil majors because its managers had already considered their responses to dramatically lower prices. Arie De Geus sees scenarios as central to the role of strategic planning as a vehicle for institutional learning.

Sources: J. P. Leemhuis, "Using Scenarios to Develop Strategies," *Long Range Planning* 18 (April 1985): 30–37; Pierre Wack, "Scenarios: Uncharted Waters Ahead," *Harvard Business Review* (September–October 1985): 72 and "Scenarios: Shooting the Rapids," *Harvard Business Review* (November–December 1985): 139; Arie de Geus, "Planning as Learning," *Harvard Business Review* (March–April 1988): 70–4; Paul Schoemacher, "Multiple Scenario Development: Its Conceptual and Behavioral Foundation," *Strategic Management Journal* 14 (1993): 193–214.

SUMMARY

Strategy is about establishing an identity and a direction for the development of a business into the future. How can we formulate a strategy for the future if the future is unknown and difficult to predict?

In this chapter we have learned that some regularities are evident in the evolutionary paths that industries follow. The life cycle model is a useful approach to exploring the impact of temporal processes of market saturation and technology development and dissemination and their impact on industry structure and the basis of competitive advantage. Classifying industries according to their stage of development can in itself be an insightful exersise:

- It acts as a shortcut in strategy analysis. Categorizing an industry according to its stage of development can alert us to the type of competition likely to emerge and the kinds of strategy likely to be effective.

- Classifying an industry encourages comparison with other industries. By highlighting similarities and differences with other industries, such comparisons can help us gain a deeper understanding of the strategic characteristics of an industry.

- It directs attention to the forces of change and direction of industry evolution, thereby helping us to anticipate and manage change.

The dual nature of strategy – maximizing competitive performance in the present while preparing for the future – is a central dilemma for strategic management. If the industry environment is subject to fundamental change, the more successful a company is in achieving fit between its resources and capabilities and the current key success factors, the greater the difficulties of adapting to the requirements of the future. Despite Gary Hamel urging managers to take up the cause of strategic revolution, the fact remains that organizational change is painful and difficult. However, by recognizing the barriers that they face in adapting to internal change, companies become better placed to overcome the "core rigidities."[34]

In the next two chapters, we discuss strategy formulation and strategy implementation in industries at different stages of their development: emerging industries, those characterized by technology-based competition, and mature industries.

---

[34] Dorothy Leonard-Barton, "Core Capabilities and Core Rigidities: A Paradox in Managing New Product Development," *Strategic Management Journal* 13 (Summer 1992): 111–26.

APPENDIX: ALTERNATIVE APPROACHES TO INDUSTRY CLASSIFICATION

Industries can be classified in many ways: by type of customer (producer goods and consumer goods), by the principal resources used (capital-intensive, technology-intensive, and marketing-intensive professional skill industries), or by the geographic scope of the industry (local, national, global). The critical issue is whether a particular approach to industry classification can offer insight into the similarities and differences among industries for the purposes of formulating business strategies. Here are two useful approaches.

BCG's Strategic Environments Matrix

In the industry life cycle, the stage of maturity of an industry determines its key structural characteristics, which, in turn, determine the nature of competitive advantage. The Boston Consulting Group's Strategic Environments Matrix reverses this direction: it is the nature of competitive advantage in an industry that determines strategies that are viable, which in turn determine the structure of the industry.

Two variables are used:

1. *The number of viable strategy approaches that are available.* This depends on the complexity of the industry in terms of the diversity of sources of competitive advantage. Complex products (automobiles, restaurants) offer more scope for differentiation than do commodities. Among commodities, the potential for competitive advantage depends on whether there are opportunities for cost advantage.

2. The size of potential competitive advantage. How big is the advantage available to the industry leader? This may derive from economies of scale, or brand leadership, or controlling the industry standard.

The two variables define four industry types (see Figure 10.7):

1. *Volume businesses* are those where the sources of advantage are few, but the size of advantage (typically resulting from scale economies) is considerable.

2. *Stalemate businesses* are those where the sources of advantage are few and the size of potential advantage is small. The result is a highly competitive industry where firms compete with similar strategies, but none is able to obtain significant advantage. Once a business is embroiled in a stalemate industry, survival and profitability require operational efficiency, low administrative overheads, and a cost-conscious corporate culture.

FIGURE 10.7 BCG's strategic environments matrix

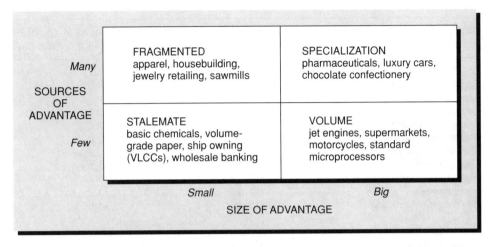

3. *Fragmented businesses* are those where the sources of competitive advantage
    are many, but the size of advantage is small. They typically supply differentiated
    products where brand loyalty is low, technology is well diffused, and scale
    economies are small. Success factors may include low costs through operational
    efficiency, focusing on an attractive market segment, responding quickly to
    change, and establishing novel forms of differentiation. Successful companies
    tend to be entrepreneurial. Franchising is one way of matching the advantages
    of size with those of flexibility and decentralization. An alternative strategy is
    to attempt to transform the business into a specialization or volume business.
    McDonald's transformed the fast-food industry from a fragmented industry
    into a specialized/volume industry. Starbucks is achieving a similar feat among
    gourmet coffee shops.

4. *Specialization businesses* are those where the sources of advantage are many
    and the size of the potential advantage is substantial. Specialization busi-
    nesses feature varied customer needs, first-mover advantages, brand loyalty,
    scale economies, and few economies of scope (hence, there are no major
    advantages to firms with a broad market or product scope). Specialization
    businesses require strategic differentiation – each firm focuses on a particular
    approach to product design, innovation, or branding.

Classifying Industries According to Competitive Dynamics

The extent to which different industries are affected by intense technological
competition is not entirely a result of their level of maturity. Some industries are
comparatively stable right through their life cycles, others seem to be in a state of
permanent revolution. Focusing on dynamic aspects of competition – the rate of

TABLE 10.2 Classifying Industries According to Rate of Productivity Growth (as Indicated by Decline in Real Prices)

INDUSTRY	PERIOD	AVERAGE ANNUAL REAL CHANGE IN PRODUCER PRICE INDEX (%)
Local monopoly industries		
Surgical, orthopedic, and prosthetic appliances	1983–89	+4.9
Boot repair	1981–88	+2.8
General job printing	1982–89	+2.6
Musical instruments	1985–89	+2.6
Map, atlas, and globe cover printing	1982–89	+2.3
Entertainment	1980–87	+1.8
Highway construction	1970–88	+1.7
Burial caskets	1982–89	+1.7
Residential construction	1970–88	+1.6
Traditional manufacturing industries		
Passenger cars	1982–89	+0.3
Wheeled tractors	1982–89	0.0
Metal cans	1981–89	−0.1
Electric lamps	1983–89	−0.7
Gasoline engines (under 11hp)	1982–89	−0.8
Household refrigerators	1981–89	−0.9
Dynamic Schumpeterian industries		
Home electronic equipment	1982–89	−3.6
Microprocessors	1981–89	−4.6
Microwave cookers	1982–89	−4.6
Analog integrated circuits	1981–89	−4.8
Digital PBXs	1985–89	−4.9
Color TVs (more than 17-inch)	1980–89	−6.0
Memory-integrated circuits	1981–89	−6.0
Digital computers	1985–89	−10.3

new product introduction, duration of product life cycles, the rate of decline of unit costs, geographical scope, and the stability of supplier–customer relations – Jeffrey Williams identifies three industry types:[35]

1. *Local monopoly markets* sell specialized products to meet the specific requirements of small groups of customers. Examples include defense and other government contractors, professional service companies that rely on close client contact (corporate law firms, private bankers), and exclusive consumer product companies (designer clothes, Rolls-Royces, and Ferraris). Product differentiation

---

[35] This section draws on several papers by Jeffrey R. Williams: "The Productivity Base of Industries," working paper 1983–84 (Graduate School of Industrial Administration, Carnegie-Mellon University, May 1984); "I Don't Think We're in Kansas Any More . . . : How Market Settings Influence CIM Strategies," *Long Range Planning* 23 (February 1990); "How Sustainable Is Your Competitive Advantage," *California Management Review* (Spring 1992).

tends to be high: customers are resistant to standardization and elasticity of demand is low, reflecting customers' preference for specialty products. High-quality, low-volume production with lack of competition encourages craft-based production that is vertically integrated with little emphasis on economies of scale or experience.

2. *Traditional industrial markets* are large, not heavily segmented, and feature modest rates of product innovation. Competition is a quest for the benefits of size – economies of scale and brand leadership – but rival products are close substitutes and market domination is seldom achieved. The typical strategy is based on cost leadership, brand awareness, and product variety (e.g., Unilever, General Motors, Toyota, General Electric, Citigroup).

3. *Schumpeterian markets*, driven by a "gale of creative destruction," are "hypercompetitive" in nature (see Chapter 3). Product innovation is the dominant form of competition, with established products continually displaced by new products. Imitation means that speed in exploiting new products is essential. Product innovation must be supported by the manufacturing and marketing capabilities required to move quickly down the experience curve. Semiconductors, telecommunications, computers, consumer electronics, financial derivatives, recorded music, and some fashion goods are Schumpeterian in character. Annual reductions in real unit costs in excess of 8 percent are common for these products (see Table 10.2).

Some industries may be hybrids: thus, in the personal computer industry, components such as keyboards and power supplies are traditional industries, other components such as microprocessors are Schumpeterian industries, while some applications software and customer support are craft-based, sheltered industries. These hybrids pose considerable difficulties for strategy and organization.

11

Technology-based Industries and the Management of Innovation

Whereas a calculator on the ENIAC is equipped with 18,000 vacuum tubes and weighs 30 tons, computers in the future may have only 1,000 vacuum tubes and perhaps weigh only 1.5 tons.
—**Popular Mechanics, March 1949**

I can think of no conceivable reason why an individual should wish to have a computer in his own home.
—**Kenneth Olsen, Chairman, Digital Equipment Corporation, 1977**

OUTLINE

Introduction and Objectives

Industries where competition centers on innovation and the application of technology provide some of the most fascinating and complex competitive environments in which to apply the concepts of strategy analysis. Consider the upheaval that wireless communication and internet protocols have caused in the telecom sector:

- In 1993, the world's three most valuable telecom companies were AT&T, Nippon Telephone and Telegraph (NTT), and British Telecom (BT), accounting for 55 percent of the combined stock market value of the world's top 10 telecommunications companies. By 2000, these three accounted for only 24 percent of the valuation of the telecom top 10, a group now led by newcomers Vodafone and NTT DoCoMo.

- A similar upheaval occurred on the manufacturing side of the telecom industry. In 1993, AT&T, Alcatel, NEC, Siemens, GTE, and Motorola were the leading producers of telecom equipment and possessed the highest market valuations among the industry group. By 2000, only the AT&T spinoff, Lucent, remained in the top tier. In terms of market valuation, Cisco Systems, Nokia, LM Ericsson, and Nortel Networks were the dominant players. Also riding the wave of new digital technologies was Qualcomm, with a market value far in excess of the electronics and telecom giant NEC, despite having less than 10 percent of NEC's sales.

- But technological change isn't simply a story of agile startups beating the stuffing out of established giants. Tire-maker Pirelli has emerged as Italy's biggest telecom company, while former pulp and paper company, Nokia, became the world's leading supplier of telecom equipment.

There are few industries that have seen as much technological upheaval as has the telecom industry over the past five years. At the same time, technological change has been a feature of almost every sector of the economy, due to the pervasive influence of microelectronics, digitization, new materials, and new forms of communication. In this chapter, we concentrate on technology-intensive industries. These include both *emerging industries* (those in the introductory and growth phases of their life cycle) as well as long-established industries (such as pharmaceuticals, chemicals, telecommunications, and electronics) where technology continues to be the major driving force of competition. The issues we examine, however, are also relevant to a much broader range of industries. Although industries such as food processing, fashion goods, domestic appliances, and financial services are not technology based to the same extent as consumer electronics or pharmaceuticals, innovation and technology utilization are, nevertheless, important sources of competitive advantage. Hence, the management of technology is, potentially, an important strategic issue for all companies.

Our emphasis is the role of technology in creating competitive advantage. The central focus is innovation. Innovation involves the creation of new products and new industries (biotechnology, fiber-optics, digital wireless communication), the enhancement of existing products (driverless automobiles, laser surgery), and the application of technology to industrial and business processes (virtual prototyping, internet-based business-to-business auctions).

By the time you have completed this chapter, you will be able to:

■ Analyze how technology affects industry structure and competition.

■ Identify the factors that determine the returns to innovation, and evaluate the potential for an innovation to establish competitive advantage.

■ Formulate strategies for exploiting innovation and managing technology focusing in particular on:
 —the relative advantages of being a leader or a follower in innovation;
 —identifying and evaluating strategic options for exploiting innovation;
 —how to win standards battles;
 —how to manage risk.

■ Design the organizational conditions needed to implement such strategies successfully.

This chapter is organized as follows. First, we examine the links among technology, industry structure, and competition in technology-intensive industries. Second, we explore the potential for innovation to establish sustainable competitive advantage. Third, we deal with key issues in designing technology strategies, including timing (to lead or to follow), alternative strategies for exploiting an innovation, setting industry standards, and managing risk. Finally, we examine the organizational conditions for the successful implementation of technology-based strategies.

COMPETITIVE ADVANTAGE IN TECHNOLOGY-INTENSIVE INDUSTRIES

Our focus is innovation. Innovation is responsible for industries coming into being, and innovation creates competitive advantage. The role of innovation in creating competitive advantage was discussed in Chapter 7. Let's look more closely at the linkage between innovation and profitability.

The Innovation Process

Invention is the creation of new products and processes through the development of new knowledge or from new combinations of existing knowledge. Most inventions are the result of novel applications of existing knowledge. Samuel Morse's telegraph, patented in 1840, was based on several decades of research into electromagnetism from Ben Franklin to Orsted, Ampere, and Sturgion. The compact disc embodies knowledge about lasers developed several decades previously.

Innovation is the initial commercialization of invention by producing and marketing a new good or service or by using a new method of production. Once the innovation has occurred, it diffuses: on the demand side, through customers purchasing the good or service; on the supply side, through imitation by competitors. An innovation may be the result of a single invention (most product innovation in chemicals and pharmaceuticals involve the discovery of a new chemical compound) or it may combine many inventions (the first automobile embodied a multitude of inventions, from the wheel, invented some 5,000 years previously, to the internal combustion engine). Not all invention progresses into innovation: among the patent portfolios of most technology-intensive firms are numerous inventions that have yet to find a viable commercial application. Many innovations may involve little or no new technology: the personal computer brought together existing components and technologies, but no fundamental scientific breakthroughs; most new types of packaging – including the vast array of anti-tamper packages – involve clever design but little in the way of new technology. Most business process patents are process innovations with little technological content.

Figure 11.1 shows the pattern of development from knowledge creation to invention and innovation. The tendency over time has been for the lags between each stage to contract:

- Chester F. Carlson invented xerography in 1938 by combining established basic knowledge about electrostatics and printing. The first patents were awarded in 1940. Patent rights were purchased by Xerox Corporation, which launched its first office copier in 1958. By 1974, the first competitive machines were introduced by IBM, Kodak, Ricoh, and Canon.

- The jet engine, employing Newtonian principles of forces, was patented by Frank Whittle in 1930. The first commercial jet airliner, the Comet, flew in 1957. Two years later, the Boeing 707 was introduced.

FIGURE 11.1 The development of technology: from knowledge creation to diffusion

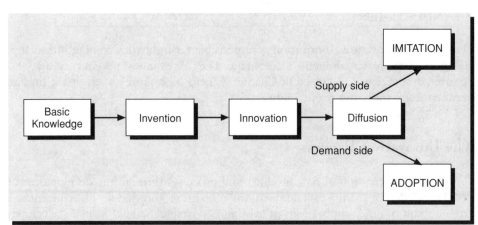

- The mathematics of *fuzzy logic* were developed by Lofti Zadeh at Berkeley during the 1960s. By the early 1980s, Dr. Takeshi Yamakawa of the Kyushu Institute of Technology had registered patents for integrated circuits embodying fuzzy logic, and in 1987, a series of fuzzy logic controllers for industrial machines was launched by Omron of Kyoto. By 1991, the world market for fuzzy logic controllers was estimated at $2 billion.[1]

- During the 1990s, a number of consumer electronics and software companies were working on the problem of how to compress digital audio and video files. When, in 1996, David Bowie posted a sound file of his new single on his website, the file was more than 40Mb and took over an hour to download. The agreement by the Motion Picture Expert Group-1 of the Audio Level 3 standard for audio file compression (better known as MP3) was quickly followed in 1998 by the launch of the first MP3 player, Diamond Multimedia's Rio. In 1999, 18-year-old Shawn Fanning came up with the idea of networking PCs to share MP3 files. Despite the legal battle over Fanning's Napster, system, by mid-2000 30 million people were estimated to be using Napster, including 75 percent of US college students.[2]

Innovation is responsible for the creation of new industries and, as we saw in the last chapter, is the basis of competition and competitive advantage throughout the early phases of industries' life cycles. Chapter 10 outlined typical patterns of technology development and their implications for products, industry structure, and the shifting basis of competitive advantage. However, just because innovation is important, that does not necessarily mean that pursuing innovation will be profitable for the firm. Let us explore the returns to innovation.

[1] "The Logic that Dares Not Speak its Name," *Economist* (April 16, 1994): 89–91.
[2] "Music Wars on the Web," *Independent*, magazine supplement (November 18, 2000): 8–9.

FIGURE 11.2   Appropriation of value: who gets the benefits from innovation?

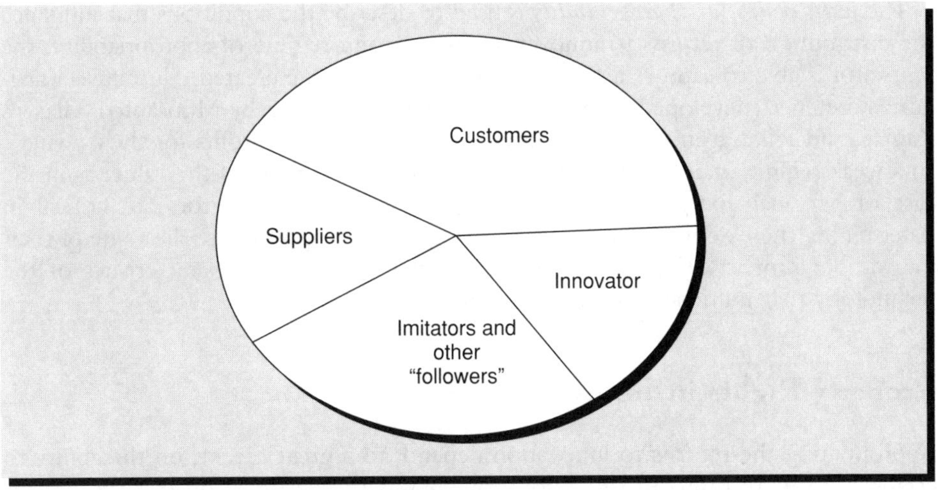

The Profitability of Innovation

"If a man . . . make a better mousetrap than his neighbor, though he build his house in the woods, the world will make a beaten path to his door," claimed Emerson. Yet, the inventors of new mousetraps, and other gadgets too, are more likely to be found at the bankruptcy courts than in the millionaires' playgrounds of the Caribbean or the French Riviera. Certainly, innovation is no guarantor of fame and fortune, either for individuals or for companies. The empirical evidence on technological intensity, innovation, and profitability confirms this mixed picture. PIMS data show R&D intensity and the rate of new product introductions to be negatively related to profitability, although lags between expenditure on innovation and returns may obscure the relationship.[3] Over the longer term, high market share companies in research-intensive industries earned above-average returns, although firms in these industries with above-average patents-to-sales ratios did not earn significantly higher returns.

The key determinant of the profitability of an innovation to the innovator is the share of the value created by that innovation that the innovator is able to appropriate. The value created by an innovation is distributed among a number of different parties (see Figure 11.2). The innovators gain profits from the innovation. So too do the imitators who are able to copy and modify it: Dell, Compaq, Acer, and other followers into the personal computer industry earned far more profit than the innovators, MITS and Apple. Suppliers may also be key beneficiaries: in personal computers, the suppliers of components (Intel and AMD in microprocessors, Seagate Technology and Quantum Corp. in disk drives, Sharp in flat-panel displays) and operating software (Microsoft). Finally, customers also are major recipients of the

---

[3]   R. D. Buzzell and B. T. Gale, *The PIMS Principles* (New York: Free Press, 1987): 274.

value created: presumably, the value each of us derives from our PCs is far in excess of the $900 or so that we spent on purchasing it.[4]

The term *regime of appropriability* is used to describe the conditions that influence the distribution of returns to innovation. In a strong regime of appropriability, the innovator is able to capture a substantial share of the value created: NutraSweet artificial sweetener (developed by Searle, subsequently acquired by Monsanto), Glaxo's Zantac, and Pilkington's float glass process generated huge profits for their owners. In a weak regime of appropriability, other parties derive most of the value: as in the case of personal computer industry described above. Four factors are critical in determining the extent to which innovators are able to appropriate the value of their innovation: property rights, complementary resources, those characteristics of the technology that influence its imitability, and lead time.

Property Rights in Innovation

Appropriating the returns to innovation depend, to a great extent, on the ability to establish property rights in the innovation. It was the desire to protect the returns to inventors that prompted the English Parliament to pass the 1623 Statute of Monopolies, which established the basis of patent law. Since then, the law has been extended to several areas of *intellectual property*, including:

- *Patents* are exclusive rights to a new and useful product, process, substance, or design. Obtaining a patent requires that the invention is novel, useful, and not excessively obvious. Patent law varies from country to country. In the United States, a patent is valid for 17 years (14 for a design).

- *Copyrights* are exclusive production, publication, or sales rights to the creators of artistic, literary, dramatic, or musical works. Examples include articles, books, drawings, maps, photographs, and musical compositions.

- *Trademarks* are words, symbols, or other marks used to distinguish the goods or services supplied by a firm. In the United States, they are registered with the Patent Office. Trademarks provide the basis for brand identification.

- *Trade secrets* offer less well-defined legal protection. Their protection relates chiefly to chemical formulae, recipes, and industrial processes.

The effectiveness of these legal instruments of protection depends on the type of innovation being protected. For some new chemical products and basic mechanical inventions, patents can provide effective protection. For products that involve new configurations of existing components or new manufacturing processes, patents may be less effective due to opportunities to innovate around the patent. Patents granted

---

[4] The excess of the benefit received by the consumer over the price paid by the consumer is called *consumer surplus* in the economics literature (it is closely related to the term *delivered value* used in the marketing literature). See: D. Besanko, D. Dranove, and M. Shanley, *Economics of Strategy* (New York: Wiley, 1996): 442–3.

on dubious grounds may later be revoked or challenged in the courts. The US courts and Patent Office have continually broadened the scope of the patent laws. In 1980 patent law was extended to biotechnology, in 1981 patenting of software was allowed, and in 1998 patents were allowed on business processes. Thus, Dell Computer has 77 patents protecting its build-to-order system, while Amazon holds a patent on its "one-click-of-a-mouse" buying through a web site.[5] While patents and copyright establish property rights, their disadvantage (from the inventor's viewpoint) is that they make information public. Hence, companies may prefer secrecy to patenting as a means of protecting innovations.

Whatever the imperfections of patents and copyrights, companies have become increasingly attentive to the economic value of their intellectual property and, in the process, more careful about protecting and exploiting these knowledge assets. During the 1950s and 1960s, the leading companies in electronics research – RCA, IBM, and AT&T – pursued liberal patent licensing policies, almost to the point of giving away access to their patent portfolios. When Texas Instruments began exploiting its patent portfolio as a revenue source during the 1980s, the technology sector as a whole woke up to the value of its knowledge assets. From 1990–95, TI's royalty income exceeded its operating income from other sources. Over 150,000 patents were granted by the US Patent Office in each of 1998 and 1999 – more than double the annual rate during the 1980s.

As Grindley and Teece show, licensing is used not only to generate income, but to gain access to other companies' technologies. In semiconductors and electronics, cross-licensing arrangements, whereby one company gives access to its patents across a field of use in exchange for access to another company's patents, play a key role in permitting "freedom to design": the ability to design products that draw on technologies owned by different companies.[6]

Complementary Resources

Innovation brings new products and processes to market. This requires more than invention, it requires the diverse resources and capabilities needed to finance, produce, and market the innovation. These are referred to as *complementary resources* (see Figure 11.3). Chester Carlson invented xerography, but was unable for many years to bring his product to market because he lacked the complementary resources needed to develop, manufacture, market, distribute, and service his invention. Conversely, Searle (and its later parent, Monsanto) was able to provide almost all the development, manufacturing, marketing, and distribution resources needed to exploit its NutraSweet innovation. As a result, Carlson was able to appropriate only a tiny part of the value created by his invention of the plain-paper Xerox copier, while Searle/Monsanto was successful in appropriating a major part of the value created by its new artificial sweetener.

---

[5] "Knowledge Monopolies: Patent Wars," *Economist* (April 8, 2000): 95–9.
[6] Peter Grindley and David Teece, "Managing Intellectual Capital: Licensing and Cross-Licensing in Semiconductors and Electronics," *California Management Review* 39 (Winter 1997).

FIGURE 11.3　Complementary resources

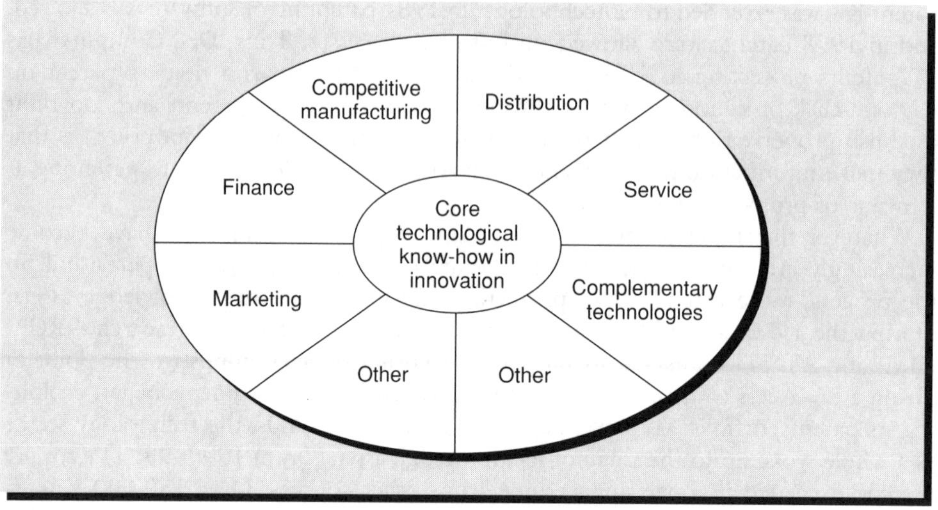

The division of value between an innovator and the suppliers of complementary resources depends on their relative power. A key determinant of this is whether the complementary resources are *specialized* or *unspecialized*. Airbus's A380 superjumbo airliner promises to be a significant innovation in air transport. However, to the extent that this innovation depends on the development of new engines by Rolls-Royce and Pratt & Whitney, specially developed composite materials for fuselage and wings, and specialized mechanical servicing and baggage handling by the airlines, then the suppliers of these complementary resources will have the potential to capture a significant proportion of the value created by the innovation.

Where complementary resources are generic, the innovator is in a much stronger position to capture value. If I develop an innovative new lightbulb that is cheaper, longer lasting, and converts electricity into light more efficiently, I will make more money from it if it can fit into any standard lamp socket. If the bulb requires a specialized lamp, it is likely that the manufacturers of the specialized lamps will capture part of the value of my innovation.

The presence of specialized complementary resources means that the innovator has to share his or her gains with the suppliers of these assets, but the innovator may benefit from the fact that these specialized complementary resources also create a barrier to imitation. Suppose a startup company develops an operating system for PCs that is more efficient, more functional, and more reliable than Microsoft Windows. The challenge for the new company is not simply that Windows is installed on 92 percent of the world's PCs, but the fact that the manufacturers of microprocessors, data storage products, applications software, modems, and many other components have specialized their products to be compatible with Windows, which reinforces Microsoft's incumbency advantage.

The Characteristics of the Technology

The extent to which an innovation can be copied depends not just on legal protection through patents and copyrights, but also on the characteristics of the technology. Two characteristics are especially important. The first is the extent to which the knowledge embodied in the innovation is tacit or codifiable. *Codifiable knowledge,* by definition, is that which can be written down. Hence, if it is not effectively protected by patents or copyright, diffusion is likely to be rapid and the competitive advantage not sustainable. Financial innovations such as mortgage-backed securities, zero-interest bonds, and new types of index options embody readily codifiable knowledge and are not patentable. As such, they only confer sustainable competitive advantage if supported by complementary resources such as human skills in designing and trading them, and the ability to offer liquidity by developing secondary markets with sufficient volumes of trade. Similarly, Coca-Cola's recipe is codifiable and, in the absence of trade secret protection, is easily copied. On the other hand, innovations based on *tacit knowledge*, such as Toyota's systems for developing and producing its cars, and AOL's developments in online entertainment and building virtual communities, cannot be codified: they are built on the know-how, intuition, and insight of employees and the organizational routines and values that link employees. Such innovations are not easily imitated.

The second characteristic is *complexity*. Some innovations are more complex than others. Even without patent and copyright protection, a Pentium III microprocessor is very difficult to copy. Conversely, every new toy, from the hula hoop of 1958 to the Pokemon toys of 2000, and every new fashion, from the Mary Quant miniskirt of 1962 to the Dior fur-trimmed duffle coat of winter 2000, has been very easy to imitate.

Lead Time

Tacitness and complexity do not provide lasting barriers to imitation, but they do offer the innovator *time*. The implication is that innovation offers a competitive advantage that is only temporary: it is a window of opportunity where the innovator can build on the initial advantage. The innovator's *lead time* is the time it will take followers to catch up. The challenge for the innovator is to use initial lead time advantages to build the capabilities and market position to entrench industry leadership. The critical issue is to exploit it effectively and not allow the opportunity to pass. Microsoft, Intel, and Cisco Systems were brilliant at exploiting lead time advantage to build product development, efficient production, and strong customer base. By contrast, a number of innovative British companies have squandered their initial lead time advantage: DeHaviland with the Comet (the world's first jet airliner), EMI with its CT scanner, Clive Sinclair and the home computer, all failed to capitalize on their lead time with large scale investments in production, marketing, and continued product development.

A key advantage of lead time is the ability to move down the learning curve ahead of followers. Despite AMD and Cyrix's successful cloning of Intel's microprocessors with very little time lag, Intel has used its time advantage and its 82 percent world market share to move quickly down its experience curve, cut prices, and so pressure the profit margins of its competitors. The ability to turn lead time into cost advantage is thus a key aspect of the innovator's advantage.[7]

The Effectiveness of Different Mechanisms for Protecting Innovation

How effective are these different mechanisms in protecting technological advantage and permitting innovators to appropriate the returns on their innovations? Empirical evidence shows tremendous variability across industries, but the principal conclusion is that patent protection is of limited effectiveness in most industries. One survey found that across 12 industries, patents were judged essential to the development of commercially important inventions in:

- 65 percent of pharmaceutical inventions;

- 30 percent of chemical inventions;

- 10–20 percent of petroleum, machinery, and metal products inventions;

- less than 10 percent of electrical equipment, instruments, primary metals, office equipment, motor vehicles, rubber, and textiles inventions.[8]

A landmark study of the appropriability of the returns to R&D by researchers at Yale and Columbia found that patents were less effective at protecting both process and product innovations than were lead time advantages, learning curve advantages, and sales and service networks (see Table 11.1). The study also found that lead times before competitors could duplicate new products and processes also tended to be short, with patents offering little lead time advantage (see Table 11.2).

Strategies to Exploit Innovation: How and When to Enter

Now that we understand some of the factors that determine the potential for innovation to establish and sustain competitive advantage, what are the implications for how we manage technology and innovation?

---

[7] We associate rapidly falling prices and costs primarily with electronics, although, such a phenomenon is common with almost all new products. The ballpoint pen, invented by Ladislao Biro, is a classic example. At Christmas 1945, Biro pens sold at Gimbel's New York store for $12.50; by 1950, ballpoint pens were being sold for 15 cents. "Bic and the Heirs of Ball-Point Builder Are No Pen Pals," *Wall Street Journal* (May 27, 1988): 1, 27.

[8] David J. Teece, "Profiting from Technological Innovation: Implications for Integration, Collaboration, Licensing and Public Policy," in *The Competitive Challenge: Strategies for Industrial Innovation and Renewal* (Cambridge, MA: Ballinger, 1987): 190.

TABLE 11.1 Protecting Innovation: The Effectiveness of Different Barriers to Imitation

	OVERALL SAMPLE MEANS	
METHOD OF APPROPRIATION	PROCESSES	PRODUCTS
Patents to prevent duplication	3.52	4.33
Patents to secure royalty income	3.31	3.75
Secrecy	4.31	3.57
Lead time	5.11	5.41
Moving quickly down the learning curve	5.02	5.09
Sales or service efforts	4.55	5.59

Note: The means show responses from 650 individuals across 130 lines of business. The range was from 1 (= not at all effective) to 7 (= very effective).
Source: R. C. Levin, A. K. Klevorick, R. R. Nelson, and S. G. Winter, "Appropriating the Returns from Industrial Research and Development," *Brookings Papers on Economic Activity* 3 (1987): 794.

TABLE 11.2 The Time Required to Duplicate an Innovation

	LESS THAN 6 MONTHS	6–12 MONTHS	1–3 YEARS	3–5 YEARS	MORE THAN 5 YEARS	TIMELY DUPLICATION NOT POSSIBLE
Major patented new product	2	6	64	40	8	9
Major unpatented new product	3	22	89	12	1	2
Major patented new process	0	4	72	37	9	7
Major unpatented new process	2	20	84	17	2	4

Source: R. C. Levin, A. K. Klevorick, R. R. Nelson, and S. G. Winter, "Appropriating the Returns from Industrial Research and Development," *Brookings Papers on Economic Activity* 3 (1987).

Alternative Strategies to Exploit Innovation

How should an innovating firm maximize the returns to its innovation? Several alternative strategies are available. Figure 11.4 ranks then according to increasing involvement by the innovator in commercialization. Thus, licensing requires very little involvement by the innovator in subsequent commercialization; internal commercialization – possibly through creating a new enterprise or business unit – involves much greater involvement. In between, there are various opportunities for collaboration with other companies. This may take the form of an informal alliance, subcontracting certain activities to outside companies (e.g., outsourcing manufacturing or appointing an agent to handle all marketing and sales within a designated geographical area), or a joint venture, a new company created and owned

FIGURE 11.4 Alternative strategies for exploiting innovation

	Licensing	Outsourcing certain functions	Strategic alliance	Joint venture	Internal commercialization
Risk and return	Very small investment risk, but small returns also limited (unless patent position very strong). Some legal risks	Limits capital investment, but may create dependence on suppliers/partners	Benefits of flexibility, risks of informal structure	Shares investment and risk. Risk of partner disagreement and culture clash	Biggest investment requirement and corresponding risks. Benefits of control
Competing resources	Few	Permits accessing of outside resources and capabilities	Permits pooling of the resources and capabilities of more than one firm		Substantial requirements in terms of finance, production capability, marketing capability, distribution, etc.
Examples	Konica licensing its digital camera to Hewlett-Packard	Pixar's computer animated movies (e.g., *Toy Story*) marketed and distributed by Disney Co.	Apple and Sharp build the "Newton" PDA	Microsoft and NBC formed MSNBC	TI divestment of its Digital Signal Processing Chips

by two or more partners. Figure 11.4 summarizes some of the key distinctions among these strategic alternatives in terms of risk and resource requirements.

The choice of strategy mode depends on two main sets of factors: the character-istics of the innovation, and the resources and capabilities of the firm.

Characteristics of the Innovation

The key issue here is the extent to which the firm can establish property rights through patents. The licensing option is only viable where an innovation has clearly defined patent rights. Thus, in pharmaceuticals, licensing is widespread. Because patents are clear and defensible, specialist R&D companies can appropriate a major part of the potential value of their inventions through license agreements. Similarly, Dolby's sound-reduction business is built entirely on licensing the Dolby technology. On the other hand, Steve Jobs and Steve Wozniak, developers of the Apple I and Apple II computers, had little option other than to go into business themselves – the absence of proprietary technology ruled out licensing as an option.

The advantages of licensing are, first, that it relieves the company of the need to develop the full range of complementary resources and capabilities needed for com-mercialization, and second, that it can allow the innovation to be commercialized quickly. If the lead time offered by the innovation is short, multiple licensing can allow for a fast global rollout. The problem, however, is that the success of the innovation in the market is totally dependent on the commitment and effectiveness of the licensees. When Raisio developed its innovate cholesterol-lowering margarine, Benecol, it chose to launch it outside of Scandinavia through a licensing arrange-ment with Johnson & Johnson. The slow rollout of the product and indecision over how to market Benecol in the US resulted in Raisio's losing much of its lead time advantage; when the market launch finally occurred in the US, Unilever and other competitors were close behind.[9]

Resources and Capabilities of the Firm

As Figure 11.4 shows, the different strategic options require very different capabilities. Developing the innovation requires research, development, and creativity. Thus, a high proportion of major inventions are associated either with individuals or small organizations. Of the major innovations of the first seven decades of the twentieth century, most were contributed by individual inventors – frequently working in their garage or garden shed.[10] Among 27 key inventions of the post-war period, only seven emerged from the R&D departments of established corporations.[11] Hence, the organizations that are best at innovation are often small firms and startup enterprises that do not possess the range of resources required for commercialization. These companies resort typically to licensing, outsourcing, or strategic alliances in order to

[9] "Raisio," *Financial Times* (July 18, 1997): 13; "Raisio to Widen Benecol Range," *Financial Times* (December 6, 2000): 24.
[10] J. Jewkes, D. Sawyers, and R. Stillerman, *The Sources of Invention*, 2nd ed. (London: Macmillan, 1969).
[11] D. Hamberg, *Essays in the Economics of Research and Development* (New York: John Wiley, 1966).

access the complementary resources needed to take their innovation to market. Alternatively, they may seek to be bought out by a larger concern. In biotechnology and electronics, a two-stage model for innovation is common: the technology is developed initially by a small, technology-intensive startup, which then licenses to a larger concern.

Large, established corporations, which can draw on their wealth of resources and capabilities, are better placed for internal commercialization. Companies such as Sony, GE, Siemens, Hitachi, and IBM have traditionally developed innovations internally – yet, as technologies evolve, converge, and splinter, so these companies have increasingly resorted to joint ventures, strategic alliances, and outsourcing arrangements in order to access technical capabilities outside their corporate boundaries.

Alternative Development Models: Corporatism versus Silicon Valley

Recognition that different types of company have resources and capabilities that are suited to different stages of the innovation and business development process raises interesting questions as to the type of industry structure (or "system of innovation") most conducive to successful innovation. The debate has centered around two rival models:

1. The *corporate model* typical of technology-based industries in Japan and Germany and of the chemical and aerospace sectors in the United States, in which the innovation process from R&D to production and marketing is nurtured and controlled within large, technologically diverse, mature corporations.

2. The *entrepreneurial (or "Silicon Valley") model*, named after the semiconductor–computer hardware–computer software cluster based in the San José area of California. This model is also apparent in the biotechnology industries of the United States and Britain and in the cluster of communications and internet companies in the Greater Washington area. This model features loose corporate control. Innovation is associated with small, startup companies, many of them spun off from earlier startups. These innovations are exploited through various collaborative relationships, ranging from loose networks of strategic alliances to more formalized joint ventures. Finance is provided initially by venture capitalists, and subsequently through initial public offerings of stock.[12]

These alternative approaches to technological development have given rise to a lively debate. George Gilder, techno-guru of the internet age, has praised the dynamism and inventiveness of the Silicon Valley model. He emphasizes its ability to harness

[12] A. Saxenian, "Regional Networks and the Resurgence of Silicon Valley," *California Management Review* 33 (Fall 1990): 89–112.

creativity and entrepreneurial drive, its flexibility, and its diversity in permitting different types of companies to exploit their distinctive capabilities in undertaking different stages of the innovation process.[13] Charles Ferguson, on the other hand, sees these freewheeling entrepreneurial startups as permitting the individual exploitation of the technologies developed within large corporations, which ultimately stunts their development of broad-based innovative capabilities.[14] The key arguments here are: first, to develop and exploit innovation effectively, technology and the full range of complementary resources needed to exploit the innovation have to be brought together within the same company; second, technological development is not about single innovations but a *technological trajectory* comprising a stream of related innovations. Alfred Chandler provides historical support for the corporate model, arguing that the superior industrial development of Germany and the US as compared to Britain during the twentieth century was due to the presence of large, stable industrial corporations in the US and Germany that were lacking in Britain.[15]

Different development models may be appropriate to different industries and different national cultures. There is no doubt that the entrepreneurial approach of California's Silicon Valley, based on startups, spinoffs, and interfirm networks, has been outstandingly successful in fostering creativity. It has also encouraged knowledge transfer among universities (notably Stanford and Berkeley), corporate research labs (e.g., Bell Labs and Xerox PARC), established corporations (Hewlett-Packard, IBM, and Microsoft), and entrepreneurial startups. It is also apparent that the corporate model has worked outstandingly well in the Japanese consumer electronics industry (notably for companies such as Matsushita, Canon, Toshiba, and Sony) and in the world's chemical industry.

To what extent is it possible to combine the benefits of an established corporation's well-marshaled resources and the drive and flexibility of an entrepreneurial startup? During the 1990s, many large corporations established business development units whose role was to identify, fund, and foster new business opportunities. Such corporate venturing tended to be driven primarily by innovations emerging from corporate R&D departments. More recently, they have evolved into *corporate incubators* – corporate units designed to provide infrastructure and venture capital funding for new business ideas, both from within and outside the corporation. Thus, Ford's Consumer Connect was created to identify and develop new ways to leverage the company's capabilities, consumer base, and purchasing power in the new economy. Covisint – an online B2B parts exchange for the auto industry – was an early outcome of Consumer Connect.[16] British Telecom established Brightstar in December 2000 with a view to creating new businesses that will exploit BT's portfolio of over 14,000 patents.[17] Entries by established ("bricks-and-mortar") companies into e-commerce have often

[13]   George Gilder, "The Revitalization of Everything: The Law of the Microcosm," *Harvard Business Review* (March–April 1988): 49–66.
[14]   Charles H. Ferguson, "From the People Who Brought You Voodoo Economics," *Harvard Business Review* (May–June 1988).
[15]   A. D. Chandler, *Scale and Scope: The Dynamics of Industrial Capitalism* (Cambridge: Belknap Press, 1994).
[16]   M. T. Hansen, H. W. Chesborough, N. Nohria, and D. N. Sull, "Networked Incubators: Hothouse of the New Economy," *Harvard Business Review* (September–October 2000): 74–88.
[17]   "How to Make the Most of a Brilliant Idea," *Financial Times* (December 6, 2000): 21.

followed a corporate venturing model – the new e-business unit established with in-house resources, but in a separate location largely free from the parent company's systems, rules, procedures, and behavioral norms.

Timing Innovation: To Lead or to Follow?

To gain competitive advantage in emerging and technologically intensive industries, is it best to be a leader or a follower in innovation? As Table 11.3 shows, the evidence is mixed: in some products the leader has been the first to grab the prize, in others the leader has succumbed to the risks and costs of pioneering. Optimal timing of entry into an emerging industry and the introduction of new technology are complex issues. The extent of first-mover advantages (or disadvantages) associated with pioneering depends on the following factors:

1. *The extent to which innovation can be protected by property rights or lead time advantages.* If an innovation is appropriable through patent or copyright protection or through a lead time advantage such as learning, there is likely to be advantage in being an early mover. This is especially the case where patent protection is important, as in pharmaceuticals. Here, competition can take the form of a patent race where the rewards are winner-takes-all.

2. *The importance of complementary resources.* The more important are complementary resources in exploiting an innovation, the greater the costs and risks of pioneering. Several firms have already failed in their attempts to develop and market an electric automobile. The problem of the pioneer, as General Motors is discovering, is that the development costs are huge, partly because of the need to orchestrate the development of a number of technologies (batteries and other power-storage devices, electric motors, and weight-reducing new materials), and partly because of the need to establish facilities for service and recharging. Meanwhile, it is not clear what will be the dominant electrical vehicle technology, or even if there will be a mass market for such vehicles. Resource requirements change as an industry evolves: as industry infrastructure develops, so firms can access complementary resources from specialist firms. In the British frozen foods industry, Birds Eye, the pioneer, was forced to make huge investments in a frozen foods distribution network, including the leasing of frozen food cabinets to retailers. However, by the mid-1970s, the growth of public cold stores and refrigerated trucking companies meant that companies introducing new frozen food products could enter with much smaller investments.

3. *The potential to establish a standard.* As we shall see later in this chapter, markets vary as to whether they converge toward a technical standard or not. For the time being, let us simply note that the greater the importance of product standards, the greater the advantages of being an early mover in order to influence those standards. Once a standard has been set, displacing it becomes exceptionally difficult. IBM had little success with its PS2 operating

TABLE 11.3 Leaders, Followers, and Success in Emerging Industries

PRODUCT	INNOVATOR	FOLLOWER	THE WINNER
Jet airliner	De Haviland (Comet)	Boeing (707)	Follower
Float glass	Pilkington	Corning	Leader
X-ray scanner	EMI	General Electric	Follower
Office PC	Xerox	IBM	Follower
VCRs	Ampex/Sony	Matsushita	Follower
Diet cola	R. C. Cola	Coca-Cola	Follower
Instant camera	Polaroid	Kodak	Leader
Pocket calculator	Bowmar	Texas Instruments	Follower
Microwave oven	Raytheon	Samsung	Follower
Plain-paper copier	Xerox	Canon	Not clear
Fiber-optic cable	Corning	Many companies	Leader
Video games player	Atari	Nintendo/Sega	Followers
Disposable diaper	Procter and Gamble	Kimberley-Clark	Leader
Web browser	Netscape	Microsoft	Follower
MP3 music players	Diamond Multimedia	Sony (& others)	Followers
Operating systems for hand-held digital devices	Palm and Symbian	Microsoft (CE/Pocket PC)	Leaders

Source: Based in part on David Teece, *The Competitive Challenge: Strategies for Industrial Innovation and Renewal* (Cambridge, Ballinger, 1987): 186–8.

system against the entrenched position of Microsoft Windows. However, in establishing a technical standard, there may also be some risk of entering too early before the direction of technological development is clear. Although IBM's 1981 entry into personal computers was comparatively late, a dominant technology or design had not emerged, despite the strength of Apple and Commodore in the market. Hence, IBM was able to establish a dominant *de facto* standard for the industry.

Optimal timing depends not only on the characteristics of the technology and the industry, but also on the resources and capabilities that the individual firm has at its disposal. Different companies have different *strategic windows* – periods in time when their resources and capabilities are aligned with the opportunities available in the market. A small, technology-based firm may have no choice but to pioneer the introduction of an innovation. Given its lack of complementary resources, its only chance of building sustainable competitive advantage is to grab first-mover advantage and use this to develop the necessary complementary resources before more powerful rivals appear. For the large, established firm with financial resources and strong production, marketing, and distribution capabilities, the strategic window is likely to be both longer and later. The risks of pioneering are greater for an established firm with a reputation and brands to protect, and to exploit its complementary resources effectively typically requires a more developed market. Consider the following examples:

- In personal computers, Apple was a pioneer, IBM a follower. The timing of entry was probably optimal for each. Apple's resources were its imagination and its technology. Its strategic window occurred at the very beginning of the industry when these strengths could make the biggest impact. IBM had enormous strengths in manufacturing, distribution, and reputation. It could use these resources to establish competitive advantage even without a clear technological advantage. What was important for IBM was to delay its entry to the point when market and technological risks had been reduced and the industry had reached a stage of development where strengths in large-scale manufacturing, marketing, and distribution could be brought to bear.

- In the browser war between Netscape and Microsoft, Microsoft had the luxury of being able to follow the pioneer, Netscape. Microsoft's huge product development, marketing, and distribution capabilities, and – most important – its vast installed base of the Windows operating system allowed it to overhaul Netscape's initial lead.

- Although General Electric entered the market for CT scanners some four years after EMI, GE was able to overtake EMI within the space of three years because of its ability to apply vast technological, manufacturing, sales, and customer service capabilities within the field of medical electronics.

Managing Risks

Emerging industries are risky. There are two main sources of uncertainty:

- *Technological uncertainty* arises from the unpredictability of technological evolution and the complex dynamics through which technical standards and dominant designs are selected. Hindsight is always 20/20, but at the end of 2000, for example, it was difficult to predict how electronic money would develop, the extent to which internet access would migrate to mobile devices, or the implications of the human genome project for the pharmaceuticals industry.

- *Market uncertainty* relates to the size and growth rates of the market for a new products. When Xerox introduced its first plain-paper copier in 1959, Apple its first personal computer in 1977, or Sony its Walkman in 1979, none had any idea of the size of the potential market. Forecasting demand for new products is hazardous since all forecasting is based on some form of extrapolation or modeling based on past data. One approach is to use analogies.[18] Another is to draw on the combined insight and experience of experts through the *Delphi technique*.[19]

---

[18] For example, data on rates of market penetration and price decline for household appliances such as electric toothbrushes and compact disc players were used to forecast the market demand for high-definition TVs in the United States (B. L. Bayus, "High-Definition Television: Assessing Demand Forecasts for the Next Generation Consumer Durable," *Management Science* 39 (1993): 1319–33.

[19] See B. C. Twiss, *Managing Technological Innovation*, 2nd edn (New York: Longman, 1980).

If forecasting is impossible, the keys to managing risk are alertness to emerging trends, flexibility, and reducing vulnerability to mistakes. Useful strategies include the following:

- *Cooperating with lead users.* During the early phases of industry development, careful monitoring of and response to market trends and customer requirements is essential to avoid major errors in technology and design. Von Hippel argues that lead users provide a vital source of market data for developing new products.[20] As well as providing an "early warning system" for emerging needs and technological trends, lead users can assist in the conception and development of new products and processes[21] and achieve an early cash flow to contribute to further development expenditures. In computer software, "beta versions" are released to computer enthusiasts for testing; in footwear, Nike test markets new product ideas with inner-city street gangs; in communications and aerospace, government defense contracts play a crucial role in developing new technologies.

- *Limiting risk exposure.* The high level of risk in emerging industries requires that firms adopt financial practices that minimize their exposure to adversity. Uncertainties over development costs and the timing and amount of future cash flows require a strong balance sheet with limited debt financing. Restricting risk exposure also requires economizing on capital expenditure commitments and other sources of fixed cost. Smaller players in high-tech, high-risk industries from biotechnology to computer games typically concentrate on research and development and rely upon larger companies for manufacture, marketing and distribution. Even large companies are resorting increasingly to strategic alliances and joint ventures in developing major new initiatives.

- *Flexibility.* The high level of uncertainty in emerging industries makes flexibility critical to long-term survival and success. Because technological and market changes are difficult to forecast, it is essential that top management closely monitor the environment and respond quickly to market signals. For Sichiro Honda, the founder of Honda Motor Company, a key aspect of flexibility was learning from failure: "Many people dream of success. To me success can only be achieved through repeated failure and introspection. In fact, success represents the 1 percent of your work that only comes from the 99 percent that is called failure."[22] Such flexibility and responsiveness were evident in Honda's initial entry into the US motorcycle market when, after its failure to attract interest in its bigger models, the Honda sales team recognized the market potential of its 50cc Supercub.[23] Flexibility also means keeping options open and delaying commitment to a specific technology for as long as possible. Microsoft is well known for its strategy of investing in alternative technologies (see Exhibit 11.1).

[20] Eric von Hippel, "Lead Users: A Source of Novel Product Concepts," *Management Science* 32 (July 1986).
[21] In electronic instruments, customers' ideas initiated most of the successful new products introduced by manufacturers. See Eric Von Hippel, "Users as Innovators," *Technology Review* no. 5 (1976): 212–39.
[22] Tom Peters, *Thriving on Chaos* (New York: Knopf, 1987): 259–66.
[23] Richard T. Pascale, *Honda (B)*, Case No. 384-050 (Boston: Harvard Business School): 5–6.

EXHIBIT 11.1 Keeping Your Options Open: Microsoft in Operating Systems

In 1988, as I wandered about the floor of Comdex, the computer industry's vast annual trade show, I could feel the anxiety among the participants. Since the birth of the IBM PC, six years earlier, Microsoft's Disk Operating System (DOS) had been the *de facto* standard for PCs. But DOS was now starting to age. Everyone wanted to know what would replace it.

Apple Computer, at the peak of its powers, had one of the largest booths showcasing the brilliantly graphical Macintosh operating system . . . Two different alliances of major companies, including AT&T, HP, and Sun Microsystems, offered graphical versions of Unix . . . And IBM was touting its new OS/2.

Amid the uncertainty, there was something very curious about the Microsoft booth . . . [which] resembled a Middle Eastern bazaar. In one corner, the company was previewing the second version of its highly criticized Windows system . . . In another, Microsoft touted its latest release of DOS. Elsewhere it was displaying OS/2, which it had developed with IBM. In addition, Microsoft was demonstrating new releases of Word and Excel that ran on Apple's Mac. Finally, in a distant corner, Microsoft displayed SCO Unix . . .

"What am I supposed to make of this?" grumbled a corporate buyer standing next to me. Columnists wrote that Microsoft was adrift, that its chairman and chief operating officer, Bill Gates, had no strategy.

Although the outcome of this story is now well known, to anyone standing on the Comdex floor in 1988 it wasn't obvious which operating system would win. In the face of this uncertainty, Microsoft followed the only robust strategy: betting on every horse.

Source: E. D. Beinhocker, "Robust Adaptive Strategies," *Sloan Management Review* (Spring 1999): 95–106.

COMPETING FOR STANDARDS

In the previous chapter, I noted that the establishment of standards is a key event in industry evolution. The ability to influence and, ideally, to own a standard may be critical to a company's competitive advantage. The adoption of key parts of Qualcomm's CDMA technology in emerging global standards for digital wireless communications resulted in Qualcomm's market value increasing from $2.4 billion to $49.2 billion between May 1998 and May 2000. Table 11.4 lists a number of companies whose success is closely associated with their control of standards within a particular product category.

Why Standards Appear: Network Externalities

Why do standards emerge in some product markets and not in others? As we noted in Chapter 10, most products tend to develop a dominant design: a convergence of different companies' product offerings around a common configuration that sets the standard for further product development. The Ford Model T in cars, the Boeing 707 in passenger jet aircraft, the IBM PC in microcomputers are all examples of

TABLE 11.4   Examples of Companies that Control Industry Standards

COMPANY	PRODUCT CATEGORY	STANDARD
Microsoft	Personal computer operating systems	Windows
Intel	PC microprocessors	*86 series
Matsushita	Videocassette recorders	VHS system
Iomega	High capacity PC disk drives	Zip drives
Intuit	Software for on-line financial transactions	Quicken
AMR	Computerized airline reservation system	Sabre
Rockwell and 3Com	56K modems	V90
Qualcomm	Digital cellular wireless communication	CDMA
Adobe Systems	Common file format for creating and viewing documents	Acrobat Portable Document Format

dominant designs. Some product markets, however, go beyond dominant design to the establishment of uniform technical standards.

A network externality exists whenever the value of a product to an individual customer depends on the number of other users of that product. The classic example of network externality is the telephone. Since there is little satisfaction to be gained from talking to oneself on the telephone, the value of a telephone to each user depends on the number of other users connected to the same telephone system. This is different from most products. When I pour myself a class of Glenlivet after a couple of exhausting MBA classes, my enjoyment is independent of how many other people in the world are also drinking Glenlivet. Indeed, some products may have *negative* network externalities – the value of the product is less if many other people purchase the same product. If I spend $3,000 on an Armani silver-lamé tuxedo and find that half my colleagues at the faculty Christmas party are wearing the same jacket, my satisfaction is lessened. Figure 11.5 compares such "exclusivity" products with "network externality" products.

Network externalities do not require everyone to use the same product or even the same technology, but rather that the different products are *compatible* with one

FIGURE 11.5   Positive and negative network externalities

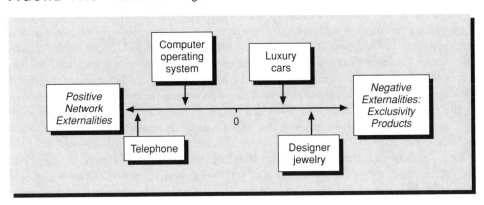

another through some form of common interface. In the case of wireless telephone service, it doesn't matter (as far as network externalities are concerned) whether we purchase service from AT&T, Nextel, or Sprint – the key issue is that every supplier's system is compatible with everyone else's. Similarly with railroads, if I am shipping coal from Wyoming to New Orleans, my choice of railroad company is not critical since I know that, unlike the 1870s, every railroad company uses a standard gauge and is required to give "common carrier" access to other companies' rolling stock. Network externalities arise from several sources:

- *Products where there are network links between users.* Telephone, railroad systems, and e-mail instant messaging groups are networks where users are linked together. Applications software, whether spreadsheet programs or video games, also link users – they can share files and play games interactively. User-level externalities may also arise through social identification. I watch *Friends* and the Hollywood Oscar presentations on the TV not because I enjoy them, but in order to have some topics of conversation with my fellow human beings.

- *Availability of complementary products.* Where products are consumed as systems, the availability of complementary products and services depends on the number of customers for that system. The key problem for Apple Computer is that, because the Macintosh accounts for only 9 percent of the installed base of personal computers, fewer and fewer producers of applications software are writing Mac-based applications. I choose to drive a Ford Taurus rather than a Ferrari Testerossa because I know that, should I break down 200 miles from Bismarck, North Dakota, spare parts and a repair service will be more readily available.

- *Economizing on switching costs.* By purchasing the product or system that is most widely used, there is less chance that I shall have to bear the costs of switching. By using Microsoft Office rather than Lotus SmartSuite, it is more likely that I will avoid the costs of retraining and file conversion when I become a visiting professor at another university.

The implication of network externalities is that they create *positive feedback*. The technology or system that has the largest installed base attracts the greatest proportion of new buyers because of the benefits of going with the market leader. Conversely, the more a technology is perceived to have a minority of the market, the more new and existing users will defect to the market leader. The result is a tendency toward a *winner-takes-all* market. The markets for computer operating systems, suites of office software, and web sites for online auctions tend toward domination by a single supplier (Microsoft in the case of operating and office software, eBay in the case of internet auctions). Rival technologies may coexist for a time, but after one company appears to be gaining the upper hand, the market may then "tip" very quickly.

Once established, technical and design standards tend to be highly resilient. Standards are difficult to displace due to learning effects and collective lock-in. Learning effects cause the dominant technology and design to be continually improved and refined.

A new technology, even though it may have the potential to overtake the existing standard, will initially be inferior. Such was the fate of the Wankel rotary engine. Continued refinement over 100 years has given the standard four-cycle engine a remarkable combination of efficiency, economy, and reliability. Although the Wankel rotary engine is believed by many to be potentially superior, the fact that it was only adapted by a single manufacturer (Mazda) meant that there has never been the continuous development needed to overcome its initial technical problems.

Even where the existing standard is inherently inferior, switching to a superior technology may not occur because of collective lock-in. The classic case is the QWERTY typewriter layout. Its 1873 design was based on the need to *slow* the speed of typing to prevent typewriter keys from jamming. Although the jamming problem was soon solved, the QWERTY layout has persisted, despite the patenting in 1932 of the faster and more efficient Dvorak Simplified Keyboard (DSK). The investments of millions of people in touch typing based on the QWERTY keyboard makes it costly for individual keyboard users or keyboard manufacturers to switch.[24]

Who Sets Standards?

Standards may be set by governments, international agencies, voluntary associations, or markets:

- Governments set standards in many areas where the public interest is involved. In 1953, the Federal Communications Commission adopted RCA's color TV broadcasting system in preference to CBS's system. A host of government-determined standards exist in relation to product safety.

- The American National Standards Institute (ANSI), British Standards Institute (BSI), and International Standards Institute (ISO) are nongovernment, voluntary bodies that agree standards across a wide range of products, services, and practices.

- *De facto* standards are those that arise in markets through the operation of competitive markets.

Such standards may be *proprietary*, where a company possesses patents or other proprietary technology that gives it ownership and control of the standard. Or a standard may be *open*, where the firm makes access to the standard available to all. Thus, in computer operating systems, Windows is a proprietary standard, owned and tightly controlled by Microsoft; Unix is an open standard, developed by Bell Labs and subsequently acquired by Novell – but freely licensed to any company or user.

---

[24]   P. David, "Clio and the Economics of QWERTY," *American Economic Review* 75 (May 1985): 332–7; and Stephen Jay Gould, "The Panda's Thumb of Technology," *Natural History* 96 no. 1 (1986). For an alternative view see S. J. Leibowitz and S. Margolis, "The Fable of the Keys," *Journal of Law and Economics* 33 (1990): 1–26.

The problem of *de facto* standards is that they may take a long time to emerge, resulting in duplication of investments and delayed development of the market. It was 40 years before a standard railroad gauge was agreed in the US.[25] The slow transition of US wireless telephone systems from analog to digital technology may be attributed in part to uncertainty created by continuing competition between TDMA and CDMA standards. By contrast, Europe officially adopted GSM (a close relative of TDMA) back in 1992.[26] Delayed emergence of a standard may kill the technology altogether. The failure of quadraphonic sound to displace stereophonic sound during the 1970s resulted from incompatible technical standards among manufacturers of audio equipment. The absence of a dominant standard discouraged recorded music companies from investing in quadraphonic records and tapes, and consumers from investing in quadraphonic systems.[27] Similar uncertainty has arisen over high-definition television (HDTV).[28]

An *architectural standard* may combine a number of closely linked technical standards. Thus, the standard for personal computers is often referred to as the "Wintel" (Windows–Intel) standard. In fact, the standard is even broader: Intel owns the microprocessor design, Microsoft the Windows operating system, Novell or Microsoft owns the networking software, Adobe or Hewlett-Packard owns the printer page description system, Norton or McAfee owns the anti-virus software.[29]

Winning Standards Wars

If network externalities exist in a market, setting the standard is the basis of competitive advantage. Apple Computer's failure to establish the standard in personal computers reduced it to the role of a bit player struggling for survival. Intel, Microsoft, Qualcomm, Sony (Playstation), and Oracle have reaped fortunes from their ownership of key standards. By identifying the extent and nature of network externalities in a particular market and the dynamics of how standards emerge, we can develop a strategy that can maximize our chances of setting the industry standard.

The single most important strategic issue in standards setting is recognition of the role of positive feedback: the technology that can establish early leadership will tend to attract new adopters. Building a "bigger bandwagon," according to Shapiro and Varian,[30] requires the following:

---

[25] A. Friedlander, *The Growth of Railroads* (Arlington, VA: CNRI, 1995).
[26] C. Shapiro and H. R. Varian, *Information Rules: A Strategic Guide to the Network Economy* (Boston: Harvard Business School Press, 1999): 264–7.
[27] Steve Postrel, "Competing Networks and Proprietary Standards: The Case of Quadraphonic Sound," *Journal of Industrial Economics* 24 (December 1990): 169–86.
[28] Shapiro and Varian, op. cit.: 218–23.
[29] C. R. Morris and C. H. Ferguson, "How Architecture Wins Technology Wars," *Harvard Business Review* (March–April 1993): 86–96.
[30] C. Shapiro and H. R. Varian, "The Art of Standards Wars," *California Management Review* 41 (Winter 1999): 8–32.

- *Before you go to war, assemble allies.* You'll need the support of consumers, suppliers of complements, even your competitors. Not even the strongest companies can afford to go it alone in a standards war.

- *Preempt the market* – enter early, achieve fast-cycle product development, make early deals with key customers, and adopt penetration pricing.

- *Manage expectations.* The key to managing positive feedback is to convince customers, suppliers, and the producers of complementary goods that you will emerge as the victor. These expectations become a self-fulfilling pro-phecy. The massive pre-launch promotion and publicity built up by Sony prior to the American and European launch of Playstation 2 in October 2000 was an effort to convince consumers, retailers, and game developers that the product would be the blockbuster consumer electronics product of the new decade, thereby stymieing Sega and Nintendo's efforts to establish their rival systems.

The lesson that has emerged from the classic standards battles of the past is that in order to create initial leadership and maximize positive feedback effects, a company must share the value created by the technology with other parties (customers, com-petitors, complementors, and suppliers). If a company attempts to appropriate too great a share of the value created, it may well fail to build a big enough bandwagon to gain market leadership (see Exhibit 11.2). Thus, most of the standards battles being waged currently involve broad alliances, where the owner uses liberal licensing in order to attract as many customers and allies as possible. For example, the battle being fought between Palm, Microsoft, and Symbian for leadership in operating systems for hand-held digital devices involves broad alliances including consumer electronics manufacturers, telecommunications hardware companies, software companies, and

---

EXHIBIT 11.2 Building a Bandwagon by Sharing Value: Lessons from VCRs and PCs

Profiting from standards requires two elements: first, setting the standard; second, retaining some proprietary interest in the standard in order to appropriate part of its value. There is a tradeoff between the two – the more value a company tries to appropriate, the greater the difficulty in building early support for its technology. Consider the standards wars in VCRs and PCs:

- In VCRs, Matsushita's VHS format won against Sony's Betamax format not because of the technical superiority of VHS, but because Matsushita did not insist on such tight ownership of its technology and was more effective in gaining acceptability in the mar-ket. The key here was Matsushita's encouragement of adoption through licensing of the VHS system to Sharp, Philips, GE, RCA, and other competitors.

- In personal computers, IBM was highly successful in setting the standard, partly because it did not restrict access to its technology. Its product specifications were openly available to "clone makers," and its suppliers (including Microsoft and Intel) were free

EXHIBIT 11.2 *(cont'd)*

to supply them with microprocessors and the MS-DOS operating system. IBM was remarkably successful at setting the standard, but failed to appropriate much value because it retained no significant proprietary interest in the standard – it was Intel and Microsoft that owned the key intellectual property. For Apple, the situation was the reverse. It kept tight control over its Macintosh operating system and product architecture, it earned high margins during the 1980s, but it forfeited the opportunity of setting the industry standard.

The tradeoff between market acceptance of a technology and appropriating the returns to a technology is shown below:

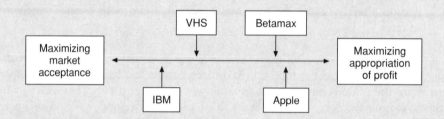

The innovator who enforces no ownership rights and gives away the innovation to anyone who wants it will probably maximize market penetration. On the other hand, the innovator who is most restrictive in enforcing ownership rights will maximize margins in the short run, but will probably have difficulty building a bandwagon big enough to establish market leadership. In recent battles over technical standards, the desire to gain market leadership has encouraged firms to be less and less restrictive over ownership in the interests of building their market bandwagon. Thus, in the battle for dominance of internet browser software, both Microsoft (Internet Explorer) and Netscape (Navigator) offered their products for free in the interests of wresting market leadership. When attacking an existing standard, there may be no alternative to giving the technology away: the only chance for Unix and Sun Microsystems' Java to establish themselves against Microsoft's Windows was by committing to an open standard.

Increasingly, companies are trying to reconcile market acceptance with value appropriation: Adobe gives away its Acrobat Reader in order to broaden the user base, but charges for the software needed to create pdf documents in Acrobat.

Where competition is weak, a company may be able to set the dominant standard while also appropriating most of the value: Nintendo in video games during the late 1980s and early 1990s is the classic example. However, once Nintendo met competition from Sega and Sony, its strategy backfired, as games developers and retailers welcomed competitors that offered a better deal.

Sources: *The World VCR Industry*, Case No. 9-387-098 (Boston: Harvard Business School, 1990); *Apple Computer – 1992*, Case No. 9-792-081 (Boston: Harvard Business School, 1994); *The Browser Wars, 1994–1998*, Case No. 9-798-094 (Boston: Harvard Business School, 1998); "The Video Game Industry," in R. M. Grant, *Cases in Contemporary Strategy Analysis*, 3rd edn (Oxford: Blackwell Publishers, 2001).

telecommunication suppliers. The alliances overlap: thus, Ericsson is a member of Psion's Symbian alliance and has linked with Microsoft to include Microsoft software in its internet-accessing phones.[31]

Achieving compatibility with existing products is a critical issue in standards battles. Advantage typically goes to the competitor that adopts an *evolutionary strategy* (i.e., offers compatibility with existing technology) rather than one that adopts a *revolutionary strategy*.[32] Microsoft Windows won the PC war against the Apple Macintosh for many reasons. Both companies offered an operating system with a graphical user interface. However, while Windows was designed for compatibility with the DOS operating system, the Apple Mac was incompatible both with DOS and the Apple II. Similarly, a key advantage of the Sony Playstation 2 over the Sega Dreamcast and Nintendo Cube is its compatibility with the Playstation 1.

What are the key resources needed to win a standards war? Shapiro and Varian emphasize:

- Control over an installed base of customers.

- Owning intellectual property rights in the new technology.

- The ability to innovate in order to extend and adapt the initial technological advance.

- First-mover advantage.

- Strength in complements, e.g., Intel has preserved its standard in microprocessors by promoting standards in busses, chipsets, graphics controllers, and interfaces between motherboards and CPUs.

- Reputation and brand name.[33]

However, even with such advantages, standards wars are costly and risky. The best strategy may be to reach an agreement over standards with potential competitors. Thus, in CDs, Philips and Sony avoided a standards war by pooling their CD patents and agreeing to a common standard.

IMPLEMENTING TECHNOLOGY STRATEGIES: CREATING THE CONDITIONS FOR INNOVATION

As we have noted previously, strategy formulation cannot be separated from its implementation. Nowhere is this more evident than in technology-intensive businesses.

---

[31] "If at First You don't succeed . . . ," *Business Week* (April 24, 2000): 62–5.
[32] Shapiro and Varian, "The Art of Standards Wars," op. cit.: 15–16.
[33] Ibid.: 16–18.

From Strategy Formulation to Promoting Innovation

Our analysis so far has taught us about the potential for generating competitive advantage from innovation and about the design of technology-based strategies, but has said little about the conditions under which innovation is achieved. The danger is that strategic analysis can tell us a great deal about making money out of innovation, but this isn't much use if we cannot generate innovation in the first place. If the essence of innovation is creativity and one of the key features of creativity is its resistance to planning, it is evident that strategy formulation must pay careful attention to the organizational processes through which innovations emerge and are commercialized. Because the features of new products and processes are unknown when resources are committed to R&D and there is no predetermined relationship between investment in R&D and the output of innovations, the productivity of R&D depends heavily on the organizational conditions that foster innovation. Hence, the most crucial challenge facing firms in emerging and technology-based industries is: How does the firm create conditions that are conducive to innovation?

To answer this question, we must return to the critical distinction between invention and innovation. Invention is dependent on creativity. Creativity is not simply a matter of individual brilliance; it depends on the organizational conditions that foster ideas and imagination at the individual and group levels. Similarly, innovation is not just a matter of acquiring the resources necessary for commercialization; innovation is a cooperative activity that requires interaction and collaboration between technology development, manufacturing, marketing, and various other functional departments within the firm.

The Conditions for Creativity

Invention has two primary ingredients: knowledge and creativity. Only by understanding the determinants of creativity, then fostering it through an appropriate organizational environment, can the firm hope to innovate successfully. The creativity that drives innovation is typically an individual act that establishes a meaningful relationship between concepts or objects that had not previously been related. This reconceptualizing can be triggered by accidents: an apple falling on Isaac Newton's head or James Watt observing a kettle boiling. Creativity also requires personal qualities. Research shows that creative people share certain personality traits: they are curious, imaginative, adventurous, assertive, playful, self-confident, risk taking, reflective, and uninhibited.

Motivating creativity presents a further challenge. Creatively oriented people are typically responsive to different incentives than those that are effective in motivating other members of the organization:

> They desire to work in an egalitarian culture with enough space and resources to provide the opportunity to be spontaneous, experience freedom, and have fun in the performance of a task that, they feel, makes a difference to the strategic performance of the firm. Praise,

recognition, and opportunities for education and professional growth are also more important than assuming managerial responsibilities.[34]

Creativity is likely to be stimulated by human interaction. Michael Tushman's research into communication in R&D laboratories concludes that developing communication networks is one of the most important aspects of the management of R&D.[35] An important catalyst of interaction is *play*, which creates an environment of inquiry, liberates thought from conventional constraints, and provides the opportunity to establish new relationships by rearranging ideas and structures at a safe distance from reality. Apple Computer placed considerable emphasis on creating an atmosphere of playfulness:

> Almost every building had its own theme, so meeting and conference rooms . . . are named by employees who decide upon the theme of their building. In our "Land of Oz" building, the conference rooms are named "Dorothy" and "Toto." Our Management Information Systems Group has meeting rooms named "Greed," "Envy," "Sloth," "Lust," and the remaining deadly sins. It's not an accident that many of these are the symbols of childhood (popcorn included). William Blake believed that in growing up, people move from states of innocence to experience, and then, if they're fortunate, to "higher innocence" – the most creative state of all.[36]

These conditions for creativity have far-reaching organizational implications. Anita Roddick of Body Shop cultivated a culture of "benevolent anarchy – encouraging questioning of established ways and going in the opposite direction to everyone else."[37] In particular, creativity requires an organizational structure and management system that are quite different from those appropriate to the pursuit of cost efficiency. Table 11.5 contrasts some characteristics of the two types of organization.

Although innovation requires creativity, creativity needs to be stimulated by and directed toward *need*. Few important inventions have been the result of spontaneous creative activity by technologists; almost all have resulted from grappling with practical problems. James Watt's redesign of the steam engine was conceived while repairing an early Newcomen steam engine owned by Glasgow University. The basic inventions behind the Xerox copying process were the work of Chester Carlson, a patent attorney who became frustrated by the problems of accurately copying technical drawings. These observations reaffirm the notion that "necessity is the mother of invention," which explains why customers are such fertile sources of innovation – they are most acutely involved with matching existing products and services to their needs.[38] The relocation of R&D from corporate research departments to

[34] Louis W. Fry and Borje O. Saxberg, "Homo Ludens: Playing Man and Creativity in Innovating Organizations," discussion paper (Department of Management and Organization, University of Washington, 1987).
[35] Michael L. Tushman, "Managing Communication Networks in R&D Laboratories," *Sloan Management Review* (Winter 1979): 37–49.
[36] John Scully, *Odyssey* (Toronto: Fitzhenry and Whiteside, 1987): 187–8.
[37] L. Grundy, J. Kickel, and C. Prather, "Building the Creative Organization," *Organizational Dynamics* (Spring 1994): 22–37.
[38] Eric Von Hippel, *The Sources of Innovation* (New York: Oxford University Press, 1988), provides strong evidence of the dominant role of users in the innovation process.

TABLE 11.5　The Characteristics of "Operating" and "Innovating" Organizations

	OPERATING ORGANIZATION	INNOVATING ORGANIZATION
Structure	Bureaucratic. Specialization and division of labor. Hierarchical control	Flat organization without hierarchical control. Task-oriented project teams.
Processes	Operating units controlled and coordinated by top management, which undertakes strategic planning, capital allocation, and operational planning.	Processes directed toward generation, selection, funding, and development of ideas. Strategic planning flexible, financial and operating controls loose.
Reward systems	Financial compensation, promotion up the hierarchy, power, and status symbols.	Autonomy, recognition, equity participation in new ventures
People	Recruitment and selection based on the needs of the organization structure for specific skills: functional and staff specialists, general managers, and operatives.	Key need is for idea generators that combine required technical knowledge with creative personality traits. Managers must act as sponsors and orchestrators.

Source:　Based on Jay R. Galbraith and Robert K. Kazanjian, *Strategy Implementation: Structure, Systems and Processes*, 2nd edn (St. Paul, MN: West, 1986).

operating businesses is motivated by the desire to link technology development more closely with the needs of the business. It also permits the businesses to be better positioned to utilize the output of R&D units, so avoiding the fate of Xerox Corporation's PARC facility during the 1980s.[39]

From Invention to Innovation: The Challenge of Cross-functional Integration

The commercialization of new technology requires linking creativity and technological expertise, with capabilities in production, marketing, finance, distribution, and customer support. As we noted in Chapter 5, the challenge of new product development is that it draws upon every area of functional and technical expertise within the company. The organizational challenge is considerable: there are substantial differences between an organization that conceives and designs an innovative product and one that makes it and takes it to market. It is the classic dichotomy between knowledge generation (or *exploration*) and knowledge application (or *exploitation*).[40]

---

[39]　"The Lab That Ran Away from Xerox," *Fortune* (September 5, 1988); "Barefoot into PARC," *Economist* (July 10, 1993): 68.

[40]　J. March, "Exploration and Exploitation in Organizational Learning," *Organization Science* 2 (1991): 71–87.

Operating functions such as production and sales must be organized differently from technology and product development functions, giving rise to the need for differentiation and integration among departments.[41]

Tension between the operating and the innovating parts of organizations is inevitable. Innovation upsets established routines and threatens the status quo. The more stable the operating and administrative side of the organization, the greater the resistance to innovation. A classic example is the opposition by the US naval establishment to continuous-aim firing, a process that offered huge improvements in gunnery accuracy.[42]

Two organizational innovations have helped reconcile creativity and knowledge development with operational efficiency and knowledge application:

- *Cross-functional product development teams.* Cross-functional product development teams have proven to be highly effective mechanisms for integrating the different functional capabilities required to develop a new product, and for developing communication and cooperation across functional divisions. Japanese companies in automobiles, electronics, and construction equipment have been the most prominent pioneers of product development teams. Imai, Nonaka, and Takeuchi show how the structure of product development teams facilitates knowledge integration, learning, and swift development of innovative and defect-free new products.[43] The US auto producers have adopted many of these features in the redesigns of their own new model development processes. The Ford Taurus was one of Detroit's first team-based product development efforts (see Exhibit 11.3). Clark and Fujimoto's study of new automobile development in Japan, the United States, and Europe provides fascinating insight into the organization of product development efforts and the advantages derived from "overlapping" the different stages of product development rather than simply sequencing them, and from providing strong leadership through "heavyweight" product managers.[44]

- *Product champions* provide a means by which individual creativity and the desire to make a difference can be reconciled within organizational processes. The key is to permit the same individuals who are the creative forces behind an innovation or business idea also to be the leaders in commercializing those innovations. Companies that are consistently successful in innovation have

---

[41] P. Lawrence and S. Lorsch, *Organization and Environment: Managing Differentiation and Integration* (Cambridge, MA: Harvard University Press, 1967).

[42] Elting Morrison, "Gunfire at Sea: A Case Study of Innovation," in Michael Tushman and William L. Moore (eds), *Readings in the Management of Innovation* (Cambridge, MA: Ballinger, 1988): 165–78.

[43] K. Imai, I. Nonaka, and H. Takeuchi, "Managing the New Product Development Process: How Japanese Companies Learn and Unlearn," in K. Clark, R. Hayes, and C. Lorenz (eds), *The Uneasy Alliance* (Boston: Harvard Business School Press, 1985).

[44] Kim Clark and Takahiro Fujimoto, *Product Development Performance: Strategy, Organization, and Management in the World Auto Industry* (Boston: Harvard Business School Press, 1991).

EXHIBIT 11.3   Product Development at Ford: From a Sequential to a Team Approach

The Sequential Approach: Pre-Taurus

Designers designed a car on paper, then gave it to the engineers, who figured out how to make it. Their plans were passed on to the manufacturing and purchasing people . . . The next step in the process was the production plant. Then came marketing, the legal and service departments, and finally the customers. If a glitch developed, the car was bumped back to the design stage for changes. The farther along in the sequence, however, the more difficult it was to make changes.

The Team Approach: The Taurus

With Taurus . . . we brought all disciplines together, and did the whole process simultaneously as well as sequentially. The manufacturing people worked with the design people, engineering people, sales and purchasing, legal, service and marketing. In sales and marketing we had dealers come in and tell us what they wanted in a car to make it more user-friendly . . . We had insurance companies – Allstate, State Farm, American Road – tell us how to design a car so when accidents occur it would minimize the customer's expense in fixing it . . . We went to all stamping plants, assembly plants and put layouts on the walls. We asked them how to make it easier to build . . . It's amazing the dedication and commitment you can get from people.

Source: Taurus project leader, Veraldi, quoted by Mary Walton, *The Deming Management Method* (New York: Mead & Co., 1986): 130–1.

the ability to capture and direct individuals' drive for achievement and success within their organizational processes; creating product champion roles is the most common means for achieving this. Given resistance to change within organizations and the need to forge cross-functional integration, leadership by committed individuals can help overcome vested interests in stability and functional separation. Schön's study of 15 major innovations concluded that: "the new idea either finds a champion or dies."[45] A British study of 43 matched pairs of successful and unsuccessful innovations similarly concluded that a key factor distinguishing successful innovation was the presence of a "business innovator" to exert entrepreneurial leadership.[46] 3M Corporation is exemplary in its use of product champions to develop new product ideas and grow them into new business units (see Exhibit 11.4).

[45]   D. A. Schön, "Champions for Radical New Inventions," *Harvard Business Review* (March–April 1963): 84.
[46]   R. Rothwell et al., "SAPPHO Updated – Project SAPPHO Phase II," *Research Policy* 3 (1974): 258–91.

EXHIBIT 11.4   Innovation at 3M: The Role of the Product Champion

---

Start Little and Build

We don't look to the president, or the vice-president for R&D to say, all right, now Monday morning 3M is going to get into such-and-such a business. Rather, we prefer to see someone in one of our laboratories, or marketing or manufacturing, or new products bring forward a new idea that he's been thinking about. Then, when he can convince people around him, including his supervisor, that he's got something interesting, we'll make him what we call a "project manager" with a small budget of money and talent, and let him run with it.

In short, we'd rather have the idea for a new business come from the bottom up than from the top down. Throughout all our 60 years of history here, that has been the mark of success. Did you develop a new business? The incentive? Money, of course. But that's not the key. The key . . . is becoming the general manager of a new business . . . having such a hot project that management just has to become involved whether it wants to or not. (Bob Adams, vice president for R&D, 3M Corporation)

Scotchlite

Someone asked the question, "Why didn't 3M make glass beads, because glass beads were going to find increasing use on the highways?" . . . I had done a little working in the mineral department on trying to color glass beads we'd imported from Czechoslovakia and had learned a little about their reflecting properties. And, as a little extra-curricular activity, I'd been trying to make luminous house numbers – and maybe luminous signs as well – by developing luminous pigments.

Well, this question and my free-time lab project combined to stimulate me to search out where glass beads were being used on the highway. We found a place where beads had been sprinkled on the highway and we saw that they did provide a more visible line at night . . . From there, it was only natural for us to conclude that, since we were a coating company, and probably knew more than anyone else about putting particles onto a web than anybody, we ought to be able to coat glass beads very accurately on a piece of paper.

So, that's what we did. The first reflective tape we made was simply a double-coated tape – glass beads sprinkled on one side and an adhesive on the other. We took some out here in St. Paul and, with the cooperation of the highway department, put some down. After the first frost came, and then a thaw, we found we didn't know as much about adhesives under all weather conditions as we thought . . .

We looked around inside the company for skills in related areas. We tapped knowledge that existed in our sandpaper business on how to make waterproof sandpaper. We drew on the expertise of our roofing people who knew something about exposure. We reached into our adhesive and tape division to see how we could make the tape stick to the highway better.

The resulting product became known as "Scotchlite." Its principal application was in reflective signs; only later did 3M develop the market for highway marking. The originator of the product, Harry Heltzer, interested the head of the New Products Division in the product, and he encouraged Heltzer to go out and sell it. Scotchlite was a success and Heltzer became the general manager of the division set up to produce and market it. Heltzer later went on to become 3M's president.

Source: "The Technical Strategy of 3M: Start More Little Businesses and More Little Businesses," *Innovation* no. 5 (1969).

SUMMARY

In emerging industries and other industries where technology is the primary medium of competition, the nurturing and developing of innovation is the fundamental source of competitive advantage and the focus of strategy formulation. Does this mean that the principles of strategic management are fundamentally different in technology-based industries from other types of business environments? Many of the strategy issues we have discussed in this chapter are the same as those we covered in the previous chapters of the book. For example, the analysis of the determinants of the returns to innovation covered almost the same factors as our analysis of the returns to resources and capabilities: relevance to customer needs, barriers to imitation, and appropriability through well-established property rights.

At the same time, some aspects of strategic management in technology-based industries are distinctive. An issue with technology-based industries is the rapid rate of change and the difficulty of forecasting change. Conditions of Schumpeterian "creative destruction" (or, in Rich D'Aveni's terminology, *hypercompetition*) mean that traditional approaches to strategy formulation based on forecasting must be abandoned in favor of strategic management approaches that combine a clear sense of direction based on vision and mission, with the flexibility to respond to and take advantage of the unexpected.

Despite this turbulence and uncertainty, the principles of strategic analysis are critical in guiding the quest for competitive advantage in technology-intensive industries. Our analysis has been able to guide us on key issues such as:

- whether an innovation has the potential to confer sustainable competitive advantage;

- the relative merits of licensing, alliances, joint ventures, and internal development as alternative strategies for exploiting an innovation;

- the factors that determine the comparative advantages of being a leader or a follower in innovation.

This chapter also pointed to the central importance of strategy implementation in determining success. The key to successful innovation is not resource allocation decisions, but creating the structure, integration mechanisms, and organizational climate conducive to innovation. No other type of industry environment reveals so clearly the inseparability of strategy formulation and strategy implementation. Strategies aimed at the exploitation of innovation, choices of whether to be a leader or a follower, and the management of risk must take careful account of organizational characteristics.

Technology-based industries also reveal some of the dilemmas that are a critical feature of strategic management in complex organizations and complex business environments. For example, technology-based industries are unpredictable, yet some investments in technology have time horizons of a decade or more. Successful strategies must be responsive to changing market conditions, but successful strategies also require long-term commitment. The fundamental dilemma is that innovation is an unpredictable process that requires creating a nurturing organizational context, whereas strategy is about resource-allocation decisions. How can a company create the conditions for nurturing innovation while planning the course of its development? As John Scully of Apple has observed:

> Management and creativity might even be considered antithetical states. While management demands consensus, control, certainty, and the status quo, creativity thrives on the opposite: instinct, uncertainty, freedom, and iconoclasm.[47]

Fortunately, the experiences of companies such as 3M, Sony, Merck, Cisco Systems, and Canon point to solutions to these dilemmas. The need for innovation to reconcile individual creativity with coordination points toward the advantages of cross-functional team-based approaches over the isolation of R&D in a separate "creative" environment. Moreover, the need to reconcile innovation with efficiency points toward the advantage of parallel organizational structures where, in addition to the "formal" structure geared to the needs of existing businesses and products, an informal structure exists, which is the source of new products and businesses. The role of top management in balancing creativity with order and innovation with efficiency becomes critical. The success of companies in both Japan and Silicon Valley in managing technology (especially compared with the poor innovation performance of many large, diversified US and British corporations) points to the importance of technological knowledge among senior managers.

The increasing pace of technological change and intensifying international competition suggests that the advanced, industrialized countries will be forced to rely increasingly on their technological capabilities as the basis for international competitiveness. Strategies for promoting innovation and managing technology will become more important in the future.

---

[47]   John Scully, op. cit.: 184.

12

Competitive Advantage in Mature Industries

We are a true "penny profit" business. That means that it takes hard work and attention to detail to be financially successful – it is far from being a sure thing. Our store managers must do two things well: control costs and increase sales. Cost control cannot be done by compromising product quality, customer service, or restaurant cleanliness, but rather by consistent monitoring of the "vital signs" of the business through observation, reports, and analysis. Portion control is a critical part of our business. For example, each Filet-O-Fish sandwich receives 1 fluid ounce of tartar sauce and 0.5 ounces of cheese. Our raw materials are fabricated to exacting tolerances, and our managers check them on an ongoing basis. Our written specification for lettuce is over two typewritten pages long. Our French fries must meet standards for potato type, solid and moisture content, and distribution of strand lengths.
—Edward H. Rensi, President and Chief Operating Officer, McDonald's U.S.A.[1]

Outline

- INTRODUCTION AND OBJECTIVES
- KEY SUCCESS FACTORS IN MATURE ENVIRONMENTS
   Cost Advantage
   Segment and Customer Selection

---

[1] Edward H. Rensi, "Computers at McDonalds," in J. F. McLimore and L. Larwood (eds), *Strategies . . . Successes . . . Senior Executives Speak Out* (New York: Harper & Row, 1988): 159–60.

Introduction and Objectives

Although technology-based enterprises provide some of the most exciting examples of real-world strategy, if importance is measured by share of GDP rather than share of press commentary, mature industries – food processing, automobiles, financial services, hotels and restaurants – continue to be the primary sources of income and employment in the industrialized nations.

Despite their heterogeneity – mature industries range from insurance to steel – they present several similarities from a strategic perspective. The purpose of this chapter is to explore the characteristics of mature industries, the strategies through which competitive advantage can be established within them, and the implications of these strategies for structure, systems, and leadership style. As we shall see, maturity does not imply lack of opportunity. Companies such as Home Depot (hardware retailing), Nike (sports footwear and apparel), Virgin Group (music, airlines, financial services), Nucor (steel), and Enron (energy) have prospered on the basis of innovative strategies. Coca-Cola and General Electric have achieved combinations of profitability and growth that would make most high-tech companies envious. Nor does maturity imply an absence of technological change: the internet has the potential to revolutionize retail banking; the fuel cell may reshape the automobile industry.

By the time you have completed this chapter, you will be able to:

■ Recognize the principal strategic characteristics of mature industries.

■ Identify key success factors within mature industries and formulate strategies directed toward their exploitation.

■ Locate and analyze opportunities for strategic innovation in mature industries to establish competitive advantage.

■ Design organizational structures and management systems that can effectively implement such strategies.

Key Success Factors in Mature Environments

Maturity has two principal implications for competitive advantage: first, it tends to reduce the number of opportunities for establishing competitive advantage; second, it shifts these opportunities from differentiation-based factors to cost-based factors.

Diminishing opportunities for competitive advantage in mature industries stem from:

- Less scope for differentiation advantage resulting from increased buyer knowledge, product standardization, and less product innovation.

- Diffusion of process technology means that cost advantages based on superior processes or more advanced capital equipment methods are difficult to obtain and sustain.

- A highly developed industry infrastructure together with the presence of powerful distributors makes it easier to attack established firms that occupy particular strategic niches.

- The vulnerability of cost advantage to exchange rate movements and the emergence of low-cost overseas competitors.

Warren Buffett – "The Sage of Omaha" – notes that the profit potential of mature businesses tends to deteriorate as they transform from "franchises" into "businesses":

> An economic franchise arises from a product or service that (1) is needed or desired; (2) is thought by customers to have no close substitute; and (3) is not subject to price regulation. Franchises earn high rates of return on capital . . . [and] can tolerate mismanagement . . . In contrast, "a business" earns exceptional profits only if it is a low-cost operator or if supply of its product or service is tight. And a business, unlike a franchise, can be killed by poor management.[2]

Buffett observes that the profitability of the media business – newspapers, television, and magazines – "continues to erode as retailing patterns change and entertainment choices proliferate." The problem is that as the businesses have transformed from "franchises" into "businesses," consumers "enjoy greatly broadened choices as to where to find them." Unfortunately, demand can't expand in response to the new supply: 500 million American eyeballs and a 24-hour day are all that's available. The result is that competition has intensified, markets have fragmented, and the media industry has lost some – though far from all – of its franchise strength.

This trend toward deteriorating industry profitability is a constant threat in mature industries. As rivalry encourages overinvestment in capacity, international competition increases, and differentiation is undermined by commoditization, attaining a competitive advantage becomes essential to achieving positive economic profits.

---

[2]   Letter to shareholders, *The 1991 Annual Report of Berkshire Hathaway Inc.*

Cost Advantage

If cost is the overwhelmingly important key success factor in most mature industries, what are the primary sources of low cost? Three cost drivers tend to be especially important:

- *Economies of scale.* In capital-intensive industries, or where advertising, distribution, or new product development is an important element of total cost, economies of scale are important sources of inter-firm cost differences. The increased standardization that accompanies maturity greatly assists the exploitation of such scale economies. The significance of scale economies in mature industries is indicated by the fact that the association between ROI and market share is stronger in mature industries than in emerging industries.[3]

- *Low-cost inputs.* Where small competitors are successful in undercutting the prices of market leaders in mature industries, it is frequently through their access to low-cost inputs. Established firms can become locked into high-cost positions through unionization of their workforces or through inertia. The decline in the market share of the US steel majors over the past three decades is partly the result of union agreements over wages, benefits, and working practices that guaranteed high-cost production. During the 1970s and 1980s they steadily lost ground to overseas suppliers and domestic minimills, both of which benefited from lower labor costs. New entrants into mature industries may gain cost advantages by acquiring plant and equipment at bargain-basement levels. The emergence of Tosco as one of the largest and most profitable oil refiners in the United States has been based on its acquisition of refineries sold off by the majors as unprofitable assets. Depressed stock markets can also allow assets to be acquired cheaply: during the Asian financial crisis of 1997–99, Citigroup and GE Capital acquired a number of Asian banks and investment companies at bargain-basement prices.

- *Low overheads.* During the early 1990s, some of the most profitable companies in mature industries tended to be those that had achieved the most substantial reductions in overhead costs. In discount retailing, Wal-Mart is famous for its parsimonious approach to overhead cost. Among the oil majors, Exxon is known for its rigorous control of overhead costs. Exxon's headquarters cost (relative to net worth) was estimated at less than one-quarter that of Mobil's.[4] When Exxon merged with Mobil, it was able to extract huge cost savings from Mobil. Excess overhead costs in mature firms can be pervasive and institutionalized and their elimination may require shock therapy. In the oil industry, it was the oil price collapse of 1986 that triggered a wave of cost reduction and restructuring.[5] Among the Korean *chaebols*, the financial crisis of 1998 led to extensive reductions in overheads.

[3]   Robert D. Buzzell and Bradley T. Gale, *The PIMS Principles* (New York: Free Press, 1987): 279.
[4]   T. Copeland, T. Koller, and J. Murrin, *Valuation: Measuring and Managing the Value of Companies,* 3rd edn (New York: Wiley, 2000): 305.
[5]   R. Cibin and Robert M. Grant, "Restructuring among the World's Leading Oil Companies," *British Journal of Management* 7 (December 1996): 283–308.

While cost efficiency will not necessarily provide for sustainable competitive advantage, cost inefficiency can be fatal. Research into performance turnarounds among mature businesses points to the critical role played by aggressive cost cutting. Hambrick and Schecter identified three successful turnaround strategies:

- *Asset and cost surgery* – aggressive cost reduction through reduction of excess capacity; halting of new investment in plant and equipment; and cutbacks in R&D, marketing expenditures, receivables and inventories.

- *Selective product and market pruning* – refocusing on segments that were most profitable or where the firm possessed distinctive strength.

- *Piecemeal productivity moves* – adjustments to current market position rather than comprehensive refocusing or reorganizing, including reductions in marketing and R&D expenditures, higher capacity utilization, and increased employee productivity.[6]

The importance of cost reduction in boosting profitability is confirmed by Grinyer, Mayes, and McKiernan's study of turnarounds among British companies (most of which were long-established companies in mature industries). The two factors that most frequently distinguished the "sharpbenders" from a control group of companies were, first, changes in top management and, second, intensive efforts to reduce production costs.[7]

Segment and Customer Selection

Sluggish demand growth, lack of product differentiation, and international competition tend to depress the profitability of mature industries. Yet, even unattractive industries may offer profitable niche markets. Not only do growth rates of demand vary between segments, but the structure of segments with regard to concentration, buyer power, and potential for differentiation varies considerably. As a result, segment selection can be a key determinant of differences in the performance of companies within the same industry. Wal-Mart's profitability was assisted by locating its stores in small and medium-sized towns where it faced little competition. In chemicals, ICI has followed several other major chemical producers in exiting bulk chemicals and concentrating on specialty chemicals where margins are higher.

In the auto industry, all the major companies have sought to improve their profitability by shifting into higher-margin segments, notably luxury cars, light trucks, sport-utility vehicles (SUVs), and passenger vans. As these segments have become overcrowded, so companies have sought to create new segments through developing hybrid vehicles. Japanese carmakers have pioneered compact SUVs, the US Big

[6] Donald C. Hambrick and Steven M. Schecter, "Turnaround Strategies for Mature Industrial-Product Business Units," *Academy of Management Journal* 26, no. 2 (1983): 231–48.
[7] Peter H. Grinyer, D. G. Mayes, and P. McKiernan, *Sharpbenders* (Oxford: Basil Blackwell, 1988).

Three offer five-seater pick-up trucks, DaimlerChrysler has pioneered new segments with its ultra-micro Smart car and its retro-look PT cruiser.

The logic of segment focus implies further disaggregation of markets – down to the level of the individual customer. Information technology increasingly makes it possible to identify those customers that contribute the greatest profit contribution to the firm. In the same way that Las Vegas casinos have long recognized that the major part of their profits derives from a tiny minority of customers – the "high rollers" – so banks, supermarkets, credit card companies, and hotels increasingly use transactions data to identify their most attractive customers, and those that yield no contribution.

The next stage in this process is to go beyond customer selection actively to target more attractive customers and transform less valuable customers into more valuable customers. Alan Grant and Leonard Schlesinger point to the need for companies to optimize their *value exchange* – the relationship between the investment a company makes in a customer relationship and the return that investment generates. For example:

- Credit card issuer First Direct uses IT to allocate customers into hundreds of different segments, which it targets with over 750 different credit offers with varying fees, credit limits, interest rates, and add-on features.

- AT&T uses information on customer call volumes and patterns to analyze carefully each customer's profit contribution and tailors its incentives, service offering, and sales approach accordingly.[8]

The Quest for Differentiation

Cost leadership, we noted in Chapter 9, is difficult to sustain, particularly in the face of international competition. Hence, differentiating to attain some insulation from the rigors of price competition is particularly attractive in mature industries. The problem is that the trend toward commoditization narrows the scope for differentiation and reduces customer willingness to pay a premium for differentiation. For example, in the tire and domestic appliance industries, many companies have sought differentiation advantage through product innovation, quality, and investing in brand reputation. For most tire and appliance companies, such differentiation has not yielded superior margins: in these competitive markets with price-sensitive customers and strong, aggressive retailers, these approaches to differentiation support only modest price premiums. Hence, creating meaningful differentiation represents one of the greatest challenges to managers in mature industries.

Standardization of the physical attributes of a product and convergence of consumer preferences constrain but do not eliminate the potential for differentiation. Product standardization is frequently accompanied by increased differentiation of

[8]   A. W. H. Grant and L. A. Schlesinger, "Realize Your Customer's Full Profit Potential," *Harvard Business Review* (September–October 1995): 59–72.

TABLE 12.1   Large Retailers with the Highest and Lowest Valuation Ratios

COMPANY	COUNTRY	VALUATION RATIO*	SALES ($, BILLIONS)
Top 15			
Amazon.com	US	62.6	1.6
Intimate Brands	US	18.9	3.9
Hennes & Mauritz	Sweden	18.3	3.1
Seven-Eleven Japan	Japan	16.9	16.3
Gap	US	13.4	11.6
Home Depot	US	12.4	38.4
Best Buy	US	11.7	12.5
CDW Computer Centers	US	10.7	2.6
Wal-Mart	US	9.9	166.8
Kohl's	US	9.4	4.6
Dixons Group	UK	9.3	4.7
Bed, Bath & Beyond	US	9.2	1.9
Carrefour	France	8.7	47.8
Pinault-Printemps-Redoute	France	7.9	17.5
Castorama Dubois Investissements	France	7.0	6.8
Bottom 15			
J. C. Penny	US	0.7	32.5
Federated Department Stores	US	1.2	18.2
J. Sainsbury	UK	1.3	26.3
Marks & Spencer	UK	1.5	12.3
Great Universal Stores	UK	1.7	5.5
Marui	Japan	1.8	4.8
Jusco	Japan	1.9	23.4
Sears Roebuck	US	2.0	41.1
May Department Stores	US	2.6	13.9
Ito-Yokado	Japan	2.7	29.9
Albertson's	US	2.7	37.5
Tesco	UK	2.9	28.9
Boots	UK	2.9	7.5
George Weston	Canada	3.2	13.9
Metro	Germany	3.5	43.5

*   Ratio of market value of equity to the book value of the company.
Source: *Business Week Global 1000* (July 10, 2000): 45–77.

complementary services. In the auto industry, greater similarity among the competing models of different manufacturers has encouraged firms to compete on financing terms, leasing arrangements, warranties, after-sales services, and the like. In consumer goods, maturity is often associated with the focus of differentiation shifting from physical product characteristics to image. Deeply entrenched consumer preferences for Coke or Pepsi and Marlboro or Camel cigarettes are a tribute to the capacity of brand promotion over long periods of time to create distinct images among near-identical products.

The intensely competitive retail sector produces particularly interesting examples of differentiation strategies. The dismal profitability earned by many retail chains (Kmart, J. C. Penny, and Federated Department Stores in the US; J. Sainsbury,

FIGURE 12.1 Innovation over the life cycle: from technological to strategic innovation

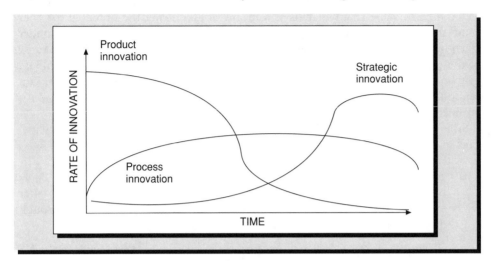

Selfridges, and Storehouse in the UK) contrasts sharply with the sales growth and profitability of stores that have established clear differentiation through variety, style, and ambiance (The Gap, Pier 1, TJX, and Bed, Bath and Beyond in the US; New Look Group, Next, and Dixons in the UK). Table 12.1 lists the retailers among the world's 1,000 most biggest companies with the highest and lowest performance (measured by valuation ratio). However, the competitive process means that competitive advantage is difficult to sustain: fallen stars include British retailers such as Laura Ashley, Body Shop, Conran Stores, and Marks & Spencer; and US retailers such as Barney's, Macy's, Saks, and Montgomery Ward.

Innovation

We have characterized mature industries as industries where the pace of technical change is low. Yet, the quest for differentiation in mature industries requires innovation: finding new approaches to uniqueness in terms of features, image, distribution, and bundling. Such innovation extends beyond technical innovation. In most mature industries – steel, textiles, food processing, insurance, and hotels – R&D expenditure is below 1 percent of sales revenue.[9] However, the pressure of competition and the limited opportunities for technology-based advantage create impetus for innovation in marketing, product design, customer service, and organization. This quest for new ways of doing business is what we referred to in Chapter 6 as "strategic innovation." In relation to the innovation cycles identified by Abernathy and Utterback, it is possible that there is a third phase of innovation – *strategic innovation* – which becomes most prominent once product and process innovation have begun to slacken (see Figure 12.1).

---

[9] United States Department of Commerce.

Because every strategic innovation requires strategic initiatives that are new and unique, it is difficult to adopt a systematic approach to their design. In Chapter 6, we pointed to value chain analysis as a means of identifying the potential for "new game strategies." Understanding the sequence of activities currently being undertaken by the firm (and by competitors) may facilitate the search for a reconfiguration of the sequence of activities in new strategic format. Benetton and Dell Computer may both be viewed as companies whose success has involved reconfiguring the conventional value chain in terms of establishing novel systems for the production of products and their distribution to the customer.

Strategic innovation may also involve redefining markets and market segments.[10] This may involve:

- *Embracing new customer groups.* In the same way that Henry Ford extended car ownership to ordinary families, AOL extended online information and entertainment to the mass market, and Donna Karan and Paul Smith have brought designer clothes to a new market.

- *Adding products and services that perform new but related functions.* In the US, Arco was an innovator in recreating the gas station as a convenience store. In book retailing, large stores such as Barnes and Noble and small stores such as Kramers in Washington DC have expanded the traditional bookstore into a place to meet, eat and drink, and listen to readings.

Baden Fuller and Stopford's analysis of strategic innovation in mature industries focuses on the reconciliation of multiple (often opposing) performance goals in order to create new options. Based on in-depth case analysis of successful mature companies, they conclude:

1. Maturity is a state of mind, not a state of the business; every enterprise has the potential for rejuvenation.

2. It is the firm that matters, not the industry. The industry sets a context, not a prison for the firm. Not only can the creative firm achieve success within a hostile industry environment, it can transform its industry environment. Look what Honda did to the motorcycle markets of North America and Europe during the 1960s.

3. Strategic innovation is the basis for competitive advantage in industries where the potential for competitive advantage seems limited. The essence of strategic innovation is reconciling alternatives: quality at low cost (Toyota), variety at low cost (Courtaulds), speed at low cost (Benetton), and so on.

4. Businesses should be selective in choosing their strategic territory. An island kingdom is more defensible than the Hapsburg Empire. The firm's market scope needs to be limited by its resources and capabilities.

---

[10]   Derek Abell, *Managing with Dual Strategies* (New York: Free Press, 1993): 75–8.

5. The pursuit of strategic innovation requires an entrepreneurial organization with freedom to experiment and the capacity to learn.

6. Rejuvenation requires a sequence of strategic and organizational development. The key stages are to galvanize top management commitment, to simplify by eliminating outdated and unnecessary activities and control systems, to build the strategic infrastructure and capabilities needed to implement the new vision, and to leverage advantages and maintain the momentum.[11]

Rejuvenation represents as formidable a challenge to a mature enterprise as it does to an aging university professor. Indeed, change is likely to be even more difficult for organizations than for individuals. In Chapter 10, we noted the resistance to change caused by organizational inertia. Resistance to innovation and renewal also arises from the propensity for the managers of long-established firms to be trapped within their industry's conventional thinking about key success factors and business practices. Chapter 4 noted how established firms' responses to competitive threats may be limited by industry-wide systems of belief. J.-C. Spender refers to these common cognitive patterns as "industry recipes."[12] Studies of cognitive maps – the mental frameworks through which managers perceive and think about their environments and their companies – yield insights into why some firms are able to adapt better than others. A study of organizational renewal among railroad companies found that the ability of managers to learn in the form of changing their mental models of the business was critical to their capacity to renew themselves.[13]

The ability to break away from conventional wisdom and establish a unique positioning or novel form of differentiation may be critical in mature industries. Costas Markides identifies several examples of such contrarian thinking, including the following:

■ Most US brokerage houses have embraced economies of scale, diversification, integration with investment banks, and new approaches to delivering services. Edward Jones has almost 2,000 offices, mostly in the US but also in Canada and the UK. Each office has just one investment adviser, there are no proprietary investment products, and no online investing. Edwards Jones strategy has been built on face-to-face relationships, motivating its office mangers to develop their local business, and ambitious growth targets. Its business model is based more on McDonald's or Holiday Inns than on Goldman Sachs or Merrill Lynch. Between 1995 and 1999, its revenues doubled from $720 million to $1.8 billion.[14]

---

[11] Charles Baden Fuller and J. Stopford, *Rejuvenating the Mature Business* (London: Routledge, 1992): especially Chapters 3 and 4.

[12] J.-C. Spender, *Industry Recipes: The Nature and Sources of Managerial Judgment* (Oxford: Basil Blackwell, 1989). On a similar theme, see also Anne S. Huff, "Industry Influences on Strategy Reformulation," *Strategic Management Journal* 3 (1982): 119–31; and Gerry Johnson, "Strategic Frames and Formulae," *Strategic Management Journal* 8 (1987).

[13] P. S. Barr, J. L. Stimpert, and Anne S. Huff, "Cognitive Change, Strategic Action, and Organizational Renewal," *Strategic Management Journal* 13, Summer special issue (1992): 15–36.

[14] "A Lesson in Small Town Economics," *Financial Times* (November 30, 2000): 16.

- Enterprise Rent-A-Car has adopted a location strategy that is quite different from its major competitors Hertz and Avis. Rather than concentrate on serving the business traveler through locating at airports and downtown, Enterprise concentrates on suburban locations, where it caters primarily to the consumer market.[15]

- The difficulty that established firms have in identifying and exploiting opportunities for strategic innovation is indicated by the fact that novel strategies in mature sectors are the work of newcomers. In long-established industries with well-entrenched incumbents – steel and autos, for example – it is only when challenged by new competitors – minimills in steel, Toyota and Honda in autos – that the established embark on change.[16]

Gary Hamel has identified the challenge facing established firms in even starker terms: evolutionary change will not be enough; established companies must embrace radical change. "In the new industrial order . . . it's the insurgents versus the incumbents . . . Somewhere out there there's a bullet with your company's name on it. Somewhere out there is a competitor, unborn and unknown, that will render your strategy obsolete."[17]

How do companies break away from their traditional mindsets and achieve strategic innovation? According to Hamel, the role of strategy should be to foster revolution through reorganizing the strategy-making process. This means breaking top management's monopoly over strategy formulation, bringing in younger people from further down the organization, and gaining involvement from those on the periphery of the organization.[18] Increasingly, however, Hamel appears to be recognizing that companies and their top management teams cannot rely on their internal processes alone. Strategic innovation goes well beyond rethinking strategies, it also requires delivering new strategies through new approaches to structuring the mature business.

STRATEGY IMPLEMENTATION IN MATURE INDUSTRIES: STRUCTURE, SYSTEMS, AND STYLE

If the key to success in mature industries is achieving operational efficiency and reconciling this with innovation and customer responsiveness, achieving competitive advantage in mature businesses requires implementing structures, systems, and management styles that can mesh these multiple performance goals.

---

[15] C. C. Markides, *All the Right Moves* (Boston: Harvard Business School Press, 1999).
[16] Paul R. Lawrence and Davis Dyer, *Renewing American Industry* (New York: Free Press, 1983): Chapter 2, "Autos: On the Thin Edge," and Chapter 3, "Steel: The Slumping Giant."
[17] G. Hamel, *Leading the Revolution* (Boston: Harvard Business School Press, 2000): 8, 11.
[18] G. Hamel, "Strategy as Revolution," *Harvard Business Review* 96 (July–August 1996): 69–82.

Efficiency through Bureaucracy

If maturity implies greater environmental stability, slower technological change, and an emphasis on cost efficiency, what types of organization and management approaches are called for? As we observed in Chapter 6, the conventional prescription for stable environments at the beginning of the 1960s came from Burns and Stalker, who argued that, whereas dynamic environments require "organismic" organizational forms characterized by decentralization, loosely defined roles, and a high level of lateral communication, stable environments require a "mechanistic" organization characterized by centralization, well-defined roles, and predominantly vertical communication.[19] Henry Mintzberg describes this highly formalized type of organization dedicated to the pursuit of efficiency as the *machine bureaucracy*.[20] Efficiency is achieved through standardized routines, division of labor, and close management control based on bureaucratic principles. Such forms of organization were typical in mature industries with large-scale production and heavy reliance on Frederick Taylor's principles of scientific management. Division of labor extends to management as well as operatives. Mechanistic structures typically display high levels of vertical and horizontal specialization. Vertical specialization is reflected in the concentration of strategy formulation at the apex of the hierarchy, while middle and junior management supervise and administer through the application of standardized rules and procedures. Horizontal specialization in the company is organized around functional departments rather than product divisions.

The machine bureaucracy as described by Mintzberg is a caricature of actual organizations – probably the closest approximations are found in government departments performing highly routine administrative duties (e.g., the Internal Revenue Service or departments of motor vehicle licensing). However, in most mature industries, the features of mechanistic organizations are evident in highly routinized operations and application of highly detailed rules and procedures. McDonald's may not be a typical bureaucracy, but it certainly operates with highly standardized and refined operating procedures that govern virtually every aspect of how it does business (see the quotation that introduces this chapter). The characteristics of mechanistic organization and principles of bureaucracy are prominent among the large enterprises found in most mature industries, whether we are looking at DaimlerChrysler, Walt Disney Company, Exxon-Mobil, or HSBC. The key features of these mature organizations are summarized in Table 12.2.

---

[19] T. Burns and G. M. Stalker (*The Management of Innovation*, London: Tavistock Institute, 1961) argued that dynamic environments required *organismic* structures characterized by decentralization, loosely defined roles, and extensive lateral communication, while stable environments required *mechanistic* structures.

[20] Henry Mintzberg, *Structure in Fives: Designing Effective Organizations* (Englewood Cliffs, NJ: Prentice-Hall, 1983): Chapter 9.

TABLE 12.2 Strategy Implementation in Mature Industries: Traditional Features of Organization and Management

STRATEGY
Primary goal is cost advantage through economies of scale, capital-intensive production of standardized product/service. Dichotomization of strategy formulation (the preserve of top management) and strategy implementation (carried down the hierarchy).

STRUCTURE
Functional departments (e.g., production, marketing, customer service, distribution). Distinction between line and staff. Clearly defined job roles with strong vertical reporting/delegation relationships.

CONTROLS
Performance targets are primarily quantitative and short term and are elaborated for all members of the organization. Performance is closely monitored by well-established, centralized management information systems and formalized reporting requirements. Financial controls through budgets and profit targets particularly important.

INCENTIVES
Incentives based on achievement of individual targets and are in the form of financial rewards and promotion up the hierarchy. Penalties exist for failure to attain quantitative targets, for failure to adhere to the rules, and for lack of conformity to company norms.

COMMUNICATION
Primarily vertical for the purposes of delegation and reporting. Lateral communication limited often achieved through interdepartmental committees.

MANAGEMENT
Primary functions of top management: control and strategic decision making. Typical top management styles: the politician – the organizational head who can effectively wield power through understanding and manipulating organizational processes and building consensus (e.g., Alfred Sloan Jr. of General Motors); and the autocrat – the CEO who is able to lead and control through aggressive use of power and sheer force of personality (Lee Iacocca of Chrysler and Al Dunlap of Sunbeam).

Beyond Bureaucracy

As was noted in Chapter 6, the past two decades have seen growing unpopularity of bureaucratic approaches to management, especially in mature industries. Factors contributing to this trend include:

- *Increased environmental turbulence.* Bureaucracy is conducive to efficiency in stable environments. However, the centralized, structured organization cannot readily adapt to change. Achieving flexibility to respond to external change requires greater decentralization, less specialization, and looser controls.

- *Increased emphasis on innovation.* The organizational structure, control systems, management style, and interpersonal relationships conducive to efficiency are likely to hinder innovation. As mature enterprises sought new opportunities for competitive advantage, so the disadvantages of formalized, efficiency-oriented organizations became increasingly apparent.

- *New process technology.* The efficiency advantages of bureaucratized organizations arise from the technical virtues of highly specialized, systematized production methods. The electronics revolution has changed the conditions for efficiency. Computer-integrated manufacturing processes permit cost efficiency with greater product variety, shorter runs, and greater flexibility. As automation displaces labor-intensive, assembly-line manufacturing techniques, there is less need for elaborate division of labor and greater need for job flexibility. Simultaneously, the electronic revolution in the office is displacing the administrative bureaucracy that control and information systems once required.

- *Alienation and conflict.* The dependence of bureaucracy on departmentalization, layering, and the control of some employees by others is conducive to alienation and conflict.

Companies in mature industries have undergone substantial adjustment over the past decade. Among large, long-established corporations management hierarchies have been pruned, decision making decentralized and accelerated, and more open communication and flexible collaboration fostered. The trend began in North America, spread to Continental Europe, and is now evident in Japan and Korea. The changes are apparent in:

- Strategic decision processes that increase the role of business-level managers and reduce the role of corporate management; an emphasis on the strategy formulation process as more important than strategic plans *per se.*

- This shifting of decision-making power to the business level has been accompanied by shrinking corporate staffs.

- Less emphasis on economies of large-scale production and increased responsiveness to customer requirements together with greater flexibility in responding to changes in the marketplace.

- Increased emphasis on teamwork as a basis for organizing separate activities to improve interfunctional cooperation and responsiveness to external requirements.

- Wider use of profit incentives to motivate employees and less emphasis on controls and supervision.

These trends amount to a closer convergence between the organizational and managerial characteristics of firms in mature industries and those located in the newer, more technologically oriented industries. At the same time, the primary emphasis on cost efficiency remains. It is not that the goal of cost efficiency has been superseded, rather that the conditions for cost efficiency have changed. The most powerful force for organizational change in mature industries has been the inability of highly structured, centralized organizations to maintain their cost efficiency in an increasingly turbulent business environment. As we observed in Chapter 9, the requirements for dynamic efficiency are different from the requirements for static efficiency. Dynamic efficiency requires flexibility, which necessitates higher levels of autonomy and non-hierarchical coordination. A feature of the revitalization efforts of Jack Welch at General Electric, Ferdinand Piech at Volkswagen, John Browne at British Petroleum, and Sandy Weill at Citigroup has been combining strong central direction with increased decision-making autonomy at the business level. By relying more on performance targets and less on approvals and committees, the old corporate empires have become more flexible and responsive while maintaining a strong focus on efficiency.

STRATEGIES FOR DECLINING INDUSTRIES

The transition from maturity to decline can be a result of technological substitution (typewriters, railroads), changes in consumer preferences (men's suits), demographic shifts (babyware in Italy), or foreign competition (cutlery in Sheffield, England). Shrinking market demand gives rise to acute strategic issues. Among the key features of declining industries are:

- Excess capacity.

- Lack of technical change (reflected in a lack of new product introduction and stability of process technology).

- A declining number of competitors, but some entry as new firms acquire the assets of exiting firms cheaply.

- High average age of both physical and human resources.

- Aggressive price competition.

Despite the inhospitable environment offered by declining industries, research by Kathryn Harrigan has uncovered declining industries where at least some participants earned surprisingly high profits. These included electronic vacuum tubes, cigars, and leather tanning. However, elsewhere – notably in prepared baby foods, rayon, and meat processing – decline was accompanied by aggressive price competition, company failures, and instability.[21]

What determines whether or not a declining industry becomes a competitive blood-bath? Two factors are critical: the balance between capacity and output, and the nature of the demand for the product.

Adjusting Capacity to Declining Demand

The smooth adjustment of industry capacity to declining demand is the key to stability and profitability during the decline phase. In industries where capacity exits

---

[21] Kathryn R. Harrigan, *Strategies for Declining Businesses* (Lexington, MA: D. C. Heath, 1980).

from the industry in an orderly fashion, decline can occur without trauma. Where substantial excess capacity persists, as has occurred in the steel industries of America and Europe, in the bakery industry, in gold mining, and in long-haul bus transportation, the potential exists for destructive competition. The ease with which capacity adjusts to declining demand depends on the following factors:

■ *The predictability of decline.* If decline can be forecast, it is more likely that firms can plan for it. The problems of the steel industry, oil refining, and petro-chemicals during the 1970s and 1980s were exacerbated by the unpredicted oil price shocks of 1974 and 1980. The more cyclical and volatile the demand, the more difficult it is for firms to perceive the trend of demand even after the onset of decline.

■ *Barriers to exit.* Barriers to exit impede the exit of capacity from an industry. The major barriers are:
—Durable and specialized assets. Just as capital requirements impose a barrier to entry into an industry, those same investments also discourage exit. The longer they last and the fewer the opportunities for using those assets in another industry, the more companies are tied to that particular industry. The intensity of price competition in steel, acetylene, and rayon during the 1970s was partly a consequence of the durability and lack of alternative uses for the capital equipment employed.
—Costs incurred in plant closure. Apart from the accounting costs of writing off assets, substantial cash costs may be incurred in redundancy payments to employees, compensation for broken contacts with customers and suppliers, and dismantling and demolishing the plant.
—Managerial commitment. In addition to financial considerations, firms may be reluctant to close plants for a variety of emotional and moral reasons. Resistance to plant closure and divestment arises from pride in company traditions and reputation, managers' unwillingness to accept failure, loyalties to employees and the local community, and the desire not to offend government.

■ *The strategies of the surviving firms.* Smooth exit of capacity ultimately depends on the decisions of the industry players. The sooner companies recognize and address the problem, the more likely it is that independent and collective action can achieve capacity reduction. In the European petrochemical industry, for example, the problem of excess capacity was partially solved by a series of bilateral exchanges of plants and divisions – ICI swapped its polyethylene plants for BP's PVC plants, for example.[22] Stronger firms in the industry can facilitate the exit of weaker firms by offering to acquire their plants and take over their after-sales service commitments.

---

[22] Joe Bower, *When Markets Quake* (Boston: Harvard Business School Press, 1986).

The Nature of Demand

Where a market is segmented, the general pattern of decline can obscure the existence of pockets of demand that are not only comparatively resilient, but also price inelastic. For example, despite the obsolescence of vacuum tubes after the adoption of transistors, Harrigan observed that GTE Sylvania and General Electric earned excellent profits supplying vacuum tubes to the replacement and military markets.[23] As late as 1994, it was noted that the US system of air traffic control depended on vacuum tubes supplied by a few specialist companies. In fountain pens, survivors in the quality pen segment such as Cross and Mont Blanc have achieved steady sales and high margins through appealing to high-income professionals and executives. Decline may be punctuated by periodic upswings of demand: during 1996–99 the quality cigar market was revived by a sudden return to fashion.

Strategies for Declining Industries

Conventional strategy recommendations for declining industries are either to divest or to harvest, i.e., to generate the maximum cash flow from existing investments without reinvesting. However, these strategies assume that declining industries are inherently unprofitable. If profit potential exists, then other strategies may be attractive. Harrigan and Porter[24] identify four strategies that can profitably be pursued either individually or sequentially in declining industries.

- *Leadership.* By gaining leadership, a firm is well placed to outstay competitors and play a dominant role in the final stages of the industry's life cycle. Once leadership is attained, the firm is in a good position to switch to a harvest strategy and enjoy a strong profit stream from its market position. Establishing leadership can be done by acquiring competitors, but a cheaper way is to encourage competitors to exit (and then acquire their plants). Inducements to competitors to exit may include showing commitment to the industry, helping to lower their exit costs, releasing pessimistic forecasts of the industry's future, and raising the stakes – e.g., by supporting more stringent environmental controls that make it costly for them to stay in business.

- *Niche.* Identify a segment that is likely to maintain a stable demand and other firms are unlikely to invade, then pursue a leadership strategy to establish dominance within the segment. The most attractive niches are those that offer the greatest prospects for stability and where demand is most inelastic.

---

[23]   Kathryn R. Harrigan, "Strategic Planning for Endgame," *Long Range Planning* 15 (1982): 45–8.
[24]   Kathryn R. Harrigan and Michael E. Porter, "End-Game Strategies for Declining Industries," *Harvard Business Review* (July–August 1983): 111–20.

- *Harvest.* By harvesting, a firm maximizes its cash flow from existing assets, while avoiding further investment. A harvesting strategy seek to boost margins wherever possible through raising prices and cutting costs by rationalizing the number of models, number of channels, and number of customers. Note, however, that a harvest strategy can be difficult to implement. In the face of strong competition, harvesting may accelerate decline, particularly if employee morale is adversely affected by a strategy that offers no long-term future for the business.

- *Divest.* If the future looks bleak, the best strategy may be to divest the business in the early stages of decline before a consensus has developed as to the inevitability of decline. Once industry decline is well established, finding buyers may be extremely difficult.

Choosing the most appropriate strategy requires a careful assessment both of the profit potential of the industry and the competitive position of the firm. Harrigan and Porter pose four key questions:

- Can the structure of the industry support a hospitable, potentially profitable decline phase?

- What are the exit barriers that each significant competitor faces?

- Do your company strengths fit the remaining pockets of demand?

- What are your competitors' strengths in these pockets? How can their exit barriers be overcome?

Selecting an appropriate strategy requires matching the opportunities remaining in the industries to the company's competitive position. Figure 12.2 shows a simple framework for strategy choice.

FIGURE 12.2 Strategic alternatives for declining industries

COMPANY'S COMPETITIVE POSITION		Strengths in remaining demand pockets	Lacks strength in remaining demand pockets
INDUSTRY STRUCTURE	Favorable to decline	LEADERSHIP or NICHE	HARVEST or DIVEST
	Unfavorable to decline	NICHE or HARVEST	DIVEST QUICKLY

Summary

Mature industries present challenging environments for the formulation and implementation of business strategies. Competition – price competition in particular – is usually strong and competitive advantage is often difficult to build and sustain: cost advantages are vulnerable to imitation, differentiation opportunities are limited by the trend to standardization. Stable positions of competitive advantage in mature industries are traditionally associated with cost advantage from economies of scale or experience, and differentiation advantage through brand loyalty. Such strategies are typically implemented through hierarchical organizations, with high levels of specialization and formalization, and centralized decision making directed toward maximizing static efficiency.

    Increased dynamism of mature industries resulting from international competition, economic turbulence, and greater pressure for innovation has had two consequences. First, the conditions for cost efficiency have changed. In a dynamic environment, cost efficiency is less dependent on scale, specialization, and rigid control, and more on rapid adjustment to change. Second, as competition has become more intense, companies (especially those in the advanced industrialized countries) have been forced to seek new sources of competitive advantage through innovation and differentiation. Reconciling the pursuit of scale economies with the need for responsiveness and flexibility, and the requirements of cost efficiency with the growing need for innovation and differentiation, poses complex strategic and organizational challenges. Some of the most successful companies in mature industries – Wal-Mart in retailing, BP in oil and gas, Nike in shoes and sportswear, and Coca-Cola in beverages – are companies that have achieved flexibility through dismantling bureaucratic structures and procedures, exploited new technology to combine variety and flexibility with efficiency, encouraged high levels of employee commitment, and relentlessly pursued financial targets. We return to some of these challenges and firms' responses to them in Chapter 17.

V

Corporate Strategy

13

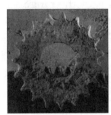

Vertical Integration and the Scope of the Firm

The idea of vertical integration is an anathema to an increasing number of companies. Most of yesterday's highly integrated giants are working overtime at splitting into more manageable, more energetic units – i.e., de-integrating. Then they are turning around and re-integrating – not by acquisitions but via alliances with all sorts of partners of all shapes and sizes.

—*Tom Peters*, **Liberation Management**

OUTLINE

INTRODUCTION AND OBJECTIVES

Chapter 2 introduced the distinction between *corporate* strategy and *business* strategy. Corporate strategy is concerned primarily with the decisions over the *scope* of the firm's activities, including:

- *Product scope.* How specialized should the firm be in terms of the range of products it supplies? Coca-Cola (soft drinks), Cummins Engine (diesel engines), The Gap (fashion retailing), and Swiss Re (reinsurance) are specialized companies: they are engaged in a single industry sector. General Electric, Vivendi, and Siemens are diversified companies: each is engaged in a number of different industries.

- *Geographical scope.* What is the optimal geographical spread of activities for the firm? In the restaurant business, most businesses serve their local markets. McDonald's, on the other hand, operates in close to 100 countries throughout the world.

- *Vertical scope.* What range of vertically linked activities should the firm encompass? Walt Disney Company is a vertically integrated company: it produces its own movies, distributes them itself to cinemas and through its own TV networks (ABC and Disney Channel), and uses the movies' characters in its retail stores and theme parks. Dell Computer is much more vertically specialized: it outsources many activities in its value chain, including components, assembly, logistics, and customer service to other companies.

Business strategy (also known as *competitive strategy*) is concerned with how a firm competes within a particular market. The distinction may be summarized as follows: corporate strategy is concerned with *where* a firm competes; business strategy is concerned with *how* a firm competes.[1] The major part of this book has been concerned with issues of business strategy. For the next four chapters, the emphasis is on corporate strategy: decisions that define the *scope of the firm*.

We begin with vertical integration because it takes us to the heart of many of the issues relevant to determining the optimal scope of the firm and, in particular, the role of transaction costs in drawing the boundaries of the firm and the types of relationships between firms. Also, vertical integration has been a central issue in corporate strategy in recent years as outsourcing, alliances, and e-commerce have caused companies to rethink which parts of their value chains they wish to include within their organizational boundaries.

---

[1] In practice, determining where business strategy ends and corporate strategy begins is far from clear. When Dell Computer expanded from PCs into servers, was this diversification or simply product line extension within the same business? It all depends on where we draw industry and market boundaries.

By the time you have completed this chapter, you will be able to:

- Identify the relative efficiencies of firms and markets in organizing economic activity and apply the principles of *transaction cost economics* to determining the boundaries of firms.

- Assess the relative merits of vertical integration and market transactions in organizing vertically related activities and understand the circumstances that influence their comparative advantages.

- Identify a range of possible relationships among vertically related firms, including spot market transactions, long-term contracts, franchise agreements, and alliances.

- Explain why some types of vertically related activities are integrated within a single company, whereas others are performed by separate companies.

- Identify the critical considerations pertinent to make-or-buy decisions and the extent to which a firm should vertically integrate.

- Design the most advantageous form of relationship between a firm and its suppliers and customers.

TRANSACTION COSTS AND THE SCOPE OF THE FIRM

In Chapter 6, we noted that firms came into existence because they were more efficient in organizing production than were market contracts between independent workers. Let us explore this issue in more detail and consider the determinants of firm boundaries.

Firms, Markets, and Transaction Costs

Although the capitalist economy is frequently referred to as a "market economy," in fact, it comprises two forms of economic organization. One is the *market mechanism*, where individuals and firms make independent decisions that are guided and coordinated by market prices. The other is the *administrative mechanism* of firms, where decisions over production, supply, and the purchases of inputs are made by managers and imposed through hierarchies. The market mechanism was characterized by Adam Smith, the eighteenth-century Scottish economist, as the "invisible hand" because its coordinating role does not require conscious planning. Alfred Chandler has referred to the administrative mechanism of company management as the "visible hand" because it is dependent on coordination through active planning.[2]

---

[2] Alfred Chandler Jr., *Strategy and Structure* (Cambridge: MIT Press, 1962); Alfred Chandler Jr., *The Visible Hand: The Managerial Revolution in American Business* (Cambridge: MIT Press, 1977).

FIGURE 13.1 The scope of the firm: specialization versus integration

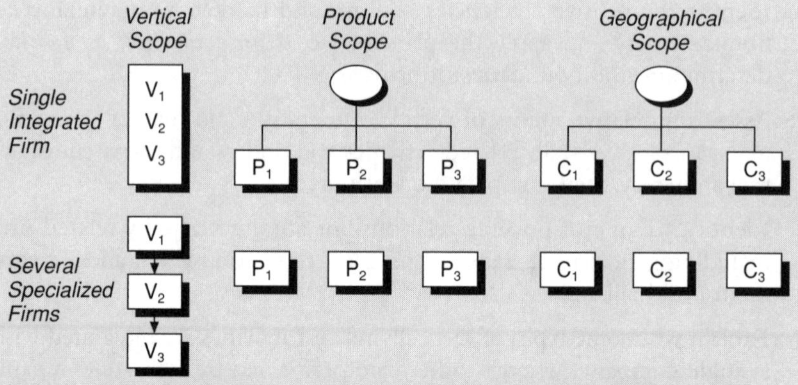

In the integrated firm there is an administrative interface between the different vertical units (V), product units (P), and country units (C). Where there is specialization, each unit is a separate firm linked by market interfaces.

Why do institutions called "firms" exist in the first place? The firm is an organization that consists of a number of individuals bound by employment contracts with a central contracting authority. But firms are not essential for conducting complex economic activity. When I recently remodeled my basement, I contracted with a self-employed builder to undertake the work. He in turn subcontracted parts of the work to a plumber, an electrician, a joiner, a drywall installer, and a painter. Although the job involved the coordinated activity of several individuals, these self-employed specialists were not linked by employment relations but by market contracts ("$4,000 to install wiring, lights, and sockets").

What determines which activities are undertaken within a firm, or between individuals or firms coordinated by market contracts? Ronald Coase's answer was *relative cost*.[3] Markets are not costless: making a purchase or sale involves search costs, the costs of negotiating and drawing up a contract, the costs of monitoring to ensure that the other party's side of the contract is being fulfilled, and the enforcement costs of arbitration or litigation should a dispute arise. All these costs are types of *transaction costs*.[4] If the transaction costs associated with organizing across markets are greater than the *administrative costs* of organizing within firms, we can expect the coordination of productive activity to be internalized within firms.

This situation is illustrated in Figure 13.1. With regard to vertical scope, which is more efficient: three independent companies, one producing steel, the next rolling

[3] R. H. Coase, "The Nature of the Firm," *Economica* 4 (1937): 386–405.

[4] The term *interaction costs* has also been used to describe the "the time and money expended whenever people and companies exchange goods, services or ideas." See J. Hagel and M. Singer, "Unbundling the Corporation," *Harvard Business Review* (March–April 1999): 133–44.

the steel into sheet, and the third producing steel cans, or having all three stages of production within a single company? In the case of geographical scope, which is more efficient: three independent companies producing cans in the US, UK, and Italy, or a single multinational company owning and operating the can-making plants in all three countries? In the case of product scope, should metal cans, plastic packaging, and domestic appliances be produced by three separate companies, or are there efficiencies to be gained by merging all three into a single company?

The Shifting Boundary between Firms and Markets

The answers to these questions have changed over time. During the nineteenth and for most of the twentieth century, companies grew in size and scope, absorbing transactions that had previously taken place across markets. Figure 13.2 shows changes in *aggregate concentration* – the proportion of total output contributed by the largest companies – for the US industrial sector. As we observed in Chapter 6, companies that once were specialized in a single product and local market grew vertically, geographically, and across different business sectors. Such growth can be attributed to a fall in the administrative costs of the firm as compared with the transaction costs of markets. Two factors have greatly increased the efficiency of firms as organizing devices: technology and management techniques. The telegraph, telephone, and computer have played an important role in facilitating communications within firms and expanding the decision-making capacity of managers. At the same time, the principles and techniques of management have greatly expanded the organizational and decision-making effectiveness of managers. Beginning with the dissemination of double-entry bookkeeping in the nineteenth century,[5] and the introduction of scientific management in the early twentieth century,[6] the past 50 years have seen massive advances in management theories and methods, ranging from human resource management and organizational design to corporate finance and total quality management. By the mid-1960s, this displacement of the coordinating role of markets by the internal management systems of vertically integrated, diversified, multinational corporations had amounted to the replacement of the *market* economy by the *corporate* economy. In 1969, J. K. Galbraith predicted that the inherent advantages of firms over markets in allocating resources and permitting long-term planning would result in increasing dominance of capitalist economies by a small number of giant corporations.[7]

During the 1980s and 1990s, these predictions were refuted by a sharp reversal of the trend toward increased corporate scope. Although the majority of large companies have continued to expand internationally, the dominant trends of the last

---

[5] Although double-entry bookkeeping was invented in the fifteenth century, its use as a tool of management control did not become widespread until the nineteenth century (K. Hoskin and L. Zan, "A first *Discourso del Maneggio*: Accounting and the Production of Management Discourse at the Venice Arsenal," EIASM Working Paper 97-01 (1997).

[6] F. W. Taylor, *The Principles of Scientific Management* (Bulletin of the Taylor Society, 1916).

[7] J. K. Galbraith, *The New Industrial State* (Harmondsworth: Penguin, 1969).

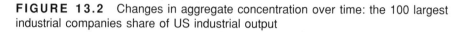

FIGURE 13.2 Changes in aggregate concentration over time: the 100 largest industrial companies share of US industrial output

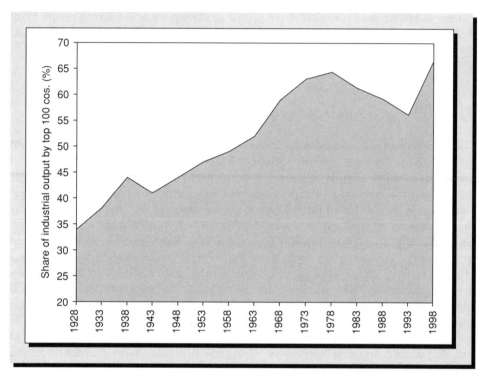

15 years have been "downsizing" and "refocusing," as large industrial companies have reduced both their product scope through focusing on their core businesses, and their vertical scope through outsourcing activities. The result, as shown in Figure 13.2, was a decline in aggregate concentration. These changes seem to be associated with the more turbulent business environment that followed the oil shocks of 1973 and 1979, the end of fixed exchange rates (1972), the invention of the integrated circuit, and the upsurge of international competition. The implication seems to be that during periods of instability, the costs of administration within firms tend to rise as the need for flexibility and speed of response overwhelms traditional management systems.

Oliver Williamson's contribution to economics has been his analysis of the nature and sources of the transaction costs, which form the basis for a theory of economic organization.[8] His analysis offers penetrating insights into corporate strategy decisions concerning the scope of the firm and the design of relationships among firms. We

---

[8] Oliver E. Williamson, *Markets and Hierarchies: Analysis and Antitrust Implications* (New York: Free Press, 1975); Oliver E. Williamson, *The Economic Institutions of Capitalism: Firms, Markets and Relational Contracting* (New York: Free Press, 1985).

proceed by applying his analysis to vertical integration and, in doing so, introduce concepts and ideas that are also relevant to decisions concerning multinational growth and product diversification.

THE COSTS AND BENEFITS OF VERTICAL INTEGRATION

Changing ideas about the efficiency of large corporations as organizers of economic activity have exerted a strong influence on firms' vertical integration strategies. Thirty years ago the dominant belief was that vertical integration offered superior coordination as well as protection from the vagaries of the market. The prevailing wisdom today is that any benefits of vertical integration tend to be outweighed by the greater advantages of specializing in a narrow range of vertical activities. Such vertical specialization is conducive to flexibility and the development of core competencies moreover, most of the coordination associated with vertical integration benefits can be achieved through inter-firm collaboration. Let's explore some of these issues.

Defining Vertical Integration

Vertical integration refers to a firm's ownership of vertically related activities. The greater the firm's ownership and control over successive stages of the value chain for its product, the greater its degree of vertical integration. The extent of vertical integration is indicated by the ratio of a firm's value added to its sales revenue. Highly integrated companies – such as the major oil companies that own and control their value chain from exploring for oil down to the retailing of gasoline – tend to have low expenditures on bought-in goods and services relative to their sales.

Vertical integration can occur in two directions:

■ *Backward integration* – where the firm takes ownership and control of producing its own inputs (e.g., Henry Ford's upstream expansion from automobile assembly to the production of his own components, back to the production of basic materials including steel and rubber).

■ *Forward integration* – where the firm takes ownership and control of its own customers (e.g., Coca-Cola acquiring its local bottlers).

Vertical integration may also be *full* or *partial*:

■ *Full integration* exists between two stages of production when all of the first stage's production is transferred to the second stage with no sales or purchases from third parties. Thus, before IBM entered PCs, all its microprocessors were produced in its own semiconductor plants and none was supplied to other customers.

- *Partial integration* exists when stages of production are not internally self-sufficient. Thus, in manufacturing TV receivers, Philips obtains cathode ray tubes (CRTs) both internally and from external suppliers of CRTs. Similarly, a major share of Philips' production of CRTs is sold to other TV manufacturers.[9] Partial integration is also typical among integrated oil companies. "Crude-rich" companies (such as Statoil) produce more oil than they refine and are net sellers of crude oil; "crude-poor" companies (such as Exxon-Mobil) have to supplement their own production with purchases of crude to keep their refineries supplied.

Technical Economies from the Physical Integration of Processes

Analysis of the benefits of vertical integration has traditionally emphasized the *technical economies* of vertical integration: cost savings that arise from the physical integration of processes. Thus, most steel sheet is produced by integrated producers of steel and sheet in plants that first produce steel, then roll hot steel into sheet. Linking the two stages of production at a single location reduces transportation and energy costs. Similar technical economies arise in pulp and paper production and from linking oil refining with petrochemical production.

However, although these considerations explain the need for the co-location of plants, they do not explain why vertical integration in terms of *common ownership* is necessary. Why can't steel and steel sheet production or pulp and paper production be undertaken by separate firms owning facilities that are physically integrated with one another? To answer this question, we must look beyond technical economies and consider the implications of linked processes for transaction costs.

The Sources of Transaction Costs in Vertical Exchanges

Consider the value chain for steel cans, which extends from mining iron ore to delivering cans to the canning company. Between the production of steel and steel strip, most production is vertically integrated. Between the production of steel strip and steel cans, there is very little vertical integration: can producers such as Crown, Cork and Seal are specialist packaging companies that purchase steel strip from steel companies.[10]

The absence of significant benefits from vertical integration between steel companies and can companies reflects low transaction costs in the market for steel strip: competitive supply, conditions, and information are readily available, and the switching costs for buyers and suppliers are low. The same is true for many other commodity

---

[9]   R. Johnston and P. R. Lawrence, "Beyond Vertical Integration – The Rise of the Value-Adding Partnership," *Harvard Business Review* (July–August 1988): 94–101.
[10]   The situation is somewhat different in aluminum cans where aluminum producers such as Reynolds and users such as Coca-Cola and Anheuser Busch are major producers of beverage cans.

products: few jewelry companies own gold mines; few flour-milling companies own wheat farms.

Although steel is also a commodity product with potentially competitive supply conditions, the fact that there are technical economies from integrating steel production and steel rolling effectively destroys the potential for a competitive market for bulk steel and changes the market into a set of *bilateral monopolies*. These situations, where a single steel maker is tied to a single steel roller through separately owned but physically linked plants, create big problems.

To begin with, economic theory tells us that where there is a monopoly supplier and a monopoly buyer – or just a few suppliers and buyers – there is no equilibrium price: it all depends on relative bargaining power. Such bargaining is likely to be costly: the mutual dependency of the two parties is likely to give rise to *opportunism* and *strategic misrepresentation* as each company seeks to both enhance and exploit its bargaining power at the expense of the other but to the detriment of their mutual benefit. Hence, once we move from a competitive market situation to one where individual buyers and sellers are locked together in close bilateral relationships, the efficiencies of the market system are lost.

The culprits in this situation are *transaction-specific investments*. When a can maker is buying steel strip, the relationship between buyer and seller is one where neither party needs to invest in equipment or technology that is specific to the needs of the other party. In the case of the steel producer and the steel roller, each company's plant is built to match the other party's plant. Once built, the plants have little value without the existence of the partner's complementary facilities. Once transaction-specific investments are significant then, even though there may be a number of suppliers and buyers in the market, it is no longer a competitive market – it is a series of local bilateral monopolies that encourage opportunism because of the potential for one party to "*hold up*" the other.

Hence, where a vertical relationship between companies requires one or both companies to make investments that are specific to the needs of the other party, a market contract will tend to be inefficient in coordinating the activities of the two parties. These inefficiencies arise from the negotiation and enforcement of contracts, including bargaining, monitoring, investing in activities whose only purpose is to improve bargaining power, and dispute resolution. These are key sources of transaction costs. The basic case for vertical integration is that by bringing both sides of the transaction into a single administrative structure, transaction costs may be avoided.

Empirical research gives considerable support to these arguments:

- In electricity generation, coal-fired power plants built adjacent to coal mines tend to be vertically integrated (i.e., the electricity utility also owns the coalmine).[11]

- In the automobile industry, components that are designed to meet the specific needs of a particular auto manufacturer are more likely to be manufactured

---

[11] P. Joskow, "Vertical Integration and Long-term Contracts: The Case of Coal-Burning Electricity Generating Plants," *Journal of Law, Economics, and Organization* 33 (Fall 1985): 32–80.

in-house than low-tech, commodity items such as tires and spark plugs, where the components supplier did not need to make transaction-specific investments.[12]

■ In aerospace, components that are designed specifically to meet the needs of an aerospace company are more likely to be produced in-house rather than purchased externally.[13]

■ In the semiconductor industry, some companies specialize either in semiconductor design or in fabrication, while other companies are vertically integrated across both stages. Which is more efficient? Again, it depends on the characteristics of the transaction between the designer and the fabricator. The more technically complex the integrated circuit and, hence, the greater the need for the designer and fabricator to engage in technical collaboration, the better the relative performance of integrated producers.[14]

Why is it not possible to anticipate the potential for transaction-specific investments to give rise to opportunism and to write a contract that covers these risks? The problem is uncertainty about the future. If at the time that the steel producer and the steel sheet roller were agreeing to build their integrated plant all eventualities over the 30-year life of the plant could be anticipated, a contract could be written to take account of these and opportunistic behavior by either party would not be possible. The problem is that all eventualities cannot be anticipated, hence contracts are inevitably incomplete.

Administrative Costs of Internalization

Just because there are transaction costs in intermediate markets does not mean that vertical integration is necessarily an efficient solution. Vertical integration avoids the costs of using the market, but internalizing the transactions means that there are now costs of administration. The efficiency of the internal administration of vertical relations depends on several factors.

Differences in the Optimal Scale of Operation between Different Stages of Production

Suppose that Federal Express requires trucks and vans that are specialized to its particular needs and requires the manufacturer to invest in designs and equipment

---

[12]   K. Monteverde and J. J. Teece, "Supplier Switching Costs and Vertical Integration in the Automobile Industry," *Bell Journal of Economics* 13 (Spring 1982): 206–13.

[13]   S. Masten, "The Organization of Production: Evidence from the Aerospace Industry," *Journal of Law and Economics* 27 (October 1984): 403–17.

[14]   J. Macher, "Vertical Disintegration and Process Innovation in Semiconductor Manufacturing Foundries vs. Integrated Producers," working paper (Haas School of Business, University of California, Berkeley, 2000).

specific to those needs. Such a relationship would involve transaction costs that could be avoided by Federal Express building its own vehicles. Would this be an efficient solution? Almost certainly not: the transaction costs associated with Federal Express are likely to be trivial compared with the inefficiencies incurred in its manufacturing its own requirements. Although Federal Express purchases over 40,000 trucks and vans each year, these purchases are far below the output needed for efficiency as a manufacturer. Ford produced two million commercial vehicles in 1999.

The same logic explains why specialist brewers such as the Boston Brewing Company are not backward integrated into aluminum cans like Anhauser Busch or Miller. Dedicated can-manufacturing plants involve specific investments, creating problems of opportunism that vertical integration can avoid. However, small brewers simply do not possess the scale needed to establish a scale-efficient can-manufacturing line.

Managing Strategically Different Businesses

Problems of differences in the optimal scale of different vertical activities are compounded by the difficulties of coordinating vertical activities that are strategically very different. A major disadvantage to FedEx of owning a truck-manufacturing company is that the management systems and organizational capabilities required for truck manufacturing are very different from those required for express delivery. These considerations may explain why vertical integration between manufacturing and retailing companies is rare. Manufacturing and retailing are quite different types of businesses: manufacturing requires product development and operational capabilities; retailing requires rapid response capability, astute buying, and constant attentiveness to managing the customer interface. The difficulties of reconciling the management needs of its retailing and manufacturing divisions was a key problem faced by the ailing British fashion retailer Laura Ashley.

Strategic dissimilarities between businesses have encouraged a number of companies to vertically de-integrate. Marriott's decision to split into two separate companies, Marriott International and Host Marriott, was influenced by the belief that *owning* hotels is a strategically different business from *operating* hotels. Similarly, the decision by the British brewer and catering company, Whitbread, to divest its breweries was based on the belief that it was difficult for it to be successful both as a brewer and as an operator of pubs and restaurants.

Developing Distinctive Capabilities

A key advantage of a specialized company over one that is diversified across a number of vertically linked businesses is the specialized company's ability to develop distinctive capabilities. In particular, vertical specialization encourages flexibility and the development of core competencies, while most of the benefits of vertical integration can be achieved through collaboration between vertically related, specialized companies. Even large, technology-based companies such as Xerox, Kodak, and Unilever cannot maintain IT capabilities that match those of IT specialists such as EDS, IBM, and Accenture. However, this assumes that organizational capabilities in different vertical activities are independent of one another. Where one capability builds on capabilities in vertically adjacent activities, vertical integration may help develop distinctive capabilities. Thus, Motorola's success in wireless communication equipment rests to a significant extent on its technical capabilities in semiconductors. In the semiconductor industry itself, a key debate is over the merits of integrating design and fabrication as compared to "fab-less" semiconductor companies. Where complementarities exist between design capability and manufacturing capability, vertical integration is desirable. In the case of digital logic integrated circuits, design and manufacturing capabilities are largely independent, and such activities are commonly undertaken by separate design and fabrication companies.[15]

The Incentive Problem

An important difference between relationships across markets and relationships within firms relates to *incentives*. We noted that in any administrative structure there is the *agency problem*. How does the owner of the firm encourage employees to work for the maximization of profits? In relation to vertical integration, this may be a major source of inefficiency. Market contracts, on the other hand, provide for high-powered incentives – each party to the contract is primarily interested in maximizing his or her own returns. Hence, in gasoline where there are benefits from vertically integrating refining, wholesaling, and retailing, many oil companies prefer to have their gas stations operated by profit motivated independent retailers. Similarly with clothing manufacturer and distributor Benetton. There are advantages from integrating manufacture, distribution, and retailing but, like many other chains, Benetton prefers to have its retail businesses operated by independent franchisees rather than by salaried managers.

Competitive Effects of Vertical Integration

Monopolistic companies have used vertical integration as a means of extending their monopoly positions from one stage of the industry to another. The classic cases are Standard Oil, which used its power in transportation and refining to foreclose markets to independent producers; and Alcoa, which used its monopoly position in aluminum production to squeeze independent fabricators of aluminum products in order to advantage its own fabrication subsidiaries. Such cases are rare. As economists have shown, once a company monopolizes one vertical chain of an industry, there is no further monopoly profit to be extracted by extending that monopoly position to adjacent vertical stages of the industry. A greater concern is that vertical integration may make independent suppliers and customers less willing to do business

---

[15]   K. Monteverde, "Technical Dialogue as an Incentive for Vertical Integration in the Semiconductor Industry," *Management Science* 41 (1995): 1624–38.

with the vertically integrated company, because it is now perceived as a competitor rather than as a supplier or customer. Such implications followed Disney's acquisition of ABC. Other studios (e.g., Dreamworks) became less interested in collaborating with ABC in developing new programming and shifted their advertising on new movies from ABC to other TV networks.

Flexibility

Both vertical integration and market transactions can claim advantage with regard to different types of flexibility. Where the required flexibility is rapid responsiveness to uncertain demand, there may be advantages in market transactions. The lack of vertical integration in the construction industry reflects, in part, the need for flexibility in adjusting both to cyclical patterns of demand and to the different requirements of each project. Vertical integration may also be disadvantageous in responding quickly to new product development opportunities that require new combinations of technical capabilities. Ever since IBM outsourced most of the components for its PC in 1981, fast-cycle product development in electronics has involved extensive outsourcing and technical collaboration. During the 1990s, some of the most rapidly growing companies in the electronics sector have been contract electronics manufacturers. However, where system-wide flexibility is required, a vertically integrated set of activities may offer a more effective means of achieving simultaneous adjustment at every level. For example, the recent merger between AOL and Time-Warner may assist the companies in responding quickly and effectively to changes in the technologies for distributing entertainment content, to a degree that Time-Warner's music and movies can be adapted to meet to the technical needs of internet distribution.

Compounding Risk

To the extent that vertical integration ties a company to its internal suppliers, vertical integration represents a compounding of risk insofar as problems at any one stage of production threaten production and profitability at all other stages. When union workers at a General Motors brake plant went on strike in 1997, the company's US assembly plants were quickly brought to a halt. Such problems are particularly acute when technology or customer preferences are changing quickly. The problems caused by Ford's outmoded automobile designs during the late 1920s and early 1930s were exacerbated by Ford's high-level vertical integration.

What we observe is that the overall balance of costs and benefits associated with vertical integration depends on the costs associated with the internalization of vertical transactions, as compared with the costs of undertaking them in separate companies linked by market transactions. Whether there are net benefits to vertical integration depends on many factors relating both to the industry and the individual firm. Table 13.1 summarizes some of these.

TABLE 13.1 Vertical Integration (VI) versus Market Transactions: Some Relevant Considerations

CHARACTERISTICS OF THE VERTICAL RELATIONSHIP	IMPLICATION
How many firms are there in the vertically related activity?	The fewer the number of firms the greater are transaction costs of market contracts
Do transaction-specific investments need to be made by either party?	The more important are transaction-specific investments, the greater the advantage of VI relative to market contracts
How well distributed is information between the vertical stages?	The greater are information asymmetries, the more likely is opportunistic behavior and the greater the advantages of VI relative to market contracts
Are market transactions in intermediate products subject to tax regulations?	Taxes and regulations increase the advantages of VI relative to market transactions
How uncertain are the circumstances prevailing over the period of the relationship?	Greater uncertainty increases the problems of incomplete contracts, hence increasing the advantages of VI relative to market contracts
Are two stages similar in terms of the optimal scale of operation?	The greater the dissimilarity, the greater the advantages of market contracts as compared with VI
Are the two stages strategically similar (e.g., similar key success factors, common resources/capabilities)?	The greater the strategic dissimilarity, the greater the advantages of market contracts as compared with VI
How great is the need for continual investment in upgrading and extending capabilities within individual activities?	The greater the need to invest in capability development, the greater the advantages of vertical specialization over VI
How great is the need for entrepreneurial flexibility and drive in the separate vertical activities?	The greater the need for entrepreneurial drive, the greater the advantages of high-powered incentives provided by market contracts between independent businesses
How uncertain is market demand?	The greater the unpredictability of demand, the more costly is VI
Does VI increase risk through requiring heavy investment in multiple stages and compounding otherwise independent risk factors?	The heavier the investment requirements and the greater the independent risks at each stage, the more risky is VI

FIGURE 13.3   Different types of vertical relationship

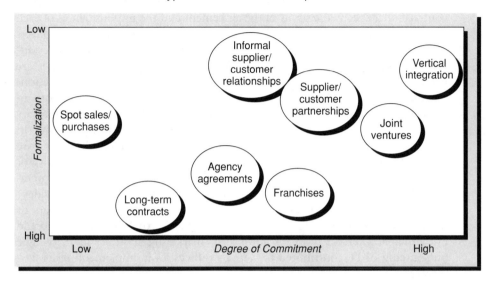

DESIGNING VERTICAL RELATIONSHIPS

Our discussion so far has compared vertical integration with arm's-length relationships between buyers and sellers. In practice, there is a variety of relationships through which buyers and sellers can interact and coordinate their interests. Figure 13.3 shows a number of different types of relationship between buyers and sellers. These relationships may be classified in relation to two characteristics. First, the extent to which the buyer and seller commit resources to the relationship: the arm's-length nature of spot contracts means that there is no significant commitment; vertical integration involves substantial investment. Second, the formalization of the relationship: long-term contracts and franchises typically involve complex written agreements, spot contracts may involve little or no documentation, but are bound by common law, collaborative agreements between buyers and sellers are by definition informal, while the formality of vertical integration is at the discretion of the firm's management.

Different Types of Vertical Relationship

Different types of vertical relationship offer different combinations of advantages and disadvantages. Consider for example the following:

■ *Long-term contracts.* In the discussion so far, I have implicitly equated market transactions with *spot contracts* – a single, current transaction such as a shopper buying a loaf of bread, a broker selling 100 IBM shares on the NYSE, or

Shell purchasing a cargo of crude oil from Kuwait Oil Corporation. However, the majority of business-to-business market transactions are under long-term contracts that specify the terms of the agreement and the responsibilities of each party. Spot transactions work well under competitive conditions – many buyers and sellers and a standard product – where there is no need for transaction-specific investments by either party. Where closer supplier–customer ties are needed – particularly when one or both parties need to make transaction-specific investments – then a longer-term contract may be needed both to avoid opportunism and to provide the security needed to make the necessary investment. However, long-term contracts introduce their own problems. In particular, they cannot anticipate all the possible circumstances that may arise during the life of the contract and run the risk either of being too restrictive or being incomplete, and giving rise to opportunism and conflicting interpretation. The inflexibility problems of long-term contracts are particularly evident in IT outsourcing when the agreement may be for a period of 10 years or more. Thus, the 10-year IT outsourcing deal that Xerox signed in 1994 could not anticipate Xerox's reorganization of its marketing and sales in 1999. The outsourcing of IT contributed to Xerox's difficulties in implementing its new marketing structure.[16]

- *Vendor partnerships.* The greater the difficulties of specifying complete contracts for long-term supplier–customer deals, the more likely it is that vertical relationships will be based on trust and mutual understanding. Such relationships can allow the security needed to encourage transaction specific investment, the flexibility to meet changing circumstances, and the trust needed to avoid opportunism.[17] Such arrangements may be entirely *relational contracts* with no written contract at all. The model for vendor partnerships has been the close collaborative relationships that many Japanese companies have with their suppliers. During the late 1980s, Toyota and Nissan directly produced about 20 to 23 percent of the value of their cars, whereas Ford accounted for 50 percent of its production value and GM for about 70 percent. Yet, as Jeff Dyer has shown, the Japanese automakers have been remarkably successful in achieving close collaboration in technology, quality control, design, and scheduling of production and deliveries.[18] The relationships that the British retailer Marks & Spencer has with its suppliers are similarly based on long-term relational contracts (see Exhibit 13.1).

---

[16] L. Willcocks and C. Sauer, "High Risks and Hidden Costs in IT Outsourcing," *Financial Times* Mastering Risk (May 23, 2000): 2–4.

[17] These arrangements have been described as "value adding partnerships." See R. Johnston and P. R. Lawrence, op. cit.

[18] J. H. Dyer, "Effective Interfirm Collaboration: How Firms Minimize Transaction Costs and Maximize Transaction Value," *Strategic Management Journal* 18 (1997): 535–56; J. H. Dyer, "Specialized Supplier Networks as a Source of Competitive Advantage: Evidence from the Auto Industry," *Strategic Management Journal* 17 (1996): 271–92.

EXHIBIT 13.1   Managing Supplier Relations at Marks & Spencer

Marks & Spencer plc is undoubtedly the most successful retailer in Britain in the twentieth century. Established in the 1890s, M&S has achieved near continuous growth in revenue and profit over the last half-century. The company is primarily a supplier of clothing, but in the 1970s expanded into gourmet and convenience foods. Central elements of M&S strategy are its commitment to high quality and value for money and its policy that all its merchandise is sold under its own brand name and is exclusive to M&S. The foundation of M&S's achievement of unique products of high quality and moderate prices is its system of supplier relations.

The interesting feature of these relationships is that they are long term (often extending over decades), and they are based on a common understanding, but there is no written contract. The absence of a formal contract permits a high degree of flexibility, and the potential for highly sophisticated patterns of cooperation between M&S and its suppliers. For example, M&S involves itself in numerous aspects of the supplier's business including product design, quality control, purchasing of inputs, manufacturing methods, human resource policies, and delivery schedules. The supplier is encouraged to make substantial investments in equipment and know-how that are specific to the needs of M&S. Why is it that suppliers are willing to become dependent on M&S and invest in adapting their business system to meet the specific needs of this single customer? Surely this is very risky for the supplier. The critical factor is the incentive structure. M&S procurement policies have been developed over a century. They are well known, and M&S has developed an unparalleled reputation for fair dealing. Any new supplier has the knowledge that previous suppliers have been treated well, and the long-term relationship that M&S is willing to build has made many of its suppliers highly profitable. Because M&S's reputation is its greatest asset, it is unlikely to engage in behavior that might put that reputation at risk.

At the same time, M&S's long-term supplier relationships are a source of inflexibility with regard to exchange rates. The problems that M&S experienced during 1999–2000 were, in part, the result of its UK-based supply chain at a time of overvaluation of the British pound. As M&S also has terminated several long-established UK supply arrangements in favor of offshore sourcing, there is a risk that the trust and incentives that have supported its informal relationship with manufacturers may be destroyed.

Source: K. K. Tse, *Marks & Spencer: Anatomy of Britain's Most Efficiently Managed Company* (New York: Pergamon, 1985).

■ *Franchising.* Like other vertical forms that are intermediate between external market contracts and internal management hierarchy, franchising is an organizational form that aims to combine advantages of both. In particular, the franchising systems of companies such as McDonald's Restaurants, Domino's Pizza, Hilton Hotels, Blockbuster, and Seven-Eleven convenience stores are designed to facilitate the close coordination and investment in transaction-specific assets that vertical integration permits, with the high-powered incentives, flexibility, and cooperation between strategically dissimilar businesses that market contracts make possible. The key feature of multinational service chains in fast foods, hotels, and retailing is the strategic difference between managing brands, product development, and IT, and managing operations in local outlets. Franchising reconciles the need for large-scale management of brands, products, and IT, while leaving individual entrepreneurs to start up and manage individual outlets.

Choosing between Alternative Vertical Relationships

In selecting among different types of relationships and designing the contractual form, all the advantages and disadvantages that we have discussed in relation to market contracts and vertical integration are relevant. What is the optimal type of vertical relationship? As with almost all strategic decisions, it all depends. Even within the same industry, what is best for one company will not make sense for another company whose strategy and capabilities are different. While most food and beverage chains have expanded through franchising, Starbucks, anxious to replicate precisely its unique "Starbucks experience," directly owns and manages its retail outlets.[19] While most banks have been outsourcing IT to companies such as IBM and EDS, Nick Morris, president of US credit card group Capital One, see IT as a key source of competitive advantage: "IT is our central nervous system . . . if I outsourced tomorrow I might save a dollar or two on each account, but I would lose flexibility and value and service levels."[20]

In addition to the factors that we have already considered, the design of vertical relationships needs to take careful account of the following:

1. *Allocation of risk.* Any arrangement beyond a spot contract must cope with uncertainties over the course of the contract. A key feature of any contract is that its terms involve, often implicitly, an allocation of risks between the parties. How risk is shared is dependent partly on bargaining power and partly on efficiency considerations. In franchise agreements, the franchisee (as the weaker partner) bears most of the risk – it is the franchisee's capital that it at risk and the franchisee pays the franchiser a flat royalty based on sales revenues. In oil exploration, outsourcing agreements between the oil majors (such as Chevron, Exxon-Mobil, and ENI) and drilling companies (such as Schlumberger and Halliburton) have moved from fixed-price contracts to risk-sharing agreements where the driller often takes an equity stake in the project.

2. *Incentive structures.* For a contract to minimize transaction costs it must provide an appropriate set of incentives to the parties. Thus, unless a contract for the supply of ready-mixed concrete to construction projects specifies the proportions of cement, sand, and gravel, there is an incentive to supply substandard concrete. However, achieving completeness in the specification of contracts also bears a cost. The $400 toilet seats supplied to the US Navy may reflect the costs of meeting specifications that filled many sheets of paper. Very often, the most effective incentive is the promise of future business. Hence, in privatizing public services – such as passenger rail services or local refuse collection – the key incentive for service quality is a fixed-term operating contract with regular performance reviews and the prospect of competition at contract renewal time. Toyota and Marks & Spencer's vendor partnerships depend on the incentive that satisfactory performance will lead to a long-term business relationship.

---

[19] M. Schilling and S. Kotha, "Starbucks Corporation (A)" in R. M. Grant and K. Neupert, *Cases in Contemporary Strategy Analysis*, 2nd edn (Oxford: Blackwell, 1999): 218–43.
[20] L. Willcocks and C. Sauer, "High Risks and Hidden Costs in IT Outsourcing," *Financial Times* Mastering Risk (May 23, 2000): 3.

Recent Trends

Decisions about vertical scope are no longer binary choices of "make or buy." There is a spectrum of vertical relationships that lie between the polar cases of pure market contracts and vertical integration. However, even this view does not truly reflect the complexity of vertical relationships. The form of a vertical relationship in terms of contractual terms, ownership, and incentive structure only partly determines how the interaction will occur between the two activities. Thus, a company may be integrated across two adjacent vertical activities, but this tells us little about how the relationship between the two stages is managed.

The main feature of recent years has been a growing diversity of intermediate vertical relationships that have attempted to reconcile the flexibility and incentives of market transactions with the close collaboration that is typical of vertical integration. The tendency has been to regard collaborative vertical relationships as a recent phenomenon, closely associated with Silicon Valley and Japanese supplier networks. In fact, closely linked value chains comprising many small, specialist enterprises are a long-time feature of craft industries in Europe, India, and elsewhere. The close collaboration evident in manufacturing industry in northern Italy – notably in textiles,[21] packaging equipment,[22] and motorcycles[23] – has its roots in family-based business relationships that can be traced back to the sixteenth century. The ability for networks of small firms to access the economies of scale and scope typically associated with large companies while avoiding the transactions costs of spot contracts has encouraged the strong trend away from vertical integration across many industries in western Europe and North America.

The success of Japanese manufacturing companies in forging close collaborative relationships with suppliers – including extensive knowledge sharing[24] – has encouraged a shift from arm's-length supplier relationships to closer vertical relationships across the manufacturing and service sectors of North America and Europe. Long-term collaboration and single-supplier agreements have increasingly replaced competitive tendering and multiple sourcing. Most large manufacturers have drastically reduced their number of vendors and have introduced supplier certification programs as frameworks for quality management and technical collaboration.

At the same time, increasing outsourcing has resulted in most companies specializing in fewer activities within their value chains. Companies have focused on a smaller number of vertical activities and increasingly outsourced components and business services. As a result, the fundamental issue in vertical strategy is deciding in which activities the company wishes to specialize. This choice requires, first, examining

---

[21] G. Lorenzoni, "Benetton," in C. Baden-Fuller and M. Pitt (eds), *Strategic Innovation* (London: Routledge, 1996).
[22] G. Lorenzoni and A. Lipparini, "The Leveraging of Interfirm Relationships as Distinctive Organizational Capabilities: A Longitudinal Study," *Strategic Management Journal* 20 (1999): 317–38.
[23] G. Lorenzoni and A. Lipparini, "Relational Strategies and Learning by Interacting Mechanisms in the Italian Motorcycle Industry," paper presented at Strategic Management Society Conference, Barcelona (October 1997).
[24] J. H. Dyer and K. Nobeoka, "Creating and Managing a High-performance Knowledge-Sharing Network: The Toyota Case," *Strategic Management Journal* 21 (2000): 345–68.

the relative attractiveness of different vertical stages of the value stages and, second, examining the company's potential for competitive advantage at each stage. In relation to attractiveness, the relative profitability of different vertical stages may shift over time. Thus, in the media industry, spectrum – access to the final consumer through broadcasting channels and cables – was considered key. With the vast expansion of spectrum – media distribution through broadcasting, cable, fixed-line telephone, and the internet – power has shifted to the producers of content.[25] In relation to competitive advantage, the critical issue is the location of the company's key strengths in resources and capabilities. If the strengths of Richard Branson's Virgin Group are in business startups and brand management, then it is sensible that Virgin's new ventures should be joint ventures in which the joint-venture partner takes primary responsibility for operations management.

The combination of outsourcing and long-term collaboration with suppliers transformed the strategies and the performance of many traditionally integrated manufacturing companies.[26] As companies have increased their dependence on one another, so the need to protect against opportunism becomes more critical. Increasingly, vertical relationships between companies have involved minority ownership stakes. For example, Commonwealth Bank of Australia took an equity stake in its IT supplier, EDS Australia, and pharmaceutical companies often acquire equity stakes in the biotech companies that undertake much of their R&D. Such equity stakes offer a channel of influence and, more importantly, an alignment of incentives. Thus, where engineering companies are required to take an equity stake in projects they are less likely to require incentive payments and penalty clauses.

The extent of outsourcing and vertical de-integration has given rise to a new organizational form: the *virtual corporation,* where the primary function of the company is coordinating the activities of a network of suppliers.[27] Such extreme levels of outsourcing reduce the strategic role of the company to that of a systems integrator. The critical issue is whether a company that outsources most functions can retain the capabilities needed to adapt to changing technologies and market conditions. In the same way that the company that outsources its IT functions may lack the IT capability to adapt its strategy effectively to a digital world, so the virtual corporation may degenerate into a "hollow corporation."[28] The key issue is whether a company's *architectural capabilities* can develop without simultaneously developing at least some of the *component capabilities* that are integrated within the overall architecture. If, as Hamel and Prahalad argue, core competences are embodied in "core products" that in most cases are the components that embody critical technologies, then reducing a company to a mere assembler and marketer may jeopardize the capacity to innovate and develop.[29]

---

[25] "Another Link in the Chain," *Financial Times Creative Business Supplement* (November 21, 2000): 15.

[26] See J. H. Dyer, "How Chrysler Created an American Keiretsu," *Harvard Business Review* (July–August 1996): 42–56.

[27] "The Virtual Corporation," *Business Week* (February 8, 1993): 98–104; W. H. Davidow and M. S. Malone, *The Virtual Corporation* (New York: HarperCollins, 1992).

[28] H. W. Chesborough and D. J. Teece, "When is Virtual Virtuous? Organizing for Innovation," *Harvard Business Review* (May–June 1996): 68–79.

[29] C. K. Prahalad and Gary Hamel, "The Core Competences of the Corporation," *Harvard Business Review* (May–June 1990): 79–91.

The development of the internet has had a major impact on reducing the transaction costs of markets – particularly in reducing search costs. The rapid growth in business-to-business e-commerce hubs involves a major revival in arm's-length competitive contracting. One of the biggest e-commerce hubs for purchasing components is the Covisint venture, launched in 2000 by Ford, GM, and DaimlerChrysler.[30]

Summary

Deciding which parts of the value chain to engage in presents companies with one of their most difficult strategic decisions. The conventional analysis of vertical integration has looked simply at the efficiency of markets as compared to the efficiency of firms: if the cost of transacting through the market is greater than the cost of administering within the firm, then the company should vertically integrate across the stages. Transaction cost analysis does not, however, provide the complete answer. In the first place, vertical strategies are not simply make-or-buy choices – there are a wide variety of ways in which a company can structure vertical relationships. Secondly, the most critical long-run consideration is the development of organizational capability. If a company is to sustain competitive advantage, it must restrict itself to those activities where it possesses the capabilities that are superior to those of the other companies that perform those activities. If my company's data-processing capabilities are inferior to those of IBM and its logistics capabilities are inferior to those of Federal Express, I should consider outsourcing these activities. The most difficult issues arise where there are linkages between value chain activities. Even though a contract manufacturer may be able to manufacture my remote-controlled lawnmower more efficiently than I can internally, what would be the implications for my new product development capability if I no longer have in-house manufacturing?

Ultimately, vertical integration decisions revolve around two key questions. First, which activities will we undertake internally and which will we outsource? Second, how do we design our vertical arrangements with both external and internal suppliers and buyers? In the case of external relations, these may be conducted through spot contracts, long-term contracts, or some form of strategic alliance. Similar ranges of alternatives face the vertically integrated firm – including the option of arm's-length negotiated contracts. Both types of decision are critically dependent on the firm's competitive strategy and the capabilities it possesses. As we have already noted, the critical issue for the individual business is not to follow conventional wisdom but carefully to evaluate its strategic needs, its resources and capabilities at different stages in the value chain, the characteristics of the transactions involved, and the relative attractiveness of different stages of the value chain.

[30] www.covisint.com.

14

Global Strategies and the Multinational Corporation

ABB is a company with no geographic center, no national ax to grind. We are a federation of national companies with a global coordination center. Are we a Swiss company? Our headquarters is in Zurich, but only 100 professionals work at headquarters and we will not increase that number. Are we a Swedish company? I'm the CEO, and I was born and educated in Sweden. But our headquarters is not in Sweden and only two of the eight members of our board of directors are Swedes. Perhaps we are an American company. We report our financial results in US dollars and English is ABB's official language. We conduct all high-level meetings in English. My point is that ABB is none of those things – and all of these things. We are not homeless. We are a company with many homes.
—Percy Barnevik, CEO, Asea Brown Boveri

OUTLINE

INTRODUCTION AND OBJECTIVES

Internationalization is the most important and pervasive force changing the competitive environment of business in recent decades. It has opened national markets to new competitors and created new business opportunities for both large and small firms. Internationalization has occurred through two mechanisms: trade and direct investment. The growth of world trade has consistently outstripped the growth of world output, increasing export/sales and import penetration ratios for all countries and all industries. For the United States, the share of imports in sales of manufactured goods rose from less than 4 percent in 1960 to 26 percent in 1999. Trade in commercial services (transportation, communications, information, financial services, and the like) grew even faster than merchandise trade. From 1994 to 1999, world exports of services grew at an annual rate of about 14 percent, compared to 7 percent for merchandise exports. The second aspect of internationalization has been overseas direct investment by corporations. By 1999, the total stock of foreign direct investment by all companies in the world was $3.6 trillion – 12 percent of world GDP.

The forces driving both trade and direct investment are, first, the quest to exploit market opportunities in other countries, and, second, the desire to exploit production opportunities by locating production activities wherever they can be conducted most efficiently. The resulting "globalization of business" has created networks of international transactions comprising merchandise trade, flows of services (including technology), flows of people (especially those with highly developed skills), flows of factor payments (interest, profits, and licensing and royalty income), and flows of capital.

The implications for industry structure are far reaching. During the 1960s, local companies dominated most domestic markets in the industrialized countries. Internationalization has changed all that. Consider the US market for television sets. Many of the leading brands of yesteryear are still around, but all are now owned by overseas companies: General Electric and RCA by the French company Thomson, Magnavox by Philips of the Netherlands, Motorola's television business by Matsushita, and Zenith by LG of South Korea. Manufacture is not for the most part in these companies' home countries – most assembly of televisions is carried out in lower labor cost locations in Southeast Asia and Latin America.

Similarly with investment banking in London. The same global giants that dominate investment banking in New York and Frankfurt – Citigroup, Merrill Lynch, Goldman Sachs, Deutsche Bank, and SBC – are also the kingpins in London. The venerable investment banks that once financed Britain's imperial might have now been absorbed by these international players: Warburg by SBC, Barings by ING Group, Hambros by Societe Generale, and Kleinwort-Benson by Dresner.

The ability to take advantage of the opportunities made available by internationalization has been a key factor in the success or failure of companies. The industry leadership of Citigroup in financial services, Honda in motorcycles, Crown Cork and Seal in metal containers, Vodafone in wireless communication, and Philip Morris in cigarettes owes much to these companies' ambitious global strategies. Not that commitment to internationalization is a guarantee of success: for Saatchi & Saatchi in advertising, Daewoo in automobiles, and Laura Ashley in fashion retailing, ambitious internationalization was a critical source of failure. For countries too, harnessing the forces of internationalization has been a prime determinant of relative economic performance. In 1950, Hong Kong's GDP per head of population lagged slightly behind that of the Philippines. By 2000, Hong Kong's development as a hub for international trade and commerce had given it a per capita GDP of $26,000, compared with $4,500 for the Philippines (at purchasing power parity rates of exchange). Within the European Union, Ireland's ability to take advantage of international trade and inward direct investment has resulted in real GDP growth of 84 percent during 1993–2000, as compared with 12 percent for Italy.

This chapter examines the implications of the internationalization of the business environment for the formulation and implementation of company strategy. In doing so, we extend our strategy framework to take account of the firm's national environment as a critical dimension of its competitive environment. By the time you have completed this chapter, you will be able to:

- Apply the tools of industry analysis to global industries, including identifying the impact of trade and direct investment on industry structure and competition and appraising the critical differences between national markets within the same industry.

- Analyze how the national environment of the firm influences its competitive advantage, in particular how the national context affects the resources and capabilities of the firm and the choice of strategies through which the firm can best exploit these national conditions.

- Formulate strategies for exploiting overseas business opportunities, including overseas entry strategies and overseas production strategies, and determine the appropriate degree of globalization or national differentiation.

- Design organizational structures and management systems appropriate to the pursuit of international strategies.

We begin by exploring the implications of international competition, first for industry analysis, and then for the analysis of competitive advantage.

IMPLICATIONS OF INTERNATIONAL COMPETITION FOR INDUSTRY ANALYSIS

Patterns of Internationalization

Internationalization occurs through trade and direct investment. On this basis we can identify different types of industry according to the extent and mode of their internationalization (see Figure 14.1):

- *Sheltered industries* are national, even local, in terms of firms' market scope. Most of the industries that were once sheltered from international competition by regulation, public ownership, or physical barriers to trade – banking, insurance, electricity generation, telecommunications, cement – are now well on the road to internationalization. Industries left in this category are primarily fragmented service industries (dry cleaning, hairdressing, auto repair), some small-scale manufacturing (handicrafts, homebuilding), and industries producing products that are nontradable because they are perishable (fresh milk, bread) or difficult to move (four-poster beds, garden sheds).

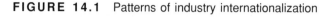

FIGURE 14.1 Patterns of industry internationalization

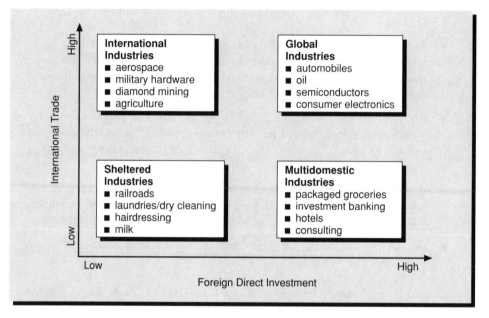

- *Trading industries* are those where internationalization occurs primarily through imports and exports. If a product is transportable, not nationally differentiated, and subject to substantial scale economies, exporting from a single location is the most efficient means to exploit overseas markets, which would apply for example with commercial aircraft, shipbuilding, and defense equipment. Trading industries also include products whose inputs are available only in a few locations: diamonds from South Africa, caviar from Iran and Azerbaijan.

- *Multidomestic industries* are those that internationalize through direct investment – either because trade is not feasible (as in the case of service industries such as banking, consulting, or hotels) or because products are nationally differentiated (e.g., frozen dinners, recorded music).

- *Global industries* are those in which both trade and direct investment are important. Most large-scale manufacturing industries tend to evolve towards global structures: in automobiles, consumer electronics, semiconductors, pharmaceuticals, and beer, levels of trade and direct investment are high.

By which route does internationalization typically occur? In the case of services and other nontradable products, there is no choice. The only way that Marriott, Starbucks, and Goldman Sachs can serve overseas markets is by creating subsidiaries (or acquiring companies) within these markets. In the case of manufacturing companies, internationalization typically begins with exports from the home base. Later a sales and distribution subsidiary is established in the overseas country. Eventually the company develops a more integrated overseas subsidiary that undertakes manufacturing and product development as well.

Implications for Competition

The consequences of internationalization for competition and industry attractiveness are mostly adverse. Although internationalization offers increased investment and marketing opportunities to companies, such opportunities mean increased intensity of competition. Consider the US markets for automobiles in 1970 and 2000. In 1970, the US automobile industry was dominated by the Big Three – GM, Ford, and Chrysler, with American Motors and Volkswagen as minor producers. By the end of 2000 there were 11 companies with auto plants within the US.[1] The overall impact has been intensified price competition and lower profitability – though for the US, the adverse impact of increased international competition was offset during the 1990s by the upswing in overall profitability.

The impact of internationalization on competition and industry profitability can be analyzed within the context of Porter's Five Forces of Competition framework. For the purposes of our analysis, let us take our unit of analysis as national markets where the relevant "industry" comprises the firms supplying that national market. Hence, for the purposes of analyzing competition, the US auto industry includes all companies supplying autos to the US automobile market, whether they are domestic or overseas companies. Within this context, internationalization affects competition in three major ways: through reducing entry barriers, increasing rivalry, and enhancing the bargaining power of domestic buyers.

Competition from Potential Entrants

The growth of international trade indicates a substantial lowering of barriers to entry into national markets. Multilateral tariff reduction during successive GATT rounds, falling real costs of transportation, the removal of exchange controls, internationalization of standards, and convergence between customer preferences have made it much easier for producers in one country to supply customers in another. Many of the entry barriers that were effective against potential domestic entrants may be ineffective against potential entrants that are established producers in overseas countries.

Rivalry among Existing Firms

Internationalization increases internal rivalry within industries because it lowers seller concentration and increases the diversity of competing firms.

---

[1] GM, Ford, DaimlerChrysler, Honda, Toyota, Nissan, Suzuki, Mitsubishi, BMW, Fuji (Subaru), and Isuzu.

Seller Concentration

International trade typically means that more suppliers are competing for each national market. Consider the US auto market. In 1970, GM, Ford, and Chrysler together held 84 percent of total sales, and there were just five manufacturers with market shares greater than 2 percent. By 2000, the combined share of the Big Three had fallen to 61 percent, and there were eight manufacturers with market shares greater than 2 percent. In European countries, the fall in market share of the national leaders (Fiat in Italy, Renault and Peugeot-Citroën in France, British Leyland in the United Kingdom, Seat in Spain) was even more dramatic. While internationalization decreases concentration in national markets, it increases concentration at the global level as competition forces smaller companies to either exit or merge.

Diversity of Competitors

Lower entry barriers and concentration ratios only partly explain the increasing intensity of competition between established firms. Equally important is the increasing diversity of competitors, which causes them to compete more vigorously while making cooperation more difficult. The cozy collusiveness observed in domestic oligopolies during the 1960s (e.g., in autos, steel, and banking) was possible because of the similarities among domestic companies in their costs, strategies, goals, and perceptions. The entry of overseas competitors into domestic markets upset these patterns of coordination – their different costs, goals, and strategies made tacit collusion much less likely.[2]

Excess Capacity

When internationalization occurs through direct investment, the result is likely to be increased capacity. To the extent that direct investment occurs through investment in new plants, industry capacity increases with no corresponding increase in market size. The automobile industry is a classic example of this – the investment by Japanese and Korean manufacturers in the US and Europe, and by US manufactures in Latin America and Asia, added substantially to global excess capacity during the 1990s.

The Bargaining Power of Buyers

A further implication of the internationalization of business is that large customers can exercise their buying power far more effectively. Global sourcing provides a key tool for cost reduction by manufacturers. The growth of internet-based markets for components and materials enhances the power of industrial buyers.

---

[2] Collusion in international industries is not unknown. During the 1930s, Standard Oil of New Jersey (now Exxon) and the Royal Dutch/Shell Group effectively regulated competition in the international oil industry. The world cigarette industry for much of the twentieth century was neatly divided between American Tobacco and the Imperial Tobacco Group of Britain. American Tobacco agreed not to compete within the former British Empire, Imperial agreed to keep outside the Americas, while exports to other countries were handled by a jointly owned subsidiary British American Tobacco (BAT). See M. Corina, *Trust in Tobacco* (London: Michael Joseph, 1975).

ANALYZING COMPETITIVE ADVANTAGE IN AN INTERNATIONAL CONTEXT

The growth of international competition has been associated with some stunning reversals in the competitive positions of different companies. RCA in consumer electronics, Atari in video games, and Xerox in office copiers were all leaders in their industries before being decimated by international competition. Conversely, international market opportunities have made it possible for Honda in motorcycles, Microsoft in computer software, and IKEA in furniture retailing to achieve success that has exceeded their founders' wildest dreams.

To understand how internationalization has shifted the basis of competition, we need to extend our framework for analyzing competitive advantage to include the influence of firms' national environments. Competitive advantage, we have noted, is achieved when a firm matches its internal strengths in resources and capabilities to the key success factors of the industry. In relation to competitive advantage, global industries differ from domestic industries. When firms are located in different countries, their potential for achieving competitive advantage depends not only on their internal stocks of resources and capabilities, but also on the conditions of their national environments – in particular, the resource availability within the countries where they do business (see Figure 14.2).

FIGURE 14.2 Competitive advantage in an international context

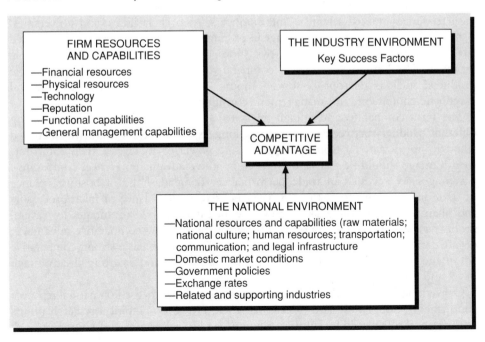

TABLE 14.1   Indexes of Revealed Comparative Advantage for Certain Broad Product Categories

	USA	CANADA	GERMANY	ITALY	JAPAN
Food, drink, and tobacco	.31	.28	−.36	−.29	−.85
Raw materials	.43	.51	−.55	−.30	−.88
Oil and refined products	−.64	.34	−.72	−.74	−.99
Chemicals	.42	−.16	.20	−.06	−.58
Machinery and transportation equipment	.12	−.19	.34	.22	.80
Other manufacturing	−.68	−.07	.01	.29	.40

Note: Revealed comparative advantage for each product group is measured as: (Exports less Imports)/Domestic Production.
Source: OECD.

National Influences on Competitiveness: Comparative Advantage

The role of national resource availability on international competitiveness is the subject of the *theory of comparative advantage*. The theory states that a country has a comparative advantage in those products that make intensive use of those resources available in abundance within that country. Thus, Bangladesh has an abundant supply of unskilled labor. The United States has an abundant supply of technological resources: trained scientists and engineers, research facilities, and universities. Bangladesh has a comparative advantage in products that make intensive use of unskilled labor, such as clothing, handicrafts, toys, shoes, and assembly of consumer electronic products. The United States has a comparative advantage in technology-intensive products, such as microprocessors, computer software, pharmaceuticals, medical diagnostic equipment, and management consulting services.

The term comparative advantage refers to the relative efficiencies of producing different products between countries. So long as exchange rates are well behaved (they do not deviate far from their purchasing power parity levels), then comparative advantage should be translated into competitive advantage. Hence, comparative advantages are revealed in trade performance: Bangladesh has a positive balance of trade in shoes and toys; the US has a positive trade balance in microprocessors and pharmaceuticals. Table 14.1 shows revealed comparative advantages for several product groups and several countries. Positive values show comparative advantage, negative values show comparative disadvantage. Thus, Japan has a strong comparative advantage in machinery and transportation equipment, and a strong disadvantage in oil and refined products.

Conventionally, the theory of comparative advantage has focused on natural resource endowments, population, and the capital stock. However, empirical research points to the critical role played by cultural, religious, and social factors, and "home-grown" resources such as technology, human capital, management capabilities, and infra-structure (e.g., transportation and communications facilities, and the legal system).[3] The remarkable transformation in the pattern of comparative advantage (and real incomes) of the "tiger economies" of South Korea, Taiwan, Hong Kong, Malaysia, and Singapore demonstrate importance of internally developed resources. Lacking natural resources, these countries invested heavily in capital, education, technology, and communications and transportation infrastructure and, in the process, became leading exporters of sophisticated electronic products.[4] Increasingly, knowledge is emerging as a critical determinant of patterns of national advantage. In order to remain at the top of the "knowledge pyramid," Lester Thurow points to the key roles of social organization, entrepreneurship, and education.[5]

The size of a country's domestic market influences comparative advantage in industries where the minimum efficient size of operation is large or where demand is so segmented that a large total market is required for niches to be of a viable size.[6] Size of home market has been a traditional advantage for US firms and has been a key motivation for the creation of free trade areas such as the European Union, Mercosur, and NAFTA.

Porter's National Diamond

Based on a detailed study of the patterns of comparative advantage among 13 indus-trialized nations, Michael Porter offers an important extension of our understanding of the impact of national conditions on firms' international competitive advantage.[7] Porter's analysis is built on three principles:

1. The competitive performance of a country depends on the performance of the firms within it. However, the national environment exerts a powerful influence on the performance of the firm: it provides the home base within which firms develop their identity, resources and capabilities, and critical man-agerial behaviors.[8]

---

[3] A key finding was that *human capital* (knowledge and skills) was more important than *physical capital* in explaining the pattern of US trade – the so-called *Leontief Paradox*. See W. W. Leontief, "Domestic Production and Foreign Trade," in Richard Caves and H. Johnson (eds), *Readings in International Economics* (Homewood, IL: Irwin, 1968).
[4] Paul Krugman, "What happened to the Asian miracle?," *Fortune* (August 18, 1997): 18–19.
[5] L. C. Thurow, *Building Wealth: The New Rules for Individuals, Companies and Nations* (New York: Harper Collins, 1999).
[6] Paul Krugman, "Increasing Returns, Monopolistic Competition, and International Trade," *Journal of International Economics* 9 (November 1979): 469–79.
[7] Michael E. Porter, *The Competitive Advantage of Nations* (New York: Free Press, 1990).
[8] Porter's view differs sharply from those observers who point to the emergence of the "stateless corporation" (ABB's Percy Barnevik among them). Although the national market is comparatively unimportant to a number of MNCs (ABB, Nestlé, Royal Dutch/Shell Group, Philips, and Hoffman-La Roche) that is not to say that their capabilities, strategy, and management style are not influenced by their national home base. See "The Stateless Corporation," *Business Week* (May 14, 1990): 98–106.

FIGURE 14.3   Porter's national diamond framework

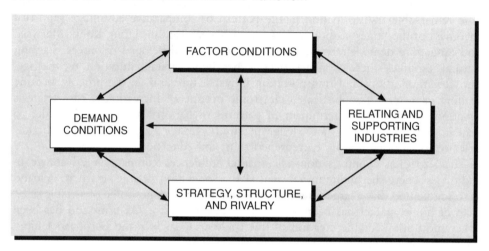

2. For a country to sustain a competitive advantage in a sector over time requires *dynamic* advantage: its firms must broaden and extend the basis of their competitive advantage by innovation and upgrading their resources and capabilities. Thus, Japanese success in automobiles reflects its companies' ability continuously to advance the basis of their competitive advantage. By contrast, Britain's dismal performance in many manufacturing sectors during the second half of the 20th century resulted from the tendency for many of its leading industrial companies to allow their competitive advantages to atrophy through a lack of continuous innovation and upgrading.

3. The impact of the national environment on firms' competitive performance is less about national resource availability and more about the *dynamic conditions* that influence innovation and the upgrading.

Porter's analysis is summarized in his national diamond framework (see Figure 14.3).[9]

Factor Conditions

Whereas the conventional advantage of comparative analysis focuses on endowments of broad categories of resource, Porter's analysis emphasizes, first, "home-grown" resources and, second, the role of highly specialized resources. For example, in analyzing Hollywood's preeminence in film production, Porter points to the local concentration of skilled labor, including the roles of UCLA and USC schools of film. Also, resource constraints may encourage the development of substitute capabilities: in Japan, lack of raw materials has spurred miniaturization and low-defect manufacturing; in Italy, restrictive labor laws have stimulated automation.

[9]   For a review of the Porter analysis, see Robert M. Grant, "Porter's *Competitive Advantage of Nations*: An Assessment," *Strategic Management Journal* 12 (1991): 535–48.

Related and Supporting Industries

For many industries, a critical resource is the presence of related and supporting industries. One of the most striking of Porter's empirical findings is that national competitive strengths tend to be associated with "clusters" of industries. One such cluster is US strength in semiconductors, computers, and computer software. For each of these industries, critical resources are the other related industries. In Germany, a mutually supporting cluster exists around chemicals, synthetic dyes, textiles, and textile machinery.

Demand Conditions

Demand conditions in the domestic market provide the primary driver of innovation and quality improvement. For example:

- The preeminence of Swiss and Belgian chocolate makers may be attributed to their highly discerning domestic customers.

- The dominance of the world market for cameras by Japanese companies owes much to Japanese consumers' enthusiasm for amateur photography and their eager adoption of innovation in cameras.

- German companies' (Mercedes, BMW, Porsche) dominance of the high-performance segment of the world automobile industry, as compared to their much weaker position in mass-produced autos, may be linked to German motorists' love of quality engineering and their irrepressible urge to drive on autobahns at terrifying speeds.

Strategy, Structure, and Rivalry

National competitive performance in particular sectors is inevitably related to the strategies and structures of firms in those industries. Porter puts particular emphasis on the role of competition between domestic companies in driving innovation and the upgrading of competitive advantage. Domestic competition is usually more direct and personal than that between companies from different countries. As a result, the maintenance of strong competition within domestic markets is likely to provide a powerful stimulus to innovation and efficiency. The most striking feature of the Japanese auto industry is the presence of nine companies, all of which compete fiercely within the domestic market. The same can be said for cameras, consumer electronic products, and facsimile machines. This lack of domestic competition may help explain why the efforts of European governments to create "national champions" in so many industries has been so unsuccessful.[10]

---

[10] This analysis also suggests that measures to support local industries through subsidies, currency devaluation, or import protection, to the extent that they reduce competitive pressure, may discourage efficiency, innovation, and quality upgrading.

Consistency between Strategy and National Conditions

Establishing competitive advantage in global industries requires congruence between business strategy and the pattern of the country's comparative advantage. For example, in the British cutlery industry, competition from South Korean manufacturers benefiting from low wage and low steel costs meant that it was virtually impossible for companies such as J. Billam to survive in the mass market for stainless steel cutlery. The only firms to prosper, or even survive, were those that relied on technology (such as Richardson in kitchen knives), or focused on the high-quality silverware segment. In stereo systems and other audio products, US and European companies (such as Bose and Bang & Olufsen) have survived by focusing on skill-intensive and design-intensive products; Sony, Matsushita, and other Japanese producers compete on the basis of product innovation and highly automated assembly; the low end of the market (e.g., retailers' own brands) is supplied by companies in Thailand, Malaysia, and China.

The linkage between the firm's competitive advantage and its national environment is not a simple one of consistency between the strategy pursued and the resources and capabilities available within the national economy. It also relates to the development of the firm's organizational capabilities. The firm's development of its internal capabilities is closely linked to the characteristics of the culture and social structure of the country in which these capabilities are being developed. The capabilities of Japanese companies in integrating diverse technologies into innovative new products (electronic musical instruments, color copying machines), and in quality enhancement through continuous improvement, owes much to Japanese traditions of assimilating outside ideas and cooperative social behavior. Similarly, the excellence of US firms in financial management and pioneering new industries through entrepreneurship may link with US traditions of individualism and quest for material wealth. Thus, the design of long-term strategies that simultaneously develop market positions and organizational capabilities need to recognize the potential for harnessing national characteristics.

APPLYING THE FRAMEWORK: INTERNATIONAL LOCATION OF PRODUCTION

To examine the role of firm resources and country resources in international strategy decisions, we look at two types of decision that face internationalizing companies: first, the decision of where to locate their production activities and, second, the decision of how to enter a foreign market.

So far, our discussion of the linkage between the competitive advantage of the firm and its national environment has assumed, implicitly, that each firm is based within its home country. In fact, a primary motivation of multinational strategies is to access the resources and capabilities available in other countries. Whether a firm markets its product in many countries or only in its domestic market, it must decide where it is to produce it. Some firms market globally but concentrate production in their home country (Honda, Toyota, and Matsushita were like this for most of the 1970s; Boeing and Microsoft are like it today). Other multinationals, especially in service industries, establish stand-alone country subsidiaries, where each country unit produces for its own national market. Such companies have been called "multidomestic" corporations (examples include the tobacco company BAT and the French utilities and media company Vivendi). Other companies have geographically dispersed locations where each location plays a specialized role within a global network.

Determinants of Geographical Location

The decision of where to manufacture requires consideration of three sets of factors:

■ *National resource availability.* Where key resources differ between countries in their availability or cost, then firms should manufacture in countries where resource supplies are favorable. For the oil industry this means exploring in Kazakhstan, Angola, and Venezuela. For Nike and Reebok, it means locating shoe assembly where labor costs are low: China, Thailand, India, and the Philippines. (Table 14.2 shows differences in employment costs between countries.) For semiconductor and computer companies, it means establishing R&D facilities in California's Silicon Valley in order to exploit US microelectronics expertise.[11]

■ *Firm-specific competitive advantages.* For firms whose competitive advantage is based on internal resources and capabilities, location depends on where those

TABLE 14.2 Hourly Compensation Costs in US Dollars for Production Workers in Manufacturing

	1975	1980	1985	1990	1995	1998	1999
United States	6.36	9.87	13.01	14.91	17.19	18.66	19.20
Mexico	1.47	2.21	1.59	1.58	1.51	1.84	2.12
Australia	5.62	8.47	8.20	13.07	15.27	14.92	15.89
Hong Kong	.76	1.51	1.73	3.20	4.82	5.47	5.44
Israel	2.25	3.79	4.06	8.55	10.54	12.02	11.91
Japan	3.00	5.52	6.34	12.80	23.82	18.29	20.89
Korea	.32	.96	1.23	3.71	7.29	5.39	6.71
Taiwan	.40	1.00	1.50	3.93	5.94	5.27	5.62
Denmark	6.28	10.83	8.13	18.04	24.07	22.69	22.96
France	4.52	8.94	7.52	15.49	20.01	18.28	17.98
Germany (former west)	6.31	12.25	9.53	21.88	31.58	27.52	26.93
Italy	4.67	8.15	7.63	17.45	16.22	17.11	16.60
Spain	2.53	5.89	4.66	11.38	12.88	12.14	12.11
Sweden	7.18	12.51	9.66	20.93	21.44	22.02	21.58
Switzerland	6.09	11.09	9.66	20.86	29.30	24.38	23.56
United Kingdom	3.37	7.56	6.27	12.70	13.67	16.43	16.56

Source: US Department of Labor, Bureau of Labor Statistics, September 2000.

---

[11] P. Almeida, "Knowledge Sourcing by Foreign Multinationals: Patent Citation Analysis in the US Semiconductor Industry," *Strategic Management Journal* 17 (December 1996): 155–65.

resources and capabilities can best be deployed. The competitive advantages of Toyota, Nissan, and Honda rest primarily on their own technical, manufacturing, and product development capabilities. Traditionally, these companies concentrated production within Japan where they could exploit scale economies. During the 1980s, they demonstrated the ability to transfer these competitive advantages to overseas locations.

■ *Tradability.* The ability to locate production away from markets depends on transportability. High transportation costs may necessitate local production, and differences in national customer preferences may encourage local production. Production close to the market may also result from governments' import restrictions as a means of forcing global corporations to establish manufacturing operations in local markets.

Location and the Value Chain

Location decisions must take account of the fact that the production of any good or service is composed of a vertical chain of activities and that the input requirements of each vary considerably. The result is that different countries are likely to offer differential advantage at each stage of the value chain. Table 14.3 shows the pattern of international specialization within textiles and apparel and consumer electronics. In textiles and apparel, the resource requirements for the different production stages are very different. Fiber production is concentrated in the countries with comparative advantage in agricultural production (for cotton and wool) and chemicals (for synthetic fibers). The production of yarn and cloth is capital intensive and occurs in both newly industrialized and mature countries. Apparel is labor intensive – here the developing countries have a clear comparative advantage. Similarly with consumer electronics: component production is research and capital intensive and is concentrated in the US, Japan, Korea, and Malaysia; assembly is labor intensive and is concentrated in China, Thailand, and Latin America.

Identifying the Optimal Location for Each Individual Activity

To determine the best location for each activity, the firm needs to identify the principal inputs into each stage and then match these to the costs and availability of these inputs in different countries.[12] Nike is a classic example of a company exploiting national comparative advantages at each stage of its value chain: its R&D and design are located within the US; the production of fabric, rubber, and plastic shoe components in Korea, Taiwan, and China; assembly in India, China, the Philippines, Thailand, and other low-wage locations; marketing and distribution in the United

---

[12]   The linking of value-added chains to national comparative advantages is explained in B. Kogut, "Designing Global Strategies and Competitive Value-Added Chains," *Sloan Management Review* (Summer 1985): 15–38.

TABLE 14.3 Comparative Advantage in Textiles and Consumer Electronics by Stage of Processing

INDUSTRY	COUNTRY	STAGE OF PROCESSING	INDEX OF REVEALED COMPARATIVE ADVANTAGE
Textiles and apparel	Hong Kong	1	−0.96
		2	−0.81
		3	−0.41
		4	+0.75
	Italy	1	−0.54
		2	+0.18
		3	+0.14
		4	+0.72
	Japan	1	−0.36
		2	+0.48
		3	+0.78
		4	−0.48
	USA	1	+0.96
		2	+0.64
		3	+0.22
		4	−0.73
Consumer electronic products	Brazil	1	−0.62
		2	+0.55
	Hong Kong	1	−0.41
		2	+0.28
	Japan	1	+0.53
		2	+0.97
	S. Korea	1	−0.01
		2	+0.73
	USA	1	+0.02
		2	−0.65

Notes: Revealed comparative advantage is measured as: (Exports − Imports)/(Exports + Imports). For Textiles and apparel, the stages of processing are: 1. fiber (natural and manmade), 2. spun yarn, 3. textiles, 4. apparel. For consumer electronics, the stages of processing are: 1. components, 2. finished products.
Source: United Nations.

States, Europe, and other affluent countries.[13] The costs of different locations may be strongly influenced by government subsidies and tax breaks.

Linkages between Activities

The benefits derived from breaking the value chain and locating individual activities in different countries must be traded off against the costs of weaker linkages between stages in the chain. Transportation costs are one consideration. Another is increased inventory costs. Where learning curves are steep, the time costs of shipping

---

[13] *Nike: International Context*, HBS Case Services Case 9-385-328 (Boston: Harvard Business School, 1985); and *Nike in China*, HBS Case Services Case 9-386-037 (Boston: Harvard Business School, 1985).

TABLE 14.4 The Cost of Producing a Compact Automobile, US and Mexico

	US ($)	MEXICO ($)
Parts and components	7,750	8,000
Labor	700	140
Shipping costs	300	1,000
Inventory	20	40
Total	8,770	9,180

Source: US Office of Technology Assessment, October 1992.

components can be great: semiconductors can lose 5 percent of their value while being shipped from Asia to the United States. Just-in-time scheduling has increased the attraction of geographically concentrated component manufacture and assembly. As Table 14.4 shows, the labor cost advantages of producing cars for the US market in Mexico are offset by the costs of importing components, shipping finished cars, and increased inventory. Dispersed activities also mean increased problems of coordination and control. The importance of close linkages through geographical proximity depends on the strategy of the company. Dell Computer, with its emphasis on fast delivery and customizing to meet customer specifications, must manufacture close to its markets. Acer (which also owns Packard Bell) competes primarily on price and produces mainly in Southeast Asia.

Figure 14.4 summarizes the relevant criteria in location decisions.

FIGURE 14.4 Determining the optimal location of value chain activities

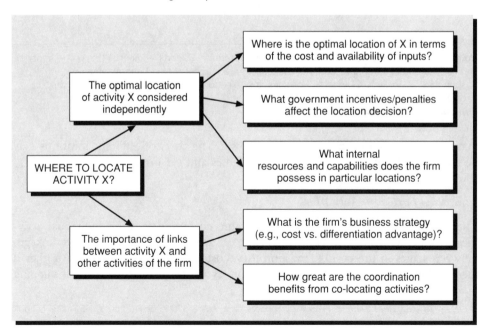

FIGURE 14.5   Alternative modes of overseas market entry

TRANSACTIONS				
Exporting: Spot transactions	Exporting: Long-term contract	Exporting: with foreign distributor/agent	Licensing technology and trademarks	Franchising

DIRECT INVESTMENT			
Joint venture		Wholly owned subsidiary	
Marketing and distribution only	Fully integrated	Marketing and sales only	Fully integrated

APPLYING THE FRAMEWORK: FOREIGN ENTRY STRATEGIES

Many of the considerations relevant to locating production activities also apply to choosing the mode of foreign market entry. A firm enters an overseas market because it believes that it will be profitable. This assumes not only that the overseas market is attractive – that its structure is conducive to profitability – but also that the firm can establish a competitive advantage vis-à-vis local producers and other multinational corporations (MNCs). We discussed the analysis of industry and market profitability in Chapters 3 and 4. Our focus here is on how the firm can best establish competitive advantage in a foreign market.

In exploiting an overseas market opportunity, a firm has a range of options with regard to mode of entry. These correspond closely to the firm's strategic alternatives with regard to exploiting innovation (see Chapter 11). The basic distinction is between market entry by means of *transactions* and market entry by means of *direct investment*. Figure 14.5 shows a spectrum of market entry options arranged according to the degree of commitment by the firm. Thus, at one extreme there is exporting through individual spot-market transactions; at the other, there is the establishment of a fully owned subsidiary that undertakes a full range of functions.

How does a firm weigh the merits of different market entry modes? Among the critical considerations are the following.

Is the firm's competitive advantage based on firm-specific or country-specific resources?

If the firm's competitive advantage is country based, the firm must exploit an overseas market by exporting. Thus, to the extent that Hyundai's competitive advantage in the US car market is its low Korean wage rates, it must produce in Korea and export to the United States. If Toyota's competitive advantage is company specific, then assuming that advantage is transferable within the company, Toyota can exploit the US market either by exports or by direct investment in US production facilities.[14]

Is the product tradable and what are the barriers to trade?

If the product is not tradable because of transportation costs or import restrictions, then accessing that market requires entry either by investing in overseas production facilities or by licensing the use of key resources to local companies within the overseas market.

Does the firm possess the full range of resources and capabilities for establishing a competitive advantage in the overseas market?

Competing in an overseas market is likely to require that the firm acquire additional resources and capabilities, particularly those related to marketing and distributing in an unfamiliar market. Accessing such country-specific resources is most easily achieved by establishing a relationship with firms in the overseas market. The form of relationship depends, in part, on the resources and capabilities required. If a firm needs marketing and distribution, it might appoint a distributor or agent with exclusive territorial rights. If a wide range of manufacturing and marketing capabilities is needed, the firm might license its product and/or its technology to a local manufacturer. In technology-based industries, firms frequently exploit their innovations internationally by licensing their technology to local companies. In marketing-intensive industries, firms may offer their brands to local companies through trademark licensing. Alternatively, a joint venture might be sought with a local manufacturing company. The difficulties that US companies faced when entering the Japanese market encouraged many to form joint ventures with local companies (e.g., Fuji-Xerox, Caterpillar-Mitsubishi). Typically, such joint ventures combined the technology and brand names of the overseas partner with the local market knowledge and manufacturing and distribution facilities of the local partner.

Can the firm directly appropriate the returns to its resources?

Whether a firm licenses the use of its proprietary resources or chooses to exploit them directly (either through exporting or direct investment) depends partly on appropriability considerations. In chemicals and pharmaceuticals, the patents protecting product innovations tend to offer strong legal protection, in which case patent licenses to local producers can be an effective means of appropriating their returns. In computer software and computer equipment, the protection offered by patents and copyrights is looser, which encourages exporting rather than licensing as a means of exploiting overseas markets.

---

[14]   The role of firm-specific assets in explaining the multinational expansion is analyzed in Richard Caves, "International Corporations: The Industrial Economics of Foreign Investment," *Economica* 38 (1971): 1–27.

With all licensing arrangements, key considerations are the capabilities and reliability of the local licensee. This is particularly important in licensing brand names, where the licenser must carefully protect the brand's reputation. Thus, Cadbury-Schweppes licenses to Hershey the trademarks and product recipes for its Cadbury's range of chocolate bars for sale in the United States. This arrangement reflects the fact that Hershey has production and distribution facilities in the US that Cadbury cannot match, and that Cadbury views Hershey as a reliable business partner. The need to exert close control over the use of one's trademarks, technologies, and trade secrets is reflected in the design of international franchising systems.

What transaction costs are involved?

A key issue that arises in the licensing of a firm's trademarks or technology concerns the transaction costs of negotiating, monitoring, and enforcing the terms of such agreements as compared with internationalization through a fully owned subsidiary. It is notable that the first outlets opened by McDonald's in the United Kingdom were directly managed rather than franchised. The primary reason was that given British traditions of poor service and indifferent cuisine, direct management avoided the difficulties of monitoring and guiding British franchisees.

Issues of transaction costs are fundamental to the choices between alternative market entry modes. Barriers to exporting in the form of transport fees and tariffs are forms of transaction costs; other costs include exchange rate risk and information costs. Transaction cost analysis has been central to theories of the existence of multinational corporations. In the absence of transaction costs in the markets either for goods or for resources, companies exploit overseas markets either by exporting their goods and services or by selling the use of their resources to local firms in the overseas markets.[15] Thus, multinationals tend to predominate in industries where:

- firm-specific intangible resources such as brands and technology are important (transaction costs in licensing the use of these resources favor direct investment);

- exporting is subject to transaction costs (e.g., through tariffs or import restrictions);

- customer preferences are reasonably similar between countries.

Strategy Alternatives for Overseas Production

This analysis has examined alternative strategies for exploring overseas *market* opportunities. The same type of analysis can be performed by analyzing overseas *production* opportunities. A firm can access the resources and capabilities available for producing in an overseas country either by *transactions* (e.g., importing) or by *direct*

---

[15] The role of transactions cost is explained in D. J. Teece, "Transactions Cost Economics and Multinational Enterprise," *Journal of Economic Behavior and Organization* 7 (1986): 21–45. See also "Creatures of Imperfection," in "Multinationals: A Survey," *Economist* (March 27, 1993): 8–10.

investment. Thus, Exxon-Mobil accesses the crude oil production of the North Sea both by importing oil purchased on long-term contracts with Statoil, BP, and other producers, and on spot contracts through the London and Rotterdam oil markets. At the same time, Exxon-Mobil also has production facilities in the North Sea – some of which are wholly owned, and some of which are joint ventures with Shell and other companies. Nike's production of shoes in Asia is entirely through long-term contracts with local production companies.

Multinational companies have traditionally been interested in overseas production for two main reasons: to access raw materials and cheap labor, and to provide local production to overseas markets. Increasingly, however, direct investment by multinational firms is driven not only by the quest for overseas markets, raw materials, and lower-cost labor, but also by the desire to access technology. Kenichi Ohmae's view that multinational firms need to be based in all three of the world's leading industrial centers – North America, Japan, and Europe – in order to be "where the action is" is supported by evidence that a key role of the foreign subsidiaries of multinational corporations is gaining access to locally available technological knowledge.[16]

International Alliances and Joint Ventures

During the last decade and a half, one of the most striking features of the development of international business has been the upsurge in the numbers of joint ventures and other forms of strategic alliance across national borders. Consider for example the US and Japanese automobile companies: despite the intense competition between them – which extends from the marketplace into government policies and international relations – there has been a remarkable growth in collaborative arrangements between them. Figure 14.6 shows GM's network of alliances with other automakers.

The traditional reason for cross-border alliances and joint ventures was the desire by multinational companies to access the market knowledge and distribution capabilities of a local company, together with the desire by local companies to access the technology, brands, and product development of the multinationals. Such arrangements were supported by the policies of the host government in China, India, and other countries, where foreign companies were obliged to take a local partner. In technology-based industries – computers, semiconductors, telecom equipment, pharmaceuticals, and aerospace – the rapid growth of international collaboration reflects companies' desire to access other companies' different technological capabilities. Local partners can also facilitate the rapid global rollout of new products and technologies.

The success of international joint ventures and other forms of strategic alliance has been mixed. There are plenty of examples of international joint ventures that

---

[16] Kenichi Ohmae, *Triad Power: The Coming Shape of Global Competition* (New York: Free Press, 1985); Paul Almeida, "Knowledge Sourcing by Foreign Multinationals: Patent Citation Analysis in the US Semiconductor Industry," *Strategic Management Journal* 17, Winter special issue (1996): 155–65.

FIGURE 14.6 General Motors: alliances with competitors

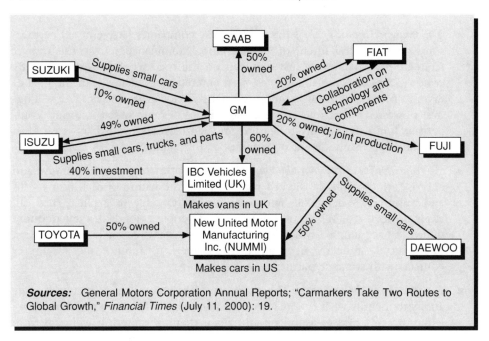

Sources: General Motors Corporation Annual Reports; "Carmarkers Take Two Routes to Global Growth," *Financial Times* (July 11, 2000): 19.

have been spectacular failures. Joint ventures that share management responsibility are far more likely to fail than those with a dominant parent or with independent management.[17] The greatest problems arise between firms that are also competitors: reconciling cooperation with competition requires a tolerance for ambiguity that is has proved difficult for some North American companies. Achieving a balanced distribution of benefits between alliance partners is a general problem. In alliances between Japanese and western firms, a frequent pattern has been for the western partner to make available its key resources of technology or distribution to its Japanese partner in return for short-term benefits, only to see its Japanese collaborator reemerge as a resurgent competitor.[18] Typically, however, technology flows are two-way: the revival of Xerox Corporation during the 1990s was greatly assisted by the flow of technology, product designs, and management techniques from its Japanese joint venture, Fuji-Xerox.[19]

The effective strategic management of international alliances, argue Hamel, Doz, and Prahalad, depends on a clear recognition that collaboration is competition in a

[17] J. Peter Killing, "How to Make a Global Joint Venture Work," *Harvard Business Review* (May–June 1982): 120–7.
[18] See Robert Reich and Eric Mankin, "Joint Ventures with Japan Give Away our Future," *Harvard Business Review* (March–April 1986).
[19] *Xerox and Fuji Xerox* Case 9-391-156 (Boston: Harvard Business School, 1992).

different form.[20] Though both partners must benefit if the alliance is to continue, sharing benefits depends on three key factors:

- *The strategic intent of the partners.* Japanese companies have entered partnerships with the clear intent of gaining global dominance, and in this respect strategic partnerships are just one step on the road to global expansion. By contrast, western companies have often entered partnerships with the goal of giving up manufacturing to more efficient Japanese producers. The willingness of western companies to yield major items of value added to former competitors limits their ability to learn from their partners and is likely to lead to a cumulative abandonment of activities and capabilities.

- *Appropriability of the contribution.* The ability of each partner to capture and appropriate the skills of the other depends on the nature of each firm's skills and resources. Where skills and resources are tangible or explicit, they can easily be acquired. Where they are tacit and people embodied, they are more difficult to acquire. To avoid the unintended transfer of know-how to partners, Hamel et al. argue the need for a "gatekeeper" to monitor and administer contacts with strategic partners.

- *Receptivity of the company.* The more receptive a company is in terms of its ability to identify what it wants from the partner, to obtain the required knowledge or skills, and to assimilate and adapt them, the more it will gain from the partnership. In management terms, this requires the setting of performance goals for what the partnership is to achieve for the company and managing the relationship to ensure that the company is deriving maximum learning from the collaboration.[21]

MULTINATIONAL STRATEGIES: GLOBALIZATION VERSUS NATIONAL DIFFERENTIATION

So far, we have viewed international expansion, whether by export or by direct investment, as a means by which a company can exploit its competitive advantages not just in its home market but also in foreign markets. However, there is more to internationalization than simply extending the geographical boundaries of a company's market. International scope may also be a source of competitive advantage over nationally based competitors. In this section, we explore whether, and under what conditions, firms that operate on an international basis, either by exporting or by direct investment, are able to gain a competitive advantage over nationally focused firms. If such "global strategies" have potential for creating competitive advantage, in what types of industry are they likely to be most effective? And how should they be designed and deployed in order to maximize their potential?

---

[20] Gary Hamel, Yves Doz, and C. K. Prahalad, "Collaborate with Your Competitors – and Win," *Harvard Business Review* (January–February 1989): 133–9.
[21] Ibid.

The Benefits of a Global Strategy

A global strategy is one that views the world as a single, if segmented, market. Theodore Levitt of Harvard Business School has argued that companies that compete on a national basis are highly vulnerable to companies that compete on a global basis.[22] The superiority of global strategies rests on two assumptions:

- *Globalization of customer preferences.* National and regional preferences are disappearing in the face of the homogenizing forces of technology, communication, and travel. "Everywhere everything gets more and more like everything else as the world's preference structure is relentlessly homogenized," observes Levitt. Nor is this trend restricted to technology-based products such as pharmaceuticals, aircraft, and computers; it is just as prevalent in branded consumer goods such as Coca-Cola, Ralph Lauren menswear, and McDonald's hamburgers.

- *Scale economies.* Firms that produce standardized products for the global market can access scale economies in product development, manufacturing, and marketing that offer efficiency advantages that nationally based competitors cannot match. In automobiles, consumer electronics, investment banking, and many other industries, domestic firms have increasingly lost ground to global competitors.

Pursuing a global strategy does not necessarily imply that a company becomes multinational: indeed, maximizing the benefits of scale economies favors geographically concentrated production and serving world markets through exporting. This was the traditional strategy of Japanese companies in motorcycles, consumer electronics, and office equipment during the 1960s and early 1970s. Conversely, many European and American multinational corporations (MNCs) used *multidomestic* rather than global strategies: each country was served by a fairly autonomous national subsidiary that managed a full range of functional activities. For example, until the late 1970s, each of General Motors' main overseas subsidiaries (Opel in Germany, Vauxhall in Britain, and Holden in Australia) produced its own range of models under its own brand names for its own domestic market. The advantage of this strategy was that it permitted flexibility in relation to local conditions, particularly in allowing differentiation on the basis of local preferences, while avoiding the administrative complexities associated with centralized control from a remote corporate head office.

Levitt's thesis is not that customers are the same the world over – national and regional differences in customer preferences do exist. However, underlying national differences is a commonality of people's goals. When presented with a choice between a lower-priced, globally standardized product and a higher-priced, nationally differentiated alternative, most customers favor the former.

The evidence of the past decade is that national differences in customer preferences continue to exert a powerful influence in most markets: products that are

---

[22] Theodore Levitt, "The Globalization of Markets," *Harvard Business Review* (May–June 1983): 92–102.

designed to meet the needs of the "global customer" often fail to be popular in any market. Ford's first world car, the Mondeo/Contour, is an example of this. Moreover, costs of national differentiation can be surprisingly low if common basic designs and common major components are used. Flexible manufacturing systems have reduced the costs of customizing products to meet the preferences of particular customer groups.

Domestic appliances provide an interesting test of the globalization hypothesis. In washing machines, Levitt pointed to the success of Italian companies' mass-produced standardized products over Hoover's nationally differentiated washing machines. Subsequent analysis has shown that national preferences have remained remarkably durable: French and US washing machines are primarily top loading, elsewhere in Europe they are mainly front loading; the Germans prefer higher spin speeds than the Italians, US machines feature agitators rather than revolving drums, and Japanese machines are small. The result is that some nationally focused companies (such as Hotpoint in the UK) were more profitable than the pioneers of globalization, Electrolux and Whirlpool.[23]

Even the most ardent advocates of globalization must take account of local preferences and customs if they are to be internationally successful. McDonald's Big Mac is a standard global product. But McDonald's also offers McChicken Korma Nan in Britain, CroquMcDo (a grilled ham and cheese sandwich) in France, teriyaki chicken burgers in Japan, noodles in Korea, cappuccino in Italy, and beer in Germany.[24] The key to successful globalization lies in ensuring uniformity in components and activities where important scale economies are present, while catering to cultural and language differences that do not impede scale efficiency. Thus, the 2001 Honda Accord is a global car, but one whose dimensions, accessories, trim, and paintwork are adapted to meet different national preferences. Ultimately, companies must find ways to reconcile the benefits of globalization with the need to address the specifics of local markets in terms of regulation, competition, distribution, and customer preferences – what Sony's former chairman described as "global localization."[25]

Strategic Strength from Global Leverage

The argument so far is that the key competitive advantage derived from a global strategy is cost advantage from scale economies. However, this is not the only benefit of a global strategy. George Yip identifies four major benefits from global market participation:

- Cost reduction (from scale economies, avoiding duplication of facilities, and exploiting differences in factor costs between countries).

---

[23]   Charles Baden Fuller and John Stopford, "Globalization Frustrated," *Strategic Management Journal* 12 (1991): 493–507; "Rough and Tumble Industry," *Financial Times* (July 2, 1997): 13.
[24]   See McDonald's individual country web sites, e.g., www.mcdonalds.com (US), www.mcdonalds.co.uk (UK), www.mcdonalds.fr (France).
[25]   A. Morita, "Global Localization," in *Genryn* (Tokyo: Sony, 1996): Chapter 8.

- Improved quality through exposure to demanding customers and a wide range of competitors.

- Enhanced customer preference through global availability and global recognition.

- Competitive leverage through providing multiple bases for competitive attacks and the potential to use global resources in competitive initiatives within individual countries.[26]

Let's focus on the last of these benefits, the ability to gain competitive leverage from a market position in multiple countries. The key aspect of such leveraging is *cross-subsidization*: using the cash flow from countries where market position is strong to finance competition against nationally focused competitors in other markets. While the classic form of cross-subsidization – predatory pricing – is likely to contravene both GATT antidumping rules and national antitrust laws, cross-subsidization also occurs through heavy advertising, sales promotion, and dealer support.[27]

Faced with aggressive competition from the local subsidiary of a foreign MNC, the domestic competitor is in a weak position: it has no overseas revenues to finance aggressive competition in its home market. Such was the position US television manufacturers faced against strong Japanese competition in the 1970s. The most effective response to competition in one's home market may be to retaliate in the foreign MNC's own home market. Thus, when Kodak was attacked by Fuji in the US market – an attack that was symbolized by Fuji's sponsorship of the 1984 Olympic Games in Los Angeles – Kodak responded by attacking Fuji in Japan.[28] To effectively exploit such opportunities for national leveraging, some overall global coordination of competitive strategies in individual national markets is required.

MNCs are increasingly recognizing the advantages of strong market positions in the world's largest economies. During the 1990s, European and Japanese companies scrambled to establish positions within the United States. Companies such as British Petroleum, Siemens, Thomson, Sony, ICI, and Unilever all made large US acquisitions, while Japanese banks and auto companies built US subsidiaries from scratch. Similarly, US companies (especially in financial services) have been developing their market positions in Europe and Asia. The head of McKinsey & Co.'s Tokyo office, Kenichi Ohmae, argues the case for *triad power* – that the need to access technology, developing customer preferences, and scale economies requires global players to become true insiders within all of the world's major markets: the United States, Europe, and Japan.[29]

---

[26]   G. S. Yip, *Total Global Strategy: Managing for Worldwide Competitive Advantage* (Englewood Cliffs, NJ: Prentice Hall, 1995).
[27]   Gary Hamel and C. K. Prahalad, "Do You Really Have a Global Strategy?," *Harvard Business Review* (July–August 1985): 139–48.
[28]   R. C. Christopher, *Second to None: American Companies in Japan* (New York: Crown, 1986).
[29]   Kenichi Ohmae, *Triad Power: The Coming Shape of Global Competition* (New York: Free Press, 1985).

FIGURE 14.7 The development of the multinational corporation: alternative parent–subsidiaries relations

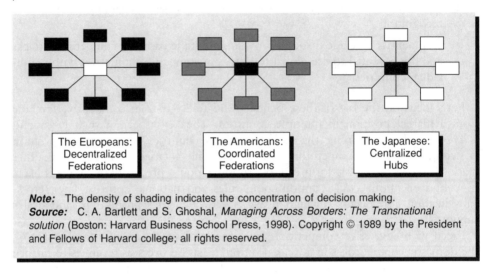

The Europeans:
Decentralized
Federations

The Americans:
Coordinated
Federations

The Japanese:
Centralized
Hubs

Note: The density of shading indicates the concentration of decision making.
Source: C. A. Bartlett and S. Ghoshal, *Managing Across Borders: The Transnational solution* (Boston: Harvard Business School Press, 1998). Copyright © 1989 by the President and Fellows of Harvard college; all rights reserved.

STRATEGY AND ORGANIZATION WITHIN THE MULTINATIONAL CORPORATION

The Evolution of Multinational Strategies and Structures

Balancing the benefits of globalization against those of adaptation to national market conditions is a central issue not only for the strategy of multinational firms but also for their organizational structures. As we have already observed, strategy and structure are not easily changed in the short or medium term and the strategy–structure configurations adopted by today's MNCs tend to reflect the choices made by the companies at the time of their international expansion. Because of their size and international spread, MNCs are likely to find fundamental changes in their organizational structure especially difficult: once an international distribution of functions, operations, and decision-making authority has been determined, reorganization can be difficult and costly, particularly when host governments become involved. The result is that early choices with regard to strategy and structure have a lasting impact on the development of organizational capability.

Bartlett and Ghoshal identify three phases in the development of MNCs, each associated with a different choice with regard to globalization/centralization versus national differentiation/decentralization. The allocation of decision making between the parent company and overseas subsidiaries associated with each phase is shown in Figure 14.7.

Pre World War I: The Era of the European Multinationals

During the early decades of the twentieth century, European multinationals – companies such as Unilever, Royal Dutch/Shell, ICI, and Philips – were pioneers of multinational expansion. These companies are described by Bartlett and Ghoshal as *multinational federations*: each national subsidiary was permitted a high degree of operational independence from the parent company, undertaking its own product development, manufacturing, and marketing.[30] The "hands-off" approach of the corporate head office to its overseas subsidiaries was a response to conditions at the time of internationalization: international transportation and communication were slow, costly, and unreliable, and national markets were highly differentiated. Parent company control of the subsidiary involved the appointment of senior managers to subsidiaries, the authorization of major capital expenditures, and the flow of dividends from subsidiary to parent.

Post World War II: The Era of the American Multinationals

The emergence of the United States as the world's dominant industrial nation at the end of World War II was followed by two decades during which companies such as GM, Ford, IBM, Coca-Cola, Caterpillar, Gillette, and Procter & Gamble became clear international leaders in their respective industries. Although the subsidiaries of these US multinationals typically operated with a high degree of autonomy in terms of product introduction, manufacturing, and marketing, the US parent companies occupied a dominant position within the groups. Because the United States was the largest and most affluent market in the world, the US base acted as the source of new products and process technology for the companies. The primary competitive advantage of overseas national subsidiaries was their ability to utilize new products, process technology, and marketing and manufacturing know-how developed in the United States.

The 1970s and 1980s: The Japanese Challenge

During the 1970s, Japanese companies emerged as leading global players across a number of manufacturing industries, from steel and shipbuilding to electronics and automobiles. A distinguishing feature of the Japanese multinationals was their pursuit of global strategies from centralized domestic bases. Companies like Honda, Toyota, Matsushita, and NEC concentrated R&D and manufacturing in Japan, while overseas subsidiaries were initially for sales, distribution, and customer support. By building plants of unprecedented scale to service growing world demand, Japanese companies were able to exploit substantial scale and experience advantages.

---

[30] Christopher A. Bartlett and Sumantra Ghoshal, *Managing Across Borders: The Transnational Solution*, 2nd edn (Boston: Harvard Business School Press, 1998).

EXHIBIT 14.1 Matching Multinational Strategy to Industry Characteristics

Consumer Electronics

During the 1980s, Matsushita was highly globally integrated, Philips was the most multinational in terms of international spread and responsiveness of national subsidiaries to local requirements, whereas GE was primarily US-based and oriented toward the requirements of the North American market. During the 1980s, customer preferences for consumer electronic products were highly uniform across countries, and competitive advantage was strongly determined by the ability of companies to access global economies in product development and manufacturing, and coordinate the global marketing of new products and new models. By the end of the 1980s, Matsushita was the clear winner, Philips was still hanging on (despite dismal profitability), and GE had exited from the industry.

Branded, Packaged Consumer Goods

In branded, packaged consumer goods, national differences remained strong during the 1980s. Unilever, with its locally responsive multinational spread, and Procter & Gamble, despite its strong US and European bases, increased their global leadership. Meanwhile Kao, the leading Japanese soaps and personal hygiene products supplier, largely failed in its attempts to penetrate international markets.

Telecommunications Equipment

In contrast to electronics and branded, packaged consumer goods, telecommunications equipment is subject to substantial global scale economies in R&D and manufacturing, *and* requires responsiveness to the specific requirements of national telecommunication companies. ITT, the most international of the major players, was increasingly unable to achieve the integration necessary to leverage its global position. NEC, despite its technological capabilities and dominant position in Japan, has so far failed to develop a strong position in Europe or North America. One of the most successful companies has been Ericsson, which, despite its small domestic market, has effectively combined global integration with national responsiveness (see Figure 14.8).

FIGURE 14.8

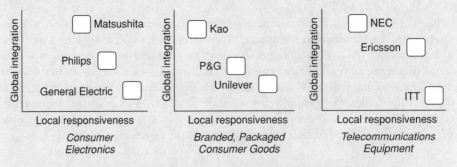

Source: Adapted from: C. A. Bartlett and S. Ghoshal, *Managing Across Borders: The Transnational solution* (Boston: Harvard Business School Press, 1989) and S. Ghoshal, Presentation at IAFE, Castelgandolfo, 1990.

Matching Global Strategies and Structures to Industry Conditions

Although global preeminence in manufacturing industries passed from European to American to Japanese companies between 1920 and 1980, it is not possible to point to any particular strategy/structure combination as uniquely successful for MNCs. The strength of European multinationals was their adaptation to the conditions and requirements of individual national markets. The strength of the US multinationals was their ability to transfer technology and proven new products from their domestic strongholds to their national subsidiaries. That of the Japanese global corporations was the efficiency advantages derived from global integration.

The relative merits of each configuration depend on market and competitive conditions – and hence the key success factors – in different industries. In semi-conductors, electronics, and motorcycles, the importance of scale economies and the lack of national differences in customer requirements underscore the benefits of global strategies and structures. Where scale economies are more modest relative to the size of national markets and where national market differences are important – such as in processed foods, recorded music, beer, children's clothing, and furniture – responsiveness to national customer preferences takes precedence. In a number of industries, there are considerable benefits from global integration, and also the need to respond to differentiated national requirements. Capital- and technology-intensive products (such as telecommunications equipment, military hardware, and power-generating equipment) supplied to public authorities in different countries are typical examples. Exhibit 14.1 shows how different strategy/structure configurations have had different success in three different industry environments.

Emergence of the "Transnational Corporation"

During the 1990s, multinational firms tried to reconcile the scale economies of global integration with the differentiation benefits of national adaptation. Increased competitive pressure forced companies to seek cost efficiency through globally integrating their manufacturing and technology development. At the same time, the resilience of national market differences and the need for swift response to local circumstances has required greater decentralization. Accelerating technological change further exacerbates these contradictory forces: despite the cost and "critical mass" benefits of centralizing research and new product development, innovation occurs at multiple locations within the MNC and requires nurturing of creativity and initiative throughout the organization. A key tradeoff is the decentralization conducive to generating innovation, and the global centralization needed to efficiently exploit these innovations – the familiar *exploration versus exploitation* dilemma once again. Thus, Philips, with its decentralized, nationally responsive organization structure, was extremely successful in encouraging company-wide innovation. In its TV business, its Canadian subsidiary developed its first color TV, its Australian subsidiary developed its first stereo sound TV, and its British subsidiary developed teletext TVs. However, lack of global

FIGURE 14.9   The transnational corporation

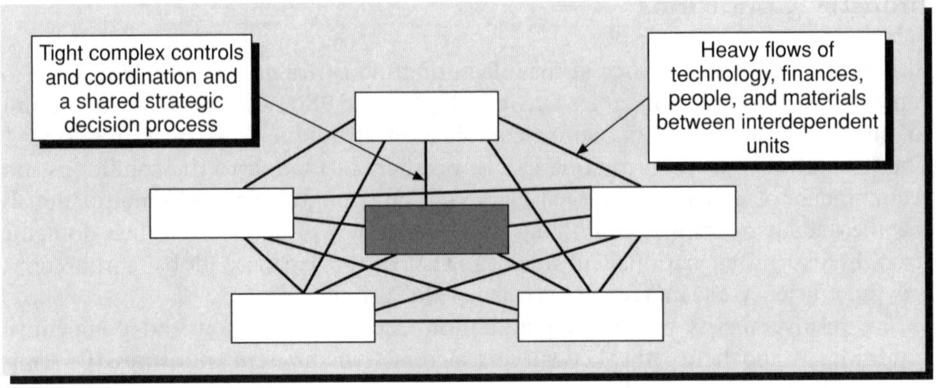

integration has constrained its ability successfully to exploit its innovation on a global scale. During the 1980s and 1990s, Philips was on the losing side of a number of key standards battles: its V2000 VCR system lost out to Matsushita's VHS system and its digital audio tape lost out to other digital recording formats.

Developing the organizational capability to pursue both responsiveness to national markets and global coordination simultaneously requires, according to Christopher Bartlett, "a very different kind of internal management process than existed in the relatively simple multinational or global organizations. This is the 'transnational organization.'"[31] The distinguishing characteristic of the *transnational* is that it becomes an integrated network of distributed and interdependent resource and capabilities (see Figure 14.9). Features of the transnational corporation include the following:

- Each national unit is a source of ideas, skills, and capabilities that can be harnessed for the benefit of the total organization.

- National units achieve global scale economies by designating them the company's world source for a particular product, component, or activity.

- The center must establish a new, highly complex managing role that coordinates relationships among units but does so in a highly flexible way. The key is to focus less on managing activities directly and more on creating an organizational context that is conducive to the coordination and resolution of differences. Creating the right organizational context involves "establishing clear corporate objectives, developing managers with broadly based perspectives and relationships, and fostering supportive organizational norms and values."[32]

---

[31]   Christopher Bartlett, "Building and Managing the Transnational: The New Organizational Challenge," in Michael E. Porter (ed.), *Competition in Global Industries* (Boston: Harvard Business School Press, 1986): 377.
[32]   Ibid.: 388.

The transnational form is more of a direction of development than a clear organizational form. It represents a convergence of the different strategy configurations of MNCs. Thus, traditional "decentralized federations" such as Philips and Royal Dutch/Shell have reorganized to achieve greater integration within their far-flung empires of national subsidiaries, whereas Japanese global corporations such as Toyota and Matsushita are drastically reducing the role of their Japanese headquarters and increasing the roles of their national subsidiaries. Meanwhile, American multinationals such as Ford and GM are moving in two directions: while they reduce the role of their US bases they are simultaneously increasing integration among their different national subsidiaries.

A critical task for the top managers of MNCs is to establish structures and systems that allow local adaptation and initiative while maintaining the close linkages that diffuse innovations and best practices and integrate the knowledge generated in different locations. Where overseas subsidiaries have the autonomy and the leadership to take the initiative in product development and new investment proposals, they can make an important contribution to the competitive advantage of the MNC.[33] The distinctive capabilities that individual subsidiaries develop are likely to be strongly influenced by the national resources and markets within their host countries. Among multinational semiconductor companies, the development of capabilities reflect the international patterns of competitive advantage in customer industries – European subsidiaries have developed strong capabilities in integrated circuits for digital wireless communication, Japanese subsidiaries have developed strength in the microprocessors and memory chips required by the consumer electronics industry, US subsidiaries have been lead developers of computers chips. Firms need to establish the organizational structures and management systems that permit decentralization while creating the tight linkages to diffuse innovations and best practices and integrate the different types of knowledge generated in different locations.[34]

Exhibit 14.2 discusses the move toward the integrated, global network form at Ford and Unilever.

EXHIBIT 14.2 Building the Transnational Corporation: Unilever and Ford

Unilever

Unilever was formed in 1930 from the merger of the Dutch company Margarine Unie, and the British soap company Lever Brothers. Over the following seven decades, the company evolved through a process of trial and error into a global food, cleaning products, and toiletries group. A key aspect of this evolution was the changing relationship between the parent company and the national subsidiaries. During the 1940s and 1950s, each national subsidiary became locally managed with a high degree of autonomy. This decentralization was balanced by heavy investment in management education and development designed not only to train managers, but also to create a common culture. In 1955, the Four Acres management training center

---

[33] J. Birkinshaw, N. Hood and S. Jonsson, "Building Firm-specific Advantages in Multinational Corporations: The Role of Subsidiary Initiative," *Strategic Management Journal* 19 (1998): 221–42.
[34] Jay R. Galbraith, *Designing the Global Corporation* (San Francisco: Jossey-Bass, 2000).

EXHIBIT 14.2 *(cont'd)*

near London was opened. Unilever seeks the best and brightest university graduates who are trained in groups of 25 to 30 for similar managerial positions. This shared experience creates an informal network of equals who continue to meet and exchange information and ideas across different companies and countries. Coherence and coordination is further enhanced by an extensive system of attachments whereby a manager is placed for a short or long period of time at the head office or in another subsidiary. These cross-postings help build managers' worldwide informal networks, and establish unity and a common sense of purpose across national cultures. Managers' personal networks are an important mechanism for the transfer of ideas.

Unilever is organized primarily on a geographical basis with subsidiaries in each country responsible for a particular business. Thus, in Britain, Lever Brothers Ltd supplies soaps and household detergents, Walls Ice Cream Ltd supplies ice cream, and Birds Eye Foods Ltd produces and distributes frozen foods. In addition there are worldwide product groups. Thus, food products are divided into five strategic groups: edible fats, ice cream, beverages, meals and meal components, and professional markets. The balance between centralized requirements and local adaptability varies by function and product. Thus, in the food category there are *global fast foods* (hamburgers, fried chicken, soft drinks), *international foods* (Indian, Chinese, and Italian foods sold in many national markets), and *national foods* (steak and kidney pies in Britain).

According to CEO Floris Maljers, flexibility in a matrix organization is essential for it to operate as a transnational: "I like to use an analogy with a dance called the quadrille. This is an old-fashioned dance in which four people change places regularly. This is also how a good matrix should work, with sometimes the regional partner, sometimes the product partner, sometimes the functional partner, and sometimes the labor-relations partner taking the lead. Flexibility rather than hierarchy should always be a transnational's motto – today and in the future."

Ford

In 1970, Ford was an archetypal US multinational with a dominant North American core and more-or-less stand-alone subsidiaries in Britain, Germany, Australia, and elsewhere, each of which designed, manufactured, and marketed its own line of autos. For example, in Britain, Ford's most popular car was the British-made Cortina, in Germany it was the German-built Taunus.

The quest for scale economies in engineering and design and component manufacture encouraged increasing international integration. This began with the formation of Ford of Europe, and continued with the consolidation and integration of new product development and manufacturing. Small car design was located primarily in Ford of Europe and in Mazda in Japan; large car design was centered in Dearborn. Ford's smallest car, the Festiva/Fiesta, is manufactured in South Korea and Spain; its Escort is manufactured in Michigan, Mexico, Britain, and Germany; the Mercury Capri is made in Australia. Similar global specialization occurred in engines and other major subassemblies.

Under chairman Alex Trotman, the Ford 2000 initiative aimed at greatly increasing the extent of international integration. The Mondeo/Contour was Ford's first serious attempt at developing a world car. The primary challenge of Ford 2000 was to develop global models of automobile faster and at a much lower cost than the $6 billion that the Mondeo/Contour had cost.

Sources: Floris A. Maljers, "Inside Unilever: The Evolving Transnational Company," *Harvard Business Review* (September–October 1992): 46–51; Maryann Keller, *Collision: GM, Toyota, Volkswagen and the Race to Own the 21st Century* (New York: Doubleday, 1993); Ford Motor Company Annual Reports.

The Cultural Dimension

Designing multinational structures that take account of different national environments is not simply about adapting to local market differences. Organizational structures and management systems also need to be consistent with national cultures. Any of the problems encountered in international expansion have arisen from imposing structures and management systems on overseas subsidiaries that were developed within the home country. When Lincoln Electric expanded overseas in the late 1980s, the system of individual compensation based on piecework that had driven Lincoln's exceptional performance within the US was a source of server problems in Europe, Asia, and Latin America, where society was less individualist and less tolerant to individual differences in compensation levels.[35] A critical issue in cross-border mergers has been reconciling the different compensation systems of the merging companies. With the BP-Amoco merger and the Daimler Benz-Chrysler merger, some of the biggest integration problems were the result of the much higher levels of salary and bonus received by US executives compared to their European counterparts.

Research into national culture has attempted to classify national cultures according to a few characteristics. Geert Hofstede has used two cultural dimensions: *individualist versus collectivist* and *egalitarian versus hierarchical*. Countries with high levels of both individualism and egalitarianism include the US and Australia. Countries with high levels of collectivism and acceptance of hierarchy include India, China, and Venezuela. Countries with high levels of both individualism and hierarchy include France and South Africa, while Costa Rica combines collectivism with egalitarianism.[36]

SUMMARY

Moving from a national to an international business environment represents a quantum leap in complexity. In an international environment, a firm's potential for competitive advantage is determined, not just by its own resources and capabilities, but also by the conditions of the national environment in which it operates, including input prices, exchange rates, and a host of other factors. The extent to which a firm is positioned in a single or multiple national markets also influences its competitive position.

Our approach in this chapter to simplify the complexities of international strategy by applying the same basic tools of strategy analysis that we developed in earlier chapters. For example, in analyzing international expansion, the critical issue in determining whether a firm should enter an overseas market is an analysis of the profit implication of such an entry. This requires an analysis

[35]   *Lincoln Electric: Venturing Abroad*, Case Number 9-398-095 (Boston: Harvard Business School, 1998).
[36]   G. H. Hofstede, *Cultures and Organizations: Software of the Mind* (New York: McGraw-Hill, 1997).

of (a) the attractiveness of the overseas market using the familiar tools of industry analysis; and (b) the potential of the firm to establish competitive advantage in that overseas market, which requires consideration of whether the firm can transfer its resources and capabilities from its home base to that overseas market, and whether these resources and capabilities can yield a competitive advantage in the same way as they did at home.

However, establishing the potential for a firm to create value from internationalization is only a beginning. Subsequent analysis needs to design an international strategy: Do we enter an overseas market by exporting, licensing, or direct investment? If the latter, should we set up a wholly owned subsidiary or a joint venture? Once the strategy has been established, then a suitable organizational structure needs to be designed.

The fact that so many companies that have been outstandingly successful in their home market have failed so miserably in their overseas expansion demonstrates the complexity of international management. In some cases, the companies have failed to recognize that the resources and capabilities that underpinned their competitive advantages in their home market could not be readily transferred or replicated in overseas markets. In others, the problems were in designing the structures and systems that could effectively implement the international strategy.

As the lessons of success and failure from international business become recognized and distilled into better theories and analytical frameworks, so we advance our understanding of how to design and implement strategies for competing globally. We are at the stage where we recognize the issues and the key determinants of competitive advantage in an international environment. However, there is much that we do not fully understand. Designing strategies and organizational structures that can reconcile critical tradeoffs between global scale economies versus local differentiation, decentralized learning and innovation versus worldwide diffusion and replication, and localized flexibilities versus international standardization remain key challenges for senior managers.

15

Diversification Strategy

Telephones, hotels, insurance – it's all the same. If you know the numbers inside out, you know the company inside out.
    —*Harold Sydney Geneen, Chairman of ITT, 1959–78, and instigator of 275 company takeovers*

OUTLINE

- INTRODUCTION AND OBJECTIVES
- TRENDS IN DIVERSIFICATION OVER TIME
  - Postwar Diversification
  - Factors Driving Diversification
  - Refocusing during the 1980s and 1990s
  - Factors that Cause Refocusing
- MOTIVES FOR DIVERSIFICATION
  - Growth
  - Risk Reduction
  - Profitability
- COMPETITIVE ADVANTAGE FROM DIVERSIFICATION
  - Market Power
  - Economies of Scope
  - Economies from Internalizing Transactions
  - The Diversified Firm as an Internal Market
  - Information Advantages of the Diversified Corporation
- DIVERSIFICATION AND PERFORMANCE
  - The Findings of Empirical Research
  - The Meaning of Relatedness in Diversification
- SUMMARY

INTRODUCTION AND OBJECTIVES

The decision over the businesses in which the firm is to operate is fundamental to its strategy and its very identity. It is guided by the firm's mission statement. Xerox defines itself as "The Document Company," Eastman Kodak as a "picture company," while Enron "operates networks throughout the world to develop and enhance energy and broadband communication services," and "The Philip Morris family of companies is the largest and most profitable producer and marketer of consumer packaged goods in the world." These statements of identity provide the context and boundaries that guide choices over the businesses in which the companies will participate.

A company's conceptualization of its business scope may change radically over time. Many companies have dramatically reduced their range of business interests through the years. Hanson, the Anglo-American conglomerate, spun off most of its main subsidiaries – Imperial Tobacco, Millennium Chemicals, Peabody Coal – leaving Hanson plc as a comparatively specialized supplier of building materials. Other companies have moved in the opposite direction. Microsoft began as a supplier of microcomputer operating software, expanded into application and networking software, and is now emerging as a broad-based supplier of software, information services, and entertainment. Tyco International began as a semiconductor and applied material sciences company but grew into a highly diversified manufacturing and service company, with 650 profit centers in four major areas: electrical and electronic components, healthcare and specialty products, fire and security services, and flow control.

Faced with radical technological and regulatory change, a company may be forced continually to redefine its business scope. Consider AT&T's struggle to define its corporate strategy in the turbulent environment of telecommunications. Until 1984, AT&T was an integrated supplier of local and long-distance telephone services, as well as being the largest producer of telecom equipment in the US.

- After the 1984 divestiture, AT&T was reduced to its long-distance telephone business and a technology and equipment company (AT&T Network Solutions/Bell Labs).

- Between 1991 and 1994, AT&T expanded into computer and wireless communication with the acquisitions of NCR and McCaw Cellular.

- In 1995 AT&T spun off its computer business (NCR) and its hardware activities (as Lucent Technologies) to refocus on its core communications services company, which it extended into cable TV with the acquisition of TCI.

- In January 2001, AT&T was in the process of splitting into four separate companies: AT&T Wireless (wireless telecommunication),

AT&T Broadband (cable TV and broadband services), AT&T Business (telecommunications and networking), and AT&T Consumer (consumer communications and marketing).

How do companies determine the range of industries in which they should participate? At first glance, diversification decisions appear impossibly complex:

- Which is better: to remain as a clearly focused, specialized company such as Coca-Cola, or – like PepsiCo – to exploit growth opportunities and business complementarities by diversifying from soft drinks into snack foods (FritoLay), fruit juices (Tropicana), and breakfast cereals and other packaged foods (Quaker Oats)?[1]

- How does Richard Branson decide whether his Virgin Group should add wireless communications and auto retailing to his sprawling Virgin empire that extends from airlines to financial services?

- How can Westinghouse Electrical (now renamed CBS) weigh the merits of transforming itself from a manufacturer of turbines and power equipment into a TV and radio broadcaster?

In practice, we make these types of decision every day in our personal lives. If my car doesn't start in the morning, should I try to fix it myself or have it towed directly to the garage? There are two considerations. First, is repairing a car an attractive activity to undertake? If the garage charges $60 an hour, but I can earn $400 an hour consulting, then car repair is not attractive to me. Second, am I any good at car repair? If I am likely to take twice as long as a skilled mechanic, then I possess no competitive advantage in car repair.

Diversification decisions by firms involve the same two issues:

- How attractive is the industry to be entered?

- Can the firm establish a competitive advantage within the new industry?

These are the very same factors we identified in Chapter 1 (see Figure 1.3) as determining a firm's profit potential. Hence, no new analytic framework is needed for appraising diversification decisions: diversification may be justified either by the superior profit potential of the industry to be entered, or by the ability of the firm to create competitive advantage in the new industry. The first issue draws on the industry analysis developed in Chapter 3; the second draws on the analysis of competitive advantage developed in Chapters 5 through 8.

---

[1] "Pepsico to Acquire the Quaker Oats Company," Pepsico Inc. Press Release. December 4, 2000 (www.pepsico.com).

Our primary focus is on the latter question: Under what conditions does operating multiple businesses assist a firm in gaining a competitive advantage in each? This leads into exploring linkages between different businesses within the diversified firm, what has often been referred to as "synergy."

By the time you have completed this chapter, you will be able to:

■ Appreciate the factors that have determined diversification of companies in the past and the recent trend toward "refocusing."

■ Identify the conditions under which diversification creates value for shareholders.

■ Evaluate the potential for creating value across businesses by sharing and transferring resources and capabilities within the diversified firm.

■ Appraise the conditions that determine whether diversification or inter-firm collaboration is more effective in exploiting the linkages between different businesses.

■ Recognize the organizational and managerial issues to which diversification gives rise and why diversification so often fails to realize its anticipated benefits.

TRENDS IN DIVERSIFICATION OVER TIME

As a background to our analysis of diversification decisions, let's begin by examining the factors that have influenced diversification strategies in the past.

Postwar Diversification

In Chapter 13, we saw how the development of the modern corporation since the mid-nineteenth century had involved an expansion in their geographical, vertical, and product scope. During the period 1950 to 1980, diversification – the expansion of companies across different product markets – was an especially important source of corporate growth. Research at the Harvard Business School documented the diversification trend among large US corporations.[2] Over time, the number of single-business companies among the ranks of the Fortune 500 declined steadily, whereas the most diversified companies – both related business and unrelated

---

[2] A. D. Chandler Jr., *Strategy and Structure: Chapters in the History of the Industrial Enterprise* (Cambridge, MA: MIT Press, 1962); L. Wrigley, *Divisional Autonomy and Diversification*, doctoral dissertation (Boston, Harvard Business School, 1970); R. P. Rumelt, *Strategy, Structure and Economic Performance* (Cambridge, MA: Harvard University Press, 1974).

TABLE 15.1   Changes in the Diversification Strategies of the Fortune 500, 1949–74

	1949 %	1954 %	1959 %	1964 %	1969 %	1974 %
Single-business companies	42.0	34.1	22.8	21.5	14.8	14.4
Vertically integrated companies	12.8	12.2	12.5	14.0	12.3	12.4
Dominant-business companies	15.4	17.4	18.4	18.4	12.8	10.2
Related-business companies	25.7	31.6	38.6	37.3	41.4	42.3
Unrelated-business companies	4.1	4.7	7.3	8.7	18.7	20.7
	100.0	100.0	100.0	100.0	100.0	100.0

Note: Single-business companies have more than 95 percent of their sales within their main business. Vertically integrated companies have more than 70 percent of their sales in vertically related businesses. Dominant-business companies have between 70 and 95 percent of their sales within their main business. Related-business companies have more than 70 percent of their sales in businesses that are related to one another. Unrelated-business companies have less than 70 percent of their sales in related businesses.
Source: Richard P. Rumelt, "Diversification Strategy and Profitability," *Strategic Management Journal* 3 (1982): 359–70.

business – increased in number (see Table 15.1). Similar trends occurred in Europe (see Table 15.2) and also in Japan.[3] The 1960s and 1970s saw the height of the diversification boom with a flurry of mergers and acquisitions between unrelated companies and the emergence of a new form of corporate entity – the conglomerate – represented in the US by ITT and Allied-Signal, and in the UK by Slater-Walker and BTR.

Factors Driving Diversification

The diversification trend of the 1960s and 1970s was a consequence of several factors. Chapter 13 pointed to the developments in management techniques and organizational forms that reduced the costs of internal administration compared to the transaction costs of markets. Foremost among these developments was the multi-divisional structure, which allowed companies to add divisions without overloading corporate management. During the 1950s and 1960s, multidivisional structures spread rapidly across North America and Europe, assisted by the efforts of McKinsey & Co. and other management consultants in reorganizing large corporations. The rapid advancement of the "science of management" propagated the view that the essence of management was not the deployment of industry-specific, experiential knowledge, but the application of the tools and principles of general management. The universality of the principles of management implied that professional managers could run

[3] H. Itami, T. Kagono, H. Yoshihara, and S. Sakuma, "Diversification Strategies and Economic Performance," *Japanese Economic Studies* 11, no. 1 (1982): 78–110.

TABLE 15.2 Changes in the Diversification Strategies of Large European Companies, 1950–93

	1950 %	1960 %	1970 %	1983 %	1993 %
France					
Single business	45	35	20	24	20
Dominant business	18	22	27	11	15
Related business	31	36	41	53	52
Unrelated business	5	5	9	12	14
Germany					
Single business	37	27	27	18	13
Dominant business	22	24	15	17	8
Related business	31	38	38	40	48
Unrelated business	9	11	19	25	32
UK					
Single business	24	18	6	7	5
Dominant business	50	36	32	16	10
Related business	27	48	57	67	62
Unrelated business	–	–	6	11	24

Notes:
1. Some column totals do not equal 100 due to rounding.
2. The categorization of firms by strategies is consistent for each country over time, but is not consistent between countries.

Sources: R. Whittington, M. Mayer, and F. Curto, "Chandlerism in Post-war Europe: Strategic and Structural Change in France, Germany and the UK, 1950–1993," *Industrial and Corporate Change* 8 (1999): 519–50. Updating earlier research by data D. Channon, *The Strategy and Structure of British Enterprise* (Cambridge: Harvard University Press, 1973) and G. Dyas and H. Thanheiser, *The Emerging European Enterprise* (London: Macmillan, 1976).

widely diversified corporations through the application of a common set of financial controls, capital appraisal systems, human resource management policies, and decision rules. The development of the concepts and techniques of corporate strategy during the late 1960s and early 1970s added further weight to the view that professional managers were not constrained by industry boundaries. The simple logic that had driven the opportunistic growth of conglomerates was refined into a more sophisticated analysis of corporate strategy decisions concerning industry choice and competitive positioning. New techniques of corporate strategy – including portfolio-planning matrices – facilitated performance analysis and resource allocation across multiple businesses by providing top management with a "helicopter view" of the company.[4]

Corporate motives were also important. From the 1950s into the early 1980s, large corporations in North America, Europe, and Japan were driven more by a quest for

---

[4] Michael Goold and Kathleen Luchs, "Why Diversify? Four Decades of Management Thinking," *Academy of Management Executive* 7, no. 3 (August 1993): 7–25.

growth than by the desire to maximize profitability. In the benign economic environment of the 1950s and 1960s, earning returns in excess of the cost of capital was
easy and shareholders were quiescent. Under these circumstances, many corporate
CEOs became rampant empire builders, whose bold, diversifying acquisitions were
seldom matched by their strategic logic.

Refocusing during the 1980s and 1990s

The last two decades of the century saw a sharp reversal in the trend toward diversification. In Britain, companies that had diversified most extensively during previous years
became less diversified during the late 1970s and early 1980s.[5] Between 1980 and
1990, the average index of diversification for the Fortune 500 declined from 1.00 to
0.67.[6] Among US companies, unprofitable "non-core" businesses were increasingly
being divested during the later 1980s, and a number of diversified companies fell prey
to leveraged buyouts.[7] Despite the fact that acquisition activity was extremely heavy
during the 1980s – some $1.3 trillion in assets were acquired, including 113 members
of the Fortune 500 – only 4.5 percent of acquisitions during the 1980s represented
unrelated diversification.[8] Moreover, acquisitions by the Fortune 500 were outnumbered
by dispositions. Diversified companies have tended to divest unrelated businesses,
then restructure around fewer, more closely related businesses.[9]

Factors that Cause Refocusing

Increased industrial specialization by companies is the result of three principal factors:
management's emphasis on shareholder value rather than growth, increased turbulence
in the business environment, and new ideas about corporate strategy and the nature
of the firm.

Emphasis on Shareholder Value

The forces causing companies to narrow their corporate scope were reviewed in
Chapter 13. In relation to product scope, the overwhelmingly important factor

---

[5] A. P. Jammine, *Product Diversification, International Expansion and Performance: A Study of Strategic
Risk Management in U.K. Manufacturing*, doctoral dissertation (London Business School, 1984).
[6] G. F. Davis, K. A. Diekman, and C. F. Tinsley, "The Decline and Fall of the Conglomerate Firm in the
1980s: A Study in the De-Institutionalization of an Organizational Form" (Evanston, IL: Northwestern
University, September 1993).
[7] For a discussion of restructuring of diversified companies, see R. E. Hoskisson and M. A. Hitt,
Downscoping: How to Tame the Diversified Firm (New York: Oxford University Press, 1994).
[8] A. Shleifer and R. W. Vishny, "The Takeover Wave of the 1980s," *Science* 248 (July–September 1990):
747–9.
[9] J. R. Williams, B. L. Paez, and L. Sanders, "Conglomerates Revisited," *Strategic Management Journal*
9 (1988): 403–14.

driving the retreat from diversification and the refocusing around core businesses was the reordering of corporate goals from growth to profitability. The new emphasis on profitability was the result of several factors. The economic downturns and interest-rate spikes of the mid-1970s, the early 1980s, and 1989–90 revealed the inadequate profitability of many large, diversified corporations. A second factor was increased pressure on incumbent management from shareholders and financial markets. Share-holder activism has been led by institutional shareholders, especially by pension funds such as California's Public Employees Retirement System. The result of such pressure has been to increase the influence of independent members of boards of directors and to unseat incumbent management. The increasing insecurity of top management positions is indicated by rising CEO turnover. During 2000, 39 of the top-200 US companies replaced their CEO (up from 23 in 1999). Ousted CEOs included Douglas Ivester at Coca-Cola, Michael Hawley at Gillette, Durk Jager at Procter & Gamble, and Richard Thoman at Xerox.[10]

The surge in leveraged buyouts during the 1980s was a key ingredient in a more active market for corporate control. Where an incumbent management team had destroyed shareholder value, corporate raiders saw the opportunity to use debt financing to mount a takeover bid, and then to oust existing management in favor of a team that would embark on aggressive restructuring. Kohlberg Kravis Roberts' $25 billion takeover of the tobacco and food giant RJR Nabisco in 1989 is the most renowned of these buyouts.[11] The RJR Nabisco buyout demonstrated that even the largest US companies were not safe from acquisition. Since then, diversified companies have voluntarily embarked on spinoffs and breakups, without the need for corporate raiders to get involved. ITT sold off its telecom interests, then split into separate hotel (Sheraton), insurance (Hartford), and automotive businesses. Philips, the Dutch consumer electronics giant, disposed of its domestic appliance division, Polygram music business, Grundig consumer electronics company, and many other "peripheral" businesses. The British chemicals company ICI spun off its Zeneca pharmaceuticals business and sold its bulk chemicals businesses in order to become a specialty chemicals company. As top management has become increasingly appraised in terms of returns to shareholders, so the pressure to reverse earlier diversification has increased. Not only do companies tend to earn lower rates of return in their diversified businesses than in their core businesses, but widely diversified firms have been subject to a "conglomerate discount" – the market valuations of the whole is less than the sum of the parts.

Turbulence and Transaction Costs

The increased turbulence of the business environment may also have caused large, diversified corporations to be less efficient as mechanisms for allocating resources than are specialized companies coordinated by financial and labor markets. Dynamic market conditions expose the sluggishness of the complex corporate planning and capital

---

[10] "The CEO Trap," *Business Week* (December 11, 2000): 44–9.
[11] B. Burrough, *Barbarians at the Gate: The Fall of RJR Nabisco* (New York: Harper & Row, 1990).

budgeting systems of diversified corporations, and overload the decision-making capacity of corporate top management. As a result, the performance of diversified corporations appears to have deteriorated compared to more specialized companies. The shifting balance between the relative efficiencies of large diversified corporations and specialized companies accessing resources through factor markets may also have been influenced by the increasing efficiencies of the markets for finance and labor. The trend toward corporate spinoffs has been influenced by the belief that these businesses could better exploit their growth opportunities by drawing directly on external markets for finance, human resources, and technology.

The "back to basics" trend is certainly strong in North America and western Europe, but is less evident elsewhere in the world. In Asia and Latin America, there is little evidence of any divestment trend among the diversified corporations that continue to dominate their national economies – Samsung and Hyundai in South Korea, Charoen Pokphand in Thailand, Lippo in Indonesia, Keppel Group in Singapore, and Tata in India. The continued dominance of large conglomerates outside of North America, Japan, and western Europe may be the result of transaction costs. Less efficient markets for finance, information, and labor may offer internalization advantages to diversified companies.[12]

Trends in Management Thinking

New ideas about corporate strategy have also influenced patterns of corporate evolution. There is less confidence over the applicability of a common set of management principles and techniques to many different business, and greater emphasis has been given to the role of resources and capabilities as the basis of the competitive advantage. This encourages firms to focus on their major strengths in resources and capabilities and avoid the risks of spreading themselves too thinly. If deploying core resources and capabilities requires diversification into new product markets, this is more likely to occur through collaborative arrangements with other companies rather than through internal diversification or outright acquisition.

This is not to imply that ideas concerning synergies from operating in multiple product markets are dead. Indeed, the 1990s have seen continuing interest in economies of scope and the transferability of resources and capabilities across industry boundaries. The major change is that strategic analysis has become much more precise about the circumstances in which diversification can create value from multibusiness activity. Mere linkages between businesses are not enough: the key to creating value is the ability of the diversified firm to share resources and transfer capabilities more efficiently than alternative institutional arrangements, where the additional costs of management do not outweigh the value created. Figure 15.1 summarizes some of the key developments in diversification strategy over the past 40 years.

---

[12]   T. Khanna and K. Palepu, "Why Focused Strategies May Be Wrong for Emerging Markets," *Harvard Business Review* (July–August 1997): 41–51; T. Khanna and K. Palepu, "The Right Way to Restructure Conglomerates in Emerging Markets," *Harvard Business Review* (July–August 1999): 47–57; "South-East Asia's Octopuses," *Economist* (July 17, 1993): 61.

FIGURE 15.1 Diversification: the evolution of management thinking and management practice

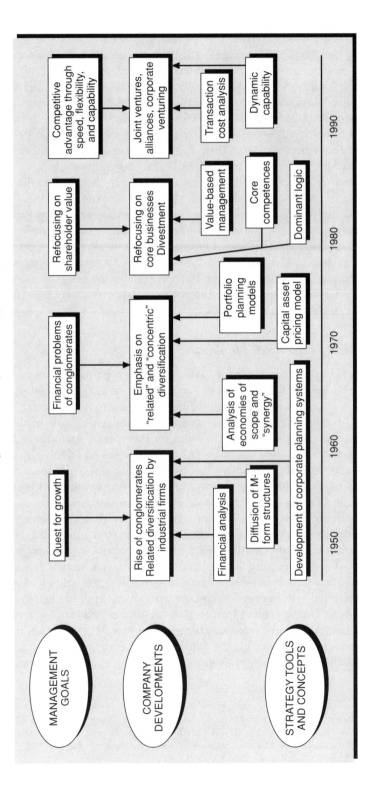

MOTIVES FOR DIVERSIFICATION

Diversification strategies tend to be driven by three major goals: growth, risk reduction, and profitability. As we shall see, although growth and risk reduction have been prominent motives for diversification, they tend to be inconsistent with the creation of shareholder value.

Growth

We noted that an important factor in the reversal of the postwar diversification trend was a reordering of corporate objectives. To the extent that managers' status, security, and power are closely linked to the size of enterprise they control, there are good reasons to expect that they will pursue *growth* at the expense of profitability. Such tendencies were reinforced by the fact that top management salaries and prestige have tended to be correlated more closely with company size than profitability. The tendency for managers to invest at a greater rate than is consistent with profit maximization is constrained by the tendency for such overinvestment to reduce the market value of the firm, making it vulnerable to acquisition.[13]

For firms in declining industries, managers' aversion to contraction provides a pressing motive for diversification. Thus, diversification by tobacco companies and oil companies during the 1970s and 1980s was driven by the fear of declining sales in domestic markets, and was undeterred by the fact that the diversification was into less profitable industries and had the effect of destroying shareholder value.[14] The propensity for managers to pursue their own goals rather than those of company owners is one aspect of the *agency problem*: the problem faced by a *principal* (in this case, the owners of a firm) ensuring that his *agent* (in this case, the top management team) operates in the principal's interest.

Top management's ability to pursue objectives other than profitability is constrained by at least two factors. First, over the long term a firm must earn a return on capital greater than its cost of capital or it will not survive. Second, if management sacrifices profitability for other objectives, managers run the risk of losing their jobs, either from a shareholders' revolt or from acquisition. This explains why companies sell off diversified businesses when their independence is threatened by a takeover bid or by a fall in profitability that attracts potential predators.[15]

[13] R. Marris, *The Economic Theory of Managerial Capitalism* (London: Macmillan, 1964).

[14] R. M. Grant and R. Cibin, "Strategy, Structure and Market Turbulence: The International Oil Majors, 1970–1991," *Scandinavian Journal of Management* 12, no. 2 (1996): 165–88.

[15] David A. Ravenscraft and F. M. Scherer, "Divisional Selloff: A Hazard Analysis," in *Mergers, Selloffs and Economic Efficiency* (Washington, DC: Brookings Institute, 1987); and Michael E. Porter, "From Competitive Advantage to Corporate Strategy," *Harvard Business Review* (May–June 1987): 43–59.

Risk Reduction

A second motive for diversification is the desire to spread risks. To isolate the effects of diversification on risk it is useful to consider "pure" or "conglomerate" diversification, where different businesses are brought under common ownership but, because these businesses are unrelated, their individual cash flows remain unchanged. So long as the cash flows of the different businesses are imperfectly correlated, then the variance of the cash flow of the diversified company is less than the average of that of the individual businesses. Since individuals are risk averse, such risk reduction would seem to be consistent with shareholder interests. However, this ignores a critical factor: to achieve diversification of risk, shareholders can hold diversified portfolios or invest through mutual funds. Not only does this achieve wider diversification than even the most diversified corporations can attain, it can also be achieved at lower cost. The transaction costs to shareholders of diversifying their portfolios are far less than the transaction costs to firms diversifying through acquisition. Not only do acquiring firms incur the heavy costs of using investment banks and legal advisers, they must also pay an acquisition premium in order to gain control of an independent company.

The *capital asset pricing model* (CAPM) formalizes this argument. The theory postulates that the risk that is relevant to determining the price of a security is not the overall risk (variance) of the security's return, but *systematic risk*: that part of the variance of the return that is correlated with overall market risk. Systematic risk is measured by the security's *beta coefficient*. Corporate diversification does not reduce systematic risk: if three separate companies are brought under common ownership, in the absence of any other changes, the beta coefficient of the combined company is simply the weighted average of the beta coefficients of the constituent companies. Hence, the simple act of bringing different businesses under common ownership does not create shareholder value through risk reduction.[16]

Empirical studies are generally supportive of the absence of shareholder benefit from diversification that simply combines independent businesses. Studies of conglomerates in the United States have shown that their risk-adjusted returns to shareholders are typically no better than those offered by mutual funds or by matched portfolios of specialized companies.[17] Another study found that unrelated diversification failed to lower either systematic or unsystematic risk, though moderate, closely related diversification did reduce both.[18]

Hence, so long as securities markets are efficient, diversification whose sole purpose is to spread risk will not benefit shareholders. However, risk spreading through

---

[16]   These principles are outlined in any standard corporate finance text. See, for example, R. A. Brealey and S. Myers, *Principles of Corporate Finance*, 6th edn (McGraw-Hill, 2000): Chapter 8.

[17]   See, for example, H. Levy and M. Sarnat, "Diversification, Portfolio Analysis and the Uneasy Case for Conglomerate Mergers," *Journal of Finance* 25 (1970): 795–802; R. H. Mason and M. B. Goudzwaard, "Performance of Conglomerate Firms: A Portfolio Approach," *Journal of Finance* 31 (1976): 39–48; F. W. Melicher and D. F. Rush, "The Performance of Conglomerate Firms: Recent Risk and Return Experience," *Journal of Finance* 28 (1973): 381–8; J. F. Weston, K. V. Smith, and R. E. Shrieves, "Conglomerate Performance Using the Capital Asset Pricing Model," *Review of Economics and Statistics* 54 (1972): 357–63.

[18]   M. Lubatkin and S. Chetterjee, "Extending Modern Portfolio Theory into the Domain of Corporate Strategy: Does It Apply?," *Academy of Management Journal* 37 (1994): 109–36.

diversification may benefit other stakeholders. If cyclicality in the firm's profits is accompanied by cyclicality in employment, then so long as employees are transferable between the separate businesses of the firm, there may be benefits to employees from diversification's ability to smooth output fluctuations. Managers appear to be especially enthusiastic about the risk-spreading benefits of diversification. Their risk aversion is motivated by their desire to protect their independence and their jobs. Downturns in profit, even if only temporary, can stimulate concern among shareholders and stock analysts. Downturns may make the company temporarily dependent on financial markets for borrowing and may encourage takeover bids.

Special issues arise once we consider the risk of bankruptcy. For a marginally profitable firm, diversification can help avoid cyclical fluctuations of profits that can push it into insolvency. It has been shown, however, that diversification that reduces the risk of bankruptcy is beneficial to the holders of corporate debt rather than to equity holders. The reduction in risk that bondholders derive from diversification is the *coinsurance effect*.[19] Managers and other employees are also likely to have strong interests in any strategy that reduces the risk of bankruptcy.

Are there circumstances where reductions in unsystematic risk can create shareholder value? If there are economies to the firm from financing investments internally rather than resorting to external capital markets, the stability in the firm's cash flow that results from diversification may reinforce independence from external capital markets. Among the major oil companies (Exxon-Shell, Shell, BP-Amoco), one of the benefits of extending across upstream (explorations and production), downstream (refining and marketing), and chemicals is that the negative correlation of the returns from these businesses increases the overall stability of the companies' cash flows. This in turn increases their capacity to undertake huge risky investments such as offshore oil production, transcontinental pipelines, and natural gas liquefaction plants.

Profitability

If we return to the assumption that corporate strategy should be directed toward the interests of shareholders, what are the implications for diversification strategy? We have already revisited our two sources of superior profitability: industry attractiveness and competitive advantage. For firms contemplating diversification, Michael Porter proposes three "essential tests" to be applied in deciding whether diversification will truly create shareholder value:

1. *The attractiveness test.* The industries chosen for diversification must be structurally attractive or capable of being made attractive.

2. *The cost-of-entry test.* The cost of entry must not capitalize all the future profits.

3. *The better-off test.* Either the new unit must gain competitive advantage from its link with the corporation, or vice versa.[20]

[19] S. A. Ross and R. W. Westerfield, *Corporate Finance* (St. Louis: Times Mirror/Mosby College, 1988): 681.
[20] Michael E. Porter, "From Competitive Advantage to Corporate Strategy," *Harvard Business Review* (May–June 1987): 46.

The Attractiveness and Cost-of-entry Tests

A critical realization in Porter's "essential tests" is that industry attractiveness is insufficient on its own. Although diversification is a means by which the firm can access more attractive investment opportunities than are available in its own industry, it faces the problem of entering the new industry. The second test, *cost of entry*, recognizes that the attractiveness of an industry to a firm already established in an industry may be different from its attractiveness to a firm seeking to enter the industry. Industries such as pharmaceuticals, management consulting, or investment banking offer above-average profitability – but this occurs because they are protected by barriers to entry. Firms seeking to enter investment banking or pharmaceuticals have a choice. They may enter by acquiring an established player, in which case not only does the market price of the target firm reflect the superior profit prospects of the industry, but the diversifying firm must also offer an acquisition premium of around 25 to 50 percent over the market price to gain control.[21] Alternatively, entry may occur through establishing a new corporate venture. In this case, the diversifying firm must directly confront the barriers to entry protecting that industry. This typically involves high risk and low returns over a long period.[22]

The "Better-off" Test

Porter's third criterion for successful diversification – *the better-off test* – addresses the basic issue of competitive advantage: If two businesses producing different products are brought together under the ownership and control of a single enterprise, is there any reason why they should become any more profitable? Diversification has the potential to enhance the competitive advantage of the diversified business, the original core business, or both businesses. Combining the different businesses in separate, but related product areas can enhance the competitive advantages of the businesses of both the acquired company and the acquiree. For example:

- In acquiring Quaker Oats, PepsiCo believes that combining its FritoLay snack foods business with Quaker Oats' breakfast cereals and convenience foods businesses will permit operating economies, enhance marketing capability, and offer greater distribution clout with supermarkets. Combining Pepsi's Pepsi-Cola and Tropicana drinks businesses with Quaker's Gatorade will offer economies in distribution as well as enhanced brand management.

- AOL's merger with Time Warner is intended to exploit the opportunities for linking AOL's internet-based distribution presence and capabilities with

---

[21] The history of diversification is littered with companies that overpaid in order to gain a position in a seemingly attractive industry. During the 1980s, the eagerness for movie studios resulted in Sony, Matsushita, and Viacom paying excessive acquisition prices for Columbia Pictures, MCA, and Paramount. During the 1990s, the commercial banks acquired investment banks at hugely inflated prices.

[22] A study of 68 diversifying ventures by established companies found that, on average, breakeven was not attained until the seventh and eighth years of operation: R. Biggadike, "The Risky Business of Diversification," *Harvard Business Review* (May–June 1979).

Time Warner's strong position in cable TV and print media distribution, while better exploiting Time Warner's content creation through its studios and publishing operations.

Yet, although the potential for value creation from exploiting linkages between the different businesses may be considerable, the practical difficulties of exploiting such opportunities have made diversification a corporate minefield. Let us examine the issues systematically.

COMPETITIVE ADVANTAGE FROM DIVERSIFICATION

If the primary source of value creation from diversification is exploiting linkages between different businesses, what are the linkages and how are they exploited? As we shall see, the primary means by which diversification creates competitive advantage is through the sharing of resources and capabilities across different businesses. Before addressing this issue, let us look first at the potential for diversification to enhance a firm's market power.

Market Power

The potential for diversification to enhance profitability by increasing a firm's market power has interested antitrust authorities in the United States and Europe for several decades. It has been claimed that large diversified companies could exercise market power through three mechanisms:

- *Predatory pricing.* Just as global corporations derive strength from their ability to finance competitive battles in individual markets through cross-subsidization, so multibusiness companies can use their size and diversity to discipline or even drive out specialized competitors in particular product markets through predatory pricing – cutting prices to below the level of rivals' costs. The Justice Department's desire to split Microsoft into separate companies was based on the fear that Microsoft's monopoly in PC operating systems allowed Microsoft to squeeze rivals in other software markets in the same way that it was able to overcome Netscape's initial leadership in internet browsers.

- *Reciprocal buying.* A diversified company can leverage its market share across its businesses by reciprocal buying arrangements with customers. This means giving preference in purchasing to firms that become loyal customers for another of the conglomerate's businesses. Although reciprocal buying arrangement have been seen as a risk in several mergers,[23] the potential is greatest in those emerging market countries whose business sectors are dominated by a few large conglomerates.

---

[23]   See, for example, E. Blackstone, "Monopsony Power, Reciprocal Buying and Government Contracts: The General Dynamics Case," *Antitrust Bulletin* 17 (Summer 1972): 445–62.

■ *Mutual forbearance.* Corwin Edwards argued that:

> When one large conglomerate enterprise competes with another, the two are likely
> to encounter each other in a considerable number of markets. The multiplicity
> of their contacts may blunt the edge of their competition. A prospect of advant-
> age in one market from vigorous competition may be weighed against the danger
> of retaliatory forays by the competitor in other markets. Each conglomerate may
> adopt a live-and-let-live policy designed to stabilize the whole structure of the
> competitive relationship.[24]

Through modeling *multimarket competition* among diversified firms, game
theory has permitted more rigorous analysis of mutual forbearance. In repeated
games involving players that meet in multiple markets, companies are likely
to refrain from aggressive action in any one market for fear of triggering
more generalized warfare.[25] Such behavior is most likely among companies that
meet in multiple geographical markets for the same product or service – the
airline industry, for example[26] – though such tendencies may also exist where
diversified companies meet in multiple product markets.[27]

Economies of Scope

The most general argument concerning the benefits of diversification focuses on the
presence of economies of scope in common resources. If a certain input is used in
the production of two products and this input is available only in units of a certain
minimum size, then a single firm producing both products is able to spread the cost
of the input over a larger volume of output and so reduce the unit costs of both
products.[28] Thus, economies of scope exist for similar reasons as economies of scale.
The key difference is that the economies of scale relate to cost economies from
increasing the scale of production for a single product; economies of scope are cost

---

[24]   US Senate, Subcommittee on Antitrust and Monopoly Hearings, *Economic Concentration*, Part 1,
Congress, 1st session (1965): 45.
[25]   B. D. Bernheim and M. D. Whinston, "Multimarket Contact and Collusive Behavior," *Rand Journal
of Economics* 2 (1990): 1–26.
[26]   In the US airline industry, extensive multimarket contact resulted in a reluctance to compete on routes
dominated by one or other of the airlines. See J. A. C. Baum and H. J. Korn, "Competitive Dynamics
of Interfirm Rivalry," *Academy of Management Review* 39 (1996): 255–91.
[27]   H. J. Korn and J. A. C. Baum "Chance, Imitative and Strategic Antecedents to Multimarket Contact,"
Academy of Management Journal 42 (1999): 171–93.
[28]   The formal definition of economies of scope is in terms of "sub-additivity." Economies of scope exist
in the production of goods $x_1, x_2, \ldots x_n$, if $C(X) < \Sigma_i C_i(x_i)$

Where: $X = \Sigma_i(x_i)$
         $C(X)$ is the cost of producing all n goods within a single firm
         $\Sigma_i C_i(x_i)$ is the cost of producing the goods in n specialized firms.

See W. J. Baumol, John C. Panzar, and Robert D. Willig, *Contestable Markets and the Theory of Industry
Structure* (New York: Harcourt Brace Jovanovich, 1982): 71–2.

economies from producing increasing numbers of products. The nature of economies of scope vary between different types of resources and capabilities.

Tangible Resources

Tangible resources – such as distribution networks, information technology systems, sales forces, and research laboratories – offer economies of scope by eliminating duplication between businesses through creating a single shared facility. The greater the fixed costs of these items, the greater the associated economies of scope are likely to be. Entry by cable TV companies into telephone services, and telephone companies into cable TV, are motivated by the desire to spread the costs of networks and billing systems over as great a volume of business as possible. A variety of companies, including gas and electricity utilities, envisage becoming single-point suppliers of a full range of electricity, gas, telephone, and TV services to households.

Economies of scope also arise from the centralized provision of administrative and support services by the corporate center to the different businesses of the corporation. Among diversified companies, accounting, legal services, government relations, and information technology tend to be centralized – often through *shared service organizations* that supply common administrative and technical services to the operating businesses. Similar economies arise from centralizing research activities in a corporate R&D lab. In aerospace, the ability of leading US companies to spread research expenditures over both defense and civilian products has given these companies an advantage over overseas competitors with more limited access to large military contracts.[29]

Intangible Resources

Intangible resources such as brands, corporate reputation, and technology offer economies of scope primarily due to the ability to transfer them from one business area to another at low marginal cost.[30] Thus, when American Express diversified its range of financial services by acquiring Shearson, Lehman Brothers, IDS Financial Services, and Trade Development Bank, the new subsidiaries adopted the American Express blue and white corporate logo and the suffix "An American Express Company." The intention was "to focus on individual brand names, multiple distribution channels and carefully targeted market segments . . . [while] continuing to draw on the marketing power and identification of the American Express name."[31]

---

[29] More generally, research intensity is strongly associated with diversification. For the US, see C. H. Berry, *Corporate Growth and Diversification* (Princeton: Princeton University Press, 1975); for the UK, see Robert M. Grant, "Determinants of the Interindustry Pattern of Diversification by U.K. Manufacturing Companies," *Bulletin of Economic Research* 29 (1977): 84–95.

[30] Among service companies, the ability to transfer corporate reputation across different markets was found to be an important influence on the profitability of diversification. See P. R. Nayyar, "Performance Effects of Information Asymmetry and Economies of Scope in Diversified Service Firms," *Academy of Management Journal* 36 (1993): 28–57.

[31] American Express Company 1984 Annual Report: 3.

Organizational Capabilities

Organizational capabilities can also be transferred within the diversified company. For example:

- Philip Morris leveraged Miller Brewing Company from seventh to second in terms of US market share by applying the same brand management, advertising, and market segmentation skills that had proved so successful with Marlboro cigarettes. In both cases, Philip Morris repositioned the brand toward the mass market, increased advertising and promotional expenditure, segmented the market through sub-branding, improved packaging, and invested in production capacity.

- Motorola's success in electronic components and wireless products over the past 60 years has been built on a set of core technological capabilities that are transferred and integrated across a number of different business areas. These technological capabilities relate to the development of microelectronic and communications technology, the embodiment of new technology into innovative, carefully designed new products, and quality-based manufacturing.[32]

Some of the most important capabilities in influencing the performance of diversified corporations are general management capabilities located at the corporate level. Consider the case of General Electric. In an era when conglomerates are being dismantled, GE has achieved remarkable shareholder returns. Although it does a remarkable job of transferring best practices between its different businesses, its core capabilities lie at the corporate level. These include GE's ability to motivate and develop its managers, its reconciling of decentralized decision making with centralized financial control, and its management of international expansion. Similar observations could be made about 3M. While 3M's capabilities in technical know-how, new product development, and international marketing reside within the individual businesses, it is the corporate management capabilities and the systems through which they are exercised that maintain, nourish, coordinate, and upgrade these competitive advantages.

Economies from Internalizing Transactions

Although economies of scope provide cost savings from sharing and transferring resources and capabilities, does a firm have to diversify across these different businesses in order to exploit those economies? The answer is no. Economies of scope in resources and capabilities can be exploited simply by selling or licensing the use of the resource or capability to another company. In Chapter 11, we observed that a firm can exploit proprietary technology by licensing it to other firms. In Chapter 14, we noted how technology and trademarks are licensed across national

---

[32] "Keeping Motorola on a Roll," *Fortune* (April 18, 1994): 67–78.

frontiers as an alternative to direct investment. The same can be done to exploit resources across different industries. Harley-Davidson exploits its brand name across many products. However, it sticks to manufacturing motorcycles and licenses its brand name to the manufacturers of T-shirts, clothing, key rings, cigarettes, and studded leather underwear. Walt Disney exploits the enormous value of its trademarks, copyrights, and characters partly through diversification into theme parks, live theater, cruise ships, and hotels; and partly through licensing the use of these assets to producers of clothing, toys, music, comics, food, and drinks, as well as to the franchisees of Disney's retail stores. Disney licensing fees and royalties comprise the major part of the $2.6 billion in revenue earned by its consumer products division in 2000.

Even tangible resources can be shared across different businesses through market transactions. Airport and railroad station owners exploit economies of scope in their facilities not by diversifying into catering and retailing, but by leasing out space to specialist retailers and restaurants. Caterpillar exploits economies of scope in its parts distribution network not by diversifying into the supply of a wider range of parts, but by distributing parts for Chrysler, Hyundai, Hewlett-Packard, and Siemens.[33]

What determines whether economies of scope are better exploited internally within the firm through diversification, or externally through market contracts with independent companies? The key issue is relative efficiency: What are the transaction costs of market contracts, as compared with the costs of managing economies of scope within the diversified enterprise? Transaction costs include the costs involved in drafting, negotiating, monitoring, and enforcing a contract. The costs of internalization consist of the management costs of establishing and coordinating the diversified business.[34]

Let's return to the Walt Disney Company. Why does Disney choose to license Donald Duck trademarks to a manufacturer of orange juice rather than set up its own orange juice company? Why does it own and operate its own Disneyland and DisneyWorld theme parks rather than license its trademarks to independent theme park companies? And why, in the case of Tokyo Disneyland, did it choose a licensing arrangement with the Oriental Land Company, which owns and operates Tokyo Disneyland?

These issues are complex. Much depends on the characteristics of the resource or capabilities. Though the returns to patents and brand names can often be appropriated efficiently through licensing, complex general management capabilities may be near impossible to exploit through market contracts. There is little scope for Sony to deploy its new product development capabilities other than within its own business. A similar situation occurs with Berkshire Hathaway and its skills in identifying attractive acquisition candidates then nurturing the management of these companies. The more deeply embedded a firm's capabilities within the management systems and the culture of the organization, the greater the likelihood that these capabilities can

[33] "A Moving Story of Spare Parts," *Financial Times* (August 29, 1997): 7.
[34] This issue is examined more fully in David Teece, "Towards an Economic Theory of the Multiproduct Firm," *Journal of Economic Behavior and Organization* 3 (1982): 39–63.

only be deployed internally within the firm. Even with simpler resources, market contracts may not be effective in protecting the value of the resources in question. Texaco chose to exploit its coal gasification technology internally by developing its own power-generation plants rather than license the technology, for fear that licensing would not adequately safeguard its proprietary interests.

The Diversified Firm as an Internal Market

We see that economies of scope on their own do not provide an adequate rationale for diversification – they must be supported by the presence of transaction costs. However, the presence of transaction costs in any nonspecialized resource can offer efficiency gains from diversification, even where no economies of scope are present. Consider the case of financial capital. Where significant costs are incurred in using external capital markets (the margin between borrowing and lending rates, and the underwriting costs of issuing securities), diversified companies can benefit from lower costs of capital by building a balanced portfolio of cash-generating and cash-absorbing businesses. A central role of the corporate head office in diversified corporations is to allocate capital among the different businesses according to the profit prospects of the different investment opportunities. In this respect, the diversified corporation represents an internal capital market in which the different businesses compete for investment funds.

Some companies operate highly sophisticated internal financial markets. Since 1985, British Petroleum Finance International has managed the financing of BP's 50+ operating companies, undertaken standard accounting functions, traded in foreign exchange, managed leasing, and offered 24-hour trading in short-term instruments through offices in London, New York, and Melbourne.[35] A key advantage of internal corporate banks is that they are not subject to the myriad regulations that raise the costs of using external financial institutions.[36]

Efficiencies also arise from the ability of diversified companies to transfer employees – especially managers and technical specialists – between their divisions, and to rely less on hiring and firing. As companies develop and encounter new circumstances, so different management skills are required. The costs associated with hiring include advertising, the time spent in interviewing and selection, and the costs of "headhunting" agencies. The costs of dismissing employees can be very high where severance payments must be offered. A diversified corporation has a pool of employees and can respond to the specific needs of any one business through transfer from elsewhere within the corporation. Not only are such internal transfers less costly than external transfers, they are also much less risky because of the superior information the firm possesses on internal job candidates. The broader set of opportunities available in the diversified corporation as a result of internal transfer may also result in attracting a higher caliber of employee. Graduating students compete intensely for entry-level positions with diversified corporations such as Matsushita,

---

[35] "Inside the New In-House Banks," *Euromoney* (February 1986): 24–34.
[36] Robert K. Ankrom, "The Corporate Bank," *Sloan Management Review* (Winter 1994): 63–72.

General Electric, Unilever, and Nestlé in the belief that these companies can offer richer career development than more specialized companies.

Information Advantages of the Diversified Corporation

An important benefit of internal capital and labor markets within the diversified corporation is that the corporate head office of the diversified corporation has better access to information than is available to external capital and labor markets. As a result, the diversified corporation may be more efficient in reallocating labor and capital among its divisions than are external capital and labor markets in allotting labor and capital among independent businesses. In the case of capital, these information advantages may be especially great for new ventures. Despite a well-developed market for venture capital in the United States and Europe, the risks associated with such ventures are compounded by the limited information available to potential lenders and investors. A diversified company such as 3M or Hewlett-Packard has full access to the information on performance and prospects for each of its business units.

These information advantages may be even greater in the case of labor. A key problem of hiring from the external labor market is not just cost but limited information. A resume, references, and a day of interviews are a poor indicator of how an otherwise unknown person will perform in a specific job. The diversified firm that is engaged in transferring employees between business units and divisions has access to much more detailed information on the abilities, characteristics, and past performance of each of its employees. This informational advantage exists not only for individual employees but also for groups of individuals working together as teams. As a result, in diversifying into a new activity, the established firm is at an advantage over the new firm, which must assemble a team from scratch with poor information on individual capabilities and almost no information on how effective the group will be at working together. As a result, in an economy where new industries are constantly arising, there are reasons to expect that diversification by established firms offers some advantages over exploiting new opportunities than entirely new ventures.[37]

┤ DIVERSIFICATION AND PERFORMANCE

We have established that diversification has the potential to create value for shareholders where it exploits economies of scope and where transaction costs in the markets for resources offer efficiencies from their internal exploitation. Diversification motivated by the desire to reduce risk or achieve growth is likely to destroy rather than create shareholder value. How do these predictions work in practice?

---

[37] A. A. Alchian and H. Demsetz, "Production, Information Costs, and Economic Organization," *American Economic Review* 62 (1972): 777–95, argue that the collection and processing of information is the basic role of management and provides the primary rationale for the existence of the firm.

FIGURE 15.2 The relationship between diversification and profitability among British manufacturing companies

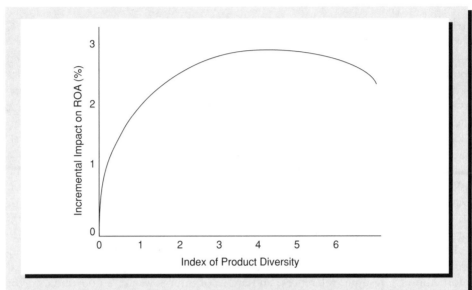

Source: R. M. Grant, A. Jammines, and H. Thomas, "Diversity, Diversification, and Profitability among British Manufacturing Companies," *Academy of Management Journal,* 31 (December, 1988): 771–801.

The Findings of Empirical Research

Empirical research into diversification has concentrated on two major issues: first, how do diversified firms perform relative to specialized firms and, second, does related diversification outperform unrelated diversification?

The Performance of Diversified and Specialized Firms

To the extent that diversified companies face a wider range of investment opportunities and can readily shift resources from less attractive to more attractive industries, they should be able to achieve higher profitability and higher growth than specialized firms. On the other hand, the ability of specialized firms to focus on building excellence across a narrow range of capabilities may give them a competitive advantage over diversified companies.

No consistent, systematic relationships have emerged between performance and the degree of diversification. However, there is evidence that high levels of diversity are associated with deteriorating performance – possibly because of the problems of complexity that diversification creates. Among British companies, diversification was associated with increased profitability up to a point, after which further diversification was associated with declining profitability (see Figure 15.2). Other studies have also detected a curvilinear relationship between diversification and profitability.[38] As with most studies of strategy and performance, a key problem is distinguishing association from *causation*. If diversified companies are generally more profitable than specialized firms, is it because diversification increases profitability or because profitable firms channel their cash flows into diversifying investments?

It is also likely that the performance effects of diversification depend on the mode of diversification. There is a mass of evidence pointing to the poor performance of mergers and acquisitions in general. Among these, mergers and acquisitions involving companies in different industries appear to perform especially poorly.

Some of the most powerful evidence concerning the relationship between diversification and performance relates to the refocusing initiatives by a large number of North American and European companies. The evidence, ranging from conglomerates such as ITT and Hanson, to the oil majors, tobacco companies, and engineering companies such as Daimler-Benz, is that narrowing business scope leads to increased profitability and higher stock market valuation. This may reflect a changing relationship between diversification and profitability over time: the growing turbulence of the business environment may have increased the costs of managing complex, diversified corporations. The stock market's verdict on diversification has certainly shifted over time: the high price–earnings ratios attached to conglomerates during the 1960s and 1970s have been replaced by a "conglomerate discount."[39] The result is that diversified companies have come under attack from leveraged buyout specialists seeking to add value through dismembering these companies. Markides points to the performance gains to diversified companies divesting their noncore activities.[40]

Related and Unrelated Diversification

Because of the importance of economies of scope in shared resources, it seems likely that diversification into *related* industries should be more profitable than diversification into *unrelated* industries. Empirical research initially supported this prediction. Richard Rumelt discovered that companies that diversified into businesses closely related to their core activities were significantly more profitable than those that pursued unrelated diversification.[41] At the same time, the primary exponents of unrelated diversification – conglomerates such as LTV, ITT, and Allegheny International – were experiencing deteriorating performance. By 1982, Tom Peters

[38] L. E. Palich, L. B. Cardinal, and C. C. Miller, "Curvilinearity in the Diversification–Performance Linkage: An Examination of over Three Decades of Research," *Strategic Management Journal* 22 (2000): 155–74.
[39] Indeed, by the 1980s, acquisition announcements generally were greeted by a negative stock market reaction, see G. A. Jarrell, J. A. Brickly, and J. M. Netter, "The Market for Corporate Control: Empirical Evidence Since 1980," *Journal of Economic Perspectives* 2, no. 1 (Winter 1988): 49–68.
[40] C. C. Markides, "Consequences of Corporate Refocusing: Ex Ante Evidence," *Academy of Management Journal* 35 (1992): 398–412; C. C. Markides, "Diversification, Restructuring and Economic Performance," *Strategic Management Journal* 16 (1995): 101–18.
[41] R. P. Rumelt, *Strategy, Structure and Economic Performance* (Cambridge, MA: Harvard University Press, 1974).

and Robert Waterman were able to conclude: "virtually every academic study has concluded that unchanneled diversification is a losing proposition."[42] This observation provided the basis for one of Peters and Waterman's "golden rules of excellence" – *Stick to the Knitting*:

> Our principal finding is clear and simple. Organizations that do branch out but stick very close to their knitting outperform the others. The most successful are those diversified around a single skill, the coating and bonding technology at 3M for example. The second group in descending order, comprise those companies that branch out into related fields, the leap from electric power generation turbines to jet engines from GE for example. Least successful, as a general rule, are those companies that diversify into a wide variety of fields. Acquisitions especially among this group tend to wither on the vine.[43]

Subsequent evidence shattered this consistent picture. The apparent superior performance of related diversifiers could be explained in terms of other factors such as risk and industry membership.[44] Other studies even found unrelated diversification to be more profitable than related.[45]

The lack of clear performance differences between related and unrelated diversification is troubling. Two factors may help explain the confused picture. First, related diversification may offer greater potential benefits, but may also pose more difficult management problems for companies such that the potential benefits are not realized. The issues concerning the management of the diversified corporation are addressed in Chapter 16. Suffice it to say at this point that economies of scope from sharing and transferring resources and capabilities among different businesses within the diversified corporation need to be managed and such management is not costless. Second, the distinction between "related" and "unrelated" diversification is not entirely clear – the key resource and capability linkages that we have emphasized do not necessarily correspond to the measures of industry relatedness used in the empirical literature.

The Meaning of Relatedness in Diversification

The issue of what we mean by relatedness is critical in determining the product scope of the company. Our discussion of economies of scope has defined relatedness in terms of the sharing and transfer of resources and capabilities between

---

[42]   Tom Peters and Robert Waterman, *In Search of Excellence* (New York: Harper & Row, 1982): 294.

[43]   Ibid.

[44]   H. K. Christensen and C. A. Montgomery, "Corporate Economic Performance: Diversification Strategy versus Market Structure," *Strategic Management Journal* 2 (1981): 327–43; R. A. Bettis, "Performance Differences in Related and Unrelated Diversified Firms," *Strategic Management Journal* 2 (1981): 379–83.

[45]   See, for example, A. Michel and I. Shaked, "Does Business Diversification Affect Performance?," *Financial Management* 13, no. 4 (1984): 18–24; G. A. Luffman and R. Reed, *The Strategy and Performance of British Industry, 1970–80* (London: Macmillan, 1984).

businesses. Distinguishing the potential for exploiting economies of scope between businesses is no easy matter and researchers have used simple criteria to determine whether businesses are related. Typical criteria are similarities between industries in terms of technologies and markets. Using the first criterion, oil exploration, medical diagnostic imaging, and electronic arcade games would be related through their common dependence on 3D computer imaging. Under the second criterion, gasoline, automobile repair, and fast food are related because they are sold to the same customers through the same retail outlets (service stations).[46]

These types of link tell us little about the potential for economies of scope in resources and capabilities. Moreover, similarities in technology and markets refer primarily to relatedness at the *operational* level – in manufacturing, marketing, and distribution activities. These operating-level commonalities may not offer substantial economies in resource sharing: the management costs of common systems of purchasing and distribution tend to be high relative to the savings. Conversely, some of the most important sources of value creation within the diversified firm are the ability to apply common general management capabilities, strategic management systems, and resource allocation processes to different businesses. Such economies depend on the existence of *strategic* rather than *operational* commonalities among the different businesses within the diversified corporation.[47]

- Berkshire Hathaway is involved in insurance, candy stores, furniture, kitchen knives, jewelry, and footwear. Despite this diversity, all these businesses have been selected on the basis of their ability to benefit from the unique style of corporate management established by chairman Warren Buffett and CEO Charles Munger.

- ABB comprises a wide range of businesses. Yet, they share certain strategic similarities: they tend to be international, capital intensive, and engineering based. All fit with ABB's decentralized, but closely integrated, system of corporate management.

The essence of such strategic-level linkages is the ability to apply similar strategies, resource allocation procedures, and control systems across the different businesses within the corporate portfolio. Table 15.3 lists some of the strategic factors that determine similarities among businesses in relation to corporate management activities.[48]

---

[46] The role of capabilities in diversification is discussed in C. C. Markides and P. J. Williamson, "Related Diversification, Core Competencies and Corporate Performance," *Strategic Management Journal* 15 (special issue, 1994): 149–65.

[47] For a discussion of relatedness in diversification, see J. Robins and M. F. Wiersema, "A Resource-Based Approach to the Multibusiness Firm: Empirical Analysis of Portfolio Interrelationships and Corporate Financial Performance," *Strategic Management Journal* 16 (1995): 277–300; and J. Robins and M. F. Wiersema, "Measurement of Related Diversification: Are the Measures Valid for the Concepts?," discussion paper (Graduate School of Management, Irvine, CA: University of California, November 1997).

[48] For a discussion of the role of strategic linkages between businesses in affecting the success of diversification, see Robert M. Grant, "On Dominant Logic, Relatedness, and the Link Between Diversity and Performance," *Strategic Management Journal* 9 (1988): 639–42.

TABLE 15.3 The Determinants of Strategic Relatedness between Businesses

CORPORATE MANAGEMENT TASKS	DETERMINANTS OF STRATEGIC SIMILARITY
Resource allocation	Similar sizes of capital investment projects Similar time spans of investment projects Similar sources of risk Similar general management skills required for business unit managers
Strategy formulation	Similar key success factors Similar stages of the industry life cycle Similar competitive positions occupied by each business within its industry
Performance management and control	Targets defined in terms of similar performance variables Similar time horizons for performance targets

Source: R. M. Grant, "On Dominant Logic, Relatedness, and the Link Between Diversity and Performance," *Strategic Management Journal* 9 (1988): 641.

Unlike operational relatedness, where the benefits of exploiting economies of scope in joint inputs are comparatively easy to forecast, and even to quantify, relatedness at the strategic level may be much more difficult to appraise. The short, unhappy life of Allegis Corporation is just one example of managers' propensity to identify synergies between businesses that in practice prove either elusive or nonexistent (see Exhibit 15.1).

Diversification decisions are determined more by perceived relatedness than by actual relatedness. Prahalad and Bettis use the term *dominant logic* to refer to managers' cognition of the rationale that links their different business activities.[49] Certainly, a dominant logic in the form of a common view within the company as to its identity and rationale is a critical precondition for effective integration across different businesses. (This issue is discussed further in Chapter 16.) There is a danger, however, that dominant logic may not be underpinned by any true economic synergies. In the same way that Allegis Corporation attempted to diversify around serving the needs of the traveler, so General Mills diversified into toys, fashion clothing, specialty retailing, and restaurants on the basis of "understanding the needs and wants of the homemaker."

[49] C. K. Prahalad and R. A. Bettis, "The Dominant Logic: A New Linkage Between Diversity and Performance," *Strategic Management Journal* 7 (1986): 485–502.

EXHIBIT 15.1 The Rise and Fall of Allegis Corporation

On May 1, 1987, Richard J. Ferris, chief executive of UAL Inc., inaugurated a fresh era in the company's history under the new name of Allegis Corporation. The name change symbolized the metamorphosis of UAL from an airline into a diversified travel company. Ferris explained the company's mission as follows:

> Allegis is United, the airline industry leader. It is Hertz, the top car-rental company. It is Westin, a luxury hotel group. Allegis is Covia whose Apollo product is a multinational computer reservations network. It is MPI, a full-service direct marketing agency. It is United Vacations, a wholesale travel tour operator. And Allegis will soon be Hilton International, when we complete our purchase of that leading company with 88 luxury hotels in 42 countries.
>
> Allegis Corporation . . . caring for travelers worldwide . . . a distinctive partnership of companies . . . where people are pledged to service and quality.
>
> Allegis will be the world's premier travel-related corporation – recognized by customers, employees, and investors as the source of superior quality and value.
>
> Allegis customers will prefer the services of its worldwide operating partnership because they represent the best in dependability, comfort, and convenience . . . and because they are delivered by people whose attention to detail enhances every aspect of the travel experience . . . Allegis will also be unwavering in its dedication to bring quality and care back into the total travel experience. So we pledge to you, our customers, value, convenience, dependability, security, comfort – in sum, ease of travel that no other single corporation can match.

On June 9, only six weeks after formally adopting the Allegis name, Dick Ferris was ousted by the board. The car rental and hotel subsidiaries were sold, and the company reverted to its name of United Airlines Inc.

What had gone wrong? Allegis broke two out of three of Porter's "essential tests" of a diversification strategy. First, its cost of entry, in terms of the prices it paid for companies during its two-year, $2.3 billion acquisition binge, was too high. Second, in terms of the "better-off" test, it appeared that Ferris had greatly overestimated the synergies to be exploited in bringing together airlines, hotels, and car rental under a common ownership. Indeed, it was not apparent that the chief benefit, providing one-stop shopping for the business traveler through an integrated reservations system, could not be achieved equally well by collaboration among independent companies.

If market relatedness provided the benefits from diversification, the stumbling block anticipated was strategic dissimilarity between the different businesses. While Allegis's upmarket hotel chains competed on service and reputation, success in the deregulated airline industry required rigorous cost cutting and maintaining high load factors through quick-footed operational management. Allegis's focus on servicing the needs of the business traveler deflected its attention from its critical need: reducing costs and increasing efficiency at United Airlines.

Sources: Richard J. Ferris, "From Now On," *Vis-à-Vis* (March 1987): 13; "Allegis: Is a Name Change Enough for UAL?," *Business Week* (March 2, 1987): 54–8; "The Unraveling of an Idea," *Business Week* (June 22, 1987): 42–3.

SUMMARY

Diversification is like sex. Its attractions are obvious, often irresistible. Yet, the experience is often disappointing. For top management it is a minefield. The diversification experiences of large corporations are littered with expensive mistakes: Exxon with Exxon Office Systems, GE with Utah International and Kidder Peabody, American Express with Shearson Lehman, Daimler-Benz in aerospace, AT&T with NCR. Despite so many costly failures, the urge to diversify continues to captivate senior managers. Part of the problem is the divergence between managerial and shareholder goals. While diversification has offered meager rewards to shareholders, it is the fastest route to building vast corporate empires. A further problem is hubris. A company's success in one line of business tends to result in the top management team becoming overconfident of its ability to achieve similar success in other businesses.

Nevertheless, if companies are to survive and prosper over long periods of time they must change, and this change inevitably involves redefining the businesses in which the company operates. Hewlett-Packard and Motorola are among the longest-established companies in the fast-paced US electronics industry. The success and longevity of both have been based on their ability to adapt their product lines to changing market opportunities. While Motorola has moved from car radios to TVs to semiconductors to wireless communication equipment to communication services, HP has shifted from measuring instruments to computers and printers, to cameras and other imaging products. Enron's successful, ambitious diversification from pipelines into power generation and now into trading gas, electricity, and wireless spectrum has earned it the mantle of the world's most innovative company.[50] Although many firms appear to have rejected diversification in favor of "refocusing" and "downsizing," ultimately, long-term survival requires that companies develop new areas of business. As new technologies and deregulation continue to reshape the telecommunications industry, firms such as AT&T and British Telecom must develop wireless networks, digital technologies, data transfer, internet support, information services, and the like.

The critical issue for managers is to avoid the errors of the past through better strategic analysis of diversification decisions. The objectives of diversification need to be clear and explicit. Shareholder value creation has provided a demanding and illuminating criterion with which to appraise investment in new business opportunities. Rigorous analysis may also counter the tendency for diversification to be a diversion, a form of escapism resulting from the unwillingness of top management to come to terms with difficult competitive circumstances in the firm's core businesses.

The analytic tools at our disposal for evaluating diversification decisions have developed greatly in recent years. Twenty years ago, diversification decisions were

---

50 "The World's Most Admired Companies," *Fortune* (October 2, 2000): 182–8.

based on vague concepts of synergy that involved the identification of linkages between different industries. More specific analysis of the nature and extent of economies of scope in resources and capabilities has given greater precision to our analysis of synergy. At the same time, we recognize that economies of scope are insufficient to ensure that diversification creates value. The critical issue is the optimal organizational form for exploiting these economies. The transaction costs of markets must be compared against the management costs of the diversified corporation. These management costs depend heavily on the top management capabilities and management systems of the particular company. This type of analysis has caused many companies to realize that economies of scope often can be exploited more efficiently and with less risk through collaborative relationships with other companies rather than through diversification.

16

Managing the Multibusiness Corporation

Some have argued that single-product businesses have a focus that gives them an advantage over multi-business companies like our own – and perhaps they would have, but only if we neglect our own overriding advantage: the ability to share the ideas that are the result of wide and rich input from a multitude of global sources.

GE businesses share technology, design, compensation and personnel evaluation systems, manufacturing practices, and customer and country knowledge. Gas Turbines shares manufacturing technology with Aircraft Engines; Motors and Transportation Systems work together on new propulsion systems; Lighting and Medical Systems collaborate to improve x-ray tube processes; and GE Capital provides innovative financing packages that help all our businesses around the globe. Supporting all this is a management system that fosters and rewards this sharing and teamwork, and, increasingly, a culture that makes it reflexive and natural at every level and corner of our Company.

—*Jack Welch, Chairman, General Electric Company, 1981–2001.*

Outline

- Introduction and Objectives
- The Structure of the Multibusiness Company
  The Theory of the M-Form Corporation
  The Divisionalized Firm in Practice
- The Role of Corporate Management

Introduction and Objectives

In the last chapter, we argued that the case for diversification rests ultimately on the ability of the diversified corporation to exploit sources of value from operating across multiple businesses more effectively than can specialized firms linked by markets. Chapters 13 and 14 arrived at the same conclusion in relation to vertical integration and multinational operations. Hence, multibusiness companies[1] – whether vertically integrated, multinational, or diversified across multiple products – face two critical issues. First, can value be derived by operating across the different activities and markets in which they are engaged? Second, how should the multibusiness company be structured and managed to ensure that these sources of value are exploited more efficiently than under any other type of organizational arrangement? Chapters 13, 14, and 15 addressed the first question in relation to vertical, multinational, and multiproduct scope. This chapter addresses the second question.

Multibusiness corporations face the challenge of managing multiple activities in multiple markets. Their common characteristic is that they are *multidivisional*:

---

[1]   I use the term *multibusiness company* to refer to a company that engages in multiple vertical activities, national markets, or product areas.

they comprise a number of divisions or subsidiaries, and these divisions and subsidiaries are typically divided into a number of separate business units. The separate parts of the company are coordinated and controlled by a corporate headquarters. Our emphasis here is on the organizational structures, management systems, and leadership styles through which strategy is *formulated* and *implemented* within these multibusiness companies. As we will see, corporate strategy is not simply a matter of answering the question: "What businesses should we be in?" Some of the most difficult issues of corporate strategy pertain to the roles and activities of the corporate head office and the relationships between the businesses and the corporate center. We are concerned with five main areas of corporate-level strategic management:

1. The composition of the company's portfolio of businesses (decisions about diversification, acquisition, and divestment).

2. Resource allocation among the company's different businesses.

3. The role of head office in the formulation of business unit strategies.

4. Controlling business unit performance.

5. Coordinating business units and creating overall cohesiveness and direction for the company.

By the time you have completed this chapter you will be able to:

■ Recognize the central issues of formulating and implementing corporate strategy.

■ Deploy the concepts and techniques necessary for making judgments about these issues.

■ Evaluate the relationships between the resources and capabilities of the firm, its corporate strategy, and the implementation of the strategy through an appropriate organization structure, management system, and leadership style.

THE STRUCTURE OF THE MULTIBUSINESS COMPANY

Chapter 1 introduced the distinction between business strategy and corporate strategy and observed that, within the multibusiness company, corporate management takes primary responsibility for corporate strategy, and divisional management takes primary responsibility for business strategy. This corporate/divisional distinction is the most characteristic feature of the multibusiness corporation. Whether we are referring to a multiproduct company (such as TRW), a multinational company (such as Coca-Cola), or a vertically integrated corporation (such as Alcoa), almost all multibusiness companies are organized as multidivisional structures where business-level decisions are located at the business level and the corporate center exercises overall coordination and control. Indeed, we saw in Chapter 6 that the development of the multidivisional structure during the early part of the twentieth century was instrumental in facilitating the strategies of diversification and multinational expansion that then characterized large corporations.

The corporate/divisional distinction within the multidivisional firm provides the basic structure for the formation and implementation of corporate strategy. The initial rationale for the multidivisional firm was the separation of strategic and operational decision making. Over time the boundary has shifted: increasingly, business-level strategic decision making has become the responsibility of the divisions, while the corporate headquarters has taken responsibility for corporate strategy and overall corporate performance. Our key task here is to analyze and understand the role of the corporate center in managing the multibusiness company.

The Theory of the M-form Corporation

Once Alfred Chandler had documented the origin and diffusion of the multidivisional form, it was up to Oliver Williamson to theorize about its efficiency advantages.[2] Williamson identified four key features of the divisionalized firm (or, in his terminology, the *M-form*) that are the basis of its superiority as an organizational form:

1. *Adaptation to bounded rationality.* Managers are limited in their cognitive, information-processing, and decision-making capabilities. Thus, the top management team cannot be responsible for all coordination and decision making within a complex organization, and the multidivisional corporation permits management responsibilities to be decentralized.

2. *Allocation of decision making.* Decision-making responsibilities should be separated according to the frequency with which different types of decisions are made. Thus, decisions that are made with high frequency (e.g., operating decisions) need to be separated from decisions that are made infrequently (e.g., strategic decisions).

3. *Minimizing coordination costs.* In the functional organization, decisions concerning a particular product or business area must pass up to the top of the company where all the relevant information and expertise can be brought to bear. In the divisionalized firm, so long as close coordination between different business areas is not necessary, most decisions concerning a particular business can be made at the divisional level. This eases the information and decision-making burden on top management.

[2] This section draws on Oliver E. Williamson, *Markets and Hierarchies: Analysis and Antitrust Implications* (New York: Free Press, 1975); and Oliver E. Williamson, "The Modern Corporation: Origins, Evolution, Attributes," *Journal of Economic Literature* 19 (1981): 1537–68.

4. *Global rather than local optimization.* In functional organizations, senior managers tend to emphasize functional goals over those of the organization as a whole. In multidivisional companies, divisional heads, as general managers, are more likely to identify with the performance goals of the company as a whole.

These features result in the multidivisional firm offering possible solutions to two key problems of the large, managerially controlled corporation:

■ *Allocation of resources.* Resource allocation within any administrative structure is a political process in which power, status, and influence can triumph over purely commercial considerations.[3] To the extent that the multidivisional company can create a competitive internal capital market in which capital is allocated according to financial and strategic criteria, it can avoid much of the politicization inherent in purely hierarchical systems. The multidivisional company can achieve this through operating an internal capital market where budgets are linked to past and projected divisional profitability, and individual projects are subject to a standardized appraisal and approval process. The efficiency of this process is enhanced by the extent and quality of information that is available within the divisionalized company.

■ *Resolution of agency problems.* A second shortcoming of the modern corporation is the tendency for salaried top managers to pursue personal goals that conflict with the wealth-maximizing goals of owners. To the extent that the multibusiness, multidivisional company places a layer of corporate management between the shareholders and operating management, this organizational form might be expected to exacerbate the agency problem. However, Williamson argues to the contrary that, given the limited power of shareholders to discipline and replace managers, and the tendency for top management to dominate the board of directors, the multidivisional form may act as a partial remedy to the agency problem. The rationale is as follows: The corporate management of the multidivisional company acts as an interface between the stockholders and the divisional managers and can ensure adherence to profit goals. Because divisions and business units are typically profit centers, financial performance can readily be monitored by the head office, and divisional managers can be held responsible for performance failures. The multidivisional corporation thus creates the discipline of the capital market within the diversified corporation. So long as corporate management is focused on shareholder goals, the informational and control advantages of the multidivisional company can provide a particularly powerful system for enforcing profit maximization at the divisional level. The key tools are corporate management's ability to allocate funds, threaten divestiture, and reward or fire divisional presidents. General Electric under Jack Welch, Hanson under Lord Hanson, Emerson Electric under Charles Knight, and British Petroleum under John Brown are all companies where the multidivisional structure proved to be highly effective in imposing a strong profit motivation among business-level managers.

---

[3] J. L. Bower, *Managing the Resource Allocation Process* (Boston: Harvard Business School Press, 1986).

Oliver Williamson explains these merits of the multidivisional corporation as follows:

> The M-form conglomerate can be thought of as substituting an administrative inter-face between an operating division and the stockholders where a market interface had existed previously. Subject to the condition that the conglomerate does not diversify to excess, in the sense that it cannot competently evaluate and allocate funds among the diverse activities in which it is engaged, the substitution of internal organization can have beneficial effects in goal pursuit, monitoring, staffing, and resource allocation respects. The goal-pursuit advantage is that which accrues to M-form organizations in general: since the general management of an M-form conglomerate is disengaged from operat-ing matters, a presumption that the general office favors profits over functional goals is warranted. Relatedly, the general office can be regarded as an agent of the stockholders whose purpose is to monitor the operations of the constituent parts. Monitoring benefits are realized in the degree to which internal monitors enjoy advantages over external monitors in access to information – which they arguably do. The differential ease with which the general office can change managers and reassign duties where performance failures or distortions are detected is responsible for the staffing advantage. Resource allocation benefits are realized because cash flows no longer return automatically to their origins but instead revert to the center, thereafter to be allocated among competing uses in accordance with prospective yields.[4]

The assumption that the corporate management of diversified, multidivisional companies is better able to allocate capital efficiently and more likely to operate their companies in the interests of shareholders is not wholly consistent with the evidence. Some of the most notorious examples of chief executives operating their com-panies as personal fiefdoms are found among diversified, divisionalized corporations. Armand Hammer at Occidental Petroleum, Russ Johnson at RJR Nabisco, Howard Hughes at Hughes Corporation, and the Saatchi brothers at Saatchi & Saatchi all pursued empire building at the expense of shareholder return.[5] Corporate executives of diversified companies may be less emotionally committed to particular businesses, but this does not necessarily mean that they are more predisposed to shareholder return than to Napoleonic personal grandeur.

The proposition that the multidivisional structure is more efficient for the man-agement of diversified firms has been tested in a number of studies. Most studies have found that among diversified firms, those with multidivisional structures have outperformed both looser holding companies and more centralized unitary forms.[6]

[4] Williamson, "The Modern Corporation," op. cit.
[5] E. J. Epstein, *Dossier: The Secret History of Armand Hammer* (New York: Carroll & Graf, 1999); B. Burrough, *Barbarians at the Gate: The Fall of RJR Nabisco* (New York: Harper & Row, 1990); K. Goldman, *Conflicting Accounts: The Rise and Crash of the Saatchi & Saatchi Advertising Empire* (New York: Touchstone Books, 1998).
[6] See, for example, Peter Steer and John Cable, "Internal Organization and Profit: An Empirical Analysis of Large UK Companies," *Journal of Industrial Economics* 21 (September 1978): 13–30; Henry Armour and David Teece, "Organizational Structure and Economic Performance: A Test of the Multidivisional Hypothesis," *Bell Journal of Economics* 9 (1978): 106–22; and David Teece, "Internal Organization and Economic Performance," *Journal of Industrial Economics* 30 (1981): 173–99.

The Divisionalized Firm in Practice

Despite the theoretical arguments in favor of the divisionalized corporation and empirical evidence of its efficacy, close observation reveals that its reconciliation of the benefits of decentralization with those of coordination is far from perfect. Henry Mintzberg points to two important rigidities imposed by divisional structures:[7]

- *Constraints on decentralization.* Although operational authority in the M-form firm is dispersed to the divisional level, the individual divisions often feature highly centralized power that is partly a reflection of the divisional president's personal accountability to the head office. In addition, the operational freedom of the divisional management exists only so long as the corporate head office is satisfied with divisional performance. Monthly financial reviews typically mean that variances in divisional performance precipitate speedy corporate intervention.

- *Standardization of divisional management.* In principle, the divisional form permits divisional management to be differentiated by their business needs. In practice, there are powerful forces for standardization across divisions through common control systems, common management development processes, common corporate culture, and the tendency of the corporate center to promote similar types of managers to top divisional positions. The imposition by Exxon of its standard financial control systems and hierarchical culture on its entrepreneurial IT subsidiary, Exxon Office Systems, was a key factor in the venture's eventual failure. The problems of coexisting with different internal cultures and management systems also arises from mergers and acquisitions; for example, Daimler Benz's merger with Chrysler and American Express's acquisition of Shearson and Lehman point to the difficulties associated with conflicting cultures among different businesses.

THE ROLE OF CORPORATE MANAGEMENT

We have looked at the structure of the multibusiness corporation and observed how the multidivisional structure is conducive to the efficient management of multi-market activity. However, we have yet to consider the bigger question of how the corporate center manages value creation. The fundamental issue is this: The multibusiness corporation brings together a number of separate businesses that are placed under the control of a corporate headquarters. If this arrangement is to add value, then the additional profits generated within the different businesses must more than offset the costs of the corporate headquarters. To explore the potential for corporate management to add value, we must consider the role and functions of corporate managers. In Chapter 1, corporate strategy was defined by the answer to the question:

---

[7] Henry Mintzberg, *Structure in Fives: Designing Effective Organizations* (Englewood Cliffs, NJ: Prentice-Hall, 1983): Chapter 11.

"What business are we in?" This encompasses issues of diversification, acquisition, divestment, and the allocation of resources. It should be apparent from the last three chapters that the functions and responsibilities of corporate management extend much further. Corporate strategy is certainly concerned with defining and shaping the business portfolio. Equally important, however, are the administrative and the leadership roles of corporate management in terms of implementing corporate strategy, participating in divisional strategy formulation, coordinating the different divisions, and fostering cohesion, identity, and a sense of direction within the company. These functions extend beyond what is normally thought of as "corporate strategy." For this reason, Goold, Campbell, and Alexander refer to the role of the corporate headquarters in the multibusiness company as "corporate parenting."[8]

If the purpose of corporate management in the multibusiness company is to add value to the businesses it manages, there are three main areas where this can occur:

■ Managing the corporate portfolio, including acquisitions, divestments, and resource allocation.

■ Exercising guidance and control over individual businesses, including the formulation of business strategy and the imposition of financial incentives and controls.

■ Managing linkages among businesses by sharing and transferring resources and capabilities.

Let us consider each of these three sets of corporate management activity and identify the conditions under which they can create value.

MANAGING THE CORPORATE PORTFOLIO

The fundamental question we posed in order to identify corporate strategy was: "What business are we in?" This question points us directly to the composition and balance of the portfolio of businesses that the company holds. The key issues are extensions of the portfolio (acquisitions, mergers, new ventures, and market entries), deletions from the portfolio (divestments), and changes in the balance of the portfolio through the allocation and reallocation of investment funds and other resources. While additions to and deletions from the corporate portfolio are typically major but infrequent corporate strategy decisions, resource allocations among businesses are an ongoing strategic responsibility of corporate management. Although the resource allocation process focuses on capital budgeting, the assignment and transfer of senior divisional managers are also vital corporate management activities, as is reassignment of responsibilities and "strategic mandates" between business units. These portfolio management roles of the corporate center have been closely associated in the strategic management literature with the development and deployment of portfolio planning models and,

[8] M. Goold, A. Campbell, and M. Alexander, *Corporate-Level Strategy: Creating Value in the Multibusiness Company* (New York: Wiley, 1994).

more recently, with restructuring strategies based on shareholder value analysis. Let's consider both these sets of tools.

GE and the Development of Strategic Planning Techniques

The development of portfolio planning techniques for multibusiness corporations is closely associated with one company, General Electric. Indeed, of all the world's great corporations, General Electric has been a leading source of corporate strategy concepts and innovations and a pioneer of corporate management techniques. GE has been among the top five members of *Fortune* magazine's "America's Most Admired Corporations" since the listings began. Peer admiration for GE is linked primarily to its highly effective and constantly evolving system of corporate management. As one executive remarked, "When Japanese managers come to visit us, they don't ask to see our research centers or manufacturing facilities. All they want to know is about our management system."[9]

In response to the challenges of managing a widely diversified corporation organized into 46 divisions and over 190 businesses, GE launched a series of initiatives aimed at developing a more effective system of corporate planning backed by better analytic techniques. Working with the Boston Consulting Group, McKinsey & Co., Arthur D. Little, and the Harvard Business School, GE spawned three innovations that were to transform the formulation and implementation of corporate strategy:

- *Portfolio planning models* – two-dimensional, matrix-based frameworks to evaluate business unit performance, formulate business unit strategies, and assess the overall balance of the corporate portfolio.

- *The strategic business unit (SBU)* – the basic organizational unit for which it is meaningful to formulate a separate competitive strategy. Typically, an SBU is a business consisting of a number of closely related products and for which most costs are not shared with other businesses. McKinsey recommended the reorganization of GE into SBUs for formulating and monitoring business strategies.

- *The PIMS database* – an internal database that comprises strategic, market, and performance data on each of GE's businesses for assisting strategy formulation by providing analysis of the impact of market structure and strategy variables on profitability.[10]

Portfolio Planning: The GE/McKinsey Matrix

The best-known products of GE's corporate planning initiatives of 1969–72 are the portfolio planning models developed by McKinsey, BCG, and A. D. Little. The

---

[9] *General Electric: Strategic Position – 1981*, Case 381-174 (Boston: Harvard Business School, 1981): 1.
[10] The PIMS database is referred to extensively in Chapter 3.

basic idea is to represent the businesses of the diversified company within a simple graphical framework that can be used to assist strategy analysis in four areas:

1. *Allocating resources.* Portfolio analysis examines the position of a business unit in relation to the two primary sources of profitability: industry attractiveness and the competitive advantage of the firm. These indicate the attractiveness of the business for Future investment.

2. *Formulating business unit strategy.* The current positioning of the business in relation to industry attractiveness and potential competitive advantage indicates the strategic approach that should be taken with regard to capital investment and can point to opportunities for repositioning the business.

3. *Analyzing portfolio balance.* The primary usefulness of a single diagrammatic representation of the company's different businesses is the ability of corporate management to take an overall view of the company. This permits planning the overall balance of:
   —*cash flows*: by balancing cash-generating businesses against cash-absorbing businesses, the diversified company can achieve independence from external capital markets;
   —*growth*: by balancing a mix of businesses in different stages of their life cycles, the diversified company can stabilize its growth rate and achieve continuity over time.

4. *Setting performance targets.* To the extent that positioning with regard to industry attractiveness and competitive position determine profit potential, portfolio-planning matrices can assist in setting performance targets for individual businesses.

The two axes of the GE/McKinsey matrix (see Figure 16.1) are the familiar sources of superior profitability for a firm: *industry attractiveness* and *competitive advantage.* Industry attractiveness is computed on the basis of the following factors:

■ Market size.

■ Market growth (real growth rate over 10 years).

■ Industry profitability (three-year average return on sales of the business and its competitors).

■ Cyclicality (average annual percentage trend deviation of sales).

■ Inflation recovery (ability to cover cost increases by higher productivity and increased prices).

■ Importance of overseas markets (ratio of international to US market).

Business unit competitive advantage is computed on the basis of the following variables:

■ Market position (as indicated by share of the US market, share of world market, and market share relative to that of leading competitors).

FIGURE 16.1   The GE/McKinsey portfolio planning matrix

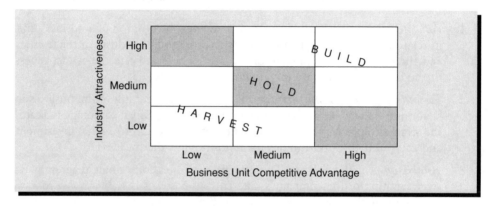

- Competitive position (superior, equal, or inferior to competitors) with regard to quality, technology, manufacturing, distribution, marketing, and cost.

- Return on sales relative to that of leading competitors.

Strategy recommendations are shown by three regions of Figure 16.1:

- Business units that rank high both on both dimensions have excellent profit potential and should be *grown*.

- Those that rank low on both dimensions have poor prospects and should be *harvested* (managed to maximize cash flow with little or no new investment).

- In-between businesses are candidates for a *hold* strategy.

The value of this technique is its simplicity: even for a complex and diverse company such as General Electric, which in 1980 consisted of 43 SBUs, all the firm's SBUs can be shown on a single diagram. Thus, though the matrix may be simplistic, its power lies in its ability to display the relative strategic positions of all the company's businesses and to compress a large amount of data into two dimensions.

Portfolio Planning: BCG's Growth–Share Matrix

The Boston Consulting Group's matrix is similar: it also uses industry attractiveness and competitive position to compare the strategic positions of different businesses and draw strategy inferences. However, unlike the McKinsey matrix, it uses single variables for each axis: industry attractiveness is measured by *market growth rate*, competitive advantage by *relative market share* (the business unit's market share relative to that of its largest competitor).

The four quadrants of the BCG matrix predict patterns of profits and cash flow and offer strategy recommendations as to appropriate strategies. These are summarized in Figure 16.2.

FIGURE 16.2   The BCG growth–share matrix

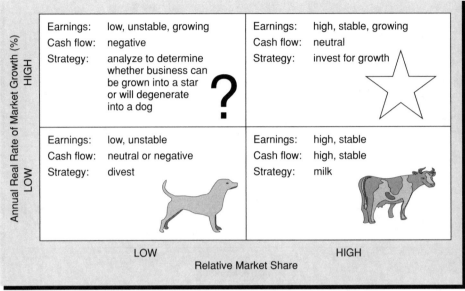

The BCG growth–share matrix is even more elementary than the McKinsey matrix and at best can provide only a rough, first-cut analysis. Nevertheless, the BCG matrix has been widely used by companies who have found virtues in its very simplicity:

■ Because information on only two variables is required, the analysis can be prepared easily and quickly.

■ It assists senior managers in cutting through vast quantities of detailed information to reveal key differences in the positioning of individual business units.

■ The analysis is versatile – it can be applied not only to business units, but also to analyzing the positioning and performance potential of different products, brands, distribution channels, and customers.

■ It provides a useful point of departure for more detailed analysis and discussion of the competitive positions and strategies of individual business units.

The value of combining several elements of strategically useful information in a single graphical display is illustrated by the application of the BCG matrix to a diversified food-processing company (see Figure 16.3). Not only does the display show the positioning of the business units with regard to market growth and relative market share, it also indicates the relative sales revenues of the units, their patterns of distribution, and movements in their strategic position over time.

Since the 1980s, portfolio planning matrices (including those of BCG and McKinsey) have lost their popularity as analytic tools. Among their weaknesses are the following:

FIGURE 16.3   Applying the BCG matrix to BM Foods Inc.

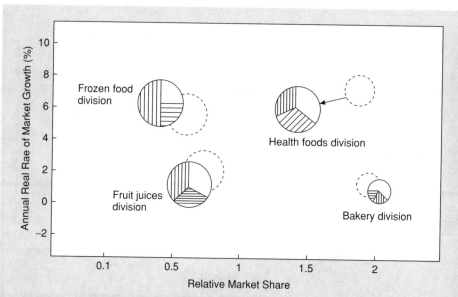

Notes:
1. The continuous circles show the position of each division in 1996; the broken circles show the position in 1994.
2. The sizes of the circles are proportional to sales revenue at 1996 prices.
3. The vertically shaded segments show sales to supermarket chains, the horizontally shaded segments show sales to other retailers, and the unshaded segments show sales to wholesalers and caterers.

- Both are gross oversimplifications of the factors that determine industry attractiveness and competitive advantage. This is especially true of the BCG matrix, which uses just two variables: market share is not a good indicator of competitive advantage; market growth is a poor proxy for market profit potential.

- The positioning of businesses within the matrix is highly susceptible to measurement choices. For example, relative market share in the BCG matrix depends critically on how markets are defined. Is BMW's North American auto business a "dog" because it holds about 2 percent of the total auto market, or a cash cow because BMW is market leader in the luxury car segment?

- The approach assumes that every business is completely independent. Where linkages exist between business units, viewing each as a standalone business inevitably leads to suboptimal strategy choices. Texaco's European heating oil business appears to be a "dog," but to the extent that the business helps in the utilization of the company's European refineries, the heating oil business contributes to the competitive positions of Texaco's other European businesses.

FIGURE 16.4   The McKinsey restructuring pentagon

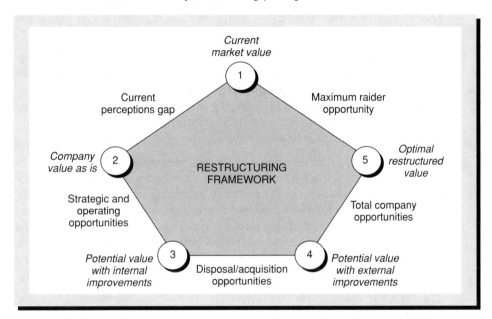

Value Creation through Corporate Restructuring[11]

If portfolio analysis was a key framework for strategy analysis during the diversification era of the 1970s, the refocusing of the 1990s has been closely associated with the application of shareholder value analysis to corporate strategy decisions. In appraising the business portfolio of a company, the fundamental criterion to be applied to each business is whether the market value of the company is greater *with* that business or *without* it (i.e., selling it to another owner or spinning it off as a separate entity).

The application of value-based management tools has been salutary for the top management teams of many multibusiness corporations. As noted in the previous chapter, the majority of diversifying acquisitions have destroyed shareholder wealth: the acquisition premiums paid have greatly exceeded the value added by the acquired businesses. Conversely, stock market valuations have responded positively to divestments, or even to the anticipation of divestment.

Applying the techniques of shareholder value analysis outlined in Chapter 2, McKinsey & Co. has proposed a systematic framework for increasing the market value of multibusiness companies through corporate restructuring. McKinsey's *Pentagon Framework* consists of a five-stage process, illustrated in Figure 16.4. The five stages of the analysis are:

[11] This section draws on T. Copeland, T. Koller, and J. Murrin, *Valuation: Measuring and Managing the Value of Companies*, 3rd edn (New York: Wiley, 2000).

1. *The current market value of the company.* The starting point of the analysis is the current market value of the company, which comprises the value of equity plus the value of debt. (As we know from Chapter 2, this equals the net present value of the anticipated cash flow to the company.)

2. *The value of the company as is.* Even without any changes to strategy or operations, it may be possible to value simply by managing external perceptions of a company's future prospects. Over the past ten years, companies have devoted increasing attention to managing investor expectations by increasing the flow of information to shareholders and investment analysts and establishing departments of investor relations.

3. *The potential value of the company with internal improvements.* As we shall see in the next section, the corporate head office of a company has opportunities for increasing the overall value of the company by making strategic and operational improvements to individual businesses that increase their cash flows. Strategic opportunities include exploring growth opportunities such as investing in global expansion, repositioning a business in relation to customers and competitors, or strategic outsourcing. Operating improvements would include cost-cutting opportunities and taking advantage of the potential to raise prices.

4. *The potential value of the company with external improvements.* Once top management has determined the value of its constituent businesses and of the company as a whole, it is in a position to determine whether changes in the business portfolio will increase overall company value. The key issue is whether an individual business, even after strategic and operating improvements have been made, could be sold for a price that is greater than its potential value to the company.

5. *The optimum restructured value of the company.* This is the maximum value of a company once all the potential gains from changing investor perceptions, making internal improvements, and taking advantage of external opportunities have been exploited. The difference between the maximum restructured value and the current market value represents the profit potential available to a corporate raider from taking advantage of the restructuring opportunities.

This type of analysis has been traditionally associated with leveraged buyout specialists and other corporate raiders. However, faced with the increasing threat of acquisitions, such analysis is increasingly being undertaken by corporate senior managers themselves. The restructuring measures undertaken by the oil majors during 1986–92 exemplify this process: increasing the value of existing businesses through cost cutting, while taking advantage of external opportunities for trading assets and selling businesses.[12]

---

[12] R. Cibin and R. M. Grant, "Restructuring Among the World's Largest Oil Companies," *British Journal of Management* 7 (December 1996): 411–28.

MANAGING INDIVIDUAL BUSINESSES

Despite the emphasis given to economies of scope and other types of linkage among the businesses within the multibusiness firm, some of the most important opportunities for corporate headquarters to create value arise from what Goold, Campbell, and Alexander call "standalone influence." This relates to the corporate parent's ability to:

> appoint the general manager of each business and influence management develop-
> ment and succession planning within the businesses. It can approve or reject budgets,
> strategic plans, and capital expenditure proposals and it can influence the shape and
> implementation of these plans and proposals. It can provide advice and policy guidance
> to the businesses. The parent also influences the businesses by the hints and pressures
> passed on through both formal and informal line management meetings and contacts,
> and, more indirectly, through the corporate culture.[13]

There are two primary means by which the corporate headquarters can exert control over the different businesses of the corporation. It can control decisions, through requiring that particular categories of decision – typically those involving significant resource commitments – are referred upward for corporate approval. Thus, a company may require that all capital expenditure decisions involving a commitment of funds of over $20 million are approved by the executive committee. Alternatively, corporate may seek to control businesses through controlling performance targets, backed by incentives and penalties to motivate the attainment of these targets. The distinction is between *input* and *output* controls: the company can control the inputs into the process (i.e., the decisions) or it can control the outputs (the performance). Although most companies use a combination of input and output controls, there is an unavoidable trade-off between the two: more of one implies less of the other. If a company exerts tight control over divisional decisions, it must accept the performance outcomes that arise from those decisions. If the company exerts rigorous controls relating to performance in terms of annual profit targets, it must give divisional managers the freedom to make the decisions necessary to achieve these targets. Here, we concentrate on two aspects of corporate influence: influence over business strategy formulation, and financial control.

Business Strategy Formulation

In Chapter 1, I identified corporate strategy as being set at the corporate level and business strategy as set at the business level. In reality, business strategies are formulated jointly by corporate and divisional managers. In most diversified, divisionalized companies, business strategies are initiated by divisional managers and the role of corporate managers is to probe, appraise, amend, and approve divisional strategy proposals. The critical issue for corporate management is to create a strategy-making process that reconciles the decentralized decision making essential

---

[13] Goold, Campbell, and Alexander, op. cit.: 90.

to fostering flexibility, responsiveness, and a sense of ownership at the business level, with the ability of the corporate level to bring to bear its knowledge, perspective, and responsibility for the shareholder interest. Achieving an optimal blend of business-level initiative and corporate-level guidance and discipline is a difficult challenge for the multibusiness corporation. Common to the success of General Electric, Exxon, Tyco International, Enron, and Unilever is a system of strategic management that has managed this difficult tradeoff between business initiative and corporate control. Exhibit 16.1 describes key elements of the strategic planning process at Exxon Corporation.

EXHIBIT 16.1   Strategic Planning at Exxon

In terms of profitability and shareholder return, Exxon has been one of the most successful of the oil and gas majors as well as being one of the world's largest and most international companies. Exxon's strategic planning system has been especially successful at reconciling the critical dilemmas facing the large multibusiness corporation: notably the conflict between long-term strategic planning and rigorous, short-term financial control; and between strong centralized direction and flexible, responsive, business-level decision making. Exxon's strategic planning process flows an annual cycle that is similar to the "generic" strategic planning process outlined in Chapter 6 (see Figure 6.5).

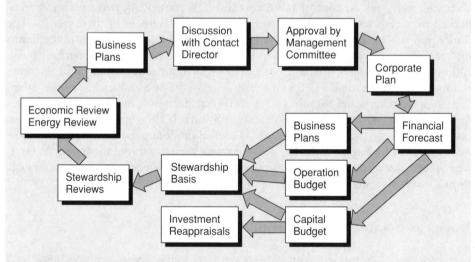

The principal stages of the planning cycle are as follows:

1. *Economic Review and Energy Review* are forecasts of the economy and energy markets prepared in spring by the Corporate Planning Department to provide a basis for strategic planning.

2. *Business Plans* are developed during the spring and summer by individual businesses and are aggregated and refined at the divisional level. Their time horizon is ten years for upstream, five years for downstream and chemicals. Prior to discussion,

EXHIBIT 16.1   *(cont'd)*

negotiation, and approval by the Management Committee, the plans are discussed with each division's contact director and evaluated by Corporate Planning Department (during October).

3. *The Corporate Plan* results from the aggregation of individual business plans. The approved business and corporate plans then provide the basis for the financial and performance plans (formulated during November).

4. *The Financial Forecast* comprises forecasts of revenues, operating costs, capital expenditures, interest and other expenses, income, and cash flow for divisions and for the company as a whole over a two-year period.

5. *The Operating and Capital Budgets* are set for the upcoming year (the first year of the plans).

6. *The Stewardship Basis* is a statement of annual targets against which the next year's performance by each division will be judged. The objectives include financial objectives, operating targets (e.g., wells drilled, contracts signed, capacity utilization, throughput), safety and environmental objectives, and strategy mileposts. A key aspect of the stewardship process is to identify performance measures that reflect *controllable* aspects of the business. Thus, profit performance targets are set such that they can be adjusted for unforecasted price and exchange rate movements.

7. *Stewardship Reviews.* In February of each year, each division's performance for the previous year is evaluated against its stewardship objectives. These reviews involve presentations by the divisional top management to the Management Committee.

8. *Investment Reappraisals* occur in August and September and involve the divisions reporting back on the outcomes of specific investment projects.

In addition to this annual strategic planning cycle, *Strategic Studies* are *ad hoc* projects by the Corporate Planning Department that address specific issues such as country and product studies and responses to major market, technological, and political changes.

In terms of the ability to link and reconcile expertise and influence at both the corporate and business level, Exxon's strategic management system features clearly defined corporate, divisional, and business unit responsibilities (with matching accountability), together with close communication and coordination between these levels. Thus, despite the clear division of responsibilities between corporate strategy and corporate performance and business strategy and performance – the former is the responsibility of the Management Committee (composed of Exxon's executive board members), the latter is the responsibility of the Divisional Presidents and their management teams – close linkage exists between the two, to the extent that each member of the Management Committee is "Contact Director" for two or three divisions. The ongoing dialog between the Divisional Presidents and the Contact Directors is a mechanism for knowledge sharing and initiating strategic changes that adds flexibility to the formal strategic planning process. The result is a system of strategy formulation and performance management that is simultaneously top down and bottom up – strategy is a result both of top-down priorities and guidelines and bottom-up decision making from those closest to the individual businesses.

Strategy formulation and financial control are linked by the close integration of budgeting and performance management with strategic planning. This is reinforced by Exxon's emphasis on *stewardship* – a doctrine of managerial responsibility and accountability that makes each executive responsible in a personal way to the corporation and its shareholders.

Performance Control and the Budgeting Process

Most multidivisional companies operate a dual planning process: strategic planning concentrates on the medium and long term, financial planning controls short-term performance. Typically, the first year of the strategic plan includes the performance plan for the upcoming year in terms of an operating budget, a capital expenditure budget, and strategy targets relating to market share, new product introductions, and output and employment levels. Annual performance plans are agreed between senior business-level and corporate-level managers. They are monitored on a monthly or quarterly basis, and are reviewed more extensively in meetings between business and corporate management after the end of each financial year.

The corporate head office is responsible for setting, monitoring, and enforcing performance targets for the individual divisions. Performance targets may be financial (return on invested capital, gross margin, growth of sales revenue), strategic (market share, rate of new product introduction, market penetration, quality), or both. Performance targets are primarily annual, but also longer term – most companies set targets for between two and five years. However, the monitoring of these targets to detect deviations from annual performance targets results in considerable weight being placed on monthly and quarterly performance data.

Incentives for achieving target performance include financial returns (salary, bonuses, stock options), promotion, and intangible rewards that enhance organizational status and self-image (e.g., praise, recognition). Sanctions include blame and loss of reputation, demotion, and, ultimately, dismissal. Some diversified companies have proved to be highly effective in using performance monitoring and a combination of incentives and sanctions to create an intensely motivating environment for divisional managers. At ITT, Geneen's obsession with highly detailed performance monitoring, ruthless interrogation of divisional executives, and generous rewards for success developed a highly motivated, strongly capable group of young, senior executives who were willing to work unremittingly long hours. They demanded as high a standard of performance from their subordinates as Geneen did of them.[14] The existence of precise, quantitative performance targets that can be monitored on a short-term (monthly or quarterly) basis can provide an intensely competitive internal environment that is highly effective in motivating a business unit and divisional managers. PepsiCo's obsession with monthly market share results nourishes an intense and aggressive, marketing-oriented culture. As one PepsiCo executive explained, "The place is full of guys with sparks coming out of their asses."[15] At Tyco International, CEO Dennis Kozlowski focuses on deal making while giving his business managers enormous autonomy. This autonomy is matched by exceptionally demanding performance goals with powerful incentives for reaching them. The result is an organization with 215,000 employees and a tiny head office in Oxford, New Hampshire.[16]

---

[14] Geneen's style of management is discussed in Chapter 3 of Richard T. Pascale and Anthony G. Athos, *The Art of Japanese Management* (New York: Warner Books, 1982).
[15] "Those Highflying PepsiCo Managers," *Fortune* (April 10, 1989): 79.
[16] "Dennis Kozlowski, Tyco International," *Business Week* (January 8, 2001): 48.

As I discussed in Chapter 2, reconciling short-term financial targets with longer-term strategic goals represents a dilemma for many companies. For example, in technology-based industries, financial targets may stunt innovation. I introduced the *balanced scorecard* as one solution to this problem (see pp. 56–58). Another approach to reconciling long-term strategic goals with on-going performance control is to establish a series of *milestones* that set dates for achieving specific stages in the development of products, projects, or the business as a whole. Milestones might include the signing of particular contacts, the production of a product prototype, the market launch of a new product, achieving a particular level of market penetration, or reducing costs by a specific level. High-tech companies may also achieve high levels of financial awareness and responsibility, not through tight formal control, but though a culture that emphasizes commitment to profitability and fiscal prudence. AOL is a company that has continuously made big financial bets and been willing to forgo short-term profitability for longer-term strategic goals, yet maintains a strong financial discipline primarily through a culture that emphasizes financial returns and disciplined investment decisions.

Implementing performance management typically means the introduction of performance-related pay. Over time, top management compensation has become increasingly closely tied to company performance. This has occurred through the growing size of performance-related annual bonuses as a percentage of salary, and the increasing role of stock options. Moreover, performance bonuses and options packages are being extended down corporate hierarchies to increasing numbers of employees. In the UK, salary comprised 54 percent of total executive compensation as compared with bonuses 24 percent, and options and long-term incentive plans 22 percent.[17]

Strategic Management Styles

One implication of the tradeoff between *input control* (controlling decisions) and *output control* (controlling performance) is that companies must choose how far to emphasize strategic planning relative to financial planning as their primary control system. A study of corporate strategy by Michael Goold and Andrew Campbell found that large, British, multibusiness companies could be classified according to whether their management systems emphasized strategy or finance as the basis of planning and control.[18] Their research identifies three strategic management styles:

- *Strategic planning* was associated with substantial involvement by corporate headquarters in business-level planning. Strategies emphasized strategic objectives (market share, innovation, quality leadership) over financial objectives, and the long term over the short term. Strong corporate involvement in

---

[17] M. J. Conyon, S. I. Peck, L. E. Read, and G. V. Sadler, "The Structure of Executive Compensation Contracts: The UK Evidence," *Long Range Planning* 33 (August 2000): 478–503.
[18] M. Goold and A. Campbell, *Strategies and Styles* (Oxford: Blackwell, 1987).

business-level planning limits the independence of divisional top management, thereby undermining their initiative and sense of ownership. This may also slow strategic decision making and limit responsiveness to new circumstances and opportunities. Strong corporate influence may also impose a unitary view of the world. A strategic planning style is appropriate for companies whose businesses are small in number, do not span too wide a range of products and industries, and with strong linkages between them. The style is more appropriate to companies that compete in international and technology-intensive markets where longer-term strategic goals are more important than short-term profit targets.

■ *Financial control* implied limited involvement by corporate management in business strategy formulation, which was the responsibility of divisional and business unit managers. The primary influence of headquarters was through short-term budgetary control. By setting profit targets that were ambitious, short term, and easily measured, managers were strongly motivated to increase efficiency and expand business into profitable areas. Careful monitoring of performance by headquarters – with rigorous questioning of managers responsible for deviations from target – maintained constant pressure on divisional management and created a challenging working environment. The benefits of the financial control style were in the autonomy it gave to business units, including the sense of ownership and personal commitment it engendered among divisional managers.[19] This autonomy also encouraged managers to break away from ineffective strategies at an early stage. The key drawbacks of financial control arose from the tendency to neglect long-term strategic development and difficulties in managing cooperation between different divisions. Hence, the financial control style is suited to companies characterized by broad business diversity, with investment projects that are mainly short and medium term in fruition, and in low-tech industries with limited international competition.

Table 16.1 summarizes key features of the two styles.

Using PIMS in Strategy Formulation and Performance Appraisal

The PIMS program grew out of General Electric's internal database and was subsequently extended and developed by the Strategic Planning Institute, which conducts research and provides advisory services to the member companies. The PIMS database comprises information on over 5,000 business units that is used to estimate

---

[19]   J. Roberts points to the role of the "psychological contract" between divisional and corporate management as a key motivating device. See "Strategy and Accounting in a U.K. Conglomerate," *Accounting, Organizations and Society* 15 (1990): 107–26.

TABLE 16.1 Characteristics of Different Strategic Management Styles

	STRATEGIC PLANNING	FINANCIAL CONTROL
Business Strategy Formulation	Business units and corporate center jointly formulate strategy. Center responsible for coordination of strategies among business units.	Strategy formulated at business unit level. Corporate HQ largely reactive, offering little coordination.
Controlling Performance	Primarily strategic goals with medium- to long-term horizon.	Financial budgets set annual targets for ROI and other financial variables with monthly and quarterly monitoring.
Advantages	Can exploit linkages among businesses. Can give appropriate weight to innovation and longer-term competitive positioning.	Business units given autonomy and initiative. Business units can respond quickly to change. Encourages development of business unit managers. Highly motivating.
Disadvantages	Loss of divisional autonomy and initiative. Conducive to unitary view. Resistance to abandoning failed strategy.	Short-term focus discourages innovation, building longer-term competitive position, and sharing resources and skills among businesses. Businesses may be willing to give ground to determined competitors.
Style suited to:		
Portfolio Structure	Small number of businesses across narrow range of sectors with close interrelations.	Many businesses across wide range of industries. Linkages ideally few.
Type of Investment	Large projects with long-term paybacks.	Small capital investments with short payback periods.
Environmental Features	Industries with strong technological and global competition.	Mature industries (technical change modest or slow). Stable industry environment without strong international competition.
UK Examples	BP, BOC, Cadbury-Schweppes, Lex Group, STC, United Biscuits.	Hanson, BTR, General Electric Company, Ferranti, Tarmac

Source: Based on M. Goold and A. Campbell, *Strategies and Styles* (Oxford: Blackwell, 1987).

the impact of strategy and market structure on business-level profitability. Table 16.2 shows an estimated PIMS equation.

PIMS data is used by multibusiness companies to assist in three areas of corporate management:

■ *Setting performance targets for business units.* Using the regression coefficients in the PIMS profitability equations, it is possible to plug into the PIMS regression the actual levels of the strategic and industry variables for a particular business and thereby calculate its "Par ROI" – the level of ROI that would

TABLE 16.2   The PIMS Multiple Regression Equations: The Impact of Industry and Strategy on Profitability

PROFIT INFLUENCES	IMPACT ON:	
	ROI	ROS
Real market growth rate	0.18	0.04
Rate of price inflation	0.22	0.08
Purchase concentration	0.02	N.S.
Unionization (%)	−0.07	−0.03
Low purchase amount:		
low importance	6.06	1.63
high importance	5.42	2.10
High purchase amount:		
low importance	−6.96	−2.58
high importance	−3.84	−1.11
Exports–Imports (%)	0.06	0.05
Customized products	−2.44	−1.77
Market share	0.34	0.14
Relative quality	0.11	0.05
New products (%)	−0.12	−0.15
Marketing, percentage of sales	−0.52	−0.32
R&D, percentage of sales	−0.36	−0.22
Inventory, percentage of sales	−0.49	−0.09
Fixed capital intensity	−0.55	−0.10
Plant newness	0.07	0.05
Capital utilization	0.31	0.10
Employee productivity	0.13	0.06
Vertical integration	0.26	0.18
FIFO inventory valuation	1.30	0.62
R^2	0.39	0.31
F	58.3	45.1
Number of cases	2,314	2,314

Note: For example, if Real Market Growth Rate of a business was to increase by one percentage point, the equation predicts that its ROI would rise by 0.18 percent.
Source: Robert D. Buzzell and Bradley T. Gale, *The PIMS Principles: Linking Strategy to Performance* (New York: Free Press, 1987): 274.

be expected for the business given its profile of strategic and industry characteristics if its performance were typical of the sample as a whole. "Par ROI" represents a benchmark that can be used as the basis for profitability targets or for evaluating actual profitability.

■ *Formulating business unit strategy.* Because the PIMS regression equations estimate the impact of different strategy variables on ROI, these estimates can indicate how a business can adjust its strategy in order to increase its profit performance.

■ *Allocating investment funds between businesses.* Past profitability of business units is a poor indicator of the return on new investment. PIMS' "Strategic Attractiveness Scan" indicates investment attractiveness based on (a) estimated future real growth rate of the market, and (b) the "Par ROI" of the business. The analysis offers predictions as to the "strategic attractiveness" of investment in the business, and the cash flow that can be expected from it.

MANAGING INTERNAL LINKAGES

As we saw in the previous chapter, the main opportunities for creating value in the multibusiness company arise from sharing resources and transferring capabilities among the different businesses within the company. This sharing occurs both through the centralization of common services at the corporate level and through direct linkages between the businesses.

Common Corporate Services

The simplest form of resource sharing in the multidivisional company is the centralized provision of common services and functions. These include corporate management functions such as strategic planning, financial control, cash and risk management, internal audit, taxation, government relations, and shareholder relations. They also include services that are more efficiently provided on a centralized basis, such as research, engineering, human resources management, legal services, management development, purchasing, and any other administrative services subject to economies of scale or learning. By 2000, shared corporate services accounted for 43 percent of headquarters staff among large UK corporations.[20]

In practice, the benefits of centralized provision of common services tend to be smaller than many corporate managers anticipate. Although there is little doubt that centralized provision can avoid costs of duplication, the key problem tends to be a lack of incentive among corporate headquarters staff and specialized corporate units to exploit cost efficiencies or to meet the needs of their business-level customers. During the 1960s and 1970s, many companies found that their corporate staffs tended to grow under their own momentum with few obvious economies from central provision and no obvious benefits to the businesses in terms of superior services.

As a result, many companies separated their corporate headquarters into two groups: a corporate management unit responsible for supporting the corporate management team in core support activities such as strategic planning, finance, and legal, and a *shared services organization* responsible for supplying common services such as research, engineering, training, and information technology to the businesses. The tendency has been to create market incentives for these shared service organizations by requiring them to supply services on an arm's-length basis to internal operating units, frequently in competition with independent suppliers of the same services. For example, prior to its merger with British Petroleum, Amoco' split its head office between a Corporate Roles group – comprising the Controller, Treasurer, Financial

---

[20] M. Goold and A. Campbell, "Redesigning the Corporate Center," *Long Range Planning* (forthcoming, 2001).

Operations, Corporate Planning, Corporate Secretary, and Quality Management – and a Shared Services Organization, including Human Resources, IT, Government Relations, Public and Government Affairs, Purchasing, Facilities and Services, Business Processing, Analytical Services, Environment–Health–Safety, Supply, Engineering and Construction, Tax, Auditing, and Legal Services. These 14 service groups initially had a three-year "monopoly" on supplying services to the business groups, after which the businesses were free to obtain services from inside or outside the Amoco group. In 1999, DuPont followed a similar route. It combined its common corporate services into a separate organization called Global Services Business, which was required to supply services on an arm's-length basis to the different DuPont businesses.[21]

Business Linkages and Porter's Corporate Strategy Types

Exploiting economies of scope doesn't necessarily mean centralizing resources at the corporate level. Resources and capabilities can also be shared between the businesses. Michael Porter has argued that the way in which a company manages these linkages determines its potential to create value for shareholders. He identifies four corporate strategy types.

■ *Portfolio management*. The most limited form of resource sharing is where the parent company simply acquires a portfolio of attractive, soundly managed companies, allows them to operate autonomously, and links them through an efficient internal capital market. This corresponds to the traditional holding company, a contemporary example of which is Berkshire Hathaway. Value is created by acquiring companies at favorable prices, closely monitoring their financial performance, and operating a highly effective internal capital market.

■ *Restructuring*. British conglomerates BTR and the former Hanson, and US leveraged buyout operators such as KKR, have created value by restructuring: acquiring poorly managed companies, then intervening to dispose of underperforming businesses and assets, restructure liabilities, and change management and reduce costs in ongoing businesses.

■ *Transferring skills*. Organizational capabilities can be transferred between business units. Philip Morris transfers brand management and distribution capabilities among its tobacco, beer, and Kraft–General Foods businesses. Sharp transfers its microelectronics and miniaturizational capabilities across a number of consumer, electronic and office equipment products. Creating value by sharing skills requires that the same capabilities are applicable to the different businesses, and also that mechanisms are established to transfer these skills through personnel exchange and best practice transfer.

---

[21]   Ibid.

- *Sharing Activities.* Porter argues that the most important source of value arises from exploiting economies of scope in common resources and activities. For these economies to be realized, corporate management must play a key co-ordinating role, including involvement in formulating business unit strategies and intervention in operational matters to ensure that opportunities for sharing R&D, advertising, distribution systems, and service networks are fully exploited. Such sharing is facilitated by:
  —a strong sense of corporate identity;
  —a corporate mission statement that emphasizes the integration of business-level strategies;
  —an incentive for cooperation among businesses;
  —inter-business task forces and other vehicles for cooperation.

The Corporate Role in Managing Linkages

The closer the linkages among businesses, the greater the opportunities for creating value from sharing resources and transferring capabilities, and the greater the need for corporate headquarters to manage the coordination of divisional strategies and activities. In the conglomerate, the independence of each business limits the opportunities for managing linkages. The coordinating role of the head office is restricted to managing the budgetary process and establishing "framework conditions" for divisional planning in the form of economic forecasts, scenarios, and a common format for strategic plans.

In more closely related companies such as the highly vertically integrated oil companies, or companies with close market or technological links (such as IBM, Procter & Gamble, American Express, and Alcoa), corporate management is likely to play a much greater coordinating role. This is likely to involve not only coordination of strategies but also operational coordination in order to exploit the economies of scope and transferable skills discussed in Chapter 15. One indicator of the impact of divisional interrelationships on the coordinating role of corporate management is the size of the corporate headquarters in different types of companies. Berkshire Hathaway, which has almost no linkages among its businesses, has a corporate staff of about 50. Hewlett-Packard, with about the same sales but much closer linkages between its divisions, has close to 3,000 employees at its Palo Alto head office. Goold and Campbell note that the companies that are closely involved with creating value in their businesses through "*value-added corporate parenting*" tend to have significant numbers of headquarters staff involved in developing key technical and functional capabilities. Thus, Pfizer and Corning have strong corporate R&D groups; Dow has a strong corporate manufacturing function; and Virgin's corporate team plays a key role in managing the brand.[22]

The need to marry decentralized decision making with multiple dimensions of coordination gives rise to complex issues of organizational design within the

---

[22] Ibid.

multibusiness company. Virtually all multibusiness companies are organized around some form of matrix; even companies that are based on product divisions tend to have a geographical organization through country managers who coordinate government relations, taxation, and legal affairs within each country, and functional heads responsible for coordination and best practice transfer in manufacturing, marketing, and other functions across the corporation.

Opportunities for sharing and transferring resources and capabilities may also be accessed through various types of *ad hoc* organizational arrangements such as *cross-divisional task forces*. Such task forces might be formed for the introduction and dissemination of total quality management, to reengineer financial management practices, to promote fast-cycle new product development, to coordinate business development in Vietnam, and so on.

Corporate management may also encourage divisional managers to exploit inter-business linkages through exhortations to divisional managers. A key aspect of the top-down aspect of corporate planning is for the CEO to identify company-wide issues for divisional managers to take account of in their strategies and operating decisions. The annual planning cycle typically begins with the CEO issuing corporate priorities and performance targets, which might include cross-divisional issues such as expansion into China, increasing inventory turnover, integrating IT networks, and the like. In many companies, the periodic launching of company-wide initiatives provides a key mechanism for disseminating strategic changes, best practices, and management innovations. At General Electric, Jack Welch has been an especially effective exponent of corporate initiatives as a means of driving organizational change. These have been built around communicable and compelling slogans such as "GE's growth engine," "boundarylessness," "six-sigma quality," and "destroy-your-business-dot-com."

Exploiting linkages between businesses requires careful management, and this imposes costs. Though Porter may be right that the *potential* for value creation increases as a company moves from a loose, "portfolio management" strategy toward the more integrated, "shared activity" strategy, it is not apparent that this potential is always realized. For example, most attempts at exploiting the potential for cross-selling across different businesses have yielded disappointing results, especially in financial services.[23] A study by Lorsch and Allen offers insight into the corporate management implications of exploiting close linkages between businesses. They compared three conglomerates with three vertically integrated paper companies.[24] The coordination requirements of the paper companies resulted in greater involvement of head office staff in divisional operations, larger head office staffs, more complex planning and control devices, and lower responsiveness to change in the external environment. By contrast, the conglomerates made little attempt to exploit linkages even if they were present:

---

[23] "Cross-selling's Elusive Charms," *Financial Times* (November 16, 1998): 21.
[24] Jay W. Lorsch and Stephen A. Allen III, *Managing Diversity and Interdependence: An Organizational Study of Multidivisional Firms* (Boston: Harvard Business School Press, 1973).

The conglomerate firms we had studied seemed to be achieving appreciable degrees of financial and managerial synergy but little or no operating synergy. Some of the firms saw little immediate payoff in this operating synergy; others met with little success in attempting to achieve it.[25]

The success with which the corporate headquarters manages linkages between businesses depends on top management's understanding the commonalities among its different businesses. As we noted in the last chapter, the mindset and underlying rationale that give cohesiveness to the diversified company has been defined by C. K. Prahalad and Richard Bettis as the dominant logic of the enterprise.[26] They define *dominant logic* as "the way in which managers conceptualize the business and make critical resource allocation decisions." For a diversified business to be successful, they argue, there must be sufficient strategic similarity among the different businesses so that top management can administer the corporation with a single dominant logic. For example:

- Emerson Electric comprises a number of different businesses (electric motors, air conditioning, electrical appliances, control instruments), but the common goal of being a low-cost producer in each of its businesses provides a unifying thread.[27]

- Unilever's dominant logic is that it is an international manufacturer and marketer of branded, packaged consumer goods. Pursuing this logic has encouraged Unilever to exit animal feeds, transportation, packaging, and chemicals, and build on its core businesses of processed foods, household detergents and cleaning supplies, and toiletries.

- Jack Welch's restructuring of GE's business portfolio was preceded by his conceptualizing of GE as three intersecting circles, each containing 15 businesses. One circle was GE's core businesses (such as lighting, appliances, and turbines), the second was high-technology businesses (such as aerospace, medical equipment, and electronics), the third was service businesses (such as financial and information services).[28]

These strategic similarities can promote learning across the company, as strategies that prove successful in one business can be applied in others. At the same time, the tendency for headquarters to encourage uniformity in the strategies applied in different businesses can cause a failure to fit strategy to the circumstances of the individual business. Although Philip Morris successfully transferred its marketing capabilities from its cigarette business to Miller Brewing, the deployment of these same capabilities and approaches at its Seven-Up soft drink subsidiary was a costly failure.[29]

[25] Ibid.: 168.
[26] C. K. Prahalad and R. Bettis, "The Dominant Logic: A New Linkage Between Diversity and Performance," *Strategic Management Journal* 7 (1986): 485–502.
[27] "Shades of Geneen at Emerson Electric," *Fortune* (May 22, 1989): 39.
[28] "General Electric – Going with the Winners," *Fortune* (March 26, 1984): 106.
[29] *The Seven-Up Division of Philip Morris Inc.*, Case no. 9-385-321 (Boston: Harvard Business School, 1989).

RECENT TRENDS IN THE MANAGEMENT OF MULTIBUSINESS CORPORATIONS

The past decade and a half has seen major changes in our thinking about the multibusiness corporation and the role played by its corporate center. At the basis of this shift has been a focus on value creation. As a result, corporate strategy has been seen less in terms of the effective control of vast corporate empires and much more about identifying the means by which the corporate center can create value for the individual businesses. The discussion of corporate management styles in terms of "parenting roles" as compared to "systems of corporate control" reflects this shift of thinking. Key elements of the current approach include:

- A view of corporate headquarters less as the apex of a hierarchy and more as a support service for the businesses.

- Less emphasis on formal systems and techniques, and more on relationships and informal interaction.

- Decentralization of both operational and strategic decisions from corporate to divisional levels.

- Emphasis on the role of headquarters, and the CEO in particular, as a catalyst and driver of organizational change.

The Lessons from General Electric

In the same way that General Electric was the pioneer in the development of formalized approaches to corporate strategy and control, it has also been a prime mover in the dismantling of these formal controls in favor of a more flexible, informal, and dynamic approach to corporate strategy. The "reinventing" of GE has been closely associated with the role of CEO Jack Welch, who took over in 1981 and retired in 2001. Welch's tenure began with an intensive period of restructuring, which transformed the composition of GE's business portfolio through acquisitions and disposals and extended the conglomerate's global reach. Toward the mid-1980s, Welch's attention shifted from the business portfolio to the structure, systems, and style of GE. Among the changes he initiated were the following.

Delayering

Welch's fundamental criticism of GE's management was that it was slow and unresponsive. A precondition for a more nimble enterprise was fewer levels of management. Welch eliminated GE's sector level of organization (which combined a number of businesses) and within each business pressed for the flattening of management pyramids through reducing the layers of hierarchy from nine or ten to four or five:

We used to have things like department managers, subsection managers, unit managers, supervisors. We're driving those titles out . . . We used to go from the CEO to sectors, to groups, to businesses. We now go from the CEO to businesses. Nothing else.[30]

Changing the Strategic Planning System

During the 1970s, GE had developed a systematic and formalized approach to strategy formulation and appraisal. Welch believed that not only was the system slow and inefficient, it also stifled innovation and opportunism. A Harvard case study outlines the changes:

> Nowhere was the change more striking than in the area of strategic planning and operational reviews. Although the basic processes were retained, the old staff-led, document-driven process of the 1970s was largely replaced by a more personal, less formal, but very-intensive face-to-face discussions and small meetings. To cut through the bureaucracy Welch asked each of his 13 business heads to reduce the complex, multivolume planning documents to a slim "playbook" that summarized key strategic issues and actions. On each page, they provided concise answers to questions about their global, market dynamics, key competitive activity, major competitive risks, and proposed GE business responses. These documents became the basis for a half-day shirtsleeve review in mid-summer. Business heads and their key people (usually from three to ten in total) met with the Office of the CEO members and their key staff in an open dialogue on core plans and strategies.[31]

Redefining the Role of Headquarters

The changes in the strategic planning system are indicative of a broader set of changes in the role of the corporate headquarters. Welch viewed headquarters as interfering too much in the businesses, generating too much unnecessary paper, and failing to add value. His objective was to "turn their role 180 degrees from checker, inquisitor, and authority figure to facilitator, helper, and supporter of the 13 businesses. Ideas, initiatives, and decisions could now move quickly." Welch explained his view of corporate HQ as follows:

> What we do here at headquarters . . . is to multiply the resources we have, the human resources, the financial resources, and the best practices . . . Our job is to help, it's to assist, it's to make these businesses stronger, to help them grow and be more powerful.[32]

The Coordinating Role of Corporate

Placing increased emphasis on informal aspects of corporate–business relations increased the role of corporate in facilitating coordination across GE's businesses.

[30] "GE Chief Hopes to Shape Agile Giant," *Los Angeles Times* (June 1, 1988): D1.
[31] *General Electric: Jack Welch's Second Wave (A)*, Case 9-391-248 (Boston: Harvard Business School, 1991).
[32] Jack Welch, "GE Growth Engine," speech to employees (1988).

The Corporate Executive Council was reconstituted to include the leaders of GE's 13 businesses and several key corporate executives. It met two days each quarter to discuss common problems and issues. The Council became an important vehicle for identifying and exploiting synergies. By 1990, Welch had formulated his notions of coordination and integration within his view of the "boundaryless company." A key element of this concept was a blurring of internal divisions so that people could work together across functional and business boundaries. Welch aimed at "integrated diversity" – the ability to transfer the best ideas, most developed knowledge, and most valuable people freely and easily between businesses.

> Boundaryless behavior is the soul of today's GE . . . Simply put, people seem compelled to build layers and walls between themselves and others, and that human tendency tends to be magnified in large, old institutions like ours. These walls cramp people, inhibit creativity, waste time, restrict vision, smother dreams and, above all, slow things down . . . Boundaryless behavior shows up in the actions of a woman from our Appliances business in Hong Kong helping NBC with contacts needed to develop satellite television service in Asia . . . And finally, boundaryless behavior means exploiting one of the unmatchable advantages a multibusiness GE has over almost any other company in the world. Boundaryless behavior combines 12 huge global businesses – each number one or number two in its markets – into a vast laboratory whose principal product is new ideas, coupled with a common commitment to spread them throughout the Company.[33]

GE's hard-driving, performance-focused management style and its systems of strategy formulation, financial control, and human resource management have become models for many other corporations in the Anglo-Saxon world, and have become increasingly influential in guiding organizational change in continental Europe, Japan, and South Korea.

Corporate Managers as Drivers of Organizational Change

Devolution of decision-making authority from corporate to business level does not imply a passive role for the corporate HQ. In many respects, corporate management has become more interventionist in attempting to influence business operations. A critical role for corporate management is in driving large-scale organizational change. This has required new organizational structures. For example, GE's "Work-Out" initiative set up forums where employees could speak their minds about management and propose changes in business structures and operating practices. Work-Out was a vehicle for cultural change in which the relationship between manager and subordinate was redefined and the creativity of employees was unleashed.

Achieving large-scale organizational change requires chief executives whose primary role is that of change maker. In the oil sector, Lucio Noto at Mobil, James Kinnear at Texaco, John Browne David Simon at BP, Serge Tchuruk at Total, and Franco

---

[33] "Letter to Share Owners," *General Electric Company 1993 Annual Report* (Fairfield, CT, 1994): 2.

Bernabe at ENI were all pioneers of fundamental organizational change that embraced strategy, structure, and culture.[34] Intel's former CEO, Andy Grove, has emphasized the important role of chief executives in identifying and responding to *strategic inflection points* – instances where seismic shifts in a firm's competitive environment require a fundamental redirection of strategy.[35] At Intel, such inflection points included the transition from DRAM chips to microprocessors, the decision to focus on its X86 series of microprocessors in favor of RISC architecture, and the decision to replace its faulty Pentium chips.[36]

The role of corporate management in the large, multibusiness company has been shaped by the challenges that these corporate executives have faced. These include the overriding need to establish competitive advantage within each of the business areas in which the firm competes, the need for responsiveness to external change, the need to foster innovation, and the need for cost efficiency. The problem for top management is that these challenges require conflicting adjustments. For example:

- Rigorous financial controls are conducive to cost efficiency and autonomy; flexible controls are conducive to responsiveness and innovation.

- Multibusiness companies have typically been based on the advantages of exploiting existing resources and capabilities across different markets, yet competitive advantage in the future is dependent on the creation of new resources and capabilities.

- Active portfolio management based on the maximization of shareholder value is best achieved with independent businesses; the creation of competitive advantage increasingly requires the management of business interdependencies.

The common dilemma is this: How can the resource advantages of the large company be exploited, while achieving the responsiveness and creativity associated with small companies? The key is to reconcile the flexibility of decentralized decision making with high levels of coordination that can harness the resources, capabilities, and learning potential of the large organization. In Chapter 14, we noted how conflicting pressures for globalization and local adaptability were resolved by multinationals moving toward a "transnational" structure. Similar tendencies are observable in managing the tensions within diversified corporations. At IBM, CEO Lou Gerstner resisted stock market pressures to break up the company in favor of internal changes that would transform its performance and adapt it to a new era of networked IT. The changes involved:

[34] R. M. Grant, "The Chief Executive as Change Agent," *Planning Review* 24 no. 1 (December 1995): 9–11.

[35] A. S. Grove, *Only the Paranoid Survive: How to Exploit the Crisis Points that Challenge Every Company* (New York: Bantam, 1999).

[36] R. A. Burgelman and A. Grove, "Strategic Dissonance," *California Management Review* 38 (Winter 1996): 8–28.

- ■ Aggressive cost cutting and employee reduction.

- ■ Encouraging responsiveness and flexibility through greater autonomy, while more effectively exploiting internal resources and capabilities through internal coordination.

- ■ A breaking down of corporate boundaries and an increased willingness to learn from other companies and to collaborate with other companies in strategic alliances.

Achieving coordination in terms of sharing capabilities, transferring capabilities, harmonizing market initiatives in different countries, and collaborating to develop new products and exploit new technologies requires horizontal communication and cooperation rather than hierarchically designated initiatives. For such coordination to be effective in creating value in the multibusiness company requires that divisions are identified not only with their particular businesses, but also with a corporate identity. Just as the single-business company needs clarity of purpose to provide its strategy with direction and its employees with commitment, so the diversified firm typically needs an identity and a rationale that give meaning to its strategy beyond the composition of its portfolio. Hence, key roles of corporate management in co-ordinating the diversified company are providing *leadership*, defining *mission*, and establishing a set of values and beliefs that create a unifying *corporate culture*.

Strategic similarities and *dominant logic* across the different businesses may not be adequate as an integrating force – especially in developing the loyalty and commitment needed to mobilize the talents and creativity of employees. At the same time, the very diversity of the multibusiness corporation may make it difficult to establish a common culture that unifies the various businesses and their different employees. LVMH, the French producer of Moët & Chandon champagne, Hennessy cognac, Dior and Givenchy perfumes, and Louis Vuitton luggage is a company that has made great efforts to establish a unifying set of values and traditions:

> The common cultural trunk is based on the permanent search for quality of the products and the management, human relations based on responsibility and initiative, and rewarding competences and services.[37]

A major theme in American Express's "one enterprise" program aimed at integrating its various financial service companies was the development of a common set of values oriented around quality, outstanding customer service, and marketing excellence.

Asea Brown Boveri (ABB), the diversified Swiss–Swedish engineering company, has been seen as a model of multibusiness management. Despite very high levels of product and geographical diversification, it has reconciled decentralization with a strong corporate culture that facilitates flexible integration. Key features of ABB's management system are:

---

[37]   Roland Calori, "How Successful Companies Manage Diverse Businesses," *Long Range Planning* 21 (June 1988): 85; "LVMH Tries to Adjust After a Life of Luxury," *Financial Times* (June 11, 1993): 26.

- *Matrix organization.* ABB's matrix comprises both global business chiefs and country and regional managers. Yet, ABB has avoided the problems of bureaucracy, complexity, and diffused accountability that have dogged the matrix structures of many diversified multinationals.

- *Radical decentralization.* The fundamental units of organization in ABB are not product divisions, as assumed in the traditional M-form model, but individual businesses within each country, of which ABB possesses 1,300. These are free-standing legal entities with average employment of 200. These businesses are where strategic and operating decisions are made. Between them and the corporate headquarters is a single management layer formed by worldwide business area managers and country managers. However, the intermediate layer is exceptionally lean, and corporate HQ employs fewer than 100 people.

- *Bottom-up management.* The M-form presupposes that decision-making power has been devolved from corporate down to the divisions. In ABB, authority lies with the individual businesses. Its 1,300 local operating companies each prepare their own financial statements and are able to retain one-third of their net income. The primary role of front-line managers is as entrepreneurs – not implementers of corporate and divisional decisions.

- *Informal collaboration and integration.* The traditional view of the diversified corporation views the corporate HQ as managing the exploitation of economies of scope in joint resources. In ABB, it is horizontal linkages between the front-line business units facilitated by country and business area managers through which capabilities are transferred and common resources are shared.[38]

Based on their observations of ABB, 3M, Corning, Komatsu, and other companies, Bartlett and Ghoshal argue that combining flexible responsiveness with integration and innovation requires rethinking the role of management and the distribution of management roles within the company.[39] They identify three central management processes: the *entrepreneurial process* (decisions about the opportunities to exploit and the allocation of resources), the *integration process* (how organizational capabilities are built and deployed), and the *renewal process* (the shaping of organizational purpose and the initiation of change). Conventionally, all three processes have been concentrated within the corporate HQ. Bartlett and Ghoshal propose a distribution of these functions between three levels of the firm: corporate ("top management"), the business and geographical sector coordinators ("middle management"), and the business units ("front-line management"). The critical feature of the relationships between these management levels and between the individual organizational members form a social structure based on cooperation and learning. Figure 16.5 illustrates their framework.

[38] C. A. Bartlett and S. Ghoshal, "Beyond the M-Form: Toward a Managerial Theory of the Firm," *Strategic Management Journal* 14, Winter special issue (1993): 23–46.
[39] C. A. Bartlett and S. Ghoshal, "The Myth of the General Manager: New Personal Competencies for New Management Roles," *California Management Review* 40 (Fall 1997): 92–116; and "Beyond Structure to Process," *Harvard Business Review* (January–February 1995).

FIGURE 16.5 Management processes and levels of management

	RENEWAL PROCESS	
Attracting resources and capabilities and developing the business	Developing operating managers and supporting their activities. Maintaining organizational trust	Providing institutional leadership through shaping and embedding corporate purpose and challenging embedded assumptions
	INTEGRATION PROCESS	
Managing operational interdependencies and personal networks	Linking skills, knowledge, and resources across units. Reconciling short-term performance and long-term ambition	Creating a corporate direction. Developing and nurturing organizational values
	ENTREPRENEURIAL PROCESS	
Creating and pursuing opportunities. Managing continuous performance improvement	Reviewing, developing, and supporting initiatives	Establishing performance standards
Front-line Management	*Middle Management*	*Top Management*

SUMMARY

The formulation and implementation of corporate strategy present top management with a tangle of issues of almost impenetrable complexity. Increasing globalization of multiproduct companies adds further layers of complexity. It is almost impossible to establish generic recommendations for how multibusiness companies should implement their corporate strategies: each firm possesses a unique portfolio of products and markets; each owns a unique set of resources and capabilities; each has developed a distinct administrative structure, management style, and corporate culture. As might be expected, empirical research offers little clear guidance as to the correlates of superior performance – close relationships between businesses may or may not lead to higher profitability, sharing resources and capabilities offers economies but also imposes management costs, and there are no consistent relationships between a company's performance and the characteristics of its structure, control system, or leadership style.

Designing the appropriate organizational structure, management systems, and leadership style of a multibusiness corporation depends critically on *fit* with the corporate strategy of the company. Fundamental to this fit is the *rationale* for the firm. Diversification – both across product markets and across geographical markets – can create value in different ways. Each source of gain from diversification is likely to imply a quite different approach to managing the firm.

For a conglomerate firm, value can be created through the strategic judgment of the CEO with regard to business prospects and company valuation, and the ability to operate a highly efficient internal capital market. Hence, organization and management systems should be oriented toward a clear separation of business levels on corporate decisions and a highly effective system for budgetary control and project evaluation. For a technology-based diversified corporation, value is created through the transfer and integration of knowledge, ideas, and expertise. The company must be organized in order to facilitate the transfer and application of knowledge. Corporate HQ is likely to play a critical role in technological guidance and in divisional integration.

At a more detailed level, the design of structure and systems, and the allocation of decision-making responsibilities, depends on specific issues such as:

- *The characteristics of the resources and capabilities that are being exploited within the multibusiness corporation.* If capital is the primary common resource, then the corporate system must be established to ensure its efficient allocation. If common corporate services such as information technology and administrative services are the primary sources of economies of scope, then these activities need to be grouped together at the corporate level. If the brand marketing capability is the key common resource, then systems need to be established that facilitate the transfer of marketing capabilities between businesses.

- *The characteristics of the businesses.* If the businesses are highly diverse in terms of their industry characteristics and competitive positions, then a high degree of divisional autonomy is required, as well as the establishment of corporate systems that are sufficiently flexible to accommodate that flexibility. If the businesses are more similar (e.g., P&G's diversification across branded, packaged consumer goods), then a greater uniformity of systems and style is desirable.

Ultimately, finding the appropriate structure, systems, and style with which to manage a multibusiness corporation is dependent on establishing an identity for the company. The failure of most of the conglomerates of the 1960s and early 1970s came about either because they did not establish a clear identity, or because their identity was so closely linked with a single person (e.g., Geneen at ITT) that the companies found difficulty surviving the demise of that person. In other cases, the rationale on which the identity was based was found to be flawed (e.g., Allegis Corp.). Conversely, the success of diversified corporations such as General Electric, Matsushita, Canon, Emerson Electric, and ABB reflects a cohesiveness between the businesses of the company, the strategies being pursued, the structure of the organization, and its management style. This permits a sense of identity and clarity of vision with regard to the fundamental strategic question: *"What kind of company are we seeking to become?"*

17

Current Trends in Strategic Management

I sometimes feel like I'm behind the wheel of a race car . . . One of the biggest challenges is that there are no road signs to help navigate. And in fact, no one has yet determined which side of the road we're supposed to be on.

—Stephen M. Case, chairman,
AOL Time Warner[1]

OUTLINE

[1] Quoted in Jeffrey E. Garten, *The Mind of the CEO* (New York: Perseus, 2001).

INTRODUCTION

The 1990s was a time of unprecedented turbulence: accelerating techno-logical change, the worldwide collapse of communism, the coexistence of US boom and Japanese recession, global financial contagion, and volatile currency and commodity prices. What does the first decade of the new millennium have in store? The simple answer – we don't know. However, the evidence to date suggests one sure bet: the turbulence that has characterized the past decade and a half will continue. The same forces of technological innovation, post-cold war political instability, global interdependence, and volatile market conditions will continue to be key sources of uncertainty both for the managers responsible for formulating and implementing strategy, and for the academics who develop the tools and techniques for strategy analysis.

The challenges of the current decade may be even greater than those of the past decade. The uncertainty and volatility of the 1990s were made bearable for business by two factors. First, the booming US economy underpinned pro-sperity and growth for most of the world. Second, the corporate restructuring – downsizing, refocusing, cost reduction – that dominated the strategies of large western corporations provided a major boost to profitability and shareholder return. During the decade 2001–10, both these cushions have been lost. The Great American Boom, if not dead, is unlikely to maintain its prior vigor, while Europe and Japan are poorly positioned to become locomotives of the world economy. In relation to corporate restructuring, the benefits were probably one-time-only. In Japan, South Korea, and Southeast Asia, gains from applying the basic disciplines of financial control and shareholder value have yet to be fully exploited, but for most North American and European companies, there is little fat left to trim.

So, where will the next major sources of value be located? The emergence of new technologies, new products, and new markets presents companies with a dazzling array of new opportunities. But, through what strategies, business models, and organizational forms should these opportunities be exploited, and – most important – will they create value for shareholders as well as for customers? The evidence from the internet boom of 1999–2000 is hardly encouraging: few of the investments of this period are showing reasonable returns.

The quest for new sources of value and new approaches to exploiting that value has had a powerful effect on strategic thinking. The major themes of the 1990s – shareholder value maximization, resource-based theory, and the role of organizational capability – continue to influence companies' thinking about their strategies. At the same time, emerging ideas about the role of knowledge, the implications of digital technologies and the networked economy, and applications of recent thinking about complexity, mathematics, ethics, and human behavior provide a continual pull toward experimentation and innovation in strategy and the quest for new business models and organizational forms.

Unlike the other chapters of this book, this chapter will not equip you with tools and frameworks that you can deploy directly in your own companies or in case analysis. My approach is exploratory: to introduce you to some of the ideas that are reshaping our thinking about business strategy and business enterprise during this era of uncertainty and rapid change. Let us begin by examining the state of our economic system.

A NEW ECONOMY?

The period of intense economic and technological change beginning in the latter part of the 1990s has been described as the "third industrial revolution" – following the first industrial revolution that began in Britain at the end of the eighteenth century and was associated with the mechanization of production, and the second industrial revolution that began in the US at the end of the nineteenth century and was associated with the rise of the modern corporation and the introduction of the telephone, automobile, and electrical power. As with prior industrial revolutions, the period 1995–2000 was one of prosperity and opportunity, especially for companies in North America and western Europe. These opportunities have been closely associated with new technology. Although the microelecronics revolution dates back to the invention of the integrated circuit and the rise of the personal computer industry, it was not until the 1990s when the full impact of the digital revolution was felt by the world of business – not least because of the revolutionary impact of the internet. New opportunities for trade, investment, and entrepreneurship have also sprung from rapid globalization: worldwide privatization and deregulation, increased freedom of trade following the creation of the World Trade Organization, and the formation of regional free-trade areas (NAFTA, Mercosur, and the enlarged European Union).

The telecommunications sector reflects the combined impact of these forces more clearly than almost any other industry. Beginning with the breakup of AT&T, the privatization of British Telecom, and the advent of wireless telephony at the beginning of the 1990s, the industry has been propelled into a hypercompetitive ferment. Globalization, digitalization and fiber optics, the development of the internet and internet protocols, privatization and deregulation, and the convergence of telecommunications with entertainment and information technology have created a state of permanent revolution. Giants such as AT&T have been slain, upstarts such as Vodafone, DoCoMo, and Worldcom have emerged as leading players, and there is little consensus as to what the industry will look like at the end of this decade.

During the late 1990s, the term "New Economy" was used to refer to this emerging industrial revolution. In its narrower sense, the New Economy was associated with the industries most heavily affected by digital technologies and knowledge-based production – primarily the TMT sector (technology, media, and telecommunications) – as opposed to the "Old Economy" of mature, established industries. In its wider sense, the New Economy referred to the new economic conditions that resulted from the diffusion of new technologies and new business models and the transition to a

FIGURE 17.1 US labor productivity: changes in nonfarm output per hour worked from year ago quarter, 1995–2000.

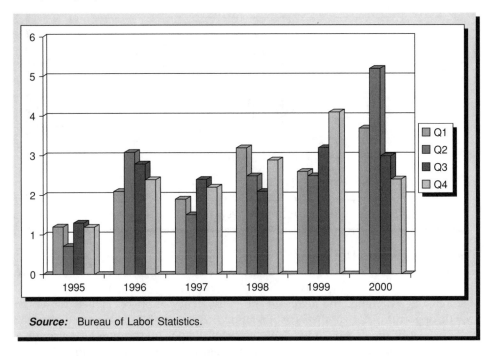

Source: Bureau of Labor Statistics.

knowledge-based economy. The resulting surge in labor productivity (see Figure 17.1) – especially in the US – permitted an unprecedented combination of growth and price stability.

However, by early 2001, it was evident that the promise of the New Economy had been greatly overhyped. Surging productivity appeared to be primarily a US phenomenon, with little follow-on in Europe and even less in Asia. As for a new era of profitable growth, virtually all the evidence pointed toward the New Economy generating profitless growth. As was discussed in Chapter 3 (see "Competition in the New Economy"), most of the TMT sector was associated with intense price competition resulting from low entry barriers, lack of product differentiation, and extreme scale economies. The telecommunications sector is a classic case of phenomenal growth and rapid erosion of margins. By February 2001, long-distance prices in the US had fallen to 2 cents a minute, from 15 cents a minute four years earlier. During 2001, few of the world's leading telecom companies were expected to earn positive economic profits. Meanwhile, in e-commerce it was looking as though even the biggest and best established of the new internet businesses, including Amazon, Webvan, and Ameritrade, would be unable to generate economic profit in the foreseeable future.

The impact of the New Economy on profitability in the Old Economy also seemed to be mainly negative. The internet provided a new avenue for communication and distribution that facilitated new entry into existing markets, lowered consumers' costs

FIGURE 17.2 US corporate profitability

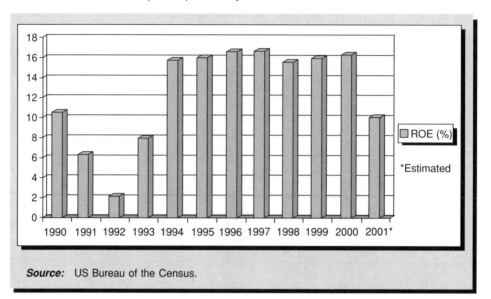

Source: US Bureau of the Census.

of search and switching, and increased the transparency of prices. Hence, for all the growth opportunities that the New Economy made possible, it appeared that the major impact of the new economic conditions of the new millennium was a tougher economic environment for most companies in terms of greater competition, greater uncertainty, and lower profitability.

NEW DIRECTIONS IN STRATEGIC THINKING

Beyond Downsizing

If the impact of digital technologies, the internet, and internationalization has been to increase the intensity of competition, how do we explain the upsurge of profitability that occurred during the latter part of the 1990s (see Figure 17.2)? Certainly, the benign macroeconomic environment of low interest rates, subdued inflation, and buoyant consumer demand boosted corporate profitability. At least as important were the corporate strategies that dominated top management thinking and action during most of the 1990s: shareholder value focus, cost reduction, refocusing, outsourcing, reengineering, and delayering. The bottom-line impact of these practices has been substantial (see Figure 17.2).

The problem for senior management is that the principal sources of increased profitability in the past (cost cutting, divesting underperforming assets, and reengineering processes) are no longer available. The "low-hanging fruit" has been picked and, in the future, value creation is likely to require access to sources of value that are more difficult to reach.

For many companies, the simple answer was to shift from cost-cutting mode to revenue-growing mode. However, the evidence so far suggests that translating revenue growth into profit growth is increasingly difficult – especially where growth has been achieved through acquisition. Looking ahead to the future, it is not apparent that, across the business sector as a whole, the returns available to new investments will match those that have been earned on previous investments. As we have already observed, across both old and new economies, the dominant trends are for more excess capacity, greater price-sensitive buyers, and growing intensity of competition. Even if the US productivity boom continues and diffuses to the rest of the industrialized world, the beneficiaries are likely to be customers rather than stockholders.

Under these circumstances, the challenge to top management is to identify and access new sources of profitability. The recent upsurge of interest in strategic management reflects the importance and complexity of this task. What is lacking, however, is any clear sense of direction as to what the primary sources of value are likely to be during this first decade of the new millennium. This is certainly a change from the past. If the mantras of the 1980s were market share, economies of experience, and portfolio management, and those of the 1990s were restructuring, refocusing, and core capabilities, no such unison is apparent in the current decade. This lack of consensus as to appropriate strategies for the current environment is appropriate in the strategic direction of large companies. At one level, companies have responded to the turbulent environments by increasing their agility, response speed, and innovation. At another level, they have resorted to defensive strategies. In oil, automobiles, banking, insurance, aluminum, airlines, and alcoholic beverages, the primary thrust of strategy has been consolidation through mergers and acquisitions. While business commentators sing the praises of entrepreneurship and the vibrant hurly-burly of business creation and destruction in e-commerce and high-tech, the corporate response to the harsh uncertainties of competition has often been to merge with competitors. Thus, automobiles are evolving toward (perhaps) six major global players (GM, Ford, Toyota, DaimlerChrysler, Renault-Nissan, and VW), investment banking to a "bulge bracket" comprising Citigroup, Goldman Sachs, MSDW, and Merrill Lynch, and liquor to a big-three comprising Diageo, Pernod-Ricard, and Allied Domecq. This urge to consolidate has driven the greatest wave of mergers and acquisitions in history (see Figure 17.3).

The primary justification for these amalgamations has been to access scale economies and global reach. Yet, evidence on the outcomes of horizontal acquisitions reveals that only a minority achieve significant asset rationalization, cost savings, or competency transfer, although the majority did result in increased sales, profitability, and geographical coverage.[2] The suspicion remains that the primary driver of concentration is the desire to escape the uncertainty and misery of intense competition. As British economist J. R. Hicks observed: "The best of all monopoly profits is a quiet life." There is little doubt that acquiring competitors moderates the pressure of competition, but these amalgamations also exacerbate the problems of managing large, international corporations. Traditional conglomerates such as GE have resolved

---

[2]   L. Capron, "The Long-term Performance of Horizontal Acquisitions," *Strategic Management Journal* 20 (1999): 987–1018.

FIGURE 17.3   The value of mergers and acquisitions worldwide

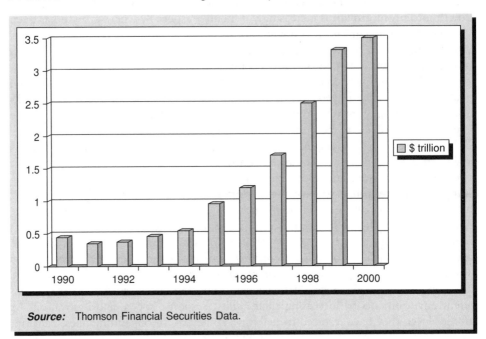

Source: Thomson Financial Securities Data.

the problem of complexity through differentiating the roles of corporate and business management so that all operating decisions and most business strategic decisions are located at divisional level. For less diversified industrial giants – General Motors, Wal-Mart, Siemens, and Matsushita – the problem of defining the role of top management is more acute. "You've gotta know what the hell is going on in your business," says Rick Waggoner, president and CEO of General Motors. "If you've got a problem in China, you've gotta get into it and make sure that it's getting fixed. You've got to be on top of your business enough to know where are the problems, where are the opportunities."[3] The problem of such top-level involvement is that it places tremendous strain on top management.

New Concepts of the Firm

The spectacular success of the corporate sector in generating shareholder value during the 1990s and the resurgence of US business over this same period owes much to a model of the firm built on shareholder sovereignty, resolution of agency problems through financial incentives and individual insecurity, and performance-based management built around an integrated system of metrics. If the success of this model has focused on undoing the inefficiencies, lethargy, and self-indulgence

---

[3]   "Critical Mass: As the Companies Keep Growing, CEOs Struggle to Keep Pace," *Wall Street Journal* (February 8, 2001): A1, A6.

of the corporatism that flourished in the 1960s and 1970s, it is not apparent that this management model will foster competitiveness under a post-downsizing era.

The critical requirements of the future are likely to be accessing more complex sources of advantage and achieving more effective reconciliation of the contradictions between short-run vs. long-run optimization, individual initiative vs. coordinated response, cost efficiency vs. innovation, and global integration vs. local responsiveness. Attaining these performance goals is likely to require a model of the firm that embodies a richer set of human relationships. The ascendancy of the shareholder-oriented, economically rational model of the firm has left alternative approaches to management – notably the human relations, sociotechnical systems, and stakeholder approaches – in the shadows. There is current evidence that management concepts based on a socially richer conception of the firm may be reappearing.

A number of recent approaches view the firm not just as a legal and social institution, but as a social organism that develops over time. The concept of the business as a *learning organization* – closely associated with the ideas of Peter Senge – regards the firm as a social organism whose central characteristic is as a knowledge system.[4] Arie de Geus extends this concept of the firm as organism to draw more heavily on biological analogies. The key to survival and prosperity in the long run, he notes, is adaption. Based on a study of the world's longest-living companies (including Stora, a Swedish paper company founded in the thirteenth century, Japan's 400-year old Sumitomo, 195-year old DuPont, and Pilkington, the British glass maker founded in the 1820s), de Geus identifies longevity with *financial conservatism*; *sensitivity* to the external environment reinforced by organizational mechanisms that promote adaptation (such as "flocking"); and *cohesion* in terms of a strong sense of identity infused through a strong corporate culture, yet with significant *tolerance* for individuality.[5]

Biological analogies have exerted strong influences on organizational design and the role of management among Japanese companies. Kao Corporation bases its philosophy and management systems on the concept of the company as a living organism. For example, when facing localized problems, employees are expected to act as an immune system, focusing their attention on the threat to the system and mobilizing to contain and eliminate the "infection." Kyocera, the multinational manufacturer of ceramic semiconductor components, bases its structure around some 400 "amoebas" – cells comprising a single self-organizing team of 3–50 members that can divide as its work expands or as it develops internal specialties.

The idea of the firm as an organism rather than a machine is central to Margaret Wheatley and Myron Kellner-Rogers' concept of self-organization.[6] As with other living organisms, organizations have the capacity to self-organize, to sustain themselves, to adapt to change, to develop leadership as and when needed, to create new structures and systems. Examples of self-organization include communities reorganizing

[4] Peter Senge, *The Fifth Discipline* (London: Century, 1990); Peter Senge, AA Kleiner, Charlotte Roberts, Richard Ross, George Roth, and Bryan Smith, *The Dance of Change: The Challenges to Sustaining Momentum in Learning Organizations* (New York: Doubleday, 1999).

[5] A. de Geus, *The Living Company* (Boston: Harvard Business School Press, 1997). See also "How to Live Long and Prosper," *Economist* (May 10, 1997): 59.

[6] M. J. Wheatley and M. Kellner Rogers, *A Simpler Way* (Berrett-Koehler, 1996).

after a natural disaster, the World Wide Web, crowds of 100,000 or more attending impromptu rock festivals, or the densely packed humanity navigating the sidewalks of Hong Kong. Synchronized behavior is common to social insects, flocks of birds, and schools of fish. Computer simulations of such coordinated behavior require only two or three rules for individuals to follow. In the case of organizations, there are three essential requirements for self-organization:

- *Identity.* Organizations need to be founded on an intent that drives the sense-making process within the organization.

- *Information.* Information provides the medium through which an organization relates to its environment and through which the individuals within the organization know how to react to external changes.

- *Relationships.* Relationships are the pathways through which information is transformed into intelligent, coordinated action. The more access individuals have to one another, the greater the possibilities for organized activity. Responsiveness to a wide range of external circumstances necessitates every individual having a wide range of connections to other individuals, with the potential for unplanned connections.[7]

Complexity

By resorting to concepts of self-organization we are acknowledging the limits to management. If the environment of business is complex and unpredictable, the chief executive, no matter how experienced or well trained in the art and science of strategic management, is unable to formulate strategy based on a rational, objective analysis of the firm and its environment. This idea that the dynamics of the business environment are too complex to be analyzed by the human brain is a challenge that complexity theory addresses. Research into complex systems – whether natural (weather patterns and earthquakes), biological (evolution), or social (crowd behavior, group dynamics) – have established common features of these *complex adaptive systems* that are susceptible to modeling using the tools of cybernetics, general systems theory, chaos theory, catastrophe theory, and fractal mathematics.[8]

The technical aspects of modeling complex, nonlinear, adaptive systems are daunting, especially since stable equilibrium are absent. Nevertheless, emerging from a wide diversity of studies are some common features of environments where cascades of change are constantly interacting and reshaping competitive landscapes. A result that has attracted particular attention in the strategic management literature is the existence of a *power law distribution* whereby small exogenous changes typically result in small consequences but may also trigger major movements. The typical

[7]   M. J. Wheatley and M. Kellner Rogers, "Self-Organization: The Irresistible Future of Organizing," *Strategy and Leadership* 24 (July–August 1996): 18–25.
[8]   For a review of the development of complexity theory and its applications to management, see P. Anderson, "Complexity Theory and Organizational Science," *Organization Science* 10 (1999): 216–32.

example is dropping grains of sand onto a sand pile where small sand movements are interspersed by major landslides.[9] These results point to the advantages of systems that evolve to the *edge of chaos* – they are capable of small, localized adaptations, but also have the potential to make larger leaps toward higher *fitness peaks* while avoiding tumbling off the fitness edge into chaos.

Shona Brown and Kathy Eisenhardt have applied the concepts and results of complexity theory to the problems of strategic management in hypercompetitive environments.[10] They argue that companies can scale the performance peaks associated with locating at the edge of chaos by imposing organizational processes that guide the behavior of the organization. These include:

- Establishing a few simple, hard-and-fast rules that define direction without confining it. Companies such as Enron, AES, Vodafone, Cemex, and Yahoo! do not plan integrated strategies in any conventional sense. Indeed, they cannot: their markets are too chaotic. Rather than formulating a strategy in terms of selecting a market position or focusing around a particular set of capabilities, these companies pick a few strategically significant processes and craft simple rules that can help locate the company where the opportunities are richest. These key processes might include product innovation, new market entry, or partnering. The simple rules can help companies cope with complexity in several ways. First, they can act as rules of thumb in screening opportunities (*boundary rules*). Thus, Cisco's acquisitions strategy is guided by the rule that it will acquire companies with fewer than 75 employees of which 75 percent are engineers. Second, rules can designate a common approach to how the company will exploit opportunities (*how-to rules*). Thus, as Enron develops new risk management products in areas such as electricity derivatives, weather futures, and bandwidth trading, it keeps to two basic rules: every trade must be offset by another trade that allows the company to hedge its risk; and every trader must complete a daily profit-and-loss statement. Third, companies have rules to determine priorities in resource allocation (*priority rules*). Thus, Intel allocates manufacturing capacity according to each product's gross margin. It was this role that allowed it to evolve from a memory chip company to a microprocessor company even before such a transition had been determined by top management.[11]

- Adopting a co-evolutionary approach to managing business units can permit the more effective exploitation of synergies than a directed, top-down approach. As we found in Chapter 15, opportunities for sharing resources and capabilities between businesses are easy to identify but difficult to access. Rather than attempt to manage business unit linkages from the corporate level, it may be better for corporate to create a context within which businesses can co-evolve.

[9] P. Bak, *How Nature Works: The Science of Self-organized Criticality* (New York: Copernicus, 1996).
[10] S. L. Brown and K. M. Eisenhardt, *Competing on the Edge: Strategy as Structured Chaos* (Boston: Harvard Business School Press, 1998).
[11] For discussion of the role of rules in strategy making, see K. M. Eisenhardt and D. Sull, "Strategy as Simple Rules," *Harvard Business Review* (January–February 2001): 107–16.

The key elements of such a context are, first, linking rewards to individual business performance rather than to reward collaborative efforts, second, maintaining porous boundaries to each business such that a multiplicity of voluntary collaborations can thrive between individuals across the businesses. Walt Disney Company exemplifies co-evolution between different internal divisions. Disney's *Lion King* movie spawned videos, theme park attractions, a stage musical, and over 150 kinds of merchandise. These spinoffs were not planned by corporate, they occurred through voluntary cooperation across Disney's different divisions.[12]

Applications of complexity theory to strategy management promises to add analytic support to the argument of Mintzberg and others in favor of *emergent* rather than *planned* approaches to strategy making. Mintzberg's critique of the "planning" and "design" schools of strategy making was based on the argument that intuition and decentralized processes were better ways to make strategy than rational frameworks and systematic decision processes.[13] At the intuitive level, David Hurst argues that rational objectivity limits the capacity for adaptation and shows how, in human terms, objectivity creates a dangerous distance between the senior managers who perpetrate change programs and those being managed.[14] However, by establishing a body of theory that shows how self-organization and localized adaptation can take an organization toward the edge of chaos, complexity theory provides a sound intellectual basis for Mintzberg's intuition.

Dynamic Capabilities

Adapting to a changing environment poses a critical challenge for the development of firm capabilities. As we have observed (Chapter 5), firms develop distinctive capabilities by perfecting organizational routines through repetition. As a result, core capabilities tend also to be core rigidities: once Wal-Mart has become the most brilliant discount retailer on the planet, it is likely to have difficulties becoming a luxury-goods retailer or an online retailer. Once we accept that capabilities are based on organizational routines and these routines are developed through repetition and learning, it follows that most capabilities tend to be static in nature. So what are the *dynamic capabilities* to which many strategy scholars have referred? According to David Teece and colleagues, dynamic capabilities are "the firm's ability to integrate, build, and reconfigure internal and external competences to address rapidly changing environments."[15] Eisenhardt and Martin also point to firms' capability in reconfiguring

---

[12]   K. M. Eisenhardt and D. C. Galunic, "Coevolving: At Last, a Way to Make Synergies Work," *Harvard Business Review* (January–February 2000): 91–101.

[13]   H. Mintzberg, *The Rise and Fall of Strategic Planning* (New York: Free Press, 1994); H. Mintzberg, B. Ahlstrand, and J. Lampel, *Strategy Safari: A Guided Tour through the Wilds of Strategic Management* (New York: Free Press, 1998).

[14]   D. K. Hurst, "When It Comes to Real Change, Too Much Objectivity May Be Fatal to the Process," *Strategy and Leadership* 25 (March–April 1997): 7–11.

[15]   D. J. Teece, G. Pisano, and A. Shuen, "Dynamic Capabilities and Strategic Management," *Strategic Management Journal* 18 (1997): 509–33.

their existing pools of resources and capabilities: "Dynamic capabilities are the organizational and strategic routines by which firms achieve new resource combinations as markets emerge, collide, split, evolve, and die."[16]

Certainly, it is possible to identify companies that have displayed remarkable adaptability and, presumably, possess such dynamic capabilities – Hewlett-Packard, AOL, Sony, 3M, and Nokia. However, specifying precisely what these dynamic capabilities are, where they are located, and what their internal architecture looks like represents a formidable challenge. Eisenhardt and Martin suggest that the critical feature is a process that allows the firm to alter its resource base. Thus, 3M's new product development capability represents a fairly standardized approach to how the company nurtures new product ideas and develops and commercializes them. However, the process is dynamic to the extent that it allows 3M to develop a vast range of products drawing on very different areas of technology and meeting the needs of very different markets. The nature of these dynamic capabilities may vary according to the dynamism of market situation. In high-velocity environments, dynamic capabilities rely extensively on new knowledge created for specific situations. In these circumstances, routines need to be simple and adaptable through being semi-structured.

REDESIGNING THE ORGANIZATION

As business environments become more complex and more competitive, so a business enterprise's survival requires it to perform at a higher level with a broader repertoire of capabilities. Achieving this kind of performance requires managing dilemmas that cannot be resolved as simple tradeoffs: a company must be efficient today, while also adapting for tomorrow; it must produce at low cost, while also innovating; it must deploy the massed resources of a large corporation, while showing the entrepreneurial flair of a small startup; it must achieve high levels of reliability and consistency, while also being flexible in adapting to change. Reconciling these conflicts within a single organization presents huge management challenges. We know how to devise structures and incentive systems that drive cost efficiency, we also know the organizational conditions conducive to innovation. But how on earth do we do both simultaneously?

Among the multiplicity of innovations and new developments in organizational design, two major trends may be discerned. The first is the design of organizations to facilitate the development and deployment of organizational capability. The second is the design of organizations to permit rapid adaptability.

Capability-based Structures

In Chapter 6, we noted that organizational design has been dominated by the requirements of cooperation rather than coordination. As a result, hierarchical structures have emphasized control and the need for unitary lines of command. Once we acknowledge

---

[16] K. M. Eisenhardt and J. A. Martin, "Dynamic Capabilities: What are They?," *Strategic Management Journal* 21 (2000): 1105–21.

that building outstanding capabilities is the primary goal of organizational design, then the emphasis shifts to the need to achieve effective coordination. If we accept that most enterprises need to deploy multiple capabilities and the coordination needs of different capabilities vary, it follows that our organizational structure must encompass different patterns of interaction. Hence, most business enterprises are unlikely to be successful with a unitary structure and will need to encompass multiple structures.

Beyond Unitary Structures

The principles of knowledge management offer one approach to understanding how different capabilities require different types of structure. Knowledge management distinguishes between activities directed toward building the firm's stock of knowledge and those directed toward deploying the existing stock of knowledge. James March refers to the former as *exploration* and the latter as *exploitation*.[17] The observation that exploratory capabilities (R&D and market research, for example) need to be organized differently from knowledge-exploiting capabilities (operations and finance, for example) is well known. A more difficult challenge is the fact that the same people undertake both exploratory and exploitation activities as part of their same jobs. Thus, a plant manager may be primarily engaged in knowledge exploration, but when she is involved in training activities, new product development, and benchmarking studies, her emphasis is exploitation.

The solution is the simultaneous deployment of different structures for different tasks.[18] Thus, the primary structure of the firm is established for the basic tasks of knowledge exploitation – purchasing, producing, selling, distributing. However, exploratory activities, such as new product development, typically require interacting with different people within a different type of collaborative relationship. Here, a multifunctional product development team is more conducive to developing and applying product development capability. Similarly, for identifying and transferring manufacturing best practices, an informal cooperative group comprising different plant managers is likely to be most effective.

Separate structures for pursuing the exploratory activities required for developing and adapting the organization have been described as *parallel learning structures*. While operational tasks typically require high levels of specialization and coordination through rules and routines, activities oriented toward innovation and adaptation require lower levels of specialization and coordination through planning and mutual adjustment, both of which are likely to be communication intensive. Examples of parallel structures include:

- At 3M, the formal structure exists in terms of business units, and divisions within which individuals have clearly defined job tasks. In addition, there is an informal structure for the purpose of new product development whereby

---

[17]   J. G. March, "Exploration and Exploitation in Organizational Learning," *Organization Science* 2 (1991): 71–8.
[18]   J. Ridderstråle, "Business Moves Beyond Bureaucracy," *Financial Times* Mastering Management (November 6, 2000): 14–15.

individuals are permitted, indeed encouraged, to "bootleg" time, materials, and use of facilities to work on new product ideas. If new products that emerge from the informal structure are deemed promising, they are taken within the formal structure to be launched, and ultimately may form the basis for a business unit within the formal structure.

■ Total quality management is a tool for changing work practices in order to eliminate defects and improve performance. Implementing TQM is typically through the creation of a parallel structure of quality circles, often coordinated by quality management committees and task forces. Thus, Texaco's "Star Quality" program created a hierarchy of quality management groups extending up to the corporate-level quality team chaired by the CEO.

■ GE's "Work-Out" program is a classic example of a parallel structure effecting change within the formal structure. The essence of Work-Out is a distancing of the parallel structure formed around "town-hall" type Work-Out sessions from the formal structure. To achieve this, Work-Out sessions were held at venues outside the company, all norms regarding hierarchical positions and authorities were suspended, and free interchange of ideas was encouraged. The outcome was a powerful device for initiating change within the formal structure in unusually short periods of time.

■ Business process reengineering and other radical change initiatives are typically initiated and implemented by task forces operating outside the formal structure. Thus, Chevron's "breakthrough teams" were formed from multiple functions and multiple vertical levels in the company and were challenged to devise ways of finding substantial reductions in costs. The result was a series of far-reaching proposals for reorganizing and outsourcing information technology, restructuring the corporate head office, and reducing operating costs.

Some of these parallel structures may be entirely informal. Informal networks where individuals share experience and expertise are called *communities of practice*.[19] Although existing entirely informally within most organizations in some form or another, the experience of the World Bank, American Management Systems, Hewlett-Packard, and many other organizations shows that such communities of practice can be nurtured deliberately as social networks for developing organizational capabilities, upgrading individuals' technical skills, retaining talented employees, and initiating innovation.[20]

Nonaka and Takeuchi's concept of a *hypertext organization* similarly involves meshing the "business-system layer" with flexible project teams that can address development needs.[21] Thus, Sharp Corporation has a formal structure that is organized around

[19]   J. S. Brown and P. Duguid, "Organizational Learning and Communities of Practice," *Organizational Science* 2 (1991): 40–57.
[20]   E. C. Wenger and W. M. Snyder, "Communities of Practice: The Organizational Frontier," *Harvard Business Review* (January–February 2000).
[21]   I. Nonaka and H. Takeuchi, *The Knowledge-Creating Company* (New York: Oxford University Press, 1995).

business groups and specialist functions, but for innovative priorities it has an "urgent project system" in which employees from particular businesses and functions are assigned to project teams for a limited period of time. The electronic organizer team set up on June 1, 1985 with a goal of bringing to market the world's first electronic organizer in October 1986 was one example of this system. The team comprised five engineers from the calculator division, one from integrated circuits, and one from liquid crystal displays.

Team-based, Project-based, and Process-based Structures

Creating structures that foster the kinds of coordination conducive to the functioning of organizational capabilities may require different patterns of interaction than are normal within conventional structures. The move toward team-based structures reflects the observation that building effective routines may be better undertaken by leaving a team to develop patterns of interaction and integration for themselves rather than relying on management direction. Although it is widely recognized that team-based structures can achieve the kinds of flexible integration that are fundamental to dynamic capabilities, how teams should be designed, their optimal sizes, and how different teams should interact with one another remain unresolved issues.

An increasing number of companies are organizing their activities less around functions and continuous operations and more around time-designated projects where a team is assigned to a specific project with a clearly defined outcome and a specified completion date. Some enterprises – construction companies and management consulting firms – have always been project based. Increasingly, these project-based organizations, which feature temporary cross-functional teams, have become viewed as models for organizing the dynamic, innovative, ambidextrous organization. One of the most extreme and interesting examples of project-based organization is Oticon A/S, the Danish manufacturer of hearing aids. CEO Lars Kolind abolished Oticon's formal organization and introduced a project-based company in which over 100 self-directed projects competed to attract employees. The ten-person top management team acted as project owners, but with few decision-making responsibilities other than to enforce basic rules such as "no paper-based communication."[22]

The desire to improve coordination has also encouraged companies to design their structures more closely with their internal *processes*. While business process re-engineering directs attention to the micro-structure of processes, interest in organizational capabilities has fostered a more integrated view of processes that focuses on how individual processes fit together in sequences and networks of complementary activities. For example, a company's order fulfillment process would span the whole chain of activities, from supplying information to potential customers, to customer selection and ordering, to manufacturing, through to distribution. Similarly, the customer relations process embraces the entirety of a company's interactions with

---

[22] For description and analysis of the Oticon experiment, see "This Organization Is Disorganization," *Fast Company* (April 1997): 77–83; and N. J. Foss, "Internal Disaggregation in Oticon: An Organizational Economics Interpretation of the Rise and Decline of the Spaghetti Organization," (Department of Industrial Economics and Strategy, Copenhagen Business School, October 2000).

its customers through marketing and after-sales services. In many cases, these macro processes extend beyond the company. Thus, supply-chain management involves linking internal logistics with those of suppliers and suppliers' suppliers. Effecting coordination and change within these processes for companies organized around functions and business units requires painful adjustment. Volvo's reorganization of its order fulfillment process in order to achieve a 14-day cycle between customer order and customer receipt of a customized automobile involved a Herculean effort to reorganize and reintegrate all the component processes: the order process, the production planning process, the distribution process, and the delivery to dealers process.[23]

Organizing for Adaptability

One of the implications we drew from our brief review of complexity theory was the idea that, in order to cope with a complex environment, an enterprise might have to resort to simple rules. A similar implication may be drawn in relation to internal organization. To the extent that organizations are required to perform tasks whose complexity and variety require structures and systems that we cannot design for the simple reason that we do not have the knowledge, then the optimal response may be to simplify the formal structure to allow the individuals within the organization to self-organize. Loosening the structure may be a critical step toward building the *ambidextrous organization* – one that can combine gradual evolutionary change with occasional revolutionary leaps.[24]

Consider Jack Welch's system of management at General Electric. Welch has continually emphasized the "3Ss" – "Speed, Simplicity, Self-confidence." His quest for simplicity has involved a minimalist approach to formal control systems. Thus, GE's once elaborate strategic planning system was cut back to a focus on a few issues with a minimal degree of documentation, formal presentation, and reporting. Welch's own leadership emphasized short slogans: *boundarylessness, six-sigma, work-out, destroy-your-company-dot-com*. Yet, paradoxically, this emphasis on greater simplicity of formal systems permitted more complex patterns of coordination and collaboration within GE. Recognizing that it is impossible to devise a formal management system that can reconcile efficiency with innovation, and rapid-response adaptability with relentless cost reduction and vigorous bottom-line accountability, Welch guided the corporation less by formal controls and more by exhortations that directly influenced attitudes and behaviors.[25]

Thus, the principle that strategy making in a complex, dynamic environment involves establishing direction and a decision-making context rather than a formulating a

---

[23] Suzanne Hertz and Johny Johansson, "Process Management in Networks: The New Volvo Story," discussion paper (Stockholm School of Economics/Georgetown University, 1997).

[24] M. L. Tushman and C. A. O'Reilly III, "The Ambidextrous Organization: Managing Evolutionary and Revolutionary Change," *California Management Review* 38 no. 4 (Summer 1996): 8–30.

[25] "General Electric: End of the Welch Era," in R. M. Grant, *Cases in Contemporary Strategy Analysis*, 3rd edn (Oxford: Blackwell, 2002).

detailed plan can also be applied to the internal organization of the firm. In order to create an organization that can coordinate in complex ways and resolve conflicts between efficiency and creativity and short term and long term, the optimal approach may be to concentrate on context – organizational culture and modes of behavior – and to allow coordination to occur voluntarily and spontaneously. As a result, management becomes less concerned with the creation of formal systems and control processes, and more with developing and maintaining a social system defined by behavioral norms and attitudes. As Herb Kelleher of Southwest airlines affirms: "We hire attitudes." Three concepts may be of practical use in formulating such an approach: *identity*, *modularity*, and *networks*.

Identity

What does it mean to "manage the organizational context" to influence how the employees of the firm collaborate and interact? Clearly, this is something about social norms and common values, but all of these depend on some shared concept of what the organization *is*. The editors of an *Academy of Management Review* forum on "Organizational Identity and Identification" argue that:

> as conventional organizational forms are dismantled, so too are many of the institutionalized repositories of organizational history and method and the means by which organizations perpetuate themselves. Increasingly an organization must reside in the heads and hearts of its members.[26]

The power and usefulness of such identities may lie in quite simple conceptualizations of what the enterprise is about. For example, managers at America Online often make the observation that "AOL is an entertainment company." Although this statement does not appear in any of AOL's mission or values statements, it is clear that it acts as a powerful guide to its strategic direction amidst the chaos of its business environment. Implicit in this statement is that AOL targets the mass consumer market, that the value it provides to its customers are fun and family enjoyment, and that AOL is not a technology company, nor is it oriented toward the business sector.

Modularity

If the essence of dynamic capability is in building over time strong capabilities in technologies and specific functions, and in reconfiguring these to meet the requirements of a changing environment, what kind of structure can achieve such a combination of continuity and flexibility? In Chapter 6, we examined the argument that hierarchical structures based on loosely coupled, semi-autonomous modules possessed considerable adaptation advantages over more tightly integrated structures. Such modular structures may be particularly useful in reconciling the need for close

---

[26] S. Albert, B. E. Ashcroft, and J. E. Dutton, "Organizational Identity and Identification: Charting New Waters and Building New Bridges," *Academy of Management Review* 25 (2000): 13–17.

collaboration at the small group level with the benefits of critical mass.[27] Thus, the key to Microsoft's success in designing huge software programs such as Windows NT, Internet Explorer, and Microsoft Office, which require the coordinated efforts of close to 500 software developers, is to modularize these programs using its "synch and stabilize" system.[28]

Networks

A key feature of the changes in strategy, structure, and management systems has been less distinction between what happens within the firm and what happens outside it. Organization theory emphasizes the distinction between the organization and its environment, while economics distinguishes between markets and hierarchies as alternate organizational mechanisms. The growth of inter-firm collaboration and the development of the "contingent workforce" – people who work for companies but who are not covered by long-term employment contracts – has blurred this distinction, and theory has recognized a continuum of organizational forms and a multiplicity of contractual forms that make it clear that spot markets and unitary firms are just two specific organizational forms. As "command and control" modes of management give way to less formal patterns of coordination, so internal relationships within the firm are less differentiated from external relationships. The immediate implication is that the boundaries of the firm are less distinct and more permeable. Jack Welch's concept of the *boundaryless firm* is one where neither the internal divisions within the firm nor the external boundaries are barriers to cooperation and communication. If cooperation across individuals and small enterprises can achieve the close coordination conventionally associated with corporations, the large, integrated company may disappear as the dominant organizational form in many industries. We have already noted how in the Italian clothing industry networks of small firms simultaneously achieve integration, flexibility, and innovation. The potential for networks of small firms to emulate the advantages of large corporations is evident in the Italian motorcycle industry, where comparatively small players such as Aprilia, Italjet, and Ducati have used integrated networks of suppliers to take market share from the dominant Japanese manufacturers.[29]

Internet technology provides a key tool in increasing the efficiency of firm networks. Indeed, using intranets to link together the different parts of the enterprise and outside companies has the effect of blurring the distinction between internal units and external companies. At Cisco Systems, for example, internet systems not only link

---

[27] R. Sanchez and T. Mahoney "Modularity, Flexibility and Knowledge Management in Product and Organization Design," *Strategic Management Journal* 17, Winter special issue (1996): 63–76; M. A. Schilling, "Toward a General Modular Systems Theory and its Application to Inter-firm Product Modularity," *Academy of Management Review* 25 (2000): 312–34.
[28] M. A. Cusumano, "How Microsoft Makes Large Teams Work Like Small Teams," *Sloan Management Review* (Fall 1997): 9–20.
[29] Gianni Lorenzoni and Andrea Lipparini, "Relational Strategies and Learning by Interacting Mechanisms in the Italian Motorcycle Industry," paper presented at Strategic Management Society Conference, Barcelona (October 7, 1997).

customers and suppliers for the purposes of ordering and invoicing, but also provide common systems technological change and joint product development. In addition, the same systems facilitate internal management systems ranging from employee performance reviews to budgeting and strategic planning.[30]

An important feature of firm networks is that they can help companies address the problems of complexity and rapid change in their business environments. In producing complex products that require a wide range of technical and commercial capabilities, such as automobiles, aircraft, and telecom equipment, networks allow each firm to specialize in a few capabilities while providing the close linkages needed to integrate these different capabilities. Furthermore, the flexibility of these linkages offers the potential for the capabilities resident within an inter-firm network to be reconfigured in order to adapt quickly to external change.[31]

NEW MODES OF LEADERSHIP

New organizational structures and strategic priorities point to new models of leadership. The era of restructuring and shareholder focus has been associated with "change-masters"[32] – visible, individualistic, often hard-driving management styles of CEOs such as Al Dunlap at Sunbeam, Lee Iacocca at Chrysler, Cor Boonstra at Philips, Franco Bernabe at ENI, and Tom O'Malley at Tosco Corporation. These leaders have first and foremost been strategic decision makers, charting the direction and redirection of their companies, and making key decisions over acquisitions, divestments, and cost cutting.

The responses that have been suggested to the problems of complex business environments in terms of both strategy formulation and organizational design imply a very different role for the chief executive than the "buck-stops-here" peak decision-making role traditionally associated with corporate leadership. The guidelines for strategy and organization design that we have discussed so far point to management leadership as directed more toward the creation and maintenance of the organizational environment rather than decision making *per se*.

If the foundation of strategy is a sense of organizational identity, then a key role of top management is to clarify and communicate that identity. James Collins and Jerry Porras, in their influential study of successful companies *Built to Last*,[33] emphasize the critical and complementary roles of:

- *Core values* – such as Walt Disney Company's emphasis on imagination and wholesome family entertainment.

---

[30] P. J. Brews, "The Challenge of the Web-Enabled Business," *Financial Times* Mastering Management (November 27, 2000): 4–7. See also D. Tapscott, D. Ticoll, and A. Lowry, *Digital Capital: Harnessing the Power of Business Webs* (Boston: Harvard Business School Press, 2000).

[31] R. Gulati, N. Nohria, and A. Zaheer, "Strategic Networks," *Strategic Management Journal* 21 (2000): 203–15, reviews recent research into inter-firm networks.

[32] R. M. Kanter, *The Change Masters* (New York: Simon & Schuster, 1983).

[33] J. C. Collins and J. I. Porras, *Built to Last* (New York: Harper Business, 1996).

- *Core purpose* – the organization's reason for being, which for successful companies typically goes beyond the goal of making money for shareholders. As David Packard, co-founder of Hewlett-Packard, observed: "You can look around in the general business world and see people who are interested in money and nothing else, but the underlying drives come largely from the desire to do something else – to make a product, to give a service – generally to do something which is of value."[34]

- *Envisioned future* – a view of the future that comprises *BHAGs* (Big, Hairy, Audacious Goals), such as Boeing's 1950 goal of becoming the dominant producer of commercial aircraft and bringing the world into the jet age, and Honda's declared intention of the 1970s to destroy Yamaha ("Yamaha wo tsubusu!").

The role of values and purpose is not just to provide a foundation for strategy, but also to unify and inspire the efforts of organizational members. To this end, the purpose and values of the enterprise must be consistent with those of its employees. To the extent that our lives are a search for meaning, the satisfaction that our work offers will depend critically on the congruence between organizational purpose and our own aspirations. British Petroleum's rebranding in 2000 included the theme "beyond petroleum," an attempt to communicate a more meaningful and resonant image to its stakeholders than the production of petroleum products. Ultimately, creating a common identity between the organization and those who work within it may require the organization to recognize the existence of human emotion and, ultimately, the human soul.[35]

What do these considerations imply about the job of the chief executive and the top management team? If the managers are making decisions, what are they doing? Mark Youngblood identifies the key responsibilities of leaders as:

- Clarifying shared vision.

- Enriching the culture.

- Developing alignment between the different parts of the organization and among shared vision, strategy, organizational design, and human resources.

- Promoting understanding in interpreting information and events within the context of the shared vision.

These roles are likely to require different types of management skills:

> The balance has clearly shifted from attributes traditionally thought of as masculine (strong decision-making, leading the troops, driving strategy, waging competitive battle) to more

---

[34] Quoted by J. C. Collins and J. Porras, "Building Your Company's Vision," *Harvard Business Review* (September–October 1996): 68.
[35] L. Grattan, "Building Companies Founded on People" *Financial Times* Mastering Management (November 27, 2000): 14–15; L. Grattan, *Living Strategy: Putting People at the Heart of Corporate Purpose* (London: Prentice Hall, 2000).

FIGURE 17.4   New models of leadership: implications for top management competencies

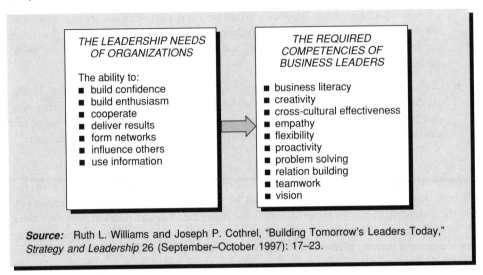

Source: Ruth L. Williams and Joseph P. Cothrel, "Building Tomorrow's Leaders Today," *Strategy and Leadership* 26 (September–October 1997): 17–23.

feminine qualities (listening, relationship-building, and nurturing). The model today is not so much "take it on your shoulders" as it is to "create the environment that will enable others to carry part of the burden." The focus is on unlocking the organization's human asset potential.[36]

Figure 17.4 identifies the kinds of skills that such a role requires.

What kinds of personality attributes are such leadership competencies founded on? Recent research points to the key role of a set of characteristics commonly referred to as *emotional intelligence*. These comprise:

■ *Self-awareness* in terms of the ability to read and understand one's emotions and assess one's strengths and weaknesses, underlain by the confidence that stems from positive self-worth.

■ *Self-management* in terms of control, integrity, conscientiousness, initiative, and achievement orientation.

■ *Social awareness* in relation to sensing others' emotions (empathy), reading the organization (organizational awareness), and recognizing customers' needs (service orientation).

■ *Social skills* in relation to influencing and inspiring others; communicating, collaborating, and building relationships with others; and managing change and conflict.[37]

[36]   Ruth L. Williams and Joseph P. Cothrel, "Building Tomorrow's Leaders Today," *Strategy and Leadership* 26 (September–October 1997): 17–23.

[37]   D. Goleman, "What Makes a Leader?," *Harvard Business Review* (November–December 1998): 93–102.

Goleman argues that these competencies are apparent in all leadership styles. Certainly, empirical studies of managerial competency offer robust association between these characteristics and superior performance across a wide range of situations. While effective leaders may share common individual competencies, what kind of leadership styles are appropriate to the complex, high velocity environments of today? Green and Cooper look at leadership in terms of different approaches to managing personal and organizational knowledge. Are leaders reflexive or nonreflexive, controlling or empowering? They identify four styles and draw on religious analogies to label them "prophet," "sage," "priest," and "visionary."[38] Building on the *Built to Last* study, Jim Collins identifies "level 5" leadership: a combination of humility and resolve that, according to Collins, has characterized transformational leaders from Abraham Lincoln to Philip Morris's Joseph Cullman and Nucor's Ken Iversen.[39] Among the most successful companies, this leadership characteristic was exercised through specific management practices:

- Priority given to building the right team over creating the right strategy.

- Willingness to confront reality while maintaining faith in the future.

- Building organizational momentum.

- Depth of knowledge about the key strategic issues of the economics of the business, what the company is best at, and how to ignite the passions of its people.

- Pioneering a few carefully selected technologies while maintaining skepticism over technology bandwagons.

- Maintaining discipline of thought, action, and people.

SUMMARY

While the future remains unknowable, its roots are in the present and the past. From what we observe today, we can identify many of the key developments of the next few years. The trends that we discern in science and technology, economic development, government policies, social structure, demographics, and lifestyles will shape the business environment for the remainder of the decade. We have reviewed some of the sources of competitive advantage in the emerging business environment and the capabilities that companies will need to develop and deploy.

[38]   S. Green and P. Cooper, "Sage, Visionary, Prophet and Priest Leadership Styles of Knowledge Management and Wisdom," in G. Hamel, C. K. Prahalad, H. Thomas, and D. O'Neal (eds), *Strategic Flexibility* (New York: Wiley, 1998): 173–94.
[39]   J. Collins, "Level 5 Leadership: The Triumph of Humility and Fierce Resolve," *Harvard Business Review* (January 2001): 67–76.

Some of the most critical, and difficult, issues concern the structures, systems, and styles needed to build and exercise these capabilities. The configurations that were so successful during the last two decades of the twentieth century are unlikely to serve enterprises so well in this first decade of the twenty-first.

Emerging theories of complexity, self-organization, knowledge management, and leadership can augment our existing standard tools of strategic management. Even more encouraging is the fact that experimentation and innovation at the coal-face of managerial practice offer lessons that are yielding solutions capable of wider application and the seeds of new principles and frameworks. AES's "honeycomb" structure, Sun Microsystems' networks of alliances, Kao Corporation's system of "biological self-control," and Yahoo!'s approach to strategic management through "structured emergence" suggest novel approaches to managing within complex, high-velocity environments.

Strategic management remains highly dependent on concepts and theories drawn from the basic disciplines of economics, sociology, psychology, biology, and systems theory. However, the encouraging feature of the past few years has been greater synthesis across these disciplines and between theory and practice. One indicator of progress is that strategic management is less obviously a net importer of ideas and findings from its contributing disciplines. In areas such as the analysis of competition, determinants of long-run profitability, organizational design, and the management of technology, it is strategic management scholars who are breaking new ground and influencing thinking in the underlying disciplines.

Formidable challenges lie ahead. As the opportunities for creating value from downsizing, refocusing, restructuring, and reengineering have become mined out, so managers have been forced to explore new territory seeking new sources of competitive advantage. The end of the e-commerce boom points to the reality that new sources of value are elusive. While our basic tools of strategy analysis – industry analysis and the analysis of resource and capabilities – remain valid and robust, it is clear what we shall need to continually develop our concepts and frameworks to meet the circumstances of tomorrow. The challenge is to apply what we know, recognize what we don't know, and engage in reflective observation in order to extend our domain of understanding.

Index